VRIJE UNIVERSITEIT TE AMSTERDAM

THE SAYINGS OF JESUS IN THE EPISTLE OF JAMES

ACADEMISCH PROEFSCHRIFT

ter verkrijging van de graad van doctor aan
de Vrije Universiteit te Amsterdam,
op gezag van de rector magnificus
dr. C. Datema,
hoogleraar aan de faculteit der letteren,
in het openbaar te verdedigen
ten overstaan van de promotiecommissie
van de faculteit der godgeleerdheid
op 1 September 1989 te 13:30 uur
in het hoofdgebouw van de universiteit, De Boelelaan 1105

door
DEAN B. DEPPE
geboren te Grand Rapids, Michigan, USA

Bookcrafters, Chelsea, Michigan
1989

Promotor:

Prof. Dr. Bastiaan Van Elderen
Vrije Universiteit

Copromotor:

Prof. Dr. Tjitse Baarda
Universiteit Utrecht

Referent:

Prof. Dr. H. Leene
Vrije Universiteit

ACKNOWLEDGEMENTS

The pursuit of graduate studies has unexpectedly brought me back to the home of my grandparents, the Netherlands. My wife and I have found it tremendously rewarding to view the land and culture of our ancestors, to learn the Dutch language and converse with our relatives, and to be introduced first hand to the rich history of the European environment. We have been especially undergirded by the caring and hospitality of our neighbors and church friends in the village of Bodegraven. Furthermore, we appreciate the financial assistence of the Dutch government to support our study leave in the Netherlands.

I want to offer high praise and great respect to my promoters, Professors Tjitze Baarda and Bastiaan Van Elderen. Prof. Baarda's high standards of critical scholarship have heightened the demands of scientific accuracy and intellectual persistence which I have placed upon myself. His careful attention to the primary texts has deepened my appreciation and knowledge of the Jewish and Christian documents of antiquity. These qualities have been matched by his cheerful support and valuable friendship. Having completed my undergraduate work in the United States under the supervision of Prof. Van Elderen, it was indeed a pleasant surprise to again receive his guidance as a mentor and friend. Seeing the respect which he has received in the international community of Biblical scholars, I am now grateful for the previous opportunities I have had to reap from the abundance of his exegetical gifts and teaching experience. Thanks again to both of you. Without the combination of your critical comments and supportive enthusiasm this dissertation may have never seen the light of day.

We returned to Grand Rapids, Michigan, in the summer of 1984 in order to fill a teaching vacancy at Calvin Theological Seminary. I want to thank the faculty of Calvin Seminary for this opportunity for teaching experience as well as the earlier years of training which have equipped me for a ministry in Biblical teaching. The difficult and energy-draining experience of reworking this manuscript in the midst of pastoral and preaching responsibilities was made lighter by the companionship and emotional support of my wife, Julie, and our family. I am especially indebted to the unselfish and diligent effort of my mother, Bernice Deppe, who saved me hours of work by the typing and retyping of this thesis. I am also thankful for the supportive push of reassurance which my father, Frank Deppe, offered me in my initial decision to study in a foreign country.

Finally, God's continual care through the presence of his Holy Spirit is the primary cause and the continuing reason why I pursue theological studies and desire a teaching ministry. May his kingdom come and his will be done on earth as it is in heaven.

PREFACE

Increasingly in recent years I have been captivated and enriched by gospel studies. In writing my masters dissertation at Calvin Theological Seminary on the Salt Sayings of Jesus, the transmission of the dominical sayings particularly caught my attention. Since volumes of literature have been written on most of the problems connected with the Synoptic tradition, I have chosen to concentrate my efforts upon the Epistle of James and approach the gospels through a study of the paraenetic tradition encountered in James. I will not rehearse the outline of this dissertation here in the preface since the more natural location for such a description is at the conclusion of an introductory chapter dealing with a history of the problems connected with interpreting the Epistle of James.

I began my study of the Epistle of James with the common evangelical assumption that James of Jerusalem was the author. An especially enlightening experience (which I recommend to all my readers) was the comparative study of the documements of James, 1 Peter, 1 Clement, and the Shepherd of Hermas. Through this project (which is outlined in Appendix II) I became convinced that some important type of relationship ties together the similar content and vocabulary of this early Christian literature. This was confirmed by the research of Sophie Laws whose commentary was just entering the shelves of the Dutch libraries as I was completing my research. Whether the explanation for these similarities is the common Jewish-Christian background of the authors, a provenance in Rome, or the particular genre of paraenesis, I will leave this difficult question to the judgment of the reader.

Regarding the bibliographical data, I have basically followed the format presented by Kate Turabian in her volume entitled A Manuel of Writers of Term Papers, Theses, and Dissertations (Chicago: Un. Press, 1973). I have departed from her example in not including the information about publication in the first footnote of a particular book since this data is easily accessible in the bibliography. Furthermore, I have placed articles found in dictionaries and encyclopedias under the author rather than under the title in the bibliography. I prefer the American method of including the first name of the author and the name of the publisher in the bibliography which I contend will benefit the reader in his search for these materials. I have included publishing data in the footnotes only when I have not read a particular book or when its subject matter is foreign to our discussion. Rather than continually quoting from certain standard works of ancient literature, I have decided to mention these works here in the preface. For the NT Greek I have employed Nestle-Aland 26; for the English, The Revised Standard Version; for the OT LXX, Rahlf's edition of the Septuaginta; for the apocrypha, Goodspeed's volume entitled The Apocrypha: an American Translation; for the OT pseudepigrapha, Charles' work, The Apocrypha and Pseudepigrapha of the Old Testament in English, Vol. II; for the Qumran writings, Vermès' book, The Dead Sea Scrolls in English; for the Apostolic Fathers in Greek, Patrum Apostolicorum Opera; for the Apostolic Fathers in English, Harmer's edition of Lightfoot's series The Apostolic Fathers; and finally for the Mishnah, Danby's book under the same name, The Mishnah.

Hopefully this study on the relationship between the Epistle of James and the sayings of the Jesus-tradition will stimulate additional literature on the transmission of the sayings of Jesus. In addition to our dissertation we have accumulated in recent years significant studies of the sayings of Jesus in the Epistle of James by Kittel, Shepherd, and more recently Davids, articles describing the Jesus-tradition in 1 Peter by Gundry and Best, and comparisons of the gospels and Pauline literature by Allison, Furnish, and Davies which alter Resch's conclusions of a century ago; we have a dissertation on the Synoptic traditions in the Apocalypse by Vos, books on the sayings of Jesus in the Apostolic Fathers by Köster and the 1905 Oxford Society's report, and Bellinzoni's helpful contribution on the *logia* of Jesus in Justin Martyr. What would be extremely helpful at this time is a scholarly overview of this literature in one volume tracing the history of the transmission of the sayings of Jesus outside the genre of gospel.* Maybe a reader of this dissertation will be stimulated to adopt such a project.

*During the reworking of this thesis an excellent contribution toward this goal appeared, i.e. Gospel Perspectives, Vol. 5, subtitled, "The Jesus Tradition Outside the Gospels," ed. David Wenham.

THE SAYINGS OF JESUS IN THE EPISTLE OF JAMES

TABLE OF CONTENTS

OUTLINE OF THE CONTENTS

Chapter 1

Introduction: A History of the Problems

1.1 The Problems With Regard to Background

Probably the most concise description of the history of interpretation of the Epistle of James in the modern era is the title of Meyer's book, Das Rätsel des Jacobusbriefes.[1] The book of James has become an enigma. Toxopeus laments, "Over weinige brieven van het N.T. werden in den loop des tijds zo verschillende meningen geuit als over den Jacobusbrief."[2] Decisive questions over the authorship, date, readers, provenance, genre, and canonicity of this writing lie like an unsolved puzzle, an unanswered riddle in the hands of the exegete. Almost every James mentioned in the NT has been posited at one time or another as the author of this epistle. Some interpreters jump back and forth swayed in divergent directions by the ambiguous quality of the literature,[3] while others finally choose the solution of a pseudonymous document.[4] The possible date of origin has ranged all the way from the early years of Christ's life to the latter half of the second century.[5] With regard to audience Jülicher and von Soden[6] contend that not a word in the entire letter points to Jewish readers, while Spitta[7] attempts to prove that every word can be better applied to a Jewish audience. Furthermore, there has been a long-standing argument whether James is an epistle, a homily, a series of diatribes, wisdom literature, or paraenesis.[8] Finally, even the certainty of James' canonicity has remained an unfinished argument.[9] Everyone remembers Luther's designation of James as "an epistle of straw"[10] as compared with the pure gold of the gospel found in John, Romans, Galatians, and 1 Peter.

---

[1] Arnold Meyer, Das Rätsel des Jacobusbriefes, title page.

[2] Hendrik J. Toxopeus, Karakter en Herkomst van den Jacobusbrief, 1.

[3] Friedrich H. Kern argued for pseudonymity in his 1835 article, "Der Charakter und Ursprung des Briefs Jakobi," TZTh, zweites Heft, 1-132, but changed his position in his 1838 commentary, Der Brief Jakobi.

[4] A typical example is Martin Dibelius and Heinrich Greeven, James: A Commentary on the Epistle of James, 18ff.

[5] Toxopeus, Jacobusbrief, contains thorough lists of the 19th century writers: pp. 2-3 prePauline date, 40-41 end of the apostolic period, 59-61 second century date.

[6] Adolf Jülicher, Einleitung in das Neue Testament, 188; Hermann von Soden, Hebraerbrief, Brief des Petrus, Jakobus, Judas, 171.

[7] Friedrich Spitta, "Der Brief des Jakobus," Zur Geschichte und Literatur des Urchristentums, II: 155-183.

[8] Cf. ch. 5, sections 3.1-3.5 for the various proponents of these views.

[9] Cf. ch. 6, section 2.4e.

[10] See Willibald Beyschlag, Der Brief des Jacobus, 22 for the primary references in Luther and his grounds for such a conclusion. Cf. also Charles L. Mitton, The Epistle of James, 221.

1.2 The Literary Relationships

Where do we find the leading clues to this unsolved riddle? What method of investigation can uncover the design and pinpoint the interconnected pieces of the Jamesian[11] puzzle? The key, as testified by many scholars,[12] will only be discovered when one investigates the relationship of the Epistle of James to other literature, both Christian and Jewish. Shepherd, for instance, states, "Since the Epistle does not appear designed to meet a specific crisis or situation in the life of the Church, any determination of its date and place of origin must depend upon whatever evidence can be drawn from its literary relationships with other Jewish and Christian documents."[13]

Prominent attention has been given to Peter's first epistle where surprisingly close parallels in wording, content, common quotations from the OT, and order of material have been discerned with the Epistle of James.[14] The following list by Carrington[15] is representative:

James	General Description	1 Peter
1:1	the diaspora	1:1
1:2	various temptations	1:6
1:3	testing of faith	1:7
1:11	reference to Is. 40:6	1:24
1:12	receiving the crown	5:4
1:18	begotten by a word	1:23
1:21	salvation and putting off	2:2
1:27	spiritual worship	2:5
3:13	honest "walking"	2:12
4:1	lusts producing war	2:11

---

[11]Just as we employ the adjectives Pauline, Petrine, and Johannine, we should also use an adjective form for the Epistle of James. Some authors have employed Jacobean (cf. Peter Davids, "James and Jesus," Gospel Perspectives 5: 79-80, n. 20,25; Everett F. Harrison, Introduction to the New Testament, 387; George E. Ladd, A Theology of the New Testament, 588; John A. T. Robinson, Redating the New Testament, 132) but this can be confused with the adjective used to designate King James of England (cf. Jack Lewis, The English Bible: From KJV to NIV (Grand Rapids: Baker, 1981), 331). Jacobine is employed by James Moffatt, The Historical New Testament, 576, but we prefer Jamesian (cf. Paul S. Minear, "Yes and No: The Demand for Honesty in the Early Church," NovT 13(1971): 7) because of its similarity to the English title of the epistle.

[12]A.H. Blom, De brief van Jacobus, 133-216 dedicates two of his five chapters to the question of literary relationships; Toxopeus, Jacobusbrief, 133-243, one of four chapters; Paul Feine, Der Jakobusbrief nach Lehranschauungen und Entstehungsverhaltnissen, 100-138, one of five chapters; Spitta, Zur Geschichte II: 155-236, one of three chapters.

[13]Massey H. Shepherd, "The Epistle of James and the Gospel of Matthew," JBL 75(1956): 40. Cf. also Robert R. Williams, The Letters of John and James, 84.

[14]Extended discussions can be found in Blom, Jacobus, 208-243; Arthur T. Cadoux, "The First Epistle of St. Peter," The Thought of St. James, 39-43; Feine, Jakobusbrief, 125-131; Meyer, Rätsel, 72-82; Adolf Schlatter, Der Brief des Jakobus, 67-73; Edward G. Selwyn, The First Epistle of St. Peter, 365-466, esp. 462ff; Spitta, "Der erste Petrusbrief," Zur Geschichte, II: 183-202; Ernst Vowinkel, Die Grundgedanken des Jakobusbriefes verglichen mit den ersten Briefen des Petrus und Johannes; Albert Wifstrand, "Stylistic Problems in the Epistles of James and Peter," STh 1(1948): 170-182.

[15]Philip Carrington, The Primitive Christian Catechism, 28. See Appendix II, section 2.1 for a chart of the similarities of wording in the original language.

4:6	reference to Prov. 3:34	5:5b
4:7	submit to authority	5:5a
4:7	resist the devil	5:9
4:10	be humbled	5:6

Yet what seems at first sight to be a promising method yields in the end only contradictory results. Many distinguished scholars conclude that Peter utilized the Epistle of James in his composition process,[16] but an equal number argue that James employed the contents of 1 Peter in the setting forth of his thoughts.[17] A third position posits the presence of a primitive Christian catechism which both James and Peter enlisted to serve their individual purposes. Carrington explains,

> 1 Peter is nearer in general outline to James than to any Pauline writing, yet differences in vocabulary and general theme are so great as to preclude the explanation that one borrowed from the other. Both exhibit a succession of thought and terminology which is best thought of as prior to either.[18]

Carrington develops the thesis that the common background is a primitive Christian catechism containing at least four sections based on common expressions in NT literature:

1) Deponentes igitur omne malum	Putting off all evil
2) Subiecti estote	Submit yourselves
3) Vigilante (et orate)	Watch and pray
4) Resistito diabolo	Resist the devil

Not only do James and 1 Peter fit this pattern but also the later Pauline writings of Colossians and Ephesians.[19] Inspired by Carrington's suggestions, Selwyn drew up a more detailed outline of contents comprising two baptismal catechisms based on a Christian holiness code as well as a persecution source for preparing disciples for times of trial.[20] A fourth solution typified by Dibelius insists that literary dependence is unfounded and that the kinship of style found among paraenetic writings is the basis of every parallel.[21] Lohse

---

[16]For instance, Blom, Cadoux, Mayor, Meyer, Rendall, Schlatter, Sidebottom, Spitta, and Zahn. The usual arguments for James' earlier dating include: 1) In quotes from the OT Peter's wording is more exact, indicating a correcting tendency; 2) It is easier to envision a transformation whereby Jesus is substituted for the OT prophets as a model of a believer's attitude toward suffering than the reverse process; 3) James has a less developed Christology; 4) In 1 Peter separation between Christians and Jews has become final (2:8), whereas in James Christians still meet in the synagogue (2:2); 5) The common thought finds fuller expression in 1 Peter.

[17]Brückner, Holtzmann, Jülicher, Moffatt, von Soden, B. Weiss etc. Similarities with the Apostolic Fathers (esp. 1 Clement and the Shepherd of Hermas) cause them to place 1 Peter chronologically prior to James. Cf. T.E.S. Ferris. "The Epistle of James in Relation to 1 Peter," CQR 129(1939): 303-308 for an elaborately worked-out proposal on how James supposedly used Peter's epistle.

[18]Carrington, Catechism, 22.

[19]This thesis of a primitive catechism also accounts for the puzzling similarities between Paul's epistles and 1 Peter.

[20]Selwyn, "Essay II," First Peter, 363-466. His fourteen tables of parallel material clearly make visible the striking similarities of expression, content, and order of material in the NT literature.

[21]Dibelius and Greeven, James, 30, n. 101.

has adopted Dibelius' conclusion and applied it to other primitive documents.[22] Therefore, since an investigation into the relationship between James and 1 Peter has not resulted in the expected consensus of opinion, we need to look elsewhere to locate the key to the enigma of James.

A comparison between the writings of Paul and James has also received much attention. The themes of justification[23] and faith/works[24] have been carefully studied and a long series of possible parallels in wording and content has been enumerated.[25] The following list indicates the numerous parallels which have been suggested.[26]

James	General Description	Paul
1:2-4	beneficial results of suffering	Rom. 5:3-5
1:6	not waver through unbelief	Rom. 4:20
1:13	God and temptations	1 Cor. 10:13
1:15	sin brings death	Rom. 5:12; 6:23
1:18	first fruits	Rom. 8:23
1:21	put aside evil	Rom. 13:12
1:22	hearing the law is not enough	Rom. 2:13
1:26	deceived religion	1 Cor. 3:18; Gal. 6:3
2:2-4	conduct toward outsiders	1 Cor. 14:23; Rom. 14:1
2:5	the poor are rich in faith	1 Cor. 1:27-28
2:6	bringing to court	1 Cor. 6:2,4
2:8	loving neighbor as oneself	Rom. 13:8-9; Gal. 5:14
2:10	keeping the whole law	Gal. 5:3
2:11	breaking the commandments	Rom. 2:22-23
2:19	one God and demons	1 Cor. 8:4; 2 Cor. 11:14
2:21,23	Abraham and righteousness	Gal. 3:6; Rom. 4:2-3
2:24	justification and works	Gal. 2:16; Rom. 3:28
3:15	worldly and spiritual wisdom	1 Cor. 2:6,14
3:16	jealousy and disorder	1 Cor. 3:3; 14:33

---

[22]Eduard Lohse, "Glaube und Werke: Zur Theologie des Jakobusbriefes," ZNW 48(1957): 14-15.

[23]Bernhard Bartmann, St. Paulus und St. Jacobus über die Rechtfertigung (Freiburg: Herder, 1897); Ernst Kühl, Die Stellung des Jakobusbriefes zum alttestamentlichen Gesetz und zum paulinischen Rechtfertigungslehre (Konigsberg: Koch, 1905); E. Tobac, "Le problème de la justification dans Saint Paul et dans Saint Jacques," RHE 22(1926): 797-805.

[24]Georg Eichholz, Glaube und Werke bei Paulus und Jakobus; Lohse, "Glaube und Werke," 1-22; Albert Köhler, Glaube und Werke im Jakobusbrief, BJGZ (Zittau: Menzel, 1913); Robert Kübel, Über das Verhaltnes von Glauben und Werken bei Jakobus (Tübingen: Un. Schr., 1880) Henry P. Hamaan, "Faith and Works in Paul and James," LThJ 9(1975): 33-41; Leonhard Usteri, "Glaube, Werke, und Rechtfertigung im Jakobusbrief," ThSKr 62(1889): 211-256.

[25]General articles comparing Paul and James include: Feine, Jakobusbrief, 100-122; Joachim Jeremias, "Paul and James," ET 66(1955): 368-371; Charles Johnson, "The Controversy between St. Paul and St. James," CQ 3(1915): 603-619; Ulrich Luck, "Der Jakobusbrief und die Theologie des Paulus," ThG 61(1971): 161-179; P. Schanz, "Jakobus und Paulus," ThQ 62(1880): 3-46,247-286; Walter Schmithals, Paulus und Jakobus.

[26]This list is a combination of the parallels enumerated by Heinrich J. Holtzmann, "Jakobusbrief," Bibel-Lexikon III: 187; James Moffatt, An Introduction to the Literature of the New Testament, 466; and Toxopeus, Jacobusbrief, 168-173. Paul's later letters are not included in this list but may be found in Appendix II, section 4.0.

4:1	the inner battle	Rom. 6:13; 7:23
4:4	enemies of God	Rom. 8:7
4:5	the spirit within us	Gal. 5:17; Rom. 8:9,11
4:11	against judging	Rom. 2:1; 14:4
4:15	if it is the Lord's will	1 Cor. 4:19

After examining this list of possible parallels, scholars are again divided in their opinions. One group contends that Paul polemicized against James;[27] a second set argues that James polemicized against Paul;[28] a third group insists that there is no real encounter between James and Paul at all in Jas. 2:14-26.[29]

Other investigators have searched the Apostolic Fathers to discover key parallels with the Epistle of James. 1 Clement and the Shepherd of Hermas have yielded a rich harvest of striking resemblances.[30] The list of Mußner[31] comparing James and the Shepherd of Hermas is representative.

James	General Description	Shepherd of Hermas
1:5	asking in prayer	Sim. 5,4,3
1:7	double-minded doubters do not receive	Mand. 9:5
1:21	commandment able to save the soul	Sim. 6,1,1
1:27	widows and orphans	Sim. 1:8
2:7	invoke a name over someone	Sim. 8,6,4
3:2-4	put away evil desires	Mand. 12,1,1
3:15	spirit from above	Mand. 11:5
4:5	indwelling spirit	Mand. 3:1
4:7	resist the devil and he will flee	Mand. 12,5,2
4:11	concerning slander	Mand. 2:2
4:12	fear him who can save and destroy	Mand. 12,6,3
5:4	groans of destitute heard by Lord	Vis. 3,9,6

Again, in interpreting these similarities analogous divisions appear. For most the Shepherd of Hermas is dependent upon the Epistle of James so that "Hermas furnishes a *terminus ad quem* for the composition of James."[32] However, Pfleiderer and Holtzmann arrive at the opposite opinion,[33] while a third group accepts the contention that James exhibits the same spirit as the Apostolic Fathers but places the date earlier than Hermas, discerning no literary dependence either way.[34]

---

[27]Theodore Zahn, Einleitung in das Neue Testament, I: 52ff; Joseph B. Mayor, The Epistle of St. James, xci (We will use the 1897 ed.); Gerald H. Rendall, The Epistle of St. James and Judaic Christianity, 86.

[28]Willi Marxsen, Introduction to the New Testament, 230.

[29]Eichholz, Glaube und Werke, 39,41. For our conclusions see Appendix II, section 3.3.

[30]For parallels with 1 Clement and Hermas in the original language see Appendix II.

[31]Franz Mussner, Der Jakobusbrief, 37-38.

[32]Moffatt, Introduction, 467. Cf. Sophie Laws, A Commentary on the Epistle of James, 22-25; Mayor, James, cxlv-cxlvi.

[33]Otto Pfleiderer, Das Urchristentum: seine Schriften und Lehren II: 539; Heinrich J. Holtzmann, Lehrbuch der historisch-kritischen Einleitung in das Neue Testament, 336.

[34]Dibelius and Greeven, James, 31; Lohse, "Glaube und Werke," 15-17; James A. Brooks, "The Place of James in the New Testament Canon," SWJTh 12(1969): 46-47.

1.3 The Four Strands of Jamesian Interpretation

In sorting out the considerable gamut of conclusions with regard to the relationship of James to other literature, one discovers that when a certain literary relationship is emphasized all the corresponding questions of authorship, date, readers, origin, etc. are answered in precisely the same way. Thus we acquire four main categories or strands of interpretation. An exposition of James is seemingly locked into solving all the particular problems of background within one of these specific strands. As a result there is seemingly no touchstone between the four worlds of Jamesian interpretation listed below.

	I	II	III	IV
emphasized relationship	OT and Jewish writings	personal hearing of Jesus	gospels esp. Matthew	Apostolic Fathers
date	preChristian authorship	early first century	late apostolic	second century
author	Christian redactor of Jewish work	James, brother of Jesus	another James	pseudonymous
readers	originally Jews	Jewish Christians	Jewish Christians	Hellenistic Christians
relationship to 1 Peter	1 Peter dependent upon James	1 Peter dependent upon James	independent; catechetical material	James dependent upon 1 Peter
relationship to Paul	Paul polemicized against James[35]	prePauline or independent	formal similarities of phraseology[36]	James polemicized against Paul
relationship to Apostolic Fathers	Christianized during this time	Apostolic Fathers utilize James	common emphases of thought	James uses Apostolic Fathers or common environment
relationship to sayings of Jesus	common Jewish concepts	reminiscences from personal memory	oral tradition or Matthew's community	written gospels or oral tradition
prime examples	Spitta Massebieau Meyer	Mayor Grosheide Guthrie	Shepherd Gryglewicz	Brückner Holtzmann Pfleiderer, Laws Aland

The aim of this dissertation is to investigate the kinship between the Epistle of James and the Synoptic traditions. Yet one might ask: "Can we expect that an exploration of the inter-

[35]Spitta, Zur Geschichte, II: 216 posits another possibility that Paul and James are dependent upon a third Jewish author.

[36]In categories II and III some maintain that James polemicized against a misunderstanding of Paul.

connections with the Synoptic traditions will hold the key to unlocking the enigma of the Epistle of James?" Based upon past research, one might expect that emphasizing the relationship with the Synoptic tradition would inevitably "lock us in" to one of these categories just discussed. Possibly exegetes must face an ongoing lack of consensus. The divergent roads of these categories may never meet. A comparative investigation of the Epistle of James with the Synoptic gospels at least offers us an opportunity to evaluate these divergent routes. Furthermore, it may shed new light on an old difficult problem and reveal what Herder had in mind when he quipped,

> If the Epistle is "of straw,"
> then there is within that straw
> a very hearty, firm, nourishing
> but as yet uninterpreted and unthrashed, grain.[37]

2.0 The Problems Connected with the Transmission of the Sayings of the Jesus-tradition[38]

Not only do we approach this subject with a set of problems connected with the interpretation of the Epistle of James, there is also an extended complicated history of the transmission of the sayings of Jesus that transports its problems into our discussion. Windisch believes that, "das Problem 'Jesus und der Jakobusbrief' erscheint fast noch schwierger und ratselhafter als das bekannte Problem 'Jesus und Paulus.'"[39] The questions set before us are these: Are there *logia* of Jesus cited in the Epistle of James? If so, what has influenced the form in which these sayings are transmitted? Must the principal determinant governing the particular wording of these sayings be assigned to the influence of one of the gospels, to a prior first stage in the transmission of the Jesus-tradition, or is the peculiar genre of James the piece of ground requiring excavation to uncover the valuable clue to an age-old problem?

2.1 The Vital Connection Between James and the Sayings of Jesus

Countless exegetes have pointed to the Epistle of James as a veritable gold mine for the sayings of the Jesus-tradition. This position has a long history: already in 1886 Weizsäcker noted that the presence of similarities between the Epistle of James and the sayings in the Synoptic gospels was a long observed fact.[40] Throughout the European continent and the English speaking world this position has found support from scholars of varied theological traditions. Holtzmann summarized the findings of 19th century German exegetes:

---

[37]Johann G. Herder, Briefe zweener Brüder Jesu in unserem Kanon, in Herder's Sammliche Werke VII, ed. Bernhard Suphan (Berlin: Weidmann, 1884), 500, n. 2 quoted in Dibelius and Greeven, James, 1.

[38]I do not seek to distill the "historical Jesus" from the remembered interpretations of Jesus' first followers. Therefore, I employ the phrases "the sayings of Jesus" and "the sayings of the Jesus-tradition" as synonyms.

[39]Hans Windisch, Gnomon X, 380 quoted in Gerhard Kittel, "Der geschichtliche Ort des Jakobusbriefes," ZNW 41(1942): 84, n. 31.

[40]Carl Weizsäcker, Das apostolische Zeitalter der christlichen Kirche, 378.

> Man behauptet augenfällige Uebereinstimmung des Lehrgehaltes mit der einfachen Verkündigung Jesu, weil unser Brief verhältnismäßig mehr Anklänge an synopt. Herrnworte bietet, als irgendeine andere neutest. Schrift.[41]

Twentieth century German introductions to the NT have continued this appraisal. Wikenhauser concludes, "Der Brief weist aber so zahlreiche Anklänge an Herrenworte auf wie sonst kiene andere ntl. Schrift."[42] Even when James' lack of Christology is emphasized, a close connection with the sayings of the Jesus-tradition is still posited. Rendtorff states,

> Obwohl der Name 'Jesus Christus' nur zweimal ausdrücklich zitiert wird (1,1 und 2,1), lassen sich doch zahllose sachlich und wörtlich enge Berührungen mit den Worten Jesu in den ersten drei Evangelien feststellen.[43]

Moreover, this conclusion not only permeates introductions and encyclopedia articles which tend to follow past authorities in the field but also is found in dissertations dealing in depth with this subject.[44] A similar close connection with the words of Jesus has been assumed by the Dutch Reformed exegete Grosheide who states, "Wie den brief van Jakobus doorleest, wordt telkens herinnerd aan uitspraken van Jesus, die ons in de Evangelien zijn bewaard en wel met name aan de Bergrede."[45] In France the conclusions of Reuss[46] are cited as an authority on the subject, as in this quote from Patry's dissertation: "Cette courte épitre de Jacques contient à elle seule plus de réminiscences des discours de Jésus que tous les autres écrits du Nouveau Testament pris ensemble."[47] Chaine investigates the parallels with greater precision than most French scholars, dividing them into three distinct categories, and yet arrives at a similar contention: "Dans un écrit aussi juif que l' Épitre de Jacques on est surpris de trouver un si grand nombre de rapprochements avec l' enseignement de Jésus."[48] Finally, in the English-speaking world there is a long series of authors who agree with the above conclusions. In 19th century England, Mayor claims that James has preserved more of the teaching of our Lord than all the other epistles put together.[49] A host of 20th century English and American theologians support the less dramatic claim that James contains more allusions to Jesus' words than any of the remaining NT epistles. Thc comments of Kugelman are typical of commentaries written in the English-speaking world:

> Almost half of James' Epistle, forty-six of one hundred and eight verses, echoes Jesus' teaching as it is recorded in the gospels. Twenty-two of these forty-six verses are very similar in language and concepts to sayings of Jesus recorded in Matthew or in Luke

---

[41]Heinrich J. Holtzmann, Lehrbuch der neutestamentlichen Theologie, II: 383 follows the conclusions of Kern, Schmid, and Bunsen.

[42]Alfred Wikenhauser, Einleitung in das Neue Testament, 343.

[43]Heinrich Rendtorff, Hörer und Täter: Einer Einführung in den Jakobusbrief, 11.

[44]Cf. Felix Eleder, Jakobusbrief und Bergpredict, 186.

[45]Frederick W. Grosheide, De brief aan de Hebreën en de brief van Jakobus, 342. We will quote the 1955 ed.

[46]Eduard Reuss, Die Geschichte der Heiligen Schriften Neuen Testament, 130.

[47]Raoul Patry, L'Epitre de Jacques dans ses rapports avec la prédication de Jésus, 12.

[48]Joseph Chaine, L'Épitre de Saint Jacques, LXVIII.

[49]Mayor, James, xliv-xlv.

.... With the exception of the gospels, there is no other New Testament writing which rings with so many echoes of Jesus' sayings as does Jas.[50]

The standard procedure for indicating similarities between James and the Synoptic gospels consists of an enumeration of parallels. In Appendix I we have tabulated over 180 different parallels with the average interpreter listing between 15 and 20. Since in the whole of the Pauline corpus only about 10-30 parallels are enumerated,[51] many have contended that the overabundance of reminiscences to the Jesus-tradition in James must be of some significance. On the other hand, an equally striking result of the research is the lack of consensus in the cataloging of these equivalents: three-fourths of the exegetes agree on only three parallels, two-thirds on only six.[52] How can we account for both this similarity in the authors' contentions and the dissimilarity of their results?

A second means of exhibiting the interconnection between the teaching of James and Jesus consists in a systematic critique of the similarities of content. A few authors such as Patry use the important themes of James to structure their entire discussion.[53] More frequently, commentators like Dibelius and Mayor summarize the basic parallels of content in their introduction to the book.[54] Many interpreters emphasize that the primary points of similarity lie in the content of the ethical exhortations rather than in the closeness of verbal expressions. Rendall, for instance, concludes that the teachings of the Synoptic gospels and the Epistle of James "agree closely in substance and content, yet with a marked absence of verbal borrowing or reproduction."[55]

In addition to the areas of wording and content, numerous scholars draw attention to the formal equivalence of style. Schaff, the church historian, states that the Epistle of James "echoes the Sermon on the Mount in the fresh, vigorous, pithy, proverbial, and sententious style of oriental wisdom."[56] The common use of imperatives is also striking.[57] Especially emphasized by Dibelius is the kinship of various sets of metaphors: "the metaphors of the soil and the plants (5:7; 3:12), of the moths and rust (5:2f), and points of contact with the Watching and Waiting group of metaphors (5:9) are encountered in Jas as well as in the Gospels."[58] A final similarity lies in the lack of organization and the

---

[50]Richard Kugelmann, James and Jude, 8-9. Cf. Donald Guthrie, New Testament Introduction, 743; Simon Kistemaker, The Gospels in Current Study, 92; Alexander Ross, The Epistles of James and John; William D. Davies, The Setting of the Sermon on the Mount, 402.

[51]Cf. below, p. 169.

[52]For additional statistics see Appendix I, section 2.0.

[53]Chapter 1. Les Riches et les Pauvres (pp. 20-46) Jas. 2:1-4; 2:5-9; 5:1-6; 4:4-10; 1:9-11.
Chapter 2. Les Épreuves et les Tentations (pp. 47-63) Jas. 1:2-4,13-18; 5:7-11.
Chapter 3. La Foi et les Oeuvres (pp. 64-75) Jas. 2:14-26.
Chapter 4. La Prière (pp. 76-82) Jas. 1:2-8; 3:13-18; 4:1-4; 5:15-18.
Chapter 5. La Loi (pp. 83-99) Jas. 2:8-13; 1:19-27; 4:11-12.
Chapter 6. Le Sermet, le Fruit de la Justice et les Projets téméraires (pp. 100-104) Jas. 5:12; 3:18; 4:13-14,16-17.

[54]Dibelius and Greeven, James, 28; Mayor, James, xliii-xliv.

[55]Rendall, James and Judaic Christianity, 68. Cf. Alan H. McNeile and C.S.C. Williams, An Introduction to the Study of the New Testament,208 and Zahn, Einleitung, I:81.

[56]Philip Schaff, History of the Christian Church (Grand Rapids: Eerdmans, 1910), I: 743.

[57]In 108 verses James employs 54 imperatives (provided one counts participles which follow imperatives in a series).

[58]Dibelius and Greeven, James, 28. Cf. ch. 4, section 3.3.

catchword connection between the various exhortations.[59] These points of contact have led many exegetes to attach the descriptive adjective "significant" to any enumeration of the parallels between the Epistle of James and the sayings of the Jesus-tradition.

2.2 Opposition to any Close Connection Between James and the Sayings of the Jesus-Tradition

Opposition to this dominant opinion has arisen along three fronts, one denying dependence upon the Jesus-tradition and two minimizing any close association. Without knowledge of each other's work, both Massebieau (1895) and Spitta (1896) published writings denying the original Christian character of the Epistle of James. Whereas Massebieau argues for a Jewish background from the thought patterns of the epistle,[60] Spitta presents a host of possible parallels to the sayings of Jesus and then one by one offers what he thinks are better parallels from Jewish literature.[61] Agreeing with this thesis, Meyer has called special attention to the parallels with The Testaments of the Twelve Patriarchs arguing that the Epistle of James is really an allegory based on Jacob's farewell address to his twelve sons (Gen. 49).[62] Subsequently Christian interpolations were added (1:1; 2:1; 5:12,14) and the epistle was accepted by the Christian church into its canon. In these analyses the Jewish background takes prominence over the Jesus-tradition.

Nineteenth century Dutch adherents to the Tübingen school of theology minimized the connection between James and the Synoptic traditions by emphasizing a decisive gap between the proclamation of Jesus and the teaching of James. Structuring church history along the lines of the Hegelian thesis-antithesis-synthesis pattern, the Tübingen school (Baur, Schwegler, Strauss) emphasized distinctions and dichotomies rather than following the traditional approach of harmonizing the dissimilarities in NT history and thought. Following this tradition the Dutch exegetes, Blom and Riedel,[63] concentrated on the antithesis between James and Jesus rather than Baur's distinction between Peter and Paul. Blom believed that the list of textual parallels could just as easily be traced to Jewish literature or Paul as to the teaching of Jesus.[64] Furthermore, James' complete omission of the deeds of Jesus and the significance of his death and resurrection for theological reflection dramatically separates the content of the book of James from the Jesus-tradition.

> Geen woord van Jezus' optreden, prediking of dood. Geen vermaning wordt aangedrongen door de herinnering van hetgeen hij gedaan heeft. De oude profeten, niet hij, worden tot voorbeelden van geduld onder het lijden gesteld (5:10). Een wonder van Elia, maar geen, dat door hem verrigt is, moet ten bewijze strekken van de kracht des gebeds (vs. 17,18). En zelfs, dat de regte kennis van de wet Gods een

---

[59] Cf. below, pp. 32-33 and Dibelius and Greeven, James, 7-11.

[60] L. Massebieau. "L'Épitre de Jacques est-elle l'oeuvre d'un Chrétien," RHR 32(1895): 249-283. Cf. below, section 3.4.

[61] Spitta, Zur Geschichte, II: 155-183. His alternatives to the major parallels will be discussed in detail in ch. 3.

[62] Meyer, Rätsel, esp. 240-307.

[63] Blom, Jacobus, 191-207; Petrus A. Riedel, De zedeleer van den Brief van Jacobus vergeleken met de zedeleer van Jezus.

[64] The only parallels he speaks positively about are 1:2=Mt. 5:11-12; 1:10-11=Mt. 13:6; 5:12=Mt. 5:33-37. He produces these alternatives: Jas. 1:5 and 4:13=1 Kings 3:5,12 not Mt. 7:7,11; 1:22=Rom. 2:13 not Mt. 7:24; 3:1=Rom. 13:2 not Mt. 23:14 par.; 3:12=Is. 5:2 not Mt. 7:16; 5:2=Job 13:28 and Is. 51:8 not Mt. 6:19; 4:4=Rom. 8:7 not Mt. 6:24; 5:17=1 Kings 17:1 and 18:1 not Lk. 4:25.

vrucht zijner prediking is, word wel stilzwijgend ondersteld, maar neit uitdrukkelijk en met dankbaarheid aan hem geroemd.[65]

Riedel, even more than Blom, presents a stark contrast between the ethical teaching of James and Jesus. The following table summarizes the differences:

page	Jesus	James
24	the rudimentary principle is the inner religious conscience	the controlling principle is obedience to the law
25	emphasis on God as loving father	emphasis on the demands of God
35	God's will is the foundation of the moral life	knowledge of the law is the foundation
34	the neighbor is anyone and everyone	the neighbor is only the partner in faith with a similar religious perspective
57	the welcoming of all peoples into the kingdom	Jewish particularism
92	emphasis on moral freedom whereby it is impossible for a person to be anything other than good	emphasis on an unbroken series of good works where at any moment someone's moral equilibrium could be disturbed
92	demands cleanness of heart and holiness towards God	demands unceasing acceptance of the prescriptions of the law
92	the impetus for good works comes from within	reward and punishment is the goad for good works
92	the goal is not reward but one's relationship with God	the goal of good works is the reward

This antithesis between the thought of James and Jesus functions as a methodological apriori or axiomatic presupposition throughout this analysis. Riedel is mistaken in his observations since he has unwittingly pulled Jesus out of his Jewish environment into the 19th century and at the same time forced James back into a certain legalistic stereotype of Judaism.

A third proposal minimizing the parallels with the Synoptic gospels is offered by the form critic Dibelius who proposes that James' use of the genre of paraenesis is the key to unlocking the enigma of the Epistle of James.[66] The formal similarities, harmony of style, and the shared ethical convictions are all traced back by Dibelius to the use of similar paraenetic traditions. In this way the influence of the Jesus-tradition upon the Epistle of James is thrust into the background.

---

[65]Blom, Jacobus, 201.
[66]Cf. below, section 3.5.

2.3 Suggested Explanations for the Similarities with the Synoptic Tradition

The most prominent cause for these different evaluations is the fact that the so-called "sayings of the Jesus-tradition" are nowhere introduced by James as *logia* of Jesus. His pen never begins a sentence with "For our Lord said" or "As Jesus said." Instead the apparent references to sayings of Jesus are incorporated among James' exhortations. Furthermore, the resemblance of wording is too indistinct to demonstrate any direct literary dependence upon one of the gospels. This, of course, does not prove that James neither knew nor employed the gospels. Yet the terms "citation" or "quotation" are too strong to describe these parallels. James never quotes in exact phraseology a known tradition of Jesus nor does he validate his exhortations by citing the authority of Jesus. What then is the precise connection between James' exhortations and words of the Jesus-tradition? Four regularly cited answers are given: 1) The similarities and divergencies with Jesus' sayings can only be explained by a common Jewish background. 2) James was familiar with the teaching of Jesus through his personal recollections as the brother of Jesus. 3) James was familiar with the sayings of Jesus through the oral tradition preserved by the church. 4) The author was familiar with one of the Synoptic gospels or a pre-edition of the gospel and quoted it freely in his writing.

2.4 The Relationship of Matthew and Luke to James

Before describing how these various suggestions arose historically in the record of interpretation, we will raise the additional problem concerning which gospel tradition most resembles the exhortations of the Epistle of James. The usual preference is for Matthew and in particular the Sermon on the Mount. This premise has been repeated regularly so that Adamson in 1976 quotes Schmid from 1853.

> James not only agrees in numerous passages with Matthew's gospel, which appear to be but the echo of the discourses of Jesus ... but also with that great body of precepts which Matthew gives as a whole, the Sermon on the Mount, which in its whole spirit may be looked upon as the model of the Epistle of James.[67]

On the other hand, several scholars of the 19th century place James closer to the special material of Luke discerning in each Ebionite influence. As a prominent proponent of this view Weizsäcker states,

> Dem Verfasser liegt schon die ebionitische Umbildung des Einganges der Bergpredigt vor, wie er sich denn überhaupt in einer offenbaren Verwandtschaft der Gedanken mit den jenigen Theilen des Lukasevangeliums bewegt, welche wir auf eine ebionitische Quelle zurückzuführen berechtigt sind.[68]

Schenkel as well consistently assigns the closest parallels to Luke so that even Jas. 5:12 is considered closer to Lk. 6:37 than to Mt. 5:33-37.[69] Since Feine's research the Epistle of

---

[67]James A. Adamson, The Epistle of James, 21.
[68]Weizsäcker, Apostolische Zeitalter, 379.
[69]Daniel Schenkel, Das Christusbild der Apostel und der nachapostolischen Zeit, 117.

James has for the most part been separated from Ebionite thought,[70] yet such scholars as Moffatt and Streeter have still argued for a closer verbal proximity to the Lucan parallels. Streeter even posits the likelihood that "the author of James had read Q in the recension known to Luke."[71] A third group of interpreters contends that this epistle is an independent primitive source of the sayings of Jesus. Patry even calls James a fifth gospel although short and incomplete.[72] The possibility of another source for the sayings of Jesus has always intrigued scholars. The ending of Halson's article is typical:

> Could it be, then, that like the Synoptic writers ... the compiler of our Epistle drew some of his basic material from orally preserved "sayings of the Lord" -- sayings preserved for the instruction of the churches, and that we have here traditions written down in literary independence of the synoptic Gospels?[73]

Who is right in this debate? Is our author completely independent of the Synoptic traditions or can he be linked with the community of Luke or tied to the school of Matthew?

3.0 The History of Interpretation of the Relationship Between James and the Jesus-Tradition

A rehearsal of the main events in the history of interpretation provides the clearest means of elucidating the problems that have arisen in determining the relationship between the Epistle of James and the Synoptic traditions.

3.1 The dominant oldest tradition identifies the author of this epistle with James, the brother of Jesus, and maintains that James' personal memory is the source from which he draws various sayings spoken by Jesus. The problem here, of course, is the testimony within the gospels that Jesus' brothers did not believe in him during his lifetime (Mk. 3:21,31ff; Jn. 7:5) and, therefore, would not have followed him around the countryside listening to him preach and teach. This objection is tempered by the confusion in the history of interpretation over the exact relationship between Jesus and his brothers. Ever since Jerome the Catholic tradition has equated one of the disciples named James with James, the brother of Jesus.[74] It appears that Jerome was influenced by The Gospel of the

---

[70]Feine, Jakobusbrief, 69-70. Hans J. Schoeps, "Exkurs I: Die Stellung des Jacobusbriefes," Theologie und Geschichte des Judenchristentums, 343 still follows the interpretation of the Tübingen school as in F.C. Baur, Das Christentum und die christliche Kirche der ersten drei Jahrhunderte (Tübingen: Mohr, 1860), 123 that James is "ebionitische." Schoeps, however, emphasizes the antignostic quality of the Epistle of James.

[71]Burnett H. Streeter, The Primitive Church: Studied with Special Reference to the Origins of the Christian Ministry, 193.

[72]Patry, Jacques, 112. For a similar evaluation see R.S.T. Haslehurst, "The Fifth Gospel," Th 35(1937): 102-103.

[73]B.R. Halson, "The Epistle of James: 'Christian Wisdom?'" SE 4:314.

[74]The exact nature of the relationship between James of Jerusalem and Jesus has divided scholars throughout the history of interpretation. The Epiphanian theory (from Epiphanius, bishop of Salamis, died 403) states that James was an elder half brother of Jesus from Joseph's first marriage. Thus the virginity of Mary was safeguarded. The Helvidian theory (from Helvidius, died 384) contends that all Jesus' brothers and sisters were children of Joseph and Mary, hence all younger than Jesus. The Hieronymian theory (from Jerome, died 420) refuted the position of Helvidius by holding that Jesus' brethren were really his cousins, the offspring of Clopas and Mary, the sister of the mother of Jesus. Cf. D. Edmond Hiebert, The Epistle of James, 30-34. The second view is rightly accepted by most modern scholars since the brothers of Jesus appear with their mother in the gospels (Mk. 3:21,31) and because of the late date of Jude.

Hebrews which portrays the brother of Jesus as participating in the last supper during which he swears to abstain from all nourishment until he sees the resurrected Jesus.[75] After Jesus appears to him (as in 1 Cor. 15:7), he becomes the most important witness of the resurrection. Thus we encounter in the early traditions a confusion between James of Jerusalem, the brother of Jesus, and James the apostle, the son of Alphaeus. This confusion of identity may have helped to create the dominant tradition that personal memory is the source of the Jesus-sayings in the Epistle of James. The popularity of this opinion has continued beyond the rise of the critical period in Biblical scholarship. This is especially true in the evangelicalism of the English-speaking world. Mayor, for instance, believes that our author "grew up under his Brother's influence, and that his mind was deeply imbued with his Brother's teaching."[76] Knowling likewise finds in the Epistle of James "references of such a kind as might have come from the fullness of a faithful memory, a memory retentive not merely of oral tradition but of words actually heard from the lips of Jesus."[77] The Dutch Reformed tradition as represented by Grosheide also fits here: "Jakobus moet kennis gedragen hebben van de woorden van Jezus, geen wonder hij had ze zelf zoo vaak gehoord."[78] This emphasis has thrived to the present day as will become apparent in the final section of this rehearsal of the main points of the history of interpretation.

3.2 In the 19th century a lively discussion of the problems of the Epistle of James took place within German scholarly periodicals.[79] In this series of discussions Brückner offered a quite radical solution, positing the dependence of the sayings in James upon the Gospel of Matthew itself. He states, "So ist es auch leichter in allen stellen, an die hier gedacht werden kann, die unmittelbare Abhängigkeit vom Matthäus evangelium vorauszusetzen."[80] Since Brückner also accepted a dependence of James upon Romans, Hebrews, and Revelation, he became a prominent proponent of assigning a late date to the Epistle of James. With the assumption of a late date a relationship with the written Synoptic gospels was, of course, easier to accept.[81]

3.3 Although many detailed source theories were being spun by the authors of this period, even these source critics separated themselves from Brückner's conclusion of dependence upon the Gospel of Matthew. Instead they looked to the oral tradition as can be seen in Huther's model argument:

> es läßt sich sogar nicht nachweisen, daß der Briefsteller jenes Schriftstück selbst gekannt habe: nicht nur finden sich in jedem der beiden Schriftstücke manche Beziehungen, die dem andern fremd sind, sondern auch, wo jene zusammentreffen, ist bei gleichem Gedanken der Ausdruck doch meistens verschieden. Die Ver-

---

[75]For more detailed information over Jerome's opinions see Dibelius and Greeven, James, 12-13, n. 29-30.

[76]Mayor, James, xlv.

[77]Richard J. Knowling, The Epistle of St. James, xxi.

[78]Grosheide, Jakobus, 342.

[79]From its first issue the Zeitschrift für wissenschaftliche Theologie wrestled with these issues: Adolf Hilgenfeld, "Das Urchristenthum und seine neuesten Bearbeitungen," ZWTh 1(1858): esp. 405ff; Eduard Zeller, "Ueber Jakobus 1,12," ZWTh 6(1863): 93-96; Wilibald Grimm, "Zur Einleitung in den Brief des Jacobus," ZWTh 13(1870): 377-394; Adolf Hilgenfeld, "Der Brief des Jakobus," ZWTh 16(1873): 1-33; Wilhelm Brückner, "Zur Kritik des Jakobusbriefes," ZWTh 17(1874): 530-541; Heinrich J. Holtzmann, "Die Zeitlage des Jakobusbriefes," ZWTh 25(1882): 292-310.

[80]Brückner, "Kritik Jakobusbriefes," 537.

[81]In the Netherlands Blom, Jacobus, 199 supported a knowledge of Matthew by the Epistle of James.

> wandtschaft besteht vielmehr darin, daß die ethisch-praktische Auffassung des Christenthums, wie sie in dem Briefe hervortritt, in völliger Uebereinstimmung mit den Gedanken steht, welche Christus in der Bergrede -- wie auch in anderen Reden -- ausgesprochen hat, und die sich -- ehe sie schriftlich verzeichnet wurden -- in ihrer ursprünglichen Ausdrucksform in der Gemeinde durch mündliche Tradition lebendig erhielten.[82]

This position quickly became the dominant position in German scholarship when it was accepted by such men as Beyschlag, Holtzmann, and Feine,[83] who criticized the findings of Brückner.

3.4 In 1896 Spitta provoked a landslide of literature and renewed interest in the problems of the Epistle of James when he proposed that this letter was not initially a Christian document at all. As was mentioned earlier, the Frenchman, Massebieau, and the German, Spitta, independently concluded that James was a Jewish document which was transformed into Christian literature by the addition of interpolations at Jas. 1:1 and 2:1.[84] In support of this theory they claimed that the grammatical problem of the Greek genitives in Jas. 2:1 could best be solved only by interpolation. Both also pointed to the lack of Christology in the letter in order to prove its compatability with preChristian Jewish writers. Spitta methodically discussed numerous parallels to the Synoptic gospels and everywhere offered other alternatives. Massebieau, on the other hand, argued more generally that if the author were a Christian, he would certainly have distinguished his own words from those of the gospel tradition. Although using a different approach, both concur that "an eine Abhängigkeit von dem Worte Jesu nicht zu denken sei."[85]

An immediate negative response to their conclusions was recorded in the scholarly literature throughout Europe. Already in 1896 Haupt argued that most of the parallels adduced by Spitta were completely arbitrary, having little or no significance, often either losing the original sense James had in mind or inserting conceptions which were completely strange to the nature of his letter. For Spitta's thesis to be proven acceptable, Haupt contended that one must show that all the contents of this letter could be grasped by a Jewish writer. Haupt credited Spitta with choosing the one book of all the NT writings that offered the best possibility for such a thesis. However, he then called attention to the similarities with the moral teaching of Jesus and emphasized the certain Christian references of Jas. 1:18,21; 2:7; 3:9 and 5:7-8 to discredit Spitta's hypothesis.[86] Other German scholars have agreed with Spitta's interpolation theory but denied his major conclusions. Hauck explains, "Das Christliche ist dabei keineswegs nur in zwei kurzen äußerlichen Erwähnungen (1,1: 2,1) dem Schreiben äußerlich angeklebt sondern es durchdringt das ganze Schreiben."[87] Dibelius specifically cites three such indisputable Christian passages:

> A. It is impossible to interpret 1:18 as a reference to mankind (as "first fruits") vis-à-vis creation ....
> B. A Jewish understanding of the passage in 2:7 is out of the question. The addressees are readers over whom the "honorable name" is invoked .... So the "honorable

---

[82]Johannus E. Huther, Kritisch exegetisches Handbuch über den Brief des Jakobus, 19.

[83]Willibald Beyschlag, "Der Jakobusbrief als urchristliches Geschichtsdenkmal," ThSKr 47(1874): 143; Holtzmann, Bibel-Lexikon III: 180; Feine, Jakobusbrief, 134.

[84]Spitta omits the words "and of the Lord Jesus Christ" in 1:1 while Massebieau omits only "Jesus Christ".

[85]Spitta, Zur Geschichte, II: 165. Cf. Massebieau, "Jacques," 256.

[86]Erich Haupt, "F. Spitta, Der Brief des Jakobus," ThSKr 69(1896): 767.

[87]Friedrich Hauck, Der Brief des Jakobus, 17.

name" cannot be a designation for Judaism at all, but must refer to a far more limited group which does not include the rich -- thus it must refer to the Christians.
C. In the second Excursus on 2:26, I attempt to show that the contrast "faith-works" which is presupposed and contested in 2:14ff is not conceivable prior to Paul ....[88]

In Switzerland Steck thanked Spitta for his enumeration of the widespread parallels between James and the Jewish literature but insisted that the letter is of Christian origin.[89] He argued that Spitta's parallels, even if accepted, do not prove that the author was a preChristian Jew but only that he knew certain Jewish writings. He contested Spitta's view that Paul polemicized against James, contending that such a thoroughly integrated teaching as Paul's instruction on righteousness could never be dependent on such an unsystematic, spiritually poor perception as James. In France a negative reaction was registered by Rose[90] in the very year in which Spitta's conclusions were published. A more thorough rebuttal, however, is found in Patry's dissertation where he emphasized the relationship between the teaching of James and Jesus, thus refuting the conclusions of Massebieau and Spitta without denying their emphasis on the Jewish background. In the Netherlands van Manen[91] had difficulty accepting Spitta's theory that a Christian interpolator would be satisfied to merely insert the name of Jesus Christ in two places. Certainly this would not make up for all the lack of references to the incarnation, atonement, suffering, death, and resurrection of Jesus or the fact that not Jesus but Abraham, Rahab, Job, and Elijah are models for ethical behavior. On the other hand, Toxopeus accepted Spitta's claim that Jas. 1:1 and 2:1 were interpolations but still insisted against Spitta that James was written by and for Christians.[92]

Off the continent in England Mayor published a completely new 1897 edition of his commentary to refute the findings of Spitta.[93] Spitta's conclusions also provoked Knowling to argue that "this theory of interpolation is so entirely arbitrary that it is severely criticized and condemned by critics who in many other respects differ widely from each other."[94] Cone argued that the eschatological terminology of Jas. 5:7-8 is decisively closer to Christian parallels than to the parallels from the book of Enoch emumerated by Spitta.[95] It was the important commentary of Ropes, however, which succinctly summarized the major arguments.

(1) The interpolation of the words referring to Christ in 1:1 is not suggested by anything in the sentence. In 2:1 the phrase is, indeed awkward, but is not intolerable.
(2) The passages of the epistle interpreted above as Christian are an integral part of the structure of the letter, and in the case of most of them Spitta's attempt to show that the language was equally possible for a Jew is unsuccessful. Note also the surely Christian reference to "the elders of the church" (5:14). Again, if the discussion of faith and works in 2:14-26 implies a polemic against Paul or Paulinists, that is conclusive for the Christian origin of the epistle; and the position of recognised primary significance assumed for faith in 1:3 and 2:5 is both characteristic of Christian thinking and unlikely for a non-christian Jewish writer.

---

[88]Dibelius and Greeven, James, 23.

[89]R. Steck, "Die Konfession des Jakobusbriefes," ThZS 5(1898): 188.

[90]Vincent P. Rose, "L'Épitre de Saint Jacques est-elle un ecrit chretién?" RB 5(1896): 534.

[91]W.C. van Manen, "Jacobus geen Christen?" ThT 31(1897): 424.

[92]Toxopeus, Jacobusbrief, 285, *Stelling* 1.

[93]In his 1897 edition Mayor adds Chapter VII entitled "Harnack and Spitta on the Date of the Epistle," cliv-clxxviii.

[94]Knowling, James, xv.

[95]Orello Cone, "James (Epistle)," Encyclopaedia Biblia II: 2325.

> (3) The epistle contains nothing whatever which positively marks it as distinctively Jewish. There is no sentence which a Jew could have written and a Christian could not; its Jewish ideas are without exception those that a Christian could hold.[96]

Even though the theories of Massebieau and Spitta have been resolutely rejected, derivations from their thinking have lived on in the history of interpretation. Von Soden presents a newly-minted postulation of partial Jewish authorship. He believes that Jas. 3:1-18 and 4:11-5:6 indicate no sort of accord with Christian writings but are complete discourses in themselves. Assuming that these two sections betray a different mood from the rest of the epistle in time, language, and manner of apprehending things, von Soden conjectures that the former section is an essay by an Alexandrian scribe while the latter constitutes a fragment from a Jewish apocalypse. As evidence he points out that of the forty words in James foreign to the NT only six fall outside these two sections.[97]

It is interesting that especially Jewish interpreters have leaned in the direction of Spitta's theories. Looking for parallels in contemporary Jewish writings, Köhler argues that no valid reasons can be given for holding that "the brethren" addressed in the Epistle of James may not have been Jews of a particular frame of mind, such as the Essenes, who formed a strong brotherhood in the Diaspora. Specifically concerning Jas. 5 he retorts, "To ascribe these instructions to a believer in Jesus as the Savior and Hearer of men is absolutely without foundation."[98] Schoeps, another Jew, also concludes that there is "keinen besonderen christlichen Lehrertrag"[99] in the Epistle of James. He does not rule out the possibility that it is merely a Jewish document but prefers to classify it as a document in the antignostic camp of the early Catholic church during the first half of the second century.

Finally, Meyer has revised Spitta's hypothesis, positing that James is really an allegory on Gen. 49. Just as Jacob addressed his twelve sons, so James (the Greek form of the name Jacob) addresses the twelve tribes who are now dispersed. Meyer accounts for the apparent disorder of ethical injunctions by insisting that this epistle consists of twelve exhortations each based on the name of one of the twelve patriarchs. He finds references to Simeon in 1:19-24 (hearing and not being angry based on Gen. 49:5-7), Levi in 1:26-27 (Levitical purity), Judah in 2:5-8 (the royal tribe), and Dan in 2:12-13 and 3:1 (Dan means judge). Meyer especially probes the intertestamental book, The Testaments of the Twelve Patriarchs, finding countless hidden references in the Epistle of James. With regard to James' relationship to the sayings of the Jesus-tradition, he naturally minimizes any significance given to them.

> Es liegt also kein Grund vor, Jac von den Evangelien abhängen zu lassen und zeitlich später zu setzen. Ja, die Selbständigkeit von Jac 5,12; 3,12; 4,3 läßt uns annehmen, daß Jac. entweder vor unsern Evangelien oder so entfernt von ihnen schrieb oder so selbständig nach Tradition und Anschauung war, daß keine Kenntnis ihres Wortlautes ihn beeinflußte.[100]

---

[96]James H. Ropes, Epistle of St. James, 32-33.

[97]Von Soden, Jakobus, 173. ῥυπαρια and ἔμφυτος in 1:21 and χρυσοδακτύλιος, προσωπολήμπτες, ἀνέλεος, and ἐφήμεπος in ch. 2.

[98]Kaufmann Köhler, "James, General Epistle of," A Jewish Encyclopedia, 1925 ed., VII: 69.

[99]Schoeps, Theologie des Judenchristentums, 344. He finds gnostic catchwords in 1:18,25; 2:20. Other allusions to gnostic tendencies have been detected in the antithesis between true and false wisdom (3:13-18) as well as in the terms φυχική (3:15) and τελείος (1:4,17,25; 3:2). But as Robinson, Redating, 123 points out, "None of these need imply anything more than can be found in the Jewish wisdom literature or in Philo or, for example, in 1 Cor. 2:12-14; 15:44-46."

[100]Meyer, Rätsel, 86.

Meyer's hypothesis has met with some approval,[101] yet the majority of writers have quietly dismissed his conclusions. Shepherd articulates well the majority opinion when he writes, "But his theory of a Jewish *Urschrift* on the Patriarch Jacob, as a basis for the Epistle of James, is fantastic."[102]

3.5 After the epoch-making preChristian hypothesis of Massebieau and Spitta, the next momentous event in the history of research is the commentary by Dibelius in 1921. He was in agreement with the dominant German tradition that the oral transmission of the sayings of Jesus by the church was the key to understanding the similarities and differences between the dominical sayings and the instruction of James. His additional contribution concerned the role of the genre of paraenesis in explaining certain peculiarities in the Epistle of James. For Dibelius the particular genre explained the lack of continuity and structure in the book (p. 5), the pervasive eclecticism of various sources by the author (p. 2), the repetition of identical motifs in different places within the writing (p. 11), the combination of Jewish and Hellenistic material (p. 26), the lack of explicit quotation formulas (p. 29), the relationship to 1 Peter (p. 30), Hermas, 1 Clement, and Hebrews (p. 32), the lack of Christology and specific Christian references (p. 46), our inability to determine the geographical localization of James (p. 47), its late and gradual dissemination into the canon (p. 53), and finally also the problem we are chiefly concerned with, the relationship between the Synoptic traditions and the Epistle of James (p. 17). On this subject Dibelius states,

> For this relationship is not due primarily to characteristics shared exclusively by the Letter of James and the sayings of Jesus, but rather it corresponds to the fact that they belong to a common literary genre: our text and the collections of sayings in the Gospels both belong to the genre of paraenesis.[103]

Dibelius' conclusion about genre has won large support. Windisch, for example, soon followed Dibelius' suggestion: "Der Autor ist ein Sammler von Schriftlich und mündlich überlieferter Paränese."[104] On the other hand, many have disagreed with the implications which Dibelius drew from his supposition of genre. In reviewing the book Kittel strongly objects to Dibelius' contention that the genre of paraenesis is the reason the Epistle of James lacks a concrete historical background, has various verses and pericopes with no connection of content, and alludes to sayings from the Jesus-tradition without any introductory formulations.[105] Likewise Hauck refuses to explain all the references to the words of Jesus merely as similarities of genre; he does not want to eliminate James' personal choice and individual contribution:

> Daß es sich bei Jac vielfach nur um Anklänge, nicht um ausdrückliche Zitate handelt, entspricht einesteils, wie Dib richtig beobachtet hat, der Art paränetischer Literatur, es zeigt aber andrerseits, daß Jac dem uberlieferten Spruchgut frei gestaltend gegenübersteht. Sein eigenes geistiges Schaffen ist hier zu beobachten.[106]

---

[101]Burton S. Easton, "The Epistle of James," The Interpreter's Bible, XII: 12; Marxsen, Introduction to NT, 231.

[102]Shepherd, "James and Matthew," 40, n. 2.

[103]Dibelius and Greeven, James, 17.

[104]Hans Windisch, Die katholischen Briefe, 4. For further support see below in ch. 5, section 3.5.

[105]Gerhard Kittel, "Der Brief des Jakobus," ThLBl 44(1923): 3-7. Cf. Kittel, "Der geschichtliche Ort," 71.

[106]Hauck, Jakobus, 10. Cf. also pp. 21-22 for further warnings about inferring too many implications from Dibelius' conclusions.

Stronger disagreement has issued forth from more conservative scholars. In the Dutch Reformed tradition Grosheide questions how paraenesis could explain why James, out of all the possibilities of exhortation, would choose those which he remembered from Jesus.

> Deze reeks van overeenstemmende plaatsen is te groot, dan dat er niet een bijzondere reden voor zou zijn. Die reden kan moeilijk wezen, dat zoowel de woorden van Jezus als die van Jakobus tot de paraenese behooren, want dan blijft onverklaard, waarom Jakobus uit de vele vermaningen, die er te geven waren, juist zulke keist, die tot in de woorden toe aan die van Jezus herinneren en m.n. aan die uit de Bergrede.[107]

These divergent reactions to Dibelius' proposal of genre betray the different conclusions reached by authors on the question of the relationship between the Epistle of James and the sayings of the Jesus-tradition.

3.6 Kittel became a major voice in this discussion in 1941 when he published an article with the thesis "daß der Jakobusbrief die älteste uns erhaltene christliche Schrift ist; daß er seiner Platz innerhalb der palästinischen Urgemeinde, und zwar bei dem Herrnbruder Jakobus had."[108] Kittel coupled his view of an early date in Palestine with a particular explanation concerning our problem of the relationship between the sayings of Jesus and the ethical exhortations of James. He postulated that the peculiar form in which the sayings of Jesus are transmitted in James (without introduction and simply as reminiscences) betrays a first stage in the process of transmission. By examining the transmission of the sayings of Jesus in James, Paul, and the Apostolic Fathers, Kittel discovers a process which begins with the passing on of living words from a living person applied freely to various situations in the early church, which then passes through a second stage where Jesus' words are specifically quoted as an authoritative reference to a person in the past, and which concludes in a final stage where the sayings of Jesus are referred to as scripture with a fixed wording.[109] James is then a representative of the first stage where the words of Jesus occur without ackowledgement or direct citation.[110] It is therefore not the genre of paraenesis which explains the similarities and divergencies from the sayings of Jesus in the Synoptic tradition as Dibelius had maintained.

Strong opposition has arisen against Kittel's perceptions. Already in 1944 Aland endeavored, as he says, to understand Kittel and Dibelius together.[111] Finding that task impossible, he rejects Kittel's findings, arguing that 1) the Apostolic Fathers' references to the sayings of Jesus are not Scripture citations, as Kittel insisted, but Lord-citations[112] which do not equate Jesus' words with the authority of the OT; 2) there is also a large number of reminiscences (which Kittel assigned to the early stages) in the Apostolic Fathers;[113] and therefore 3) the Epistle of James could just as easily have originated during the time of the Apostolic Fathers and need not be the earliest Christian document as Kittel had proposed.[114] After investigating the evidence Davies concurred in the dismissal of Kittel's thesis, stating that "the attempt to distinguish distinct stages in the use of the sayings of

---

[107]Grosheide, Jakobus, 342.

[108]Kittel, "Der geschichtliche Ort," 71.

[109]Cf. ch. 5, sections 2.1-2.2.

[110]Kittel, "Der geschichtliche Ort," 94.

[111]Kurt Aland, "Der Herrenbruder Jakobus und der Jakobusbrief," ThLZ 69(1944): 97.

[112]1 Cl. 13:2; 46:8; Did. 1:3f; Pol. Phil. 2:3; Herm. Sim. 3,1,1-3.

[113]Did., 48 times; Barn., 19; 1 Cl., 14; Herm., 52; 2 Cl., 30; Ig., 32; Pol. Phil., 17.

[114]Aland, "Herrenbruder Jakobus," 104. See also Wolfgang Schrage, "Der Jakobusbrief," in Horst Balz und Wolfgang Schrage, Die katholischen Briefe, 11.

Jesus ... must be regarded as questionable."[115] Noticing that it is precisely within paraenetic sections that reminiscenses and allusions (rather than direct citations) are encountered, Lohse proposed the alternative solution that the genre and not the date of the writing explains the particular form of transmission used by the author.[116]

3.7 Recently the history of interpretation has witnessed a renewal of the thesis that James availed himself of the Gospel of Matthew in transmitting the sayings of the Jesus-tradition. Already in 1937 Goodspeed had considered the possibility,[117] but the arguments of Shepherd in 1956 provided the driving force for the reconsideration of this theory. The new twist added by Shepherd was the supposition that James was acquainted with the Gospel of Matthew only from hearing it read during worship services.

> It would be absurd to maintain that the author of the Epistle had a written copy of the Gospel of Matthew in front of him when he put together his discourses. The lack of precise quotation indicates this much. But his familiarity with the Gospel was far greater than a vague reminiscence. We suspect that the Gospel of Matthew was known to him from hearing it read in his Church.[118]

Shepherd believes that like the letters of Ignatius of Antioch and the Didache, the Epistle of James indicates a special relationship to the Gospel of Matthew.[119] From these connections he argues for a place of origin in greater Syria ("inclusive of Phoenicia and even Palestine -- not in the narrower limits of Antioch and its environs") and a date just after the composition of Matthew's gospel. Five years after the appearance of Shepherd's proposal, Gryglewicz also posited a dependence upon Matthew, but this time upon a written Greek version of Matthew which had already existed in a Hebraic form around the year 50.[120] In the common occurrence of certain phrases and concepts Gryglwicz perceives a literary dependence:

Jas.	1:5f = Mt. 7:1; 21:21-23	(ἐν πίστει)
	1:22 = Mt. 7:24	(ποιητὴς λόγου)
	3:10 = Mt. 15:18f	(ἐξέρχεσθαι, στόμα)
	3:12 = Mt. 7:15f	(σῦκα)
	4:10 = Mt. 18:3f; 23:12	(humiliation, exaltation)
	5:2f = Mt. 6:19f	(θησαυρίζειν, σής, βρῶσις)
	5:12 = Mt. 5:34-36	(on swearing oaths)
	5:15 = Mt. 12:31f	(ἀφεθήσεται αὐτῷ)[121]

As with Brückner in the 19th century, the thesis of Shepherd and Gryglewicz has encountered stiff opposition. Mußner exemplifies the attitude of most commentators when he states,

> Eine kenntnis des Mt-Ev durch Jak, wie sie SHEPHERD und GRYGLEWICZ annehmen, kann nicht nachgewiesen werden, vielmehr nur gemeinsames Traditions-

---

[115]Davies, Setting, 404.

[116]Lohse, "Glaube und Werke," 9-13. He calls attention to Rom. 12 and 13 and 1 Thess. 5.

[117]Edgar J. Goodspeed, An Introduction to the New Testament, 291. Cf. also Robert M. Cooper, "Prayer: a Study in Matthew and James," Encounter 29(1968): 270.

[118]Shepherd, "James and Matthew," 47.

[119]Ibid., 49. For our evaluation of Shepherd's conclusions see ch. 4, section 1.2.

[120]Feliks Gryglewicz, "L'Épitre de St. Jacques et l'Évangile de St. Matthieu," RTK 8,3(1961): 55.

[121]Ibid., 43-56. For our critique see ch. 4, section 2.3.

> gut. Es gilt hier dasselbe wie für die Didache, in der auch eine ev. tradition verarbeitet ist, dieser des Mt verwandt, aber nicht mit ihr identisch ist.[122]

Mußner continues in the established German tradition explaining the correspondence and variance of James with the Synoptic gospels through the oral transmission of the sayings of Jesus by the church.

3.8 Throughout this unstable history of interpretation the thesis that James, the brother of Jesus, drew from his personal memory various sayings from the teaching of Jesus has continually surfaced. Recently in the English-speaking world it has received extensive support in the commentaries. In 1954 Ross, following the lead of Robertson, almost romantically exclaims,

> We can in fact scarcely resist the conclusion that we are listening to the reproduction of the thoughts from a mind that had lived and laboured for years alongside the Master-mind which created and gave them perfect utterance. They drop out freely and spontaneously, as from a mind that had so absorbed them that they had become part and parcel of its very self. Had James not listened to Jesus' talk, as they wrought side by side, at the bench in Nazareth, and half-unconsciously, half-reluctantly, all his thinking had become moulded by it.[123]

The same explanation is offered by Adamson when in 1976 he writes,

> We ourselves believe that this is at least mainly due not merely to James's early sharing some of the oral and written evidence to which those Gospels sooner or later were indebted, but to his own personal witness of the life and teaching of Jesus.[124]

This position is being passed on to the future generation through the use of Guthrie's NT introduction in many evangelical English-speaking seminaries.[125] Numerous examples could be added to argue that this is the dominant position in the English-speaking world today, even though the NT record (Mk. 3:21,31ff; Jn. 7:5) clearly teaches that Jesus' brothers did not believe in him during his lifetime.

3.9 If we were to catalogue systematically the various options given to solve the relationship between the exhortations of James and the *logia* of Jesus, we could enumerate these five solutions:[126]

1) Dependence upon various Jewish writings and traditions. The similarities to the sayings of Jesus are accounted for by a common environment of thought and background of tradition.
Support: Massebieau (1895), Spitta (1896), von Soden -- partial agreement (1899), Köhler (1925), Meyer (1930), Hartmann (1942), Thyen (1955), Easton (1957), Marxsen (1963).

---

[122]Mußner, Jakobusbrief, 51.

[123]J.A. Robertson, Hidden Romance of the New Testament quoted in Ross, James and John, 17.

[124]Adamson, James, 21.

[125]Guthrie, NT Introduction, 743.

[126]This synopsis is an elaboration of the alternatives mentioned on page 14. Here we have subdivided the oral tradition possibility into transmission by the church and transmission by community paraenesis based upon the conclusions of Dibelius.

2) Dependence upon the Gospel of Matthew. Here the disparity is accounted for by an oral hearing of the gospel at worship services (Shepherd) or by an interweaving of these sayings into the epistle to further James' particular literary purposes.
Support: Blom (1869), Brückner (1874), Grafe (1904), Goodspeed -- a possibility (1937), Shepherd (1956), Gryglwicz (1961), Cooper (1968). The possibility of dependence is postulated by most writers who accept a second century dating for James.[127]

3) Dependence upon James' personal memory of the oral teachings of Jesus. The divergencies are accounted for by differing personal recollections between James and the Synoptic writers or James' particular style.
Support: Schmid (1853), Mayor (1892), Patry (1899), Knowling (1904), Grosheide (1927), Ross (1954), Guthrie (1962), Kistemaker (1972), Adamson (1974).

4) Dependence upon the oral transmission of the sayings of Jesus in the churches. The reason for dissonance is the existence of separate communities of Christians who transmitted the sayings in slightly different forms or the positing of particular stages of transmission where constancy of form and the presence of introductory formulas were modified (Kittel).
Support: Huther (1865), Holtzmann (1871), Beyschlag (1874), Feine (1893), Kittel (1942), McNeile (1953), Eleder (1964), Williams (1965), Davies (1966), Mußner (1967), Laws (1980).

5) Dependence upon the genre of paraenesis, the passing on of traditional material from various authorities (thus similarities) within the vocabulary and purposes of the individual author (thus differences).
Support: Dibelius (1921), Windisch (1930), Aland (1944), Lohse (1957), Schrage (1973).

4.0 It is interesting to note that the interpretation of the relationship between James and the Synoptic tradition has been substantially affected by the changing climate of gospel criticism, from source and literary criticism, through form criticism, to the emphasis upon redaction criticism. At the high tide of source criticism there was a great search for the literary connections between James and other writings. Detailed studies were undertaken on the relationship between James and 1 Peter, the Shepherd of Hermas, and 1 Clement. Brückner even posited a direct relationship to the Gospel of Matthew. With the rise of form criticism the emphasis switched from literary sources to the oral traditions at work before the gospels were written. Therefore literary relationships were minimized. As Dibelius explains,

> In a paraenetic text, which to a large extent hands down tradition, it is difficult to prove with certainty any dependence upon other writers. For no literary conclusions at all can be drawn from many of the parallels ....[128]

Instead the writings, including James, were seen to derive from a conglomeration of traditions in which the author's individuality consisted only in his selection and arrangement of traditional material. As the gospel writers were "scissors and paste" men, so James was a transmitter of community paraenesis; his own role in the process was therefore minimized. Dibelius even contends that James had no theology,[129] that he "is not a thinker, a prophet, or an intellectual leader, but rather a pedagogue, one among many, who appropriates and distributes from the property common to all."[130] The emphasis of the form critic did not fall

---

[127]Cf. Toxopeus' list, Jacobusbrief, 59-61.
[128]Dibelius and Greeven, James, 26.
[129]Ibid., 21.
[130]Ibid., 25.

upon the author's purpose in presenting the material to a certain audience but rather upon a whole series of audiences and sets of circumstances from the tradition. Therefore Dibelius can say, "The admonitions in James do not apply to a single audience and a single set of circumstances; it is not possible to construct a single frame into which they will fit."[131]

With the rise of redaction criticism again the tide changed in scholarship dealing with the Epistle of James. The role of the author has again come to the forefront. It is now contended that James presents his own legitimate theology which can be investigated and compared with other NT theologies, as that of Matthew, for instance. Such research might even lead to certain discoveries about basic background information to this epistle. Therefore it is not the tradition, but James himself, tied historically to his religious community, who has chosen what material to include from the Jesus-tradition. In a tide-swinging article defending redaction criticism applied to James, Soucek explains "daß der Jakobusbrief gewiße eigene zusammenhängende innere Linien aufweist, daß er nicht bloß eine ganz lose Auslese paränetischer Stücke darstellt."[132] Thus in our day we are seeing an increasing number of books and articles aimed at the various emphases of James' theology.[133]

5.0 The purpose of this introductory chapter was to acquaint the reader with the problems involved in a discussion of the relation between the Epistle of James and the Synoptic tradition. From our review of the highpoints of the history of interpretation two sets of problems emerge: 1) those connected with the background questions of James, i.e. problems of authorship, date, origin, readers, etc. and 2) those associated with the transmission of the sayings of Jesus. With regard to the first set of problems we need to ask the question: What further information about the date and place of origin can be gleaned from a discussion about the relationship of the Epistle of James to the Synoptic gospels? Could we, for instance, substantiate the presence of a similar community of origin between James and Matthew by establishing an interconnection between their theologies? With the second set of problems involving the transmission of the sayings of Jesus we need to likewise ask: Did James consciously cite this Jesus-tradition, and if so, how many allusions to these sayings do we encounter? Is there one tradition of transmission (Matthew, Luke, Q) that is noticeably closer to the wording of James, or do the Jamesian allusions form a completely independent testimony alongside the Synoptic gospels? In addition, what accounts for the particular similarities and differences with these Synoptic traditions? Is it the application of a written tradition (gospel) to a specific situation, the personal memory of the author, the development of divergent oral traditions of transmission, or the use of a common genre of literature (paraenesis, for example)? Finally, we must inquire whether the sayings in the Epistle of James support the hypothesis that stages of transmission have developed in the passing on of the sayings of Jesus.

In order to investigate these questions in a systematic format, we will first take up (in chapters 2 and 3) the issue of preexistent material in the Epistle of James. In chapter 2 we will survey how and in what form James has incorporated known preexistent material from the OT and intertestamental literature. We will investigate whether the author quotes preexistent material in a verbatim manner or by merely offering allusions and freely-composed recollections of the tradition. Having answered this question, we can then in chapter 3 compare these conclusions with James' manner of transmitting the material from the Synoptic traditions to determine whether he employs source material in a consistent manner. Chapter 3 will consist of a descriptive analysis of the various parallels

---

[131]Ibid., 11.

[132]Josef B. Soucek, "Zu den Problemen das Jakobusbriefes," EvTh 18(1958): 463.

[133]Georg Braumann, "Der theologische Hintergrund des Jakobusbriefes," ThZ 18(1962): 401-410; Rudolf Hoppe, Der theologische Hintergrund des Jakobusbriefes.

between the sayings of the Jesus-tradition and the Epistle of James. It is unnecessary to examine each reference since in many cases we are only talking about minor similarities of content or wording. Yet it is important to analyze sufficient cases to be able to arrive at valid well-evidenced conclusions. Therefore, we have elected to discuss those parallels that are listed by at least one-third of the 60 authors whose research has been documented in Appendix I. This will mean the investigation of twenty parallels between the Epistle of James and the Synoptic gospels.[134]

In chapter 4 we will turn from discussing the presence of sayings from the Jesus-tradition to their specific relationship to the documents of Matthew, Luke, and Q along with the possible communities behind these documents. We will ask the question whether the sayings in James are connected with one of the communities that produced these documents or whether an independent tradition alongside the gospels is evident.

In chapter 5 we will scan one particular problem connected with the transmission of these sayings. Is the explanation for the divergencies of form and the lack of introductory formulas found in the positing of different stages in the transmission process, or does the common genre of paraenesis explain these changes? First we will investigate Kittel's hypothesis of three progressive stages of development. Here it will be important to compare the transmission of the sayings of the Jesus-tradition in James, Paul, and the Apostolic Fathers to determine whether the history of transmission is 1) fixed; 2) fluid; or 3) in stages. Then we will turn to Dibelius' solution of the genre of paraenesis. Here the question of the genre of James (epistle, homily, diatribe, wisdom literature, paraenesis) will be tackled followed by a closer examination of the manner in which sayings are passed on in paraenetic literature and its implications for the Epistle of James.

In chapter 6 we will explore whether the results of our study facilitate the resolving of certain long-lasting problems in the interpretation of the Epistle of James, including the lack of Christology, the problem of Jewish or Hellenistic background, the place of origin, the date, and finally authorship. Thus in our discussion there will be a movement from the sayings of the Jesus-tradition in James, to the transmission of the sayings in general, and finally, to the problems of background associated with the Epistle of James. A short chapter surveying our conclusions (chapter 7) will bring this dissertation to its climax.

---

[134]Parallels listed by at least one-tenth of the authors are included in Appendix I.

Chapter 2

THE MANNER IN WHICH JAMES EMPLOYS PREEXISTENT MATERIAL

1.0 In order to discern whether James utilizes sayings from the Jesus-tradition, it is important first to establish how preexistent material can be detected. The most obvious indication is the positioning of an introductory formulation prior to a group of words closely or exactly resembling those in some other body of literature. Six such *formulae citandi* appear in the Epistle of James, either introduced with a form of the word γραφή (2:8,23; 4:5) or a verb of saying (ὁ εἰπών 2:11; εἶπεν καί 2:11; διὸ λέγει 4:6) with the implied subject being either God or scripture.

Other less obvious introductory formulas can also be discerned in the Epistle of James. The conjunction ὅτι receives basically three functions in NT Greek: 1) the explicative ὅτι; 2) the recitative ὅτι; and 3) the causative ὅτι.[1] The recitative ὅτι introduces direct discourse and "serves the function of our quotation marks"[2] with regard to preexistent sayings. However, with verbs of mental perception (esp. γινώσκω and οἶδα) the explicative ὅτι can also refer to already known preexistent material.[3] Familiar ethical instruction from the church's teaching tradition is alluded to in this manner through such common phrases as οὐκ οἴδατε ὅτι,[4] οἴδαμεν ὅτι,[5] and γινώσκοντες ὅτι.[6] These phrases occur five times in the Epistle of James introducing popular religious wisdom sayings known to the early church.[7]

1:3 (γινώσκοντες ὅτι) "The testing of faith works endurance."
3:1 (εἰδότες ὅτι) "The teacher will be judged with greater strictness."
4:4 (οὐκ οἴδατε ὅτι) "Friendship with the world is enmity with God."
5:11 (εἴδετε, ὅτι) "The Lord is compassionate and merciful."[8]

---

[1]Cf. BAGD, s.v. ὅτι, 588-589.

[2]BDF 470.

[3]In Pol. Phil. the phrase εἰδότες ὅτι has become a standard means to refer to Paul's letters: 1:3; 4:1; 5:1; 6:1; 11:2 (in Latin), and 9:2 with πεπεισμένους ὅτι. In 1 Peter a form of γραφή with ὅτι is used in 1:16 and 2:6 and ὅτι or διότι by itself in 1:16, 24; 2:3; 3:9 ?; 4:8,14; 5:5 to introduce an OT quote in a recitative manner. Likewise, ὅτι is employed to allude to apocryphal material (5:7=Wis. 12:13), hymns (1:18; 2:21; 3:18 -- all indented in Nestle-Aland 26), and a group of sayings connected with times of trial and persecution (4:16,17; 5:9 in p[72]; 2:15 which is paraphrased by Peter without ὅτι in 2:20; 3:6,17; 4:19 using in each case a form of the word ἀγαθοποίεω).

[4]Rom. 6:16; 1 Cor. 3:16; 5:6; 6:2,3,9,15,16,19; 9:13,24.

[5]Rom. 2:2; 3:19; 7:14; 8:22,28; 1 Cor. 8:4; 2 Cor. 5:1; 1 Tim. 1:8; 1 Jn. 3:2; 5:18; οἴδατε ὅτι in 1 Thess. 5:2; 1 Jn. 3:5, 15. Bruce M. Metzger, A Textual Commentary on the Greek New Testament, 514 confirms our conclusion when he states, "The plural οἴδαμεν is a typical expression which the apostle uses when he refers to a commonly acknowledged truth."

[6]Rom. 6:6; 2 Pet. 1:20; 3:3; cf. Rom. 7:1.

[7]Twice a probable saying is referred to without attaching the ὅτι to οἶδα: 1:19; 4:17.

[8]Even though the verb εἴδετε fits grammatically with the preceding phrase "the purpose of the Lord", with regard to content the addition that "He is compassionate and merciful" is a thematic equivalent to this phrase.

5:20 (γινωσκέτω ὅτι) "Whoever brings back a sinner covers a multitude of sins."[9]

When ὅτι is used alone, it is more doubtful that James is employing preexistent material,[10] although the use of γνῶναι with ὅτι in 2:20 probably indicates that "faith without works is useless" was a well-known proverbial saying in the early church as evidenced by the similar expressions with ὅτι in 2:22,24. In two instances ὅτι is used to preface hypothetical sayings which James places in the mouth of a straw man whom he afterwards contradicts: 1:13 "I am tempted by God" and 2:19 "God is one".

We cannot speak as confidently about allusions to preexistent material without any introductory formulation since the detection of such source material is always somewhat biased and more in the realm of probability than conclusive reality. Yet we can offer a few suggestive comments for identifying preexistent material. Frequently James employs catchwords to weave source material into his writing. Two sentences are tied together not by a sequence of logical thought but by the presence of similar vocabulary.[11] Either before or after the allusion to preexistent material the author repeats one or more of the words of this particular saying and thus stitches or attaches the saying to the new context.[12] By using this technique we can detect the presence of preexistent material in Jas. 1:3 (ὑπομονήν / ὑπομονὴ) 5 (λειπόμενοι / λείπεται), 6 (αἰτείτω / αἰτείτω; διακρινόμενος / διακρινόμενος), 12 (πειρασμόν / πειραζόμενος), 13b (πειράζομαι / πειράζει), 20 (ὀργήν / ὀργὴ); 2:13 (κρίνεσθαι / κρίσις / κρίσεως); 3:2a (πταίομεν / πταίει), 5b (πῦρ / πῦρ), 18 (εἰρηνική / εἰρηνη; καρπῶν / καρπὸς); 4:10 (ταπεινοῖς / ταπεινώθητε), and 12a (νόμου / νομοθέτης ; κριτὴς / κριτὴς).[13] Secondly, wisdom sayings are commonly prefaced with the term "blessed". Therefore, it is possible that the μακάριος sayings of 1:12,25; 5:11 are derived from preexistent wisdom traditions.[14] Furthermore, often embedded in a rhetorical question is a popular slogan or well-known piece of wisdom;[15] James is probably reminding his readers of these familiar truths in 2:5; 3:11,12; 4:1,4a. The presence of preexistent material is also disclosed when a saying fails to fit well into the new context to which it is inserted[16] as evidenced by the grammatical construction[17] or by the presence of divergent

---

[9]1 Pet. 4:8 and 1 Cl. 49:5 employ this saying with "love" as the subject.

[10]A causal usage is likely at 1:10,12,23; 5:8 (cf. NIV); the explicative use at 1:7; 4:5. Even the causal ὅτι can introduce an OT allusion in Jas. 1:10.

[11]The use of catchwords was also a technique for memorization. Cf. Vincent Taylor, The Gospel according to St. Mark, 408.

[12]Therefore it is possible to distinguish between catchwords and stitchwords. The stitchword is not within the quote itself but is used by the author to stitch the preexistent material into his own context. Catchwords are found in the quote itself, and often two quotes originally unconnected are placed one after the other, attached only formally by similar words. This is a common device in the Synoptic gospels, especially in the discourses of Matthew. Cf. Dibelius and Greeven, James, 7-11.

[13]Dibelius and Greeven, James, 7 detect additional connections between 1:26 and 27; 5:9 and 12; and 5:13ff, 16ff, and 19f. However, the connection between 1:26 and 27 is more than just a formal catchword; there is also a thematic contrast between vain religion and pure religion. The best explanation for the interconnection of material in Jas. 5:7-20 is not the use of catchwords but rather the grouping together of paraenetic material into a primitive Christian catechism. Cf. ch. 3, section 6.0.

[14]Shepherd, "James and Matthew," 42 believes that "most of James' discourses are built around, or contain, a central *macarism* or gnomic saying, adopted by the author to his particular theme."

[15]In a rhetorical question the writer assumes that his audience knows or should know the answer.

[16]Cf. Gryglewicx, "Jacques et Matthieu," 54.

[17]Possibly the dative εἰδότι in 4:17, the future tense in 5:3b, the referent to πρὸ πάντων in 5:12, and the singular ἀφεθήσεται in 5:15.

vocabulary and forms in the same context.[18] Finally, terminology which coincides with the vocabulary of a well-known source could reveal the presence of an allusion, especially if an identical thematic emphasis is present. As we now examine the Epistle of James, we will determine if these methods of detecting preexistent material are helpful in discovering what sources were employed in the writing of James' epistle.

2.0 Citations of the Old Testament as Scripture

First we will examine the six quotations[19] which begin with an introductory formula. Then in the next section we will turn to possible instances where James only alludes to the OT or merely utilizes similar terminology.

2.1

Jas. 2:8	Lev. 19:18b LXX	Lev. 19:18 MT
Εἰ μέντοι νόμον τελεῖτε		
βασιλικὸν κατὰ τὴν γραφήν·		
ἀγαπήσεις	καὶ ἀγαπήσεις	וְאָהַבְתָּ
τὸν πλησίον σου	τὸν πλησίον σου	לְרֵעֲךָ
ὡς σεαυτόν,	ὡς σεαυτόν·	כָּמוֹךָ
καλῶς ποιεῖτε·	ἐγώ εἰμι κύριος.	אֲנִי יְהוָה

A positive identification of Jas. 2:8 as a quote from the OT is based both on the presence of an introductory formulation and the exact representation of the LXX. The phrase κατὰ τὴν γραφήν is not a typical formula of introduction in the NT,[20] but is similar to the expression ἡ γραφὴ λέγει which is Paul's second most frequently used means of referring to the OT.[21] There is sufficient identical vocabulary to verify a quotation of the OT, although it is impossible to determine from this reference alone whether James regularly quoted from memory or followed either the LXX or MT.[22]

The love command as exemplified in Lev. 19:18 played an important role in both Judaism and Christianity. Hillel emphasized that love was the path of entrance to the Torah: "Hillel used to say: 'Be Thou of the disciples of Aaron, loving peace and pursuing peace; [Be Thou] one who loveth [one's fellow-] creatures and bringeth them nigh to the Torah'" (Aboth 1:12). Rabbi Akiba in Sifra Qedoshim to Lev. 19:18 labels the command to

---

[18]Possibly the switch from middle (αἰτεῖσθαι) to active (αἰτεῖτε) and back to middle again (αἰτεῖσθε) in 4:2-3 or the presence of δέησις in 5:16b when a form of εὔχομαι is used in both 5:16a and 5:17. However, these changes could be merely for the sake of variety.

[19]Most authors categorize Jas. 2:11a and b together and report the presence of five OT quotations in James (cf. Daniel S. Gotass, The Old Testament in the Epistle to the Hebrews, the Epistle of James, and the Epistle of Peter, 282; William O.E. Oesterley, "The General Epistle of James," The Expositor's Greek Testament, IV: 389; and Guthrie, NT Introduction, 741 who includes Jas. 1:11 while omitting Jas. 4:5). Because the introductory formula is slightly different, we distinguish six OT citations (cf. Richard Longenecker, Biblical Exegesis in the Apostolic Period, 196).

[20]This phrase is used in Dt. 10:4; 1 Chr. 15:5; 2 Chr. 30:5; 35:4; 1 Esd. 1:4; 2 Esd. 6:18 (LXX) and the similar wording κατὰ τὰς γραφάς in 1 Cor. 15:3-4 although not as an introductory formula to an OT citation.

[21]It is used on six occasions whereas "it is written" is employed 29 times. Cf. E. Earle Ellis, Paul's Use of the Old Testament, 22.

[22]At the end of this chapter we will offer a conclusion based upon the cumulative total of James' citations and allusions from the OT.

love one's neighbor a comprehensive rule of the Torah.[23] The commandment of love embedded in Lev. 19:18 was thus more than just one of the dictates of the law for many Jewish leaders.[24] Yet Lev. 19:18 was never specifically mentioned as a summary of the Torah in Judaism,[25] although the whole of Lev. 19 was perceived as a counterpart of the Decalogue.[26] The so-called silver rule, however, was proposed by Hillel as a summary to the law.

> On another occasion it happened that a certain heathen came before Shammai and said to him, "Make me a proselyte on condition that you teach me the whole Torah while I stand on one foot." Thereupon he repulsed him with the builder's cubit which was in his hand. When he went before Hillel, he said to him, "What is hateful to you, do not do your neighbor: that is the whole Torah, while the rest is the commentary thereof; go and learn it."[27]

Therefore love of God and love of neighbor[28] are combined in Jewish literature,[29] but only in Christian writings are Dt. 6:5 and Lev. 19:18 directly tied together and given comprehensive importance.[30] James does not directly combine Lev. 19:18 with Dt. 6:5 to summarize the law and prophets as Jesus had done before him (Mk. 12:31,33 par.). Yet it is clear that in NT times the single command to love one's neighbor (as exemplified in Lev. 19:18) was estimated to be of such importance that it began to summarize the whole law.[31]

---

[23]Cf. StrB I: 357-358 and Moshe Weissman, The Midrash Says, 3:261. For the Hebrew text see Louis Finkelstein, Sifra on Leviticus: Text of Sifra acc. to Vatican Manuscript Assemani 66 (New York: Jewish Theological Seminary, 1983).

[24]Most Jewish rabbis still make all the laws of equal value. Cf. F.E. Vokes, "The Ten Commandments in the New Testament and in First Century Judaism," SE 5:151.

[25]b. Berakoth 63a, ed. Epstein, 396-397, mentions Prov. 3:6 as a short text upon which all the essential principles of the Torah depend.

[26]Rabbi Hiyya in the third century AD taught, "This section was spoken in the presence of a gathering of the whole assembly because most of the essential principles of the Torah are attached to it." Lev. Rabbah 24:5 in Midrash Rabbah, IV: 307. Pieter van der Horst, The Sentences of Pseudo-Phocylides, 66 offers other examples including Ps.-Phoc. 9-41 which is conjectured to have been written between 30 BC and AD 40 (van der Horst, 86). Cf. also Klaus Berger, Die Gesetzesauslegung Jesu, 80-81.

[27]b. Shabboth 31a, ed. Epstein, 140.

[28]Neighbor in Jewish literature meant fellow Israelite. Cf. John Piper, Love Your Enemies: Jesus' Love Command in the Synoptic Gospels and in Early Christian Paraenesis, 30-31.

[29]Rabbi Meir calls the one who occupies himself with the study of the law for its own sake both a lover of God and a lover of people (Aboth 6:1). Jub. 20 says to "love each his neighbor" (v. 2) and to "love the God of heaven" (v. 7). Commands to love each other are found in Jub. 7:20; 36:4,8; 1 QS 1:9; CD 6:20. Cf. Andreas Nissen, Gott und der Nächste im antiken Judentum, 230-244.

[30]In the Jewish Two Ways section of the Epistle of Barnabas the commands to love God and neighbor are separated (19:2,5) and given no comprehensive status. However, the Christian addition to the Two Ways in Did. 1:2b makes love of neighbor a second command to love of God whereas the original second command is given in Did. 2:2. The Testaments of the Twelve Patriarchs connect love of God and neighbor in the same context (Ben. 3:1,3) as well as even in the same verse (Iss. 5:2; 7:6; Dan. 5:3), but this command is never given the comprehensive status afforded it in the gospels.

[31]Rom. 13:9; Gal. 5:14; the precise relationship between the royal law of Jas. 2:8 and Lev. 19:18 will be discussed in ch. 3, section 3.2.

In calling it a royal law, James meant that it was the law of the kingdom.[32] Thus the whole of Christian ethics (law) was reflected in the ordinance of love.

Assuming that James has utilized Lev. 19 in the same manner as Pseudo-Phocylides,[33] Johnson has recently suggested that James engages in an halachic midrash of Lev. 19:12-18. He discovers parallels to each of the verses in this section except for Lev. 19:14: Lev. 19:12=Jas. 5:12; 19:13=5:4; 19:15=2:1,9; 19:16=4:11; 19:17b=5:20*; 19:18a=5:9*; 19:18b=2:8.[34] In our view, this extensive use of Lev. 19 is not so obvious; the thematic rather than verbal parallels indicate that James is merely using traditional Jewish themes. However, Johnson's claim that Lev. 19:15 is alluded to at Jas. 2:9 is correct, since James offers two Biblical examples (2:8-10,11) to demonstrate that just as partiality toward one law (loving the neighbor; not committing adultery) while neglecting another (not showing partiality; not killing) leads to breaking the whole law, so partiality toward the rich while neglecting the rights of the poor results in transgression. Yet this fact does not undermine James' claim that the law of love as summarized in Lev. 19:18 is of prominent significance.

2.2	Jas. 2:11a	Ex. 20:13; Dt. 5:17 LXX	Ex. 20:14; Dt. 5:18 MT
	ὁ γὰρ εἰπόν· μὴ μοιχεύσῃς	οὐ μοιχεύσεις	לֹא תִּנְאָף
	Jas. 2:11b	Ex. 20:15; Dt. 5:18 LXX	Ex. 20:13; Dt. 5:17 MT
	εἶπεν καί· μὴ φονεύσῃς·	οὐ φονεύσεις	לֹא תִּרְצָח

The introductory formulations indicate that James is quoting what God said in scripture. Similar *formulae citandi* can be found in Paul's writings: the law said (Rom. 7:7), David says (Rom. 4:6-8; 11:9-11), and God said (2 Cor. 6:16). More to the point is Paul's use of λέγει without an expressed subject where God or scripture must be the understood author.[35] The wording itself, however, shows that there is no exact quotation of the OT. In both the Hebrew Bible and the LXX it is characteristic to express the prohibitions of legal language by the negative with the future tense.[36] Paul and Matthew retain this means of expression in their quotations of the Decalogue.[37] On the other hand, James, like Mark and Luke,[38] employs the stylistically less Semitic idiom of μή with the aorist subjunctive.[39] James is, therefore, not quoting directly from the OT text but from his memory or the common usage of his time and place. However, the reversal in order from the Hebrew indicates that James was aware of the sequence found in the LXX. In most MSS of the LXX

---

[32]Cf. below, pp. 92-93.

[33]Ps.-Phoc. 10=Lev. 19:15; 16=19:12; 19=19:13; 21=19:16. Here one discovers thematic rather than verbal allusions.

[34]Luke T. Johnson, "The Use of Leviticus 19 in the Letter of James," JBL 101(1982): 399. The least likely allusions are marked by him with asterisks.

[35]Rom. 15:10; Gal. 3:16; Eph. 4:8; 5:14. It is probably a circumlocution in Jewish style to avoid the name of God (cf. Davids, James, 117).

[36]Cf. BDF 362 and Moulton and Turner, Grammar, III: 86.

[37]Rom. 13:9; Mt. 5:21,27; 19:18. Matthew employs the future as an imperative at 5:21,43,48; 6:5; 20:26; 21:3,13; 27:4,24. Paul in other passages consistently uses μή and the subjunctive.

[38]Mk. 10:19; Lk. 18:20.

[39]Cf. Charles F.D. Moule, An Idiom Book of New Testament Greek, 178-179 where οὐ and the future as a prohibition is listed as a Semitism.

the succession of commandments in Exodus is adultery, theft, murder and in Deuteronomy adultery, murder, theft,[40] while the MT reads murder, adultery, theft in both cases. Although the transposition of murder and adultery is also found in the Hebraic Nash papyrus,[41] the probable explanation for James' order is simply his recollection of the LXX text.[42] Since the more Palestinian authors choose the order of the MT[43] whereas the more Hellenistic writers opt for the order of the LXX,[44] Laws contents that a probable provenance can be derived from James' usage: "As the bulk of evidence for variety in order is in Greek literature ... we may associate it primarily with the Greek-speaking synogogues."[45] Yet no conclusion can be reached on the basis of a single piece of evidence.

2.3	Jas. 2:23	Gen. 15:6 LXX	Gen. 15:6 MT
	ἐπληρώθη ἡ γραφὴ ἡ λέγουσα·		
	ἐπίστευσεν δὲ Ἀβραὰμ	καὶ ἐπίστευσεν Ἀβραμ	וְהֶאֱמִן
	τῷ θεῷ,	τῷ θεῷ,	בַּיהוָה
	καὶ ἐλογίσθη αὐτῷ	καὶ ἐλογίσθη αὐτῷ	וַיַּחְשְׁבֶהָ לּוֹ
	εἰς δικαιοσύνην	εἰς δικαιοσύνην.	צְדָקָה
	καὶ φίλος θεοῦ ἐκλήθη.		

Both James' use of a *formula citandi* and the presence of almost exact wording indicate another quote from the OT. The text diverges from the Hebrew by expressing the subject of the first verb ("Abraham believed") and by changing the active voice of the second verb ("he reckoned it") to the passive ("it was reckoned"). James' text differs only slightly from the LXX; he stylistically improves the opening conjunction[46] and cites the

---

[40]Certain LXX texts follow the order of the MT at Ex. 20 (A, F, M, 15, 19, 29, 38, 44, 52, 55, 58, 59, 72, 85, 106, 121, 131, 134, Armenian, Bohairic, Ethiopic, Syro-hexaplar) and Dt. 5 (A, F, M, 15, 29, 38, 52, 53, 55, 59, 72, 82, 85, 120, 121, 131, Bohairic, Old Latin). Cf. Alan E. Brooke and Norman McLean, The Old Testament in Greek (Cambridge: Un. Press, 1919 and 1911), Vol. 1, pt. 2, p. 220 and Vol. 1, pt. 3, p. 570.

[41]For a photograph and reproduction of the text see Ernst Würthwein, The Text of the Old Testament, tr. Erroll F. Rhodes (Grand Rapids: Eerdmans, 1979), 132-133. Because the papyrus was acquired in Egypt, its probable provenance is not Palestine. Würthwein (p. 33) explains that "it was not derived from a Biblical scroll, but from a liturgical, devotional, or instructional collection." If it is not derived from a Hebrew Biblical scroll, then the Hellenistic environment could certainly have more easily influenced the writing of this papyrus. Cf. F. Crawford Burkitt, "The Hebrew Papyrus of the Ten Commandments," JQR 15(1903): 392-408 and S.A. Cook, "A Pre-Massoretic Biblical Papyrus," Proceedings of the Society of Biblical Archaeology 25(1903): 34-56.

[42]I. Howard Marshall, Commentary on Luke, 685 calls it an early chruch catechetical pattern, but if that were true Matthew and Mark would have also followed it. Evidence for the use of the LXX is the fact that James only deviates from the LXX on one other occasion: Jas. 5:20=Prov. 10:12. Cf. Dibelius and Greeven, James, 27.

[43]Mt. 5:21-30; 15:19; 19:18; Mk. 7:21-22; 10:19; Did. 2:2; Jos. Ant. 3:91-92.

[44]Philo, Dec. 121ff; Spec. Leg. 3:8; Rer. Div. Her. 173; Lk. 18:20; Mk. 7:21-22 D; 10:19 D; Iren.; the Latin version of Did. 2:2. For a longer list see David Flusser, "'Do not commit adultery', 'Do not murder'," Textus, IV: 220-221.

[45]Laws, James, 116. Cf. Harry A.A. Kennedy, "The Hellenistic Atmosphere of the Epistle of James," Ex 8,2(1911): 39.

[46]The Semitic introductory καί with an adversative usage is replaced by the conjunction δέ in second position in normal Greek usage (cf. Moule, Idiom Book, 178). James probably employed a standard tradition here since Philo, Mut. Nom. 33:1; Gal. 3:6; Rom. 4:3; 1 Cl. 10:6; and Justin, Dial. 92 also make the exact changes. Two LXX MSS (53, 344) have ἐπίστευσε δὲ. Cf. John W. Wevers, Genesis, Septuaginta Göttingensis, 1:168.

name "Abraham" rather than the LXX "Abram". Since Abram does not receive his new name until Gen. 17:5, the text of James is the less correct text historically speaking. However, his usage of the more familiar name "Abraham" indicates that a common tradition had established itself so that the text was no more directly consulted. The word ἐπληρώθη in the citation formula does not imply that this scripture is being fulfilled in a NT event in the manner of Matthew's formula quotations. Rather the context in James indicates that Abraham's faith and righteousness were fulfilled in his act of sacrificing Isaac.[47]

The final clause, "and he was called a friend of God," appears to be a continuation of the scriptural quote, but in reality is not found in Gen. 15:6. It is possible that James combined texts about Abraham by adding a citation from Is. 41:8 or 2 Chr. 20:7. If this is the case, then James is following the Hebrew text rather than the LXX where we find in each case a paraphrase using the verb ἀγαπάω: Abraham "whom I loved" (Is. 41:8) or "who was loved by you" (2 Chr. 20:7).[48] However, the more likely solution is that "Abraham, my friend" had become a popular expression in Judaism as well as the Christian church. We find it employed by Jewish writers in the book of Jubilees where Abraham is said to be inscribed on the heavenly tablets as a friend of God,[49] at Qumran in CD 3:2,[50] in the Testament of Abraham 13:2[51] and the Apocalypse of Abraham 10:5,[52] and by Philo in <u>Abr</u>. 273[53] as well as in an especially revealing reference (<u>Sobr</u>. 56) where within the Genesis narrative itself (Gen. 18:17 LXX) Philo changes the words "Abraham, my son" (τοῦ παιδός μου) to "Abraham, my friend" (τοῦ φιλοῦ μου).[54] The continuing popularity of this designation in the Christian church is revealed in the writings of Clement of Rome,[55] Tertullian,[56] and Irenaeus.[57] Laws' conclusion is correct: "James, then, is not strictly quot-

---

[47]Davids, <u>James</u>, 129 against Mayor, <u>James</u>, 104 and Ropes, <u>James</u>, 221.

[48]'Αβρααμ ὅν ἠγάπησα; 'Αβρααμ τῷ ἠγαπημένῳ.

[49]Jub. 19:9 "for he was found faithful, and was recorded on the heavenly tablets as the friend of God." Jub. 30:20 "and he has been recorded on the heavenly tablets as a friend and a righteous man."

[50]Abraham "was accounted friend of God because he kept the commandments of God and did not choose his own will." Eduard Lohse, <u>Die Texte aus Qumran: Hebräisch und Deutsch</u> (München: Kösel, 1964), 70 reads רֵיעַ[ל אוֹ]הֵב. The better translation is "friend" although Isaac and Jacob are called "friends of God" at CD 3:3-4.

[51]Only recension B ὅτι φίλος μου ἐστίν. <u>The Testament of Abraham: The Greek Recensions</u>, tr. Michael E. Stone, Texts and Translations 2 (Missoula: Scholars, 1972), 82, line 10. Recension A has πανόσιε (p. 32, line 4). According to Francis Schmidt, "The Two Recensions of the Testament of Abraham: In Which Way did the Transformation Take Place?" <u>Studies on the Testament of Abraham</u>, ed. George W.E. Nickelsburg Jr. (Missoula: Scholars, 1976), 80 the short recension B is prior.

[52]"Stand up, Abraham, friend of God who has loved you..." R. Rubinkiewicz, <u>OT Pseud</u>., I: 694. Only known in Old Slavonic.

[53]F.H. Colson, <u>Philo VI</u>, LCL, 133, "He no longer talked with him as God with man but as a friend (ὡς φίλος) with a familiar."

[54]F.H. Colson and G.H. Whitaker, <u>Philo III</u>, LCL, 472-473, "Shall I hide anything from Abraham, my friend?" Philo, however, follows the LXX, "my servant," on another occasion (<u>Leg. Alleg</u>. 3:27).

[55]1 Cl. 10:1 'Αβραάμ, ὁ φίλος προσαγορευθείς; 1 Cl. 17:2 'Αβραὰμ καὶ φίλος προσηγορεύθη τοῦ θεοῦ.

[56]<u>Adv. Jud</u>. 2:7 "Abraham amicus Dei deputatus" in Migne, <u>Patrologiae Latinae</u>, 2:638.

[57]<u>Adv. Haer</u>. 4,16,2 "amicus Dei vocatus est" in Migne, <u>Patrologiae Graecae</u>, 7:1016. Dibelius and Greeven, <u>James</u>, 172, n. 125 and Laws, <u>James</u>, 137 agree that these references are not quotes from the Epistle of James.

ing Scripture at this point but echoing a familiar description of Abraham which ultimately has a Scriptural background."[58] As with the other occurrences of an introductory formula, James' appeal to scripture gives authoritative backing to his argument, this time affirming the working together of faith and works in salvation (Jas. 2:14-26).

2.4 Jas. 4:5[59]	Gen. 6:1-7 ?	Num. 11:29 ?
ἢ δοκεῖτε ὅτι κενῶς		
ἡ γραφὴ λέγει·		καὶ εἶπεν αὐτῷ Μωυσῆς
πρὸς φθόνον	v. 2	μὴ ζηλοῖς σύ μοι ...
ἐπιποθεῖ τὸ πνεῦμα	vv. 3,5	ὅταν δῷ κύριος τὸ πνεῦμα
ὃ κατῴκισεν ἐν ἡμῖν	v. 3	ἀυτοῦ ἐπ᾽ αὐτούς;

Ex. 20:5 ? ἐγὼ γάρ εἰμι κύριος ὁ θεός σου, θεὸς ζηλωτὴς ...

Ps. 41:2 LXX ? ὅν τρόπον ἐπιποθεῖ ἡ ἔλαφος ἐπὶ τὰς πηγὰς τῶν ὑδάτων, οὕτως ἐπιποθεῖ ἡ ψυχή μου πρὸς σέ, ὁ θεός.

Ps. 83:3 LXX ? ἐπιποθεῖ καὶ ἐκλείπει ἡ ψυχή μου εἰς τὰς αὐλὰς τοῦ κυρίου

Up to this point the sayings prefixed with introductory formulas have been easily identified as familiar OT quotations. However, at Jas. 4:5 we run into a road block. Even though this *formula citandi* is regularly used to refer to the OT,[60] no clear allusion can be inferred here. This situation partly stems from the uncertain meaning of this "quote". Laws points out that

> it may be read as a statement or as a question; "the spirit" (*to pneuma*) may be the subject or object of the main verb; and this "spirit" indwelling men may be understood as the spirit given at creation (Gen. ii. 7, vi. 3 LXX, cf. Job xxvii. 3, xxxii. 8; 1QH iv. 31), whether seen as good or evil, or as the special endowment of the Holy Spirit (cf. Test. Sim. iv. 4; 1QH xii. 11f).[61]

Therefore translations vary. If God is the subject, then the spirit (either divine or human) is understood in a positive sense: "God jealously longs for the spirit (Spirit) that he made to live in us." If the spirit is the subject, then the sentence can be understood either positively ("The Holy Spirit, He caused to live in us, longs jealously") or negatively ("The human spirit, He caused to live in us, tends toward envy"). A question is also possible: "Does the spirit which He made to dwell in us long unto envying?"[62] Whatever the wording, three

---

[58]Laws, James, 137. John Bowker, The Targums and Rabbinic Literature, 212 recites rabbinic references and calls it "an extremely common description of Abraham." The concept of the friend of God is traced through Greek, Biblical, and early Christian literature by Erik Peterson, "Der Gottesfreund: Beiträge zur Geschichte eines religiösen Terminus," ZKG 42(1923): 161-202.

[59]Dibelius and Greeven, James, 221, n. 73 for a list of articles over the exegesis of Jas. 4:5.

[60]Paul's second most common introductory formula used six times. Ellis, Paul's Use of OT, 22.

[61]Laws, James, 174-175.

[62]With regard to English versions the following possibilities result: God as subject: RSV, NASB; Spirit as subject: KJV, ASV, NEB, JB, TEV, Living Bible, NIV; understood negatively: KJV, ASV, NEB, TEV, NIV; understood positively: RSV, JB, NASB, Living Bible; a question: ASV, NIV; the Holy Spirit: JB, NASB, Living Bible; the human spirit: KJV, ASV, RSV, NEB, TEV, NIV.

main possibilities for explaining this citation result: 1) a proverbial maxim drawn from an OT passage or combination of texts;[63] 2) a reference to an extra-Biblical source;[64] and 3) a parenthetic thought so that the introductory formula refers to Jas. 4:6 where Prov. 3:34 is cited.[65]

It is not important for the purpose of our study to discuss the source and meaning of this verse in great detail. Let us briefly explain our position. The third option listed above denies the most natural reading of this passage which would expect a quotation after "the scripture says". With regard to the second option Dibelius claims that no suitable apocryphal citation can be produced. Responding to the specific suggestion of the book of Eldad and Modad, Dibelius asks,

> But do we know that this story (i.e. Num. 11:26-30) was included in the book which purported to be the prophecy of Eldad and Modad, and whether, therefore, there was any discussion in this book about jealousy for the possession of the spirit?[66]

Sidebottom,[67] however, contends that the quote from Eldad and Modad in the Shepherd of Hermas (Vis. 2,3,4 "The Lord is nigh unto them that turn unto Him"[68]) is identical in substance with Jas. 4:8 ("Draw near to God and he will draw near to you") and that the giving

---

[63]Most posit a loose quotation of the OT. Ex. 20:5 is referred to by Hort, James, 93 and Mayor, James, 140. Sophie S. Laws, "Does Scripture Speak in Vain? A Reconsideration of James iv. 5," NTS 20(1973-74): 214-215 opts for an allusion to Ps. 41:2 or Ps. 83:3 LXX. Oesterley, "James," 459 claims that Gal. 5:17 is in James' mind, but a reference to a NT writing as scripture is unlikely within a first century milieu. Others claim that James is not referring to any particular passage but to the tenor of several OT passages (cf. Knowling, James, 99; Mitton, James, 154; Ross, James and John, 77; Rudolph V.G. Tasker, The General Epistle of James, 91). Still others suggest some unknown version of the OT. Joachim Jeremias, "Jac. 4,5: *epipothei*," ZNW 50(1959): 137-138 mentions Theodotion on Job 14:15b or the Fragmentary Targum on Gen. 2:2, but these are certainly too cryptic to have had widespread significance. Ropes, James, 262 opts for an unknown translation of Ex. 20:5.

[64]Many think James is quoting either some unknown apocryphal work (cf. Dibelius and Greeven, James, 222; Johann Michl, "Der Spruch Jakobusbrief 4,5," Neutestamentliche Aufsätze, 173-174; Mußner, Jakobusbrief, 184; Wolfgang Schrage, "Der Jakobusbrief," in Horst Balz und Wolfgang Schrage, Die katholischen Briefe, 44-45), a proverb of unknown origin (Bo Reicke, The Epistle of James, Peter, and Jude, 46), or a Christian prophecy (cf. Schlatter, Jakobus, 248). Others more specifically argue for a citation of the book of Eldad and Modad (cf. Davids, James, 162; James Moffatt, The General Epistles, 60; E.M. Sidebottom, James, Jude, and 2 Peter, 52-53; Spitta, Zur Geschichte, II: 121-123).

[65]The NIV (1978 ed.) makes 4:5-6a into a question implying that 6b is the only scriptural reference. Cf. Mayor, James, 136 for 19th century proponents of this view. On the other hand, John Calvin, Commentaries on the Catholic Epistles, 331 decides that the reference to scripture refers to the preceding verse, Jas. 4:4.

[66]Dibelius and Greeven, James, 223, n. 82. Ropes, James, 267 states that "it must be pronounced fantastic".

[67]Sidebottom, James, Jude, and 2 Peter, 52-53.

[68]ἐγγὺς κύριος τοῖς ἐπιστεφομένοις, ὡς γέγραπται ἐν τῷ 'Ελδὰδ καὶ Μωδάτ.

of greater grace mentioned in Jas. 4:6 is also applied in a rabbinical midrash[69] to Eldad and Modad on account of their humility, the very theme of Jas. 4:6-10. This hypothesis traces back to Spitta[70] who compiled remarkable evidence pointing to similarities of context, content, and vocabulary between Jas. 4 and the proposed reading of the book of Eldad and Modad.[71] First of all, the same motive of humility is given for the subsequent giving of greater grace, thus establishing the same general theme in each case. Secondly, the specific content of Jas. 4:5 as well as its context offers significant similarities. Just as the citation of scripture in Jas. 4:5 mentions envy (or jealousy) and "the spirit which God made to dwell in us", so the passage about Eldad and Modad[72] in Num. 11:29 refers to the envy[73] which seized some when Eldad and Modad received the spirit. Moreover, Hermas' quote of the book of Eldad and Modad (as cited above by Sidebottom) is similar to the emphasis of Jas. 4:8a. Furthermore, if we allow the possibility that the citations in 1 Cl. 23:3-4 entitled "this scripture" and 2 Cl. 11:2-3[74] called "the prophetic word" also derive from the book of Eldad and Modad,[75] then the theme of double-mindedness found in Jas. 4:8b is integral to both documents. Thirdly, the presence of much similar vocabulary is remarkable: γραφή (1 Cl. 23:3; Jas. 4:5), δίψυχοι 1 Cl. 23:3; Jas. 4:8), ταλαίπωροί, ταλαιπωρήσατε (1 Cl. 23:3; Jas. 4:9), ζηλοῖς, ζηλοῦτε (Num. 11:29; Jas. 4:2[76]), ἀκαταστασία (which is employed in the application of the citation of the book of Eldad and Modad in 2 Cl. 11:4 and is used with ζῆλος in Jas. 3:16 and δίψυχος in Jas. 1:8[77]), and as mentioned above the expression "greater grace" used in Rabba 15:19, Sanhedrin 17a, and Jas. 4:6.

This evidence, of course, assumes that the book of Eldad and Modad contained all this material. Yet this is the best hypothesis within the limits of our present knowledge.

---

[69]Rabba 15:19 on Num. 11:26 in The Midrash Rabbah, VI: 663. Cf. b. Sanhedrin 17a, ed. Epstein, 85, "Thereupon the Holy One, blessed be He, said, 'Because you have humbled yourselves, I will add to your greatness yet more greatness.' And how did He add to their dignity? -- In that all (the other prophets) prophesied and ceased, but their prophesying did not cease." Michael Rodkinson, The Babylonian Talmud: Jurisprudence (Boston: The Talmud Society, 1918), pt. 4, p. 39 offers the more literal translation, "I will increase your grace."

[70]Spitta, Zur Geschichte, II: 122-123. We disagree with Spitta (p. 120) that πρὸς φθόνος belongs to the citation formula and μείζονα δὲ δίδωσιν χάριν to the citation itself.

[71]The Stichometry of Nicephorus includes Eldad and Modad under the title 'apocrypha of the OT' and assigns its length as 400 lines. Cf. D.S. Russell, The Method and Message of Jewish Apocalyptic (Philadelphia: Westminster, 1974), 392.

[72]Medad is the MT spelling and Modad the LXX reading (Modat in Herm., Vis. 2,3,4).

[73]Num. 11:29 employs ζῆλος but this is a close synonym to φθόνος. Cf. 1 Mac. 8:16; Test. Sim. 4:5; 1 Cl. 3:2; 4:7; 5:2.

[74]For the wording see ch. 3, n. 323.

[75]This is the proposal of Spitta; Seitz, "Relationship of Hermas to James," 138-140; "Afterthoughts," 332-333; and Joseph B. Lightfoot, The Apostolic Fathers, Vol. 1, pt. 2 (New York: Olms, 1973), 80. Lightfoot reports that Hilgenfeld and others have suggested the Assumption of Moses but have given no reason except their own theory that Clement was acquainted with this work. Shepherd, "James and Matthew," 41, n. 3 suggests the Secrets of Elijah since he believes that 1 Cor. 2:9 comes from the same source which Origen identifies with the Secrets of Elijah. However, 1 Cor. 2:9 lacks all the vocabulary common to 1 Cl. 23:3-4 and Jas. 4 except the introductory formulation, γέγραπται. E.G. Martin, "Eldad and Modad," OT Pseud., II: 464 prefers to leave these verses anonymous.

[76]We accept Erasmus' conjecture φθονεῖτε for φονεύετε so that the φθόνον of Jas. 4:5 refers back to the envy and jealousy spoken of in Jas. 4:2. Cf. ch. 3, section 2.4.

[77]Here the adjective form ἀκατάστατος is employed as in Jas. 3:8.

All the other OT references only relate to one element in the text. Num. 11:29 has in common with Jas. 4:5 the idea of jealousy but not the theme of "greater grace" found in Rabba 15:19 and Sanhedrin 17a. Ex. 20:5 speaks of the jealousy of God in a positive sense[78] whereas Jas. 4:5 more naturally refers to the envious longing of the human spirit.[79] Laws argues convincingly for this conclusion:

> In the LXX the verb *zēloō*, with its cognate noun and adjective and the compound verb *parazēloō*, is virtually a technical term for the divine jealousy .... By contrast, despite its similar range of meanings in regard to human longings, the verb *epipotheō* is never used to translate *qnr* and is never applied to God (except perhaps in the eagle image of Deut. xxxii. 11), and the noun *phthonos*, which does not appear in the translation Greek of the LXX, is always used of base human or devilish emotion (Wisd. ii. 24; vi. 23; 1 Macc. viii. 16; 3 Macc. vi. 7).[80]

Ps. 41:2 LXX and 83:3 LXX employ the verb ἐπιποθέω along with Jas. 4:5, but there is no mention of envy or jealousy, probably the most significant word of Jas. 4:5 as indicated by its first place in the word order.

Gen. 6:1-7 demonstrates several important parallels with Jas. 4:5. In the context of 4:5 James draws distinctions between what is from God and what is only human: 3:13-17 wisdom from God vs. earthly wisdom; 4:4 friendship with God vs. worldly friendship. Reflecting on this theme, James might be reminded of the OT example in Gen. 6:1-7 where the sons of God yearn (6:1) for the daughters of this world. James might be pointing to this past example of adultery (Jas. 4:4a) to show his generation that every inclination of the human spirit tends toward evil. This explanation fits the train of thought in both contexts; the human spirit inclines towards friendship with the world, desire (envy), and pursuit of pleasure (Gen. 6:1; Jas. 4:4), putting itself at enmity with God's spirit (Gen. 6:3), but God responds to this with extra grace for the humble (Jas. 4:6). This would parallel the context immediately following Gen. 6:1-7 where Noah, the truly humble man, receives through the flood extra grace to overcome the evil inclinations of this world. The problem, however, with any supposed allusion to Gen. 6:1-7 is the lack of any specific reference to envy or jealousy (φθόνος) and the minimal links in vocabulary as compared with the proposed content of the book of Eldad and Modad. To overcome this limited similarity with any scripture, others have postulated a general reference to several texts from the OT, but the word γραφή normally cites a specific reference.[81]

---

[78]This is also the case for Ex. 34:14; Dt. 6:15; 32:16, 19ff; Is. 63:8ff; Zech. 8:2.

[79]If the Holy Spirit were in mind, it would be the only reference in the epistle, whereas the human spirit is mentioned in Jas. 2:26. Moreover, Herm., Mand. 3:1-2 speaks of the spirit which God made to dwell in this flesh, a spirit which may be corrupted and return as a lying spirit.

[80]Laws, James, 177.

[81]Joseph B. Lightfoot, St. Paul's Epistle to the Galatians (Andover: Draper, 1981), 261 states that "when γραφή is employed in the singular in the New Testament, it always means a particular passage of Scripture." In opposition to Lightfoot see the writings mentioned by James Hastings, "Scripture," A Dictionary of the Bible, ed. 1909. Knowling, James, 99 calls attention to 2 Cor. 6:16-18 which he claims uses γραφή in a general sense, but in reality one encounters there a series of specific texts. Gottlob Schrenk, s.v. γραφή, TDNT, I: 753 traces a two-fold use of γραφή with reference both to particular passages and to scripture as a whole. He claims that in the Apostolic Fathers 1 Cl. 42:5; 2 Cl. 6:8; and Barn. 6:12 refer to the entirety of scripture. However, 1 Cl. 42:5 is loosely quoting Is. 60:17 LXX (cf. Joseph B. Lightfoot, The Apostolic Fathers (New York: Olms, 1973), Vol. 1, pt. 2, p. 129) and Barn. 6:12 is obviously a loose citation of the creation account. 2 Cl. 6:8 specifically mentions Ezekiel as the source (a loose quote of Ezek. 14:14,18) and, therefore, cannot refer to all scripture in general. Therefore, even though a scriptural citation is not always word for word, a specific text is still in mind.

It has been difficult for many to accept this solution to the problematic text of Jas. 4:5 because of the presupposition that a NT author would not designate extra-canonical literature as scripture. However, the citation formula "it is written" could refer to literature outside the OT in 1 Cor. 2:9; Jn. 7:38; and Eph. 5:14. This possibility is increased by the fact that Clement of Rome, a Christian writer within the first century, designates extra-canonical literature as scripture.[82] Apparently within the earliest period of Christianity more literature was designated as scripture than those writings which have emerged as our canon.[83] Yet we do not want to be too dogmatic here! Whatever solution one arrives at regarding the meaning of this particular text, a certain degree of doubt must be admitted, so that this text is better seen as the exception than the rule in understanding how James alludes to preexistent material.

2.5 Jas. 4:6	Prov. 3:34 LXX	Prov. 3:34 MT
διὸ λέγει		
ὁ θεὸς ὑπερηφάνοις	κύριος ὑπερηφάνοις	אִם־לַלֵּצִים
ἀντιτάσσεται,	ἀντιτάσσεται,	הוּא־יָלִיץ
ταπεινοῖς δὲ	ταπεινοῖς δὲ	וְלַעֲנָיִים
δίδωσιν χάριν.	δίδωσιν χάριν.	יִתֶּן־חֵן׃

The *formula citandi* διὸ λέγει is also used in Eph. 4:8; 5:14; Heb. 3:7; 10:5. It indicates that the truth just stated (in this case the fact that God gives more grace) is substantiated by the Biblical utterance to be quoted. One can supply either "scripture" or "God" as the subject of λέγει, but the former is more likely since God is the subject within the quote itself. James definitely follows the LXX here; the Hebrew description of God as the one who "scorns the scorners" is nowhere encountered in James. Yet there is one striking variance from the LXX: here as well as in 1 Pet. 5:5; 1 Cl. 30:2; and Ig., Eph. 5:3 the general subject "he" in the Hebrew is specified as θεός rather than with the LXX addition κύριος. Oort (1885) and Gratz (1892-94) have contended that the Hebrew אִם is a corruption of אֱלֹהִים,[84] but this solution would suggest that our author utilized the Hebrew which seems very unlikely because of the divergent wording of the texts. Laws has suggested that "the tetragrammaton was written in their text and variously expressed in quotation, with *Kurios* subsequently being standardized in the MSS."[85] This is possible since the tetragrammaton was sometimes employed in this fashion, but the complete lack of any LXX MSS of Prov. 3:34 with θεός replacing the tetragrammaton argues in favor of an original κύριος. It is best to assume that this Biblical wisdom saying had become a popular quotation resulting in some word variation. Apparently, the popular oral form had θεός for its subject rather than κύριος as testified by the wording in James, 1 Peter, 1 Clement, and Ignatius' epistle to the Ephesians. The probable explanation for this as Grundmann states is that "κύριος is a term for Christ and their concern is with God's eschatological acts."[86] Having become a popular saying, this verse could be used with different emphases: thus James calls attention to the theme "grace"; Peter, the word "humble"; and Clement and Ignatius, the term "proud".

3.0 Suggested Allusions to the Old Testament

Various authors use different criteria to judge the presence of quotations and allusions. The gradation from quotation to allusion is sometimes so imperceptible that it is

---

[82] 1 Cl. 23:3; 46:2; cf. 2 Cl. 11:2.
[83] Cf. Laws, James, 177. Cf. also below, pp. 52-53.
[84] Cf. Ropes, James, 266.
[85] Laws, James, 180.
[86] Walter Grundmann, s.v. ταπείνος, TDNT, VIII: 19.

impossible to draw any certain bifurcation. We will define a citation or quotation as a reference to another source containing a *formula citandi* and/or nearly exact verbal affinity with the original text. An allusion or reminiscence, on the other hand, is here defined as a deliberate reference to another source without the use of an introductory formulation and only containing a degree of verbal affinity. A parallel (here posited as a third distinct category) contains similar terminology and/or content, but no certainty of dependence upon preexistent material can be established. We will now turn to the OT references without a scriptural *formula citandi* and attempt to determine whether these are exact quotations, allusions, or merely parallels to the OT.[87]

3.1 Jas. 1:10b-11	Is. 40:6b-8 LXX[88]	Is. 40: 6b-8 MT
	πάσα σὰρξ χόρτος,	כָּל־הַבָּשָׂר חָצִיר
ὅτι	καὶ πᾶσα δόξα ἀνθρώπου	וְכָל־חַסְדּוֹ
ὡς ἄνθος χόρτου	ὡς ἄνθος χόρτου·	כְּצִיץ הַשָּׂדֶה
παρελεύσεται.		7 יָבֵשׁ חָצִיר נָבֵל
11 ἀνέτειλεν γὰρ ὁ ἥλιος		צִיץ כִּי רוּחַ
σὺν τῷ καύσωνι		יְהוָה נָשְׁבָה בּוֹ
		אָכֵן חָצִיר הָעָם
καὶ ἐξήρανεν τὸν χόρτον	7 ἐξηράνθη ὁ χόρτος,	8 יָבֵשׁ חָצִיר
καὶ τὸ ἄνθος αὐτοῦ ἐξέπεσεν	καὶ τὸ ἄνθος ἐξέπεσεν,	נָבֵל צִיץ
καὶ ἡ εὐπρέπεια τοῦ προσώπου		
αὐτοῦ ἀπώλετο·		
	τὸ δὲ ῥῆμα τοῦ θεοῦ ἡμῶν μένει	וּדְבַר־אֱלֹהֵינוּ
	εἰς τὸν αἰῶνα.	יָקוּם לְעוֹלָם
οὕτως καὶ ὁ πλούσιος ἐν ταῖς		
πορείαις αὐτοῦ μαρανθήσεται.		

The presence of a deliberate allusion to Is. 40:6-8 is substantiated by the almost verbatim duplication of three lines from the LXX translation.[89] However, the scorching heat and the inevitable end of the rich man indicate that James is not quoting the words of

---

[87]We have drawn our list primarily from Daniel Gotaas' unpublished dissertation, The Old Testament in the Epistle to the Hebrews, the Epistle of James, and the Epistle of Peter. However, we have omitted 1)Jas. 5:2=Jer. 17:11; Job 13:28 since the Jeremiah reference contains no verbal similarities and Job 13:28 refers to a person's life rather than riches, although it speaks of a moth-eaten garment similar to James; and 2) Jas. 5:3=Prov. 1:18 which speaks of murderers storing up evil rather than riches. In both instances a saying of Jesus bears a closer resemblance. In addition, we will add Is. 5:9 to Gotaas' parallel, Jas. 5:4=Dt. 24: 14-15; Mal. 3:5. For the allusion of Jas. 2:9 ("But if you show partiality, you commit sin") to Lev. 19:15 ("You shall not be partial to the poor or defer to the great"), see instead pp. 35 and 94-95. The list in Old Testament Quotations in the New Testament, ed. Robert Bratcher, is too sparse. Wilhelm Dittmar, Vetus Testamentum in Novo: Die alttestamentlichen Parallelen des Neuen Testaments chooses too many OT allusions for each reference in James. C. Smits, Oud-Testamentliche Citaten in het Nieue Testament deals more with parallels of vocabulary than with deliberate allusions.

[88]Some versions of the LXX (Q, 86, 109, 736, 22, 48, 51, 231, 763, 46, 456, 403, 538) add with minor changes the following words: 7 ... ὅτι πνεῦμα κυρίου ἐπνεύσεν εἰς αὐτό· ἀληθῶς χορτὸς ὁ λαός. 8 ἐξηράνθη χόρτος, ἐξεπέσε τὸ ἄνθος. Cf. Joseph Ziegler, Isaias, Septuaginta Göttingensis, 14:267.

[89]James employs the active (ἐξήρανεν) in order to be consistent in his verb formation and adds αὐτοῦ.

Isaiah but only alluding to familiar Biblical language. The self-contained structure of James' description offers additional support that the structure of Is. 40 is not being followed.

a. ὅτι ὡς ἄνθος χόρτου παρελεύσεται.
    b. ἀνέτειλεν γὰρ ὁ ἥλιος σὺν τῷ καύσωνι
        c. καὶ ἐξήρανεν τὸν χόρτον
        c. καὶ τὸ ἄνθος αὐτοῦ ἐξέπεσεν
    b. καὶ ἡ εὐπρέπεια τοῦ προσώπου αὐτοῦ ἀπώλετο·
a. οὕτως καὶ ὁ πλούσιος ἐν ταῖς πορείαις αὐτοῦ μαρανθήσεται.

The concluding οὕτως clause refers back to the beginning so that the description between these two clauses is complete in itself. Thus in developing his own description of destructive weather conditions James alludes to the familiar phrases of Is. 40:6b-8. This Biblicized language is most likely derived from the LXX text since the phrases omitted by the LXX because of parablepsis[90] are likewise not included by James. Further evidence for following the LXX lies in James' repetition of a unique mistranslation of Is. 40:6, "the flower of grass" rather than "the flower of the field".[91] The addition in verse 11, "For the sun rises with its scorching heat," is then an addition to explain why the plant withers and the blossom falls since James is apparantly ignorant of the reason given in the MT for the plant's destruction: because "the breath of the Lord blows upon it."[92]

Why does James not begin his reference to Is. 40 with a *formula citandi*? One might conceivably argue that James does not dare to preface this verse with the term γραφή because he has interwoven his own words with the language of scripture. Specifically James omits the phrase "all flesh" and instead speaks about the rich. Then after citing one phrase from the LXX, he explains why the grass withers. He returns again to the LXX for two phrases but then cuts off the end of the LXX version inserting the clause "and its beauty perishes" instead of the LXX "but the word of our God abides for ever." In this way James can conveniently return to the rich man who also perishes as the flower. Does James therefore refuse to introduce an OT reference as scripture when he interweaves his own words into the language of scripture? This is an unlikely solution since we have already seen that James inserts his own thoughts at 2:23 when he adds "and he was called God's friend" to Gen. 15:6. It is our contention that James omits the *formula citandi* when he is not directly appealing to the authority of scripture in his arguments. Whenever James quotes the OT with an introductory formula, he does so to offer authoritative support to his arguments.[93] Since Is. 40:6-8 refers to the destruction of all flesh, it would not specifically support James' claim for the fading away of only the rich. Therefore James appeals to a common occurrence of nature reported in scriptural language rather than to the authority of scripture itself. We disagree with Laws' contention that "by couching his threat in the language of prophecy, James adds the suggestion that it is in some sense foreordained."[94]

---

[90]Is. 40:7 and 8 begin in Hebrew with the same four words so that the translator's eye slid down to v. 8 as he began to inscribe v. 7. However, the insertion of these words in 1QIs[a] indicates that the parablepsis had already occurred in some Hebrew MSS. Therefore this one fact alone is insufficient evidence to prove the use of the LXX.

[91]In Ps. 103(102):15 the same Hebrew is rendered more correctly ἄνθος τοῦ ἀγροῦ.

[92]One might argue for a knowledge of the Hebrew since the Greek word καύσων is used numerous times in the LXX to mean the hot southeast wind, thus similar to the breath of the Lord found in the MT. However, because καύσων is tied to the sun by the preposition "with" (σύν), the other meaning of heat is more likely, similar to Mt. 20:12; Lk. 12:55; and perhaps Is. 49:10.

[93]Cf. below, p. 52.

[94]Laws, James, 64.

Laws assumes that James is appealing to the force of scripture in both his OT quotations and allusions.[95] This particular example, however, does not substantiate this claim since James is only using familiar Biblical language and not appealing to scriptural authority.

3.2 Jas. 3:9b	Gen. 1:26 LXX	Gen. 1:26 MT
καὶ ἐν αὐτῇ καταρώμεθα	καὶ εἶπεν ὁ θεός	וַיֹּאמֶר אֱלֹהִים
τοὺς ἀνθρώπους	ποιήσωμεν ἄνθρωπον	נַעֲשֶׂה אָדָם
	κατ' εἰκόνα ἡμετέραν	בְּצַלְמֵנוּ
τοὺς καθ' ὁμοίωσιν θεοῦ γεγονότας	καὶ καθ' ὁμοίωσιν	כִּדְמוּתֵנוּ

James appeals to the OT truth that human beings are created in the likeness of God to demonstrate the corresponding fact that verbal responses (such as blessing and cursing) apply not only to one's relationship to God but also to human affairs. The word "likeness" is employed infrequently in the LXX outside Gen. 1:26[96] and is not found elsewhere in the NT. Normally it is replaced by εἰκών[97] when describing the resemblance of humankind to God or is employed with εἰκών as the second term within a series.[98] It is difficult to determine whether James chose this word for a specified purpose. Irenaeus[99] distinguished between the image of God in which all humanity participates (since reason and conscience are universal phenomena) and the likeness of God (the potentiality of moral assimilation to divine goodness) which only the redeemed inherit. It is doubtful, however, whether such a distinction can be read back into the Epistle of James. Laws argues that "he deliberately uses the more unusual of the two words in Gen. 1:26 to make a specific allusion to that passage (a technique he employs in 1:10 and 5:4) and so to add force to his argument."[100] If one were to accept this proposition, then James would be offering a two-fold argument against the person who uses the tongue to bless God and curse people: 1) inconsistency; and 2) acting against the word of God. In our opinion, Laws is assuming too much when she proposes that James is appealing to the authority of scripture by using the special word "likeness". Since this term is used as a substitute for "image" in rabbinic litera-

---

[95]Ibid., 8.

[96]It is used in contexts unconnected with the resemblance of God and human beings at Ps. 57(58):4; Ezek. 1:10; 8:10 A; 10:22; Dan. 7:5; 10:16. However, Ezek. 28:12-13 LXX ("Thou art a seal of resemblance and crown of beauty. Thou wast in the delight of the paradise of God." The Septuagint Version, Greek and English, 1016) does refer to humankind's likeness to God and thus misunderstands the Hebrew (cf. Walter Zimmerli, Ezekiel, tr. James Martin (Philadelphia: Fortress, 1983), 2:81). Since the Hebrew of v. 13 speaks of "Eden, the garden of God" and "the day that you were created" recalling the details of Gen. 1, the LXX took the liberty to insert a reference to "likeness". Cf. John W. Wevers, Ezekiel, NCBC (London: Nelson, 1969), 215 for a summary of the similarities and differences with the account of Genesis.

[97]Gen. 5:1 LXX; 9:6; Sir. 17:3; Wis. 2:23; Test. Naph. 2:6; Philo, Fug. 68; Mut. Nom. 31; 1 Cor. 11:7; 2 Cor. 3:18; cf. Aboth 3:14.

[98]Gen. 1:26; Philo, Op. Mund. 69; Conf. Ling. 169; 1 Cl. 33:5; Barn. 5:5; 6:12; cf. b. Megillah 9a.

[99]Adv. Haer. 5,16,2. Cf. The Anti-Nicene Fathers, I: 544.

[100]Laws, James, 155.

ture,[101] these words were at least interchangeable in the Jewish community.[102] Here James argues solely on the grounds of inconsistency. Blessing God and cursing humans is an inconsistent behavior -- a proposition which every wise, reasonable person would recognize. Within this argument James uses the language of Gen. 1:26, but this is very natural since all paraenetic literature employs traditional language which in the case of a Jewish-Christian mileau includes the language of the OT. Therefore, James is not arguing from the authority of scripture as he has done when employing *formulae citandi* but is only utilizing Biblical language.

3.3 Jas. 5:4	Dt. 24:15 LXX	Mal. 3:15 LXX
	αὐθημερὸν ἀποδώσεις	
ἰδοὺ ὁ μισθὸς	τὸν μισθὸν αυτοῦ	
τῶν ἐργατῶν τῶν ἀμησάντων		καὶ ἐπὶ
τὰς χώρας ὑμῶν		
ὁ ἀπεστερημένος ἀφ'		τοὺς ἀποστεροῦντας
ὑμῶν κράζει,	... καὶ οὐ	μισθὸν μισθωτοῦ
καὶ αἱ βοαὶ τῶν θερισάντων	καταβοήσεται	Is. 5:9 LXX
εἰς τὰ ὦτα	κατὰ σοῦ	ἠκούσθη εἰς τὰ ὦτα
κυρίου σαβαὼθ εἰσεληλύθασιν.	πρὸς κύριον	κυρίου σαβαὼθ ταῦτα

The similarities in terminology and content suggest that James was familiar with the language of Is. 5:9, Dt. 24:14-15, and Mal. 3:5. James' title for God, "Lord of Hosts,"[103] appears four times in Is. 5:7,9,16,28. In both Isaiah and James the Lord of Hosts is listening and will judge the offender. Moreover, the cry (κράζει) of James' poor is reminiscent of the cry (κραύγη) heard by the Lord from his vineyard in Is. 5:7.[104] However, the parallels are not exact. In James' setting and experience the rich have kept back the wages of the poor by fraud; in Isaiah the greedy have joined house to house and field to field until there is no room for anyone else. In James the day of slaughter will end the oppressor's life of luxury; in Isaiah a famine will desolate the large and beautiful homes. Besides divergencies of content one should realize that expressions describing the cry of the oppressed are common in Israel as demonstrated in the verbal similarities of Is. 5:9 and Ps. 17:7 LXX.[105] James thus employs traditional OT language and thought patterns to express his condemnation of the rich. This also applies to Dt. 24:15 and Mal. 3:5b which like Jas. 5:4 protest against holding back the wages of the poor. Here we encounter a common theology of the poor rather than a specific allusion to particular OT passages. Dibelius concurs with this opinion, "Just such motifs from the tradition were natural favorites for the expansion of paraenesis by Jewish and Christian teachers."[106] Therefore, it is likely that as James

---

[101]Cf. Sifra on Lev. 19:18 which contains Akiba's saying, "Whosoever sheddeth blood, they reckon it to him as if he diminished the likeness," a reference to Gen. 9:6 which employs the term צֶלֶם rather than דְּמוּת. b. Megillah 28a, ed. Epstein, 169 refers to the likeness of wicked men, and Epstein explains it as a reference to Gen. 1:26.

[102]For Philo (Op. Mund. 71) the addition of "likeness" after "image" clarified that it was "an accurate cast, bearing a clear impression." Colson and Whitaker, Philo I, LCL, 57.

[103]"Lord of Hosts" is the standard English translation for this divine title, although the NIV employs "Lord Almighty".

[104]Laws, James, 203.

[105]Ps. 17:7 LXX καὶ ἡ κραυγή μου ἐνώπιον αὐτοῦ εἰσελεύσεται εἰς τὰ ὦτα αὐτοῦ. Cf. also 1 En. 47:1 "And in those days shall have ascended the prayer of the righteous ... before the Lord of Spirits."

[106]Dibelius and Greeven, James, 238.

pondered a situation where the rich were oppressing their workers, his mind wandered back to other contexts where the same theme was expressed. As a result James utilizes traditional OT language applying it to a new setting. This is further substantiated by the fact that the title "Lord of Hosts" had fallen into disuse in Hebrew and Aramaic speaking Judaism; we only find one reference to this phrase in the Mishnah.[107] James' adoption of this terminology is therefore most easily explained as a deliberate "Biblicizing". There is no appeal to the authority of scripture but only a use of its language to paint a familiar prophetic picture.

3.4	Jas. 5:5	Jer. 12:3 LXX	Jer. 12:3 MT[108]
	ἐθρεψάτε τὰς καρδίας ὑμῶν	δεδοκίμακας τὴν καρδίαν μου ἐναντίον σου·	וּבָחַנְתָּ לִבִּי אִתָּךְ
		ἅγνισον αὐτοὺς	הַתִּקֵם כְּצֹאן לְטִבְחָה
	ἐν ἡμέρᾳ σφαγῆς	εἰς ἡμέραν σφαγῆς αὐτῶν.	וְהַקְדִּשֵׁם לְיוֹם הֲרֵגָה

In Jer. 12 the righteous are complaining to God about the prosperity of the wicked (12:1). God, however, sees what is happening (12:3), and the wicked will in return be judged on the day of slaughter. In James the righteous man has been cruelly killed (5:6)[109] by those who have lived in luxury upon the earth (5:5); similarly they will face a day of slaughter. The specific meaning of this day of slaughter is contested but probably refers in both cases to the day of judgment similar to 1 En. 94:9.[110] Thus James is again drawing from familiar Biblical imagery without alluding to a specific OT passage to give scriptural warrant to his argument.

3.5	Jas. 5:11	Ps. 102:8; 144:8 LXX[111]
	ὅτι πολύσπλαγχνός	8c μακρόθυμος καὶ πολυέλεος·
	ἐστιν ὁ κύριος	8b ὁ κύριος,
	καὶ οἰκτίρμων.	8a οἰκτίρμων καὶ ἐλεήμων

At 5:11 James calls attention to a fact already known by his readers (εἴδετε, ὅτι). This introductory phrase often intimates that a well-known, commonly-used wisdom saying is about to be alluded to.[112] The exact wording in Pss. 102 and 144 (both LXX) witnesses to the fact that this was an easily memorizable description of God.[113] The freqency with which the adjective οἰκτίρμος (almost always referring to God) is used in the LXX supports the conjecture that this phrase has developed into a popular creed. James' use of

---

107Cf. Laws, James, 202.

108MT: "and triest my mind toward thee. Pull them out like sheep for the slaughter, and set them apart for the day of slaughter." LXX: "thou hast proved my heart before thee; purify them for the day of their slaughter." Septuagint, Greek and English, 917.

109The murder of the righteous man has also become traditional language as witnessed by Wis. 2:20 and Prov. 1:11.

110"You have ... become ready for the day of slaughter, and the day of darkness, and the day of great judgment." Cf. also 1 En. 100:7.

111In Hebrew these two texts are divergent.
Ps. 103:8 רַחוּם וְחַנּוּן יְהוָה אֶרֶךְ אַפַּיִם וְרַב־חָסֶד
Ps. 145:8 חַנּוּן וְרַחוּם יְהוָה אֶרֶךְ אַפַּיִם וּגְדָל־חָסֶד

112Cf. above, pp. 32-33.

113Helmut Köster, s.v. σπλάγχνον, TDNT, VII: 557 calls it a common OT formula.

πολύσπλαγχνος rather than the traditional term πολυέλεος may indicate that James coined the term himself, since this is its first occurrence in our knowledge of the Greek language.[114] However, this term certainly derives from the tie between the physical organ, bowels (σπλάγχνον), and the expression of various emotions (esp. mercy) already common in the OT. The frequent presence of πολύσπλαγχνος in the Shepherd of Hermas[115] indicates that it was gaining popularity even though the term used in the Psalms (πολυέλεος) is the more familiar equivalent.[116] It is improbable that James is consciously alluding to Pss. 102:8; 144:8 LXX since the order is here reversed. Instead this description of God's character has become everyday language, and James the teacher of wisdom naturally utilizes traditional religious sayings.

3.6 Jas. 5:20[117]	1 Pet. 4:8	1 Cl.49:5 (2 Cl. 16:4)
γινωσκέτω ὅτι	ὅτι	
ὁ ἐπιστρέψας ἁμαρτωλὸν	ἀγάπη	ἀγάπη (δὲ)
... καλύψει	καλύπτει	καλύπτει
πλῆθος ἁμαρτιῶν.	πλῆθος ἁμαρτιῶν.	πλῆθος ἁμαρτιῶν.

Jas. 5:20	Prov. 10:12 LXX	Prov.10:12 MT[118]
γινωσκέτω ὅτι		
ὁ ἐπιστρέψας ἁμαρτωλὸν		12a
	12a μῖσος ἐγείρει νεῖκος,	שִׂנְאָה תְּעוֹרֵר מְדָנִים
... καλύψει	12c καλύπτει φιλία.	תְּכַסֶּה אַהֲבָה 12c
πλῆθος ἁμαρτιῶν.	12b πάντας δὲ τοὺς	וְעַל כָּל־ 12b
	μὴ φιλονεικοῦντας	פְּשָׁעִים

Although James has thus far consistently followed the LXX, here he omits the newly worded second clause of the LXX, "affection covers all that do not love strife," which is accommodated to the first phrase "hatred stirs up strife". Therefore the wording in the present instance appears at first glance to be more closely linked with the Hebrew (even more so in 1 Peter). But if James, Peter, and Clement have followed the Hebrew, then it is strange that the term "multitude" is consistently employed whereas the Hebrew states, "love covers all offenses."[119] From this discrepancy Laws has concluded,

---

[114]Cf. Laws, James, 217; Köster, TDNT, VII: 557, n. 55.

[115]Mand. 4,3,5; Sim. 5,7,4 and as a noun (πολυσπλαγχνία) in Vis. 1,3,2; 2,2,8; 4,2,3; Mand. 9:2

[116]Neither πολύσπλαγχνος nor εὔσπλαγχνος are used in the LXX; only οἰκτίρμων, ἐλεήμων, πολυέλεος, and μακρόθυμος are common.

[117]Johnson, "Lev. 19 in James," 398 argues that Jas. 5:20 is functionally much closer to Lev. 19:17b, but he has overestimated the importance of Lev. 19:12-18 for James. Cf. above, p. 35.

[118]Prov. 10:12 MT "Hatred stirs up strife, but love covers all offenses." LXX "Hatred stirs up strife, but affection covers all that do not love strife." Septuagint, English and Greek, 797.

[119]כָּל is nowhere translated by πλῆθος in the LXX. Cf. Edwin Hatch and Henry Redpath, A Concordance to the Septuagint (Grand Rapids: Baker, 1983), II: 1142-1144.

Others have posited the presence of a saying of Jesus not paralleled in the gospels, although this is impossible to prove.[121] Whatever its origin, it became a popular proverbial saying in contexts about love (1 Pet. 4:8; 1 Cl. 49:5), good deeds (2 Cl. 16:4), and the retrieving of backsliders (Jas. 5:20). James clearly adapts this saying to his context, dropping the theme of love, relating forgiveness to the work of covering sin,[122] and placing the verb in the future tense. The phrase γινωσκέτω ὅτι hints at the presence of preexistent material whose familiar terminology James uses to develop his exhortations. Here again the formal authority of scripture is not appealed to, although its familiar language is certainly utilized.

4.0 The Possible Use of Jewish Extra-Biblical Literature

Out of all the extra-Biblical literature[123] the Wisdom of Jesus Son of Sirach (Ecclesiasticus) is the most frequently recognized source for literary dependence.[124] As Ropes explains,

> Many topics referred to by James appear in it; thus, the dangers proceeding from the tongue (Eccles. 19:6-12; 20:5-8, 18-20; 22:27; 28:13-26; 35(32):7-9), wisdom the gift of God (1:1-10), prayer with a divided heart (1:27), pride (10:7-18), the uncertainty of life (10:10; 11:16-17), blaming God (15:11-20), man as made in God's image and ruling over the beasts (17:3f), the eclipse of the sun and the changes of the moon (17:31; 27:11). Other passages remind us of the conditions implied in James; so 4:10, the widow and orphan; 7:35, visiting the sick; 13:19f, oppression of the poor by the rich; 18:15, on grudging beneficence; 38:9f, prayer and confession by the sick.[125]

If we were to catagorize these parallels, they would all fall within the rubric, parallels of content alone.[126] There is only one parallel where both content and terminology are somewhat similar.

---

[121]Didascalia 2,3,3 "Et sit misericors er benevolus et caritate plenus, quia dicit Dominus: Caritas operit multitudinem peccatorum" in ed. Franciscus X. Funk, Didascalia et Constitutiones Apostolorum, 34. The later Apostolic Constitutions quote Jn. 13:35 instead. R. Hugh Connally, Didascalia Apostolorum (Oxford, Clarendon, 1969), lxxii and Alfred Resch, Agrapha: Außercanonische Schriftfragmente, 311 indicate that 1 Pet. 4:8 is recited as a dominical saying. When reciting this saying Clement of Alexandria quotes Clement of Rome (Strom. 4,11,3) or refers to citations of Paul and John in the immediate context (Dives 38:2). Although in Paed. 3,91,3 he follows the passage in question with a canonical saying of the Lord (Lk. 20:25), A. Cleveland Coxe, The Ante-Nicene Fathers, II: 293 calls our saying a NT quote from 1 Pet. 4:8. Therefore, the lone reference to the Lord in Didascalia 2,3,3 is probably a mistake.

[122]Exegetes have differed over whether the sins being covered belong to the converter, the converted, or both.

[123]I am assuming a Protestant canon here.

[124]The Wisdom of Solomon usually takes second place when the Epistle of James and apocryphal literature are compared, but Jas. 5:6 = Wis. 2:6-20 is the only important parallel. See Oesterley, "James," 405-406 for an extended list of parallels with both Sirach and the Wisdom of Solomon.

[125]Ropes, James, 19.

[126]Esp. Jas. 1:5 = Sir. 1:3,26; 1:19 = 5:11; 3:6 = 5:13-14; 5:4 = 4:6; 5:14 = 38:9.

Jas. 1:19	Sir. 5:11
ἔστω δὲ πᾶς ἄνθρωπος ταχὺς εἰς τὸ ἀκοῦσαι, βραδὺς εἰς τὸ λαλῆσαι, βραδὺς εἰς ὀργήν·	γίνου ταχὺς ἐν ἀκροάσει σου καὶ ἐν μακροθυμίᾳ φθέγγου ἀπόκρισιν.

The verbal similarities are so minimal that this parallel can in no way be classified as a deliberate allusion. The best solution to these agreements is that given by Dibelius:

> In paraenesis, ideas from Wisdom literature are often transmitted in prose form. Therefore, one who stood within the paraenetic tradition was also at home in the thought-world of Wisdom literature.[127]

Thus the conclusion of Sir. 5 and Jas. 1:19-25 both develop traditional wisdom about hearing and speaking.

In our opinion, the parallels with the pseudepigraphal book, the Testaments of the Twelve Patriarchs, should receive more scholarly attention than the parallels with Sirach since both parallels of terminology and content exist.[128] Therefore, we will list the most significant of these parallels and briefly state their relationship to the Epistle of James.[129] First of all, in both writings endurance during temptation makes one approved before God and results in numerous good things.

Jas. 1:2-3	Test. Jos. 2:7[130]
πειρασμοῖς περιπέσητε ποικίλοις ... τὸ δοκίμιον ὑμῶν τῆς πίστεως κατεργάζεται ὑπομονήν.	ἐν δέκα πειρασμοῖς δόκιμόν με ἀπέδειξε, καὶ ἐν πᾶσιν αὐτοῖς ἐμακροθύμησα· ... καὶ πολλὰ ἀγαθὰ δίδωσιν ἡ ὑπομονή.

However, the different contexts witness against any direct dependence upon the Testament of Joseph since the ten temptations faced by Joseph are surely not in the mind of James. Rather traditional language about the patient endurance of suffering is being employed.[131]

Similarly, both documents develop the reciprocal relationship between the compassion shown to others and the mercy returned by the Lord.

---

[127] Dibelius and Greeven, James, 27.

[128] In saying this, we are not recommending the allegorical use of the Testaments of the Twelve Patriarchs which characterizes Adolf Meyer's book, Das Rätsel des Jacobusbriefes.

[129] Cf. R.H. Charles, The Testaments of the Twelve Patriarchs, xc for parallels between the Epistle of James and the Testaments of the Twelve Patriarchs.

[130] Marinus de Jonge, H.W. Hollander, H.J. de Jonge, and Th. Korteweg, The Testaments of the Twelve Patriarchs: A Critical Edition of the Greek Text, 146. Charles' translation: "In ten temptations He showed me approved, and in all of them I endured; for endurance is a mighty charm, and patience giveth many good things."

[131] Cf. Marinus de Jonge and H.W. Hollander, The Testaments of the Twelve Patriarchs: A Commentary, 363.

Jas. 2:13	Test. Zeb. 8:3[132]
ἡ γὰρ κρίσις ἀνέλεος	ὅσον γὰρ ἄνθρωπος σπλαγχνίζεται εἰς τὸν πλησίον,
τῷ μὴ ποιήσαντι ἔλεος·	τοσοῦτον Κύριος εἰς αὐτόν.

Here, however, the wording is too divergent to posit any direct relationship.

The evil practice of uttering blessings and curses at the same time is condemned by both authors. Both warn against a split personality with James speaking against double-mindedness (1:8; 4:8) and the Test. Ben. 6:6 against double sight and double hearing. Both contend that a good man should not have two types of tongues or promote poverty and wealth (Test. Ben. 6:5). The Test. Ben. 6:1 contrasts the spirit of Beliar with the angel of peace similar to the manner in which Jas. 3:15-17 contrasts a peaceable wisdom from above with an earthly devilish wisdom.

Jas. 3:9	Test. Ben. 6:5[133]
	ἡ ἀγαθὴ διάνοια
ἐν αὐτῇ (ἡ γλῶσσα)	οὐκ ἔχει δύο γλώσσας,
εὐλογοῦμεν τὸν κύριον καὶ πατέρα	εὐλογίας
καὶ ἐν αὐτῇ καταρώμεθα τοὺς ἀνθρώπους	καὶ κατάρας

Because of these similarities we can be certain that similar presuppositions are at work in both documents,[134] but the lack of identical terminology forbids us to affirm a relationship of dependence of one document upon the other.

The promise that the devil will certainly flee is taught in both James and the Testament of Naphtali.

Jas. 4:7b	Test. Naph. 8:4b[135]
ἀντίστητε δὲ τῷ διαβόλῳ	καὶ ὁ διάβολος
καὶ φεύξεται ἀφ᾽ ὑμῶν.	φεύξεται ἀφ᾽ ὑμῶν

However, the condition for the flight of the devil is different in each case. In the Testament of Naphtali one must work that which is good, while in James one must submit to God and resist the devil.

Finally, in both James and the Testament of Dan there is a call to draw near to God directly preceded by a warning calling attention to the evil powers of the devil.

---

[132] de Jonge, Testaments: Critical Edition, 98. All witnesses except b, g, l, d, (m) omit this verse. However, de Jonge and Hollander, Testaments: Commentary, 254 strongly favor the longer text as original. Charles' translation: "For in the degree in which a man hath compassion upon his neighbors, in the same degree hath the Lord also upon him." Cf. also Test. Zeb. 5:3.

[133] De Jonge, Testaments: Critical Edition, 172. Charles' translation: "The good mind hath two tongues, of blessing and cursing, of contumely and of honour, of sorrow and of joy, of quietness and of confusion, of hypocrisy and of truth, [of poverty and of wealth];"

[134] De Jonge and Hollander, Testaments: Commentary, 338-341 show that these conceptions run throughout the Testaments. Cf. Ps. 61:5 LXX and its quotation in 1 Cl. 15:3.

[135] De Jonge, Testaments: Critical Edition, 122. Charles' translation: "If ye work that which is good, my children, both men and angels shall bless you; and God shall be glorified among the Gentiles through you, and the devil shall flee from you, and the wild beasts shall fear you, and the Lord shall love you, [and the angels shall cleave to you]."

Jas. 4:7b-8a	Test. Dan 6:1b-2[136]
ἀντίστητε δὲ	καὶ προσέχετε ἑαυτοῖς
τῷ διαβόλῳ	ἀπὸ τοῦ σατανᾶ
καὶ φεύξεται ἀφ' ὑμῶν,	καὶ τῶν πνευμάτων αὐτοῦ.
*ἐγγί*σατε *τῷ* *θεῷ*	*ἐγγί*ζετε δὲ *τῷ* *θεῷ*
	καὶ τῷ ἀγγέλῳ
	τῷ παραιτουμένῳ ὑμᾶς·
καὶ ἐγγιεῖ ὑμῖν.	

However, the contrast between God and Satan is a common one, and the Testament of Dan's interest in angels is not present in the Epistle of James.

Admitting the similarities between these two documents, one must confess that noticeable differences prohibit us from categorizing these as deliberate allusions. The similarities stem more from the common subject matter found in paraenetic literature (temptations instigated by the devil, endurance, mercy and judgment, the tongue) than from literary dependence. Moreover, the employment of traditional language explains all the verbal similarities. As Ropes comments, "These ideas and phrases were a part of the ever-repeated material of Jewish sermons."[137] Finally, so many questions remain about the date and the Jewish-Christian character of the Testaments of the Twelve Patriarchs that it is difficult to draw any certain conclusions about literary dependence.[138] As with James' allusions to the OT, here too we find that traditional language and common subject matter provide the solution to the question of the nature of possible parallels. The greater quantity and better quality of the OT allusions probably stems from a more frequent reading and even memorization of the OT, whereas there is insufficient evidence to claim that James is directly dependent upon this apocryphal and pseudepigraphal literature.

5.0 Conclusions

It has become evident throughout our discussion that James utilized the LXX. He follows the LXX over against the MT at 1:10b-11 (the omission of Is. 40:7 and the expression "flower of grass"), 2:11 (the order of the commandments), 2:23 (the passive verb), and 4:6 (the description of God has changed). Only at Jas. 5:20 (with Prov. 10:12) does the MT wording appear closer, but even here the better explanation proves to be an allusion to popular phraseology as evidenced by the common occurrence of the saying in James, Peter, and Clement. The differences with the LXX (2:11 aorist subjunctive, not

---

[136]De Jonge, *Testaments: Critical Edition*, 109. 'Εγγίσατε is supported by g, d, e, f, c, h, i, j and found in Robert H. Charles, *The Greek Versions of the Testaments of the Twelve Patriarchs*. Charles' translation: "And now, fear the Lord, my children, and beware of Satan and his spirits. Draw near unto God and unto the angel that intercedeth for you, for he is a mediator between God and man."

[137]Ropes, *James*, 21.

[138]De Jonge and Hollander, *Testaments: Commentary*, 83-84 argue in favor of a second century Christian document. Cf. also Marinus de Jonge, "Christian Influence in the Testaments of the Twelve Patriarchs," *Studies on the Testaments of the Twelve Patriarchs*, 183-246. On the other hand, James H. Charlesworth, *The Old Testament Pseudepigrapha and the New Testament*, 39 envisions "not a Christian composition, but a Christian redaction of earlier Jewish testaments", and H.C. Kee, *OT Pseud.*, I: 778 categorizes it as a Jewish document with ten or twelve Christian interpolations. In our opinion, the additions are Christological and not ethical: Sim. 6:5; 7:1-2; Levi 4:4; 8:5; 10:2-3; 14:2; 18:7; Zeb. 9:8; Ash. 7:3; Dan. 5:13; Naph. 8:3; Jos. 19:11-12; Ben. 3:8; 9:3.

future indicative; 2:23 Abraham, not Abram and the addition of "Abraham, a friend of God"; 4:6 θεός, not κύριος; and 5:20 several differences) can best be explained by the phenomena of quoting from memory, the employment of popular expressions, and the fitting of these sayings into new contexts. James' employment of the LXX is not surprising since the first century (esp. Hellenistic) church accepted the LXX as their Bible.[139]

James introduces six quotes with *formulae citandi* containing either a form of the word γραφή or a verb of saying with scripture or God as the understood subject. In five of these occurrences James is quoting the OT, whereas at Jas. 4:5 an extra-Biblical writing, the book of Eldad and Modad, is probably in the mind of our author. In each case James is appealing to the authority of scripture to substantiate his arguments. Against favoritism towards the rich Jas. 2:8 appeals to the royal law contained in Lev. 19:18; in favor of seeing faith and works functioning together in justification, Jas. 2:23 appeals to Gen. 15:6; the inclination of the human spirit towards jealousy (4:5) is proven by a reminder of the lesson the people of Israel learned from their criticism of Moses' dealing with Eldad and Medad; in substantiating the fact that God gives more grace (4:6), James quotes Prov. 3:34. Jas. 2:11 does not so obviously fit this pattern, yet if the flow of James' argument is rightly interpreted, this reference to scripture is also an appeal to its authority.[140] It must be admitted, however, that the sharp distinction between the canonical OT and other Jewish literature drawn by writers in the late second and third centuries AD cannot be applied to James. Not only does he probably refer to an apocryphal book, but in describing the figures of Abraham, Rahab, Job, and Elijah, he employs extra-Biblical traditions.[141] James freely utilizes contemporary expressions within this authoritative quoting of the OT and Jewish literature. Thus, as is the case with Paul,[142] James allows himself flexibility when quoting the OT. The familiarity of these OT quotations and the inexact rendering of the text lead us to the conclusion that James quoted from memory.

James also alludes to the OT in several cases. Laws has argued that even when James does not utilize a *formula citandi*, he still grounds his arguments with scriptural authority by choosing distinctive words and phrases from the OT (1:10, the grass withers and the flower fades; 3:9, the likeness of God; 3:18, fruit of righteousness[143]; 5:4, ears of the Lord of Hosts). We have found her contentions unconvincing. In his allusions to the OT James is merely recalling a commonly experienced event of nature expressed in scriptural terminology at 1:10b-11, a popular wisdom saying at 3:18,[144] and traditional Biblical language at 3:9 and 5:4. Since James' arguments are strong enough already, no outside authority is appealed to. Blessing God and cursing humans (who are made like God) is illogical; there is no need to appeal to the additional authority of scripture at Jas. 3:9.

---

[139]In Paul 51 of 93 citations are in absolute or virtual agreement with the LXX; 22 are at variance with the Hebrew; 4 follow the Hebrew against the LXX; and 38 times his text diverges from both. Ellis, Paul's Use of OT, 12.

[140]James' argument runs like this: to show that the great commandment to love one's neighbor is not fulfilled when another ordinance (not showing favoritism) is broken, James quotes two of the ten commandments explaining that each has the authority of scripture (or each is spoken by God) and, therefore, each must be obeyed. Cf. below, pp. 94-95.

[141]Cf. Peter H. Davids, "Tradition and Citation in the Epistle of James," Scripture, Tradition, and Interpretation, 113-121. Davids (p. 122) concludes that "the freedom with which James combines the canonical with the extra-canonical means that he apparently had no firm boundary in his mind between the two."

[142]Cf. Ellis, Paul's Use of OT, 11.

[143]Laws, James, 166. We have not even recognized Jas. 3:18 as an OT allusion since there is little evidence to support a combination of Prov. 11:30 and 3:7,18 as Laws contends. Its poetic structure indicates a popular wisdom saying. Cf. ch. 3, section 4.1.

[144]In 3:18 the catchwords (καρπός and εἰρήνη with καρπῶν and εἰρηνική of 3:17) stitch a widely accepted wisdom saying into James' argument.

James' condemnation of the rich at 5:4 is in traditional and well-known religious language; it is unnecessary to make a special appeal to a formal outside authority. The clue in indicating when James is appealing to some authority for conclusive support to his arguments is not found in the choice of distinctive terms or phrases (as Laws maintains) but rather by means of an introductory formula prior to an OT quotation. James' particular selection of vocabulary is governed more by the moral discourse of the church than by his desire to ground his arguments in the authority of scripture. Dibelius convincingly points to the nature of paraenesis and in particular to its use of traditional language as the key to James' choice of vocabulary and subject matter. This accounts for the similarities with apocryphal and pseudepigraphal literature as well as with the several allusions to the OT.

We now turn to the parallels between the Epistle of James and the sayings of Jesus found in the Synoptic traditions. Does James quote Jesus to appeal to the authority of the originator of the Christian faith as he has done with specific passages from the OT by means of introductory formulas? Or does James merely allude to Jesus' sayings by means of catchwords, stitching them into the flow of his teaching? Or, to posit a third alternative, have Jesus' words already become a part of the ethical tradition that James draws upon, similar to the manner in which he utilizes traditional terminology from parts of the OT? This question moves us to the heart of our study.

Chapter 3

AN INVESTIGATION OF THE SAYINGS OF JESUS IN THE EPISTLE OF JAMES

1.1 Before we investigate the primary parallels between the sayings of Jesus and the teaching of James, it is important to ask how we should organize this discussion. One could begin with the most widely recognized parallel and finish by examining the least commonly accepted. However, in order to perceive how each saying is woven into an appropriate context, it is clearly advantageous to follow the flow of the Epistle of James. What then is the logical flow of the Epistle of James? Is there a clearly identifiable structure? A prominent position states that "the entire document lacks continuity in thought."[1] Hunter calls the epistle "an ethical scrapbook", explaining that "it is so disconnected as it stands, that it is the despair of the analyst."[2] One often hears the statement that no structure exists outside the minds of the commentators. Following this view the epistle exhibits a loose structure consisting of short isolated sayings which are sometimes grouped together to form a literary paragraph called a τόπος.[3] Halson discerns 23 isolated aphorisms and 7 (possibly 8) examples of extended paraenetic discourse.[4]

1.2 A second group of interpreters has diligently endeavored to identify some intentional progression of thought unifying the themes of the Epistle of James. Cadoux exclaims, "It is strange that so many writers have found it formless, for it is probably the most completely patterned Book in the Bible."[5] He argues that there are four primary divisions each containing four subdivisions. The first two sections (1:1-27; 2:1-3:18) are analogous in order and content, each consisting of an exposition (1:2-12; 2:1-13), a warning against a possible mistake (1:13-18; 2:14-26), a practical caution as to a person's inward life (1:19-25; 3:1-12), and finally, another cautionary statement about one's Godward life (1:26-27; 3:13-18). The last two divisions (4:1-5:6; 5:7-20) likewise each contain four paragraphs, a series of four condemnations followed by four exhortations. In another attempt Forbes proposes that James introduces his prospective topics in the ten verses following the opening greeting and then in the same order elaborates more fully on these subjects.[6] Thus the proper attitude toward the trials of life is introduced in 1:2 and elaborated in 1:12-27; the testing of faith that produces perfect works is briefly touched upon in 1:3-4 and worked out more fully in chapter 2; the wisdom that God imparts to those who ask is discussed in 1:5-8

---

[1]Dibelius and Greeven, James, 2.

[2]Archibald M. Hunter, Introducing the New Testament, 96. For similar descriptions see James B. Adamson, James: the Man and his Message, 75-76.

[3]For an explanation of this term see David G. Bradley, "The *Topos* as a Form in the Pauline Paraenesis," JBL 72(1953): 238-264. We prefer the term extended paraenetic discourse.

[4]Halson, "James: 'Christian Wisdom?'" SE 4:309, n. 5. For our evaluation of the number of aphorisms and paraenetic paragraphs see the outlines introducing each major division of ch. 3.

[5]Cadoux, Thought of James, 6-7.

[6]P.B.R. Forbes, "The Structure of the Epistle of James," EQ 44(1972): 147. Adamson, James: Man and Message, 79 states that "every principle and theme in the rest of the Epistle of James is repeated, expanded, or derived from 1:2-18 on the Christian mind ... and 1:19-27 on Christian conduct."

and chapters 3-4; finally in 1:9-11 and chapter 5 we encounter a contrast between rich and poor with an emphasis on divine judgment. Francis likewise accepts this supposition that James introduces certain themes in his first chapter and subsequently develops them in the body of the epistle, but he discovers a chiastic structure preceded by a double introduction of themes, thus the reverse order of the outline advocated by Forbes.

a.	testing/steadfastness	1:2-4	12-18
b.	wisdom-words/reproaching	1:5-8	19-21
c.	rich-poor/doers	1:9-11	22-25
c.	faith and action as regards the rich and poor	2:1-26	
b.	angry passion of wisdom, words, and position	3:1-5:6	

Thus "in James the pattern is abc/abc in the opening period and then c,b in the body of the letter, with point 'a' -- testing -- underlying the whole."[7] In our estimation James does indeed use chapter 1 to foreshadow certain themes he will later discuss, but the contrasting results exhibited above indicate that the order of contents in Jas. 1 in no way structures the rest of the book.

1.3 Others have identified one central organizing theme in James. Rustler asserts that James pursues the problem of the social tensions between rich and poor "in a well-organized manner, thought through to the smallest detail".[8] Thiessen finds the central theme outlining the entire epistle to be "becoming a perfect man";[9] Hiebert calls attention to the "tests of a living faith";[10] Gromacki outlines the contents under the two motifs of the nature of true faith and true wisdom.[11] But even someone like Hiebert who advocates a well organized, intricately knit-together composition of James concedes that "the epistle obviously does not set forth a clear structural plan heralding the logical organization of its contents."[12] No one major theme reoccurs in each section; rather we encounter a series of themes such as endurance of trials, partiality, faith and works, the tongue, wisdom, riches, and prayer which are impossible to categorize under one rubric. The particular theme chosen by the various commentators can only be assigned to subjective bias.

1.4 A small fourth group of exegetes proposes that the structure of James is patterned after a previous document or group of preexistent sayings. Johnson believes that James engages in a halachic midrash on Lev. 19:12-18;[13] Gertner attempts to prove that

---

[7]Fred O. Francis, "The Form and Function of the Opening and Closing Paragraphs of James and 1 John," ZNW 61(1970): 110. Francis' findings are supported by Peter H. Davids, The Epistle of James, 25.

[8]M. Rustler, Thema und Disposition des Jakobusbriefes: Eine formkritische Studie, 84 quoted in Dibelius and Greeven, James, 6, n. 22. His outline based on the theme rich and poor is as follows: 1) fundamental dogmatics 1:2-27; 2) practical ethics 2:1-3:12; 3) eschatology 3:13-5:20, each with three subdivisions: thesis (1:2-11; 2:1-13; 3:13-4:10), antithesis (1:12-18; 2:14-26; 4:11-5:6), and synthesis (1:14-27; 3:1-12; 5:7-20).

[9]See Henry C. Thiessen, Introduction to the New Testament, 278-279 for the various subdivisions.

[10]Hiebert, James, 7. Cf. Euan Fry, "The Testing of Faith. A Study of the Structure of the Book of James." BTr 29(1978): 435.

[11]Robert G. Gromacki, New Testament Survey, 341.

[12]Hiebert, James, 41.

[13]Johnson, "Leviticus 19 in James," 401.

James is a midrash on Psalm 12;[14] and, as we saw earlier, Meyer argues for an allegory based upon the Testaments of the Twelve Patriarchs.[15] Other exegetes base the structure of James upon its use of preexistent sayings, especially those derived from the Jesus-tradition. Shepherd discerns a series of eight homiletic-didactic discourses which are built around or contain a central macarism or gnomic saying adapted by the author to his particular theme.[16]

Topic	Saying
1. Endurance of Trials (1:2-18)	1:12
2. Hearing and Doing (1:19-27)	1:25
3. Respect of Persons (2:1-13)	2:5 or 2:10
4. Faith and Works (2:14-26)	comparable to 2:20 and 2:26
5. Evil-speaking (3:1-12)	3:2
6. Factiousness (3:13-4:10)	4:4
(Recapitulation 4:11-12)	
7. Two Woes: On the Rich (4:13-5:6)	4:17
8. Patience (5:7-18)	5:11
(Summary 5:19-20)	

Woven around this central *macarism* Shepherd detects significant parallels to the sayings of Jesus, especially as found in the Gospel of Matthew. Almost each section is controlled by the teaching of Jesus: thus he reports about section 1: "the section might also be taken as a commentary upon the petition of the Lord's prayer, 'Lead us not into temptation'"; and section 2: "Underneath this whole section in James, however, is the gospel principle found in two Q sayings of Jesus: Matt. 7:21=Luke 6:46, and Matt. 7:26=Luke 6:59;" and section 5: "the whole diatribe of James on the tongue may be considered as a homiletic illustration of the saying of Jesus in Matt. 12:36."[17] Additional support for this approach comes from Michaels who explains that "the substance of his letter is a series of sermonic expansions of certain sayings of Jesus."[18] Michaels perceives four brief homilies merged into one letter:

1. on temptation (1:2-18) based upon the sixth petition of the Lord's prayer;
2. on the law of love (1:19-2:26) with Lev. 19:18 being interpreted by Jesus (Mt. 22:37-40 par.);
3. on evil speaking (3:1-4:12) based upon Mt. 15:11,17-20;
4. on endurance (4:13-5:20) based on Mk. 13:13 par.

Recently Davids affirms the truth of this approach, stating that "every section of the Epistle of James appears to have some contact with the Jesus-tradition" in such a fashion that the gospel material is found in "either the opening argument or the summarizing argument in most blocks in James".[19] This close connection of dependence between the structure of James and the sayings of Jesus appears to be forced. Each division of Michaels contains much material that is not based upon the particular saying of Jesus which is singled out.

---

[14]M. Gertner, "Midrashim in the New Testament," JSS 7(1962): 283-290. Cf. Anthony Hanson, "Seminar Report," NTS 25(1978-79): 526.

[15]Cf. above, pp. 23-24.

[16]Shepherd, "James and Matthew," 41-42.

[17]Ibid., 44-46.

[18]J. Ramsey Michaels, "James -- The Royal Law," The New Testament Speaks, 329. Michaels says this feature makes James unique among the NT epistles.

[19]Peter H. Davids, "Jesus-Paraenesis in the Catholic Epistles," paper presented at the SBL conference, Chicago, Dec., 1984, p. 3.

Because of its detail, Shepherd's outline more faithfully captures the movements in James' progression of thought, but the positing of one central *macarism* in each discourse definitely seems arbitrary. It is more accurate to suggest that James employs a series of gnomic sayings than that one prominent saying controls the development of thought in each section. Davids' view that sayings of Jesus normally introduce or summarize each section assigns material to Jesus which in certain cases (cf. 2:13; 3:12,18) has much closer parallels with Jewish sources or the everyday wisdom of the Hellenistic world. Furthermore, James' important discourse on faith and works (2:14-26) and the section denouncing the worldly merchants (4:13-17) contain no discernable Jesus-saying.

1.5 Although some view James as a series of homilies based upon specific preexistent *logia* of Jesus, it is more helpful to distinguish different types of paraenetic literature (sub-genre, if you will) within the Epistle of James. The entire epistle has been categorized as paraenesis,[20] but this genre can be used for various literary purposes.[21] In fact it is precisely these subdivisions of genre which mark off the turning points in the flow of the Epistle of James. In Jas. 1 we encounter a series of sayings loosely tied together by catchwords which can best be described as general paraenesis.[22] In Jas. 2:1-3:12 the subject matter is more ordered and logically developed around the themes of partiality (2:1-13), faith and works (2:14-26), and the tongue (3:1-12) so that the style could more appropriately be entitled, extended paraenetic discourse.[23] The paraenesis of chapter 3:13-4:10 consists of two disciplinary exhortations not addressed as usual to brethren, but rather to the adulteresses (4:4), sinners (4:8), and double-minded (4:8) of the community, calling them back to the life-style of the wise (3:13-18) and a behavior pattern not given to quarrels (4:1-10).[24] The paraenesis of the following section, 4:13-5:6, consists of two prophetic denunciations against the worldly-minded merchants (4:13-17) and the oppressive rich (5:1-6), each beginning with the same formula ἄγε νῦν. Finally, in 5:7-20 there are four loosely connected sections[25] of general paraenesis which are grouped together as a primitive church order on the topics of eschatology, oaths, healing, confession of sins, prayer, and backsliding. Thus the major divisions in the Epistle of James could be described as sub-genre of paraenesis, the movement being from general paraenesis, to extended discourse, to disciplinary exhortations, to prophetic denunciations, and finally to general paraenesis constructed into a primitive church order. Most of the sections begin with the address, "my (beloved) brethren"; this introduction is omitted when a disciplinary exhortation (3:13-4:10) or a prophetic denunciation (4:13-5:6) is employed. These various paraenetic sections are

---

[20]Ferdinard Hahn, "Die christologische Begründung urchristlicher Paränese, ZNW 72 (1981): 89, n. 13. Cf. below, ch. 5, section 3.5.

[21]Cf. Stanley K. Stowers, Letter Writing in Greco-Roman Antiquity, 23,94-96 who argues against understanding paraenesis too narrowly defined as just the stringing together of traditional exhortations.

[22]In Jas. 1 several more or less isolated sayings are developed into three paraenetic paragraphs each beginning with the address, "my (beloved) brethren" (1:2-15, 16-17, 19-27).

[23]Davids, James, 23 is correct when he states that only the context imagined for such discourse will reveal whether the Greek term "diatribe" or the Jewish expression "homily" is more applicable.

[24]Hoppe, Hintergrund des Jakobusbriefes, 10 contends that 4:1-12 should be separated from 3:13-18 and be categorized as the third diatribe of James. Yet these two series of exhortations are organized similarly. Cf. ch. 3, section 4.0.

[25]Three sections begin with the address "brethren": 5:7-11, 12, 19-20. 5:13 probably omits the address since section two (5:12) is so short. The frequency of the address in 5:7-11 (vv. 7,9,10) indicates the importance the author places upon these exhortations as in 3:10-12.

connected with isolated traditional wisdom sayings which are interspersed between the sections to serve as transitions (1:26-27 ?; 2:13; 3:18; 4:11-12; 4:17).[26] Thus there is no comprehensive structure based upon one particular theme or intentional progression of thought, yet the different sections of James' work display a strong inner consistency and together illustrate various ways in which church leaders exhorted their communities.

Because these different types of paraenetic literature reveal the inner structure of the book, it is advantageous to arrange the list of synoptic parallels into the following divisions:

1. The Synoptic parallels in the general paraenesis of Jas. 1:2-27;
2. The Synoptic parallels in the three paraenetic discourses of Jas. 2:1-3:12;
3. The Synoptic parallels in the disciplinary exhortations of Jas. 3:13-4:10 (12);
4. The Synoptic parallels in the prophetic denunciations of Jas. 4:13-5:6;
5. The Synoptic parallels in the general paraenesis of Jas. 5:7-20 developed into a primitive church order.

We now turn to the twenty parallels most often enumerated by the commentators of the 19th and 20th centuries. With each parallel we will evaluate if James is alluding to a saying in the Jesus-tradition by investigating the criteria[27] of 1) comparable subject matter and context; 2) similar phraseology and form; 3) the parallels in other literature; and 4) support from the history of interpretation.

2.0 The Synoptic Parallels in the General Paraenesis of Jas. 1

Within this division of the Epistle of James there are small paraenetic paragraphs and isolated aphorisms as illustrated below.

A. 1:2-15 Major paraenetic paragraph: On Trials. (introduced by "my brethren").

1. 1:2-4 Short paraenetic paragraph: The beneficial results of trials.
    a. 1:2 "Catechetical" exhortation about trials (possible catchword χαίρειν / χαρὰν).
    b. 1:3 Reminder of an apostolic teaching: testing produces endurance.
    c. 1:4 James' concluding exhortation (connected by stitchword ὑπομονήν / ὑπομονή). τέλειος is Jamesian vocabulary (cf. 1:17,25; 3:2).

2. 1:5-8 Short paraenetic paragraph: Asking for help in times of trial.
    a. 1:5a Exhortation (connected by stitchword λειπόμενοι / λείπεται). σοφία is a theme of James. cf. 3:13-17.
    b. 1:5b Allusion to a saying of Jesus.
    c. 1:6a Popular Christian teaching: pray in faith (catchword αἰτείτω / αἰτείτω).
    d. 1:6b Illustration from nature (connected by stitchword διακρινόμενος / διακρινόμενος).
    e. 1:7-8 James' conclusion (δίψυχος 1:8; 4:8 and ἀκατάστατος 1:8; 3:8,16 are Jamesian vocabulary).

---

[26]Mayor, James, cxxxix calls this one of the most marked characteristics of the epistle.

[27]Kittel, "Der geschichtliche Ort," 91-92, n. 39 lists four criteria for establishing allusions: 1) content (*Inhalt*); 2) selection of vocabulary (*Wahl der Vokabel*); 3) peculiar terseness of expression (*eigenartigen Prägnanz des Ausdruckes*) and 4) other allusions of Jesus' sayings in the same context (*sonstigen Jesus-anklänge im Kontext*).

3. 1:9-11 Short paraenetic paragraph: Trials can be related to wealth.
    a. 1:9-10a Exhortation to the lowly and rich.
    b. 1:10b-11a Allusion to the nature imagery of Is. 40:6-7.
    c. 1:11b James' conclusion (the condemnation of the rich is a major theme. cf. 2:1-7; 5:1-6).

4. 1:12 Aphorism: A blessing on those who endure temptations.
    (possible catchword connections: 1:4,12 ὑπομονή / ὑπομένει; 1:2,12,13 πειρασμοῖς / πειρασμόν / πειραζόμενος; 1:3,12 δοκίμιον / δόκιμος; 1:7,12 λήμψεταί / λήμψεται).

5. 1:13-15 Short paraenetic paragraph: God does not tempt.
    a. 1:13a Exhortation (connected by stitchword πειρασμόν / πειράζομαι).
    b. 1:13b Religious aphorism (connected by catchword πειράζομαι / ἀπείραστος / πειράζει).
    c. 1:14-15 James' concluding explanation (connected by stitchword πειράζει / πειράζεται).

B. 1:16-18 Major paragraph: Kerygma rather than paraenetic exhortations. (introduced by "my beloved brethren").

1. 1:16 Introductory exhortation.

2. 1:17 Teaching about the nature of God.

3. 1:18 Teaching about the word of salvation.

C. 1:19-27 Major paraenetic paragraph: Doing the word. (introduced by "my beloved brethren").

1. 1:19-21 Short paraenetic paragraph: Good and evil character qualities.
    a. 1:19 Exhortation about hearing and speaking.
    b. 1:20 Religious aphorism (connected by catchword ὀργήν / ὀργή).
    c. 1:21 "Catechetical" exhortation about putting on and putting off certain character qualities.

2. 1:22-25 Short paraenetic paragraph: Doers of the word and not hearers only.
    a. 1:22 Exhortation about hearing and doing (connected by stitchword λόγου / λόγου).
    b. 1:23-24 Illustration from everyday life.
    c. 1:25 James' concluding explanation. (The law is one of James' major emphases. cf. 2:8,13; 4:11-12).

3. 1:26-27 Short paraenetic paragraph: Vain religion vs. pure religion.
    a. 1:26 Vain religion (Teaching on the tongue is important to James. cf. 3:1-12).
    b. 1:27 Pure religion.

Jas. 1 consists of short paragraphs of ethical teaching loosely tied together. James begins almost every paragraph with an exhortation, then stitches already known material (apostolic teaching, sayings of Jesus, OT allusions, illustrations from nature etc.) into the flow of his thought, and finally offers his own conclusion or explanation. The first half of the chapter transmits material related to trials and temptations. In order to help the Christian community face the possibility of suffering, James advocates endurance, prayer, faith, wisdom, and a sure knowledge that God does not tempt human beings. In Jas. 1:9-11 we have our first hint that the wealthy are involved in the distress afflicting the church, a theme further developed in 2:5-7 and 5:1-6. In the second half of this chapter James is particularly concerned that the people of God not be deceived. The RSV and NIV translations employ the word "deceived" for three different Greek verbs (1:16 πλανάω; 1:22 παραλογίζομαι; 1:26 ἀπατάω). In 1:16-18 we encounter the only example of kerygma in the paraenesis of James. At 1:18 and 1:21 James speaks about the "word of truth" and "the implanted word which is able to save your souls". Grounded upon this word of salvation, the readers are exhorted about hearing and speaking (1:19), hearing and doing (1:22-26), and speaking and doing (1:27-28). The doing of the perfect law of liberty lies at the heart of James' theology of the Christian life.

2.1 Jas. 1:2	Mt. 5:11-12a	Lk. 6:22-23a
2b	11 μακάριοί ἐστε	22 μακάριοί ἐστε
ὅταν πειρασμοῖς	ὅταν ὀνειδίσωσιν ὑμας	ὅταν μισήσωσιν ὑμας
περιπέσητε		οἱ ἄνθρωποι καὶ
ποικίλοις.	καὶ διώξωσιν	ὅταν ἀφορίσωσιν ὑμᾶς
		καὶ ὀνειδίσωσιν
	καὶ εἴπωσιν πᾶν πονηρὸν	καὶ ἐκβάλωσιν τὸ ὄνομα
	καθ᾽ ὑμῶν ψευδόμενοι	ὑμῶν ὡς πονηρὸν ἕνεκα
2a	ἕνεκεν ἐμοῦ.	τοῦ υἱοῦ τοῦ ἀνθρώπου·
πᾶσαν χαρὰν	12 χαίρετε	23 χάρητε ἐν ἐκείνῃ τῇ
ἡγήσασθε,	καὶ ἀγαλλιᾶσθε,	ἡμέρᾳ καὶ σκιρτήσατε,
	ὅτι ὁ μισθὸς ὑμῶν	ἰδοὺ γὰρ ὁ μισθὸς ὑμων
	πολὺς ἐν τοῖς οὐρανοῖς·	πολὺς ἐν τῷ οὐρανῷ·

In both the gospel references and James we encounter an imperative requiring an attitude of joy in difficult situations. In addition Eleder contends that the same themes are considered in relatively similar progressions of thought: blessed joy, persecution or testing (Jas. 1:2; Mt. 5:11), steadfast faith, patience (Jas. 1:3; Mt. 5:11), perfection as a guide to eternal joy (Jas. 1:4; Mt. 5:12), a greater heavenly reward (Jas. 1:12; Mt. 5:12), and the prophets used as paradigms (Jas. 5:10; Mt. 5:12).[28] Regarding vocabulary, Davids contends that the common use of the root χαίρω is significant.[29] To explain the diversity of vocabulary, advocates supporting an allusion to Jesus' beatitude contend that the designation "various trials" is a summary of the more specific examples (persecuted, excluded, hated, insulted) listed in the gospels. Evidence for this theory is found in the similar descriptions of trials scattered throughout the epistle. Thus, for example, the blaspheming of the honorable name (2:7) would be similar to the "casting out of your name as evil on account of the Son of man" found in the gospels. To verify this identification one must prove that James' term πειρασμός refers to outward afflictions similar to the gospels. πειρασμός can either imply inward impulses prompting a man to evil (temptations) or outward pressures caused by persecution (afflictions). In 1:13-15, where James describes being enticed by one's own desires, he is obviously referring to temptations, not trials. Yet from this usage of πειράζω one cannot conclude that temptations are in the mind of James already in v. 2. The specific connection with endurance (1:3,12) and the context of parallel passages in the letters of Paul (Rom. 5:3-5) and Peter (1 Pet. 1:6-7) support the conclusion that Jas. 1:1-12 deals with trials rather than with temptations. The connection between these external trials and internal temptations is such that the trials of oppression feed the temptation to conclude that God is to blame (1:13). Thus by πειρασμός James means the

---

[28] Eleder, Jacobusbrief und Bergpredigt, 114.
[29] Davids, "James and Jesus," 10.

outward pressures of life (1:1-12) which test the inward character of people tempting them to despair of God's presence and working (1:13-16). James believes that an attitude of joyful endurance can overcome these afflictions and the resulting temptations. Exegetes who discern a dominical saying in Jas. 1:2 are thus justified in contending that the outward trials are the subject matter in both the gospels and James. Besides parallel content, Davids offers one additional argument for the presence of a Jesus-saying by calling attention to the amount of overlap with the beatitudes of Jesus throughout James' epistle.[30]

In arguing for a contrary conclusion we will call attention to 1) the differences with the Synoptic traditions; 2) the structuring of material throughout the first chapter of James where source material is inserted into the middle of each small paraenetic paragraph; 3) the insufficient evidence for positing a connection between Jas. 1:2 and the gospel references when compared with the superior parallels encountered in a legitimate allusion to this Jesus-logion in 1 Pet. 4:13-14; and 4) the common NT paraenetic teaching pattern with which Jas. 1:2 can be more validly compared.

The differences between Jas. 1:2 and the Synoptic traditions are substantial:
1) James does not preserve the μακάριος form of the saying, although he regularly employs it elsewhere (1:12,25; 5:11);
2) There is no reference to Jesus either as the Son of Man (Lk.) or by the phrase "on my account" (Mt.).
3) The eschatological reward is altered in James to an earthly reward of patience and wholeness.[31]
4) Only two words are identical: "joy" (an imperative in the gospels and a noun in James) and "when".
5) The order of the phrases is also reversed so that the description of the situation follows the exhortation in the Epistle of James.
6) Those who have set the highest criteria for recognizing sayings of Jesus have unanimously rejected this reference as a gospel allusion; it is not found in any author who lists less than ten parallels between the teaching of James and the *logia* of Jesus.

Eleder's series of similarities, previously mentioned, covers over these differences and misleads the reader to assume a greater uniformity than in reality is the case. James and Jesus advocate a similar perspective: rejoicing in the midst of difficult circumstances, but there the agreement ends. If the examples in James are not hypothetical, these "various trials" are mostly economic in nature. The rich drag the poor to court (2:6), defraud them of their wages (5:4), and even kill the righteous man (5:6; 4:2; 2:11). In addition, a religious dimension to the oppression is evident in 2:7 where the wealthy not only disenfranchise the Christian poor but also blaspheme the name of their Lord Jesus. Therefore the persecution (Mt.), exclusion (Lk.), hatred (Lk.), and insult (Mt. and LK.) mentioned in the gospels is roughly comparable to the situation in James. However, the lack of similar terminology and the recognition that the term "various trials" is derived from the ecclesiastical paraenetic tradition as evidence in 1 Pet. 1:6 makes it invalid to assume that ποικίλοις πειρασμοῖς is a summary of the more specific kinds of affliction found in Mt. 5:11; Lk. 6:22. Mitton has gone too far in asserting that "his injunction here might indeed be a summary of these four beatitudes from Luke."[32] In our opinion, it is far more likely that James is repeating a church catechetical teaching embedded in the paraenetic tradition.

---

[30]Ibid. Cf. ch. 3, section 3.2 below.

[31]Mußner and Davids view James' concept of perfection at 1:4 as eschatological but Laws, James, 54 offers a better explanation: "to be *teleios* is to be a complete person, having integrity, unlike the divided man of vv. 6-8." James does mention an eschatological reward in 1:12, but this is a completely different saying extracted from other source material, sometimes designated as an unknown saying of Jesus. Cf. ch. 7, n. 6.

[32]Mitton, James, 20.

In investigating the structure of the first chapter of James (cf 2.0), one notices that James regularly begins each small paraenetic paragraph with an exhortation (1:2,5,9,13,16,19, 22) and finishes with his own fitting conclusion or explanation (1:4,7-8,11b,14-15,25). Between this material James employs previously known teaching material (1:3,6a), religious aphorisms (1:13b,20), illustrations from nature (1:6b) and everyday experience (1:23-24), OT language (1:10b-11a), and allusions to sayings of Jesus (1:5b). Since James alludes to well-known teaching material at 1:3 (γινώσκοντες ὅτι), we would not expect to discover an allusion to other source material such as a dominical saying at Jas. 1:2. Instead James begins with his own exhortation as is his custom throughout the first chapter.

If we compare both 1 Pet. 4:13-14 and Jas. 1:2 with Mt. 5:11-12a; Lk. 6:22-23a, the differences between a legitimate, intentional allusion to a saying of Jesus and a mere parallel of content becomes obvious.

1 Pet. 4:13-14	Mt. 5·11-12
14εἰ ὀνειδίζεσθε ἐν ὀνόματι Χριστοῦ, μακάριοι, ὅτι τὸ τῆς δόξης καὶ τὸ τοῦ θεοῦ πνεῦμα ἐφ' ὑμᾶς ἀναπαύεται.	μακάριοί ἐστε ὅταν ὀνειδίσωσιν ὑμᾶς καὶ διώξωσιν καὶ εἴπωσιν πᾶν πονηρὸν καθ' ὑμῶν ψευδόμενοι ἕνεκεν ἐμοῦ.
13ἀλλὰ καθὸ κοινωνεῖτε τοῖς τοῦ Χριστοῦ παθήμασιν χαίρετε,	χαίρετε
ἵνα καὶ ἐν τῇ ἀποκαλύψει τῆς δόξης αὐτοῦ χαρῆτε ἀγαλλιώμενοι.	καὶ ἀγαλλιᾶσθε, ὅτι ὁ μισθὸς ὑμῶν πολὺς ἐν τοῖς οὐρανοῖς·

The striking presence of four exact terms (ὀνειδίζω, μακάριος, χαίρω, ἀγαλλιάω) as well as the parallel expression ἐν ὀνόματι Χριστοῦ = ἕνεκεν ἐμοῦ demonstrates the close tie between these two passages. The change of order can be accounted for by the paraenetic nature of 1 Pet. 4:13f where the imperative is of prime importance and is, therefore, placed at the head of the sentence (also in Jas. 1:2). The double reference to "glory" in 1 Pet. 4:13-14 as well as the allusion to Is. 11:2 where the Spirit of God rests upon the one who judges the poor with righteousness (11:4) parallels the mentioning of the reward in heaven promised to the suffering in the gospels. The corresponding vocabulary visible in 1 Pet. 4:13-14 is absent in Jas. 1:2. Instead the phraseology of Jas. 1:2 is reminiscent of 1 Pet. 1:6 and Rom. 5:3-5.

An investigation of these passages[33] reveals striking similarities of vocabulary as well as the presence of parallel concepts.

Jas. 1:2-4	1 Pet. 1:6-7	Rom. 5:3-5
Count it all joy, when you meet	In this you rejoice (ἀγαλλιᾶσθε), though now for a little while you may have to suffer	More than that, we rejoice (καυχώμεθα) in our sufferings,
various trials,	various trials,	
for you know that the testing of your faith produces endurance.	so that the genuineness of your faith ... may redound to praise	knowing that suffering produces endurance,

[33]For the Greek see Appendix II, pp. 251,256.

Jas. 1:2-4	1 Pet. 1:6-7	Rom. 5:3-5
And let <u>endurance</u> have its full effect, that you may be perfect and complete, lacking in nothing.	and glory and honor at the revelation of Jesus Christ.	and <u>endurance</u> produces character, and character produces hope, and hope does not disappoint us ...

The differences between the texts[34] indicate that the authors are not quoting each other or any standardized literary source. Instead the early church appears to have developed a common teaching pattern (probably for catechetical purposes) emphasizing the necessity of rejoicing in times of struggle.[35] Thus Davids is correct when he states, "The best explanation of both the similarities and the differences among these passages is that all three employ a common traditional form circulating in the early church."[36] When he adds, however, that this form probably stems originally from a saying of Jesus, he is making a hypothetical leap which is unwarranted by the inexact similarities of phraseology. It is more accurate to conclude that the ethical tradition of the church incorporated many of the major themes of Jesus' preaching into its paraenesis without taking over any specific sayings.

In his commentary on 1 Peter Selwyn has argued that "the thought of rejoicing in suffering for the faith is specifically Christian and goes back to our Lord's own teaching."[37] 1 Pet. 1:6 and 4:13-14 as well as Jas. 1:2 trace back according to Selwyn to a persecution source which "lies close, verbally as in substance, to some of the most authentic *verba Christi*."[38] Reviewing Selwyn's thesis, Nauck, on the other hand, concludes that the sayings about joy in tribulation neither originate with Jesus nor demonstrate direct dependence upon the gospel tradition.[39] Instead passages like 1 Pet. 1:6; 4:13f; Jas. 1:2,12; 1 Thess. 1:6; 2 Thess. 1:4-6; 2 Cor. 8:2; Rom. 5:3-5; Heb. 10:32-36; Acts 5:41 as well as the gospel references (Mt. 5:11-12 par.) have all developed out of an earlier Jewish tradition witnessed in such texts as Judith 8:25-27;[40] Wis. 3:5-6;[41] and 2 Bar. 48:48-50; 52:5-7; 54:16-18[42]

---

[34]Davids, <u>James</u>, 66 says, "James is verbally closer to 1 Peter, but his thought is closer to Paul's in that both he and Paul value the virtues produced by the trying circumstances rather than the test itself."

[35]In the book of Acts (5:41; 16:25 etc.) joy in the midst of trials is the repeated experience of the church.

[36]Davids, <u>James</u>, 66.

[37]Selwyn, <u>First Peter</u>, 450.

[38]Ibid., 455.

[39]Wolfgang Nauck, "Freude im Leiden," <u>ZNW</u> 46(1955): 73,71.

[40]"Let us give thanks to the Lord our God, who is putting us to the test as he did our forefathers." (εὐχαριστήσωμεν κυρίῳ τῷ θεῷ ἡμῶν, ὅς πειράζει ἡμᾶς καθὰ καὶ τοὺς πατέρας ἡμῶν.)

[41]"And after being disciplined a little, they will be shown great kindness. For God has tried them (ἐπείρασεν), and found them worthy of himself. He has tested (ἐδοκίμασεν) them like gold in a furnace..."

[42]The dating of 2 (Syriac) Baruch is difficult. Charles (<u>APOT</u> II, 480) contends that 2 Bar. 52:6 is dependent upon Jas. 1:2 or some common source, while this is contested by Nauck, "Freude im Leiden," 76, n. 51. Both agree (Charles, 507) that at one time all of these passages of Baruch were together, being fragments of the same address. Nauck believes they should be arranged in an order very similar to the gospel saying:
2 Bar. 48:49 And I will recount their (the righteous) blessedness
2 Bar. 48:50 ... ye have endured much labour.
2 Bar. 52:6 Rejoice ye in the suffering which ye now suffer...
2 Bar. 52:7 and prepare your souls for the reward...
In our opinion, 2 Baruch witnesses to common paraenetic teaching traditions in Judaism and early Christianity.

which originated according to Nauck in the persecution and suffering of the pious during the Maccabean revolt.[43] Nauck's list of Jewish texts definitely proves that this theme had a prehistory prior to the time of Jesus. Our position stands midway between that of Selwyn and Nauck. With Selwyn we conclude that James' teaching "goes back to our Lord's" while like Nauck we deny any direct dependence upon the gospel saying of Mt. 5:11-12 par. Here at the beginning of our search for sayings of Jesus within the exhortations of James, it is necessary to distinguish between intentional allusions to dominical sayings and the transmission of the themes of Jesus' preaching within the ethical teaching of the church. This ecclesiastical paraenetic tradition drew material from a variety of sources including OT wisdom sayings, Jewish religious aphorisms, illustrations from nature and everyday life, apostolic teaching, and the sayings of Jesus as well as the major themes in his preaching. Therefore it should not surprise us to discover both Jewish and Christian parallels to Jas. 1:2. Jesus' preaching on this theme certainly supported and reinforced the church's adoption of this exhortation, yet there is nothing to indicate that Jas. 1:2 is an allusion Mt. 5:11-12 par. When James transmits the paraenetic tradition of the early church, he indirectly repeats the themes of Jesus' preaching.

2.2 Jas. 1:4	Mt. 5:48
ἡ δὲ ὑπομονὴ ἔργον τέλειον ἐχέτω, ἵνα ἦτε τέλειοι καὶ ὁλόκληροι ἐν μηδενὶ λειπόμενοι.	 ἔσεσθε οὖν ὑμεῖς τέλειοι ὡς ὁ πάτηρ ὑμῶν ὁ οὐρανίος τέλειός ἐστιν.

The distinctive feature causing some exegetes to posit an allusion to a dominical saying is the use of the common adjective τέλειος coupled with a form of the verb "to be". Thus both Matthew and James perceive perfection as the goal of the Christian life. In Matthew the call to perfection is the summarizing command of Mt. 5:20-47; James pictures perfection as the culmination of a process of endurance stemming from the testing of one's faith.

The problem, however, is that calls to perfection are a common phenomena in NT literature (cf. Col. 1:28; Phil. 3:12; Heb. 6:1; and 1 Pet. 1:16, a call to holiness based upon God's character as in Mt. 5:48 but missing in Jas. 1:4). A similar ἵνα clause in Col. 4:12 (ἵνα σταθῆτε τέλειοι καὶ πεπληροφορημένοι ἐν παντὶ θελήματι τοῦ θεοῦ) indicates that moral completeness was the goal of many, if not all, of the early church leaders. Likewise in the OT one encounters a similar exhortation in Dt. 18:13 "You shall be blameless before the Lord your God."[44] Noah (Gen. 6:9) and Job (Job 1:1) are recognized as having achieved this quality. Closer to NT times τέλειος is an important emphasis for Philo[45] and a favorite term at Qumran where the Community Rule (1QS) employs the Hebrew equivalent some 22 times.[46] The sect even pictured themselves as the "perfect of way" (1QS

---

[43]Nauck, "Freude im Leiden," 79, n. 63 does not include Is. 35:10; 51:11; 61:7; Ps. 126:5 since they describe rejoicing after suffering and not during trials. Hans Conzelmann, s.v. χαίρω, TDNT, IX: 368 agrees that Jas. 1:2 is in the tradition of Jewish wisdom.

[44]τέλειος ἔσῃ ἐναντίον κυρίου τοῦ θεοῦ σου found in a context about sorcery.

[45] Cf. Leopold Cohn and Paul Wendland, Philonis Alexandrini Opera Quae Supersunt, 7:766-769. Specifically Spec. Leg. 4:140 and Flacc. 15 talks about a perfect person. For Philo perfection is both an intellectual road and a moral ideal (cf. Paul J. DuPlessis, ΤΕΛΕΙΟΣ : The Idea of Perfection in the New Testament, 67-68), while James consistently refers the term to conduct.

[46]1QS 1:8f; 2:2; 3:3; 4:22; 5:24; 8:1,9,18,20,21; 9:2,5, 6,8,9,19; 11:11,17. For a description of these sayings see Walter Grundmann, Das Evangelium nach Matthäus, 180.

4:22; 1QM 14:7; 1QH 1:36). Thus the OT, the writings of sectarian Judaism, and the teachings of the early church leaders could just as easily have provided the background for James' statement as the sayings of the Jesus-tradition.

The theme of perfection can best be explained as Jamesian theology since no other NT book uses the adjective "perfect" as often as this epistle (5x).[47] In addition, at several points characteristic emphases of the Epistle of James are employed precisely where the word "perfect" is utilized. In fact, the three most important themes of James are all connected with the concept of perfection: the law in 1:25, faith and works in 2:22, and the tongue in 3:1-2. Jas. 1:4 centers on the subject of endurance, another favorite emphasis of James (1:3,4,12; 5:11) but not a theme of the six antitheses of Mt. 5:21-48. Thus Jas. 1:4 should be assigned to the author's own theology rather than to source material.[48] Throughout 1:2-11 James concludes each of the short paraenetic paragraphs with one of his major themes (1:4,7-8,11b).

Finally, there is some evidence that Mt. 5:48 is an ecclesiastical theme[49] repeated by Matthew rather than a specific dominical saying. The Lucan parallel (6:36) advocates mercy instead of perfection. Manson contends that the more original vocabulary is found in Luke since "in the Old Testament the epithet 'merciful' is given to God, hardly ever to man; and the epithet 'perfect' to man, never to God."[50] Barth notes the inappropriateness of this exhortation outside of Matthew's gospel, concluding that "if the Matthaean form had stood in Q, Luke would have turned a good conclusion into a worse one."[51] It is true that some commentators such as Hill have argued that Matthew's version is more original.

> Matthew's *teleioi* (Aram. š^{e}lîm) plays on the Aramaic word for 'salute', 'ask for the peace of' (Greek *aspazō*, Aram. š^{e}lam), and that probably assures the originality of the Matthaean version. The Targ. Ps.-Jon. to Lev. 22:28 has the same word as Luke ('merciful'), and this may have influenced the Lucan variant.[52]

Hill's conclusion, however, is very doubtful since Mt. 5:48 is more structurally related to Mt. 5:20 than to the idea of "greeting" in 5:47. Just as Mt. 5:20 introduces the six antitheses by calling for a greater righteousness than the scribes and Pharisees, so 5:48 concludes this Matthean section by exhorting for perfection.[53] Since the themes of righteousness and perfection are almost identical in content for Matthew,[54] these two concepts provide an envelope technique for the six antitheses. Then in 6:1 Matthew begins a new section by

---

[47]3x in Matthew and 8x in all of Paul's epistles.

[48]DuPlessis, Perfection in NT, 240 believes that James uses OT conceptions but "applies it in his own distinct way, which is related to the basic theme of his letter, that of the profound unity of faith and works."

[49]The ecclesiastical ethical tradition added an emphasis upon perfection to the Jewish Two Ways at Did. 1:4; 6:2.

[50]Thomas W. Manson, "The Sayings of Jesus," in H.D.A. Major, T.W. Manson, and C.J. Wright, The Mission and Message of Jesus, 347.

[51]Gerhard Barth, "Matthew's Understanding of the Law," in Günther Bornkamm, Gerhard Barth, and Heinz J. Held, Tradition and Interpretation in the Gospel of Matthew, 97, n. 1.

[52]David Hill, The Gospel of Matthew, 131.

[53]Therefore, DuPlessis, Perfection in NT, 168 is incorrect in applying Mt. 5:48 to vv. 43-47. Even if 5:48 is considered the conclusion of 5:43-47, its connection with the love command in both 5:44,48 and 19:19,21 indicates that perfection is a Matthean emphasis. Cf. Robert H. Gundry, Matthew: A Commentary on his Literary and Theological Art, 100.

[54]Cf. ch. 4, sections 3.5-3.7.

repeating the exact theme of righteousness. Coupled with Matthew's unique emphasis on perfection at Mt. 19:21 (not found in Mk. 10:21; Lk. 18:22) and the fact that this word is not employed by any other evangelist, we must conclude that Matthean redaction is apparent at this point.[55] Matthew's grounding of his exhortation in terms of *imitatio Dei* (5:48) and *imitatio Christi* (19:21) is also missing in James.[56] Therefore, there is no evidence validating Mitton's claim that "indeed the reason we meet it here is probably because James knew he had behind him the greater authority of his Lord."[57] The parallels with other literature outside the gospels and the evidence of unique emphases of James precisely where this term is used indicate that James was employing his own vocabulary and developing well-known paraenetic themes of both Judaism and Christianity. There is a common environment of thought between Jas. 1:4 and Mt. 5:48, but no intentional reference to the gospel tradition is evident.

2.3 Jas. 1:5	Mt. 7:7	Lk. 11:9
ἐι δέ τις ὑμῶν λείπεται		κἀγὼ ὑμῖν λέγω,
σοφίας, αἰτείτω	αἰτεῖτε	αἰτεῖτε
παρὰ τοῦ διδόντος θεοῦ πᾶσιν		
ἁπλῶς καὶ μὴ ὀνειδίζοντος		
καὶ δοθήσεται αὐτῷ.	καὶ δοθήσεται ὑμῖν,	καὶ δοθήσεται ὑμῖν,
	ζητεῖτε καὶ	ζητεῖτε καὶ
	εὑρήσετε,	εὑρήσετε,
	κρούετε καὶ	κρούετε καὶ
	ἀνοιγήσεται ὑμῖν·	ἀνοιγήσεται ὑμῖν·

In both the gospels and James God's generous giving character is portrayed in order to substantiate the surety that prayers will be answered. In James God is described as ἁπλῶς, a term with several different shades of meaning in Hellenistic Greek.[58] When the subject matter centers on the theme of giving (as in 2 Cor. 8:2; 9:11,13; Herm., Sim. 2:4), the most appropriate meaning is "generous or without reserve". Dibelius wants to distinguish between these two translations, preferring "unreservedly, without mental reservations" (with Mayor and Mußner) to "generously, graciously" (Hort, Mitton, and Cantinat). He correctly maintains that the former definition more closely parallels the second description of God used by James, "without reproaching".[59] The point we would like to emphasize is that whichever meaning of ἁπλῶς is accepted, a parallel description of God can be discerned in the gospel accounts.[60] There (Mt. 7:9-11; Lk. 11:11-13) God is depicted as the giver of good things (Lk.: the Holy Spirit) by means of an analogy describing what a father does and does not give his children. The fatherhood of God is not specifically mentioned

---

[55]Cf. Gundry, Matthew, 233.

[56]Matthew, John, and Hebrews emphasize the Christological basis of perfection, but James does not. Cf. DuPlessis, Perfection in NT, 242-244 and H.K. LaRondelle, Perfection and Perfectionism: A Dogmatic-Ethical Study of Biblical Perfection and Phenomenal Perfectionism, diss. Vrije Universiteit (Kampen: Kok, 1971), 163.

[57]Mitton, James, 24.

[58]According to BAGD the range of meanings include 1) simply, sincerely , openly; 2) generously, without reserve; 3) simply, at all; 4) in short, in a word.

[59]Harold Riesenfeld's study of this word, "ʽΑΠΛΩΣ: Zu Jak. 1,5," Con. Neot. 9(1944): 33-41 supports Dibelius' translation (James, 78-79) "without reservation". Davids, James, 73 points out that this meaning prepares one for the description of the vacillating petitioner of v. 6.

[60]Attributes of God are similarly appealed to in a prayer for wisdom in Wis. 9:1ff, but the positive answer "and it will be given him" is missing.

in Jas. 1:5, but the description of God as one "who gives to all men generously and without reproaching" is certainly descriptive of a father's character. Moreover, the fatherhood of God is mentioned by James later in this chapter (1:17 father of lights) and specifically connected with the good things God gives (δόσις ἀγαθή instead of the δόματα ἀγαθὰ of Mt. 7:11).

Besides a similar content and context, there are also close affinities of vocabulary. In both the gospels and the Epistle of James the imperative of asking and the surety of receiving are expressed in almost the exact wording.[61] We agree with Mußner that the use of the passive form δοθήσεται in each case is striking. This indicates that James is here following an already coined tradition which in all likelihood goes back to Jesus.[62]

James repeats only one-third of the saying found in the gospel tradition. Yet this fact in no way substantiates the claim that James is transmitting a common proverb rather than the thrice repeated (asking, seeking, knocking) promise of Jesus. Likewise in John's gospel only the first exhortation with the promise is preserved. Jn. 16:23-24 explains,

> Truly, truly, I say to you, if you ask anything of the Father, he will give it to you in my name. Hitherto you have asked nothing in my name; ask, and you will receive, that your joy may be full.[63]

Secondly, outside the canonical gospels there are several instances where this thrice repeated saying is not given in its entirety. The Gospel of Thomas 94 cites only the last two parts ("Jesus [said], 'He who seeks will find, and [he who knocks] will be let in;"), while in Thomas 92 only the second promise is specifically quoted although the "asking" exhortation is possibly alluded to ("Jesus said, 'Seek and you will find. Yet, what you asked Me about in former times and which I did not tell you then, now I do desire to tell, but you do not inquire after it.'").[64] A probable allusion in The Account of Thomas the Israelite 5:3 repeats only the second part, "And the child was angry and said to him (i.e. Joseph, his father): 'It is sufficient for you to seek and not to find, and most unwisely have you acted.'"[65] Thirdly, we have evidence for the division of the gospel's triplicate tradition in the writings of the church fathers of the second and third centuries. The variety in the transmission of Mt. 7:7; Lk. 11:9 is especially evident in Clement of Alexandria where the subject matter of the context appears to control which part of the triplicate tradition is transmitted. Most frequently Clement alludes in an isolated fashion to only the first[66] or second exhortation.[67] The third command with the promise, "Knock and it will be opened to you," is never quoted in an isolated fashion but is repeated immediately following the

---

[61]The only difference is that James utilizes a third person singular imperative form instead of the second plural form of the gospels and naturally also replaces the second person pronoun with a third person form.

[62]Mußner, Jakobusbrief, 69.

[63]Jn. 16:23b,24b ἄν τι αἰτήσητε τὸν πατέρα ἐν τῷ ὀνόματί μου δώσει ὑμῖν ... αἰτεῖτε καὶ λήμψεσθε, ἵνα ἡ χαρὰ ὑμῶν ᾖ πεπληρωμένη. Cf. also 1 Jn. 3:22 καὶ ὅ ἐὰν αἰτῶμεν λαμβάνομεν ἀπ' αὐτοῦ ....

[64]Thomas Lambdin, "The Gospel of Thomas," NHL, 128.

[65]Edgar Hennecke and Wilhelm Schneemelcher, New Testament Apocrypha, I: 394. This story is also called The Infancy Story of Thomas. The Greek reads 'Αρκετὸν σοί ἐστι, ζητεῖν καὶ μὴ εὑρίσκειν as found in Giles, The Uncanonical Gospels (London: Nutt, 1852), 50.

[66]Paed. 3,40,2 (GCS 12 p. 260, line 3); Strom. 2,116,2 (GCS 52 p. 176, line 2); 3,57,3 (222, 19) 6,78,1 (470, 13); 6,101,4 (482, 26); 7,41,3 (GCS 17,2 p. 31, line 13); 7,73,1 (52, 24).

[67]Paed. 1,91,3 (GCS 12 p. 143, line 26); Strom. 1,51,4 (GCS 52 p. 33, line 24); 4,5,3 (250, 11); 5,11,1 (333, 1); 5,96,3 (389, 14).

first exhortation[68] or with all three parts together in the order: seek, knock, ask.[69] Clement never reproduces the dominical saying in the exact order of the Synoptics. Thus in well over one-third of the instances in which the gospel *logion* is quoted by Clement (7 of about 16 times[70]) only the first third of the saying is mentioned. These references substantiate the fact that individual exhortations (as in Jas. 1:5) were transmitted as well as the entire *logion* in its triplicate form. The context of "asking in prayer" explains the omission of the metaphors of seeking and knocking in James. Desiring to emphasize only the theme of "asking", James transfers to the closely related subject of asking in faith in v. 6.

If James is intentionally alluding to a saying of Jesus, how can the addition of the concept of wisdom be accounted for? In the gospels the original content of the request appears to have been quite general ("good things"). Omitting this phrase, Luke inserts his particular emphasis of asking for the Holy Spirit.[71] Similarly James freely inserts his favorite emphasis of wisdom (3:13-18). Clearly the theme of lacking wisdom is tied to James' previous material by catchword (1:4 λειπόμενοι / 1:5 λείπεται) and is, therefore, probably a phrase inserted by James to stitch these two paragraphs together.[72] This transition from perfection (1:2-4) to wisdom (1:5) could have been inspired by previous patterns in wisdom literature. Wis. 9:6 unites the two concepts, "For even if one among the sons of men is perfect, if the wisdom that comes from you is lacking, he will count for nothing."[73] Spitta contends that James is alluding precisely to this saying rather than our gospel references.[74] However, it is more likely that the popularity of this theme (asking for the gift of wisdom in prayer[75]) accounts for James' transition rather than any specific written text. The promise that God would respond positively to those who sought wisdom was an often repeated truth:

> Prov. 2:3,5-6a "Yes, if you cry out for insight (ἐὰν γὰρ τὴν σοφίαν ἐπικαλέσῃ) and raise your voice for understanding... then you will...find the knowledge of God, for the Lord gives wisdom." (ὅτι κύριος δίδωσιν σοφίαν).
>
> Wis. 6:12,14 "And she (wisdom) is easily...found by those who search for her... the man who rises early to seek her will not have to toil, for he will find her sitting at his gates."

---

[68] Paed. 3,36,3 (GCS 12 p. 257, line 31).

[69] Strom. 5,16,6 (GCS 52 p. 336, line 15); 8,1,2 (GCS 17,2 p. 80, line 9); Dives 10:2 (166, 2).

[70] Cf. Biblia Patristica (Paris: Centre National de la Recherche Scientifique, 1975), I: 244,350-351.

[71] For support see the references in Marshall, Luke, 470. Marshall himself is indecisive suggesting that the alternative is also supportable: "The form in Mt. could be a generalizing one, made in order to assimilate the second part of the saying to the first." We agree with C.S. Rodd, "Spirit or Finger," ExT 72(1960-61): 158 that the addition of the Holy Spirit in Lk. 11:13 is "due to his belief that the promise referred to God's gift of the Holy Spirit at Pentecost." Luke adds the Spirit to Markan contexts at 4:1,14 and to Q at 10:21 (Mt. 11:25). However, he deletes the Holy Spirit at 20:42 (Mk. 12:36; Mt. 22:43) since the reference is to the OT rather than the coming of the Spirit at Pentecost and possibly at 10:20 (Mt. 12:28), although a Matthean insertion of the Spirit is here more likely.

[72] Davids, James, 71 describes this clause as "an editorial technique to join originally separate units, in this case a traditional chain-saying and a short piece of instruction."

[73] κἄν γάρ τις ᾖ τέλειος ἐν υἱοῖς ἀνθρώπων, τῆς ἀπὸ σοῦ σοφίας ἀπούσης εἰς οὐδὲν λογισθήσεται.

[74] Spitta, Zur Geschichte, II: 159.

[75] Wisdom is described as a gift of God that must be entreated for in prayer in Wis. 7:7,15; 8:21; 9:4; Sir. 39:6.

Thus James reemphasizes an important element in the Jewish wisdom tradition and weaves it alongside an allusion to a saying of Jesus in a typical paraenetic fashion.

Dibelius appeals to common sentence structure patterns in denying any relationship between Jas. 1:5 and Mt. 7:7; Lk. 11:9. He endeavors to prove that the word order pattern of an imperative (ask) followed by the future tense (will give or will be given) is the natural sentence structure when talking about asking. Ps. 2:8, for instance, says, "Ask from me and I will give to you the nations." In this connection Spitta points out that even the form δοθήσεται is used in the LXX renderings of Ps. 71:15 and Is. 33:16.[76] In addition, the theme of "asking in prayer" is frequently utilized in Jewish-Christian didactic wisdom and need not be a reference to Jesus' *logion*. Dibelius detects another occurrence of this theme in James (5:16), two more in Sirach (7:10; 32:21[77]), additional examples in the gospels (Mk. 22:23f par.; Mt. 17:20), and several parallels in Mand. 9 of the Shepherd of Hermas. In arguing against Dibelius we would contend that Mand. 9 is not an independent parallel but exhibits literary dependence upon the Epistle of James. This would, of course, explain the similarities in vocabulary, content, and context.[78] Furthermore, these references mentioned by Dibelius and Spitta lack the close similarity of vocabulary and content present between Jas. 1:5 and Mt. 7:7; Lk. 11:9. It is our hypothesis that just as the teachings of James had become a part of the paraenetic tradition which Hermas passes on, so the sayings of Jesus had already become an integral dimension of the teaching tradition which James utilized. Laws is, therefore, correct when she concludes,

> It seems quite possible, then, that James draws on the tradition of the teaching of Jesus, but if so it is clear that that teaching has been absorbed without differentiation into the general stock of ethical instruction. He will have drawn on it independently of its literary fixity in either gospel....[79]

James does not employ Jesus' words as an authoritative device to support his particular emphasis as when he quotes the OT with an introductory formulation; instead, he repeats an already authoritative paraenetic tradition which had absorbed Jesus' words. In the NT epistles sayings of Jesus are frequently embedded in paraenetic sections.[80] Therefore, one does not find here support for a dependence upon Matthew, Luke, or Q; instead, the specification of "wisdom" rather than "good things" (Mt. 7:11) or the "Holy Spirit" (Lk. 11:13) indicates an independent testimony to a saying of Jesus. Contrary to Dibelius, we envision here a deliberate allusion to Jesus' teaching as indicated by the common wording, similar subject matter, and the weight of support from the history of interpretation. In the last two centuries this is the third most frequently quoted gospel parallel found in the Epistle of James.

2.4 Since Jas. 4:2c-3 is also frequently quoted as a parallel to Mt. 7:7-8; Lk. 11:9, it is logical to include a discussion of that text at this point in our presentation.

---

[76]Ps. 71:15 καὶ ζήσεται, καὶ δοθήσεται αὐτῷ ἐκ τοῦ χρυσίου τῆς 'Αραβίας. Is. 33:16 ἄρτος αὐτῷ δοθήσεται, καὶ τὸ ὕδωρ αὐτοῦ πιστόν. Spitta, Zur Geschichte, II: 159. Thus he intends to counter Brückner's claim, "Das καὶ δοθήσεται αὐτῷ stimmt doch wörtlich mit Matth. 7,7 zusammen."

[77]Sir. 7:10 "Do not be discouraged about your prayers and do not fail to give to charity." Sir. 32:21 does not apply. He probably intends 33:21, "For it is better that your children should ask from you, than that you should look to the clean hands of your sons." Neither of these parallels are as good examples as Dibelius implies.

[78]Cf. Appendix II, section 8.3.

[79]Laws, James, 56.

[80]Cf. ch. 5, section 3.6.

Jas. 4:2c-3	Mt. 7:7 / Lk. 11:9
μάχεσθε καὶ πολεμεῖτε, οὐκ ἔχετε	
διὰ τὸ μὴ αἰτεῖσθαι ὑμᾶς,	
αἰτεῖτε	αἰτεῖτε
καὶ οὐ λαμβάνετε	καὶ δοθήσεται ὑμῖν,
διότι κακῶς αἰτεῖσθε, ἵνα	
ἐν ταῖς ἡδοναῖς ὑμῶν δαπανήσητε.	
	ζητεῖτε καὶ εὑρήσετε.
	κρούετε καὶ ἀνοιγήσεται ὑμῖν·

Since the RSV translation differs from most versions, it is important at the outset to clarify the sentence structure of Jas. 4:2-3. Because the idea of coveting seems thematically disconnected from murdering, the RSV places a full stop after "you kill", thus obtaining an aabb structure.

4:2 (a) You desire and do not have; so you kill.
(a) You covet and cannot obtain; so you fight and wage war.
(b) You do not have, because you do not ask.
4:3 (b) You ask and do not receive, because you ask wrongly to spend it on your passions.

However, this structure appears contrived since there is no Greek equivalent for "so" in 4:2 and two distinct Greek words (διά and διότι) stand behind the term "because" in the last two sentences. Furthermore, the full stop in the RSV after "you kill" is unnecessary if we recognize that φονεύετε is a very early copying error (probably to harmonize "killing" with the fighting of wars in 4:1 and 4:3) and replace it with Erasmus' emendation φθονεῖτε which yields perfect sense by combining "you envy" with "you are jealous" (ζηλοῦτε).[81] This change also explains why James employs the related noun φθόνον in 4:5.[82] We thus obtain a uniform abba structural pattern.

4:2 (a) ἐπιθυμεῖτε καὶ οὐκ ἔχετε,
(b) φθονεῖτε καὶ ζηλοῦτε καὶ οὐ δύνασθε ἐπιτυχεῖν,
(b) μάχεσθε καὶ πολεμεῖτε, οὐκ ἔχετε διὰ τὸ μὴ αἰτεῖσθαι ὑμᾶς,
(a) αἰτεῖτε καὶ οὐ λαμβάνετε
διότι κακῶς αἰτεῖσθε, ἵνα ἐν ταῖς ἡδοναῖς ὑμῶν δαπανήσητε.

In order to demonstrate that passions are the cause of wars and fightings (4:1), James constructs a chain-saying which begins with desire (roughly equal to passion), builds up to wars and fightings (thus proving the point made in 4:1), and concludes with a new thought about prayer. Asking in prayer is the alternative to desire and passion for James. Thus he attaches statements about prayer after substantiating his claim that passions are the basis of conflicts. The final phrase of 4:3 brings the thought back to passions by stating that his audience prays with polluted motivations. James' message builds in intensity:

You desire and do not have;
You are envious and jealous and cannot obtain;
You fight and wage war (and) do not have.

But instead of concluding here, James appends the underlying reason why they cannot obtain, "because you do not ask." The somewhat disruptive manner in which these words fit

---

[81]These two Greek roots frequently appear together in related texts. Cf. Dibelius and Greeven, *James*, 218, n. 57 for examples.

[82]Cf. Dibelius and Greeven, *James*, 217, n. 55 for modern scholars who have followed this conjecture. Similar scribal errors are found at 1 Pet. 2:1; Gal. 5:21; and Test. Ben. 7:2 (Charles, *APOT* II, 357).

into the context is one evidence that James is alluding to source material at this point, probably as in 1:5 to a saying of Jesus. It could be objected that Jas. 4:2c-3 does not contain the imperative "ask" with the subsequent promise "it will be given you" as in Mt. 7:7; Lk. 11:9. However, as we shall see, this insertion into James' context explains the qualified form of the saying in 4:3b, the use of indicative rather than imperative in 4:3a, and the negative nature of the saying ("you do not have") in 4:2c.

Jas. 4:2c-3 combines two types of sayings about prayer, one implying unequivocally that prayers will be answered ("you do not have because you do not ask") and the other explaining realistically why some prayers are not answered ("you ask and do not receive because you ask wrongly to spend it on your passions"). As Davids explains, "The unqualified form simply encourages one to trust God and to depend upon him, while the qualified form tells one how to pray and correct abuses."[83] Dibelius claims that this qualification of the promise possesses historical significance since it indicates a later development when a highly intensified pneumatic consciousness and a strong conviction of belonging to the community of the last days have died down. He contends that only at a later time did answers to prayer become dependent upon the disposition of the petitioner[84] or upon the type of the petition.[85] However, it is more likely that qualified sayings about prayer existed alongside the unqualified form in the tradition. The conditions for answered prayer stipulated in 1 Jn. 3:22 (keeping his commandments and doing what pleases him) as well as 5:14 (asking according to his will) are thus evidence of this tradition in the early church. The unqualified and qualified forms would not be viewed as incompatible precisely because their functions differ. To a discouraged, doubting audience the unqualified form was utilized to build faith. On the other hand, when one prayed with a reckless impious disposition, the qualified form corrected abuses and taught one how to pray appropriately. James is, therefore, correcting an abuse in 4:3, whereas in 1:5 he employs the unqualified form to encourage those overcome by trials that prayer is the answer to meet their specific needs.

In order to correct a wrong understanding of the saying of Jesus, "ask and you shall receive," Jas. 4:3 places certain restricting criteria upon Jesus' promise. As Laws explains,

> Jesus' promise that prayer will be answered (Matt. vii. 7; Lk. xi. 9; cf. on Jas. i. 5) was unconditional, based upon a confidence in God as Father, but the experience of apparently unanswered prayer poses a problem for which James here supplies a second explanation.[86]

Proof that James was alluding to a saying of Jesus would be more conclusive if James had employed the imperative rather than the indicative, δοθήσεται rather than λαμβάνετε, and the promise "ask and you shall receive" rather than the negative form. However, the indicative αἰτεῖτε can be explained by the context since the completion of the chain-saying "you desire ... you are envious and jealous ... you fight and wage war" requires a statement rather than an imperative. The choice of the verb λαμβάνω rather than δίδωμι is not crucial since the Johannine versions of this dominical saying in Jn. 16:24 and 1 Jn. 3:22 replace δοθήσεται with λήμψεσθε. Furthermore, within the Synoptic gospels themselves the word

---

[83]Davids, James, 160.

[84]Dibelius and Greeven, James, 219 cite as examples Lk. 18:7 where the prayer of the "elect" is an addition to a supposedly original more general form; Herm., Vis. 3,10,6 where self-humiliation through fasting is necessary in order to make the prayer effective; and Herm., Mand. 9:4 where the requirement is purification of heart.

[85]Dibelius believes this accounts for the change from "good things" in Mt. 7:11 to the prayer for the "Holy Spirit" in Lk. 11:13, a type of prayer that is surely answered.

[86]Laws, James, 173.

λαμβάνω is employed in the following verse (Mt. 7:8; Lk. 11:10 πᾶς γὰρ ὁ αἰτῶν λαμβάνει). Finally, the negative format, "you do not have because you do not ask," is likewise explained by the parallelism in the chain-saying; the first and third parts of James' progression end with the exact wording, οὐκ ἔχετε.[87] This "not having" inevitably requires that the explanation be placed in the negative, "because you do not ask." Jesus' promise cannot be fulfilled among them.

The shift from the middle voice (αἰτεῖσθαι 4:2c), to the active (αἰτεῖτε 4:3a), and back again to the middle (αἰτεῖσθε 4:3b) has sometimes been offered as evidence that source material is being incorporated here. Kittel,[88] for instance, contends that James normally employs the middle but, because of a conscious allusion to a saying of Jesus, switches to the active voice in which this gospel saying was transmitted. This is a controversial position. Although Mußner and Davids offer tentative support to Kittel's thesis,[89] the majority of scholars refuse to see any significance in the alternation between the middle and active voice of this verb. Dibelius calls the two words "synonymous";[90] BAGD concludes that "they seem to be used interchangeably";[91] Blass-Debrunner label the distinction "arbitrary".[92] Turner suggests a deadening of linguistic sensitivity since he cannot locate any grammatical rule in either Hellenic or Hellenistic Greek to explain the alternation of forms.[93]

We will cite early Christian contexts about prayer to substantiate the majority opinion that the active and middle voices function interchangeably. Certainly this is the case with John's writings.

1 Jn. 5:14 (middle) ἐάν τι αἰτώμεθα
1 Jn. 5:15 (middle) ὃ ἐὰν αἰτώμεθα
1 Jn. 5:16 (active) αἰτήσει καὶ δώσει

One could legitimately argue that both 1 Jn. 3:22 and 5:14-15 are allusions to Mt. 7:7; Lk. 11:9, and yet 3:22 employs the active voice (ὃ ἐὰν αἰτῶμεν λαμβάνομεν) while 5:14-15 uses the middle. In John's gospel we encounter a corresponding variation: Jn. 16:24 reads αἰτεῖτε καὶ λήμψεσθε while 16:26 utilizes the middle voice (αἰτήσεσθε). A second witness is the Shepherd of Hermas where on two occasions the active form directly precedes the middle (Vis. 3,10,7 αἰτεῖς ... αἰτούμενος; Mand. 9:7 ἃ αἰτεῖς λήψῃ. καὶ ἐὰν αἰτησάμενος ... λαμβάνῃς). Outside a context of prayer we have a third witness in Mark. In the narration of the asking for the head of John the Baptizer, Mark interchanges the forms:

Mk. 6:22 (active) αἴτησον ... καὶ δώσω σοι
Mk. 6:23 (active) ὅ τι ἐάν με αἰτήσῃς δώσω σοι
Mk. 6:24 (middle) τί αἰτήσωμαι

In the pericope where the sons of Zebedee ask Jesus for positions of authority in his kingdom, the voice is again varied by Mark as well as Matthew (Mt. 20:20,22).

---

[87]The omission of the καί in 4:2c is an indication that the addition of source material has affected the wording of the context. This has caused the RSV to wrongly change the sentence structure.

[88]Kittel, "Der geschichtliche Ort," 89.

[89]Mußner, Jakobusbrief, 179; Davids, James, 160.

[90]Dibelius and Greeven, James, 219, n. 63.

[91]BAGD, s.v. αἰτέω, 25.

[92]BDF 316.2.

[93]Moulton and Turner, Grammar, III: 54-55.

Mk. 10:35 (active) ὃ ἐὰν αἰτήσωμεν
Mk. 10:38 (middle) οὐκ οἴδατε τί αἰτεῖσθε

Thus the best solution is to recognize the apparent interchangeability of the active and middle voice of αἰτέω.

Distinctions of meaning have also been suggested by various authors. Mayor explains that "when αἰτεῖτε is thus opposed to αἰτεῖσθε it implies using the words, without the spirit of prayer."[94] This suggestion can be applied meaningfully to Jas. 4:2-3 but is totally misleading if applied to Jn. 16:24,26 or 1 Jn. 5:14-16. Hort argues that the middle means "asked for" and the active "ask a person".[95] This solution would distinguish between "you have asked (active) nothing in my name" (Jn. 16:24) and "in that day you will ask (middle) in my name" (Jn. 16:26), where surely no distinction of meaning is in the author's mind. All such subtle distinctions of nuance prove ineffectual in reaching any firm exegetical results. As Turner explains,

> Every known attempt to make a distinction is no better than intellectual surmise. None has the support of sound linguistic evidence.[96]

Thus this piece of evidence should not be employed to confirm an allusion to a saying of Jesus at Jas. 4:2-3 as Kittel contends. Yet the pieces of evidence cited above remain sufficient to posit a second allusion to Mt. 7:7; Lk. 11:9 in the Epistle of James.

2.5 Jas. 1:6	Mt. 21:21	Mk. 11:23
	ἀμὴν λέγω ὑμῖν,	23aἀμὴν λέγω ὑμῖν ὅτι
αἰτείτω δὲ		ὃς ἂν εἴπῃ τῷ ὄρει τούτῳ
ἐν πίστει	ἐὰν ἔχητε πίστιν	23cκαὶ μὴ διακριθῇ
μηδὲν διακρινόμενος·	καὶ μὴ διακριθῆτε,	ἐν τῇ καρδίᾳ αὐτοῦ
ὁ γὰρ διακρινόμενος	... ἀλλὰ κἂν τῷ ὄρει	ἀλλὰ πιστεύῃ ὅτι ὃ λαλεῖ γίνεται,
	τούτῳ εἴπητε·	ἔσται αὐτῷ.
ἔοικεν κλύδωνι	ἄρθητι καὶ βλήθητι	23bἄρθητι καὶ βλήθητι
θαλάσσης	εἰς τὴν θάλασσαν,	εἰς τὴν θάλασσαν,
ἀνεμιζομένῳ καὶ	γενήσεται·	
ῥιπιζομένῳ.		

In both the gospels and the Epistle of James one encounters a similar coupling together of the themes of prayer and faith.[97] Regarding the contexts Mark has grouped together three distinct sayings after the narrative of the withered fig tree: 11:23 regarding faith and doubt; 11:24 concerning faith in prayer; 11:25 over forgiveness and prayer. Matthew includes the first two of Mark's sayings in a similar setting (Mt. 21:21-22) but inserts the saying about forgiveness into a separate context directly following the Lord's Prayer in Mt. 6:14. James' train of thought flows from the surety of answered prayer (1:5) to the condition of the petitioner when praying (1:6). A praying stance of doubt will not bring ans-

---

[94]Mayor, James, 133. Cf. Hauck, Jakobus, 192.

[95]Fenton J.A. Hort, The Epistle of St. James, 90-91.

[96]Nigel Turner, Grammatical Insights into the New Testament, 163. Cf. Gustav Stählin, s.v. αἰτέω, TDNT, I: 192.

[97]Authors have offered both an exegetical and theological argument to contend that faith is used in a broad sense here and not just in regard to prayer. Cf. Dibelius and Greeven, James, 80. Yet neither argument is convincing. If one accepts the Shepherd of Hermas (Mand. 9:3ff) as a commentary on this passage, then at least Hermas thought James was referring to faith in a context of prayer.

wered prayer since doubt indicates a condition of double-mindedness and instability (1:7-8). In a similar fashion to Jas. 4:2c-3, James explains why Jesus' promise of "ask and it shall be given to you" does not at times find fulfillment. Therefore, we encounter the same movement from an unqualified promise of answered prayer to a qualified form stressing the circumstances when this promise cannot be fulfilled. In 4:3 the problem is asking selfishly; here the wrong attitude centers upon doubt. No specifics are given about the nature of the doubt James has in mind. After first suggesting that doubt about the object of the request might be in James' mind as in 4:3, Laws rightly concludes that the doubt more likely concerns the certainty of receiving the outcome of the request.[98] It is not what they are praying for but how they are praying (without faith) which is the author's concern.

Central to the teaching of both James and Jesus is the essential role that prayer plays in the disciple's life. The direct link between prayer and faith is especially emphasized. Confident asking without doubt in one's heart is imperative to the prayer life according to James (1:5-6; 4:2c; 5:15) as it was with Jesus (Mt. 7:7-11; Lk. 11:9-13; Mk. 11:24; Mt. 21:22; 18:19-20). The basis of this asking is God's sure promise that "they will receive". A common view of God as a fatherly provider stands in the background of each one's teaching. In James the "Father of lights" gives "every good endowment and every perfect gift" (1:17) "to all men generously and without reproaching" (1:5). Jesus bases his teaching about prayer on similar descriptions of the character of God: God gives good gifts to those who ask him (Mt. 7:11); He supplies generously the needs of the birds (Mt. 6:26) and lilies (6:28-30). Prayer for both James and Jesus is the most appropriate response to a situation of need. For James these situations include times of trial when wisdom is lacking (1:5), interpersonal conflict characterized by passionate covetousness (4:2-3), and times of sickness where sin is also present (5:14-16). The gospel writers likewise attach Jesus' teaching about forgiveness of sins to contexts whose main subject is prayer (Mt. 6:14; Mk. 11:25). In fact James' exhortation for intercession in times of sickness could very well be based on the example of Jesus (Mt. 8:6-7; 9:27; Mk. 1:40; 6:56; Jn. 11:41-42) so that Jesus' healing ministry is still continuing through the church.[99] Finally, prayer is essential in determining the will of God for future plans for both James and Jesus. James instructs the merchants who are talking with each other (rather than God) about their future plans (4:15) to say, "If the Lord wills." Similarly, Jesus seeks the will of God in his Gethsemane prayer (Mk. 14:35 par.) and teaches his disciples to pray "Thy will be done" in his paradigm prayer (Mt. 6:10).[100]

Both the content and the context in the gospels and James are thus roughly parallel. There are also limited similarities of vocabulary. In each case a contrast is drawn between doubt and faith using the imagery of the sea. It is natural, therefore, to find some similar vocabulary such as the terms πίστος, διακρίνω, and θάλασσα. However, none of the forms are exactly the same. James places the word "faith" in the dative case while Matthew uses the accusative case and Mark, the verb πιστεύω. James utilizes the present participle of the term "doubt" while the gospels have the aorist passive form. Although three words are common to each, there is no evidence that James is copying the saying employed by the gospel writers.

The word order of Mt. 21:21 is closest to the Epistle of James. From this fact Davids argues that

> Surely James is reworking a concept found in Mt. 21:21 (par. Mk. 11:23), and in doing so he appears to be carrying the tendency of the Matthean redaction (where the faith-

---

[98]Laws, James, 56-57. Did. 4:4 and Barn. 19:5 echo the same theme.

[99]Cf. Appendix I, section 4.12.

[100]These two examples may reduce originally to one since Jesus' prayer in Gethsemane (Mt. 26:42) could have influenced Matthew's version of the Lord's Prayer (6:10) or vica versa.

doubt contrast is sharpened from Mark) a little further to the point where he sees behind the doubt the root distrust of God.[101]

It is our contention, however, that Matthew is not endeavoring to sharpen the faith-doubt contrast by changing the word order in Mark. Matthew only wants to clarify the chronological order of events. An attitude of faith without doubting is necessarily prior to any command to move a mountain into the sea. In order to clarify this point, Matthew makes some changes in Mark's text. Therefore, James' closer word order with Matthew does not imply that he is continuing a redaction begun by Matthew.

It is our conviction that James is not deliberately alluding to a preexistent saying of Jesus. The occurrence of three common words is caused by the similar subject matter, not by their presence in the supposed gospel parallels. It is admittedly peculiar that imagery drawn from the sea is utilized in each case. Yet upon closer examimation neither the intended theme nor the aspect of the sea being compared is the same. James pictures the theme of doubt or lack of faith by drawing on the imagery of a wave tossed up and down by the sea's billowing action or the force of the wind.[102] On the other hand, the gospels describe the theme of faith or not doubting by alluding to a mountain which is cast into the depths of the sea. There really is no vital connection between these two metaphors.[103] Sea metaphors were a common literary phenomenon.[104] Furthermore, James' imagery is unique since both Greek words occur only here in the NT.[105] Therefore any contact with another sea metaphor in the NT is doubtful.

Although their teachings about prayer are similar, the emphases of James and Jesus are not identical. Peculiar to James are his prayer for wisdom, the imagery picturing a doubting attitude, and the teaching that the prayer of a righteous man works powerful results. Both James and Jesus use the example of Elijah with the same unique time designation (three years and six months of no rain found in Lk. 4:25; Jas. 5:17), but a completely different point is stressed (Elijah as a prophet to the Gentiles in Luke; Elijah as an example of prayer in James).[106] James also omits several distinctive emphases of Jesus including his frequent criticism of hypocritical prayer,[107] his prayer for the enemy,[108] his teaching about importunity and steadfastness in prayer,[109] and his prayers of exorcism.[110] Jesus' sample prayer (Mt. 6:9-13; Lk. 11:1-4) is not transmitted here as in Did. 8:2, although some think Jas. 1:2-18 is based upon the sixth petition, "Lead us not into temptation."[111] In the Epistle

---

[101]Davids, James, 73.

[102]Dibelius and Greeven, James, 81-82 argue that the doubter is not compared with the wave but with the restless sea stirred up by the wind since κλύδων probably means "billowing, surging" in two passages from Philo. However, Hort, James, 33, based on the meaning of ῥιπίζω (to fan), argues that a fan could not raise a storm. Laws, James, 57 is correct in maintaining that surf or rough water makes better sense in describing one who wavers than the image of a tempest.

[103]The metaphor of the mountain cast into the sea is connected in the tradition with other themes besides faith (unity, for instance, in Thomas 48 and 106), but this saying about faith is never combined with other sea metaphors.

[104]Cf. Dibelius and Greeven, James, 81-82, n. 59.

[105]Mayor, James, 39 even contends that ἀνεμίζω was first coined by James. Dibelius and Greeven, James, 81, n. 56 call this suggestion "methodologically unacceptable" since the other term ῥιπίζω is used in previous literature, and James is more likely to have combined two traditional terms.

[106]Cf. Appendix I, section 3.8.

[107]Mt. 6:5-6; Mk. 12:40; Lk. 18:11ff; 20:47.

[108]Mt. 5:44; Lk. 6:28.

[109]Lk. 11:5-8; 18:1-8.

[110]Mk. 9:29 par.

[111]Cf. above, pp. 57-58.

of James we also encounter several references about prayer which indicate an historical progression beyond Jesus. In James depiction of the elders of the church as the instruments of the healing ministry (5:14), we observe both a progression to an ecclesiastical situation and an institutionalization of what was for Paul a charismatic activity (1 Cor. 12:9).[112] Furthermore, James' emphasis upon double-mindedness (1:8; 4:8) could indicate that after an initial surge of enthusiasm the Christian faith is now not held so vigorously and purely.[113] Therefore the similar teaching patterns of James and Jesus on prayer should not be emphasized without acknowledging the unique emphases of each and James' historical progression beyond the teaching of Jesus.

James' exhortation against doubting in prayer (1:6) is similar to Jesus' instruction and is surely repeated in the teaching of the early church because Jesus stressed this theme. Therefore, we can agree with Büchsel's comment that "the attention paid to doubt in the NT is obviously the reverse side of the unconditional promise which is given to faith",[114] without accepting the conclusion that a specific *logion* is in James' mind. James employs his own metaphor to express a common theme regarding prayer -- a call to faith away from doubt.[115] He only has in mind the saying of Jesus already quoted at 1:5; in 1:6 James is merely showing when this promise will not be fulfilled in a similar fashion to 4:2c-3. The theme of faith in prayer has entered into the church's teaching because of Jesus' prominent emphasis on this important point, yet there is no indication that James is alluding to a specific *logion* of Jesus such as Mt. 21:21 or Mk. 11:23.

2.6 Jas. 1:19b-20	Mt. 5:22a
ἔστω δὲ πᾶς ἄνθρωπος	ἐγὼ δὲ λέγω ὑμῖν ὅτι
ταχὺς εἰς τὸ ἀκοῦσαι,	
βραδὺς εἰς τὸ λαλῆσαι,	
βραδὺς εἰς ὀργήν·	
20 ὀργὴ γὰρ ἀνδρὸς	πᾶς ὁ ὀργιζόμενος
	τῷ ἀδελφῷ αὐτοῦ
δικαιοσύνην θεοῦ οὐκ ἐργάζεται.	ἔνοχος ἔσται τῇ κρίσει·

Jas. 1:19 contains a trio of short exhortations to be quick to hear, slow to speak, and slow to anger. The last of these is then picked up and given a specific rationale in v. 20. The angry person[116] does not work the righteousness of God. The genitive in "righteousness of God" can be categorized either as 1) a genitive of quality or subjective genitive (BDF 165); 2) a genitive of origin (BDF 162); or 3) an objective genitive (BDF 163). The genitive of quality would express the fact that anger is not an attribute of God's

---

[112]Davids, James, 57 explains, "They have *ex officio* the right to pray for the healing of disease and the forgiveness of sin."

[113]The verb, noun, and adjective forms of this word are not found in the LXX or NT outside the Epistle of James, while many parallels can be illustrated from the Apostolic Fathers, esp. the Shepherd of Hermas (Sim. 9,21,1-2).

[114]Friedrich Büchsel, s.v. διακρίνω, TDNT, III: 948.

[115]That faith in prayer is an important Jamesian emphasis is shown by Jas. 5:15.

[116]Here as in 1:7-8 ἀνήρ is used in the same setting with ἄνθρωπος, being employed interchangeable to refer to generic humanity. Mayor, James, 62 is mistaken when he explains, "the speakers would be men, and they might perhaps imagine that there was something manly in violence," as is Hort, James, 36 who states that ἀνήρ instead of ἄνθρωπος meant "the petty passion of the individual". Against Mayor see Albrecht Oepke, s.v. ἀνήρ, TDNT, I: 362 who explains that sexual differentiation is mostly expressed by ἄρσεν and θῆλυ.

character. Since God does not indulge in anger, neither should human beings.[117] Although von Soden attempted to prove this use by claiming that θεοῦ must be parallel to ἀνδρός, Dibelius has shown that it is possible to claim rhetorical parallelism in case while at the same time positing a syntactical difference.[118] A genitive of origin would imply that righteousness has its origin in our relationship with God. Because of a close connection with God (like father and son), one receives the gift of justification entailing a verdict of acquittal and the imputation of righteousness. This particular phrase, "the righteousness of God" (Rom. 1:17; 3:21f,26; 10:3; 2 Cor. 5:21), as well as the expression, "the righteousness from God" (Phil. 3:9), and the word δικαιοσύνη by itself (Rom. 5:21; 9:20; 1 Cor. 1:30; 2 Cor. 3:9) all mean for Paul the righteousness bestowed by God, thus closely approximating salvation.[119] In James this use would indicate that God's favorable verdict could never be given to the angry man. Dibelius sees here the possible influence of Paul's phrase "the righteousness of God" colored by Jewish religious language.[120] Yet it is extremely doubtful whether James is using righteousness in the same sense as Paul; here it is not in spite of actions that one is justified but precisely through human action.[121] Therefore, the third usage of an objective genitive is the most appropriate. James is speaking about the ethical demands of righteousness and not about an imputed gift of salvation. The angry person can never attain this ethical standard. The verb ἐργάζω would therefore be a synonym for ποιέω,[122] implying that the righteousness intended here is a human action. Furthermore, Jas. 2:21-23 supports this usage since the working together of faith and deeds produces righteousness. Abraham's act of offering up Isaac indicates that he has attained the ethical righteousness which God had promised would be reckoned to him. Hermas' understanding of righteousness is also in line with James' conception.[123] Using his peculiar term ὀξυχολία, Hermas warns that the working of an angry temper leads the servants of God astray from righteousness (Mand. 5,2,1).

With this as background we will now consider the ties to the gospel teaching about anger in Mt. 5:22. In each case there is similar subject matter, i.e. a moral exhortation against anger. Furthermore, one might argue that the phrase "not work the righteousness of God" could be interpreted eschatologically and seen as roughly parallel to the gospel usage "liable to the judgment".[124] Even though righteousness is not specifically mentioned in Mt. 5:22, Matthew does closely link the theme of righteousness to this context by introducing the term at the head of his six antitheses in 5:20. In addition, the concept of righteousness is infused with similar content so that both employ the term δικαιοσύνη in an unPauline sense, closer to the Jewish OT sense of moral uprightness found in human conduct.[125]

In spite of these similarities, the differences stand out more strikingly. The precise wording is nowhere the same. Matthew chooses an attributive participle for the

---

[117]The Epistle of Aristeas 254 expresses this, although righteousness is not mentioned there: "God rules ... without wrath at all, and you, O King, must of necessity copy His example." (Charles, APOT, II: 117).

[118]Dibelius and Greeven, James, 110, n. 12 use Rom. 12:10ff as evidence.

[119]BAGD, s.v. δικαιοσύνη, 196-197.

[120]Dibelius and Greeven, James, 111.

[121]Cf. Gottlob Schrenk, s.v. δικαιοσύνη, TDNT, II: 200.

[122]The variant κατεργάζεται found in C* P 0246 and the Byzantine MSS points in this direction since it means "produce".

[123]Laws, James, 81 agrees, "Hermas clearly understood James in this way" i.e. righteousness as an objective genitive.

[124]Or one might argue that we are encountering here a de-eschatologizing of a saying of Jesus. Cf. Joachim Jeremias, The Parables of Jesus, 42ff where he argues that this was a common phenomenon in the early church.

[125]Cf. ch. 4, section 3.5.

term "anger" while James prefers the noun. The word "righteousness" in Matthew is more a title of the whole section 5:21-48 than a reference to this exhortation against anger. The fact that δικαιοσύνη is only employed in contexts about John the Baptizer (3:15; 21:32), with beatitudes whose wording is peculiar to Matthew (5:6,10), and as an introduction or conclusion to material found only in Matthew (5:20; 6:1,33) is evidence that this word was particularly appropriate to Jewish audiences.[126] Secondly, Jas. 1:20 exhibits a contrast between human anger and divine righteousness while Mt. 5:22 is structured according to cause and effect so that anger results in judgment. Spitta attempts to widen the differences by claiming that Matthew is speaking about human anger against the neighbor while James is referring to anger directed at God.[127] However, Spitta is definitely mistaken here[128] since James' emphasis on human character qualities in 1:21 indicates that anger among humans is uppermost in his mind. Thirdly, the saying in James is a word to the wise and is not grounded in the fear of punishment as in the threefold reference in Matthew to retribution by judgment, the council, and the hell of fire. Although these differences argue against a Matthean comparison, an allusion to source material is evidenced by the use of catchwords and the standard pattern of James' exhortations.[129] We will argue that James is reproducing either Jewish wisdom or the catechetical teaching of the church rather than the words of Jesus.

Warnings against anger frequently occur in gnomic literature. The book of Proverbs describes anger as dangerous since it leads to evil consequences (Prov. 6:34; 15:1; 14:17; 16:14; 19:19; 27:4; 29:22). Eccles. 7:9 warns, "Be not quick to anger, for anger lodges in the bosom of fools." Although the thinking here closely resembles Jas. 1:19 ("slow to anger"), the divergent wording of the LXX[130] argues against any intentional allusion. At Qumran anger is condemned categorically: 1QS 5:25 commands, "Let no man address his companion with anger," while 1QS 7:12 records a specific punishment, "If he has spoken in anger against one of the priests inscribed in the Book, he shall do penance for one year and shall be excluded." The entire fourth chapter of the Testament of Dan is an exhortation against anger and its effects. The Mishna continues the OT wisdom tradition by exhorting against any sudden outburst of anger. Aboth 2:10, for instance, states, "be not easily provoked to anger."[131] A very intriguing parallel found in Aboth 5:11,12, 14[132] advocates being slow to anger (5:11), swift to hear (5:12), and practicing what one has learned at the house of study (5:14), just as James exhorts to be quick to hear, slow to speak, slow to anger (1:19), and doers of the word rather than hearers only (1:22). In Aboth 5:10-15 four types of people are described. The saintly person (חסיד) is "he who is slow to anger and easily pacified" (5:11),[133] the one "swift to hear and slow to lose" (5:12), and "he that goes and also practices" (5:14). This striking similarity with the descriptions of Jas. 1:19-25 indicates the close ties in content and progression of thought between Jewish wisdom literature and the Epistle of James. In the Talmud we also encounter this connection between anger and

---

[126]The one occurrence in Lk. 1:75 speaks similarly about John the Baptizer and is in a context (Lk. 1-2) filled with Semitic concepts. Mark does not employ the term.

[127]Spitta, Zur Geschichte, II: 163.

[128]Cf. Mayor, James, 63.

[129]Cf. above, section 2.0.

[130]μὴ σπεύσῃς ἐν πνεύματί σου τοῦ θυμοῦσθαι. James uses the LXX in his quotes of the OT. Cf. above, p. 52.

[131]Here we follow Epstein's translation, p. 20. Danby translates this phrase "and be not easily provoked." (נוֹחַ לִכְעוֹס).

[132]5:10,13 deal with almsgiving and 5:15 with retaining only the beneficial knowledge one has learned, neither of which are found in James' context.

[133]Here we follow Moses Mielziner, Introduction to the Talmud, 274. Danby writes "hard to provoke and easy to appease". Epstein, 67-68 translates "hard to become angry and easy to be pacified". (קָשֶׁה לִכְעוֹס).

a lack of wisdom: Pesahim 66b explains, "As to every man who becomes angry, if he is a sage, his wisdom departs from him."[134]

The Epistle of James evidences affinites with the ethical teaching of the NT church as well as with Jewish wisdom and legal literature. One of the qualifications for leadership in the church is the abstaining from anger (Tit. 1:7; Pol. Phil. 6:1). Yet anger is not categorically condemned as sin by the church. Alluding to Ps. 4:5 Paul distinguishes between temporary anger which fades before the sun has set (Eph. 4:26) and sustained anger which is categorized as a deadly sin (4:31). Similarly in James, as Stählin remarks, "There is no absolute negating of anger."[135] As with Paul, James sets side by side advice aimed at hindering the evil effects of anger (1:19)[136] with a clear condemnation of anger (1:20). In the NT anger is included in several of the lists of grievous sins (θυμοί Gal. 5:20; 2 Cor. 12:20; ὀργή and θυμός Eph. 4:31; Col. 3:8) which must be extinguished from the disciple's life. Jas. 1:21 fits into this common ecclesiastical teaching pattern of the putting off (in this case anger, filthiness, and the rank growth of wickedness) and the putting on (here, meekness) of certain character qualities. The cataloguing of vices and virtues is thus a common moral instrument of paraenesis.[137] Some even contend that the catalogue of vices allocated to Jesus (Mk. 7:21-22; Mt. 15:19) is of a secondary character inserted by the church from its teaching.[138] In fact one might even argue that Mt. 5:22 originated in the moral exhortations of the church. Jesus by his example appears not to have opposed all anger since in Mk. 3:5 he is admittedly angry with the Pharisees and in the temple-cleansing scene (Mk. 11:15-16 par.) his actions betray an attitude of anger. Furthermore, Jesus compares God to an angry master in his parables (Mt. 18:34; 22:7; Lk. 14:21). Could the Matthean church have taken a stricter moral stance than Jesus himself on this topic? On closer examination the fact that Jesus became angry or compared God to an angry master does not contradict the saying in Mt. 5:22 but rather points to an already common distinction in Judaism between God's righteous anger and human anger originating in and controlled by the passions.[139] The absolute character of the ethical demand found in Mt. 5:22 carries the irony of exaggeration which was often used by Jesus for its shock value upon his audience.[140] The fact that most of the other Matthean antitheses possess another witness supporting the saying as a *logion* of Jesus confirms the fact that Mt. 5:22 also derives from Jesus.[141] Thus both Jesus and the ethical tradition of the church transmit teachings about anger which are based upon an already established Jewish tradition.

To help determine whether James took his pattern from Jewish wisdom, Jesus' preaching, church paraenesis, or a combination of the above, we will examine the close

---

[134]b. Pesahim 66b, ed. Epstein, 337.

[135]Gustav Stählin, s.v. ὀργή, TDNT, V: 421.

[136]Paul ponders the long term effects of anger ("let not the sun go down upon it"), while James thinks about sudden outbursts of unprocessed anger ("be slow to anger").

[137]Cf. Erhard Kamlah, Die Form der katalogischen Paränese im Neuen Testament, esp. 11-38.

[138]Rudolf Bultmann, History of the Synoptic Tradition, 166; William L. Lane, The Gospel according to Mark, 256; Eduard Schweizer, The Good News According to Matthew, 328; Taylor, Mark, 347. Evidence includes the Pauline vocabulary, the symmetrical arrangement of the lists, the absence of such lists in the sayings tradition, the signs of catechetical interest in Mk. 7:1-23, and the interpretative comment of the evangelist at Mk. 7:19b. However, since such catalogues of virtues and vices are found at Qumran (1QS 4:3,9-11), Jesus himself probably employed this type of speech.

[139]Cf. Stählin, s.v. ὀργή, TDNT, V: 427.

[140]Ibid., 420.

[141]Cf. Lk. 16:18 and Mk. 10:11-12 with the third antithesis (Mt. 5:32); Jas. 5:12 with the fourth (Mt. 5:33-37); Lk. 6:29-30 with the fifth (Mt. 5:39-40,42); Lk. 6:27-28,32-36 with the sixth (Mt. 5:44-47).

parallel to Mt. 5:22 in the teaching manual of the early church, The Teaching of the Twelve Apostles. Did. 3:1-6, put into an outline format, reads like this:

3:1		My child, flee from every evil and everything that resembleth it.
3:2	A1	Be not angry, (μὴ γίνου ὀργίλος)
	2	for anger leadeth to murder, (ὁδηγεῖ γὰρ ἡ ὀργὴ πρὸς τὸν φόνον)
	3	nor jealous nor contentious nor wrathful;
	4	for of all these things murders are engendered.
3:3	B1	My child, be not lustful, (μὴ γίνου ἐπιθυμητής)
	2	for lust leadeth to fornication, (ὁδηγεῖ γὰρ ἡ ἐπιθυμία πρὸς τὴν πορνείαν)
	3	neither foul-speaking neither with uplifted eyes;
	4	for of all these things adulteries are engendered.
3:4	C1	My child, be no dealer in omens,
	2	since it leads to idolatry,
	3	nor an enchanter nor an astrologer nor a magician, neither be willing to look at them;
	4	for from all these things idolatry is engendered.
3:5	D1	My child, be not a liar,
	2	since lying leads to theft,
	3	neither avaricious neither vainglorious;
	4	for from all these things thefts are engendered.
3:6	E1	My child, be not a murmurer,
	2	since it leadeth to blasphemy,
	3	neither self-willed neither a thinker of evil thoughts;
	4	for from all these things blasphemies are engendered.

Did. 7:1 ("Having first recited all these things") suggests that the material of chapters 1-6 is a catechism to be recited before being baptized. This section, commonly entitled the "Two Ways", is also recorded in the Epistle of Barnabas 18-20.[142] The Didache, however, includes two additional sections: 1:3-2:1, a collection of Jesus' sayings, and 3:1-6, commonly called "the fences", derived from the Jewish conception of fences around the law.[143] The first two exhortations of Did. 3 are especially close parallels to Matthew's first two antitheses. Both connect anger to murder and lust to fornication. They employ similar terminology with Matthew prefering the verb forms (φονεύω, ὀργίζω, μοιχεύω, ἐπιθυμέω) and the Didache opting for the use of nouns (ὀργή, φόνος, ἐπιθυμία, πορνεία). Furthermore, both appear to be commentaries on the ten commandments, each beginning with the sixth command concerning murder.[144]

---

[142]J.M. Creed, E.J. Goodspeed, A. von Harnack (later view), K. Köhler, J.P. Audet, R. Knopf, B.H. Streeter, and C. Taylor advocate a common source. O. Bardenhower. F.X. Funk, R.D. Hitchcock, and F. Brown postulate a Didache original. F.C. Burkitt, R.H. Connally, J. Muilenburg, and J.A. Robinson perceive a Barnabas original.

[143]Cf. Aboth 1:1. Fences made it more difficult for certain forbidden acts to occur by prohibiting attitudes or actions which fostered them.

[144]The Didache speaks about killing (6th), adultery (7th), lying (9th), stealing (8th), and includes exhortations against the important subjects of idolatry and blasphemy. Matthew, after a new interpretation of the sixth and seventh commandments, includes a reference to divorce from Dt. 24:1ff which topically is closely tied with the 7th commandment, then speaks of oaths (9th or 3rd), and ends with two sayings commenting on the comprehensive OT command, "love your neighbor as yourself" (Lev. 19:18).

There is a general consensus that the Two Ways is Jewish in origin.[145] If 3:1-6 were originally a part of such a document or oral catechism, then Mt. 5:21b,22a,28 and probably Jas. 1:19b-20 all derive from Jewish wisdom. However, since Did. 3:1-6 is not found in the parallel material in Barnabas,[146] it must either be a moral teaching gathered from additional Jewish wisdom material by the church or allusions to dominical *logia* as in the other major addition to the Two Ways, Did. 1:3-2:1. Both the studies of Wohlenberg and Glover[147] omit Did. 3:2-3 when they compare the Didache to the teaching of Jesus in the gospels. Furthermore, Matthew (or an ecclesiastical tradition behind Matthew) is often seen as the formative influence upon the antithetical structuring of Jesus' teaching.[148] Therefore, Did. 3:1-6 is probably not a series of allusions to the Jesus-tradition.[149] It is true that later in the Didache (15:3) another exhortation against anger ("And reprove one another, not in anger but in peace"[150]) includes the editorial addition "as ye find in the Gospel".[151] However, from this fact we cannot deduce that Did. 3:1-6 is also an allusion to sayings of Jesus since "the fences" pericope is found in the earlier Jewish Two Ways section and has a self-contained structure of its own. The most plausible solution is that the church's paraenetic instruction which characteristically combines eclectic material such as Jewish wisdom, religious aphorisms, and the important themes of Jesus' preaching inserted both Jewish wisdom (Did. 3:1-6) and allusions to Jesus' preaching (Did. 1:3-2:1) into the teaching manual of the church. The fact that both Mt. 5:21ff and Did. 3:1-6 arrange their teaching on the pattern of the ten commandments reveals that OT organizational patterns extended into the church's paraenetic exhortations.[152]

A similar phenomenon has surely occurred in Jas. 1:19-21. The church's paraenetic tradition has taken over typical Jewish wisdom (1:19) similar to Eccles. 7:9 and Aboth 5:11-14 as well as apostolic teaching patterns (1:21). Therefore, Jas. 1:20 stands

---

[145]James Muilenburg, The Literary Relations of the Epistle of Barnabas and The Teaching of the Twelve Apostles, 98-107. Robert Kraft, The Apostolic Fathers: Barnabas and the Didache, 4 is correct in asserting that 1QH 3:18ff indicates that a similar Two Ways device was in vogue in Semitic-speaking Jewish communities in preChristian times.

[146]The self-contained structure of Did. 3:1-6 as well as the material from Barn. 19:3-6 demonstrates that it is an addition. Richard H. Connolly, "The Didache in Relation to the Epistle of Barnabas," JThS 33(1932): 241-242 states that the structure of Did. 3:1-6 "is wholly unlike anything in the rest of the Two Ways." Out of the 25 words used to describe sins and sinners, 19 of these fail to occur in the rest of the Two Ways, either in the Barnabas or Didache recensions.

[147]G. Wohlenberg, Die Lehre der zwölf Apostel in ihrem Verhältnis zum neutestamentlichen Schriftum; Richard Glover, "The Didache's Quotations and the Synoptic Gospels," NTS 5(1958-59): 12-29.

[148]For a summary of the various approaches see Robert A. Guelich, The Sermon on the Mount, 178-179.

[149]Jonathan Draper, "The Jesus Tradition in the Didache," Gospel Perspectives, 5:271-272 explains, "Apparent echoes of the Jesus tradition outside these sections (i.e. 1:3b-2:1; 8; 15:3-4; 16) should be examined with great caution, since they may well derive from a Jewish Urtext, and even if they are the product of a Christian community, they may reflect the general milieu of the earliest Christian communities rather than the Jesus tradition.

[150]ἐλέγχετε δὲ ἀλλήλους μὴ ἐν ὀργῇ, ἀλλ' ἐν εἰρήνῃ, ὡς ἔχετε ἐν τῷ εὐαγγελίῳ·

[151]This exhortation against anger probably refers to Mt. 5:22-25 (being angry followed by reconciliation) or the gospel tradition behind Matthew just as the other references to the gospel in the Didache seem to allude to specific passages (Did. 8:3 = Mt. 6:9-13; Did. 11:3 = Mt. 10:41; Did. 15:4 = Mt. 6:1-18).

[152]Cf. Vokes, "Ten Commandments in NT," SE, V: 154.

right between Jewish wisdom and ecclesiastical exhortation and could be categorized as either. The best we can say is that Jas. 1:20 is a religious aphorism transmitted by the church from concepts derived from Jewish wisdom. Exhortations against anger entered the church's paraenetic tradition both from traditional Jewish wisdom[153] and because specific *logia* of Jesus spoke against anger as in the genuine allusion to Mt. 5:22-23 in Did. 15:3. Thus already in this first chapter of James' epistle we have seen how the church combines specific sayings of Jesus (1:5), certain important emphases in Jesus' preaching (1:2,6), and traditional Jewish wisdom material (1:19-20) into its authoritative ethical instruction.

2.7 Jas. 1:22-23	Mt. 7:26	Lk. 6:49a
γίνεσθε δὲ	καὶ πᾶς ὁ ἀκούων μου	ὁ δὲ ἀκούσας
ποιηταὶ λόγου	τοὺς λόγους τούτους	
καὶ μὴ μόνον ἀκροαταὶ	καὶ μὴ ποιῶν αὐτοὺς	καὶ μὴ ποιήσας
παραλογιζόμενοι ἑαυτούς.		
ὅτι εἴ τις ἀκροατὴς λόγου ἐστὶν		
καὶ οὐ ποιητής,		
οὗτος ἔοικεν	ὁμοιωθήσεται	ὅμοιός ἐστιν
ἀνδρὶ	ἀνδρὶ μωρῷ,	ἀνθρώπῳ
κατανοοῦντι τὸ πρόσωπον	ὅστις ᾠκοδόμησεν	οἰκοδομήσαντι
τῆς γενέσεως αὐτοῦ	αὐτοῦ τὴν οἰκίαν	οἰκίαν
ἐν ἐσόπτρῳ·	ἐπὶ τὴν ἄμμον·	ἐπὶ τὴν γῆν χωρὶς
		θεμελίου

We will first present the case for a dependence of Jas. 1:22-23 upon a saying of Jesus and then develop an argument against this supposition. In both gospels the supposed parallel to Jas. 1:22-23 is located in the parable of the two houses which is placed at the end of Jesus' sermon as a vivid call to action. In general Matthew has retained the order of Q as found in Luke's gospel and only inserted additional pericopes (both Q and M) between several of Luke's sayings.[154] Only one *logion* has changed its order; Lk. 6:31, the golden rule, has been positioned at Mt. 7:12 as a summary to all the previous teaching. Following this summary saying Matthew constructs a call to action in the form of four contrasts: 1) narrow and wide gates (7:13-14); 2) fruitful and unfruitful trees (7:15-20); 3) one saying "Lord, Lord" and one doing the will of the Father (7:21-23); and 4) two houses, one built upon the rock and the other upon the sand (7:24-27). Likewise, Jas. 1:19-27 could be entitled a call to action based upon the kerygmatic proclamation of 1:18 that "he brought us forth by the word of truth". Jas. 1:19-21 talks about receiving this word. One must be quick to hear, slow to speak, and slow to anger (1:19-20). After putting off certain harmful vices, one must receive this implanted word with meekness (1:21). Then Jas. 1:22 speaks about doing this word. Jas. 1:23-24 follows with a negative example of one failing to be a doer of the word while v. 25 concludes with a positive model of one who has persevered in doing. Heeding this call to action results in a pure and undefiled religion (1:26-27). Thus we experience in James and the gospels the same emphasis on doing.[155] The commentators of the last two centuries testify to this matching perspective: this pair of sayings is the second most frequently quoted parallel (49 out of 60 authors).

---

[153]Hoppe, Hintergrund Jakobusbriefes, 5, n. 3 contends that Jas. 1:19 derives from Jewish wisdom but not 1:20 since δικαιοσύνη is not connected with ὀργή in wisdom literature. However, we have shown that similar statements about anger are common in Jewish wisdom. With regard to δικαιοσύνη we will demonstrate in our comments on Jas. 3:18 that this term was familiar to Jewish wisdom.

[154]Cf. Guelich, Sermon, 33-35. Matthew resorts to omission as well with regard to the Lucan woes (cf. below, p. 225).

[155]Cf. Mußner, Jakobusbrief, 104.

Other arguments put forward for a relationship with Mt. 7:26; Lk. 6:49 are less convincing. Davids[156] claims that Origen recited Jas. 1:22 as an agraphon of Jesus. However, there is absolutely no indication in Hom. Gen. 2:6[157] that Origen is alluding to a saying of Jesus; rather it is a reference to the Epistle of James itself.[158] Supporters of an allusion to the gospels are also forced to admit that James employs his own unique vocabulary at this point. Ποιητής occurs four of its six times in the NT in the Epistle of James,[159] and James possesses three of the four NT references to ἀκροατής.[160] However, it is precisely this uniqueness of vocabulary that causes some to claim that James himself modifies the words found in the gospels. To a classical Greek audience ποιητὴς λόγου would mean a writer, poet, or orator while the phrase ποιητὴς νόμου in Jas. 4:11 would indicate a legislator.[161] In James, however, we encounter a Semiticizing of the Greek so that the phrases mean "doer of the word" "and doer of the law" respectively. This could point to a close tie with the Jesus-tradition which by its Jewish nature often contains Semitisms. Davids even contends that "the use of 'hears these words of mine' and 'does them' is close enough to James' unusual Greek that we believe that he had this particular parable in mind."[162] Advocates of this position do admit that the metaphors used in the gospels and James are divergent: looking into a mirror vs. two houses built upon the contrasted foundations of rock and sand. Yet it is argued that a similar result is in mind; the momentary impression in a mirror which is soon forgotten is comparable to the momentary durability of a house built upon sand when a flash flood strikes its foundation.

Proponents of an allusion to a gospel saying contend that "*the Word* is the Gospel as taught by Jesus",[163] and the perfect law of freedom (1:25) is the law interpreted by Jesus and fulfilled in the love commandment.[164] To evaluate this statement we will examine the use of the term λόγος in Jas. 1:18,21,22. Jas. 1:18 states that the Father of lights "brought us forth by the word of truth that we should be a kind of first fruits of his creatures." The "word of truth" has sometimes been interpreted cosmologically[165] indicating the creating word which brought forth humankind as the first fruits, that is the preeminent part of the whole creation. Most often this verse is explained soteriologically either with the term λόγος used 1) in a mystical sense referring to the divine principle (in Hermetic texts νοῦς) which indwells all human beings and brings forth a rebirth;[166] 2) historically as the begetting of Israel (Dt. 32:18) as first fruits for God among the nations (Jer. 2:3 MT; Philo, Spec. Leg. 4:180) by the instrument of the law described as the word of truth (Ps. 119:43);[167] or 3) to refer to the gospel of Jesus Christ whereby Christians are through

---

[156]Davids, James, 97 and "James and Jesus," 82-83, n. 36.

[157]"Let us pray, however, the mercy of the omnipotent God to make us not only hearers of his word but also doers." Ronald Heine, Origen: Homilies on Genesis and Exodus, The Fathers of the Church (Washington D.C.: Catholic Un. Press, 1982), 88. Davids mistakenly refers to Hom. 2:16.

[158]Cf. ch. 6, n. 87.

[159]Jas. 1:22,23,25; 4:11; Rom. 2:13; and Acts 7:28 where the classical Greek sense of a poet is used.

[160]Jas. 1:22,23,25; Rom. 2:13. Herm., Vis. 1,3,3 and Dg. 2:1 in the Apostolic Fathers.

[161]The ποιητὴς νόμων of Pseudo-Plato Def. 415b is not the one who keeps the laws but the one who issues them.

[162]Davids, "James and Jesus," 72.

[163]Adamson, James, 82.

[164]Cf. below, section 3.2.

[165]Leonard E. Elliot-Binns, "James 1:18: Creation or Redemption?" NTS 3(1956-57): 148-161; Rendall, James and Judaic Christianity, 64; Hort, James, 31f; Laws, James, 78 attempts to combine a cosmological and soteriological interpretation.

[166]Cf. Dibelius and Greeven, James, 105.

[167]For conclusive arguments against this position see Laws, James, 77.

salvation given a position as the first fruits of the eschatological age to come.[168] The context, moving from God the creator of the heavenly bodies (1:17) to God as the Father of humankind, the culmination of all creation, supports the cosmological interpretation. The phrase "Father of lights" could refer to Gen. 1:3,14,18 and the "bringing forth" to Gen. 1:26. Furthermore, the more usual connotation assigned to τὰ κτισμάτα is nonhuman creation.[169] On the other hand, the phrase "word of truth" and the image of begetting are nowhere in the OT applied to creation.[170] In the NT Paul employs the phrase "word of truth" to refer to the gospel (Col. 1:5; Eph. 1:13; 2 Tim. 2:15).[171] 1 Peter which frequently reveals significant parallels with the Epistle of James refers to the gospel (1:25) both as the truth (1:22) and as the word (1:23) through which Christians have been born anew (ἀναγεγεννημένοι). The term "first fruits" also corresponds much better with a soteriological understanding (Rom. 16:5; 1 Cor. 16:15; Rev. 14:4). Finally, the earlier statement that sin brings forth (ἀποκύει 1:15) death would naturally follow with a corresponding teaching that the word of truth has brought forth (ἀπεκύησεν 1:18) a new soteriological birth. Therefore, there is significant evidence that James had in mind here the work of the gospel, although it is not responsible exegesis to be overly dogmatic on this point.

In 1:21 James exhorts his readers to "receive with meekness the implanted word, which is able to save your souls." The term τὸν ἔμφυτον λόγον has been understood in Stoic terms as the cosmic reason which is innately[172] apportioned to every individual (reminiscent of the λόγος σπερμάτικος).[173] In its present context it is more likely that the term indicates the deeply rooted (as in Barn. 1:2; 9:9) gospel which brings salvation. As Laws explains,

> This word would most naturally be understood as the preached word of the gospel, with both its promise of salvation and its ethical demand, and to 'receive' or 'accept' the word is a familiar description of conversion in the NT.[174]

Jas. 1:21 would then emphasize the soteriological demand and 1:22 the ethical demand of this preached word. Therefore, a reference is made to the gospel teaching in each case, v. 18 emphasizing the divine action and vv. 21-22 the human demand in response. Those who argue against this conclusion point to the parallel between 1:22 (doers of the word) and 1:25 (doers that act according to the law). Could James be speaking about the gospel in terms of hearing and doing the Jewish law? Laws has put her finger upon the key to understanding the flow of James' thought when she explains,

---

[168]Cf. Rudolf Schnackenburg, The Moral Teaching of the New Testament, 350; also Mußner, Ropes, Windisch, and Dibelius support this view.

[169]Elliott-Binns, "James 1:18," 155 perceives this argument as conclusive proof for the cosmological interpretation.

[170]Cf. Ropes, James, 116. However, in Philo, Ebr. 30 ἀποκύω appears to be used about creation. "And knowledge, having received the divine seed, when her travail was consummated bore (ἀπεκύησε) the only beloved son who is apprehended by the senses, the world which we see. Colson and Whitaker, Philo III, LCL, 334-335. Cf. Elliot-Binns, "James 1:18," 151.

[171]2 Cor. 6:7 refers to truthful speech and not the gospel while Test. Gad 3:1 indicates the law.

[172]The adjective ἔμφυτος usually implies being "implanted from birth" and, therefore, innate.

[173]These ideas arose in Christian circles in Justin Martyr's time. Cf. 2 Apol. 13:5; 8:1.

[174]Laws, James, 82. She refers to Acts 8:14; 17:11; 1 Thess. 1:6; 2:13; Lk. 8:13. Cf. Gerhard Kittel, s.v. λέγω, TDNT, IV: 116.

> Because the word demands response and action, ideas of obedience and so of law are associated with it, and in v. 25 James shifts from talking in terms of *word* to talking in terms of *law* .... This does not mean that the word and the law are identified but that the former involves the latter.[175]

As we will demonstrate at Jas. 2:8, our author understood the gospel as a new law, not one of bondage and constriction, but of perfect liberty (1:25; 2:13) fulfilled in the kingdom commandment of love (2:8). Thus James' conception of λόγος (understood as the teachings of the gospel) is employed to support the belief that Jas. 1:22-25 is alluding to the teaching of Jesus in Mt. 7:24-26; Lk. 6:46-49.

Thus far we have attempted to present objectively a good case advocating an allusion to a saying of Jesus at Jas. 1:22-23. On the other hand, the admission that Jas. 1:18,21,22 refer to the gospel does not entail that a dominical saying was in James' mind since the church constantly spoke of the gospel apart from sayings of Jesus. Moreover, there are at several points crucial differences between Jas. 1:22-25 and the gospel references. Certainly the subject matter is identical, but verbal similar-ities are minimal. Jas. 1:22 uses the adjective ἀκροάτης; the gospels the verb ἀκούω. Different forms of the central terms "doers" and "the word" are chosen.[176] Furthermore, the imperative mood (γίνεσθε) and the thought of deceiving yourselves (παραλογιζόμενοι ἑαυτούς) are unique to James. Turning to the metaphor in Jas. 1:23, more drastic dissimilarities confront the exegete: 1) different words introduce the parable (ἔοικεν in James vs. ὁμοιόω in Matthew and ὅμοιος in Luke); and 2) the imagery is obviously disparate (gazing into a mirror vs. two houses).[177] Surely it is unlikely that James would allude to a gospel saying and then recreate the imagery so that it is totally unrecognizable. Dibelius remarks that "Jas usually has borrowed such metaphors, but in this case there is as yet still no proof of any dependency."[178] Furthermore, James' so-called unique phrase "doer of the law" is already found in Dt. 28:58, 1 Mac. 2:16, and Sir. 19:20. One cannot presume from Jamesian vocabulary that he was alluding to a saying of Jesus. Since James adopts Semitic terminology, a more verifiable conclusion would be that the author is a Jewish Christian. The Semitic character of a writing can never alone prove that a saying of Jesus stands in the background.

Finally, James has in common with more parties than just Jesus this antithesis between hearing and doing. One encounters this theme in all strands of Jewish and Christian teaching: the prophets (Ezk. 33:32), the law (Dt. 30:8ff), wisdom literature (Prov. 6:3; Sir. 3:1), Jewish philosophical treatises (4 Mac. 7:9), Qumran,[179] Philo,[180] Josephus,[181]

---

[175]Laws, James, 85.

[176]In James ποιητής and the singular λόγος; in the gospels the participle form of the verb and the plural form of the noun.

[177]Gryglewicz, "Jacques et Matthieu," 46-47 believes the common term ἀνδρί links Jas. 1:22 to Matthew's gospel, but the totally different analogies demonstrate the insignificance of this parallel.

[178]Dibelius and Greeven, James, 115-116.

[179]1QS 2:25-3:12; 1QpHab 7:11; 8:1; 12:4; 4QpPs37 2:14,22.

[180]Praem. poen. 79 "If, he says, you keep the divine commandment in obedience to his ordinances and accept his precepts, not merely to hear them but to carry them out by your life and conduct, the first boon you will have is victory over your enemies." Colson, Philo VIII, LCL, 361.

[181]Ant. 20:44 "For you ought not merely to read the law but also, and even more, to do what is commanded in it." Louis H. Feldman, Josephus X, LCL, 25.

the Mishnah,[182] the Talmud,[183] Paul (Rom. 2:13), and John (1 Jn. 3:17-18). Paul's parallel is especially interesting since the amount of verbal similarity is more than that found in the gospels. Speaking in a typical Jewish fashion, Paul explains, "For it is not the hearers of the law who are righteous before God, but the doers of the law who will be justified."[184] Although Paul is addressing a slightly different problem,[185] the similar wording and emphasis point to the possibility that James could just as easily have been quoting Paul as Jesus. Furthermore, when 1 Jn. 3:18 contrasts "in word or speech" with "in deed or in truth", John reiterates James' message of doing the word without an allusion to the sayings of the Jesus-tradition. Indeed why should one choose Mt. 7:26; Lk. 6:49 as the allusion in Jas. 1:22-23 instead of Lk. 8:21 ("But he said to them, 'My mother and my brothers are those who hear the word of God and do it.")?[186] Here also the term λόγος is used together with the concepts of "hearing and doing." Therefore we have examples from Paul, John, and Luke's redaction of Mk. 3:35[187] that the theme of hearing and doing was an important topic in the church's ethical teaching. This was especially true for James who devotes a whole dis course to the related topic of faith and works (2:14-26). Every time a church leader like James taught on this theme, he was not consciously alluding to a saying of Jesus. As Laws concludes, "James shows no knowledge of the illustrative parable of the two houses, and any dependence is unlikely."[188] The similarities and differences between Jas. 1:22-23 and Mt. 7:26; Lk. 6:49 are better accounted for with the thesis that the themes of Jesus' preaching found their way into the paraenesis of the church than by the suggestion that James had a specific saying of Jesus consciously in mind.

3.0 The Synoptic Parallels Encountered in the Three Paraenetic Discourses of Jas. 2:1-3:12

A. 2:1-13 Discourse on Partiality.

1. 2:1 Introductory exhortation.

2. 2-7 Partiality to the rich.
   a. 2:1-4 Illustration of partiality.
   b. 2:5 God has chosen the poor (allusion to a saying of Jesus).
   c. 2:6-7 They have not chosen the poor.

3. 2:8-13 Partiality with regard to obeying the law.
   a. 2:8-9 Illustration from the law found in Lev. 19.
   b. 2:10 James' conclusion.
   c. 2:11 A second illustration from the ten commandments.
   d. 2:12 James' conclusion ("the law of liberty" is Jamesian).

---

[182]Aboth 2:10; 5:14; and esp. 1:17 "and not the expounding [of the Law] is the chief thing but the doing [of it]; and he that multiplies words occasions sin."

[183]b. Shabbath 88a This is a midrash on Ex. 24:7: "When Israel put 'we will do' before 'we will hear', there came 60 myriads of ministering angels, and attached to each Israelite two crowns, one corresponding to 'we will do' and the other to 'we will hear', and when they sinned there came down 120 myriads of destroying angels and tore them off." Translation from Mayor, James, 67, n. 1. Cf. also Epstein, 417-418.

[184]For the Greek see Appendix II, p. 257.

[185]Paul is confronting the Jew/Gentile problem while James is addressing the hearing/doing conflict.

[186]οἱ τὸν λόγον τοῦ θεοῦ ἀκούοντες καὶ ποιοῦντες.

[187]Mk. 3:35 does not include the addition above.

[188]Laws, James, 85.

e. 2:13 Related aphorisms (connected by catchword κρίνεσθαι / κρίσις / κρίσεως).

B. 2:14-26 Discourse on faith and works.

1. 2:14-17 Faith separated from works is insufficient (dead).
   a. 2:14 Introductory Question: Is faith alone sufficient?
   b. 2:15-16 Illustration.
   c. 2:17 James' conclusion (ending with a οὕτως clause).

2. 2:18-26 Faith and works belong together.
   a. 2:18-19 Illustration from the demons who believe in God but have no works.
   b. 2:20-24 Illustration from Abraham.
   c. 2:25 Illustration from Rahab.
   d. 2:26 James' conclusion built upon an aphorism (ending with a οὕτως clause).

C. 3:1-12 Discourse on the tongue.

1. 3:1 Warning against becoming a teacher.
   a. 3:1a Exhortation
   b. 3:1b Reminder of the apostolic teaching.

2. 3:2-5 Bridling the tongue is difficult.
   a. 3:2 Only the perfect person is able to bridle the tongue.
   b. 3:3-5 Illustrations demonstrating the power of little things like the tongue.
      1) 3:3 The bit of a horse.
      2) 3:4 The rudder of a ship.
      3) 3:5a The tongue of a person.
      4) 3:5b The match starting a forest fire.

3. 3:6-10 Evils of the tongue.
   a. 3:6 The tongue is a fire doing great damage.
   b. 3:7-8 The tongue cannot be tamed.
   c. 3:9-10 With it we bless and curse at the same time.

4. 3:11-12 Three aphorisms illustrating the contradictory nature of the tongue.
   a. 3:11 Springs do not pour forth fresh and brackish water.
   b. 3:12a Fig trees do not yield olives or grapevines, figs.
   c. 3:12b Salt water does not yield fresh.

In contrast to chapter 1, Jas. 2:1-3:12 contains pericopes with a unified theme which could more properly be called discourses than loosely-knit paraenesis. Jas. 2:1-13 expands on the concept of partiality (2:1,9) since James is concerned about the Christian community showing partiality toward the rich (2:6). He begins with a hypothetical example (ἐάν and the subjunctive) of a worship service where a rich, well-dressed person is given precedence over a poorly attired one (2:2-4). An identical attitude is reflected in the Christian community which dishonors the poor whom God has chosen to inherit the kingdom (2:5-7). To illustrate the foolishness of this action, James demonstrates through two examples that showing partiality to one commandment (Lev. 19:18 loving the neighbor; Ex. 20:14 not comitting adultery) while dishonoring another (Lev. 19:15 showing partiality; Ex. 20:13 committing murder) still condemns one as a transgressor of the whole law. James ends with an aphorism (2:13) which serves as a transition to his next theme as he does in each of these three discourses (2:26; 3:11-12). In 2:14-26 James centers his attention on the inseparable connection between faith and works. Similar to 2:1-13 this section opens with a thematic sentence (2:1,14), continues with an illustration (2:2-4,15-17), a theological argument (2:5-7,18-19), and a two part scriptural argument (2:8-12,20-25), and finishes with a summary proverbial saying (2:13,26).[189] The third discourse (3:1-12) is constructed around the theme of the tongue and again employs several illustrations.

3.1 Jas. 2:5	Mt. 5:3,5	Lk. 6:20b
ἀκούσατε,		
ἀδελφοί μου ἀγαπητοί·		
οὐχ ὁ θεὸς ἐξελέξατο	μακάριοι	μακάριοι
τοὺς πτωχοὺς τῷ κόσμῳ	οἱ πτωχοὶ τῷ πνεύματι,	οἱ πτωχοί,
πλουσίους ἐν πίστει		
καὶ κληρονόμους	ὅτι αὐτῶν ἐστιν	ὅτι ὑμετέρα ἐστὶν
τῆς βασιλείας	ἡ βασιλεία	ἡ βασιλεία
ἧς ἐπηγγείλατο	τῶν οὐρανῶν.	τοῦ θεοῦ.
τοῖς ἀγαπῶσον αὐτόν;	μακάριοι οἱ πραεῖς, ὅτι	
	αὐτοὶ κληρονομήσουσιν	
	τὴν γῆν.	

Jas. 2:5 begins with the often repeated introduction, "my beloved brethren," coupled with a call to listen (ἀκούσατε) indicating that what follows is important. After this attention getting device James continues with a rhetorical question, "Has not God chosen the poor ...?" which expects a positive response. This question is followed by two more interrogative sentences dialectically posed against the expected positive response toward the poor in 2:5. It seems that the Christian community itself has turned into a tool of oppression by siding with the rich against the poor. James thus endeavors to alter the behavior of the church by demonstrating the oppression (2:6), legal persecution (2:6), and blasphemy (2:7) which characterizes the wealthy.

The general idea of election ("Has not God chosen") is firmly rooted both in Jewish thinking (Dt. 4:37; 7:7; 14:2) and Christian theology (Acts 13:17; 15:7; 1 Pet. 2:9; Eph. 4:1). God's special care for the poor also finds a home in many OT writings[190] but is developed especially in the intertestamental period where the term "poor" becomes a designation for the pious.[191] James points to two aspects of this chosen blessedness promised to the poor: 1) the temporal blessing of being rich in faith; and 2) the eschatological blessing of being heirs of the kingdom . The two datives τῷ κοσμῷ[192] and ἐν πίστει have proven difficult to interpret. Poor "in the world" can be understood as a dative of advantage ("before the world")[193] or as a dative of respect ("in worldly goods").[194] "In faith" forms the antithesis to "in the world". If ἐν πίστει means "rich within the sphere or realm of faith",[195] then τῷ κοσμῷ is a dative of advantage. On the other hand, if ἐν πίστει means "rich with

[189]Cf. Davids, "James and Jesus," 72.

[190]Dt. 15:7-11; Pss. 9:18; 12:5; 40:18(17); 70:5; 86:1; 109:22,31; 140:13(12); Jer. 20:13.

[191]Sir. 10:22-24; Ps. Sol. 5:2,13; 1 En. 108:7-10; 1QpHab 12:3,6.

[192]The variants ἐν τῷ κοσμῷ and τοῦ κοσμοῦ offer an emendational smoothing of the text.

[193]Davids, James, 112 thus says, "The world sees only their poverty; God sees their exalted state because of his election ..." Fritz Reinecker and Cleon L. Rogers Jr, A Linguistic Key to the Greek New Testament, 382 call this an ethical dative as does Mayor, James, 82.

[194]Also called a dative of reference by Moulton and Turner, Grammar, III: 238.

[195]Dibelius, Davids, Grosheide, Mayor, Ropes.

regard to faith" then "poor in the world" would be a dative of respect, "poor in worldly goods".[196] Dibelius argues against this latter possibility saying, "for then faith would be conceived as some sort of compensation for earthly poverty, whereas this compensation actually consists in the claim to the heavenly inheritance."[197] James, however, consistently thinks in concrete realities. Therefore, he is speaking here of being rich in worldly goods themselves (dative of respect).[198] The poor not only have a prospect of reward in the future, but in fact their rich heritage is already evident in the faith they now possess.

With this as background we will discuss the relationship of Jas. 2:5 to the gospel parallels. There are some exegetical details which might initially thrust one in the direction of denying the presence of a dominical saying. If James was consciously thinking of a saying of Jesus, he nowhere makes it obvious; there is no introductory formulation as with the quotations from the OT. Secondly, the wording does not exactly parallel any known saying of Jesus. Jas. 2:5 is not set in the μακάριος format although such an introduction is familiar to James (1:12,25; 5:11). In addition to the gospel contrast between the poverty in this age and the eschatological wealth in the age to come, James inserts the additional contrast of being poor in worldly goods vs. rich in faith. Furthermore, James mentions God the Father as the subject of the sentence rather than Jesus. It is God who has chosen the poor to be heirs of the kingdom. Thirdly, the election of the poor to a blessed future was a common theme at this time in the history of Judaism.[199]

Spitta is so convinced by the similarities with Jewish thought that he confidently asserts that if one could somehow show Jas. 2:5 to be dependent upon a *logion* of Jesus, then one could legitimately be convinced that James throughout his epistle alludes to Jesus' sayings.[200] Likewise, Meyer believes that James is drawing on the teaching of the Psalms (37:11,22-23; 112:9) rather than Jesus.[201] Certainly Mt. 5:5 is based upon Ps. 37:11 ("But the meek shall possess the land"), yet Jas. 2:5 with its mention of the kingdom as the gift for the poor is closer to Jesus' beatitude in Mt. 5:3. It is important to recognize that there are no references in the OT, intertestamental literature, or the Talmud specifically saying that God is giving the kingdom to the poor. This fact makes it unlikely that a Jewish source rather than a saying of Jesus was in James' mind.

James is definitely appealing to his readers' previous knowledge; in his question, "Has not God chosen the poor ...," James assumes that his audience is already aware of the teaching being presented. If not the OT, perhaps the church's ethical teaching is the source of James' statement. The church did experience itself as the physically poor and foolish, the lowly and despised of the world. Paul's comments at 1 Cor. 1:26-28 indicate that in this condition of lowliness the churches were made mindful of their election: "God chose what is foolish ... weak ... low and despised." Paul even employs words that resemble closely those of Jas. 2:5: ἐκλέγω, θεός, κόσμος.[202] The added clause in James, "which he has promised to those who love him," could derive from a Christian hymn since this phrase already occurs at Jas. 1:12 and in a quote from an unknown source at 1 Cor. 2:9.[203] It is highly unlikely that James is dependent upon a written Pauline source such as 1 Cor. 1:27.[204] Rather the similarities of content and vocabulary point to the common experience

---

[196]Cantinat, Laws, Schoeps.

[197]Dibelius and Greeven, James, 138.

[198]The use is similar to Hermas' description of the poor as "rich in intercession" (πλούσιος ἐν τῇ ἐντεύξει) in Sim. 2:5.

[199]Cf. Ernst Bammel, s.v. πρωχός, TDNT, VI: 895 and the references we have previously mentioned.

[200]Spitta, Zur Geschichte, II: 164.

[201]Meyer, Rätsel, 85. He also refers to 1 Sam. 2:8 and Pss. Sol. 5:12; 15:2.

[202]For the Greek see Appendix II, p. 257.

[203]For similar references in the LXX and intertestamental literature see Dibelius and Greeven, James, 89, n. 110.

[204]Cf. Bammel, s.v. πτωχός, TDNT, VI: 911, n. 241.

of poverty in the early church which proved to be an unforgettable memory. In addition to Paul and James, Rev. 2:9 ("I know your tribulation and your poverty (but you are rich)") witnesses to this common experience.

As James is pondering this familiar experience of the church, he is apparently reminded of Jesus' promise of an eschatological kingdom to such a poor people as this and thus appends this afterthought to his main point that God has chosen the poor to be rich in faith. The decisive clue for the presence of a saying of Jesus lies in the fact that the word "kingdom" is not Jamesian vocabulary; Jas. 2:5 is the one and only occurrence of this term in the epistle.[205] Certainly the employment of a term particularly associated with the preaching of Jesus is evidence that James is alluding to the same saying quoted in Mt. 5:3 and Lk. 6:20. This is confirmed by the fact that even critical exegetes like Dibelius and Laws[206] admit the probability that James is consciously referring to a *logion* previously spoken by Jesus. Furthermore, exegetes who frequently perceive allusions to Jesus' sayings in the Epistle of James are sure about this particular case: "Jesus' declaration is certainly behind James's statement," states Davids;[207] "But there is no doubt that James was directly inspired by a dominical word like Luke 6:20," adds Adamson.[208]

James does not stand in the tradition of either Matthew or Luke. James' view of poverty is literal unlike Matthew's emphasis upon the religious quality of lowliness as in his expression "poor in spirit". James' perspective is closer to Luke's,[209] but the wording is divergent with Luke choosing the full expression "kingdom of God".[210] Adamson believes that "the mention of inheritance in Jas. 2:5, not so expressed in Matt. 5:3 or Luke 6:20, probably represents the more accurate form of the testimony to the words of Jesus."[211] However, the popularity of the expression "to inherit the kingdom" in the early church (Gal. 5:21; 1 Cor. 6:9-10; 15:50) as well as the distinctive wording (ἐστὶν ἡ βασιλεία) in both gospel recensions speaks against this opinion. Instead we perceive an historical development from the time of Jesus. The experience of the church is evident in the mentioning of the constituency of the group as poor, in the similarity to Paul's words at 1 Cor. 1:26, in the phrase "to those who love him", and in the two stage eschatology of James.[212] Therefore, clearly evident in this verse is a combination of the church's experience with a promise of Jesus.[213]

---

[205]א and A read ἐπαγγελίας following Heb. 6:17 according to Nestle-Aland. However, a more doctrinal reason might lie behind this change since the new reading does not limit the kingdom to the poor.

[206]Dibelius and Greeven, James, 132; Laws, James, 103-104.

[207]Davids, James, 111.

[208]Adamson, James, 110.

[209]Laws, James, 103 contends that James does not reward poverty *per se* as Luke does in Lk. 6:20 and 16:19-25 in the case of Lazarus. But this is reading too much into Luke's account.

[210]βασιλεία without the addition "of God" is employed in Mt. 4:23; 8:12; 9:35; 13:19,38; 24:14; Acts 20:35; Heb. 11:33; 12:28.

[211]Adamson, James, 109-110.

[212]The wealth of the future kingdom is already exhibited in the richness of faith among those who believe in Jesus.

[213]Davids, James, 111 concurs with this view when he explains, "That the aorist ἐξελέξατο is used might refer to some eternal election of God (Eph. 1:4) but probably refers to the declarations of Jesus and reflects the constituency of the church."

3.2 Jas. 2:8	Mt. 22:36,39 par.	Lev. 19:18b
εἰ μέντοι	36 διδάσκαλε,	
νόμον τελεῖτε βασιλικὸν	ποία ἐντολὴ μεγάλη	
κατὰ τὴν γραφήν·	ἐν τῷ νόμῳ;	
	39 δευτέρα δὲ ὁμοία αὐτῇ·	
ἀγαπήσεις	ἀγαπήσεις	καὶ ἀγαπήσεις
τὸν πλησίον σου	τὸν πλησίον σου	τὸν πλησίον σου
ὡς σεαυτόν,	ὡς σεαυτόν.	ὡς σεαυτόν·
καλῶς ποιεῖτε·		ἐγώ εἰμι κύριος.

In Jas. 2:8 one is confronted with the most complicated and controversial part of James' whole theology, i.e. his view of the law. Therefore, before attempting to compare Jas. 2:8 with the gospel parallels,[214] we will discuss and evaluate the various understandings of James' use of the law.

To understand James' conception of the law, one must examine the three terms: royal law, perfect law, and law of liberty. The description of the law as royal found in Jas. 2:8 can have various connotations: 1) the law from a king (Adamson);[215] 2) the sovereign or supreme law which governs all other laws (Hort, Mußner); 3) the law which is set for kings or the law with royal authority (Dibelius, Zahn);[216] and 4) the law of the kingdom (Davids, Mayor, Ropes, Windisch). By calling this "the law of the King of Kings", Adamson[217] may have made this passage more upbuilding for today's audience, but his interpretation goes beyond the givens of the text. As Laws explains,

> It is unlikely that the description of the law as royal involves anything so specific as a recognition of Jesus as the king who has promulgated the law, especially as it is God who is said to promise the kingdom in ii. 5 (cf. iv. 12: there is only one lawgiver, clearly God).[218]

Hort and Mußner's suggestion is attractive since it can easily be tied to Jesus' teaching of a first and second commandment. But Laws is again correct when she discerns that "this strains the meaning of the adjective, which never seems to have been used in the sense of 'governing' ..."[219] Dibelius appeals to Stoic oriented Jewish texts where law is compared to sovereign reason, royal roads, or the king's position of authority.[220] In our opinion, it seems more natural to compare the term "royal" with the kingdom concept mentioned in James' immediate context (2:5). Since Jas. 2:8 begins a Biblical argument continuing upon the trail of the experiential argument of 2:5-7,[221] it seems plausible that the adjective βασιλικὸν is related to the noun βασιλεία.[222] This is confirmed by Clement of Alexandria's

---

[214] In ch. 2, section 2.1 we have already investigated the relationship of Jas. 2:8 to Jewish thought.

[215] Karl L. Schmidt, s.v. βασιλεία, TDNT, I: 591 also states that the royal law "signifies the law as given by the βασιλεύς," but he perceives a reference to God as king rather than Jesus Christ as Adamson, James, 114-115.

[216] Knowling's view in James, 49 is unique and difficult to categorize since he speaks about the subjects as kings (royal) and not the law itself.

[217] Adamson, James, 114-115.

[218] Laws, James, 110.

[219] Ibid., 109.

[220] Cf. Davids, James, 143. He appeals to 4 Mac. 14:2; Philo, Post. Cain. 101-102; Spec. Leg. 4:147; Vit. Mos. 2:4; Cl. Alex., Strom. 7,73,5.

[221] The use of μέντοι points out that James is not beginning a new topic.

[222] Cf. Rendall, James and Judaic Christianity, 67.

substitution of "you will not be royal" for "you will never enter the kingdom of God" in Mt. 5:20.[223] Finally, Jas. 2:5 and 2:8 are connected by an emphasis on love: the kingdom is promised to those who love Him (2:5), and the love command is recited immediately following the mention of the royal law in 2:8.

The content of the royal law has been variously described as 1) the whole OT law; 2) the moral law; or 3) the specific ordinance of Lev. 19:18. This dispute traces back to the difficulty in determining the exact relationship between the royal law of 2:8a and the love command of 2:8b. The first view[224] is supported by the usual distinction between νόμος as the whole law and ἐντολή as one or more distinct commandments within the law. The term ἐντολή is employed with the love command in Mk. 12:28, Mt. 22:36, and Jn. 15:12. Since νόμος instead of ἐντολή is used in Jas. 2:8, one could conclude that the whole law rather than the single love command is intended.[225] Laws adds that τελέω (2:8) is the more appropriate verb to refer to the whole law (Rom. 2:27), while τηρέω would be expected for individual precepts (Mt. 19:17f).[226] Against this suggestion, however, is the use of τηρέω in Jas. 2:10 to refer to the whole law. Therefore, James does not work with this distinction although the scribal emendations at 2:10 show that many scribes disapproved.[227] The difficulty in ascertaining whether James employs the more important distinction between νόμος and ἐντολή stems from his failure to use the term ἐντολή anywhere in the epistle.[228] Since we do encounter exceptions to this rule at Rom. 7:2, 1 Cor. 7:39 t.r., Num. 9:12, and Jer. 31:33 (38:33 LXX), this distinction may not function in James' thinking.

Furnish, one of the foremost supporters of the second view, argues that the moral law rather than the love command is given prominence by James. He points out that the love commandment is not identified with pure religion in Jas. 1:26-27 as one might expect, nor are the clothing and feeding of a needy brother and sister (2:15-16) mentioned as an application of the love command as in 1 Jn. 3:17.[229] Rather James always refers to concrete moral deeds or exclusively ethical principles. Within the present context it is specifically the moral laws against adultery and murder (2:11) that are singled out. Furthermore, the other designations, "perfect law" and "law of liberty," can be applied more easily to the moral law in distinction from the ceremonial and civil legislation. Therefore, the background for James' thinking is often traced back to a Jewish evaluation of Lev. 19 as a counterpart of the Decalogue and as a summary of the whole Torah.[230]

The third view states that the royal law is the love command itself. Since the phrase κατὰ τὴν γραφήν is positioned immediately after βασιλικὸν, the natural implication of the preposition κατά (meaning "corresponding to") would be that the royal law and Lev.

---

[223]Strom. 6,164,2 οὐκ ἔσεσθε βασιλικοί instead of οὐ μὴ εἰσέλθητε εἰς τὴν βασιλείαν τῶν οὐρανῶν. Otto Stählin, GCS 17,2, p. 516, line 21.

[224]For a list of well-known supporters of this view see Victor P. Furnish, The Love Command in the New Testament, 178, n. 35. Walter Gutbrod, s.v. νόμος, TDNT, IV: 1081 argues against this position stating that the "general attitude of the epistle and the context of the verse are against the interpretation that it is the whole Old Testament law with all its commandments that is in mind."

[225]Cf. Davids, James, 114 and Dibelius and Greeven, James, 142.

[226]Laws, James, 107-108.

[227]τελεσει Ψ, 81, 945, 1241, 2298; πληρωσει: A, 614, 630, 1505, 2426, 2495.

[228]In 2:10 James uses the phrase ἐν ἑνί without a noun. If the phrase modifies τὸν νόμον, then James does not distinguish between νόμος and ἐντολή since νόμος would apply here to a single commandment. However, the contrast in the verse makes it likely that James is referring to one command of the law, and if he supplied a noun, it might be ἐντολή or λόγῳ as in Gal. 5:14 ὁ γὰρ πᾶς νόμος ἐν ἑνὶ λόγῳ πεπλήρωται.

[229]Furnish, Love Command, 182.

[230]Cf. ch. 2, n. 26.

19:18 correspond. In this case either 1) the distinction between νόμος and ἐντολή does not hold true for James (an exception like Rom. 7:2); or 2) a new distinction must be drawn between νόμος with the definite article referring to the whole law and the anarthrous usage indicating a particular command;[231] or 3) the precept itself (Lev. 19:18) has been accorded such an exalted position in the new law of the church that the term νόμος could without difficulty be applied to a single command.[232] In our opinion, James employs the definite and anarthrous forms interchangeably.[233] The article is lacking here as well as in 2:11,12 and 4:11, the last of which certainly refers to the whole law and not an individual precept. Therefore, the key must be seen in the fact that Lev. 19:18 was considered a comprehensive rule in Christian circles. The connection with "kingdom" in 2:5 identifies Lev. 19:18 as the law of the kingdom and assigns the text a prominence similar to that given it by Jesus (Mk. 12:28-34 par.) and Paul (Rom. 13:10; Gal. 5:14).

If the whole law were in James' mind, then royal would probably indicate surpassing significance comparable to a king's position of authority. If the moral law were meant, then royal would mean supreme and sovereign. Our dismissal of these views argues in favor of an identification of the love command with the royal law. One problem with saying that the love command summarizes or fulfils the royal law is the fact that the subject of τελεῖτε is not this scripture (τὴν γραφήν) but James' audience (second person plural). However, this argument can be dismissed if one assumes that Jas. 2:10 ("For whoever keeps the whole law") refers back to the keeping of the love command in 2:8 so that the love command would summarize the whole law. At any rate, one must admit that James nowhere explicitly states that love meets the demands of the whole law as Paul does. If such thinking is present, it can only be deduced by inference.

In our opinion, the disagreement over the content of the royal law stems from the fact that Lev. 19:18 is for James both one commandment among all the injunctions of the moral law and at the same time the most important of these commandments. Formally it occupies a place of superior rank but materially it stands only as one commandment among many.[234] James' view of Lev. 19:18 is similar to Matthew's; Matthew refers to love of God and neighbor as the summarizing command upon which the whole law and the prophets depend (Mt. 22:37-40) and yet at the same time lists Lev. 19:18 as only one command among the moral injunctions of the Decalogue (Mt. 19:18-19). With this understanding James' argument in 2:8-11 becomes clear. Jas. 2:8a ("If you really fulfil the royal law") refers to the love command found in Lev. 19:18 which during the first century had begun to summarize the whole law.[235] Jas. 2:9 ("But if you show partiality") remembers Lev. 19:15, a command in the original context of the love command. Jas. 2:10 then refers to each of these commands in order: "whoever keeps the whole law" is an allusion to the comprehensive love command of 2:8 while "but fails on one point" refers to the failure to keep

---

[231]Cf. Grosheide, Jakobus, 373; Adamson, James, 114-115; and Richard H. Poss, The Articular and Anarthrous Construction in the Epistle of James, 102. Davids, James, 114 seems to hold two contradictory opinions by both claiming that "the anarthrous νόμος indicates a particular law" and that "the use of νόμος instead of ἐντολή makes it appear decisive that the whole law rather than a single command is intended." Mußner, Jakobus, 126 explains the anarthrous noun as a Semitism. This could apply to 2:11 where a Hebrew infinitive construct can be discerned but cannot explain the anarthrous nouns at 4:11. Ropes, James, 198 claims the article is omitted because νόμος is treated as a quasi-proper noun, but this fails to explain why the article is sometimes included.

[232]Hort, James, 54.

[233]This applies to James' use of the terms "Lord" (cf. pp. 115-116) and "law". For examples in Paul see Moulton and Turner, Grammar, III: 177.

[234]Cf. Jack Sanders, Ethics in the New Testament, 124.

[235]Cf. ch. 2, section 2.1.

Lev. 19:15 alluded to in 2:9.[236] To follow the love command while breaking one of the injunctions which it summarizes makes one guilty of breaking every law. Then Jas. 2:11 employs two commands from the Decalogue as Jas. 2:8-9 had drawn two injunctions from Lev. 19, pointing out again that the failure to keep only one of these precepts results in being guilty of all the injunctions. Thus the love command is understood by James both in the OT sense as one command among many and in the contemporary NT sense as the comprehensive summary of the Torah.

There is a growing consensus that the three descriptions of the law as perfect, royal, and liberty are used synonymously in James.[237] We will now examine James' usage of "the perfect law of liberty" (1:25; 2:12) to determine whether the meaning and content of this phrase confirm the conclusions already reached about the royal law. As with the royal law, the perfect law of liberty can be understood against various backgrounds of thought. Dibelius detects a background in Stoic ideas where perfect would be understood as the demands of eternal nature and freedom as the result of a life obedient to the cosmic Reason.[238] It must be admitted that James sometimes utilizes technical religious terminology from the Graeco-Roman world,[239] but the content of these terms always remains within the Jewish-Christian world of thought. Some have discerned parallels in Pauline literature such as Rom. 8:2: "the law of the Spirit of life in Christ Jesus has set me free from the law of sin and death." But the contrast between the gospel and the bondage of the law at the heart of Pauline theology (Rom. 3:28) is nowhere evident in the Epistle of James. The term ἐλευθερία certainly does not entail independence from the law as in Paul (Gal. 5:1-4). The OT legislation provides a better conceptual background[240] since the Jewish law is called perfect[241] and the joy experienced in observing the law[242] gave the participant a sense of freedom.[243]

The weight of evidence points to a background in OT concepts supported by, but also interpreted by, the teaching of Jesus. The perfect law of liberty indicates a law based upon inward voluntariness rather than outward constraint.[244] An attitude of love (2:8) and mercy (2:12-13) which results in a voluntary action (1:25) free from outward coercion gives the OT law its perfect liberating quality. The interconnection between Jas. 2:12

---

[236]Laws, James, 108 attempts to defend the thesis that νόμος refers to the single love commandment in v. 8 by separating 2:10 from 2:1-9. The argument is faulty since Jas. 2:8-9 and 2:11 contain parallel examples from Lev. 19 and the Decalogue which both illustrate the same point. Thus keeping the law in its entirety is already in James' mind in 2:8-9.

[237]Furnish, Love Command, 180; Gutbrod, s.v. νόμος, TDNT, IV: 1082.

[238]Dibelius and Greeven, James, 116-118 refer to Philo, Op. Mund 3; Vit. Mos. 2:48; 4 Mac. 14:2; Epictetus, Diss. 4,1, 158; Cicero, Paras. 34; and Seneca, Vit. Beat. 15:7.

[239]Cf. Dibelius and Greeven, James, 21 and above, ch. 1, n. 99.

[240]Phillip Sigal, "The Halakhah of James," Intergerini Parietis Septum, 343 states the case too strongly when he contends that "there is no necessary connection between James' view of law and the Christian gospel."

[241]Ps. 19:7; Arist. 31.

[242]Ps. 1:2; 19:7-11; 40:6-8; 119; Sir. 6:23-31; 51:13-22.

[243]Ps. 119:32,45; Aboth 3:5; 6:2; Baba Kamma 8:6; b. Baba Metzia 85b. E. Stauffer, "Das 'Gesetz der Freiheit' in der Ordensregel von Jericho," ThLZ 77(1952): 527-532 claims that the same terminology "law of freedom" is evidenced in 1QS 10:6,8,11. However, Friedrich Nötscher, "'Gesetz der Freiheit' im NT und in der Mönchsgemeinde am Toten Meer," Bib 34(1953): 193-194 has proven that the better translation remains "inscribed law" as in Ex. 32:16. *Haruth*, graven, must be preferred to *heruth*, freedom.

[244]A freedom from ceremonial prescriptions in contrast to ethical obligations could also be in James' mind since nowhere does he espouse the practices of the Jewish ceremonial law.

and its preceding and following contexts is now evident. "So speak and so act as those who are to be judged under the law of liberty" refers back to 2:8 to the law of love which sets people free to show mercy to their neighbors (2:13). As illustrated in Jas. 2:8 and 2:13, the qualities of love (the royal law) and mercy are what make the law perfect and free. This does not imply, however, that the OT commands no longer need to be observed. We have seen that James like Matthew can point to love as the most important and comprehensive of commands and yet include it alongside the other injunctions of the Decalogue. James has transferred the OT commandments into the church age in order to undergird the perfect, royal law of liberty with practical implications. If one "looks into" and "perseveres" (1:25) in this Christianized law, "he will be blessed in his doing." Thus in the church's ethical instruction the moral laws of the OT are set alongside the love command of Jesus as the guide for life.

It is really a rather simple undertaking to answer the question whether Jas. 2:8 is alluding to Jesus' summary of the law found in Mt. 22:36-40 par. James states himself that he is quoting scripture; therefore, he is recalling Lev. 19:18b, not any saying of Jesus.[245] What is more difficult to determine is whether this commandment has been given prominence because of the summary position that Jesus gave to the love command. James nowhere combines the love of God (Dt. 6:5) with the love of the neighbor as Jesus had done in the gospels. Neither does he specifically state that the law of love fulfils or summarizes all the other laws as Paul in Rom. 13:8-10. Yet the special designation given to the content of Lev. 19:18 (i.e. love) as the royal law implies that the command was given special prominence. This prominence is likely accounted for by the influence that the preaching of Jesus had upon the themes of the church's ethical teaching. Jesus proclaimed God's kingdom, and James is now teaching the laws of the kingdom.[246] Therefore, once again James employs a theme of Jesus' preaching which has entered into the paraenesis of the church rather than quoting a specific dominical saying.

3.3 Jas. 2:13	Mt. 5:7
ἡ γὰρ κρίσις ἀνέλεος τῷ μὴ ποιήσαντι ἔλεος· κατακαυχᾶται ἔλεος κρίσεως.	μακάριοι οἱ ἐλεήμονες, ὅτι αὐτοὶ ἐλεηθήσονται.

Jas. 2:13 serves as a transition between paraenetic discourses in a similar fashion to 2:26 and 3:11-12. It consists of two aphorisms held together by the catchwords, mercy and judgment. It is only loosely attached to the context, again by means of a catchword connection, κρίνεσθαι / κρίσις. This verse provides no special support for the argumentation of the preceding section and, therefore, must function as a proverbial generalizing conclusion somewhat close in content to the subject matter at hand. These aphorisms probably came to the mind of James because of the conceptual connection between being judged by the law of liberty (2:12) and being judged by the "law" of mercy here illustrated. But the sudden appearance of ἔλεος along with the transition from second to third person conclusively demonstrates that we are dealing with a piece of pre-Jamesian material used as a generalizing conclusion. The first saying is a typical piece of Jewish wisdom with the eschatological outcome based upon the quality of the human action. The second is certainly not antithetical to the first and should probably be viewed as offering a ground or supplying a foundation for the truth of the first saying. However, since there is no conjunction to suggest what type of connection exists between these wis-

---

[245]Cf. Furnish, Love Command, 177.

[246]In the Markan account Jesus says to the scribe who agrees with his analysis of the greatest commandment that he is not far from the kingdom of God. We encounter a similar connection between Lev. 19:18 and the kingdom in Jas. 2:5,8.

dom sayings, it is difficult to discern their exact relationship. The obscure word κατακαυχᾶται is best translated "triumph"[247] similar to the RSV reading, "Mercy triumphs over judgment."

Turning to the relationship with the gospel parallel, we notice that both contain similar subject matter in a proverbial form. Furthermore, both couple together divine and human mercy and teach that the outcome of human mercy will be the return of divine mercy. Exegetes of the last two centuries have rated this as the sixth most popular parallel between the gospels and the Epistle of James.

However, strong evidence against an allusion to Mt. 5:7 is exhibited in the fact that these texts have only one word in common and that term, mercy, diverges in form. Whereas Mt. 5:7 is written as a blessing, Jas. 2:13a embodies the form of a threat. Furthermore, the teaching that human mercy breeds a positive divine response (Jas. 2:13a) is popular not only in Jesus' teaching (cf. also Mt. 18:23-35; 6:12; Lk. 11:4) but also outside the limits of his influence. The Test. Zeb. 8:1-3[248] declares,

> Have, therefore, yourselves also, my children, compassion towards every man with mercy, that the Lord also may have compassion upon you .... For in the degree in which a man hath compassion upon his neighbors, in the same degree hath the Lord also upon him.

In the Test. Zeb. 5:3 this same emphasis is visible: "Have, therefore, compassion (ἔλεος) in your hearts, my children, because even as a man doeth to his neighbor, even so also will the Lord do to him." In the rabbinic tradition Rabbi Barabbi explains, "He who is merciful to others, mercy is shown to him by Heaven, while he who is not merciful to others, mercy is not shown to him by Heaven."[249] Furthermore, the midrash from Sifre 93b states, "So long as you have pity on men, God will have pity on you."[250] Finally, Piska 38 quotes Rabbi Jose as saying, "You may regard your compassion as a sign that God's compassion will follow -- whenever you show compassion for your fellow man, the Lord will show compassion for other mortals as well as you."[251] In fact this principle according to Piska 38 is grounded in scripture itself: "Scripture says further, When thou art endued with mercy, He has mercy upon thee (Deut. 13:18)."[252] Thus this teaching traces back to the OT where God's mercy is emphasized (Ex. 34:5-6; Dt. 4:31; Ps. 103:8ff), and people are exhorted to show mercy (Jer. 9:16; Hos. 6:6; Mic. 6:8).

The theme of Jas. 2:13b, the triumph of mercy over judgment, also has close Jewish parallels. Already in the OT the prophet Hosea had proclaimed that judgment was the result of Israel's lack of mercy (ἔλεος Hos. 6:5,7 LXX). In the intertestamental period Tobit 4:10 states, "Charity (ἐλεημοσύνη) will save you from death and keep you from going down into darkness." Another substantial parallel is evident in Philo (Deus Immut. 76): "He tempers His judgment with mercy (τὸν ἔλεον ἀνακρίνησιν) which He shows in doing

---

[247]Cf. BAGD, s.v. κατακαυχάομαι, 401 and Rudolf Bultmann, s.v. ἔλεος, TDNT, III: 653-654. The variants in the textual tradition illustrate the confusion in understanding this word.

[248]For textual support see ch. 2, n. 132.

[249]b. Shabbath 151b, ed. Epstein, 774.

[250]Claude G. Montefiore, Rabbinic Literature and Gospel Teachings, 23.

[251]Pisikta Rabbati, tr. William G. Braude, II: 692-693. In addition Laws, James, 117 quotes Pesikta 167a as saying, "The scales are evenly balanced: the scale of iniquities on the one side and of merits on the other; the Holy One inclines the balance to mercy"; and Ropes, James, 201 cites Jer. Baba Kamma 7:10 as saying, "Every time that thou art merciful, God will be merciful to thee; and if thou art not merciful, God will not show mercy to thee," but we could not locate either quotation in the primary literature.

[252]Pisikta Rabbati, tr. Braude, II: 692. Cf. Dt. 13:17 LXX.

kindness even to the unworthy."[253] Finally the Sibylline Oracles 2:81, written around the time of Jesus, explains: "Mercy saves from death when judgment comes."[254]

Authors who claim a conscious allusion to the gospel teaching often admit that James appeals to the general teaching of Jesus rather than a specific verse. Yet Mt. 5:7 is said to be "surely of first importance",[255] or "may be said to give the key to our verse."[256] It is true that James' theme of mercy exhibits more parallels with Matthew[257] than with Luke. This is accounted for, however, by Matthew's similar interest in Jewish background material evidenced by the quoting of Hos. 6:6 on two occasions (9:13; 12:7)[258] and by their common transmission of the ethical teaching of the church.[259] This ecclesiastical emphasis upon mercy continues in the Apostolic Fathers where a saying about mercy is attributed to Jesus and written in the format of Mt. 7:1 and Lk. 6:37-38 rather than Mt. 5:7. 1 Cl. 13:2 states:

ἐλεᾶτε ἵνα ἐλεηθῆτε, ἀφίετε ἵνα ἀφεθῇ ὑμῖν·
ὡς ποιεῖτε, οὕτω ποιηθήσεται ὑμῖν·
ὡς δίδοτε, οὕτως δοθήσεται ὑμῖν·
ὡς κρίνετε, οὕτως κριθήσεσθε·
ὡς χρηστεύεσθε, οὕτως χρηστευθήσεται ὑμῖν·[260]

Polycarp (Phil. 2:3) follows the same procedure when he calls his readers to remember the words which the Lord spoke:

μὴ κρίνετε, ἵνα μὴ κριθῆτε·
ἀφίετε, καὶ ἀφεθήσεται ὑμῖν·
ἐλεᾶτε, ἵνα ἐλεηθῆτε·[261]

These quotations contain themes drawn from the preaching of Jesus and placed into well-

---

[253]Colson and Whitaker, Philo III, LCL, 48-49.

[254]ῥύεται ἐκ θανάτου ἔλεος, κρίσις ὁπόταν ἔλθῃ GCS 8, p. 30, line 81. J.J. Collins in OT Pseud., I: 330 states that this section is not part of the Christian redaction.

[255]Davids, James, 119.

[256]Knowling, James, 52.

[257]Mt. 5:7; 9:13; 12:7; 18:29,34; 24:45-46.

[258]This is similar to the above quoted parallel, Sibylline Oracles 2:81 where 2:82 continues, "God wants not sacrifice but mercy."

[259]Cf. below, p. 166.

[260]Line 1 below is similar in content to Mt. 5:7; line 2 to Mt. 6:14; line 3 to Mt. 7:12; Lk. 6:31; line 4 to Lk. 6:38; line 5 to Mt. 7:1-2; Lk. 6:37; line 6 to Lk. 35c-36 (cf. below, p. 176).

Have mercy, that ye may receive mercy.
Forgive, that it may be forgiven to you.
As ye do, so shall it be done to you.
As ye give, so shall it be given unto you.
As ye judge, so shall ye be judged.
As ye show kindness, so shall kindness be showed to you.

This is repeated as a dominical saying by Cl. Alex., Strom. 2,91,2 (GCS 52, pp. 161-162, lines 24, 1-3). Cf. also Resch, Agrapha, 197-198.

[261]Judge not that ye be not judged.
Forgive, and it shall be forgiven to you.
Have mercy that ye may receive mercy.

Polycarp continues by rehearsing two of the beatitudes but does not mention, "Blessed are the merciful."

known teaching patterns such as "Judge not that ye be not judged" for easy memorization.[262] It is therefore possible that James includes the subject of mercy in his teaching because it was an emphasis of his master. Whatever the case, Mt. 5:7 is certainly not consciously alluded to in Jas. 2:13. The best solution is to conceive of James, Jesus, intertestamental authors, and the Rabbis as drawing from a common tradition of Jewish wisdom. James concludes many of his sections with such proverbial statements (2:13,26; 3:11-12,18; 4:17; 5:20b) showing that this is an intrinsic characteristic of his style.

3.4 Jas. 3:12	Mt. 7:16	Lk. 6:44
	ἀπὸ τῶν καρπῶν αὐτῶν	ἕκαστον γὰρ δένδρον ἐκ
	ἐπιγνώσεσθε αὐτούς.	τοῦ ἰδίου καρποῦ
μὴ δύναται,	μήτι συλλέγουσιν	γινώσκεται·
ἀδελφοί μου,	ἀπὸ ἀκανθῶν	οὐ γὰρ ἐξ ἀκανθῶν
συκῆ ἐλαίας ποιῆσαι	σταφυλὰς	συλλέγουσιν σῦκα
ἢ ἄμπελος	ἢ ἀπὸ τριβόλων	οὐδὲ ἐκ βάτου
σῦκα; οὔτε	σῦκα;	σταφυλὴν τρυγῶσιν.
ἁλυκὸν γλυκὺ ποιῆσαι ὕδωρ.		

Gospel of Thomas 45a[263]

"Jesus said, 'Grapes are not harvested from thorns, nor are figs gathered from thistles, for they do not produce fruit.'"

Coptic Apocalypse of Peter 76:4-7[264]

"For people do not gather figs from thorns or from thorn trees, if they are wise, nor grapes from thistles."

Clement of Alexandria, Paed. 2,74,4[265]

"And we eat grapes from thorns (ἐξ ἀκανθῶν τρυγῶμεν σταφυλὴν) and figs from thistles (σῦκα ἀπὸ βάτων); while those to whom He stretched forth His hands -- the disobedient and untruthful people -- He lacerates into wounds."

Jas. 3:12 concludes the treatise on the tongue. James illustrates the savage nature of the tongue by pointing to its hellish properties (v. 6), its untamed unruliness (vv. 7-8), and its inconsistent behavior of blessing God while cursing those made in the likeness of God (vv. 9-10). Jas. 3:11-12 then relates two or three similitudes from nature to condemn this two-sidedness of the tongue. Typical of this middle section of the Epistle of James (three treatises from 2:1-3:12) is the frequent use of rhetorical questions. Jas. 3:11 asks about the possibility of a spring pouring forth both fresh water and brackish, sulphurous water. Jas. 3:12a speaks about the impossibility of fig trees yielding olives (along

[262] In 1 Cl. 13:2 the first two maxims employ the imperative with ἵνα and a passive verb; the following four are structured by ὡς ... οὕτως. Cf. Donald A. Hagner, "The Sayings of Jesus in the Apostolic Fathers and Justin Martyr," Gospel Perspectives, 5:235.

[263] Lambdin, "Gospel of Thomas," NHL, 123.

[264] Roger A. Bullard, "Apocalypse of Peter," NHL, 342

[265] English by William Wilson, The Ante-Nicene Fathers, II: 257; Greek from Otto Stählin, GCS 12, p. 203, lines 10ff. A better translation for ἀπὸ βάτων would be "bramble bush" as in the RSV of Luke. For Clement the thorns represent the sins from which Christ has rescued us.

with figs ?) and grapevines bearing figs (along with grapes ?). Finally, 3:12b repeats the metaphor used in 3:11 (salty and fresh water) remodeled this time after the pattern of 3:12a.[266] All the imagery does not reinforce the same point. The nature parable in v. 11 proves the unnaturalness of one spring gushing forth two types of water just as it is unnatural for the tongue to bless and curse at the same time. Jas. 3:12 proves instead the incompatibility of one type of tree or water producing another type. The metaphors of 3:12 are more difficult to relate back to James' description of the tongue; maybe the parallel would be that "inconsistency in human speech should be as much out of the question as it is for one tree to produce a different fruit."[267] Another incongruity among the metaphors is the fact that blessing and cursing as well as fresh and salt water are mixtures of good and bad, but olives and figs are both considered edible delicacies.

Comparing Jas. 3:12 with the gospel parallels, we discover a remarkable diversity of images:

Matthew and Thomas	Luke	James
grapes from thorns figs from thistles	figs from thorns grapes from bramble bush	olives from fig tree figs from grapevine

Coptic Apocalypse of Peter	Clement of Alexandria
figs from thorns or bramble bush grapes from thistles	grapes from thorns figs from bramble bush

In the Q saying, which Matthew and Luke both place in the Sermon on the Mount/Plain, the sayings stand in reverse order, and synonyms occur in one instance (τρίβολος, βάτος) instead of duplicate wording. Clement of Alexandria follows Matthew except for the substitution of bramble bush for thistles in the last phrase. The Coptic Apocalypse of Peter stands closer to the Gospel of Luke at least with regard to the order of figs followed by grapes. Yet it is important that in each case the theme is identical: something evil (thorns and thistles) cannot produce something good (figs or grapes). In James, however, the comparison is completely different: two good things are counterposed to each other. One might argue that James altered the wording of Jesus to fit the saying more appropriately into his context. Yet truthfully, the saying in the gospels would have paralleled Jas. 3:9-11 much better. Jesus' comparison of delicious grapes and figs with evil thorns and thistles would produce a congruity of images with the blessing and cursing (vv. 9-10) and the fresh and brackish water (vv. 11,12b) of James' epistle. Surely if James would have known this dominical saying, he would have employed it instead of creating an incongruous set of metaphors at 3:12. Adamson, however, suggests another alternative; he argues that "the antecedents of Jas. 3 possibly and perhaps probably are not Matthew and Luke as we have them, but personal experience or first-hand accounts at the beginning of the traditions from which Matthew and Luke are variously derived." It is true that Luke and Matthew exhibit enough divergencies from each other to conjecture the possibility that this saying was transmitted in quite variant forms. Furthermore, the *logion* is inserted into different contexts[268] by Matthew and Luke so as to leave the impression that it could as well be introduced into yet another context as we have in Jas. 3. Yet the fact that James compares two good

---

[266]ποιῆσαι makes the parallel with 12a explicit. Because of this repeated imagery and the textual problems surrounding this verse, Dibelius suggests that it is a later gloss intended to conform two images together. Laws votes for a corruption of the original text.

[267]Laws, James, 157.

[268]Luke applies the saying to the evil desires of the heart from which the mouth speaks while Matthew is concerned with false prophets. Hort, James, 79 allegorizes Jas. 3:11 so that πήγη represents the heart and thus claims a similar context with Luke.

objects while the Jesus-tradition within and outside the Biblical literature consistently compares good and evil objects argues against any conjecture of a common tradition.

The teaching of Jesus is not the only source from which James could have drawn this analogy. The discovery in Greek literature of sayings closer to the Epistle of James in both content and purpose renders it more likely that James' saying traces back to the everyday experience of the people living around the Mediterranean Sea. Widespread within contemporary literature is the use of the imagery of a plant which only produces according to its own nature.[269] The closest parallels are the statements of:

1) Plutarch: "But as it is, we do not expect the vine to bear figs nor the olive grapes." (Tranq. 13);[270]

2) Epictetus: "Such a powerful and invincible thing is the nature of man. For how can a vine be moved to act, not like a vine, but like an olive, or again an olive to act, not like an olive, but like a vine? It is impossible; inconceivable."(Diss. 2,20,18);[271]

3) Seneca: "Good does not spring from evil any more than figs grow from olive trees." (Ep. 87:25).[272]

Hunzinger and Dibelius[273] believe that such Stoic traditions are the source of the proverb spoken in Jas. 3:12. In each case two good things are compared as in James, and the thorns and thistles of the gospel parallels are not mentioned. Davids counters this suggestion with three arguments: 1) the Stoic parallels are not close enough in context; 2) similar proverbial illustrations must have been common over the whole Mediterranean area; and 3) the oral form of Jesus' teaching may have been the basis for James' ideas.[274] Against Davids, we believe that the similarities of the parallels listed above as well as their corresponding contexts prove that Dibelius has unearthed closer parallels to James than the saying of Jesus from Mt. 7:16; Lk. 6:46. To be sure none of the authors are speaking about the tongue, but both Plutarch and Epictetus are calling attention to impossible phenomena similar to Jas. 3:11-12.[275] Davids' second point, however, has weighty consequences for Dibelius's conjecture of a specifically Stoic background. Would Dibelius argue that these Stoic writers were quoting each other's literature when they mention this proverb? Of course not! Such a saying had become a common everyday expression. Laws concurs with

---

[269]Cf. Dibelius and Greeven, James, 204.

[270]W.C. Helmbold, Plutarch's Moralia VI, LCL, 212-213. νῦν δὲ τὴν μὲν ἄμπελον σῦκα φέρειν οὐκ ἀξιοῦμεν οὐδὲ τὴν ἐλαίαν βότρυς·

[271]W.A. Oldfather, Epictetus I, LCL, 376-377. οὕτως ἰσχυρόν τι καὶ ἀνίκητόν ἐστιν ἡ φύσις ἡ ἀνθρωπίνη. πῶς γὰρ δύναται ἄμπελος μὴ ἀμπελικῶς κινεῖσθαι, ἀλλ' ἐλαϊκῶς, ἢ ἐλαία πάλιν μὴ ἐλαϊκῶς ἀλλ' ἀμπελικῶς; ἀμήχανον, ἀδιανόητον ....

[272]R.M. Gummere, Seneca: Epistulae Morales II, LCL, 336-337. Bultmann, Synoptic Tradition, 202, n. 1 presents corresponding Arabic proverbs, but they are of minimal value.

[273]Claus-Hunno Hunzinger, s.v. συκῆ, TDNT, VII: 755; Dibelius and Greeven, James, 204.

[274]Davids, James, 148. We have already addressed David's third argument when we countered Adamson's claim above.

[275]Plutarch begins ch. 13 by explaining, "There are, indeed, some pursuits which cannot by their very nature exist together, but rather are by nature opposed to each other." Helmbold, Plutarch's Moralia VI, LCL, 209. Epictetus, Diss. 2,20,19 states, "Neither, then, is it possible for a man absolutely to lose the affections of a man, and those who cut off their bodily organs are unable to cut off the really important thing -- their sexual desires." Seneca's context is closer to the gospel parallels where good does not result from evil.

this line of thinking, "The drawing of images from olive, fig tree, and vine is hardly surprising in the Mediterranean area."[276] The source for James' nature parable is then directly related to the cultural experiences and everyday wisdom sayings of James' community and not any specific quote of Jesus or a Stoic writer. The paraenetic tradition of the church thus included everyday wisdom and analogies from nature as well as Jewish wisdom, specific dominical sayings, and the important themes of Jesus' preaching.

4.0 The Disciplinary Exhortations of Jas. 3:13-4:10(12)

A. 3:13-18 Disciplinary exhortation about wisdom.

1. 3:13 Question and Answer.
    - a. 3:13a Question: Who is wise?
    - b. 3:13b Answer: The one who displays works of wisdom.

2. 3:14-16 The false lifestyle: False works of wisdom.
    - a. 3:14 Characteristics: Jealousy and selfish ambition.
    - b. 3:15 Source: Wisdom that is earthly, unspiritual, devilish
    - c. 3:16 The accepted teaching: Jealousy and selfish ambition breed disorder and every vile practice.

3. 3:17 Seven characteristics of the true lifestyle.
    Seven qualities of wisdom from above: 1) pure; 2) peaceable; 3) gentle; 4) open to reason; 5) full of mercy; 6) impartial; 7) sincere.

4. 3:18 Generalizing conclusion as a transition: Righteousness is sown in peace.

B. 4:1-10 Disciplinary exhortation about humility.

1. 4:1 Question and Answer.
    - a. 4:1a Question: What causes fighting?
    - b. 4:1b Answer: Passions.

2. 4:2-6 The false lifestyle: Quarrels and lust.
    - a. 4:2-3 Characteristics: Desire, jealousy, fighting (cf. p. 71).
    - b. 4:4 Source: Friendship with the world.
    - c. 4:5-6 The accepted teaching: What scripture says.
        - 1) 4:5 Scripture warns about the envy of the human spirit.
        - 2) 4:6 God gives grace only to the humble (Prov. 3:34).

3. 4:7-10 Seven characteristics of the true lifestyle: Seven paraenetic exhortations
    - a. 4:7a Submit yourselves to God.
    - b. 4:7b Resist the devil.
    - c. 4:8a Draw near to God.
    - d. 4:8b Purify your hands and hearts.
    - e. 4:9a Be wretched and mourn and weep.
    - f. 4:9b Let your laughter be turned to mourning and joy to dejection.
    - g. 4:10 Humble yourselves.

4. 4:11-12 Transition: Exhortation about judging (cf. p. 118).

---

[276] Laws, James, 157.

It is significant that James does not begin 3:13 with his normal address, "my beloved brethren." This omission reveals a change in the literary aim of the author within the genre of paraenesis. The discourses of 2:1-3:12 are now followed by disciplinary exhortations where the audience is addressed as adulteresses (4:4) and double-minded sinners (4:8) rather than brethren. This section consists of two disciplinary exhortations with a parallel structure. Each begins with a question and answer (3:13; 4:1), the only formal difference being that the reply of 4:1b is in the form of a rhetorical question. Unchristian behavior patterns are then described under the headings false wisdom (3:14-16) and a false Christian lifestyle filled with quarrels and lust (4:2-6). In each case the negative characteristics are rehearsed (3:14; 4:2-3), the source of this counterfeit lifestyle is exposed (3:15; 4:4), and the godly alternative is supported by a quote from the accepted teaching.[277] This description of the false lifestyle is then contrasted with the characteristics of sanctioned behavior. In 3:17 seven qualites of wisdom from above are enumerated; in 4:7-10, a section enclosed by the concept of humility as an envelope technique (4:6,10), seven exhortations call the community to Christian attributes. Finally, both sections end with generalizing conclusions that function as transitional statements. Jas. 3:18 is an aphorism connected by catchword to the previous context (καρπῶν / καρπός; εἰρηνική / εἰρήνη) and by means of the thematic contrast of peace (3:18) and war (4:1) to the second disciplinary exhortation which follows. Jas. 4:10 serves as a generalizing conclusion for 4:1-10, while 4:11-12 is a transitional saying before the two prophetic denunciations against the merchants (4:13-17) and the rich (5:1-6).

4.1	Jas. 3:18	Mt. 5:9
	καρπὸς δὲ δικαιοσύνης ἐν εἰρήνῃ σπείρεται τοῖς ποιοῦσιν εἰρήνην.	μακάριοι οἱ εἰρηνοποιοί, ὅτι αὐτοὶ υἱοὶ θεοῦ κληθήσονται.

In a similar fashion to Jas. 2:13 an isolated preexistent saying is loosely tied to the previous context to give the flow of thought a parabolic type ending. If James himself had originated this material as a generalizing conclusion, then the expected subject of the sentence would have been the "fruit of wisdom" rather than the "fruit of righteousness".[278] Wisdom is the central theme of the whole paragraph, and the omission of this theme at the conclusion reveals James' use of source material. The catchword connection (καρπῶν / καρπός;[279] εἰρηνική / εἰρήνη) confirms that preexistent material is here inserted to continue James' general train of thought. As Dibelius points out, this saying "possesses an independent wholeness and inclusiveness in form".[280] This does not mean, however, that all conceptual ties are missing. The emphasis on peace in 3:18 is certainly connected with the peaceable wisdom from above in v. 17. Furthermore, just as 3:16 (following a description of earthly wisdom) indicates that jealousy and selfish ambition produce every vile practice, so here (after a description of heavenly wisdom) James teaches that peace produces righteousness. Thus 3:18 picks up previously mentioned concepts as well as offering a contrast to the lifestyle of fighting talked about in 4:1.

---

[277]Jas. 3:16 is a generally accepted apostolic teaching using Jamesian vocabulary (ἀκαταστασία 1:8; 3:8,16); 4:5-6 are quotes from sources (cf. ch. 2, sections 2.4 and 2.5).

[278]Unless one denies the presence of an epexegetical genitive and sees the fruit of righteousness as wisdom. Cf. n. 283.

[279]Although "fruit" can be employed both in its singular and plural forms to indicate the same thing, the difference here is another indication of a preexistent saying.

[280]Dibelius and Greeven, James, 208.

Every phrase in Jas. 3:18 is saturated with exegetical perplexities. καρπός usually entails the full-grown fruit which is harvested, but Prov. 11:30 LXX[281] speaks about the fruit seed rather than the ripe fruit. Since the fruit seed corresponds more appropriately with the metaphor of sowing, the meaning here might be, "The seed of righteousness is sown in peace."[282] On the other hand, an aphorism in the present tense often refers to an event which has repeatedly happened in the past and is expected in the future. The saying would then be translated, "The harvest (ripe fruit) of righteousness is always sown in peace." The complete phrase "fruit of righteousness" has also been interpreted in various ways; it is best understood either as 1) a genitive of origin (possession) whereby the fruit springs from righteousness; or 2) an epexegetical genitive (BDF 167 appositive genitive) so that the fruit consists in righteousness. If the former is postulated, then righteousness has itself a fruit. Ropes and Laws believe that this fruit is wisdom, thus tying the saying intricately with the context.[283] However, the identification of the fruit as righteousness has rightly become the most popular view[284] based on the overwhelming use of the epexegetical genitive when this phrase is employed in other contexts.[285]

The second half of the saying is likewise filled with exegetical dilemmas. The expression ἐν εἰρήνῃ can either be associated with the fruit of righteousness so that "the righteousness which springs up is a righteousness in peace"[286] or put in primary connection with sowing[287] so that the sowing happened in peace. Finally, the concluding phrase τοῖς ποιοῦσον εἰρήνην can either be connected with sowing so that the righteousness is "sown in peace by those who make peace"[288] or can be tied to the fruit of righteousness serving as a counterpart to ἐν εἰρήνῃ σπείρεται. In the latter case righteousness is pictured both as sown in peace and as a harvest (fruit) reaped for the peacemakers.[289] The advantage of the former interpretation is the emphasis which the word "sowing" receives. The purpose of this verse is definitely to emphasize how just and righteous deeds can be accomplished, and this interpretation states that such actions are sown in peace by peacemakers. No parallel metaphor concerning the reaping of a harvest is then assumed. On the other hand, this view appears to result in a tautology since the last phrase of the sentence is redundant. "The fruit of righteousness is sown in peace" seems sufficient in itself; why add "by peaceable people"? Davids attempts to counter this argument by insisting that this type of emphatic tautology is placed here for rhetorical effect.[290] However, the grammatical rule that the dative of agent is only used with verbs in the perfect tense conclusively argues

---

[281]"Out of the fruit of righteousness grows a tree of life." Septuagint, Greek and English, 798. (ἐκ καρποῦ δικαιοσύνης φύεται δένδρον ζωῆς).

[282]Cf. Dibelius and Greeven, James, 208.

[283]Ropes, James, 251; Laws, James. 166 interprets Prov. 3:18 and 11:30 together since both refer to the tree of life and James displays knowledge of Prov. 3 at Jas. 4:6. Meyer, Rätsel, 263 suggests that God grants this fruit to those who seek wisdom.

[284]Among others Cantinat, Chaine, Davids, Hort, and Mitton.

[285]This phrase certainly contains an epexegetical genitive in Heb. 12:11; Amos 6:12; Prov. 11:30; Arist. 232; and Herm., Sim. 9,19,2. Cf. Moulton and Turner, Grammar, III: 215. Phil. 1:11; Prov. 3:9 LXX; 13:2 LXX remain uncertain when the plural form is employed. The quote from Epicurus in Cl. Alex., Strom. 6,24,10 is certainly not epexegetical.

[286]Hort, James, 87.

[287]This is the usual interpretation which we also accept. The phrase ἐν εἰρήνῃ is placed before σπείρεται for emphasis and not to connect it with the "fruit of righteousness" as Hort assumes.

[288]Thus a dative of agent (RSV, Blackman, Davids, Mitton, Ropes).

[289]Thus a dative of advantage (Cantinat, Dibelius, Laws, Mayor, BDF 191.4, Moulton and Turner, Grammar, III: 238).

[290]Davids, James, 155.

against this interpretation.[291] Thus when the term "fruit" is interpreted not as a fruit seed but as the harvest of ripe fruit, then the peacemakers who sow in peace reap for themselves a harvest of righteousness. The NIV thus translates this verse, "Peacemakers who sow in peace raise a harvest of righteousness." The relationship of righteousness and peace is usually pictured with righteousness being the cause and peace the effect or result of righteousness (Is. 32:17; Aboth 2:7). Here the reverse is true: righteousness is the harvest which results when a seed is sown in peace.[292] In Heb. 12:11 the result of discipline is the peaceful fruit of righteousness (καρπὸν εἰρηνικὸν ... δικαιοσύνης); in Jas. 3:18 the fruit of righteousness results from peacemaking, not discipline.

Mt. 5:9 is often cited as the background for this wisdom saying. Davids remarks that "the phrase aptly recalls Jesus' words in Mt. 5:9,"[293] while Brückner contends that Jas. 3:18 "kann nur aus dem Wortlaut von Matth. 5,9 entstanden sein."[294] Laws agrees that Jesus' promise of a future reward is recalled even though the definition of the reward is quite different (called sons of God vs. righteousness).[295] To explain the omission of the concept of righteousness in the beatitude, authors call attention to the context of Matthew where righteousness is a major theme (5:6,10,20; 6:1,33).

Against these arguments we will point to 1) the missing eschatological situation in James; 2) the vocabulary discrepancies and new imagery presented; and 3) the similar metaphors of sowing and reaping encountered in other Jewish-Christian literature outside the Jesus-tradition. Unlike Matthew, James is not contrasting a present action with an eschatological reward. Instead James has in mind only a temporal situation where the practice of peace creates true justice in everyday human relationships. The differences with the gospel parallel become even more evident when we notice that only one word (peace) is the same in each verse. Furthermore, this one common word is employed in variant forms and the order of thought is reversed with the beneficial reward coming at opposite ends of the sentence. The climatic difference is the new imagery present in Jas. 3:18. The mention of fruit in 3:17 seems to remind James of a fitting proverb using a metaphor of sowing and harvesting (fruitbearing). It is very doubtful whether the mentioning of the word "fruit" would remind James of Mt. 5:9. Finally, when Mt. 5:9 is alluded to in Christian writings of the second or third century, the beatitude foremat is present[296] or at least other beatitudes are found in the same context.[297] In the only occurrence where this is not true (Tert. Pud. 2:2), the close connection of the terms "sons of God" and "peacemakers" disclose that Mt. 5:9 is in view: "And so it will be becoming for the sons of God too to be pitiful hearted and peacemakers."[298] This verbal resemblance is absent at Jas. 3:18. Therefore, one can only assume parallel subject matter since the shared use of

---

[291]Cf. Archibald T. Robertson, A Grammar of the Greek New Testament in the Light of Historical Research, 534. Lk. 23:15 and Jas. 3:7 are allowable since they employ the perfect tense. However, not all grammarians are completely convinced of this distinction. William W. Goodwin and Charles B. Gulick, Greek Grammar (Boston: Ginn, 1930), section 1174 state that it is rarely used with other passive tenses and Georg B. Winer, A Treatise on the Grammar of New Testament Greek (Edinburgh: Clark, 1882), 274 explains that it is usually employed with the perfect tense offering as possible exceptions 2 Cor. 12:20; 2 Pet. 3:14; Rom. 10:20 from Is. 65:1 (all with the aorist "to be found by"); (Jas. 3:18); and Lk. 24:35; Phil. 4:5; and 2 Pet. 2:19 which we find questionable.

[292]If one chooses for the fruit seed rather than the ripe fruit of the harvest, then righteousness and peace are sown together and one does not produce the other.

[293]Davids, James, 155.

[294]Quoted in Spitta , Zur Geschichte, II: 168.

[295]Laws, James, 165.

[296]Cl. Alex., Strom. 1,7,2; 4,40,2; Tert., Pud. 5:15.

[297]Tert., Pat. 11:8.

[298]S. Thelwall, The Anti-Nicene Fathers, IV: 75.

the term "making peace" would naturally be expected when two verses are rehearsing matching themes.

Similar metaphors of sowing and reaping are found in the church's ethical teaching. Paul in Gal. 6:8 states, "He who sows to the flesh will from the flesh reap corruption, but he who sows to the Spirit will from the Spirit reap eternal life." Similar terminology to Jas. 3:18 is used by Paul in 2 Cor. 9:10 in a context about sowing and reaping.[299] The particular phrase "fruit of righteousness" seems to have been fixed already in the language of the LXX. Several times the LXX (Prov. 3:9; 11:30; 13:2) employs this expression where no equivalent terminology can be found in the original Hebrew.[300] The popularization of this phrase in the Christian era is evidenced in its usage by Paul, the author of Hebrews, Hermas, and James.[301] The theme of peace is likewise regularly encountered in the exhortations of the leaders of the church.[302] Therefore the expressions and subject matter of Jas. 3:18 were of general interest to the people of that day. No specific source can be established, although it is highly likely that James drew his material from OT proverbial sayings rather than from the *logia* of Jesus.[303] The particular phrase "fruit(s) of righteousness" is employed three times in the Septuagint book of Proverbs, and the concepts of righteousness and peace are frequently combined in OT wisdom sayings.[304] Therefore, on three successive occasions at the end of James' paraenetic paragraphs (2:13; 3:12,18) we encounter wisdom sayings which have been incorporated into the church's ethical teaching.

4.2 Jas. 4:4	Mt. 6:24 / Lk. 16:13
μοιχαλίδες, οὐκ οἴδατε ὅτι ἡ φιλία τοῦ κόσμου ἔχθρα τοῦ θεοῦ ἐστιν; ὃς ἐὰν οὖν βουληθῇ φίλος εἶναι τοῦ κόσμου, ἐχθρὸς τοῦ θεοῦ καθίσταται.	οὐδεὶς (οἰκέτης) δύναται δυσὶ κυρίοις δουλεύειν· ἢ γὰρ τὸν ἕνα μισήσει καὶ τὸν ἕτερον ἀγαπήσει, ἢ ἑνὸς ἀνθέξεται καὶ τοῦ ἑτέρου καταφρονήσει. οὐ δύνασθε θεῷ δουλεύειν καὶ μαμωνᾷ.

Jas. 4:4 develops the radical ethical dualism[305] between friendship with the world and love of God. First James states the ethical dualism in the form of a principle ("Friendship with the world is enmity with God") and then applies this principle to an individualized situation ("Whoever wishes to be a friend of the world makes himself an enemy of God"). Already at 1:27 James has indicated that "to keep oneself unstained from the world" is part of the definition of pure and undefiled religion. Now he points out that the world is the false god with whom the people have committed adultery and the source of their counterfeit lifestyle of fightings and passions (4:1). The term "world" here means the perverted values of human society, especially pleasure seeking (4:3), and the various passions of the soul (3:14,16; 4:2) which set themselves against the will of God.

James introduces this verse with the words οὐκ οἴδατε ὅτι implying that his audience already knew or at least should have known what he was about to explain. This

---

[299]"The harvest of your righteousness" (τὰ γενήματα τῆς δικαιοσύνης ὑμῶν).

[300]It is found in Amos 6:12 MT. Similar phrases are encountered in Is. 32:17 (καὶ ἔσται τὰ ἔργα τῆς δικαιοσύνης εἰρήνη) and Hos. 10:12 (γενήματα δικαιοσύνης).

[301]Phil. 1:11; Heb. 12:11; Herm., Sim. 9,19,2; Jas. 3:18.

[302]Rom. 14:19; Eph. 2:14-17; 4:3; 6:15; Col. 3:15; Phil. 4:17; 1 Pet. 3:11 etc.

[303]Cf. Werner Foerster, s.v. εἰρήνη, TDNT, II: 412.

[304]Is. 32:17 (NIV) "The fruit of righteousness will be peace." Verse 20 refers to sowing seed. Cf. also Pss. 72:3,7; 85:10.

[305]This could be distinguished from Gnostic dualism (Mußner, Jakobus, 180) and the eschatological or metaphysical dualism of Paul in 1 Cor. 1:20ff (Dibelius and Greeven, James, 220).

phrase frequently indicates that preexistent material (especially familiar ethical instruction from the church's teaching tradition[306]) is about to follow.[307] Spitta, for example, explains v. 4a as a quotation and 4b as James' application of this principle to his own audience.[308] If preexistent material is present, then we must ask whether this source material originated in the Q saying of Jesus found in Mt. 6:24; Lk. 16:13? Commenting on the word οἴδατε Mayor contends that "the reference is to our Lord's words Matt. vi. 24."[309] He offers no specific proof, but one might point to the similar ethical dualism (God / world and God / mammon) as well as to the coinciding emphasis (a total commitment to God). Furthermore, the structure is reasonably parallel: James offers a general principle followed by an individualized application while the gospels state a principle in parabolic terms followed likewise with an individualized case (twice stated). The gospels add a generalizing conclusion repeating this principle in religious terms.

We will demonstrate the weakness of this line of argumentation by pointing to closer parallels than Mt. 6:24; Lk. 16:13 and by showing that such antitheses are a common phenomenon in church paraenesis. Some authors set James' view of the world in closer proximity to the Johannine picture of Jesus than to the Synoptics. Davids explains that "the first statement is conceivable as either an allusion or a citation, in which case the most likely source would be a saying of Jesus, perhaps in a Johannine type of tradition."[310] Oesterley[311] specifically claims that Jn. 15:18-19 is the text in the mind of our author:

> If the world hates you, know that it has hated me before it hated you. If you were of the world, the world would love its own; but because you are not of the world, but I chose you out of the world, therefore the world hates you.

This proposal is doubtful since Jn. 15:18-19 illustrates the world's negative relationship to the disciples (hatred by the world) rather than the disciples' overly-positive relationship to the world (friendship with the world) mentioned in Jas. 4:4. A better suggestion than either Mt. 6:24 or Jn. 15:18-19 is 1 Jn. 2:15-17 whose structure and description of the dialectic (John: Father / world; James: God / world; gospels: God / mammon) are closer to James than the gospel parallels.

Jas. 4:4	1 Jn. 2:15
μοιχαλίδες, οὐκ οἴδατε ὅτι	
ἡ φιλία τοῦ κόσμου	μὴ ἀγαπᾶτε τὸν κόσμον
ἔχθρα τοῦ θεοῦ ἐστιν;	μηδὲ τὰ ἐν τῷ κόσμῳ.
ὃς ἐὰν οὖν βουληθῇ φίλος εἶναι	ἐάν τις ἀγαπᾷ
τοῦ κόσμου,	τὸν κόσμον, οὐκ ἔστιν
ἐχθρὸς τοῦ θεοῦ καθίσταται.	ἡ ἀγάπη τοῦ πατρὸς ἐν αὐτῷ·

This type of teaching, however, is typical of the whole NT and not limited to John's writings. Such antitheses as flesh / spirit (Rom. 8:7-9; Gal. 5:16-26), the new creation / world (Gal. 6:14-15), and lovers of pleasure / lovers of God (2 Tim. 3:4) indicate that

---

[306]Rom. 6:16; 1 Cor. 3:16; 5:6; 6:2-19; 9:13-24; cf. 1 Thess, 3:3-4; 4:2; 2 Thess. 2:6.

[307]Cf. above, pp. 31-32.

[308]Spitta, Zur Geschichte, II: 117. Dibelius and Greeven, James, 220 call it a "plausible hypothesis" if it is not limited to a direct quotation but includes familiar statements from the paraenetic tradition.

[309]Mayor, James, 134.

[310]Davids, James, 161.

[311]Oesterley, "James," 458.

statements such as Jas. 4:4 were not the exception in the church's ethical teaching.[312] This emphasis in church paraenesis may very well have found its origin in the preaching of Jesus as exemplified in Mt. 6:24; Lk. 16:13. However, the fact that no common vocabulary is present argues conclusively against envisioning Jas. 4:4 as an allusion to these gospel references. Instead James and the other teachers in the church were putting Jesus' principles into practice and employing their own words to express what they had learned both from Jesus and from their own experience of the Christian faith in the first century. Therefore this is another instance where themes from Jesus' preaching have found their way into the church's ethical teaching.

4.3 Jas. 4:9	Lk. 6:21,25b
	μακάριοι οἱ <u>πεινῶντες</u> νῦν, ὅτι χορτασθήσεσθε. μακάριοι οἱ <u>κλαίοντες</u> νῦν, ὅτι <u>γελάσετε</u>.
ταλαιπωρήσατε καὶ <u>πενθήσατε</u> καὶ <u>κλαύσατε</u>.	25b οὐαί,
ὁ <u>γέλως</u> ὑμῶν εἰς <u>πένθος</u> μετατραπήτω καὶ ἡ χαρὰ εἰς κατήφειαν.	οἱ <u>γελῶντες</u> νῦν, ὅτι <u>πενθήσετε</u> καὶ <u>κλαύσετε</u>.

Jas. 4:9 lies embedded within a series of short disconnected exhortations centering upon the theme of humility which begins (4:6) and ends (4:10) this paraenetic section. Jas. 4:9 consists of three imperatives emphasizing remorse and lamentation followed by a prophetic denunciation in the style of synthetic parallelism. The first of these imperatives ταλαιπωρήσατε is a NT *hapax legomenon* and was understood in older commentaries as a call to practise voluntary asceticism.[313] Today, however, scholars agree that an exhortation to lament in an attitude of inner sorrow and wretchedness[314] is in the author's mind since this definition conforms to the series of exhortations dealing with a repentant attitude found in the context. Yet we harbor the identical "feeling" that Dibelius experienced when he wrote, "I cannot avoid the feeling that these words originally had another sense, that instead of a command, they constituted a prophetic proclamation of disaster which was worded in the form of a command."[315] Another uncertainty in this passage concerns the type of laughter to be renounced.[316] Because the brief details of the text make it difficult to determine what sort of laughter James had in mind, we should assume that he was using traditional concepts of thought. In the OT γελάω as a rendering of צָחַק is

---

[312]Already in intertestamental literature these notes were being sounded: Jub. 30:19-22; 1 En. 48:7; 108:8.

[313]Mayor, <u>James</u>, 147 following Erasmus and Grotius. E.C. Blackman, <u>The Epistle of James</u>, 135 wonders if a call to the discipline of fasting (similar to Is. 58:5) is present here.

[314]Cf. Davids, <u>James</u>, 167. The word is used this way in Herm., Vis. 3,7,1; Sim. 6,3,1; 6,2,7; 2 Cl. 19:4.

[315]Dibelius and Greeven, <u>James</u>, 227.

[316]Mitton, <u>James</u>, 162 chooses the last in a series of possible types of laughter: 1) the laughter to relieve inward stress and tension; 2) a response to an unexpected blessing; 3) a vehicle of indecency; 4) an instrument of cruelty and ridicule; 5) the flippant laughter of careless unconcern in a situation which should provoke sadness.

employed exclusively for the "true or supposed superiority towards another expressed in scorn."[317] Rengstorf points out that

> For the Gk. Bible and the Rabbis as well as the NT, laughter is an attitude which expresses human self-confidence in the face of God .... κλαίειν is opposed to it as the attitude which expresses the assurance of being, not autonomous, but for good or ill, dependent on God.[318]

This is surely the contrast stressed in Jas. 4:9.

The parallel in the Gospel of Luke lies embedded within the four woes peculiar to the Sermon on the Plain. Several differences between Jas. 4:9 and Lk. 6:25b stand in the way of immediately recognizing James' exhortation as an allusion to a saying of Jesus. First of all, the woe form of the saying is absent in James; secondly, James' order is different and an additional parallel saying is added, "and your joy to dejection." Finally, the eschatological nature of the woe is lost by the presence of imperatives which call for action now. Spitta believes that the weeping of repentance (Jas.) vs. the weeping of eschatological condemnation (Lk.) and the present summons to weeping (Jas.) vs. the holding out of the future prospect of weeping (Lk.) decisively prove that James is not alluding to the gospel saying.[319]

These differences have led exegetes to suggest other sources besides the gospels as parallels of Jas. 4:9. The OT (Is. 32:11-12; Amos 8:10; Prov. 14:13) and apocryphal literature (1 Mac. 9:41; Tob. 2:6) have been explored, but similarities of wording are completely nonexistent. In defending the Epistle of James as a Jewish document, Spitta has called attention to a different set of texts (Dt. 34:8; 2 Sam. 19:1; Sir. 22:11ff; 38:17; 2 Esd. 18:9 LXX=Neh. 8:9), but these exclusively refer to weeping and mourning while the important element of laughter is conspicuously missing. The eschatological woes of 1 En. 94ff[320] have been appealed to, but again none of these woes specifically denounce those who laugh. James' exhortation ταλαιπωρήσατε (4:9) to the δίψυχοι (4:8) bears a curious resemblance to the expression "Wretched are the double-minded" (ταλαίπωροί εἰσιν οἱ δίψυχοι) which is quoted as scripture (ἡ γραφὴ αὕτη, ὅπου λέγει) in 1 Cl. 23:3-4 and as "the prophetic word" (λέγει γὰρ καὶ ὁ προφητικὸς λόγος) in 2 Cl. 11:2-4. Could this be the source of Jas. 4:9? Based upon this similarity of terminology, Seitz[321] identified this apocryphon[322] as the source for James' use of the concept double-mindedness. Although the synonymous instruction to the double-minded could betray James' use of source material, we prefer to perceive the address as a standard moral exhortation against the specific vice of double-mindedness. Based upon the remaining subject matter in 1 Cl. 23:3-

---

[317]Karl H. Rengstorf, s.v. γελάω, TDNT, I: 659. The root שחק is sometimes employed positively (Gen. 21:6; Ps. 126:2), but the LXX employs χαρά here and not γέλως. Jesus' promise of a future laughing (Lk. 6:21) is pronounced under the influence of Ps. 126:2 MT (cf. Rengstorf, I: 662 for a thorough discussion).

[318]Karl H. Rengstorf, s.v. κλαίω, TDNT, III: 722-723.

[319]Spitta, Zur Geschichte, II: 171.

[320]Specific woes are found in 1 En. 94:6-8; 95:5-7; 96:4-8; 97:7-8; 98:9-15; 99:1-2,11-15; 100:7-9; 103:5.

[321]Seitz, "Relationship of Hermas to James," 138-140.

[322]According to Joseph A. Fischer, Die Apostolischen Väter (Darmstadt: Wissenschaftliche, 1976), I: 57, n. 139 this is a citation from the unknown book of Eldad and Modad. Cf. ch. 2, section 2.4.

4 and 2 Cl. 11:2-4,[323] it appears that no clear dependence can be established between the two passages. Laws summarizes the different content as follows, "In the 'quotation' the doubt of the *dipsuchoi* is concerned with the coming of the kingdom of God and answered in a parable of the vine, a concern and an image that have no place in the contexts of either Jas. i. 8 or iv. 8."[324] It appears that the coupling of these terms is a more general phenomenon as witnessed by Hermas' address in Sim. 1:3 "O foolish and double-minded and miserable man".[325] Therefore, no specific passage outside the NT can be identified as the source of Jas. 4:9.

Turning back to the parallel in Luke, we perceive that striking similarities exist:
1) Three major words are found in each verse: πενθέω, κλαίω, and γέλως (γελάω in Luke).
2) "Laughter" is only mentioned in these two locations in the NT.
3) The immediate context of the sayings is similar, with James speaking against the double-minded sinners (4:8) while Jesus is denouncing the rich, the well-fed, the laughing, and the people spoken well of.
4) James' saying is not prefixed with a woe, yet the word "wretched", also chosen in Jas. 5:1, appears to be the Jamesian substitute for οὐαί in both places.[326] Since the actions of weeping and mourning are frequently associated with the pronouncement of woes as in the lament over Babylon in Rev. 18:11,15,19,[327] so James' mentioning of weeping and mourning increases the possibility that he had a woe in mind.
5) By means of the three exhortations of 4:9a James fits a prophetic proclamation of disaster into a series of admonitions to the believing community. Dibelius' "feeling" that Jas. 4:9 was originally more of a judgment saying than an admonition is supported by the tie with the woe from Lk. 6:25b. Within church paraenesis the eschatological woe has been transformed into ethical instruction.
6) The change in order does not argue against Jas. 4:9 being based on a *logion* of Jesus but instead points to the development that this saying underwent in its transmission by the church. In Luke the mourning and weeping are a future result of the coming of the kingdom and therefore placed last in the sentence. But James has altered the eschatological denunciation to an exhortation for the church. The eschatological kingdom spoken about in the woes of Luke has been inaugurated in Jesus, and thus the laughter should already be turned into mourning. Since the weeping is now a present experience, the future results are transformed into exhortations and placed at the beginning of the sentence. Jesus' saying is, therefore, still eschatological, but as Dibelius says, "the prophet is calling into view the time of the End when he says 'be wretched'."[328] We can therefore reasonably conclude that Jas. 4:9 is an allusion to a saying of Jesus which is now applied to the ethical life of the church by means of a somewhat transformed word order, form, and eschatological application. Within church paraenesis James is free to explain the meaning of the saying by adding his own parallel expression, "and let your joy be turned to dejection".

---

[323]1 Cl. 23:3-4 "Wretched are the double-minded, which doubt in their soul and say, 'These things we did hear in the days of our fathers also, and behold we have grown old, and none of these things hath befallen us.' Ye fools, compare yourselves unto a tree; take a vine. First it sheddeth its leaves, then a shoot cometh, then a leaf, then a flower, and after these a sour berry, then a full ripe grape." 2 Cl. 11:2-4 with minor changes adds, "So likewise My people had tumults and afflictions: but afterward they shall receive good things."

[324]Laws, <u>James</u>, 185.

[325]ἄφρον καὶ δίψυχε καὶ ταλαίπωρε ἄνθρωπε. Cf. also Vis. 3,7,1.

[326]Thomas 87 and 112 recite almost identical statements, one with "wretched" and the other with "woe". Jer. 4:13 also demonstrates the close connection of these two words: οὐαὶ ἡμῖν, ὅτι ταλαιπωροῦμεν.

[327]The word οὐαί is utilized in each case (18:10,16,19).

[328]Dibelius and Greeven, <u>James</u>, 227.

4.4 Jas. 5:1	Lk. 6:24,25b
ἄγε νῦν οἱ πλούσιοι,	24 πλὴν οὐαὶ ὑμῖν τοῖς πλουσίοις,
κλαύσατε ὀλολύζοντες	
ἐπὶ ταῖς ταλαιπωρίαις ὑμῶν	
	ὅτι ἀπέχετε τὴν παράκλησιν ὑμῶν.
ταῖς ἐπερχομέναις.	
	25b οὐαί, οἱ γελῶντες νῦν,
	ὅτι πενθήσετε καὶ κλαύσετε.

We have positioned Jas. 5:1 after our discussion of Jas. 4:9 because of two factors that clearly tie these passages together: 1) both have been propounded as parallels to the woes of Jesus found in Lk. 6:24-26; and 2) similar wording is utilized in each case. In 5:1 James repeats the imperative κλαύσατε and chooses the rare NT term ταλαιπωρία[329] whose verb form is also used at Jas. 4:9. Thus James appears to be purposely utilizing the same imagery for the rich as he had employed for those who laugh. This link of terminology is best explained by the hypothesis that James is recalling a common source where both those who laugh and those who are rich are denounced. Since Jesus similarly warns the rich and those who laugh about the reversal of fortunes coming upon them, Lk. 6:24-25 is the most likely source.

But what are the objections to this hypothesis? First, one might protest that Jas. 5:1-6 is structurally connected with 4:13-17 rather than 4:9. Both of these sections begin with the address ἄγε νῦν οἱ ... and proceed to denounce the merchant class (4:13-17) and the landholding stratum of society (5:1-6). The literary aim of the genre is prophetic denouncement rather than the disciplinary exhortations of 3:13-4:12. The word ὀλολύζω, a NT *hapax legomenon* at 5:1, is continually enlisted by the OT prophets to proclaim the doom of foreign empires.[330] Therefore, no room is given for repentance to the rich in Jas. 5:1-6, but the laughing, double-minded, sinners of 4:1-10 are promised more grace (4:6), the flight of the devil (4:7), the drawing near of God (4:7), and exaltation (4:10) if they repent. Thus the conclusion of several commentators is that any verbal connection between 5:1 and 4:9 should be minimized. In answering this objection, we want to recognize the close structural connection between 4:13-17 and 5:1-6 as well as the change of mood from exhortation to threat. Yet the uniqueness of Jas. 4:9 within the section of Jas. 4:1-10 should be recalled. We have argued that there are clues that originally in James' source Jas. 4:9b functioned as a prophetic denunciation. Furthermore, the interconnection between 4:13-17 and 5:1-6 is not so vitally important as some maintain. Laws[331] demonstrates that "striking contrasts in content between the two sections" exist including: 1) unlike the merchants the rich are condemned even before their offense is described; 2) the merchants appear to know better and so are given instructions to act differently (4:15), while the rich are called upon only to weep and wail; 3) the merchants are not attacked for who they are but for what they have done, while the attack in 5:1ff is upon the rich *qua* rich; 4) in contrast with the "Biblicized" language employed to criticize the rich, there is a total lack of any specific OT background in 4:13-17. Based upon these considerations, one must admit that these two sections are not so structurally knit together as to disallow a comparison between Jas. 4:9 and 5:1. Many scholars at least admit that 5:1 is echoing the language used at 4:9.[332]

---

[329]It is only found in the NT at Rom. 3:16, a reference to Is. 59:7.

[330]Babylon, Is. 13:6; Philistia, Is. 14:31; Moab, Is. 15:2f; 16:7; Lebanon, Zech. 11:2.

[331]Laws, James, 195.

[332]Laws, James, 195 believes that the language of 4:9 is ironically taken up. Hoppe, Hintergrund Jakobusbriefes, 11 contends that 4:9 is "ein ursprünglich selbständiges Drohwort ... daß mit prophetischen Anklage 5,1 zu vergleichen ist."

A second objection claims that additional parallels besides Lk. 6:24 indicate that traditional language about the rich is being utilized rather than any one particular source. Already in the OT the day of the Lord is said to bring wretchedness.[333] Furthermore, 1 En. 94:8-9 announces a woe against the wealthy with the same expression "day of slaughter" employed in Jas. 5:5.

> [8] Woe to you, ye rich, for ye have trusted in your riches, and from your riches shall ye depart, because ye have not remembered the Most High in the days of your riches. [9]Ye have committed blasphemy and unrighteousness, and have become ready for the day of slaughter, and the day of darkness and the day of great judgment.[334]

Finally, 1 En. 97:5a ("And in those days the prayer of the righteous shall reach unto the Lord") resembles Jas. 5:4b ("and the cries of the harvesters have reached the ears of the Lord of Hosts"), and 1 En. 97:10 ("For ye have acquired it all in unrighteousness") parallels the specific details about fraud found in Jas. 5:4a. We have already pointed out in chapter 2 that the choice of expressions in Jas. 5:1-6 indicates that James is Biblicizing his material.[335] These similar expressions in 1 Enoch confirm that James is using traditional terminology.

There are also significant parallels in Christian literature. Rev. 3:17 employs the adjective ταλαίπωρος (wretched) to rebuke the rich: "For you say, "I am rich, I have prospered, and I need nothing;' not knowing that you are wretched, pitiable, poor, blind, and naked." Similarly Hermas (Sim. 1:3), in warning the rich about adding superfluous fields and expensive buildings to their possessions, ties the word "wretched" to his rebuke: "O foolish and double-minded and miserable (ταλαίπωρε) man, perceivest thou not that all these things are foreign, and are under the power of another?" Yet contrary to James Hermas continues with positive advice, "Therefore, instead of fields buy ye souls that are in trouble, as each is able, and visit widows and orphans, and neglect them not." Does this series of parallel sayings to Jas. 5:1 offer better evidence for the counter-hypothesis that James does not have Lk. 6:24 specifically in mind but is only employing traditional language to reproach the rich?

In evaluating this second objection, we will attempt to demonstrate that the same evidence can point in a different direction. Davids states that "only two pre-Jacobean traditions have this tone in their treatment of the rich: the apocalyptic tradition of Eth. Enoch 94-97 and the Sayings tradition in its Lucan form, i.e. Lk. 6:20-26."[336] It is possible that the woes of 1 Enoch had already influenced the sayings of Jesus[337] so that James is alluding indirctly to Enoch by referring to the gospel saying. Whatever the case, there are valid reasons for contending that Lk. 6:24 is the primary background of Jas. 5:1. In both we encounter a similar content, context, and use of eschatological language. Shortly we will argue that James is alluding in the next verse (5:2) to a gospel saying (Lk. 12:33b; Mt. 6:19-20); this increases the probability that material from the same source would occur in the immediate context.[338] This evidence coupled with the occurrence of another of the Lucan

---

[333]Joel 1:15 ὅτι ἐγγὺς ἡμέρα κυρίου καὶ ὡς ταλαιπωρία ἐκ ταλαιπωρίας ἥξει. Cf. Jer. 6:26.

[334]Since the Greek fragment begins with 97:6, this section of 1 Enoch is only preserved in Ethiopic. Woes involving riches also appear at 1 En. 96:4 and 97:8-10.

[335]Cf. ch. 2, sections 3.3 and 3.4.

[336]Davids, James, 175. He describes the tone as "a sharp, cutting cry of prophetic denouncement. Their doom is coming; woe to them."

[337]The wording of 1 En. 97:8-10 appears to have influenced Jesus' parable against the rich at Lk. 12:14-21 and therefore might also provide a background for Lk. 6:24. Cf. n. 418.

[338]See Kittel's criteria for determining an allusion in "Der geschichtliche Ort," 92, n. 39.

woes (against those who laugh) in close proximity confirms our hypothesis that a woe from Lk. 6:24 is in the mind of James at 4:9 and 5:1. The word "wretched" which ties 4:9 and 5:1 together appears in each case to be James' alternative to the Lucan term "woe". The thought of mourning and weeping in Jas. 4:9a possibly reminded James of Jesus' woe against those who laugh. Then in 5:1 he repeats the exhortation to weep as well as the coming wretchedness since he recognizes that the woes against the rich and those who laugh belong together in the Jesus-tradition.[339]

4.5 Jas. 4:10	Mt. 23:12	Lk. 14:11; 18:14b
	ὅστις δὲ ὑψώσει ἑαυτὸν	ὅτι πᾶς ὁ ὑψῶν ἑαυτὸν
	ταπεινωθήσεται καὶ	ταπεινωθήσεται, (ὁ δὲ)
ταπεινώθητε	ὅστις ταπεινώσει ἑαυτὸν	καὶ ὁ ταπεινῶν ἑαυτὸν
ἐνώπιον κυρίου		
καὶ ὑψώσει ὑμᾶς.	ὑψωθήσεται.	ὑψωθήσεται.

James concludes the series of disciplinary exhortations of 4:7-10 with a generalizing conclusion declaring that exaltation will follow the present situation of humiliation and repentance. This promise parallels the pledge of extra grace given to the humble in v. 6 so that the theme of humility serves as an envelope technique enclosing these exhortations. The humility is not connected with poverty as in Jas. 1:9 nor with oppression as in the similar expression in 1 Pet. 5:6,[340] but centers on lowliness of heart and penitence as in the attitude of the publican in Lk. 18:14. The original content of the humility in the gospel sayings is difficult to determine since the *Sitz im Leben Jesu* has probably been lost; the saying now functions as a generalizing conclusion which can be placed after various sorts of contexts. In Mt. 23:12 it concludes a description of the lowly character of the Christian community over against the practices of the Pharisees. In Lk. 14:11 it is attached to the parable about seating arrangements at a marriage feast and is not vitally necessary to understand the message of the parable. In Lk. 18:14 it is adjoined to a different parable, the Pharisee and the Publican, explaining why the latter went home justified. Thus the themes of the contexts are similar although the situation in mind is by no means identical.

Two exegetical details warn against assigning this saying uncritically to the teaching of Jesus. First of all, James completely omits the first half of the saying, "Everyone who exalts himself will be humbled." Coupled with the differences in form,[341] this fact raises the possibility that another source other than a saying of Jesus is being alluded to. Bultmann places the gospel saying in his list of secular *meshalim* made into dominical sayings[342] and would, therefore, likely set this parallel of James in the same category. The theme of the exaltation of the lowly is also a popular subject in Jewish thought during both the OT[343] and intertestamental periods.[344] Already in the NT at Lk. 1:52 ("he has put down the mighty from their thrones and exalted those (ὕψωσεν ταπεινούς) of low degree") this repeated OT theme has been utilized. Therefore, the background for Jesus' wisdom saying, "Whoever exalts himself will be humbled, and whoever humbles himself will be exalted," is certainly in such OT texts as:

339Cf. below, p. 225.

340Nor is humility connected with the humiliation and exaltation of Christ as in Phil. 2:8 or the exaltation of others as in 2 Cor. 11:7.

341The passive imperative form ταπεινώθητε and the active voice ὑψώσει are different from the gospels.

342Bultmann, Synoptic Tradition, 102-104.

343Spitta, Zur Geschichte, II: 171 chooses for Ezk. 21:26 as James' source.

344Sir. 2:17; 3:18; 7:11; Test. Jos. 10:3; 18:1; 1QH 3:20; 15:16. Cf. Walter Grundmann, s.v. ταπείνος, TDNT, VIII: 14 for references within rabbinic literature.

1 Sam. 2:7b	"The Lord ... brings low, he also exalts." (ταπεινοῖ καὶ ἀνυψοῖ)
Job 5:11	"He sets on high those who are lowly." (τὸν ποιοῦντα ταπεινοὺς εἰς ὕψος)
Ps. 87:16 LXX	"having been exalted, I was brought low ..." (ὑψωθεὶς δὲ ἐταπεινώθην)
Prov. 29:23	"A man's pride will bring him low, but he who is lowly in spirit will obtain honor." (ὕβρις ἄνδρα ταπεινοῖ, τοὺς δὲ ταπεινόφρονας ἐρείδει δόξῃ κύριος.)
Is. 2:11	"and the pride of men shall be humbled and the Lord alone will be exalted in that day." (καὶ ταπεινωθήσεται τὸ ὕψος τῶν ἀνθρώπων, καὶ ὑψωθήσεται κύριος μόνος ἐν τῇ ἡμέρᾳ ἐκείνῃ.)
Is. 10:33	"and the lofty will be brought low." (καὶ οἱ ὑψηλοὶ ταπεινωθήσονται)
Ezk. 17:24	"I the Lord bring low the high tree, and make high the low tree." (ἐγὼ κύριος ὁ ταπεινῶν ξύλον ὑψηλὸν καὶ ὑψῶν ξύλον ταπεινὸν ...)
Ezk. 21:26 (21:31 LXX)	"Things shall not remain as they are; exalt that which is low, and abase that which is high." (ἐταπείνωσας τὸ ὑψηλὸν καὶ τὸ ταπεινὸν ὕψωσας.)

Ezk. 17:24 derives from a Messianic passage where v. 23 is the background for Jesus' kingdom parable in Mt. 12:31-32 par. Therefore, this saying of Jesus (Mt. 23:12 etc.) might have its background not only in wisdom literature but also in the expectations of the eschatological age at the heart of Jesus' preaching.[345] Whatever the case, Jas. 4:10 appears to trace back to OT Jewish teaching through the saying of Jesus. Its contextual connection with Prov. 3:34 in both James and 1 Peter confirms the close tie with OT thought. In 1 Pet. 5:5-6, Prov. 3:34 and this saying on humility are positioned right next to each other. From this phenomenon Grundmann concludes that both Jas. 4:10 and 1 Pet. 5:6 are molded on the pattern of Prov. 3:34 with the exaltation being the grace which God manifests to those who submit to Him.[346] However, the connection with Prov. 3:34 does not explain the use of the word "exalt". The more likely explanation is that Prov. 3:34 and the saying of Jesus in the gospels were combined in the ethical teaching of the church which James and Peter repeat. The discovery of other allusions to the sayings of Jesus in this context of James[347] as well as the fact that both James and Jesus use this exhortation as a generalizing conclusion at the end of a pericope (unlike the OT examples) indicates that the immediate background for Jas. 4:10 includes the dominical saying.

A second exegetical detail, the addition of the expression "before the Lord", might lead one to assign church paraenesis as the source for Jas. 4:10. In this case one

---

[345]The lifting up (πληρωθήσεται) of the valleys and the lowering (ταπεινωθήσεται) of the mountains in Is. 40:4 is interpreted eschatologically in Lk. 3:5.

[346]Walter Grundmann, s.v. ταπεινός, TDNT, VIII: 18-19.

[347]Jas. 4:2c-3,9; 5:1,2. We follow the heuristic guide-line that where a cluster of allusions from one author to another exist, it is easier to argue for the probable presence of other allusions in passages which, considered alone, might seem at first unlikely candidates.

would expect that ἐνώπιον κυρίου would refer to Jesus, and the addition ὑμᾶς would designate the Christian community. Yet the referent of the word κύριος in James is not so easily determined. In 1:1 (without an article)[348] and 2:1 (with an article) κύριος is attached to the title Jesus Christ, giving us two prominent examples where Jesus is the Lord. Yet most of the occurrences of κύριος refer to God the Father (1:7; 3:9; 4:15; 5:4,10,11) as shown from their context.[349] A final group of references to the Lord in 4:10,15; 5:7,8,14,15[350] can be understood as designating either God or Jesus.

Jas. 4:10 ταπεινώθητε ἐνώπιον κυρίου (humbled and exalted by ?).
Jas. 4:15 ἐὰν ὁ κύριος θελήσῃ (seeking first the will of ?).
Jas. 5:7 ἕως τῆς παρουσίας τοῦ κυρίου (the coming of ?).
Jas. 5:8 ὅτι ἡ παρουσία τοῦ κυρίου ἤγγικεν (the coming of ?).
Jas. 5:14 ἀλείψαντες αὐτὸν ἐλαίῳ ἐν τῷ ὀνόματι τοῦ κυρίου (anointing with oil in God's name or Jesus' name).
Jas. 5:15 ἐγερεῖ αὐτὸν ὁ κύριος (God or Jesus heals the sick).

Unfortunately, the presence of the definite article does not assist us in identifying κύριος as is the case in Paul.[351] James' usage is variable especially when κύριος is found in the genitive case within or near prepositional phrases as shown above.[352] Nor does the content or context offer any conclusive evidence in most cases. In 4:15 the will of the Lord could either be the plans of God or the guidance of Christ, although the overwhelming usage in

---

348The article is commonly omitted before the title "Lord Jesus Christ" at the beginning of an epistle: Rom. 1:7; 1 Cor. 1:2; 2 Cor. 1:2; Eph. 1:2; Phil. 1:2; 1 Thess. 1:1; 2 Thess. 1:2. Poss, Articular Construction in James, 39 is mistaken when he explains, "The word for Lord with the article was a title given to the early Roman Emperors to express their deity. This makes the absence of the article in this case significant, for James no doubt did not wish to compare in this way the deity of Christ with the so-called deity of the Roman Emperors."

349The parallel expression παρὰ τοῦ θεοῦ at 1:5 demonstrates that παρὰ τοῦ κυρίου at 1:7 refers to God. At 1:12 both ὁ κύριος (C, P, 0246, M, sy[h]) and ὁ θεός (4, 33, 323, 945, 1241, 1739, vg, sy[p] etc.) are inserted. At 3:9 the Byzantine text type changes to θεός because "Lord and Father" are placed side by side. The title "Lord of hosts" at 5:4 is an OT designation for Yahweh. The OT prophets at 5:10 spoke in God's name. In 5:11 Job is rewarded by God, not Jesus, and the allusion to Ps. 103:8 would certainly indicate that ὁ κύριος refers to Yahweh. In the text under consideration (4:10) θεός is also substituted for κύριος by 945, 1241, 1739, 2298 and several versions, thus evidencing the belief of early readers that God was being spoken about.

350At 4:10 the Byzantine text tradition adds the article. In 5:10 several miniscules add the article τοῦ (69, 323, 614, 945, 1241, 1505, 1739, 2495), and A, ψ, 81 omit it from 5:14. This indicates a trend toward a uniformity which is not present in James. The omission of the article before κύριος with prepositions is especially common in the NT as testified by 1 Cor. 7:15b; 2 Cor. 3:16; 11:17; Eph. 6:8; Col. 3:24; 1 Thess. 4:17b; 2 Thess. 2:13. Cf. Moulton and Turner, Grammar, III: 174.

351Moulton and Turner, Grammar, III: 174. "As a general rule it may be said that for Paul ὁ κύριος = Christ and κύριος = Yahweh."

352Moulton and Turner, Grammar, III: 179-180 illustrate the frequent omission of the article "after prepositions" or "before a noun which governs a genitive".

the NT refers to the will of God.[353] The παρουσία of 5:7-8 is consistently applied in the NT to Jesus,[354] but coupled with the expression in v. 9, "the Judge is standing at the doors," it might indicate the coming of God the judge. In 5:14-15 the phrases "anointing him with oil in the name of the Lord" and "the Lord will raise him up" are probably references to the continuation of Jesus' earthly healing ministry by the church.[355] At the same time it could refer to anointing in the name of God, just as Jesus healed by praying in the name of his Father. Therefore, James' usage of κύριος is ambivalent. The fact that in the OT Yahweh (LXX κύριος) humbles and exalts his people (1 Sam. 2:7b; Ezk. 17:24) could favor a reference to God.[356] However, the best evidence that the κύριος of Jas. 4:10 indicates God and not Jesus is the parallel in 1 Pet. 5:6.

1 Pet. 5:6 appears in a similar context to Jas. 4:10, preceded by a quote from Prov. 3:34 (like Jas. 4:6) and including an exhortation to resist the devil (1 Pet. 5:8-9=Jas. 4:7). Put in synopsis format, the verbal parallels are striking.

Jas. 4:10	1 Pet. 5:6
ταπεινώθητε	ταπεινώθητε οὖν
ἐνώπιον κυρίου	ὑπὸ τὴν κραταιὰν χεῖρα τοῦ θεοῦ,
καὶ ὑψώσει ὑμᾶς.	ἵνα ὑμᾶς ὑψώσῃ ἐν καιρῷ

In each case there is a propositional phrase inserted between the humbling clause and the exaltation ending which describes the authority to whom the humiliation is offered. Thus "the hand of God"[357] in 1 Peter parallels "the Lord" in James. We observe, furthermore, that the differences in form between James and the gospels do not pertain to James and 1 Peter. Over against the gospels both James and 1 Peter begin with an aorist passive imperative, include the middle phrase mentioned above, place the verb ὑψόω in the active voice, and include the object ὑμᾶς referring to the Christian community. These connections cannot be accidental; the best explanation as Selwyn and Carrington observe is the postulation of a common source.[358] Yet Selwyn's intricate suggestions concerning a written persecution source require too many hypothetical leaps into the unknown area of church catechetical materials in the first century. It is more likely that the oral ethical teachings common to the leaders of the church (possibly of a particular Christian community) are the source for these striking similarities of wording and content between James and 1 Peter.

---

[353]θέλημα τοῦ θεοῦ Mk. 3:35; Rom. 1:10; 12:2; 15:32; 1 Cor. 1:1; 2 Cor. 1:1; 8:5; Gal. 1:4; Eph. 1:1; 6:6; Col. 1:1; 4:12; 1 Thess. 4:3; 5:18; 2 Tim. 1:1; Heb. 10:36; 1 Pet. 2:15; 3:17; 4:2,19. θέλημα τοῦ πέμψαντός με in John and θέλημα τοῦ πατρός μου in Matthew. When the phrase θέλημα τοῦ κυρίου is used, it is difficult to determine the referents. Cf. Acts 21:14 where the Lord Jesus is mentioned in 21:13 and Eph. 5:17 where Lord is used in v. 19 in contrast to God the Father. The same phrase (ἐὰν ὁ κύριος θελήσῃ) in 1 Cor. 4:19 does not help us since Christ is mentioned in v. 17 and God in v. 20.

[354]Mt. 24:3,27,37,39; 1 Cor. 15:23; 1 Thess. 2:19; 3:13; 4:15; 5:23; 2 Thess. 2:1,9; 2 Pet. 1:16; 3:4; 1 Jn. 2:28.

[355]Cf. Appendix I, section 4.12. Poss, Articular Construction in James, 203-204 inconsistently identifies κύριος with Jehovah in 5:14 and with Christ in 5:15.

[356]When similar phraseology to James is used in the LXX, מִלִּפְנֵי יְהוָה is translated ἐναντίον κυρίου (2 Chr. 33:23) and מִלִּפְנֵי [לִפְנֵי] אֱלֹהִים by ἀπὸ προσώπου μου (2 Chr. 34:27), ἐνώπιον θεοῦ (2 Esd. 8:21=Ezra 8:21), and ἐναντίον κυρίου τοῦ θεοῦ σου (Dan. 10:12 with Theodotion omitting κυρίου).

[357]To be humbled under the hand of someone is an OT expression: Gen. 16:9 and Ps. 105(106):42.

[358]Selwyn, First Peter, table xiv, 442-449 calls this grouping the Persecution Source. Carrington, Primitive Catechism, 42-43.

Moreover, this ecclesiastical teaching pattern is close to OT usage since the humbling is before God and not Jesus.

The fact that we have identified Jas. 4:10 and 1 Pet. 5:6 as church paraenesis using OT language does not automatically exclude this verse from being identified as a saying of Jesus. The sayings of Jesus were important to the early church's paraenesis[359] since the community would naturally give priority to Jesus' teaching on subjects such as humility. The fact that κύριος in Jas. 4:10 does not refer to Christ would indicate that little development has taken place in the content of the saying since Jesus first spoke it.[360] The fact that the wording ὅστις ταπεινώσει or ὁ ταπεινῶν has been altered to the imperative form ταπεινώθητε indicates a change in the medium of the message, since a wisdom saying would naturally change to moral exhortation if employed in the church's ethical tradition. Therefore it is probable that a saying of Jesus, which in turn has its background in OT wisdom, stands behind the similar exhortations of Jas. 4:10 and 1 Pet. 5:6. The first part of Jesus' saying could have been dropped either because James had already spoken against exalting oneself in 4:6 ("God opposes the proud") or more likely because in applying the saying to the Christian community, the more applicable upbuilding half of the saying would be transmitted. At any rate, the repetition of only half of Jesus' *logion* was a common phenomenon in the early church as witnessed by the writings of Clement of Alexandria[361] and Origen.[362] In the case of Jas. 4:10 it is difficult to decide whether only a theme of Jesus' preaching had entered into the church's ethical teaching or whether a specific saying of Jesus is being consciously alluded to. The similar function of the sayings as generalizing conclusions, the presence of other dominical *logia* in the context, the verbal and conceptual similarities, the support of many commentators in the history of interpretation,[363] and the above explanation for the divergent wording between Jas. 4:10 and Mt. 23:12; Lk. 14:11; 18:14b indicate that James is based upon a dominical saying.

4.6 Jas. 4:11-12

11 μὴ καταλαλεῖτε ἀλλήλων, ἀδελφοί.
ὁ καταλαλῶν ἀδελφοῦ ἢ κρίνων τὸν ἀδελφὸν αὐτοῦ
καταλαλεῖ νόμου καὶ κρίνει νόμον·
εἰ δὲ νόμον κρίνεις,
οὐκ εἶ ποιητὴς νόμου ἀλλὰ κριτής.
12 εἷς ἐστιν ὁ νομοθέτης καὶ κριτὴς
ὁ δυνάμενος σῶσαι καὶ ἀπολέσαι·
σὺ δὲ τίς εἶ ὁ κρίνων τὸν πλησίον;

---

[359] It is precisely in Paul's paraenetic passages that one encounters the most allusions to the sayings of Jesus: Rom. 12; 1 Thess. 5. Cf. below, p. 169.

[360] Although not specifically expressed in the gospel parallels, James and 1 Peter assume that humility before God is in the mind of Jesus.

[361] Strom. 2,132,1 (GCS 52, p. 185, line 29); Dives 1:4 (GCS 17,2, p. 160, line 3). Clement repeats the whole saying in Paed. 3,92,1 (GCS 12, p. 286, line 21) but reverses the order.

[362] Cel. 3:63 (M. Barret, SC 136(1968), p. 144, line 1).

[363] Davids, James, 168 calls the gospel parallels "the immediate background of James". Mitton, James, 163 explains that James speaks "with the full authority of Jesus".

Mt. 7:1-2a	Lk. 6:37
μὴ κρίνετε, ἵνα μὴ κριθῆτε·	καὶ μὴ κρίνετε, καὶ οὐ μὴ κριθῆτε· καὶ μὴ καταδικάζετε, καὶ οὐ μὴ καταδικασθῆτε.
ἐν ᾧ γὰρ κρίματι κρίνετε κριθήσεσθε ...	

Because of the shift in audience from adulteresses (4:4), and double-minded sinners (4:8) to the usual ἀδελφοί, we must categorize Jas. 4:11-12 as a brief, transitional, self-contained section with a different subject matter and tone from what precedes and follows it.[364] Jas. 4:11-12 contains a threefold warning against judging: judging your brother (11a), judging the law (11b), and judging your neighbor (12b). The gospel sayings are more general and do not specify what is being judged. In both James and the gospels one type of judging leads to another. In James judging another person results in judging the law; in the gospels an act of judging ends in the judgment of God being returned upon the subject.[365] Therefore we can identify certain general thematic similarities.

The specific variations between the parallels, however, cast shadows of doubt upon any thesis that identifies Jas. 4:11-12 as an allusion to a saying of Jesus. In the gospels judging results in the actor being judged, but in James there is no warning concerning the judgment of God; instead the subject of judging the law is introduced, a topic unparalleled in the context of the Sermon on the Mount.[366] Secondly, we encounter in James the emergence of one of his favorite themes, "being doers of the law." Thirdly, the structure of the passages is widely divergent. In James we encounter a step-pyramid type structure.

a Do not speak evil against one another, brethren.
  a He that speaks evil against a brother or judges his brother,
  b speaks evil against the law and judges the law.
    b But if you judge the law,
    c you are not a doer of the law but a judge.
      c (assume: But if you try to be a judge,)
      d There is one lawgiver and judge,
      d he who is able to save and to destroy.
a But who are you that you judge your neighbor?

The first line in each step repeats the previous line so that the argument builds and builds until the last line brings the reader back to the beginning. In the gospels (esp. vivid in Lk. 6:37-38a) the structure is abab throughout.

ab	Judge not,	and you will not be judged;
ab	condemn not,	and you will not be condemned;
ab	forgive,	and you will be forgiven;
ab	give,	and it will be given to you.

---

[364]Moffatt finds it so difficult to establish a connection between 4:10 and 4:11 that he transfers these verses to follow 2:13. Mitton, James, 165 suggests a contrast with 4:10, but an imperative with the vocative begins new sections at Jas. 1:2,16,19; 2:1; 3:1; 4:11; 5:7,12. Like 2:13 and 3:18 Jas. 4:11-12 is a transitional, self-contained unit.

[365]Lk. 6:37b adds that condemning reaps condemnation.

[366]Cf. Laws, James, 187; Gutbrod, s.v. νόμος, TDNT, IV: 1082.

Fourthly, the theme with which James begins this short section, slander or speaking evil against one another (καταλαλέω), is not even once utilized anywhere in the gospels. Finally, if one examines other allusions to Mt. 7:1-2 or Lk. 6:37, the similarities exhibited there are much more obvious than those experienced in Jas. 4:11-12:

> Rom. 2:1b ἐν ᾧ γὰρ κρίνεις τὸν ἕτερον, σεαυτὸν κατακρίνεις
> 1 Cl. 13:2 ὡς κρίνετε, οὕτως κριθήσεσθε·
> Pol. Phil. 2:3 μὴ κρίνετε, ἵνα μὴ κριθῆτε·

Each of the above quotations contains a similar structure as well as complementary vocabulary and subject matter to that of the gospels which seem to be the crucial criteria for evaluating whether Mt. 7:1 and Lk. 6:37 are being alluded to.

Therefore it is necessary to look elsewhere for the source of this saying in James. Since Lev. 19:18 is quoted in Jas. 2:8 in a context about judging, some contend that the expression "judge your neighbor" (κρίνων τὸν πλησίον 4:12) is a recollection of Lev. 19:18 (ἀγαπήσεις τὸν πλησίον). Davids, for instance, states, "While James may well be dependent on the Jesus *logia* cited above, Lv. 19:18, previously cited in 2:8-9, is probably foremost in his mind."[367] Because the theme of judging and being judged is familiar subject matter in James' epistle (2:4,13; 3:1; 4:11-12; 5:9), we believe that James himself is drawing upon a well-established tradition of exhortations rather than employing specific source material. Dibelius speaks of this tradition when he points out that "in Jewish as well as Christian paraenesis, slander is felt to be an especially grave sin, and one which is particularly characteristic of a life of wickedness."[368] Thus the subject of slander is especially popular in catalogues of vices.[369] As is common with most paraenetic themes in the NT, slander has a rich background in Jewish wisdom.[370] Since the subject matter of judging is also a popular teaching theme among leaders of the NT church,[371] it is highly probable that James is transmitting exhortations developed within the moral teaching of the church. Rom. 14:3-4[372] is an excellent example where the theme of judging has entered the paraenesis of the church (Rom. 12-14). Paul locates the basis for not judging in the fact that God is the master, just as James grounds his exhortation in the fact that God is law-giver and judge. Since the ethical tradition of the church often appropriates the important themes of Jesus' preaching,[373] Jas. 4:11-12 is not alluding to any specific saying of Jesus.

5.0 The Synoptic Parallels in the Prophetic Denunciations of Jas. 4:13-5:6

In 4:13-5:6 James turns from disciplinary exhortations aimed at the church to prophetic denunciations of outsiders or those only peripherally connected with the church. Jas. 4:13-5:6 consists of two sections, each introduced by the phrase ἄγε νῦν οἱ. First the

---

[367]Davids, James, 170.

[368]Dibelius and Greeven, James, 228.

[369]Rom. 1:30; 2 Cor. 12:20; 1 Pet. 2:1; Barn. 20:2; 1 Cl. 30:1,3; 35:5; Herm., Mand. 2:2-3; 8:3; Sim. 8,7,2; 9,23,2-3.

[370]Slander is a common OT theme (Pss. 50:20; 101:5; Prov. 20:13; Lev. 19:16) and used as well during the intertestamental period (Test. Iss. 3:4; Test. Gad 3:3; 5:4; Wis. 1:11; 1QS 4:9,11; 5:25-26; 6:26; 7:2-9).

[371]Cf. Rom. 2:1; 1 Cor. 4:5; 5:12; Jn. 7:24; 8:15-16.

[372]"and let not him who abstains pass judgment on him who eats; for God has welcomed him. Who are you to pass judgment on the servant of another? It is before his own master that he stands or falls."

[373]Thus Jesus' condemnation of judging as witnessed in Mt. 7:1-2 and Lk. 6:37 was taken into the paraenetic tradition and developed independently by the various teachers in the Christian community.

merchants' confidence in their own future fortunes is condemned (4:13-17), and then the wealthy oppressors are called to account (5:1-6). Sayings of Jesus as well as OT material are alluded to only in the section condemning the rich.

A. 4:13-17 Prophetic denouncement of the merchants.

1. 4:13a Address: "Come now, you who say".

2. 4:13b The merchants' claim of confidence for the future.

3. 4:14-16 James' denouncement.
   a. 4:14 The uncertainty of the future.
      1) 4:14a James' reasoning: the future is unknown.
      2) 4:14b Illustration from nature: the mist.
   b. 4:15 A positive alternative: "If the Lord wills."
   c. 4:16 James' condemnation of the merchants' boasting.

4. 4:17 Concluding aphorism: "Not doing what you know to be right is sin."

B. 5:1-6 Prophetic denouncement of the wealthy oppressors.

1. 5:1a Address: "Come now, you rich."

2. 5:1b Exhortation of woe to the rich (allusion to a saying of Jesus -- Lk. 6:24).

3. 5:2-3 Prophetic prediction of destruction.
   a. 5:2-3a Destruction of the oppressor's wealth (like rotting riches, moth-eaten garments, and rusted metals).
   b. 5:3b Future destruction of the oppressor.
   c. 5:3c Reason for destruction: they have laid up treasures in the last days (allu sion to a saying of Jesus -- Mt. 6:19-20; Lk. 12:33b).

4. 5:4 Witnesses to this evil: The wages of the laborers and the cries of the harvesters.

5. 5:5-6a A description of the injustice of the wealthy.

6. 5:6b Concluding aphorism: "The righteous one does not resist."

5.1 Jas. 5:2-3

a 2 ὁ πλοῦτος ὑμῶν σέσηπεν
a καὶ τὰ ἱμάτια ὑμῶν σητόβρωτα γέγονεν,
a 3 ὁ χρυσὸς ὑμῶν καὶ ὁ ἄργυρος κατίωται
b καὶ ὁ ἰὸς αὐτῶν εἰς μαρτύριον ὑμῖν ἔσται
b καὶ φάγεται τὰς σάρκας ὑμῶν ὡς πῦρ.
c ἐθησαυρίσατε ἐν ἐσχάταις ἡμέραις.

Mt. 6:19-21

a 19 μὴ θησαυρίζετε ὑμῖν θησαυροὺς ἐπὶ τῆς γῆς,
b ὅπου σὴς καὶ βρῶσις ἀφανίζει
b καὶ ὅπου κλέπται διορύσσουσιν καὶ κλέπτουσιν·
a 20 θησαυρίζετε δὲ ὑμῖν θησαυροὺς ἐν οὐρανῷ,
b ὅπου οὔτε σὴς οὔτε βρῶσις ἀφανίζει
b καὶ ὅπου κλέπται οὐ διορύσσουσιν οὐδὲ κλέπτουσιν·
c 21 ὅπου γάρ ἐστιν ὁ θησαυρός σου, ἐκεῖ ἔσται καὶ ἡ καρδία σου.

Lk. 12:32-34

a 32 μὴ φοβοῦ, τὸ μικρὸν ποίμνιον,
ὅτι εὐδόκησεν ὁ πατὴρ ὑμῶν δοῦναι ὑμῖν τὴν βασιλείαν.
b 33 πωλήσατε τὰ ὑπάρχοντα ὑμῶν καὶ δότε ἐλεημοσύνην·
b ποιήσατε ἑαυτοῖς βαλλάντια μὴ παλαιούμενα,
a θησαυρὸν ἀνέκλειπτον ἐν τοῖς οὐρανοις,
ὅπου κλέπτης οὐκ ἐγγίζει
οὐδὲ σὴς διαφθείρει·
c 34 ὅπου γάρ ἐστιν ὁ θησαυρὸς ὑμῶν, ἐκεῖ καὶ ἡ καρδία ὑμῶν ἔσται.

We have already established that James begins chapter 5 with an allusion to the woe against the rich in Lk. 6:24. After this introduction James proclaims (in the perfect tense) the destruction of the wealthy landowners' riches, garments, and gold and silver:

2 "Your riches have rotted
and your garments are moth-eaten.
3a Your gold and silver have rusted."

Then elaborating upon the metaphor of rust, James describes the future destruction of the oppressors themselves:

3b "and their rust will be evidence against you
and will eat your flesh like fire."

Finally, the reason for this destruction is given as a generalizing conclusion:

3c "You have laid up treasure for the last days."[374]

In our discussion below we will first survey the problems of interpretation in Jas. 5:2-3 and the gospel contexts, then compare the two sayings to determine if James is alluding to the Jesus-tradition, and finally investigate other Jewish and Christian writings to verify that no closer parallels can be discovered.

---

[374]It is also possible to put a period after ὑμῶν and have ὡς begin a causal clause, "since you have stored up fire," as found in the RSV footnote. Yet ὡς is not used this way in any of its other occurrences in Jas. 1:10; 2:8,9,12; 5:5. Dibelius and Greeven, James, 237, n. 39 mention the interpretation of Oecumenius ὁ πλοῦτος ὑμῶν, ὃν ὡς πῦρ ἐθησαυρίσατε, καταφάγεται τὰς σάρκας ὑμῶν ("Your riches, which you have treasured up as fire, will devour your flesh") which attempts to avoid the mixed metaphor of rust and fire. Yet similar mixtures of metaphors are encountered in the tradition: Judith 16:17. Furthermore, the use of the verb "to eat" with fire is not without precedent: Dibelius and Greeven, James, 237, n. 40 list as examples Is. 30:27; Amos 5:6; Is. 10:16f; Ezk. 15:7; Ps. 21:9; Rev. 11:5; 20:9.

Because of the large number of disputed exegetical details in Jas. 5:2-3, it is important at the outset to establish the meaning of the text. James appears to be making assertions about three kinds of wealth found among the oppressing rich: food,[375] fabric, and metals.[376] The precise meaning of the perfect tense used to describe this wealth has been a matter of dispute. If the perfect tense is understood in its normal sense (i.e. as something that has taken place in the past but whose ramifications continue into the present), then the disaster has already overtaken the rich.[377] Because of the change to the future tense in 3b, Laws believes that the perfect tense indicates a general proposition applying to the present. Thus the author is "here concerned to insist upon the present worthlessness of material possessions, so far as man's spiritual hope is concerned."[378] The majority of interpreters (Cantinat, Davids, Dibelius, Mayor etc.) explain the perfect tense as an expression of prophetic anticipation of future happenings. This position is substantiated by certain OT precedents[379] where the same transfer from the perfect to the future tense is evident. Thus the future destruction is so certain that it is described as an already occurring event.

A second controversy concerns the possibility whether gold and silver can rust as v. 3 appears to propound. It is unnecessary to accept 1) the conclusion that James must have belonged to a lower social class not acquainted with the properties of gold and silver[380] or 2) the contention that this unusual event will take place through a "supernatural calamity"[381] or 3) an ironical understanding of the verse ("even those things that normally keep their value in all circumstances would in this particular circumstance become valueless"[382]). It is more likely, as the majority of commentators agree, that James penned these words intending the figure of speech to be understood metaphorically as with the following description of rust eating the flesh like fire. The metaphor would then function as a proverb to describe temporality and uselessness.[383] Michel points to the Epistle of Jeremiah where rust denotes the helplessness and impermanence of silver and gold idols.[384] Apparently the tarnishing of these metals led to the use of the metaphor of rust[385] since the Epistle of Jeremiah 23 describes the rust as being wiped off so that the metal will shine again[386] (i.e. the polishing of tarnished metal).

A final difficulty involves the translation of the Greek preposition in the phrase ἐν ἐσχάταις ἡμέραις. The translation "for the last days"[387] appears to strain the meaning of the preposition ἐν.[388] Turner shows that "St. James does not use *en* when he intends no

---

[375]The rotting of wealth probably refers to perishable goods such as grain (1 En. 97:9) although it could refer generally to any product of human activity which wastes away (Bar. 6:72=Ep. Jer. 71 LXX; Sir. 14:19).

[376]Mayor, James, 149; Mitton, James, 176. Laws, James, 199 contends that this interprets the language too precisely. Davids, James, 176 suggests that "the last two terms make specific the more general first term."

[377]Cf. Tasker, James, 110.

[378]Laws, James, 198.

[379]Is. 44:23; 53:5-10; 60:1-2.

[380]Windisch, Katholischen Briefe, 31.

[381]Adamson, James, 185.

[382]Mitton, James, 177.

[383]Davids, James, 176. Cf. Bar. 6:12,24=Ep. Jer. 11,23 LXX; Sir. 29:10.

[384]Otto Michel, s.v. ἰός, TDNT, III: 335. Epistle of Jeremiah 4:11(12),23(24). The verses in parenthesis are from Charles' edition of the Apocryphal while the former numbers follow Rahlf's enumeration of the LXX.

[385]Cf. Ropes, James, 285.

[386]"Not withstanding the gold where with they are beset to make them beautiful, except one wipe off the rust, they will not shine." Charles, APOT, I: 603.

[387]JB; RSV; Ropes, James, 285.

[388]Cf. Laws, James, 200.

more than a simple dative, and he does not confuse it with *eis* (towards)."[389] Furthermore, it is inconsistent of the RSV to translate "for the last days" in v. 3 and "in the day of slaughter" at v. 5. Secondly, this phrase ἐν ἐσχάταις ἡμέραις could be taken in a proleptic sense, "to be available in the last days".[390] However, 5:8 ("the coming of the Lord is at hand") and 5:9 ("the Judge is standing at the doors") imply that James believed that the last days were close to being a present experience. Therefore, the translation "in the last days" best fits the following context as well as the prophetic anticipation of the final judgment in the perfect tenses of Jas. 5:2-3a.

Because the gospel parallels, Mt. 6:19-21 and Lk. 12:33b-34, contain completely divergent verbs (ἀφανίζει, διορύσσουσιν, κλέπτουσιν in Matthew; ἐγγίζει, διαφθείρει in Luke), disparate contexts,[391] a dissimilar order of material,[392] and a diverse emphasis in the message,[393] we must assume that they derive from different sources.[394] The additional material in Mt. 6:19 could either be an expansion by Matthew[395] or a genuine saying of Jesus derived from the M tradition.[396] Matthew has positioned this saying together with other teachings on the economic implications of discipleship (6:19-34) in the Sermon on the Mount. Mt. 6:19 begins with a negative command to not lay up treasures upon the earth followed by a pair of ὅπου clauses balanced by the inclusion of two subjects in the first clause (moth and rust) and two verbs in the second (break in and steal). A positive

---

[389]Turner, Grammatical Insights, 165.

[390]Mitton, James, 178.

[391]This section in Matthew contains M material (6:1-18) and Q sayings (6:22-24) found in Lk. 11:34-36 and Lk. 16:13. Although the exhortation against anxiety appears in close connection with this saying, it follows the saying in Mt. 6:25-34 but precedes it in Lk. 12:22-31.

[392]In Luke thief, moth; in Matthew moth and rust, thieves. Gundry, Matthew, 113 points out that in Matthew the wardrobe spoils and then the money is stolen while in Luke the drawing near of a thief precedes the moth's destruction of purses.

[393]With the addition of Mt. 6:19 Matthew's emphasis is upon the negative message to renounce earthly treasures, while Luke mentions only the heavenly treasure which can be obtained by selling possessions and giving alms.

[394]Opinions, however, differ greatly. Walter Grundmann, Das Evangelium nach Lukas, 262 and Adolf von Schlatter, Das Evangelium des Lukas, 311f claim that Matthew used Q while Luke followed his personal source L. Thomas W. Manson, The Sayings of Jesus, 114,172f and Charles F. Burney, The Poetry of our Lord, 88 believe that Luke used Q while Matthew followed his personal source M. Wilhelm Pesch, "Zur Exegese von Mt. 6, 19-21 and Lk. 12, 33-34," Bib 41(1960): 358-361 and Marshall, Luke, 531 suggest that Luke used Q and adapted it to catechetical purposes.

[395]Gundry, Matthew, 11 states, "Typically, Matthew recasts the saying on treasure for closer parallelism..." Matthew adds a negative statement to form a parallelism at 6:14-15 (vs. Mk. 11:25) and 7:13-14 (vs Lk. 13:24). Cases of antithetic parallelism peculiar to Matthew are given by Joachim Jeremias, New Testament Theology, 15, n. 3. As in Mt. 6:19-20 Matthew, unlike Luke, typically contrasts earth with heaven (receive kingdom of heaven, inherit the earth 5:3,5; salt of the earth, light of the world 5:13-14; swear by heaven or earth 5:34-35; your will be done on earth as in heaven 6:10; birds of the heavens, lilies of the field 6:26,28; bind and loose on earth and in heaven 16:19 and 18:18; agree on earth, done in heaven 18:19; no father on earth, only a heavenly father 23:9; sign of Son of Man in heaven, tribes on earth will mourn 24:30; authority in heaven and upon earth 28:18; p^{45} omits "and of the earth" in Lk. 10:21 and the negative statement of Lk. 12:9).

[396]Since Mt. 6:21 = Lk. 12:34 it could be postulated that a saying with similar imagery was spoken on two different occasions by Jesus and received separately into the Q and M traditions. The rhythmical and poetic parallelism in Matthew is a common trait in the teaching of Jesus (cf. Jeremias, NT Theology, 14-20).

injunction, using the same terminology, is then stated in v. 20 followed, as in Luke, by a generalizing conclusion: "For where your treasure is, there will your heart be also." Luke's structure contains a promise of the kingdom (12:32), followed by two commands concerning the economic life of the little flock (12:33a), and concluded with an additional promise of an unfailing treasure in the heavens which neither thief nor moth can displace (12:33b). Since the exhortation "sell your possessions and give alms" is Lucan both in theme and style,[397] it must be considered an insertion into the original context of Q. The second command to "provide yourselves with purses that do not grow old" likewise contains distinctive Lucan vocabulary since βαλλάντιον is employed only in Lk. 10:4; 12:33; 22:35,36.[398] Apparently Luke is here affected by the parallel saying in Lk. 18:22 par. where the rich ruler is also commanded to sell everything and give it to the poor to receive treasure in heaven (πάντα ὅσα ἔχεις πώλησον καὶ διάδος πτωχοῖς, καὶ ἕξεις θησαυρὸν ἐν τοῖς οὐρανοῖς). If 12:33a is a Lucan insertion, then 32 and 33b originally belonged together so that the promise of the kingdom is further identified as a treasure in the heavens.[399] Thus the catchwords "kingdom" (Lk. 12:31,32), "thief" (Lk. 12:33,39), and possibly "break in" (Mt. 6:20; Lk. 12:39)[400] held this section together in Q. It is impossible to reconstruct the original wording of the first ὅπου clause in Q, but there was certainly a parallel structure since Luke (thief approaches, moth destroys) Thomas 76 (moth comes near, worm destroys), and Matthew (moth and rust consume, thieves break in and steal) all witness to this balance of phraseology.

A discussion of the meaning of βρῶσις in Mt. 6:19 is relevant to the interpretation of Jas. 5:2-3. Its ordinary connotation is "eating" or "that which is being eaten", namely food. There are indications that a secondary meaning was derived from this denoting that which was eating some material. Therefore, the LXX of Mal. 3:11 replaces אֹכֵל [401] with βρῶσις. In the second century AD Galen uses the term to refer to the decay of teeth.[402] In the Epistle of Jeremiah 10(11)[403] a few MSS[404] have βρῶσις instead of βρῶμα with ἰός, thus setting rust (or corrosion) alongside eating. This reference demonstrates that βρῶσις

---

[397]Cf. Joseph A. Fitzmyer, The Gospel According to Luke (X-XXIV), 981; Guelich, Sermon, 326. ἐλεημοσύνη is only used in Mt. 6:2-4 (3x) but 10x in Lucan writings; ὑπάρχω is dominant in Lucan literature: Mt. 3x; Lk. 15x; Acts 25x; Paul 12x.

[398]Gundry, Matthew, 112 thinks that Matthew omitted this command because for him the old treasures are good (cf. 13:52, peculiar to his gospel). Mt. 13:52, however, is speaking about the good in Judaism, a theme not discussed in Lk. 12:33.

[399]Lk. 18:24 states that it is hard for a rich man to enter the kingdom of God, thus indicating that "treasure in heaven" (18:22) and "kingdom of God" are parallel. Thomas 76 connects the "unfailing and enduring treasure" with the "kingdom of the Father". Finally, the words kingdom and treasure are both singular, while purses in v. 33a is plural. It is disputed whether the similar Matthean phrase, "kingdom of heaven", is current language at the time of Jesus (cf. Jeremias, NT Theology, 97 vs. Dalman, Worte Jesu, 76-77 and Herman Ridderbos, The Coming of the Kingdom, 19).

[400]διαφθορά is unique to Lukan writings (6x in Acts). However, Luke's parallelism "come near ... destroy" could be from the similar Aramaic roots רקב . . . קרב (cf. Matthew Black, An Aramaic Approach to the Gospels and Acts, 178).

[401]Understood here as locusts. H. Gressmann posits מַאֲכֹלֶת (wood worm) as cited in Erich Klostermann, Das Matthäus-Evangelium, 60.

[402]Κλαύδιον Γαληνοῦ ἅπαντα (Claudii Galeni opera omnia), ed. D. Carol Gottlob Kühn, VI: 422; XII: 879. Cf. BAGD, s.v. βρῶσις, 148.2.

[403]Charles' and Goodspeed's English editions as well as the Göttingen Septuaginta (in parenthesis) number the verses different from Rahlf's LXX.

[404]L', 147, La[CLV] (*tinea*), Sy (*perditione*). The Lucian recension consists of *Hauptgruppe* 22, 36, 48, 51, 96, 231, 311, 763 and *Untergruppe* 62, 198, 407, 449.

could refer to rust at this time.[405] Charles, however, believes that the LXX reading ἀπὸ ἰοῦ καὶ βρωμάτων (βρωσέως) reveals a translation error: "If ומאכל stood in the unpointed text, the translator may be supposed to have pointed וּמַאֲכָל (= καὶ βρ...) instead of וּמֵאֹכֵל 'and from a devourer' (i.e. moth or grub; Mal. iii. 11; cf. Job xiii. 28)."[406] He believes that σὴς καὶ βρῶσις in Mt. 6:19 may represent עָשׁ וְאֹכֵל, moth and devourer. Scholars have thus become divided between understanding βρῶσις as a synonym for ἰός (rust)[407] or as a term for an insect-like worm[408] which consumes clothing like the σής (moth) with which βρῶσις is combined in Mt. 6:19. Guelich[409] suggests that the translation "rust" stems from the fact that rust is referred to in comparable contexts (Sir. 29:10[410] Jas. 5:3) where treasures of precious metals are mentioned. This is indeed an enlightening comment. A translator would naturally think of precious metals when envisioning treasures upon the earth and has thus altered the text accordingly. Originally it is likely that just as both verbs, διορύσσουσιν (break in) and κλέπτουσιν (steal), refer to the same thieves (κλέπται), so both subjects σὴς and βρῶσις would affect the identical material (precious cloth) which is being consumed (ἀφανίζει).[411] Thus the translation "rust" is excluded at Mt. 6:19-20.

Having introduced the respective contexts and the interpretive problems, we will now investigate the relationship between Jas. 5:2-3 and Mt. 6:19-21; Lk. 12:33b-34. When one places the texts in synoptic format, the divergent terminology is immediately obvious. Matthew depicts a treasure of fabric consumed (ἀφανίζω) by moth (σής) and worms (βρῶσις)[412] and a treasure of metal stolen (κλέπτουσιν) by thieves (κλέπται) who break into (διορύσσουσιν) a house. James, on the other hand, describes a treasure (πλοῦτος) of rotting (σέσηπεν) food stuffs not included in the gospels, a treasure of clothing which is moth-eaten (σητόβρωτα), and a treasure of metal which is not stolen (as in Matthew) but rusts (κατίωται) and will eat (φάγεται) the flesh of its owner. Absolutely none of the vocabulary utilized by James is exactly comparable to the gospels. In fact in each description of the different treasures James employs a NT *hapax legomenon*: σήπω, σητόβρωτος, and κατιόω. The only word that James and the gospels have in common is the term "treasure", in which case James follows the verbal form found only in Matthew. Likewise, we encounter differences in the form (Matthew, imperative; James, indicative) and order of the material (James' ending is Matthew's beginning). Finally, the concluding gnomic saying located both in Matthew and Luke is missing in James.

In spite of these verbal differences, an echo of part of the Jesus-saying in the gospels is in our opinion likely. The subject matter is identical. Both are warnings against riches; both describe the inevitable decay and deterioration of these treasures. It is possible that James omits the loss of wealth by stealing since he intends to save that description for the oppressor himself who in the next verse (5:4) is accused of stealing from the

---

[405]Goodspeed translates this verse, "And they adorn them with clothes like men, these gods of silver, gold, and wood though they cannot save themselves from being corroded with rust."

[406]Charles, APOT, I: 601.

[407]KJV, ASV, RSV, NEB, NIV, Latin Vulgate, German: Die Gute Nachricht, Dutch: Statenvertaling and NBG.

[408]RSV footnote, TEV, JB, German: Katholische Bibelanstalt, Dutch: Katholieke Bijbelstichting.

[409]Guelich, Sermon, 326.

[410]"Lose your money for the sake of a brother or a friend, and do not let it rust to ruin (ἰωθήτω ... εἰς ἀπώλειαν) under a stone."

[411]Thomas 76 has moth and worm although Craig L. Blomberg, "Tradition and Redaction in the Parables of the Gospel of Thomas," Gospel Perspectives, ed. David Wenham (Sheffield: JSOT, 1985), 5:193,186 assigns it to Gnostic redaction as in the Gospel of Truth 33:16-17 and Thomas 9.

[412]Luke includes only the moth, not the worms.

poor (literally, "kept back by fraud"). Furthermore, the dissimilar vocabulary should not be overemphasized since the language of Matthew and Luke likewise diverges at several points. Apparently both Luke and James have combined the saying of Jesus with other paraenetic teaching of the church. Luke inserts exhortations aimed at a radical lifestyle (selling your possessions) and the nourishment of the poor (giving alms), thus emphasizing the temporal conditions necessary for an unfailing treasure in the heavens. James applies the same saying to the disintegrating earthly treasure and denounces the rich who fail to live out of the eternal treasure. Therefore, Luke offers a positive example of Christian behavior, while James condemns a deplorable evil with a negative illustration. Throughout this section James interlaces his exhortations with traditional language. In 5:4-5 James alludes to OT expressions (Dt. 24:15; Mal. 3:5; Is. 5:9; Jer. 12:3 LXX),[413] while at 5:1 he addresses the rich through a woe saying of Jesus. With these allusions in the context, would one not expect to encounter similar material at 5:2-3? If so, the closest parallel is that of Mt. 6:19-20 and Lk. 12:33b. The clinching argument, we believe, is the use of the verb θησαυρίζω. In all likelihood James did not set out in v. 2 with the distinct purpose of alluding to a saying of Jesus; he is only attempting to describe the present unjust situation with traditional prophetic language. But after he has depicted the rotten food, the moth-eaten garments, and the rusting gold and silver, then he remembers that Jesus had proclaimed the same message. With Jesus' saying in mind, he concludes, "they have laid up their treasures," indicating that Jesus' saying was being fulfilled by these rich oppressors. They have laid up treasures for the last days and, therefore, there will be no treasure in heaven; instead their flesh will be eaten like fire. The contrast between eschatological fire and earthly treasures in the last days is similar to the eschatological treasure in heaven and temporal treasures on earth in Matthew. Thus James combines traditional language on the theme of wealth[414] with a reference to a saying of Jesus.

Before we can be satisfied with this conclusion, we must investigate the counter proposals of Spitta and Dibelius who contend that the woes of 1 En. 94ff are the source of Jas.5:2-3. Spitta[415] proposes 1 En. 97:8-10:

> 8 Woe to you who acquire silver and gold in unrighteousness, yet say, "We have increased in riches and have possessions and have acquired everything we have desired. 9 And now let us do what we purposed: for we have gathered silver and many are the husbandmen in our houses and our granaries are [brim] full as with water." 10 Yea, and like water your lies shall flow away; for riches shall not abide but speedily ascend from you; for ye have acquired it all in unrighteousness, and ye shall be given over to a great curse.[416]

Enoch speaks both of riches (πλούτῳ) and of gold and silver (χρυσίον καὶ ἀργύριον) like Jas. 5:3a, but this verbal similarity occurs naturally when two authors expound the same

---

[413]Cf. ch. 2, sections 3.3 and 3.4.

[414]The image of a treasure is commonplace in contexts about the judgment: Tob. 4:9; Sir. 29:11; 4 Ezr. 7:77; 8:33; 2 Bar. 14:12; 24:1; Ps. Sol. 9:5(9); cf. Rom. 2:5.

[415]Spitta, Zur Geschichte, II: 130.

[416]Charles' translation (APOT, II: 269) is from the Ethiopic version. He did not possess the Chester Beatty papyrus which contains 1 En. 97:6-104:13 and 106-107. Cf. Apocalypsis Henochi Graece. ed. M. Black, 37-38: 8 οὐαὶ ὑμῖν οἱ κτώμενοι χρυσίον καὶ ἀργύριον οὐκ ἀπὸ δικαιοσύνης, καὶ ἐρεῖτε, πλούτῳ πεπλουτήκαμεν καὶ τὰ ὑπάρχοντα ἐσχήκαμεν καὶ κεκτήμεθα, 9 καὶ πᾶν ὃ ἐὰν θελήσωμεν ποιήσωμεν, ὅτι ἀργύριον τεθησαυρίκαμεν ἐν τοῖς θησαυροῖς ἡμῶν καὶ ἀγαθὰ πολλὰ ἐν ταῖς οἰκίαις ἡμῶν. 10 καὶ ὡς ὕδωρ ἐκχυθήσεται. πεπλάνησθε, ὅτι οὐ μὴ παραμείνῃ ὁ πλοῦτος ὑμῶν, ἀλλὰ ταχὺ [ἀναπτήσεται] ἀπὸ ὑμῶν, ὅτι ἀδίκως πάντα κέκτησθε· καὶ ὑμεῖς εἰς κατάραν μεγάλην παραδοθήσεσθε.

theme. Enoch reports that the acquisition of riches has come through unjust means, and Jas. 5:4 describes a similar situation where the rich have kept back the salaries of their workers by fraud. Yet since the acquisition of wealth by unrighteous means has already become one of the most common criticisms in the ethical tradition,[417] both Enoch and James have probably drawn upon traditional material. Finally, both 1 Enoch and James employ the verb θησαυρίζω. Yet the close verbal resemblance between 1 En. 97:9 and Lk. 12:19,21 demonstrates that a Lucan dependence upon this Enoch passage is much more defensible than any allusion to it by Jas. 5:2-3.

Lk. 12:19,21	1 En. 97:8,9
19 καὶ ἐρῶ τῇ ψυχῇ μου·	8 καὶ ἐρεῖτε ...
	9 ὅτι ἀργύριον τεθησαυρίκαμεν
	ἐν τοῖς θησαυροῖς ἡμῶν
ψυχή, ἔχεις πολλὰ ἀγαθὰ	καὶ ἀγαθὰ πολλὰ
κείμενα εἰς ἔτη πολλά ...	ἐν ταῖς οἰκίαις ἡμῶν.
21 οὕτως ὁ θησαυρίζων ἑαυτῷ	
καὶ μὴ εἰς θεὸν πλουτῶν.	

Although Lk. 12:19,21 is likely dependent upon 1 En. 97:8-10,[418] nowhere in Enoch is there any description of the decay and deterioration of riches through such enemies as moths, rot, worms, rust, or robbery as we encounter in Jas. 5:2-3 and Mt. 6:19-21; Lk. 12:33b-34. Therefore the amount of divergent material is greater than the vocabulary that is congruent. Dibelius[419] claims that 1 En. 94:8 is the best parallel: "Woe to you, ye rich, for ye have trusted in your riches, and from your riches shall ye depart, because ye have not remembered the Most High in the days of your riches." This verse immediately precedes Enoch's reference to "the day of slaughter", the phrase used in Jas. 5:5, and therefore could have influenced James. However, we have determined that the presence of a similar parallel in Jer. 12:3 indicates that traditional language is chosen when the rich are upbraided.[420] Therefore, only insofar as certain themes and terminology have become traditional material for warnings against wealth can 1 En. 94:8-9 and 97:8-10 be said to function as a source for Jas. 5:2-3.

Gotaas, in his dissertation on the use of the OT in several of the Catholic epistles, suggests that "the end of verse 3 seems to be an allusion to the 'treasured up' retribution of Proverbs 1:18."[421] Gotaas is referring to the LXX translation: "For they that are concerned in murder store up evils for themselves."[422] (αὐτοὶ γὰρ οἱ φόνου μετέχοντες θησαυρίζουσιν ἑαυτοῖς κακά). Possible evidence supporting Prov. 1:18 as the source of Jas. 5:3 includes the facts that 1) James already quotes from the book of Proverbs at 4:6 (Prov. 3:34) and 5:20 (Prov. 10:12); 2) the OT references in James are based upon the LXX version;[423] 3) James' context, specifically 5:6, mentions unjust murder as does

---

[417] Amos 5:11-12; 8:4-6; Mic. 2:2; Is. 3:10(LXX),14-15; Wis. 2:10-20; Prov. 1:11; Ps. 37:14,32; 1 En. 94:6-7; 96:5,7-8; 98:12-15; 99:15; 100:7. Cf. Dibelius and Greeven, James, 239-240; Laws, James, 204.

[418] Cf. S. Aalen, "St. Luke's Gospel and the Last Chapters of 1 Enoch," NTS 13(1966-67): 4-5; George W.E. Nickelsburg, "Riches, the Rich, and God's Judgment in 1 Enoch 92-105 and the Gospel according to Luke," NTS 25(1978-79): 329-330,334-337.

[419] Dibelius and Greeven, James, 237.

[420] Cf. ch. 2, section 3.4.

[421] Gotaas, OT in James, 304.

[422] Septuagint, Greek and English, 788. Prov. 1:18 in the MT says, "but these men lie in wait for their own blood."

[423] Cf. above, p. 52.

Prov. 1:11,18; 4) it is "the just man" in each case who is taken advantage of (Prov. 1:11; Jas. 5:6); and 5) each contains a prophetic denunciation and prediction of destruction against the oppressor. On the other hand, this supportive evidence is undermined by other vital facts: 1) the OT passage speaks against murder, but James condemns the wealthy; 2) there is nothing mentioned about different types of wealth (rotten riches, moth-eaten garments, corroded gold and silver) in Prov. 1:18 as in James; and 3) Proverbs portrays a positive evaluation of wealth whereas James is consistently negative in his appraisal. For instance, in Prov. 13:22 LXX, where the same word θησαυρίζω is employed,[424] the wise sage explains, "and the wealth of ungodly men is laid up for the just." Surely James would not appeal to a book like Proverbs when he denounces wealth; the subject matter of the gospel parallels fits much better this important emphasis of James. To verify this supposition we will now investigate the close similarity of thought between James and Jesus on the subject of riches.

James develops his teaching on wealth and the wealthy in three passages: 1:9-11; 2:1-7; and 5:1-6. In summary, James' instruction includes the following elements:

1) James continues the emphasis on the pious poor begun during the intertestamental period.[425]

2) The ideal Christian for James is opposed to the lifestyle of the rich. Therefore, the term "poor" is "virtually identical in his mind with 'Christian', probably due to the community's circumstances and the traditional piety-poverty link."[426]

3) Throughout the epistle only the evil deeds of the rich (2:6-7; 5:4-6) and their condemnation (1:11; 2:5 by implication; 5:1-3) are stressed.

4) Nowhere is an attitude of repentance expected from the rich.[427] This does not entail that repentance and a changed lifestyle are not possible. Instead James' response of prophetic denunciation toward the rich is reminiscent of a long-standing tradition begun with the OT prophets.

5) The community's attitude toward the rich should exclude favoritism (2:1-4). Although James is alarmed at the advances which the rich have made into the Christian churches,[428] nowhere in the Epistle of James do we encounter any exhortations to isolation or withdrawal from the wealthy.[429] James speaks to the rich directly (5:1-6) and pictures them as participating in worship services (2:2-4).

What is the background and source of James' teaching on the subject of wealth? Certain aspects of this theme probably derive from the actual events within the community of James: the poor are those who are rich in faith (2:5); the rich are dragging the poor to court (2:6) and slandering the honorable name with which the community is identified (2:7); the rich oppress their laborers (5:4); the wealthy might be receiving the best seats at the worship services although the word "suppose" at 2:2 would more naturally imply a hypothetical situation.[430] In addition to this use of contemporary experiences, James

---

[424]Only in Proverbs does the LXX translate the Hebrew verb צָפַן by θησαυρίζω (1:18; 2:7; 13:22). This in not the case in Prov. 1:11; 10:14; 27:16.

[425]Cf. Dibelius and Greeven, James, 39ff.

[426]Davids, James, 45. Cf. Dibelius and Greeven, James, 44.

[427]James depicts the downfall of the rich in Jas. 1:11 and not an heroic act of renunciation. Supporters of the heroic view of Jas. 1:9-11 like Adamson, James, 30 contend that the description of the downfall of the rich is "to turn a sincere rich Christian to humbleness." We support the ironic interpretation based upon 1) the similarities with Jewish thought where the pious poor are contrasted with the lawless rich even though both belong to Israel; and 2) the remaining contexts within the Epistle of James which speak embitteredly against the rich and fail to extend any expectation of an alteration of lifestyle.

[428]Dibelius and Greeven, James, 44.

[429]Laws, James, 104.

[430]An anticipatory conditional sentence with ἐάν and the subjunctive is employed. Dibelius, Laws, and Davids favor a hypothetical possibility while Adamson and Reicke picture an actual experience.

chooses traditional images drawn from Jewish religious literature. He employs the language of Is. 40:6b-8 in 1:10b-11, Lev. 19:15 at 2:9, and draws from many parallel expressions in OT passages as well as intertestamental literature at 5:1-6.[431]

However, the role of the teaching of Jesus is especially important to the development of James' thinking about riches. Numerous parallels between James' and Jesus' doctrine of wealth point to James' similar involvement in the renewal of the piety-poverty tradition.[432] James and Jesus both proclaim an imminent reversal of fates for the rich and poor (Jas. 1:9-11; 2:5; Mt. 5:3 par.; Lk. 12:13-21; 16:25). These proclamations employ the language of prophetic denunciation (Jas. 5:1; Lk. 6:24). Their teaching is not based upon proletarian revolutionary ideas but upon an expectation of the coming of the kingdom.[433] Therefore, for both James and Jesus poverty and wealth are considered religious concepts. Since the rich person lives without God and acts against God (Jas. 2:5,7; Lk. 12:16ff; 16:19ff), the attack is on the rich *qua* rich (Jas. 5:1-6; Mk. 10:23-28 par.). The rich man's greater potential for doing good works with his abundance of resources is nowhere implied in their teaching; nor is there any distinction between riches and the love of riches as in 1 Tim. 6:10. Instead of extending the possibility of repentance to the rich, the difficulty of their entry into the kingdom is emphasized (Jas. 2:5; Mk. 10:25 par.). The rich, therefore, stand on the edge or outside of the community. He goes away sorrowful, since he has great possessions (Mk. 10:22 par.). The primary motive for addressing the rich is to warn disciples and potential followers of the dangers of wealth. They are cautioned about covetousness (Jas. 4:3; Lk. 12:15), a divided heart (Jas. 4:4; Mt. 6:24 par.), anxiety (Lk. 12:22ff par.), showing partiality (Jas. 2:1-4), and a delight in riches which chokes the word (Mk. 4:19 par.). The storing up of wealth is especially forbidden: Jesus tells a parable against building bigger barns (Lk. 12:15-21) and insists on the laying up of treasures in heaven (Mt. 6:19-21 par.), while James announces that the rich will be unable to enjoy any of their stored-up treasures since the last days are upon them (5:3). Finally, the extravagant lifestyle of the rich is pictured and then condemned. Jesus portrays Νεύης (p^{75}) as one "who feasted sumptously every day" (Lk. 16:19) and the rich person in Lk. 12:19 as saying, "Soul, you have ample goods laid up for many years; take your ease, eat, drink, be merry." James likewise depicts their excessive lifestyle ("You have lived on the earth in luxury and in pleasure; you have fattened your hearts in a day of slaughter." 5:5) as well as their oppression (2:6; 5:4) and murder of the just (5:6). The end of the story is always the complete destruction of what the rich valued. The overabundance of his possessions rot and tarnish (Jas. 5:2); they are moth-eaten (Jas. 5:2; Mt. 6:19 par.) and stolen (Mt. 6:19 par.). The rich man himself is consumed with fire (Jas. 5:4; Lk. 16:24-28); he withers like a parched flower (Jas. 1:11); his soul is required of him (Lk. 12:20). God has chosen the poor (Jas. 2:5); He takes their side (Mt. 5:3 par.).

In fact, contradictions between James' and Jesus' approach toward wealth are nonexistent;[434] the differences lie only in the areas of emphasis.[435] Whereas James consistently condemns the wealthy, Jesus imparts positive instructions about economic generosity, thus offering an alternative to excessive wealth (Lk. 12:33; 19:8; Mt. 19:21; 6:22-

---

431 Cf. Dibelius and Greeven, James, 44.

432 Davids, James, 44; Dibelius and Greeven, James, 42; Mußner, Jacobusbrief, 83-84.

433 Dibelius and Greeven, James, 43.

434 Mayor, James, clxxi calls attention to one apparent contradiction when James "tries to excite the anger of his readers against the rich, who had maltreated them, instead of reminding them that their duty was to love their enemies and to do good to them that hated them." However, Jesus never sets love of enemy over against an attitude of anger toward injustice and those who practice evil.

435 Of course, there is the obvious difference that Jesus preferred the medium of parables.

23).[436] James continually underscores specific evils which the rich have effectuated. They oppress, drag you to court (2:6), and blaspheme God (2:7). They are guilty of fraud against their workers (5:4) and have killed the righteous (5:6). On the contrary, the problem with the rich in the gospels is usually their negligence and inability to perceive what positive actions are required of them.[437] Thus, whereas James and Jesus maintain their individual areas of emphasis, the similarities in their teaching about wealth are of primary importance. We can therefore safely conclude that James was an "energetic representative of the ancient, recently revitalized pride of the Poor"[438] whose pioneer for the church was Jesus himself.

In order to substantiate our claim that Jesus' teaching in Mt. 6:19-21; Lk. 12:33b-34 is the source of Jas. 2:2-3, we will investigate the early church's quoting of these texts to determine the terminological precision necessary to confirm a saying as an allusion to a *logion* of Jesus. Mt. 6:19-20 is referred to by Justin Martyr in 1 Apol. 15:11. Because Justin's specified purpose in this section is to rehearse the teaching of Jesus, his quote of Mt. 6:19-20, as expected, is very close to the gospel text.[439]

1 Apol. 15:11

ὑμεῖς δὲ μὴ θησαυρίζετε
ἑαυτοῖς ἐπὶ τῆς γῆς,
ὅπου σὴς καὶ βρῶσις ἀφανίζει
καὶ λῃσταὶ
διορύσσουσι·
θησαυρίζετε δὲ ἑαυτοῖς
ἐν τοῖς οὐρανοῖς, ὅπου
οὔτε σὴς οὔτε βρῶσις ἀφανίζει.

Mt. 6:19-20

19 μὴ θησαυρίζετε
ὑμῖν θησαυροὺς ἐπὶ τῆς γῆς,
ὅπου σὴς καὶ βρῶσις ἀφανίζει
καὶ ὅπου κλέπται
διορύσσουσιν καὶ κλέπτουσιν·
20 θησαυρίζετε δὲ ὑμῖν θησαυροὺς
ἐν οὐρανῷ, ὅπου
οὔτε σὴς οὔτε βρῶσις ἀφανίζει
καὶ ὅπου κλέπται οὐ
διορύσσουσιν οὐδὲ κλέπτουσιν·

Later Clement of Alexandria quotes both Mt. 6:19 and Lk. 12:33[440] in the same context, thus indicating that he knew them as separate sayings in distinct gospels. The Gospel of Thomas 76, on the other hand, does not harmonize similar material from different gospels but merely combines this saying with other Jesus-material (in this case a version of the parable of the pearl), to give new meaning (like Luke) to the concept "unfailing treasure".

---

[436]It is possible that James hints at the neglect of almsgiving on the part of the rich in the expression "rust will be evidence against you" (5:3), but his failure to state this explicitly indicates a preference not to stress this theme. Cf. Dibelius and Greeven, James, 236.

[437]Dives, for instance, lives completely untouched by Lazarus' needs (Lk. 12:21).

[438]Dibelius and Greeven, James, 45.

[439]Cf. Arthur J. Bellinzoni, The Sayings of Jesus in the Writings of Justin Martyr, 61. For the Greek text of 1 Apol. 15:11 see Basil L. Gildersleeve, The Apologies of Justin Martyr (New York: Harper, 1877), p. 15, lines 36-39.

[440]Strom. 4,33,4 μὴ θησαυρίζετε τοίνυν ὑμῖν θησαυροὺς ἐπὶ τῆς γῆς, ὅπου σὴς καὶ βρῶσις ἀφανίζει καὶ κλέπται διορύσσουσι καὶ κλέπτουσι. Strom. 4,33,7 οὗτός ἐστι τῷ ὄντι βαλλάντιον μὴ παλαιούμενον, ἐφόδιον ζωῆς ἀιδίου, θησαυρὸς ἀνέκλειπτος ἐν οὐρανῷ. Stählin, GCS 52, p. 262, lines 30-32; p. 263, lines 8-9.

For Luke the treasure becomes like a purse that does not grow old, while for Thomas the treasure is identified with the pearl of great price.[441]

> Jesus said, "The kingdom of the Father is like a merchant who had a consignment of merchandise and who discovered a pearl. That merchant was shrewd. He sold the merchandise and bought the pearl alone for himself. You too seek his unfailing and enduring treasure where no moth comes near to devour and no worm destroys."[442]

The form of the allusion to the gospels in Jas. 5:2-3 has been affected by the development of the church's ethical teaching. In considering the similarities between such passages as Mt. 6:19-34, Jas. 5:1-6, 1 Tim. 6:6-11, 1 Pet. 5:6, and Barn. 19:2, Riesenfeld has demonstrated the influence of church paraenesis:

> So zeigt es sich, daß das Thema von Schätzesammeln und Sorgen in den neutestamentlichen Briefen an einer Anzahl von Stellen in Formen hervortritt, die in der Ausdrucksweise derartig verwandt sind, daß man mit einern verbreiteten paränetischen Stil hinsichtlich dieses Themas in der urchristlichen Gemeindepredigt zu rechnen hat.[443]

Jas. 5:2-3 is evidence that the paraenesis of the church molded the words of Jesus by mixing them with other traditional ethical material and applying them to specific settings within the life of the developing church. That a particular saying of the Jesus-tradition is in the mind of James is evidenced by 1) similar subject matter as well as some verbal connections; 2) the identical approach to the subject of wealth in the teachings of James and Jesus; 3) another allusion to a saying of Jesus at 5:1 within this traditional material; and 4) the support given by numerous exegetes in the last centuries where this is the fifth most frequently cited parallel between James and the Synoptic gospels (42 out of 60 authors).[444]

6.0 The Synoptic Parallels in the Primitive Church Order of Jas. 5:7-20

In 5:7 James returns to his customary address ἀδελφοί indicating that the prophetic denunciations of 4:13-5:6 are ended. Now James develops several loosely knit themes on the subject of eschatology and the activities of the church such as oath-taking, singing, healing the sick, confession of sins, prayer, and ministry to backsliders. Together these could be entitled a primitive church order roughly parallel to the Didache (7-16) which also discusses certain activities of the church (baptism, fasting, the eucharist, the prophetic ministry, confession of sins, church officers) and eschatology.[445]

A. 5:7-11 Eschatology.

1. 5:7-8 Patience and the eschaton (use address, "brethren").
    a. 5:7a Exhortation to patience.

---

[441]Even Clement of Alexandria can be said to have inserted his own emphasis into the meaning of treasure since in between his quotations of the gospels he says, "But our true "treasure" is where what is allied to our mind is, since it bestows the communicative power of righteousness ..." (Strom. 4,33,5-6) Wilson, The Anti-Nicene Fathers, II: 415.

[442]Lambdin, "Gospel of Thomas," NHL, 126.

[443]Harold Riesenfeld, "Vom Schätzesammeln und Sorgen -- ein Thema urchristlischer Paränese zu Mt. vi. 19-34," Neotestamentica et Patristica, 57.

[444]For strong support see especially the English-speaking authors: Knowling, James, 118; Davids, James, 44; Henry Alford, "James," The Greek Testament, IV: 321.

[445]Reicke, James, 8 calls it a "manual of discipline".

b. 5:7b Illustration from nature.
c. 5:8a Exhortation to patience and establishing your hearts.
d. 5:8b Eschatological grounding of the exhortation.

2. 5:9 Grumbling and the eschaton (repeated address, "brethren").
a. 5:9a Exhortation against grumbling.
b. 5:9b Eschatological grounding of the exhortation.

3. 5:10-11 Examples of suffering and patience (repeated address, "brethren").
a. 5:10 The example of the OT prophets.
b. 5:11a Those who endure are blessed.
c. 5:11b The example of Job and the Lord's mercy.

B. 5:12 Oaths (use address, "brethren"): Allusion to a saying of Jesus in Mt. 5:33-37.

C. 5:13-18 Prayer, confession of sins, and healing.

1. 5:13a Instruction to the suffering: pray.

2. 5:13b Instruction to the cheerful: sing.

3. 5:14-18 Instruction to the sick.
a. 5:14-15 Let the elders pray and anoint with oil.
b. 5:16a Confession of sins.
c. 5:16b Aphorism about the righteous man (like 5:6).
d. 5:17-18 The example of Elijah.

4. 5:19-20 Backsliders (use address, "brethren").

6.1 Jas. 5:10-11a	Mt. 5:11,12b	Lk. 6:22,23b
ὑπόδειγμα λάβετε,	12b οὕτως γὰρ	23b κατὰ τὰ αὐτὰ γὰρ
ἀδελφοί,		
τῆς κακοπαθίας	ἐδίωξαν	ἐποίουν
καὶ τῆς μακροθυμίας		
τοὺς προφήτας	τοὺς προφήτας	τοῖς προφήταις
οἳ ἐλάλησαν ἐν τῷ	τοὺς πρὸ ὑμῶν.	οἱ πατέρες αὐτῶν.
ὀνόματι κυρίου.		
11a ἰδοὺ μακαρίζομεν	11 μακάριοί ἐστε	22 μακάριοί ἐστε ὅταν
τοὺς ὑπομείναντας·	ὅταν ὀνειδίσωσιν ὑμᾶς	μισήσωσιν ὑμᾶς οἱ ἄνθρωποι
		καὶ ὅταν ἀφορίσωσιν ὑμᾶς
	καὶ διώξωσιν	καὶ ὀνειδίσωσιν
	καὶ εἴπωσιν πᾶν	καὶ ἐκβάλωσιν τὸ
	πονηρὸν καθ᾽ ὑμῶν	ὄνομα ὑμῶν ὡς πονηρὸν
	ψευδόμενοι ἕνεκεν ἐμοῦ.	ἕνεκα τοῦ υἱοῦ τοῦ ἀνθρώπου·

In order to recommend patience in a situation of extended waiting filled with the oppression described in 5:1-6, James appeals to the example of a farmer who patiently tarries for the rains before his harvest is ripe (5:7). He reminds his readers that the period of delay will not continue indefinitely since "the coming of the Lord is at hand" (5:8-9). Then James encourages his audience by pointing to the prophets as examples of steadfastness and to the story of Job to confirm that in the end[446] the Lord is compassionate and merciful to those who endure. This reference to OT characters is a common phenomenon in James; he has already mentioned Abraham and Rahab in chapter 2 and in a context about prayer at 5:17-18 will refer to Elijah.

When we compare Jas. 5:10-11 with the gospel parallels, it is immediately obvious that the prophets are given an exemplary role in each case. Whereas in 1 Pet. 2:21-25, 1 Thess. 1:6, 1 Cor. 11:1, and Eph. 5:2 Jesus is specified as the paradigm, in James as well as in the gospels the OT prophets are the pattern. Therefore, one might argue that James' reference to the prophets is more like Jesus' manner of speaking than that of the church. Moreover a situation of extreme suffering is assumed in both. In the gospels the disciples are reviled (Mt. and Lk.), spoken about evilly (Mt. and Lk.), persecuted (Mt.), excluded (Lk.), and hated (Lk.); in Jas. 5:10 examples of suffering are given because of the oppression of the rich. In each context the theme of wealth and poverty is also mentioned (Jas. 5:1-6; Mt. 5:3; Lk. 6:20). Besides content similarities, each saying is in the form of a μακάριος statement. Admittedly the emphasis of each beatitude is different; in James the steadfast are blessed while in the gospels the reviled, persecuted disciples are designated happy (NEB). Yet one might argue that an attitude of steadfastness is implied in each of the specifics of the gospel descriptions since persecution needs to be endured.

Upon closer examination one perceives that James and Jesus are utilizing the example of the prophets quite differently. James is looking back at the prophets for strength in present struggles. The gospels, however, speak about how the prophets have been treated by the people of Israel (cf. also Lk. 11:47,50-51; Mt. 23:37). In James the prophets are treated positively as examples to emulate, while in the gospels the prophets are negative examples of a shameful past in the history of Israel which is about to be repeated. This opposite function assigned to the prophets clearly makes it very difficult to assume any allusion to Jesus' words on the part of James. Beyond the different emphasis and use of the prophets, the specifics are in each case substantially divergent. The two main exemplary descriptions utilized to designate the prophets (examples of suffering, κακοπαθίας, and patience, μακροθυμίας) are missing in the gospels. Moreover, the μακάριος statement is better explained as an allusion to an earlier reference in the Epistle of James (1:12) where those who persevere under trial are called blessed than to the final beatitude of Mt. 5:11; Lk. 6:22. The first person plural ("We call those blessed who were steadfast") indicates that James himself or his community is designating these as blessed. The occurrence of the verb ὑπομένω at both 1:12 and 5:11 substantiates our claim that James is alluding to his own particular theme.

Finally, parallels with Jas. 5:10-11 are not limited to the gospels. Dibelius points out that "one must keep in mind how common the notion of the prophets as martyrs was during this period".[447] Furthermore, the literature of this time is replete with references to the prophets as positive paradigms similar to James' epistle.[448] The placing of

---

[446]Some authors (cf. Dibelius and Greeven, James, 247, n. 32) contend that "the end of the Lord" in 5:11 refers to the end of Jesus' life (i.e. suffering and death). Thus the plural in 5:11a ("those who were steadfast") could be accounted for by setting the example of Jesus alongside that of Job. But this interpretation breaks the continuity between the two uses of the term "Lord" in this verse. Others understand τὸ τέλος κυρίου to mean "the purpose of the Lord" (Mitton, James, 189; RSV; JB), a less usual meaning of τέλος. Since the reference is to Job, it is more likely that the happy outcome of the story is in the mind of James. Cf. Robert P. Gordon, "KAI TO ΤΕΛΟΣ ΚΥΡΙΟΥ ΕΙΔΕΤΕ (JAS. V. 11)," JThS 26(1975): 91-92.

[447]Dibelius and Greeven, James, 244.

[448]Sir. 44:1b; 2 Mac. 6:20,31; 4 Mac. 17:23; Jn. 13:15; 1 Cl. 5:1; 6:1; 46:1; 63:1; Jos. Bell. 6:103; Philo, Rer. Div. Her. 256. Cf. Davids, James, 185.

a blessing upon those who endure struggles was familiar and commonplace as well.[449] Finally, the addition of Job (Jas. 5:11b) proves that James was thinking about OT figures rather than a specific saying of Jesus.[450] Therefore, when James explains that they have already heard of the steadfastness of these figures (5:11), he is probably alluding to his readers' upbringing with the stories of the OT heroes of faith.[451] James is again reproducing traditional language.[452] Therefore, it is not "most natural to associate such words with our Lord's own Beatitudes" as Knowling contends.[453] Endurance is specifically a Jamesian emphasis. Not only is there a close parallel at 1:12, but the theme of ὑπομονή was of such importance that he begins his epistle with a rehearsal of its good qualities (Jas. 1:3-4). Therefore, no specific source is being utilized by James although the themes of endurance, blessedness, and patience are common to paraenetic literature.

6.2 Jas. 5:12	Mt. 5:33-37
	πάλιν ἠκούσατε ὅτι ἐρρέθη τοῖς ἀρχαίοις·
	οὐκ ἐπιορκήσεις,
12a	ἀποδώσεις δὲ τῷ κυρίῳ τοὺς ὅρκους σου.
πρὸ πάντων δέ, ἀδελφοί	34 ἐγὼ δὲ λέγω ὑμῖν
μου, μὴ ὀμνύετε	μὴ ὀμόσαι ὅλως·
12b μήτε τὸν οὐρανὸν	μήτε ἐν τῷ οὐρανῷ,
	ὅτι θρόνος ἐστὶν τοῦ θεοῦ,
μήτε τὴν γῆν	35 μήτε ἐν τῇ γῇ,
	ὅτι ὑποπόδιόν ἐστιν τῶν ποδῶν αὐτοῦ,
μήτε ἄλλον τινὰ ὅρκον·	μήτε εἰς Ἱεροσόλυμα,
	ὅτι πόλις ἐστὶν τοῦ μεγάλου βασιλέως,
	36 μήτε ἐν τῇ κεφαλῇ σου ὀμόσῃς,
	ὅτι οὐ δύνασαι μίαν τρίχα λευκὴν
	ποιῆσαι ἢ μέλαιναν.
12c ἤτω δὲ ὑμῶν	37 ἔστω δὲ ὁ λόγος ὑμῶν
τὸ ναὶ ναὶ καὶ τὸ οὒ οὔ	ναὶ ναί, οὒ οὔ·
12d ἵνα μὴ ὑπὸ κρίσιν πέσητε.	τὸ δὲ περισσὸν τούτων ἐκ τοῦ πονηροῦ ἐστιν.

---

[449] Laws, James, 67 refers to Dan. 12:12; Zech. 6:14 LXX; 4 Mac. 7:22; Mk. 13:13; Rev. 2:2f,10; Herm., Vis. 2,2,7. A promise is made to those who endure in Mt. 10:22; 24:13; and Lk. 21:19. Grosheide, Jakobus, 408 calls special attention to Dan. 12:12 saying, "Jakobus geeft hier wel niet een bepaald citaat, maar gebruikt toch duidelijk Dan. 12:12." For this to be true James would have to have been familiar with a type of text similar to the Theodotion version (μακάριος ὁ ὑπομένων καὶ φθάσας) since the other major documents read μακάριος ὁ ἐμμένων καὶ συνάξει. However, the apocalyptic setting of Dan. 12:12 ("Blessed is he who waits and comes to the thousand three hundred and thirty-five days") does not fit the type of literature James enlists.

[450] Another indication of the Jewish background is the fact that κακοπαθία is employed in the LXX at Mal. 1:13; 2 Mac. 2:26; and 4 Mac. 9:8 (with ὑπομονή), while in the NT it is a *hapax legomenon*. Furthermore, Laws, James, 67 points out that at 1:12 "James uses the LXX style of denoting the recipient of blessing by noun and adjectival clause rather than the participial phrase used in other NT macarisms, e.g. Matt. v. 3ff; Jn. xx. 29; Rev. i. 3."

[451] Davids, James, 186 claims that James is referring to both Jesus' words and the OT, yet we have shown that the gospel parallels treat the prophets in a different manner.

[452] Laws, James, 215.

[453] Knowling, James, 131-132.

Jas. 5:12 appears to be an isolated saying loosely attached to the preceding and following contexts. The δέ calls attention to new material as does the return to James' normal introductory formulation, ἀδελφοί μου.[454] To explain the abruptness of the change of content at Jas. 5:12 Francis has argued that oaths as well as health wishes (Jas. 5:13-18) are employed as conclusions to literary epistles.[455] He maintains that the conclusion of James (5:7-20) as well as the introduction (1:1) transforms a list of loosely connected exhortations into an epistle. We prefer to conceive the organizational arrangement of Jas. 5:7-20 as the presentation of a primitive church order less developed than Did. 7-16. Just as The Teaching of the Twelve Apostles combines instruction on baptism (Did. 7), fasting (8), prayers of thanksgiving at the eucharist (9-10), the receiving of prophets (11-13), confession of sins and reconciliation (14), the character qualities of church leaders (15), and the last things (16) into a primitive church order, so James groups together paraenetic exhortations about the last days (5:7-11), the forbidding of oaths (5:12), the healing ministry of the church (5:13-15), the confession of sins and prayer (5:16-18), and the reconciliation of the erring (5:19-20). Thus in piecing together a primitive church order, James moves from speaking about eschatology to various activities within the church, the first being oath-taking.[456]

Before specifically comparing Jas. 5:12 with Mt. 5:33-37, we will investigate the host of exegetical problems in James and Matthew. The phrase πρὸ πάντων has been interpreted in a multitude of ways. Most exegetes believe that the phrase "above all" calls attention to the importance of this saying.[457] However, it is contested whether its superior importance is to the following instructions[458] or the preceding context.[459] A second view posits πρὸ πάντων as a signal for a *verbum Christi*.[460] An interesting suggestion ties πρὸ πάντων in Jas. 5:12 to ὅλως in Mt. 5:34; "Do not swear at all" is thought to have been transposed into "above all, do not swear" at some point in the history of the transmission of this saying of Jesus.[461] A third opinion conjectures that this phrase originated in another (now irrecoverable) context where 5:12 in only a fragment of a longer quote.[462] Finally, some have given up hope of ever establishing a reason for this phrase, "above all".[463] In our opinion, the parallel expression near the end of the epistle of 1 Peter (4:8) as well as examples from papyri[464] indicate that πρὸ πάντων is a technique introducing a peculiar empha-

---

[454]Cf. Davids, James, 188-189.

[455]Francis, "Form and Function," 125.

[456]James' omission of "my brethren" at v. 13 probably indicates that the prohibition of oaths should be tied together with the church order comments on prayer etc. However, ἀδελφοί might have been omitted at 5:13 because 5:12 was so short.

[457]Laws, James, 220, however, applies this introduction to the whole context of vv. 12-18 in the same manner as 1 Pet. 4:8 does not exalt mutual love over watching and praying but emphasizes the instructions of vv. 9-11.

[458]Grosheide, Jakobus, 410.

[459]Reicke, James, 56. Adamson, James, 194-195 relates it specifically to the errors of the tongue in v. 9, e.g. boasting, grumbling, and backbiting, but Dibelius and Greeven, James, 242 believe that there is only a catchword connection with v. 9 (κριθῆτε / κρίσιν).

[460]Alfred Resch, Aussercanonische Paralleltexte zu den Evangelien, I: 99. Cf. Mayor, James, 160. Meyer, Rätsel, 253, on the other hand, discerns a hidden allusion to the tribe of Zebulun.

[461]Gryglewicz, "Jacques et Matthieu," 51.

[462]Oesterley, "James," 472-473.

[463]Dibelius and Greeven, James, 248.

[464]Cf. Jean Cantinat, Les Épîtres de Saint Jacques et de Saint Jude, 241; Knowling, James, 135.

sis of the author[465] near the conclusion of a letter. It would thus function like an asterisk in modern printing to call attention to an important theme.[466]

James' prohibition against swearing consists of two oath formulas, "either by heaven or by earth," followed by a third generalizing formula, "or with any other oath," to include every other possibility. In the second half of the verse James offers a positive alternative ("but let your yes be yes and your no be no") followed by a purpose clause ("that you may not fall under condemnation"). Mt. 5:33-37, on the other hand, introduces the oath prohibition in the form of an antithesis (5:33 as in 5:21, 27,31,38,43) drawn from OT teaching. Matthew includes four specific oath formulas each followed by a ὅτι clause indicating the reason for the prohibition:

> 34 either by heaven, for it is the throne of God,
> 35 or by the earth, for it is his footstool,
> or by Jerusalem, for it is the city of the great king,
> 36 And do not swear by your head, for you cannot make one hair white or black.

This last prohibition in 5:36 appears to be a loosely attached addition to the original saying since a subjunctive is inserted (ὀμόσῃς) rather than the infinitive (ὀμόσαι), and a singular pronoun is chosen (σοῦ) rather than the plural (ὑμῖν). Mt. 5:37a offers a positive alternative to the previously mentioned oaths similar to Jas. 5:12c. Finally, Mt. 5:37b warns that any additions to this positive alternative have their origin in evil or the evil one. In a somewhat parallel fashion Jas. 5:12d warns that condemnation will result if this instruction is not heeded.

The most knotty problem with which exegetes have wrestled is the significance given to the alteration in meaning, if any, between Matthew's ἔστω δὲ ὁ λόγος ὑμῶν ναὶ ναί, οὒ οὔ and the phrase ἤτω δὲ ὑμῶν τὸ ναὶ ναὶ καὶ τὸ οὒ οὔ in James. Because James employs the definite article before ναὶ ναὶ and οὔ οὒ, scholars are agreed that he is advocating truth-telling ("but let your yes be yes and your no be no") and not any alternative oath formulation. Over the meaning of Matthew's language, however, interpreters are sharply divided, some contending that Matthew like James advises truth-telling[467] by using a Semitic construction of intensification, while others attest that a simple oath formula[468] ("yes, yes" or "no, no") is being recommended in lieu of certain forbidden oaths. The following arguments have been employed in support of ναὶ ναί, οὒ οὔ as a surrogate oath formula:

---

[465]Paul Minear, "Yes or No, the Demand for Honesty in the Early Church," NovT 13(1971): 7 suggests that "transparent honesty may have seemed especially difficult and urgent as an expression of patience in the midst of persecution and suffering (v. 6,10,13)."

[466]Cf. Mitton, James, 191.

[467]Willoughby G. Allen, Gospel Acc. to S. Matthew, 54; Davids, James, 190; Jeremias, NT Theology, 220; Ernst Kutsch, "Eure Rede aber sei ja ja, nein, nein," EvTh 20(1960): 209; Alan McNeile, The Gospel acc. to St. Matthew, 68; Moulton and Howard, Grammar, II: 154; Mußner, Jakobusbrief, 215-216; Ernst Percy, Die Botschaft Jesus, 147; Alolf von Schlatter, Der Evangelist Matthäus, 183; Gustav Stählin, "Zum Gebrauch von Beteuerungsformeln im Neuen Testament," NovT 5(1962): 119; Charles C. Torrey, The Four Gospels, 291; Theodor Zahn, Evangelium des Matthäus, 248.

[468]Herbert Braun, Spätjüdisch-häretischer und frühchristlicher Radikalismus II: 80, n. 6; Dibelius and Greeven, James, 250-251, n. 55; Guelich, Sermon, 217; Heinrich J. Holtzmann, Die Synoptiker, 110; Klostermann, Matthäus-Evangelium, 47; Ernst Lohmeyer, Das Evangelium des Matthäus, 134; Manson, Sayings, 159; Meyer, Rätsel, 85; Julius Schniewind, Das Evangelium nach Matthäus, 63; Wolfgang Schrage, "Der Jakobusbrief," in Horst Balz und Wolfgang Schrage, Die katholischen Briefe, 11; George Strecker, Der Weg der Gerechtigkeit: Untersuchung zur Theologie des Matthäus, 133-134.

1) Matthew demands that an oath not include the name of God or a substitute for God's name. By refering to OT passages within the ὅτι clauses Matthew proves that any oath by heaven, earth, or Jerusalem is a substitute for the divine name. Is. 66:1 indicates that heaven and earth refer to God himself;[469] Ps. 48:2 demonstrates that Jerusalem alludes to God the great king.[470] Therefore, in place of these inadequate oaths, Matthew offers an alternative valid oath.

2) Matthew's addition in 5:37b "anything more than this" cannot refer to "speaking something beyond and above the truth" but must designate words that go beyond this simple oath formula "yes, yes" or "no, no".

3) It is well-known that Matthew often endeavors to supply a new law for the church based upon Jesus' words.[471] A new oath formula is another example of this Matthean tendency.

4) Evidence that Matthew does not reject all oaths is supplied by Mt. 23:16-22, where in opposition to all casuistic distinctions between oaths, it is asserted that every oath must in fact be carried out.

5) The possibility that "yes, yes" and "no, no" are oath formulas is reinforced by parallels in Jewish literature. 2 En. 49:1 (Slavonic Enoch), written according to Charles between 30 BC and 70 AD,[472] includes a remarkable parallel to Mt. 5:34-37.

> I swear to you, my children, but I swear not by any oath, neither by heaven nor by earth, nor by any other creature which God created. The Lord said: "There is no oath in me, nor injustice, but truth." If there is no truth in men, let them swear by the words "yea, yea" or else "nay, nay".

Charles calls this saying "a Jewish commonplace".[473] This opinion is supported by the Rabbinic tractate Shebuoth 36a which discusses the question whether Yes and No are oaths and finally decides that if they are repeated twice, then they are legitimate oaths: "R. Eleazar said, 'No' is an oath; 'Yes' is an oath ... Said Raba: But only if he said 'No! No!' twice; or he said 'Yes! Yes!' twice"[474] Furthermore, in the Mechilta 66a on Ex. 20:1-2 the Israelites swear an oath in response to their reception of the commandments, "The Israelites answered, 'Yea, yea' and 'nay nay' to the commands at Sinai."[475]

There are equally strong arguments supporting the thesis that Matthew is against the use of oaths for the validation of one's promise and advocates merely telling the truth:

1) Even though the grammar of Mt. 5:37 does not contain the definite article as Jas. 5:12, the two expressions have an identical meaning since the second ναί and οὔ only add

---

469"Thus says the Lord: 'Heaven is my throne and the earth is my footstool.'"

470 48:1-2 "Great is the Lord ... in the city of our God ... Mount Zion, in the far north, the city of the great King."

471 Cf Dibelius and Greeven, James, 251.

472 Charles, APOT, II: 429. It was written after 30 BC, for it makes use of Sirach, 1 Enoch, and the Book of Wisdom but before 70 AD since the temple is still standing.

473 Ibid., 460.

474 b. Shebuoth 36a, ed. Epstein, 211.

475 Montefiore, Rabbinic Literature and Gospel Teachings, 49. Cf. Joseph Z. Lauterbach, Mekhilta deRabbi Ishmael (Philadelphia, 1976).

emphasis to the first occurrence of these words. Strack, for instance, states that one should not interpret the double yes and no as a predicate, but instead view the second yes and no as an emphatic strengthening of the first.[476] Moulton and Howard[477] compare this usage to the repetition of ἀμήν for the purpose of emphasis. A second explanation for the doubling is found in the Semitic technique to express distribution. Jeremias asserts:

> Rather the doubling of the ναί or οὔ in Matt. 5:37 will be a Semitism. There is no exact equivalent in Semitic languages for our distribution "each", "on each occasion", "each time", and so they have to resort to reiteration to express a distribution. The saying therefore means: "Always consider your yes a yes and your no a no."[478]

These explanations offer an alternative to viewing this wording as an oath, with the first suggestion of added emphasis being the most likely.[479]

2) When Paul in 2 Cor. 1:17 writes τὸ ναὶ ναὶ καὶ τὸ οὔ οὔ, it is the equivalent of ναὶ καὶ οὔ in v. 18.[480] Here we have a second witness besides Mt. 5:37 that this duplication of yes and no can be understood emphatically rather than as an oath formula.[481]

3) The understanding of v. 34a (ἐγὼ δὲ λέγω ὑμῖν μὴ ὀμόσαι ὅλως) best coincides with the interpretation that Jesus is demanding absolute truth-telling without the need of an oath. Thus the introduction and conclusion of this saying fit perfectly together: "Do not swear at all. Let what you say be simply 'yes' or 'no'."

4) Just because Matthew on the basis of Biblical arguments (Is. 66:1; Ps. 48:2) certifies that inadequate oaths employ equivalents of the divine name, it does not logically follow that he supplies an alternative oath without the divine name. His alternative could simply be to speak the truth. Anything more than a simple yes or no is not necessary since a disciple's words require no additional oath to assure their veracity.

5) Mt. 23:16-22 is not asserting certain allowable oaths. Rather as Schneider maintains,

> The concern of Jesus here is simply to reduce the casuistry of the scribes and Pharisees *ad absurdum*. The basic question of the legitimacy of oaths is not at issue.[482]

---

[476]StrB I: 333; Kutsch, "Ja ja, nein, nein," 210 concurs. Davids, James, 190 believes this phrase is saying, "let your word be (an outer) yes (which is truly an inner) yes."

[477]Moulton and Howard, Grammar, II: 154.

[478]Jeremias, NT Theology, 220.

[479]The principle of distribution applies to the dublication of numbers (Gen. 7:3,9; Num. 31:4; 34:18 MT; Mk. 6:7) and groups (Ex. 8:14(10); 2 Kings 17:29; Mk. 6:39-40; Herm., Sim. 8,2,8; 8,4,2), but there is little evidence for a broader application. Considered "vulgar Greek" by Blass and Debrunner (BDF 248.1 and 493.2), it would play no part in the excellent Greek of James.

[480]p[46], 424[c], vg, Pelagius have the shorter reading in both verses, but Metzger, Textual Commentary, 576 is correct in explaining this as a scribal assimilation.

[481]Alford Plummer, A Critical and Exegetical Commentary on the Second Epistle of St. Paul to the Corinthians (New York: Scribner, 1915), 34 concurs, "The repetition gives emphasis .... Yet the difference between the way in which ναὶ ναί, οὒ οὔ is used in the saying (he means Mt. 5:37) and in this passage is so considerable that allusion is not very probable."

[482]Johannes Schneider, s.v. ὀμνύω, TDNT, V: 183.

This is verified by the fact that Mt. 23 is not an address to the disciples but a cutting polemic against the Pharisees.

6) If Matthew is advocating simply telling the truth, then James and Matthew agree over the content of this saying of Jesus. It would naturally follow that James and Matthew are two witnesses to the same *verbum Christi*.[483]

7) The early church interpreted Mt. 5:37 as a call to speaking the truth and not as a new oath formulation. Clement of Alexandria (Strom. 5,99,1) compares the messages of Matthew and Plato (Theaet. 151d: "It is quite out of the question for me to agree to a lie or to suppress the truth."[484]), thus demonstrating that he understood the gospel *logion* as a plea for truth-telling. In exegeting 2 Cor. 1:23 Didymus recites the dominical saying interpreting it as forbidding oaths: "One must not swear, but rather keep one's word above reproach, regarding his 'yes' as actually yes and his 'no' as actually being such."[485] A similar conclusion is reached in the Apostolic Constitutions:

> Wherefore it is the duty of a man of God, as he is a Christian, not to swear by the sun or by the moon, or by the stars; nor by the heaven, nor by the earth, nor by any of the elements, whether small or great. For if our Master charged us not to swear by the true God, that our word might be firmer than an oath, nor by heaven itself, for that is a piece of heathen wickedness, nor by Jerusalem, nor by the sanctuary of God, nor the altar, nor a gift, nor the gilding of the altar, nor one's own head, for this custom is a piece of Judaic corruption, and on that account was forbidden.[486] (my underlining).

As we shall discover when attempting to discern the original wording of the saying of Jesus, the early church overwhelmingly quoted Matthew's saying with the equivalent wording from James,[487] thus indicating that the two expressions conveyed exactly the same meaning for them.

8) In the Jewish tradition the call to truth-telling is also common. The Jewish expert, Montefiore, comments: "I do not think that the 'unbedingte Wahrhaftigkeit im Reden' (unqualified truthfulness in speech) which Jesus demanded was not also demanded, and was not also regarded as part of the moral ideal, by the Rabbis."[488] For example, Rabbi

---

[483]BDF 432.1, however, is incorrect when it asserts, "In Mt. 5:37 ἔστω δὲ ὁ λόγος ὑμῶν ναὶ ναί, οὒ οὒ is a corrupt variant for the well-attested and correct reading ἔστω δὲ ὑμῶν τὸ ναὶ ναὶ καὶ τὸ οὒ οὔ (θ al.)."

[484]Benjamin H. Kennedy, The Theaetetus of Plato (Cambridge: Un. Press, 1881), 15. Translation from Dibelius and Greeven, James, 250, n. 53.

[485]μὴ δεῖν ὀμνύναι, ἀλλ' ἔχειν λόγον ἀκατάγνωστον περὶ τοῦ ναὶ ὡς ὄντως ναὶ καί τοῦ οὒ ὡς ὄντως ἔχοντος. (MPG 39, 1688). Translation from Dibelius and Greeven, James, 249-250, n. 50.

[486]James Donaldson, The Ante-Nicene Fathers, VII: 443. The Greek beginning with "For if our Master" reads: εἰ γὰρ ὁ διδάσκαλος περὶ τοῦ ὄντος θεοῦ παρήγγειλεν ἡμῖν μὴ ὀμνύειν, ὅπως ὁ λόγος ἡμῶν πιστότερος ᾖ τοῦ ὅρκου, μήτε μὴν τὸν οὐρανὸν αὐτόν, ἐλληνικὸν γὰρ τὸ δυσσέβημα μήτε μὴν Ἰερουσαλήμ ἤ τὰ τοῦ θεοῦ ἅγια ἤ τὸ θυσιαστήριον καὶ τὸ δῶρον ἤ τὴν τοῦ ναοῦ χρύσωσιν ἤ τὴν οἰκείαν κεφαλήν, ἰουδαϊκῆς γὰρ παραφθορᾶς ἡ συνήθεια, διὸ καὶ ἀπαγορευτέα. Didascalia et Constitutiones Apostolorum, 5,12,6; ed. Funk, p. 269, lines 3ff.

[487]Justin Martyr, Clement of Alexandria, Eusebius, Pseudo-Clementine Homilies, Cyril of Alexandria, Gregory of Nyssa etc.

[488]Montefiore, Rabbinic Literature and Gospel Teachings, 50. He admits, however, that there is no rabbinic injunction never to swear an oath.

Hunn said, "The Yes of the righteous is Yes, and their No is No."[489] Furthermore in Baba Mezia 49a it states,

> He who punished the generations of the Flood and the Tower of Babel will also punish him who does not keep his word. Let your Yes and No be righteous. Do not speak with your mouth what you do not mean in your heart.[490]

Finally, there is compelling evidence that 2 Enoch 49:1 should not be utilized to support the Jewish oath formulation "yes, yes" since 1) this passage is missing in the shorter recension; 2) the work shows Christian influence; 3) the MSS date only from the 16th and 17th centuries; and 4) the type of swearing which is commanded ("yes, yes" or "no, no") is explicitly stated not to be an oath.[491] Therefore, based upon the close connection of Mt. 5:34a and 37 and the unanimous witness of the early church, it seems best to understand Matthew as passing on Jesus' exhortation to speak the truth without relying upon an oath.

One last exegetical problem should be examined before we specifically compare Jas. 5:12 with Mt. 5:33-37. It is disputed whether the genitive τοῦ πονηροῦ should be taken as masculine denoting the evil one or as neuter specifying that which is evil. The early church fathers understood both Mt. 5:37 and 6:13 as masculine.[492] Since then a change of climate has reversed scholarly opinion so that most modern interpreters choose for the neuter.[493] If Matthew is concerned with not speaking the truth, one might assume that the devil, the "father of lies" (Jn. 8:44), is in the mind of Matthew as at 13:19. Yet Harder in a detailed study of Matthew's use of this term concludes that "it would be more plausible in the case of lying than of mere asseveration to trace it back directly to the devil."[494] Since in the closest reference (5:39) the devil "is ruled out by the fact that the Christian must resist the devil,"[495] it is best to assume that Mt. 5:37 is designating evil in general.[496]

There are sufficient differences between Matthew and James to cause hesitation in uncritically accepting the proposition that both cite the same saying of Jesus. Mt. 5:21-48 is structured by six antitheses while Jas. 5 appears to be loosely attached paraenesis constructed much like a primitive church order. Mt. 5:33-37 includes additional examples of oaths not found in James: swearing by Jerusalem and by one's own head. Moreover, the examples common to each are used for divergent purposes. James introduces the oath formulas to elucidate the main prohibition not to swear; Matthew with the augmentation of the ὅτι clauses demonstrates in addition that to swear by heaven or earth or Jerusalem is to swear by God. Furthermore, Matthew calls attention to the source of these oaths (i.e. evil) whereas James underscores the end result of condemnation.[497] Finally, grammatical dif-

---

[489]Ruth Rabba 7:6. The Midrash Rabba: Ruth and Ecclesiastes, VIII: 85.

[490]Claude G. Montefiore and Herbert Loewe, A Rabbinic Anthology, #1088. Epstein, 292 offers an explanation rather than a literal translation.

[491]Cf. John P. Meier, Law and History in Matthew's Gospel, 153-154, n. 68; Charlesworth, Pseudepigrapha and NT, 32. F.I. Andersen in OT Pseud., I: 176 believes that "dependence on Mt. 5:34f or Jas. 5:12 appears obvious, but not certain."

[492]BAGD, s.v. πονηρός, 691.2b refers to Tertullian, Cyprian, Origen, Chrysostom, and the Pseudo-Clementine Homilies.

[493]Karl B. Bornhäuser, Die Bergpredigt: Versuch einer zeitgenössischen Auslegung (Gütersloh: Bertelsmann, 1923), 89; Günther Harder, s.v. πονηρός, TDNT, VI: 561; Klostermann, Matthäus-Evangelien, 47; RSV; Schneider, s.v. ὀμνύω, TDNT, V: 181, n. 54; Schweizer, Matthew, 128; Zahn, Matthäus, 245.

[494]Harder, s.v. πονηρός, TDNT, VI: 561.

[495]Ibid.

[496]Also in Mt. 5:11; 6:13; 8:11; 9:4; 12:35; and perhaps 13:38.

[497]P, Ψ, and the Byzantine text tradition read ὑποκρίσιν as one word. To make the verse understandable, εἰς is inserted so that the Erasmus and Tyndale translations read "lest you fall into hypocrisy".

ferences include 1) James' choice of the present tense of the verb "to swear" (implying the prohibition of an existing practice) in contrast to the aorist tense utilized in Mt. 5:34;[498] and 2) James' classical accusative construction τὸν οὐρανὸν (originally indicating the god by whom the oath was sworn) rather than the Semitic usage ἐν plus the dative found in Mt. 5:34-36; 23:16-22.[499] But acknowledging these divergencies does not minimize our strong impression that these sayings belong together. Modern authors overwhelmingly classify Jas. 5:12 as the most prominent example of a saying of Jesus alluded to by James.[500] Codex Sinaiticus appears to agree that Jas. 5:12 follows Mt. 5:37 since it adds Matthew's words ὁ λόγος to James' wording. Furthermore, the subject matter is identical: 1) two of the oath examples are alike; 2) the positive instruction about speaking the truth is worded almost precisely the same; and 3) the conclusions are similar. All these facts add validity to the thesis that Jas. 5:12 and Mt. 5:34-37 transmit the identical *logion* of Jesus. To insure the truth of this belief, we will now investigate if another source with greater similarities can be discovered.

Jesus is not unique in his antagonism against the misuses of the oath.[501] The OT was already critical of promissory oaths[502] (also called vows) which were left unfulfilled. Thus in the law oath-taking was limited to those vows which the oath-taker was convinced he could fulfil (Num. 30:2; Dt. 23:21-23). Yet it was especially the prophets who admonished against using oaths too lightly (Jer. 5:2; 7:9; Hos. 4:2; Zech. 5:3-4; Mal. 3:5). In addition swearing by other gods was classified by the prophets as idolatry (Jer. 5:7; 12:16; Amos 8:4; Hos. 4:15; Zeph. 1:5). As time passed, more and more objections were raised against oath-taking: 1) it was recognized that resorting to oaths revealed a low standard of truthfulness; 2) the third commandment could be safeguarded if oaths were disapproved of; 3) a complicated casuistic use of oaths became a means whereby the unwary could be cheated rather than a means of guaranteeing that a promise would be kept; and 4) as contact with foreign nations became more frequent, the temptation to adopt pagan oath formulas increased.[503] Sir. 23:11 is typical of Jewish examples in its rebuke:

> So the man who constantly swears (πολύορκος) and utters the Name cannot be absolved from sin. A man who swears a great deal will be filled with iniquity, and the scourge will never leave his house.

From these parallels Spitta[504] hypothesizes a Jewish source on which both Matthew and James are dependent. Yet a total prohibition of oaths did not prevail in Judaism, probably because the OT contained frequent oaths.[505] Even Montefiore, who argues for close

---

[498]Moulton and Turner, Grammar, III: 75-77.

[499]BDF 149; Robertson, Grammar, 471; Moule, Idiom Book, 183; Moulton and Howard, Grammar, II: 464.

[500]All of the authors mentioned in the chart in Appendix II view Jas. 5:12 as a possible parallel with Mt. 5:37 except for Credner who we must assume accidently omitted it.

[501]Schneider, s.v. ὅρκος, TDNT, V: 458 defines an oath as "a declaration which backs up a human statement, which guarantees its veracity, and which is affirmed by divine cooperation."

[502]Two categories of oaths can be distinguished (cf. Danby, Mishnah, 411). There are assertive oaths where one states, "I swear that I have/have not done something" and promissory oaths whereby one asserts, "I swear that I will/will not do something" (cf Guelich, Sermon, 213). An example of the former is Mt. 5:33a, "You shall not swear falsely," whereas Mt. 5:33b embodies a promissory oath, "You shall perform to the Lord what you have sworn."

[503]Cf. Laws, James, 221.

[504]Spitta, Zur Geschichte, II: 178.

[505]Cf. Dibelius and Greeven, James, 221.

similarities between the teaching of Jesus and the Rabbis on this subject, admits that "there is no Rabbinical ordinance or injunction never to 'swear' or to take an oath."[506]

In the Greek world there were warnings against any and all oaths as early as Choerilus Epicus in the fifth century BC.[507] Pythagoras and his followers were the most well-known for their stand on the prohibition of oaths.[508] As Hellenistic Judaism allowed Greek culture to shape its thought patterns, an increased opposition to oaths is encountered in Jewish circles.[509] Philo advocates avoiding oaths wherever possible:

> To swear not at all is the best course and most profitable to life, well suited to a rational nature which has been taught to speak the truth so well on each occasion that its words are regarded as oaths; to swear truly is only, as people say, a "second-best voyage", for the mere fact of his swearing casts suspicion on the trustworthiness of the man. Let him, then, lay and linger in the hope that by repeated postponement he may avoid the oath altogether. But if necessity be too strong for him, he must consider in no careless fashion all that an oath involves, for that is no small thing, though custom makes light of it.[510]

However, when faced with the problem of how to avoid the name of God, Philo suggests various types of alternative oath formulations: "But also a person may add to his 'Yes' or 'No' if he wish, not indeed the highest and most venerable and primal cause, but earth, sun, stars, heaven, the whole universe."[511] Philo believes that humans must have recourse to oaths in accord with their own unreliability, but that the words of God, on the contrary, are as certain as oaths.[512]

The Essenes[513] also offer disparate evidence over the prohibition of oaths. On the one hand, they demand a solemn oath when initiated into full membership in the ascetic community.[514] However, beyond this one-time oath of membership, all other oaths seem to have been forbidden.[515] Mitton[516] states that this contrary evidence leads to three possible conclusions: 1) the statement of Josephus that Essenes required an entrance oath is inaccurate; 2) the people of Qumran were not orthodox Essenes; or 3) the Zadokite Document does not represent the Qumran community. In our opinion none of the above conclusions are true. Is it not more likely that these two types of oaths were completely unassociated in the minds of the Essenes? The entrance oath was intricately connected with their community covenant and was viewed as a covenant promise rather than an oath.

---

[506]Montefiore, Rabbinic Literature and Gospel Teachings, 50.

[507]Stobaeus 3,27,1. See the edition by C. Wachsmuth and O. Hense, III: 611, line 3ff. Cf. also BAGD, s.v. ὀμνύω, 566.

[508]See Dibelius and Greeven, James, 248, n. 41 for references and a discussion over whether the Stoics joined the Pythagoreans in their refusal of oaths. Cf. also Schneider, s.v. ὀμνύω, TDNT, V: 179.

[509]Ps.-Phoc. 16-17 does not help us here since it only mentions perjury. Cf. van der Horst, Pseudo-Phocylides, 123-124.

[510]Philo, Dec. 84-85 in Colson, Philo VII, LCL, 48-49. J. Heinemann, "Philo's Lehre vom Eid," Judaica, 110 contends that he draws upon Stoic sources. Cf. Schneider, s.v. ὀμνύω, TDNT, V: 179, n. 31.

[511]Philo, Spec. Leg. 2:5 in Colson, Philo VII, LCL, 308-309.

[512]Cf. Sac. Abel. 93.

[513]Josephus (Ant. 15:371) believes they were following Pythagoras.

[514]CD 9:9-10; 15:1-10; 16:8-9; 1QS 2:1-18; 5:8-11. Cf. Jos. Bell. 2:139,142.

[515]Cf. Jos., Bell. 2:135; Ant. 15:371; Philo, Omn. Prob. Lib. 84.

[516]Mitton, James, 194, n. 2.

Therefore the prohibition of oaths and the establishment of an entrance promise were in their minds not contradictory.[517]

Thus we encounter in Hellenistic and ascetic Jewish literature parallels to both the demand for honesty and the refutation of oaths as found in Mt. 5:33-37 and Jas. 5:12. Furthermore, as Guelich notes, "Each of the oaths in 5:34-36 has a counterpart in Jewish literature and each is explicitly rejected as a binding oath."[518] Therefore Jesus' teaching fits generally into his cultural milieu. However, his radical hard-line approach was not the commonly accepted practice of Judaism. Because at the end of the age all people would have to render account for every careless word (Mt. 12:36),[519] Jesus advocated a radical truthfulness without the crutch of an oath.[520] James and Matthew (5:34,37) display this same attitude as supported by a wide range of scholars.[521] Therefore, Jas. 5:12 is based upon Jesus' teaching and not upon that of the Essenes or Hellenistic Judaism.

Dibelius, however, raises the possibility that both Jas. 5:12 and Mt. 5:33-37 originated in the teaching of Judaeo-Christian paraenesis. He cites three facts:

> 1) Jas does not quote the saying as a dominical saying; 2) it occurs in the Gospels only in Matthew, and it is precisely in Matthew that legal prescriptions of a Jewish origin occasionally appear as dominical sayings; 3) there are Jewish parallels to this saying.[522]

A fourth piece of evidence, the fact that honesty of speech was a popular theme in the church's ethical teaching,[523] could be added at this point. Yet after offering grounds for this thesis, Dibelius immediately decides that these arguments are inconsequential. He points out,

---

[517]We should not be too dogmatic on this point since as Davies, Setting, 244 remarks, "owing to the uncertain meaning of the pertinent texts, any conclusions we draw concerning oaths in the sect must be tentative."

[518]Guelich, Sermon, 215.

Shebuoth 4:13 "[If a man said] 'I adjure you,' or 'I command you,' or 'I bind you,' they are liable. [But if he said] 'By heaven and by earth,' they are exempt." (cf. Mt. 5:34b-35a).

Nedarim 1:3 "[If he said, 'May it be to me] as the lamb ... [or] as Jerusalem' ... it is a vow as binding as if he had uttered the word *Korban*. R. Judah says: If he said, '[May it be] Jerusalem,' he has said naught." (cf. Mt. 5:35b).

Sanhedrin 3:2 "If a man must take an oath before his fellow, and his fellow said to him, 'Vow to me by the life of thy head,' R. Meir says: He may retract. But the sages say: He cannot retract." (cf. Mt. 5:36).

[519]Thus this exhortation is in harmony with the other ethical radicalisms of Jesus which are based on the announcement of the coming of God's reign. Cf. Georg Strecker, The Sermon on the Mount, 78.

[520]Sometimes a tension is seen between Jesus' own conduct and his prohibition of oaths. Spitta, Zur Geschichte, II: 179 claims that Jesus' conduct in Mt. 26:63f proves that Mt. 5:34-37 cannot be assigned to Jesus. Arguing against this, Schneider, s.v. ὀμνύω, TDNT, V: 184-185 comments, "But the ἀμήν is not an oath. Nor does Jesus make a declaration of an oath in Mt. 26:64; this is a simple statement which ... contains an open Messianic confession on the part of Jesus." Even though b. Shebuoth 36a (ed. Epstein, 210) states that Amen sometimes implies an oath, it usually implies only the acceptance and confirmation of the words spoken.

[521]Cf. Laws, James, 222; Davids, James, 189.

[522]Dibelius and Greeven, James, 251. Cf. also Georg Strecker, "Die Antithesen der Bergpredigt (Mt. 5:21-48 par)," ZNW 69(1978): 63.

[523]Cf. Minear, "Yes and No," 8-10 for examples.

> Because of their very nature, the last two naturally prove nothing. Regarding the first argument, the absence of a quotation formula in Jas does not qualify as evidence that the saying about swearing was not regarded as a dominical saying in the time of Jas. Other sayings of Jesus whose provenance is more assured are also used in paraenetic texts without special introductory identification.[524]

Furthermore, the fourth argument would only be valid if no specific verbal parallel was reported to have been spoken by Jesus. The reason for similar teaching in the church's ethical tradition traces back to the fact that ecclesiastical paraenesis employs as one of its sources the sayings of the Jesus-tradition. Thus it can be affirmed with confidence that Jas. 5:12 and Mt. 5:34,37 trace back to a common source -- the teaching of Jesus.

Our final project is to discern if the prohibition of oaths in Jas. 5:12 or Mt. 5:33-37 has undergone development in the history of transmission. To accomplish this task we will attempt to recover the original wording of the saying of Jesus which is admittedly an effort with tentative conclusions.[525] Guelich[526] points out that both the Matthean premise (5:33) and the fourth antithesis (Mt. 5:34-37) consist of multiple elements. Mt. 5:33a is an assertive oath[527] dealing with honesty drawn from Lev. 19:12,[528] while 5:33b is a promissory oath pertaining to faithfulness to one's word taken from Ps. 50(49):14.[529] Guelich contends that Mt. 5:34a,37a corresponds to the assertive oath of 5:33a while Mt. 5:34b-36 offers several illustrations of promissory oaths as in the second half of the premise (5:33b).[530] We believe that Guelich is correct about which elements in the text correspond but incorrect in assigning the reason for this to the difference between assertive and promissory oaths. The purpose of the ὅτι clauses in Mt. 5:34b-36 is to demonstrate that certain oath formulas do not avoid God's name; therefore, these verses are not promissory oaths at all. Instead one must recognize that two divergent themes are intertwined in the Matthean passage, one advocating truth-telling instead of oaths (Mt. 5:34a, 37a) and the other protesting the use of seemingly innocent oaths such as those mentioning heaven, earth, or Jerusalem which in reality misuse the name of God (5:34b-36) as in Lev. 19:12 (5:33).

If this explanation is accepted, many of the additions in Matthew are explained, and Jas. 5:12 and Mt. 5:34a,37a correspond almost identically. The three ὅτι clauses in 34-35 were interposed to prove from the OT that God was being designated by these seemingly harmless oaths. Mt. 5:36 was then appended because its structure paralleled 34b-35 (swearing by something followed by a ὅτι clause). What remains are the three examples of oaths: neither by heaven, earth, nor Jerusalem. Guelich rejects this three-fold oath as original since James diverges in his grammatical construction and each of these oaths has counterparts within Jewish literature.[531] Yet we remain unconvinced that the parallel use of the oaths "by heaven and earth" in both Matthew and James is only a coin-

---

[524]Dibelius and Greeven, James, 251.

[525]Davids, James, 190 concludes that "priority cannot be established, especially since mixed forms were also known."

[526]Guelich, Sermon, 248-250,211-219.

[527]Lohmeyer, Matthäus, 132 and Klostermann, Matthäus-Evangelium, 46 wrongly contend that the first citation should be restricted to vows since the second citation surely refers to vows.

[528] "And you shall not swear by my name falsely, and so profane the name of your God: I am the Lord." Cf. Gundry, Matthew, 92; Gundry, OT in Matthew's Gospel, 108-109. Stendahl, School of Matthew, 137 believes that Matthew is employing catechetical material.

[529]Matthew changes "Most High" to "Lord" and "vows" to "oaths".

[530]Guelich, Sermon, 249.

[531]Ibid., 214-215.

cidence. It is more likely that we encounter here two independent witnesses to a common tradition. Both Jas. 5:12 and Mt. 5:34b-35 consist of three examples of oaths although the third instance in each case differs: Matthew mentions Jerusalem whereas James chooses a general all-embracing formula, "or with any other oath." In other passages in the Sermon on the Mount Jesus repeatedly employs two elements in his teaching: salt of the earth and light of the world (5:13-14); treasures upon earth vs. treasures in heaven (6:19-20); sound eye vs. evil eye (6:22-23); God vs. mammon (6:24); two gates (7:13-14); two trees (7:17-18); two types of lives (7:21); and two houses (7:24-27).[532] Therefore in the additions of Matthew and James we encounter a desire to include every possible situation where an oath might be used. James generalizes ("or with every other oath") while Matthew calls attention to two additional common Jewish oaths (by Jerusalem and by the hair upon one's head[533]).

It is more difficult to determine the originality of the final clause in the oath prohibition since the wording of Mt. 5:37b and Jas. 5:12d is so divergent. However, Guelich argues convincingly that the gospel conclusion contains essentially Matthean terms:

> *More than* (περισσόν) appears again in 5:47 in contrast to Luke 6:33. The *evil one* (τοῦ πονηροῦ) appears five other times in Matthew (5:39; 6:13, cf. Luke 11:4; 13:19, cf. Mark 4:15; 13:38; 5:44, with the plural) all in either the Sermon or the Parable Discourse.[534]

Therefore, Mt. 5:37b should be categorized as Matthean redaction. The eschatological threat in Jas. 5:12d, "that you may not fall under condemnation," is likewise more in accord with the well-recognized eschatological message of Jesus. The fact that the judgment is a favorite theme of James (2:4,12; 4:11-12; 5:9) might cause one to identify 5:12d as Jamesian redaction, yet an overruling piece of evidence is the resultant parallelism of structure when this clause is included in the original version.[535]

> Do not swear at all (negative prohibition)
> neither by heaven nor by earth (explanation)
> but let your yes be yes and your no no (positive affirmation)
> that you may not fall under judgment. (explanation)[536]

The most detailed attempts to reconstruct the *Traditionsgeschichte des Schwurverbots* have been undertaken by Minear and Strecker. For Minear the nucleus of the saying is Mt. 5:34a,37, "an oral tradition, highly memorable and widely current."[537] Stage I

---

[532]Jeremias, NT Theology, 14-20 (esp. the lists on pp. 15-16) has documented Jesus' preference for uttering two examples set in antithetic parallelism.

[533]See the quotations in n. 518.

[534]Guelich, Sermon, 218.

[535]Guelich, Sermon, 249 believes that the original statement included a premise (Mt. 5:33a) and antithesis (5:34a,37a) without explanatory clauses. Minear, "Yes and No," 3 suggests v. 34a and all of v. 37. George D. Kilpatrick, The Origins of the Gospel Acc. to St. Matthew, 20 concurs since then there is left a saying of approximately the same size as that of the other antithesis. Strecker, "Antithesen der Berpredigt," 63 concludes with us that James' ending is more original than Matthew's.

[536]The differences in the Greek text in the third line above are a result of Matthew's more Semitic construction. Allen, Matthew, 54 calls James' version a "graecising of the original". As we shall see, the church fathers preferred the more Greek phraseology found in James when they transmitted the gospel saying found in Matthew.

[537]Minear, "Yes and No," 3.

of the redaction would then be the addition of vv. 34b-35 giving three examples of oaths which illustrate the negative half of the original command. Stage II was the introduction of a fourth clause (5:36) illustrating both a different kind of oath and another reason for not swearing. Stage III resulted in the addition of 5:33 and the simultaneous fusing with the prohibitions of anger and lust.[538] Finally, stage IV of the redaction added the other three antitheses to establish an ethic for the church over against the synogogue. Minear defends Justin Martyr's account (1 Apol. 16:5) as nearest to the nucleus,[539] while Jas. 5:12 is located at stage I.[540] The evangelist Matthew comes upon the scene at stage IV and combines the antitheses together into their present format.[541]

Strecker's reconstruction[542] is noticeably incongruent with the explanation of Minear. He perceives a flow of traditions commencing with the criticism of an OT law and concluding with the formation of a new ecclesiastical law. The saying began as an antithetical oath prohibition (Mt. 5:33-34a) to which was attached like building blocks the following verses in the precise order they appear in Matthew. Thus step two is the addition of 5:34-35 without the grounds (ὅτι clauses) by the Hellenistic Jewish-Christian community. This is then augmented by 5:36 in the Hellenistic Gentile Christian community. Step four is accomplished by the adjoining of Mt. 5:37a in order to develop the paraenesis of the church, thus providing an ecclesiastical ordinance. Finally, before Matthew annexes the ὅτι clauses and places the saying within his gospel, 5:37b is appended making the redaction complete.

Our reconstruction differs from both of the above, but lies nearer to the history of traditions proposed by Minear. We believe that Jas. 5:12 without the additional comprehensive oath formula "or with any other oath" and his unique introduction "But above all, brethren" reiterates the saying of Jesus. The placing of this saying into the antithesis format with the other five antitheses of Mt. 5:21-48 should probably be assigned to Matthew's unique source M, assembled by the Jewish-Christian community to counter the claims of the synogogue.[543] Matthew then inserted into this antithesis vv. 34b-36 (except of course the phrases "either by heaven or by earth"). The ὅτι clauses were written to parallel

---

[538]Thus a trilogy of antitheses which Minear believes belongs to Matthew's source M.

[539]E.P. Sanders, The Tendency of the Synoptic Tradition, 57,67 believes that Justin used Matthew but intentionally omitted his examples of forbidden oaths since he "was interested only in the principle". Minear, "Yes and No," 1 unconvinced, states, "It is as credible that these illustrations should have been added during the development of oral tradition as that they should have been intentionally deleted during one of the redactional stages. Certainly, if one starts with the Justin version as the nucleus, he can readily explain the accretions." Because of the common use of two of these examples by Matthew and James, we agree more with Sanders.

[540]Minear, "Yes and No," 7.

[541]Ibid., 3.

[542]Strecker, "Antithesen der Berpredigt," 56f,69. Cf. also Gerhard Dautzenberg, "Ist das Schwurverbot Mt. 5, 33-37; Jak. 5, 12 ein Beispiel für die Torakritik Jesu?" BZ 25(1981): 48.

[543]The history of attempts to discover whether Matthew's antitheses are original is intricate and full of controversy (cf. the commentaries). The fact that each antithesis has a parallel without the antithesis form speaks against tracing the origin back to Jesus: first and second antitheses, Mt. 5:21-30=Did. 3:2-3; third, Mt. 5:31-32=Lk. 16:18; fourth, Mt. 5:33-37=Jas. 5:12; fifth, Mt. 5:38-42=Lk. 6:27-31; sixth, Mt. 5:43-48=Lk. 6:32-36. The grouping of these antitheses together probably indicates a polemic of the church against the synagogue. On the other hand, since Jesus is often involved in polemical battles in other gospel material, it is plausible that this saying was once uttered with a polemical thrust (Laws, James, 223) in a specific situation which is now impossible to recover.

the familiar *logion* of 5:36 and to reveal that these oaths used a designation equal to the name of God as prohibited in the reference to Lev. 19:12 in Mt. 5:33. Thus a triad of formulas each with a refutation backed by scripture (34b-35) came into being alongside 5:36 which Matthew adopted from the tradition.[544] Finally, Matthew reformulated the conclusion (5:37b) utilizing characteristic Matthean terminology. Thus in Matthew we encounter a combination of traditions whereas in Jas. 5:12 the saying of Jesus retains its original emphatic purity. The stages of development could be categorized as follows:

Stage I: The *logion* of Jesus roughly parallel to Jas. 5:12.

Stage II: M. The Jewish-Christian community places this saying into the antithesis format.

Stage III: To avoid the misuse of the name of God as in 5:33b, Matthew adds the ὅτι clauses according to the pattern of 5:36 which he also attaches. Then he replaces the eschatological conclusion with his own peculiar terminology in 5:37b.

Thus James preserves more of the original character of the saying than Matthew.[545] However, in the transmission of this saying in the first few centuries we encounter surprisingly a standard combination of these two versions.

Just 1 Apol.16:5[546]	Mt. 5:34-35,37	Jas. 5:12
	ἐγὼ δὲ λέγω ὑμῖν	πρὸ πάντων δέ, ...
μὴ ὀμόσητε ὅλως.	μὴ ὀμόσαι ὅλως·	μὴ ὀμνύετε
	μήτε ἐν τῷ οὐρανῷ,	μήτε τὸν οὐρανὸν
	ὅτι θρόνος ἐστὶν τοῦ	
	θεοῦ,[35] μήτε ἐν τῇ γῇ,	μήτε τὴν γῆν
	ὅτι ὑποπόδιόν ἐστιν τῶν	
	ποδῶν αὐτοῦ,	
	μήτε εἰς Ἱεροσόλυμα,	μήτε ἄλλον τινὰ ὅρκον·
	ὅτι πόλις ἐστὶν τοῦ	
	μεγάλου βασιλέυς ...	
ἔστω δὲ ὑμῶν	ἔστω δὲ ὁ λόγος ὑμῶν	ἤτω δὲ ὑμῶν
τὸ ναὶ ναί,	ναὶ ναί,	τὸ ναὶ ναὶ
καὶ τὸ οὒ οὔ·	οὒ οὔ·	καὶ τὸ οὒ οὔ,
τὸ δὲ περισσὸν τού-	τὸ δὲ περισσὸν τούτων	ἵνα μὴ ὑπὸ
των ἐκ τοῦ πονηροῦ.	ἐκ τοῦ πονηροῦ ἐστιν.	κρίσιν πέσητε.

Although Justin is purposely quoting a *logion* of the Lord (οὕτως παρεκελεύσατο where Christ is the subject), the second person plural verb in line 2 and the article in line 12 are

---

[544]Mt. 5:36 probably originated from a separate saying of Jesus similar to Mt. 23:16-22.

[545]Dibelius and Greeven, James, 251 characterize James' version as "the simpler, more unified, and ethically purer form." Cf. also Braun, Radikalismus, II: 80-81; Holtzmann, Synoptiker, 110; Klostermann, Matthäus-Evangelium, 47; Laws, James, 223; Lohmeyer, Matthäus, 131, n. 4; Shepherd, "James and Jesus," 47; Torrey, Four Gospels, 291. Others argue that Jas. 5:12 is based upon Matthew: Gryglewicz, "Jacques et Matthieu," 50-51; McNeile, Matthew, 67-68; Schlatter, Jakobus, 278; Schniewind, Matthäus, 66.

[546]From Basil L. Gildersleeve, The Apologies of Justin Martyr (New York: Harper, 1877), 16.

obviously closer to James than to Matthew. However, this does not entail that Justin is here dependent upon the Epistle of James since elements in lines 3, 11, and 14-15 are paralleled in Matthew rather than James.[547] Therefore 1 Apol. 16:5 is a harmonization of Mt. 5:34,37 and Jas. 5:12.[548] Since there are no other indications in the writings of Justin Martyr that he utilized the Epistle of James as source material, it is best to assume that there is a common, probably oral, paraenetic tradition underlying both James and Justin.[549] Evidence from other Greek Fathers indicates that this harmonization, which possibly goes directly back to Justin, grew and became widespread in the church.

1) Clem. Alex., Strom. 5,99,1[550] and 7,67,5[551] ἔστω ὑμῶν τὸ ναὶ ναὶ καὶ τὸ οὒ οὔ.

2) Epiphanius, Adversus Haereses 19,6,21[552] καὶ πάλιν ἐν τῷ εὐαγγελίῳ λέγοντος· μὴ ὀμνύναι μήτε τὸν οὐρανὸν μήτε τὴν γῆν μήτε ἕτερον τινὰ ὅρκον, ἀλλ' ἤτω ὑμῶν τὸ ναὶ ναὶ καὶ τὸ οὒ οὔ. τὸ περισσότερον γὰρ τούτων ἐκ τοῦ πονηροῦ ὑπάρχει.

3) Eusebius, Demonstratio Evangelica 3,3,103[553] ἔστω γὰρ ὑμῶν τὸ ναὶ ναί, τὸ οὒ οὔ.

4) Eusebius, Commentary on Psalms 14:4[554] ἐφ' ᾧ βεβασοῦνται τὸ ναὶ ναὶ καὶ τὸ οὒ οὔ.

5) Pseudo-Clementine Homilies 19,2,4[555] ἔστω ὑμῶν τὸ ναὶ ναὶ καὶ τὸ οὒ οὔ, τὸ δὲ περισσὸν τούτων ἐκ τοῦ πονηροῦ ἐστιν.

6) Pseudo-Clementine Homilies 3,55,1[556] ἔστω ὑμῶν τὸ ναὶ ναί, τὸ οὒ οὔ· τὸ γὰρ περισσὸν τούτων ἐκ τοῦ πονηροῦ ἐστιν.

7) Cyril of Alex., De Adoratione et Veritate VI: 212[557] ἔστω ὑμῶν τὸ ναὶ ναὶ καὶ τὸ οὒ οὔ· τὸ δὲ περισσὸν τούτων ἐκ τοῦ διαβόλου ἐστίν.

8) Gregory of Nyssa, In Canticle of Canticles, Homily XIII[558] ἔστω δὲ ὑμῶν ὁ λόγος τὸ ναὶ ναὶ καὶ τὸ οὒ οὔ· τὸ δὲ περισσότερον τούτων ἐκ τοῦ διαβόλου ἐστίν.

9) Constitutiones Apostolorum 5,12,6[559] εἶναι δὲ τὸ ναὶ ναὶ καὶ τὸ οὒ οὔ ... καὶ τὸ τούτων περισσὸν τοῦ πονηροῦ εἶναι.

---

[547]Cf. Bellinzoni, Sayings of Jesus in Justin, 65.

[548]Ibid. 66; Schneider, s.v. ὀμνύω, TDNT, V: 182, n. 60. Minear, "Yes and No," 7 contends, on the other hand, that "neither appears acquainted with the order of the teachings in Mt."

[549]Cf. Dibelius and Greeven, James, 250, n. 52. This oral tradition could possibly have had its geographical headquarters in Rome where Justin carried out his apologetic career and where James either made his home or wrote an epistle to. Cf. ch. 6, section 3.2.

[550]Stählin, GCS 52, p. 391, line 19.

[551]Stählin, GCS 17,2, p. 48, line 24.

[552]Karl Holl, GCS 25, p. 223. This is a more obvious attempt to harmonize Mt. 5:34-37 and Jas. 5:12. Cf. Bellinzoni, Sayings of Jesus in Justin, 67, n. 1.

[553]Ivar A. Heikel, GCS 23, p. 109, lines 6-7.

[554]MPG, XXIII, 152.

[555]Bernhard Rehm, GCS 42, p. 253, lines 24-25.

[556]Ibid., p. 77, lines 1-2.

[557]MPG, LXVIII, 472.

[558]MPG, XLIV, 1040. In Cyril and Gregory we encounter an interpretation which reads τοῦ πονηροῦ as masculine, i.e. the devil.

[559]Didascalia et Constitutiones Apostolorum, ed. Funk, p. 269, lines 8ff.

10) Joannis Chrysostomi, Homiliae in Matthaeum XVII: 229[560] ἔστω δὲ ὑμῖν τὸ ναὶ ναὶ καὶ τὸ οὒ οὔ· τὸ δὲ περισσὸν τούτων ἐκ τοῦ πονηροῦ ἐστι.

These references indicate that when the Greek Fathers quoted the Lord's saying, they interpreted the *ναὶ ναί, οὒ οὔ* of Matthew to mean τὸ ναὶ ναὶ καὶ τὸ οὒ οὔ. The harmonization of the Matthean and Jamesian versions demonstrates that the Church Fathers traced both back to a saying of Jesus. However, as Laws states, "This amount of difference between the two in so brief a passage makes a literary dependence of either on the other unlikely, and it is probable that they therefore represent independent crystallisations [*sic*] into literary form of the same oral tradition."[561] We will discuss the relationship between the Epistle of James and the Gospel of Matthew in more detail in the following chapter. For now it is sufficient to report that here James and Matthew are two distinct witnesses to the same *verbum Christi*. James transmits "a shorter, more classical form and Matthew a longer, more Semitic one."[562] With this discussion of Jas. 5:12 and Mt. 5:33-37 we terminate our discussion of the twenty most significant parallels between the Epistle of James and the Synoptic tradition.

---

[560]MPG, LVII, 261. There is also a reference to this standard phrase in the Coptic Gnostic writing, The Books of Jeu 43. Cf. Carl Schmidt, GCS 45, p. 305. "He charged him not to swear falsely, nor even to swear at all ... neither to slander falsely nor defame, but let their yes be yes and their no be no." Translation in Dibelius and Greeven, James, 250, n. 53.

[561]Laws, James, 223. Cf. Dibelius and Greeven, James, 250.

[562]Davids, James, 190. We disagree with David's next statement that priority cannot be established.

Chapter 4

THE SYNOPTIC GOSPELS AND THE EPISTLE OF JAMES

Many scholars regularly call attention to the relationship between the Epistle of James and the Gospel of Matthew, in particular the Sermon on the Mount.[1] Bunsen has even entitled the Epistle of James the "Bergpredigt der apostolischen Episteln".[2] Although one can validly claim that James predominantly employs Jesus-material from the Sermon on the Mount/Plain,[3] the parallels with Luke stand as visibly prominent as those of Matthew. We have discerned about an equal number of allusions to the particular material in Luke as to the unique sayings in Matthew.[4] Therefore, James does not draw exclusively from any particular strand of the gospel writings. In this chapter we will review the exegetical evidence indicating a dependence upon the teaching of Matthew and counter these claims with data which point to an independent transmission of the sayings of Jesus. We will first discuss the conclusions of Shepherd and Gryglewicz who have most vigorously contended for a Matthean source for the Epistle of James and then investigate topically the similar teachings of James and Matthew.

1.1 Shepherd[5] maintains that each of James' eight discourses[6] is build around material from the Jesus-tradition in Matthew. Since these parallels are located in both the M and Q traditions of Matthew, Shepherd argues that the finished gospel rather than a preMatthean source is employed by James. From the interconnections between James and Matthew, Shepherd draws specific conclusions about the church where the Epistle of James was composed. He explains that "it was composed in a church where Matthew, and Matthew alone, was accepted as the Gospel, insofar as 'gospel' was understood as a written transcript of traditions about Jesus and his teaching."[7] Furthermore, since the letters of Ignatius of Antioch, the Didache, and the Epistle of James all "use the Gospel freely, and use it as an authoritative guide in a way that they use no other Gospel known to us,"[8]

---

[1]Adamson, James, 21; Brückner, "Kritik Jakobusbriefes," 537; Henry W. Fulford, "James," A Dictionary of Christ and the Gospels, 847; Kistemaker, Gospels in Current Study, 92; Robinson, Redating, 125; Schmid, Biblische Theologie, II: 364; Rudolph V.G. Tasker, The Old Testament in the New Testament, 124,132; Williams, John and James, 85-86.

[2]Christian C. Bunsen, Vollständiges Bibelwerk für die Gemeinde, VIII: 588. Marcus Dods, An Introduction to the New Testament, 191 calls James "the Sermon on the Mount among the New Testament Epistles".

[3]According to our findings all of James' deliberate allusions to *logia* of Jesus correspond to passages in the Sermon on the Mount/Plain except for Jas. 4:10 which alludes to the generalizing conclusion, "whoever humbles himself will be exalted," found in various contexts in the gospels (Mt. 23:12; Lk. 14:11; 18: 14b). Davids, "James and Jesus," 78, n. 16 says, "Twenty-nine out of 45 parallels come from the Sermon tradition.

[4]Cf. ch. 7, section 1.1 for a summary of our results.

[5]Shepherd, "James and Matthew," 42.

[6]For these discourses see above, p. 57.

[7]Shepherd, "James and Matthew," 49. Shepherd (42-43) does admit two areas of convergence with Luke: 1) the length of the draught at the time of Elijah (three and a half years); and 2) James' closer reflection of the Lucan beatitude about the rich and the use of the Lucan woe upon those who laugh.

[8]Shepherd, "James and Matthew," 49.

Shepherd contends that all these documents originated in Syria. To explain the inexact rendering of Matthew's wording, Shepherd asserts that James had only heard the Gospel of Matthew read in worship services and did not have the manuscript at his disposal as he wrote the epistle.[9]

1.2 Against this hypothesis our results indicate that James did not structure each section of his epistle around a macarism or gnomic saying either specifically drawn from the Gospel of Matthew or supported by gospel parallels in the immediate context. In fact, none of the central sayings which Shepherd discovers are allusions to the Gospel of Matthew.[10] In Shepherd's list of pivotal sayings only Jas. 2:5 is a legitimate allusion to the gospels, and this verse is closer to Luke's gospel than to Matthew's. Furthermore, it is specifically in a section unique to Luke's gospel, the woes of Lk. 6:24-26, where we encounter two important parallels to James' exhortations concerning those who weep (4:9) and the rich (5:1). Nor does each section in James contain material from the Gospel of Matthew in the context surrounding the central saying as Shepherd insists. It is not true as Shepherd contends that 1) the section 1:2-18 is a commentary upon the petition in the Lord's Prayer, "Lead us not into temptation" or the Q saying on prayer, "Ask and it shall be given unto you" (p. 44); or 2) that underneath the whole section of 1:19-27 stands the gospel parable found in two Q sayings of Jesus: Mt. 7:21; Lk. 6:46 and Mt. 7:24; Lk. 6:49 (p. 45); or 3) that the discourse of James on the tongue (3:1-12) is a homiletic illustration of Mt. 12:36 (p. 46). With statements such as these Shepherd attempts to prove that Matthean parallels to James "relate to every single section of the Epistle, and to almost every major theme."[11] However, the gospel parallels do not possess the controlling function that Shepherd assigns to them. The section denouncing the worldly merchants (4:13-17) contains no discernible Jesus-saying, and Shepherd does not even claim that his central macarism (4:17) is Jesus-material. Certain sayings can more appropriately be placed in other categories rather than be identified as sayings of Jesus. There is certainly no dominical saying in James' discourse at 2:14-26 where the background is instead a theological discussion on faith and works in the early church. The metaphor of the fig tree yielding olives in 3:12 is an illustration from the broader Mediterranean world rather than from Jesus' saying in Lk. 6:44/ Mt. 7:16. Jas. 3:18 is better identified as a Jewish proverb than a dominical saying. Thus we have already listed four important pericopes lacking the presence of *logia* of Jesus. Instead allusions to the sayings of Jesus are sprinkled randomly throughout the epistle. To be sure, Jesus' sayings are important to the epistle, but they are always situated in the background, wedded to ecclesiastical teaching material or combined with traditional Jewish wisdom. They are never utilized to provide an authoritative source to ground James' teaching as with the OT quotations. Furthermore, contrary to the lengthy list of gospel parallels which one frequently encounters in an introduction to the Epistle of James, only a rather limited number of entries can be established. In most cases James transmits the paraenetic teaching of the church which had already incorporated certain emphases from Jesus' preaching into its content.

Shepherd's conclusions supporting a geographical tie between James, Matthew, the Didache, and Ignatius' epistles are also misleading. Shepherd follows in the footsteps of Streeter who championed the hypothesis that both Ignatius and the Didache utilized Matthew as their gospel.[12] Recently Glover has raised weighty objections to the supposed

---

[9]Ibid., 47.

[10]Shepherd's central gnomic sayings are Jas. 1:12,25; 2:5 or 2:10; 2:20 or 2:26; 3:2; 4:4,17; 5:11.

[11]Shepherd, "James and Matthew," 47.

[12]Burnett H. Streeter, The Four Gospels: A Study of Origins, 505-511. Cf. also Basil C. Butler, "The Literary Relations of Didache ch. XVI," JThS 11(1960): 265-283; Frederick F. Bruce, "Eschatology in the Apostolic Fathers," The Heritage of the Early Church, Festschrift for Georges V. Florovsky (Rome: Pontifical Institute, 1973), 84; F.E. Vokes, The Riddle of the Didache (London, 1938), 111.

connection between the Didache and Matthew. In the introduction to his article Glover states the problem by raising these questions:

> If Matthew was the gospel the Didachist knew and quoted, why should he so often support Luke's readings against it? Or if it is a witness to Luke also, why should he support Justin Martyr against the text of both Synoptics?[13]

After investigating 26 possible allusions to the Gospel of Matthew, Glover concludes that "the material shared by the Didache and Matthew reached their authors through different channels."[14] Therefore, "it seems necessary to sever the link that is supposed to bind the Didache and Matthew to the same place of origin, namely Syria."[15] Glover's denial of literary dependence upon Matthew is substantiated by a growing majority of scholars.[16] However, the common employment of proto-Matthean material by Ignatius[17] and the Didache does in our opinion point to a similar geographical provenance. The Epistle of James, however, demonstrates closer ties with other writings of the Apostolic Fathers, specifically 1 Clement and the Shepherd of Hermas,[18] than with the Didache and the epistles of Ignatius. Therefore, it is doubtful that the Epistle of James originated in a geographical region where Matthew's gospel was the sole authority. The hypothetical nature of Shepherd's thesis is obvious when one realizes that others like von Soden[19] and more hesitantly Feine[20]have opted for the opposite thesis that the origin and geographical location of James and Luke's special source L belong together. Although many authors have paraded forth the parallels between James and Matthew, others[21] have championed the ties with Luke's gospel. In fact, Streeter himself in another of his writings distances James from Matthew: "The verbal reminiscenses in James of sayings of Christ are also on the whole nearer to Luke than Matthew."[22] This fact indicates that a direct use of Matthew's gospel by James as well as a geographical relationship of origin are unsatisfactory hypotheses.

2.0 Shepherd's thesis has been stated in even starker terms by Gryglewicz who argues for a literary dependence upon the written Gospel of Matthew and not just upon an oral reading in worship services. He detects clues for this conclusion in James' repetition

---

[13]Richard Glover, "The Didache's Quotations and the Synoptic Gospels," NTS 5(1958-1959): 12.

[14]Ibid., 29.

[15]Ibid., 27.

[16]Jean P. Audet, La Didache. Instructions des Apôtres, 198; Paul Drews, "Untersuchungen zur Didache," ZNW 5(1904): 68-73; John S. Kloppenborg, "Didache 16:6-8 and Special Matthaean Tradition," ZNW 70(1978): 67; Helmut Köster, Synoptische Überlieferung bei den Apostolischen Vätern, 239ff; Bentley Layton, "The Sources, Date, and Transmission of Didache," HTR 61(1968): 345.

[17]Cf. Richard Bauckham, "The Study of Gospel Traditions Outside the Canonical Gospels: Problems and Prospects," Gospel Perspectives 5: 386-387; Joost Smit Sibinga, "Ignatius and Matthew," NovT 8(1966): 281; Hagner, "Sayings of Jesus in Apostolic Fathers," 239-240; On a scale of A to D the study, NT in Apostolic Fathers, 138 rates dependence upon Matthew as B and upon Luke as D. Köster, Synoptische Überlieferung, 61 contends that Ignatius is closer to Matthew because Matthew transmits the ethical tradition of the church.

[18]Cf. Appendix II, sections 7.0 and 8.0.

[19]Hermann von Soden, "Der Jakobusbrief," JrPrTh 10(1884): 171.

[20]Feine, Jakobusbrief, 76-77.

[21]Feine, Moffatt, Nösgen, Schenkel, von Soden.

[22]Streeter, Primitive Chruch, 193.

of certain characteristic expressions found only in Matthew and in the inexact manner in which certain words fit into James' context.[23]

2.1 With regard to verbal expressions Gryglewicz lists the following similarities:[24]

1) κόσμος used in a pejorative sense (Jas. 1:27; 4:4; Mt. 18:7).
2) νεκρός employed allegorically (Jas. 2:26; Mt. 8:22).
3) ἐκκλησία referring to the church (Jas. 5:14; Mt. 16:18).
4) The expression διαλογισμοὶ πονηροί (Jas. 2:4; Mt. 15:19) rather than οἱ διαλογισμοὶ οἱ κακοὶ employed in Mk. 7:21.
5) The only two commandments of the Decalogue which occur in the Sermon on the Mount are mentioned by James (Jas. 2:11; Mt. 5:21-30).
6) James' expression εἴ τις δοκεῖ (1:26) is without a doubt borrowed from the text of Matthew since the word δοκεῖν appears there frequently (Mt. 10x; Mk. 1x; Lk.-Acts 6x; Paul 10x; Jas. 1x).
7) James' wording on the themes of prayer (1:6), titles (3:1), humiliation (4:10), and oaths (5:12) derives from Matthew since the gospel parallels for these texts are found in material peculiar to Matthew.

2.2 With regard to similar subject matter Gryglewicz divides the parallels into three categories:

A. Similar subjects with a different manner of treatment (pp. 37-40).
B. Similar subject matter where no certain dependence can be established since it is impossible to determine who profited from the writing of the other (pp. 40-43).
C. Examples of direct dependence of James upon the Gospel of Matthew (pp. 43-56).

Since only the third category relates directly to the concerns of this study, we will concentrate our attention upon the following list of themes which Gryglewicz insists betray a dependence of James upon Matthew.

1) The assurance of answered prayer (Jas. 1:5; Mt. 7:7) and an explanation for unanswered prayer (Jas. 4:3; Mt. 7:8). (p. 44)
Gryglewicz believes that the passive expression δοθήσεται αὐτῷ indicates that one author has repeated the text of the other. Since Matthew consistently employs the passive voice to refrain from using the name of God, James must be repeating an expression in Matthew.

2) Faith and doubt (Jas. 1:6; Mt. 21:21-23). (p. 45)
The expression ἐν πίστει indicates James' use of Matthew since this phrase is intricately worked into the context of Matthew but is not necessary and even hinders the clarity of the thought of James. Both Matthew and James mention "doubt" immediately after the word "faith" whereas in Luke these two concepts are no longer in close proximity.

3) Hearing and doing (Jas. 1:22-25; Mt. 7:24-26). (pp. 46-47)
The more fitting expression according to Jamesian vocabulary (4:11) as well as traditional usage (1 Mac. 2:67; Rom. 2:13) would have been ποιητὴς νόμου; this expression is even transported into the text by codex C and miniscules 88, 915, 467, 242, 1518, and 378. Therefore, James' choice of ποιητὴς λόγου at 1:22 is without a doubt based upon his source, Mt. 7:24.

---

[23]Gryglewicz, "Jacques et Matthieu," 54.
[24]Ibid., 35. We will critique the use of common vocabulary in section 3.1.

4) From the mouth come both blessings and curses (Jas. 3:10; Mt. 15:18-19). (p. 47)
στόματος and ἐξέρχεται are found in both James and Matthew while in the Markan parallel (7:21-22) the word mouth is omitted and ἐκπορεύονται is employed.

5) A fig tree metaphor (Jas. 3:12; Mt. 7:16). (pp. 47-48)
Both authors offer examples drawn from nature which are placed in the form of a question in order to express a contradiction. The illustration is not well adopted to James' argumentation since he is inserting a verbum Christi drawn from Matthew's gospel.

6) Humility and exaltation (Jas. 4:10; Mt. 23:12). (pp. 48-49)

7) Storing up treasures (Jas. 5:2-3; Mt. 6:19-21). (pp. 49-50)
Three Greek words are repeated by each author (θησαυρίζω, σής, βρῶσις), but specific dependence upon Matthew is demonstrated by James' acceptance of the imprecise statement that gold and silver rust.

8) The prohibition of oaths (Jas. 5:12; Mt. 5:33-37). (pp. 50-52)
James has summed up the additional examples in Matthew by adding the phrase "or with any other oath". James' redaction has changed the Semitic expressions (the dative with an oath transformed to the accusative and ἔστω to ἤτω) and rendered Matthew's expression more comprehensible by adding the article τό.

9) Forgiveness of sins (Jas. 5:15; Mt. 12:32). (pp. 52-54)
The expression ἀφεθήσεται αὐτῷ is chosen in both James and Matthew whereas in the Markan source (3:29) οὐκ ἔχει ἄφεσιν is utilized. Jas. 5:15b employs the plural object ἁμαρτίας with a singular verb ἀφεθήσεται, a grammatical discrepancy which indicates that James must be citing source material. He appears to have deliberately left this expression in the form found in Matthew to substantiate his teaching with the very words of Jesus.

10) Clean hands (Jas. 4:7; Mt. 5:30; 18:8). (p. 55)
James softens a sharp word of Christ by referring to the cleansing of hands rather than their excision.

2.3 The weaknesses of Gryglewicz's arguments come to light when it is observed that in each of the ten instances above, arguments of equal or greater weight can be adduced against dependence of James upon Matthew. Regarding answered prayer, the wording of Mt. 7:7-11 and Lk. 11:9-13 is so close that it is impossible to determine if James employed one gospel rather than the other. In both Matthew and Luke the passive voice is employed (δοθήσεται) -- a fact not given due attention by Gryglewicz. Secondly, whereas Gryglewicz contends that the addition of the concept "faith" at Jas. 1:6 is an intrusion from a Matthean source, one can just as easily find the solution in James' use of the genre of paraenesis where the interconnection of subject matter is not always precise and logical but based instead upon catchwords. James slides easily from speaking about asking and receiving in prayer to the subject of asking in faith. Likewise in Jas. 4:3 the flow of thought is from asking and receiving to the subject matter of "how to ask". This time the positive advice of asking in faith is replaced by the negative requirement of not asking wrongly to serve one's selfish desires. In each case a saying of Jesus is followed by a Jamesian qualification. Therefore James is not consciously alluding to a new saying of Jesus at 1:6 and much less to a particular gospel. The different analogy following this exhortation (doubting compared with waves of the sea) reinforces the difference from the gospels where faith is compared to the moving of mountains. Finally the Markan omission of the phrase "if you have faith and doubt not"[25] does not indicate that James followed Matthew's

[25]Cf. also Shepherd, "James and Matthew," 44.

rendering since Mark includes the phrase μὴ διακριθῇ later in the sentence. Matthew has simplified Mark's sentence structure by placing the two concepts of faith and doubt together at the beginning of the conditional sentence rather than in separate clauses as in Mark. Although the two concepts stand in closer proximity in the word order of Matthew, this fact alone does not warrant the singling out of one particular gospel as the source behind the Epistle of James. These arguments are, of course, totally unnecessary if, as we propose, Jas. 1:6 is qualifying the saying of Jesus found in 1:5 rather than attaching an additional allusion to a Jesus *logion* about prayer.[26]

Gryglewicz argues that the use of λόγου instead of νόμου at Jas. 1:22 indicates that James borrowed phraseology from Matthew. However, if James was purposely transmitting a term from Mt. 7:24, would he not have preserved it in the plural form in which he found it? The presence of the term λόγος is easier explained by appealing to the context of James itself. The mentioning of "the word of truth" (λόγῳ ἀληθείας) at 1:18 and "the implanted word" (ἔμφυτον λόγον) at 1:21 provides the transition to the expressions "doers of the word" (ποιηταὶ λόγου) and "hearer of the word" (ἀκροατὴς λόγου) in the following verses.[27] Yet even if Gryglewicz were correct in postulating the presence of a gospel saying, it would be impossible to distinguish between Matthew and Luke since both choose the plural form of λόγος. Finally, contrary to Gryglewicz's supposition, the imagery employed within the examples does not converge. Admittedly both speak about a man (ἀνδρί), but the situations described are so totally different (James: looking into a mirror; Matthew: two houses in a storm) that the use of the common term ἀνδρί plays no significance.

The connection of Jas. 3:10 with Mt. 15:18-19 is not a very widely recognized parallel.[28] In the gospels the emphasis is placed upon the evil qualities that flow from their source in the heart. In James, on the other hand, both good and evil expressions (blessings and curses) erupt from the mouth rather than the heart. In the gospels the theme is inner defilement whereas in James the impossibility of good and evil proceeding from the same source is stressed. With these differences in mind Gryglewicz's word sequence parallel, στόματος ... ἐξέρχεται, proves to be a superficial finding. Mark's preference for the verb ἐκπορεύομαι (Mt. 6x; Mk. 11x; Lk. 3x; Jn. 2x) need not lead one to the assumption that James is dependent upon Matthew. The more likely solution is that Matthew wishes to vary the terminology after the phrase τὸ ἐκπορευόμενα in 15:18 so that two identical verbs are not needlessly repeated.

In the same context of James (3:12) Gryglewicz discerns another allusion to Matthew's gospel since James' illustration is not well adapted to the point he desires to emphasize. Gryglewicz is correct in asserting that James shifts his use of imagery at 3:12. In 3:10-11 James employs two illustrations demonstrating the impossibilty of one source producing two opposite results: a mouth producing blessing and cursing and a spring pouring forth both fresh and brackish water. Then in 3:12 the imagery shifts to examples which display the impossibility of one type of object producing a totally different sort: a fig tree yielding olives; a grapevine, figs; or salt water, fresh. This shift, however, cannot be traced back to James' use of Matthew since in James both the plants and the fruit are given positive connotations (a fig tree yielding olives or a grapevine, figs), whereas in the gospels good fruit (grapes, figs) and negatively conceived plants (thorns, thistles) are contrasted. Furthermore, only one word, σῦκα, is common to both passages. The shift in James' imagery is probably due to the quotation of source material, but that source is not Matthew but rather everyday wisdom sayings common to areas around the Mediterranean Sea where such crops are grown.[29]

Gryglewicz fails to supply any grounds supporting a connection of Jas. 4:10 with Mt. 23:12 rather than Lk. 14:11; 18:14b. In fact he does not even inform the reader of the

---

[26]Cf. ch. 3, section 2.5.
[27]Cf. above, pp. 84-85.
[28]Schlatter and Gryglewicz are the only two authors who recognize this parallel.
[29]Cf. above, p. 101 for examples.

presence of Lucan parallels. We agree that a saying of Jesus is being alluded to here, but to limit the similarities to the Matthean formulation is presumptuous. The variation in forms between Matthew and Luke supplies no clues that one version is utilized rather than the other.[30]

We agree with Gryglewicz that Jas. 5:2-3a is closer to the Matthean parallel (6:19-21) than the Lucan (12:33b-34) since both James and Matthew choose the verb form θησαυρίζω rather than the noun θησαυρός found in Luke. Yet the convergence is not so exact as to admit dependence upon the gospel. The themes of James and Matthew are similar, but the vocabulary diverges in form (σητόβρωτα vs. σής; ἰός vs. βρῶσις). Gryglewicz contends that the imprecise statement that gold and silver rust illustrates that James profited from the text of Matthew. However, the tarnishing of gold and silver was already described as rusting in earlier Jewish literature.[31] Furthermore, it is doubtful whether Matthew himself is speaking about rust since βρῶσις more likely designates the presence of worms.[32] A dependence upon Matthew is therefore excluded.

Since Jesus' prohibition of oaths is not quoted by Luke, Gryglewicz contends that Jas. 5:12 is based upon Matthew's gospel. Yet certain stark divergencies between James and Matthew[33] have caused some exegetes to assert that "the wording of the positive ruling is sufficiently dissimilar as to give a different meaning to the whole."[34] Gryglewicz fails to allow these differences in word choice to influence his conclusions about the source of this passage. The fact that Justin Martyr (1 Apol. 16:5) harmonized James and Matthew supports our conclusion that there are two separate traditions of the same *logion* of Jesus.

Gryglewicz believes that the singular verb (ἀφεθήσεται) referring back to the plural noun (ἁμαρτίας) offers a clue that source material is visible at Jas. 5:15. He locates the source in Mt. 12:32 since Matthew has exactly the same wording (ἀφεθήσεται αὐτῷ) while Mark reads οὐκ ἔχει ἄφεσιν. However, it is totally unnecessary to compare Matthew with Mark since Mt. 12:32 represents Q at this point in the narrative. Therefore Lk. 12:10a also coincides with the wording of this phrase from Jas. 5:15 although in 10b Luke omits the pronoun ἀυτῷ. Gryglewicz mentions Lk. 12:10 in a footnote[35] but fails to allow its parallel wording to affect his argument and conclusion. Furthermore, in the textual tradition the singular verb in Jas. 5:15 in only a problem for later MSS; ἀφεθήσεται is amended to ἀφεθήσονται only in Greek Biblical documents of the ninth century or later.[36] Among modern commentators this apparent grammatical discrepancy is scarcely even mentioned.[37] The presence of the singular verb might be explained by the supposition that James is referring to the fact of committing sins rather than to the sins themselves. But in all probability James is merely utilizing traditional Biblical phraseology[38] as is his custom

---

[30]Cf. ch. 3, section 4.5.

[31]Cf. above, p. 122 for references.

[32]Cf. above, pp. 124-125. It is difficult to understand how Gryglewicz (p. 49) can read "worms" in Matthew (*le ver)* and "rust" in James (*la rouille)* and still maintain that James employed Matthew as a source.

[33]Cf. above, pp. 136-137,140-141.

[34]Laws, James, 13. Cf. the arguments above, pp. 137-140.

[35]Gryglewicz, "Jacques et Matthieu," 53, n. 56.

[36]P, 69, 945, 1241, 1505, 1739, 1852, 2298, 2495. However, John Chrysostom (died 407) and a part of the Old Latin witnesses with the Vulgate appear to follow this reading.

[37]Dibelius, Mußner, Laws, and Davids fail to mention it as a problem. Maybe it is in the back of Davids' mind when he states that the perfect tense (πεποιηκώς) perhaps demonstrates that the person is in a "state of guilt".

[38]ἀφεθήσεται αὐτοῖς Lev. 4:20; Num. 15:25; ἀφεθήσεται αὐτῷ Lev. 4:26,31,35; 5:6,10,13,16,18; 6:6 (5:26 MT); 19:22; Num. 15:28A. The same form ἁμαρτίας is employed in Lev. 4:26,35; 5:10,13 but as a genitive singular. Therefore it must be admitted that a singular verb is not used in the OT with a plural referent.

throughout the epistle.[39] Therefore, the hypotheses that James has utilized a gospel source or has unintentionally included a grammatical error are inferior solutions. The above arguments are probably unnecessary, however, since there is only slim evidence pointing to a gospel allusion at Jas. 5:15. Since James is definitely not thinking about the sin against the Holy Spirit[40] mentioned in Mt. 12:32 and Lk. 12:10, the verbal contacts are only coincidental and should receive little attention.[41]

Gryglewicz offers absolutely no evidence that Mt. 5:30 and 18:8 are the source of Jas. 4:7 rather than the parallel statement in Mk. 9:43. The fact that Matthew repeats this saying about cutting off the hand on two occasions rather than the single occurrence in Mark is no indication that Matthew is the source. Moreover, the cleansing of hands in Jas. 4:8 recalls standard OT purification language[42] rather than Christ's word about amputating bodily members. The parallelism in Jas. 4:8 between "cleanse your hands, you sinners" and "purify your hearts, you men of double mind" argues against any connection with the dominical saying since the heart would not likely be excised in a time of temptation.

These counter arguments have demonstrated that Gryglewicz's conclusions are built upon insufficient evidence and at times glaring omissions of material opposing his claims. Repeatedly Gryglewicz himself admits that the common themes of James and Matthew are developed in an independent fashion.[43] Should this in itself not indicate that James' allusions to Matthean parallels are not as striking as Gryglewicz believes?

3.0 Having sufficiently refuted the claims of Shepherd and Gryglewicz, the two most convinced proponents of a Matthean source, we will now attempt a more systematic discussion of the relationship between James and Matthew. We will first discuss common vocabulary, then proceed to analyze their use of beatitudes and imagery, and finally comment upon the common themes of the law, righteousness, faith and works, perfection, and wealth and poverty.

3.1 Gryglewicz has attempted to detect the presence of Matthean wording within the Epistle of James by identifying phraseology which is out of step with James' context or normal usage.[44] He will admit only one Lucan vocabulary parallel (Jas. 4:14; Lk. 12:47). Additional vocabulary characteristic of both James and Matthew is mentioned by other authors: δικαιοσύνη (Jas. 1:20; 3:18; Mt. 3:15; 5:6,10,20; 6:1,33; 21:32), τέλειος (Jas. 1:4,17, 27; 3:2; Mt. 5:48; 19:21), and παρουσία (Jas. 5:7; Mt. 24:3,27, 37,39).[45] Discarding this list of Matthean parallels, Feine[46] demonstrates that distinctive Lucan vocabulary is paralleled in the Epistle of James:

1) ἀποτελεῖν occurs only in the NT at Lk. 13:32; Jas. 1:15.
2) σήμερον καὶ αὔριον only at Lk. 13:32,33; Jas. 4:13.

---

[39]Cf. above, pp. 53-54.

[40]James only references to πνεῦμα (2:26; 4:5) are to the human spirit. Cf. ch. 2, section 2.4.

[41]Only four other authors witness to this parallel: the exaggerated lists of Mayor and Schlatter as well as the catalog of Chaine which Gryglewicz and Feuillet have adopted.

[42]Clean hands and a pure heart are OT virtues (Ps. 24:4).

[43]Gryglewicz, "Jacques et Matthieu," 44,45,48,49,53,54.

[44]Cf. above, pp. 152-153.

[45]Laws, James, 12.

[46]Feine, Jakobusbrief, 76. Karl F. Nösgen, "Der Ursprung und die Entstehung des dritten Evangeliums," ThSKr (1880): 109 adds several minor verbal parallels to this list: ἀκαταστασία, ἀνάπτειν, ἀτιμάζειν, δαπανᾶν, ἐπιβλέπειν, ἐπέρχεσθαι, ἐπιστρέφειν, ἐφήμερος, ἡδούν, κατέρχεσθαι, κλύδων, λείπειν, παρακύπτειν, πορνεία, σοφία, ὑποδέχεσθαι. Cf. also tables 1 and 2 in Adamson, James: Man and Message, 147-149.

3) βραδύς only at Lk. 24:25; Jas. 1:19.
4) γελᾶν and γέλως only at Lk. 6:21,25; Jas. 4:9.
5) πενθήσετε καὶ κλαύσετε (Lk. 6:25) and ταλαιπωρήσατε καὶ πενθήσατε καὶ κλαύσατε (Jas. 4:9).
6) ἔλεος ποιεῖν only at Lk. 1:72; 10:37; Jas. 2:13.
7) ἐσθής only at Lk. 23:11; Acts 1:10; 10:13; 12:21; Jas. 2:2,3.
8) λαμπρός tied together with ἐσθής only in Lk. 23:11; Acts 10:30; Jas. 2:2,3.
9) μακαρίζειν only at Lk. 1:48; Jas. 5:11.
10) οἰκτίρμων only at Lk. 6:36; Jas. 5:11.
11) ταπείνωσις only at Lk. 1:48; Jas. 1:10; Phil 3:21 and the citation in Acts 8:33.
12) ὕψος only at Lk. 1:78; 24:49; Jas. 1:9 except for Rev. 21:16; Eph. 3:18; 4:8.

In our estimation the only important verbal similarities found above are 4) and 5) which point in each case to an allusion to the woe section of the Lucan Sermon on the Plain (6:24-26). The other vocabulary parallels located in Matthew and Luke tend to cancel each other out so that no great significance should be attached to either list. Furthermore, the similarities of terminology can all be explained by other solutions than that of dependence upon a gospel source. With regard to Matthew, for instance, δικαιοσύνη and τελείος have their roots in OT (LXX) vocabulary, ἐκκλησία would be encountered in any early Christian document, κόσμος is regularly employed in a pejorative sense in the NT, and παρουσία is a standard term in Christian eschatology.[47] Statistically, we discover that of the vocabulary found exclusively in James and the Synoptic gospels, 22 words are in common with Luke-Acts whereas a total of 9 coincide with the other gospels.[48] According to Adamson's findings 80 percent of the words peculiar to and characteristic of James and the Synoptic gospels are found in Luke.[49] Therefore verbal contacts with the Gospel of Matthew should not be emphasized in the manner in which Gryglewicz and others promote their significance.

3.2 The presence of beatitudes similar to those found in the gospel tradition (Mt. 5:1-11; Lk. 6:20-23) has often been discerned in the Epistle of James.[50] Riesenfeld has voiced strong support for James' knowledge of the Matthean form of the beatitudes:

> Of the eight Matthaean beatitudes, four are to be found in the Epistle of James and in the same order, a fact, by the way, which cannot be accidental. In any case the author of the epistle presupposes parts of the Sermon on the Mount as clearly well known to his readers. Indeed, we can establish that the verbal form of the sayings of Jesus which James presupposes is that of M and not of Lk.[51]

Riesenfeld is referring here to the parallels: Jas. 2:5 = Mt. 5:3,5; 2:13 = Mt. 5:7; 3:18 = Mt. 5:9; and 5:10-11a = Mt. 5:11-12a. However, Riesenfeld's definition of an allusion to a gospel saying is too broad; we have established that Jas. 2:13; 3:18; and 5:10-11 are not

---

[47]Laws, James, 13. With regard to παρουσία the Epistle of James omits Matthew's distinctive eschatological vocabulary: παλιγγενεσία (19:28) and συντελεία τοῦ αἰῶνος (24:3; 28:20; 13:40,49).

[48]Cf. Davids, James, 49; James B. Adamson, An Inductive Approach to the Epistle of James, 293-295.

[49]Adamson, James: Man and Message, 150-151. The words common to James and Luke are predominantly from peculiarly Lucan material -- 25 out of 37 instances or almost 70 percent.

[50]Recently Kugelman, James and Jude, 9 declared, "The promise of the Beatitudes is echoed again and again in the Epistle."

[51]Harold Riesenfeld, The Gospel Tradition and its Beginnings, 15.

allusions to specific *verba Christi* but only contain a common emphasis on certain themes (mercy in Jas. 2:13, righteousness and peace in 3:18, endurance in 5:10-11) and the coincidental use of vocabulary (μακαρίζω and προφήτης in Jas. 5:10-11). Furthermore, with regard to the only remaining allusion (Jas. 2:5), even Shepherd admits that this verse is closer in thought to the Lucan parallel. He states,

> In James as in Luke, the "poor" are such in the literal sense, and woes are pronounced upon their opposites, the "rich". James does not emphasize Matthew's religious distinction of "poor in spirit".[52]

Finally, Riesenfeld's contention that the order of the sayings coincides with Matthew's sequence of beatitudes is far-fetched. Riesenfeld omits from his discussion the often cited parallel Jas. 1:2=Mt. 5:11-12a[53] as well as Shepherd's additional references to beatitudes about meekness (3:13=Mt. 5:5), purity of heart (4:8=Mt. 5:8), and mourning (4:9=Mt. 5:4)[54] since the acceptance of these parallels would not fit his scheme. Therefore, Riesenfeld's thesis is completely unfounded. The only valid allusions to the beatitudes and woes of the Sermon on the Mount/Plain find their parallels in Luke (Jas. 2:5=Lk. 6:20; 4:9=Lk. 6:25; 5:1=Lk. 6:24).[55]

Shepherd attempts to establish that James was familiar with more than just the beatitudes common to both Luke and Matthew without insisting like Riesenfeld that a similar order of beatitudes is evident in James and Matthew. He suggests that "James knew a group of Beatitudes about the poor, the mourners, the merciful, and the afflicted, and possibly also macarisms upon the meek, the pure in heart, and the peacemakers."[56] Thus seven out of the eight Matthean blessing statements would be enumerated by James. Yet we have argued in chapter 3 that such themes as mercy, endurance in trials, meekness, purity, and peace originate in Jewish wisdom and/or the ethical paraenetic teaching of the church. Some authors even claim that Matthew's peculiar blessing statements trace back to the paraenetic teaching tradition of the church influenced by the themes of Jewish wisdom and Jesus' preaching.[57] Therefore there is no substantial evidence to validate the claim that James employed any of the macarisms peculiar to Matthew.

3.3 A second affinity of style within the teaching of James and Jesus is the employment of similar metaphors, analogies, and pictures.[58] First, both of these artistic orators use imagery drawn from the sea to stress practical moral lessons. James employs the tossing action of the waves to describe doubt (1:6), the huge seafaring ships overcoming violent winds with only a small rudder (3:4) as well as the contrast between salt and fresh water to expound upon the ambiguous power of the tongue (3:12), and the mist that forms from the sea and vanishes in the sunlight to describe the brevity of life (4:14). Jesus too treats the

---

[52]Shepherd, "James and Matthew," 43.

[53]This parallel has as much support as Jas. 5:10-11=Mt. 5:11-12.

[54]Shepherd, "James and Matthew," 44.

[55]Shepherd, ibid., 43 recognizes these three parallels with Luke and states that with regard to the gospel beatitudes, they "show closer affinities with the Lukan than with the Matthean form."

[56]Ibid., 44.

[57]Cf. Gundry, Matthew, 69-72.

[58]Christian F. Schmid, Biblical Theology of the New Testament, 366 states, "The form, also, of James' Epistle bears an evident similarity to the Sermon on the Mount in its sententious language and figurative style, especially in the abundance of images derived from nature and mankind." Haslehurst, "The Fifth Gospel," 101 remarks, "There is hardly a common object of the countryside that our Lord does not use to illustrate some great spiritual truth, but St. James does the same."

subject of faith by mentioning the sea[59] (either by a mountain cast into the sea at Mk. 11:23; Mt. 21:21 or a mulberry tree planted in the sea at Lk. 17:6), and the depth of the sea becomes a warning against leading astray any vulnerable disciple (Mt. 18:6; cf. Lk. 17:1-2).

Secondly, the agricultural imagery of sowing and reaping is common to both James and Jesus. James employs sowing and reaping together in Jas. 3:18 to advocate peace[60] as well as planting alone in 1:21 and the harvest alone in 5:4. Jesus' well-known parable of the sower (Mk. 4:1-9 par.) has been surrounded by other parables of sowing and reaping both in Mark (parable of the growing grain at 4:26-29 and the mustard seed at 4:30-34) and Matthew (parable of the tares at 13:24-30). In other contexts Jesus draws attention to the birds who neither sow nor reap (Mt. 6:26; Lk. 12:24) to portray God's care for his people, the farmer who reaps where he has not sown (Mt. 25:24,26) to picture God, and the eschatological harvest (Mt. 9:37-38; cf. Jn. 4:35-38) to issue a call for workers.

Other pictorial depictions beyond the category of nature imagery are commonly shared by James and Jesus. The new age is described as an eschatological door in Jas. 5:9 as well as throughout the gospels (Mt. 24:33b; 25:10; Mk. 13:29b; Lk. 13:24-25).[61] When occupations are mentioned, farm workers (Jas. 5:4; Mt. 20:1-16) or merchants (Jas. 4:13; Mt. 13:45; 25:16; Lk. 19:13) are often pictured. The standard description of the uncared for person is one without clothes and daily bread (Jas. 2:15; Mt. 25:36,41; 6:25 par.).[62] Healing and purifying procedures are also analogous: anointing with oil (Jas. 5:14; Mk. 6:13) and the washing of hands (Jas. 4:8; Mk. 7:1-4 par.).[63]

Another common feature is the repeated reference to OT paradigms. James supports his arguments by calling attention to such figures as Abraham (2:21-23), Rahab (2:25), the OT prophets (5:10), Job (5:11), and Elijah (5:17-18). In like manner Jesus refers to the lives of the prophets (Mt. 5:10 par.; 23:29,37 par.), David (Mk. 2:25 par.), Solomon (Mt. 6:29 par.; 12:42 par.), Elijah (Lk. 4:25-26), and Jonah (Mt. 12:39-41 par.). This, of course, is not unexpected since wherever the OT served as a holy book of instruction and edification, the recollection of heroes of faith has always been popular.[64]

Not only do we encounter equivalent imagery in the teaching of James and Jesus, but they also employ images to describe similar topics. Both resort to metaphors to illustrate the disciple who is a hearer but not a doer: Jesus contrasts two houses built on sand and rock (Mt. 7:24-27 par.) while James pictures the forgetting of an image in a mirror (1:24). The thought that small items (like faith or the tongue) work enormous results is conveyed by a reference to a mustard seed by Jesus (Mk. 4:30-32 par.) and to a horse's bit (3:3), the rudder of a ship (3:4), and a tiny spark (3:5) by James. To underline the impossibility of certain phenomena James illustrates from a spring spewing forth both fresh and brackish water and a fig tree yielding olives or a grapevine, figs (3:11-12), whereas Jesus highlights the fact that a good tree cannot produce evil fruit (Mt. 7:17 par.; 12:33) and thorns and thistles cannot bring forth grapes and figs (Mt. 7:16 par.). It is especially the condemnation of the rich that invited the utilization of metaphors and picturesque language. James contrasts a rich worshiper dressed in expensive clothing and gold earrings with a shabily adorned, poor disciple (2:1-4). Jesus states that a rich disciple is more peculiar than a camel passing through a needle's eye (Mk. 10:25 par.). James predicts that the wealthy will be scorched to death like the flower withering from the heat (1:11), while rot, moths, and rust will consume their stored-up assets (5:2-3a). Through the medium of parable Jesus likewise describes the downfall of the wealthy (Lk. 12:15-21; 16:19-31; Mk. 4:19 par.).

---

[59]Cf. above, pp. 75-76 for differences.
[60]Cf. above, ch. 3, section 4.1.
[61]Cf. Appendix I, section 3.7.
[62]Cf. Appendix I, section 4.7.
[63]Cf. Appendix I, sections 4.12 and 4.8.
[64]Cf. Heb. 11 and 1 Cl. 9-12,17-18.

There have been various explanations for this similar imagery in the exhortations of James and Jesus. James has been perceived as an intimate disciple of the earthly Jesus taking over his examples and mode of speaking.[65] The use of the gospels themselves could also be postulated. However, the divergencies in vocabulary and exact imagery point rather in the direction of corresponding experiences within a similar environment or a mutual affiliation with the religious expressions and cultural patterns of the Jewish faith through their religious upbringing.

3.4 Heading the list of themes where James and Matthew stand in the same theological camp is the concept of the law. Of all the NT writers the closest perspective to that of Matthew is without a doubt the Epistle of James. Both understand the teaching of the church as a new Christianized law (Mt. 5:17-20; Jas. 2:8-11; 4:11-12).[66] Both speak about the law as the way to perfection.[67] In both the law of love is, on the one hand, set alongside the other commandments which together constitute the law and, on the other hand, is given special recognition as the most important of the commandments, one which fulfils the whole law.[68] Both James and Matthew, therefore, recognize a new law summarized by Jesus without setting aside the old moral law of the OT. The gospel and the law are thus linked together for both authors. The gospel of the kingdom (Mt. 4:23; 9:35; 24:14) does not relax even the least of the commandments (5:19) for Matthew; instead, the word is completed by doing the commands of the Master (7:21). In James too the mentioning of the gospel as "the implanted word which is able to save your souls" (1:21) is followed immediately by a command to "be doers of the word", an expression which could just as easily mean "be doers of the law".[69]

Both authors emphasize the internal dimensions of the law written upon the character of a person. Matthew internalizes the commands against murder and adultery so that they become matters of the heart dealing with anger (5:22) and lust (5:28). James' reference to "the law of liberty" (1:25; 2:12) demonstrates his stress on the inward voluntariness of the law.[70] Since an attitude of mercy is for Matthew one of the weightier matters of the law (23:33), he twice repeats the ordinance of Hos. 6:6, "I desire mercy and not sacrifice" (9:13; 12:7). James, likewise, emphasizes mercy in the conclusion to his presentation of the commandments, "For judgment is without mercy to one who has shown no mercy; yet mercy triumphs over judgment" (2:13). The wisdom from above is similarly full of mercy (3:17) and other inner qualities which together constitute God's wise will for the community. Every time the law is mentioned in James it is specifically the moral law that is implied. Matthew, likewise, minimizes a strict outward observation of the ceremonial law. Although the sabbath is still observed in Matthew's community (24:20; 12:1-14) and the Jewish food laws still appear to be in force (Mk. 7:19b is omitted),[71] yet against any outward legalism Matthew calls for mercy rather than rigid slavery to this whole system of ceremonial ordinances.[72]

---

[65]Adamson, James: Man and Message, 221 says, "James speaks as Jesus speaks rather than as Jesus is spoken about."

[66]Cf. Davies, Setting, 401; Furnish, Love Command, 177. Oscar Seitz, "James and the Law," SE 2: 485 disagrees, contending that James is simply referring to the law of Moses without overtones of a new law.

[67]Hoppe, Hintergrund Jakobusbriefes, 128. Cf. also Ulrich Luck, Die Vollkommenheitsforderung der Bergpredigt, 36.

[68]Cf. above, pp. 94-95.

[69]Several MSS even substitute νόμου for λόγου: C[2], 88, 621, 1067, 1852. Cf. above, pp. 85-86.

[70]Cooper, "Prayer: a Study in Matthew and James," 275. Cf. above, pp. 95-96.

[71]Cf. Barth, "Matthew's Understanding of the Law," 89-92. But see also p. 163.

[72]Barth, ibid., 91 explains that "Matthew retains the ceremonial law, but it has undergone a reassessment under Christian motives."

Yet these similarities need not lead us to the conclusion that James was familiar with the Gospel of Matthew either in oral or written form since no specific verse to verse parallels can be identified. Nor are we forced to admit that these two documents stem from the same geographical region. The varying polemical stance in each document argues against this conclusion. Notably in chapters 5:20-6:18 and 23 Matthew polemicizes against the synagogue and calls the Pharisees to account for their alteration and defacing of the law. The Epistle of James, on the other hand, "contains no such explicit attack, nor can it be seen to be implicit in his writing at any point."[73] Within the Christian community itself Matthew is struggling against an antinomianism[74] (7:21-23; 24:10-11) which has taken on different dimensions than the libertinism which James is afraid will ensue if an overzealous "Paulinism" is not balanced with his concept of the relationship between faith and works.[75] They are "engaged in different debates".[76] Whereas "Matthew opposes a group who appeal in support of their libertinism to the fact that Christ has abolished the law,"[77] James resists a libertine view of justification. Whereas Matthew's opponents rely on their *charismata* (7:22), James' adversaries "appeal to their πίστις in support of their neglect of works."[78] Finally, the order of the commands in Jas. 2:11 follows that of Mk. 10:19, Lk. 18:20, and Rom. 13:9, whereas Mt. 19:18 and 5:21,27 follow the reverse order found in the MT.[79] Therefore, the matching outlook of James and Matthew on the subject of the law must not be accounted for with theories of literary source and common geographical origin, but rather in the similar Jewish-Christian background of the authors.[80]

3.5 The coinciding content given to the concept of righteousness is also striking. Jas. 1:20 emphasizes the fact that human anger can never work the righteousness of God. Similarly in Matthew's first example of the righteousness which exceeds that of the scribes and Pharisees (5:20), all anger will be punished (5:22) since it does not meet the standards of God's superior righteousness. Jas. 3:18 explains that righteousness will result when the way of peace is followed. Likewise, in the beatitudes of Matthew the theme of righteousness (5:6,10) is closely connected with such attributes as meekness, mercy, purity, and

---

[73]Laws, James, 15. Cf. also Robinson, Redating, 120.

[74]Barth, "Matthew's Understanding of the Law," 160,163 labels the opponents of both James and Matthew as libertines or antinomians. James E. Davison, "*Anomia* and the Question of an Antinomian Polemic in Matthew," JBL 104(1985): 628,630,634-635 argues that laxness (not practicing the law) and not antinomianism (being against the law in theory) is the problem, but both are present in Matthew with 5:16-19 against antinomianism and 7:15-23; 24:11-12 against laxness. Davison (618-619,632-634) is correct, however, in asserting that ἀνομία is used in a general, nonspecific sense.

[75]Cf. Appendix II, section 3.3 for James' relationship to Paul. There might not have been a specific group of ultra-Paulinist libertines which Matthew opposed since there is an absence of any Pauline contacts in Matthew (cf. Kilpatrick, Origins of Matthew, 130-131), but at least the fear of such a group is evident in the polemic of 5:17-19 against abolishing the law or relaxing the commandments. For the various opinions see Guelich, Sermon, 391,393 and Barth, "Matthew's Understanding of the Law," 164.

[76]Laws, James, 15.

[77]Barth, "Matthew's Understanding of the Law," 164.

[78]Ibid., 162. From these differences we should not conclude, as Barth does, that Matthew's opponents were not ultra-Paulinists. The antagonists were the same; disparate polemics occurred in different geographical locations.

[79]Cf. ch. 2, section 2.2.

[80]Benjamin W. Bacon, "Jesus and the Law," JBL 47(1928): 203 states that whereas Mark is generally conceded to exhibit the most radical point of view on his representation of Jesus' action and utterance in resistance to Jewish legislation, Matthew exhibits the most conservative or Jewish-Christian point of view.

peacemaking. This righteousness is to be pursued with the same intensity as the goal of the kingdom (6:33), since the kingdom of heaven is manifested through such attributes. A third reference in Jas. 2:23 discloses that James' view of righteousness involves the performance of religious duties. Human action is emphasized in contrast to Pauline theology where righteousness is first of all an imputed gift of God.[81] Similarly in Matthew human performance stands in the foreground.[82] Mt. 12:37 teaches that "by your words you will be justified, and by your words you will be condemned," and at Mt. 16:1 the RSV even translates the word δικαιοσύνη by the term piety: "Beware of practicing your piety before men." There is no doubt that James and Matthew possess a uniform understanding of righteousness whose degree of congruity is unparalleled by other NT writers.

3.6 In view of the definition of righteousness which both James and Matthew employ, one would expect that their understanding of the concepts good works and perfection would also be similar, and this is indeed the case. For both, faith is recognized through works (Jas. 2:18,22) as a tree by its fruit (Mt. 7:16-20). Words alone are not sufficient to fulfil the divine will (Jas. 2:15-16), and hearing must always be completed by doing (1:22-25). Likewise for Matthew it is not enough to say "Lord, Lord" (7:21); only the house built upon hearing and doing will endure the storm (7:24-27). Matthew's criticism of the Pharisees is that their teaching does not result in doing (23:3); Jesus' disciples, on the other hand, are to teach the world by doing good works (5:16). Shepherd[83] argues from this similar perspective that James follows the lead of Matthew especially since the Matthean additions to the Q statement, "And every one who hears <u>these, my words</u>, and does them" (Mt. 7:26; Lk. 6:49) is close to Jas. 1:23, "If anyone is a hearer of the <u>word</u> and not a doer." Yet we have already shown that James' terminology can be traced instead to his own context, and that the illustrations which follow bear no resemblance to each other.[84] Furthermore, there is no evidence that the antinomians of Matthew "appealed to πίστις in support of their neglect of works in the way the libertines of the Epistle of James did."[85] Therefore, the best explanation for the coinciding perspective and the similar definition of terms is the common Jewish-Christian background of James and Matthew rather than the use of a literary source.

3.7 The relationship between faith and perfection in James and Matthew is parallel to their understanding of faith and works. Abraham is held up as an example for James' audience since his faith was perfected by his works (2:22). In Jas. 1:3-4 faith, after producing the work of steadfastness, results in perfection. The goal of James' exhortations is that his recipients may be perfect and complete (1:4b), perfect people able to bridle the whole body (3:2). By calling for perfection he is not placing an imperfect attainable standard over against a higher ideal standard; there is no elitism in James. Nor is the central thrust of the term maturity as in Paul. Instead as Hort explains, "It expresses the simplest idea of complete goodness, disconnected from the philosophical idea of a τέλος."[86] James' concern is mainly ethical. Complete goodness is pictured as faith and works marching together (2:22),

---

[81]Cf. above, pp. 77-78.

[82]Schweizer, <u>Matthew</u>, 142-143 explains, "Matthew uses the term to include almsgiving, prayer, and fasting, i.e. the good works that, according to Jewish belief, go beyond the demands of the Law, earn a special reward, atone for transgressions of the Law, or even benefit others at the Last Judgment if they exceed what is required of the person himself."

[83]Shepherd, "James and Matthew," 45.

[84]Cf. above, pp. 85-86. Furthermore, the plural form in Matthew is not followed by James.

[85]Cf. Barth, "Matthew's Understanding of the Law," 162.

[86]Hort, <u>James</u>, 6.

as a person completely in charge of all the evil desires within (3:2). To help his people in this task God has given completely good gifts (1:17) along with a completely good law of liberty (1:25). In turn a disciple must strive to complete the work of endurance (1:4) and practice (τελέω) the love command (2:8).

In Matthew as in James the theme of perfection[87] is closely linked with doing the complete will of God.[88] In Mt. 5:48 the exhortation, "You, therefore, must be perfect, as your heavenly Father is perfect," is a call to put into practice all that has been said about the greater righteousness in 5:21-47.[89] Although the rich young man of Mt. 19:17-22 states that he has observed all the ordinances of the law from his youth, Jesus' call to perfection (19:21), which the young man is unable to follow (19:22), points out that his faith was not being transferred into action. The term "wholeness" probably best translates the force of τέλειος.[90] Therefore, the rich man's inability to be perfect reveals that he was unable with his whole being to be obedient to the will of God. This intimate connection between wholeness and perfection in both authors is verified by the fact that James places the terms τέλειος and ὁλόκληροι (1:4) right beside each other. For both James and Matthew perfection is "a positive and attainable object"[91] rather than something only possible for the elite.[92] The sole difference between the two lies in the fact that for Matthew perfection denotes "something more", an extra-righteousness which is the mark of the Christian congregation,[93] whereas James nowhere contrasts a Jewish and Christian view of perfection or righteousness.

3.8 The thematic similarites with Matthew vanish when we discuss the subject of wealth and poverty. Even Shepherd, a chief proponent of a Matthean source, admits that James' perspective on this subject stands closer to that of Luke.[94] The Matthean expression "poor in spirit" (5:3) "brings out more forcefully the ethical and spiritual association of poverty,"[95] while in Luke we encounter hostility to the rich *per se* (1:53; 6:24; 12:16-21; 16:19-25). This picture coincides with the portrait of James' community where riches and poverty are spoken about in a literal sense.[96] The Christian community must be warned not

---

[87]The theme of perfection is unique to Matthew's gospel and, therefore, Matthean redaction. Cf. Piper, Love Your Enemies, 63 and his footnote for other author's opinions.

[88]Cf. Schweizer, Matthew, 135; Hoppe, Hindergrund Jakobusbriefes, 139. Guelich, Sermon, 235-236 contends that Matthew emphasizes the new relationship between God and humanity as the means of perfection and righteousness. Righteousness is a gift of God (Mt. 5:6), yet Matthew's emphasis is elsewhere -- upon human conduct as the arena where perfection is displayed.

[89]Cf. above, p. 67.

[90]Guelich, Sermon, 234-235. Proof that this meaning was contemporary with the time of Jesus and the early church is shown by its frequent use at Qumran: CD 2:15; 1QM 7:5; 14:7; 1QH 1:36; 22 times in 1QS. Cf. Luck, Vollkommenheitsforderung, 30-38 for references within wisdom literature.

[91]DuPlessis, Perfection in NT, 173.

[92]Regarding James see Laws, James, 54. Regarding Matthew see Barth, "Matthew's Understanding of the Law," 96, n. 3 and Edward J. Yarnold, "Τέλειος in St. Matthew's Gospel," SE, 4: 271.

[93]Barth, "Matthew's Understanding of the Law," 97-98.

[94]Shepherd, "James and Matthew," 43.

[95]Marshall, Luke, 250.

[96]Laws, James, 103 explains that James is steering a middle course between the Matthean and Lucan versions of Jesus' promise of the kingdom to the poor. But she is mistaken in contending that Luke believes poverty will be rewarded *per se*. "Poor" in Lk. 6:20 includes a dimension of faith as witnessed in the intertestamental tie between poor and pious (cf. Dibelius and Greeven, James, 84). It cannot be deduced from the rewarding of

to follow in the footsteps of the rich since they will surely pass away (Jas. 1:10-11; 5:1-6). Nor is the church to seek the benevolence of the wealthy by showing partiality on their behalf (2:1-4) since God places himself on the side of the poor (2:5-7).[97] The community of James is struggling against rich oppressors and the corrupting evils of wealth, whereas the Gospel of Matthew according to Kilpatrick[98] precludes an affluent community. Evidence pointing in this direction include: 1) Matthew's application of the beatitude to "the poor in spirit"; and 2) the omission of the woes against the rich.[99] The divergencies on the theme of wealth and poverty sufficiently disclaim any view of a geographical connection of origin between James and Matthew.

3.9 An extended list of minor themes are often compiled to stress the coinciding emphases of James and Matthew.[100] Both contain warnings about the judgment to come (Jas. 2:12-13; 4:11-12; 5:9,12; Mt. 5:21; 10:15; 11:22,24; 12:36 etc), Gehenna (Jas. 3:6; Mt. 5:22,29,30; 10:28; 18:9; 23:15,33), and the *parousia*[101] (Jas. 5:7f; Mt. 24:3,27,37,39), yet Matthew's distinctive eschatological terms are never appropriated by James.[102] Although both define sin not merely as overt acts but also as thoughts and words (Jas. 1:19,20,26; 3:1-12; Mt. 5:22,28), the vocabulary widely diverges with James choosing ἁμαρτία throughout (1:15; 2:9; 4:17; 5:15,16,20) while Matthew employs ἁμαρτίαι, ἁμαρτήματα, παραπτώματα, and ὀφειλήματα. Both warn against anxiety over the future (Jas. 4:14f; Mt. 6:34), but James discerns the problem as overconfidence whereas Matthew cautions against over-anxiety. Both exhort against seeking the status and title of a teacher (Jas. 3:1; Mt. 23:8), yet James nowhere reflects Matthew's specific accusation against those coveting the Jewish title "Rabbi".[103] Both share a confidence in answered prayer when asked in faith[104] (Jas. 1:5-6; Mt. 7:7-11), but in Matthew "good gifts" are received whereas in James the gift of wisdom is promised. Wisdom for James is practical wisdom (1:5; 3:17), whereas in Matthew wisdom is often personified (11:19;[105] 11:28-30[106]). Both advocate speaking the truth rather than using oaths, but certain added features in Matthew's text point to emphases which are peculiarly Matthean.[107] Frequently a lengthly list of Jamesian themes are enumerated as particular parallels to Matthew's Sermon on the Mount,[108] yet the use-

---

Lazarus in Lk. 16:19-25 that it happened "only because of his misfortunes" as Laws contends. Details of Lazarus' life are omitted to concentrate on the contrast with the rich man.

[97]Cf. above, pp. 128-130.

[98]Kilpatrick, Origins of Matthew, 125f.

[99]Cf. Streeter, Primitive Church, 193. Gundry, Matthew, 68ff demonstrates how Matthew revises the beatitudes by means of the woes.

[100]Cf. Schmid, "Comparison of James with St. Matthew," Theology of NT, 365-366; Mayor, James, xliii-xliv.

[101]André Feuillet, "Le sens du mot Parousie dans l' Évangile de Matthieu. Comparaison entre Matth. XXIV et Jac. V, 1-11," Studies in the Background of the New Testament and it Eschatology, 261-280 contends that the historical judgment of Israel was forefront in the mind of both James and Matthew. However, in order to come to this conclusion, he unconvincingly presupposes that 1) Mt. 24:27 and 24:30 should be distinguished chronologically and 2) the righteous one in Jas. 5:6 is identical with Jesus.

[102]Cf. above, n. 45. For similarities with Lucan eschatology see Davids, James, 49.

[103]Cf. Laws, James, 13.

[104]Cf. Cooper, "Prayer: a Study in Matthew and James," 271.

[105]Cf. BAGD, s.v. σοφία, 760.4.

[106]Cf. Schweizer, Matthew, 268.

[107]Cf. above, pp. 140-141. Matthew's attack on Jewish casuistry is also unique (23:16-22).

[108]Schmid, Theology of NT, 365-366 refers to joy in temptation (Jas. 1:2; Mt. 5:12), the warning against wrath (Jas. 1:19-20; Mt. 5:22), the commendation of gentleness

lessness of such compilations in determining a literary source is substantiated by parallel lists which draw attention to Lucan complements.[109] The only legitimate use of these parallels would be to validate the claim that James and Jesus share many common themes. These correlative emphases are explained by the fact that "the parallels which exist between Matthew and James are in sayings which could readily be absorbed into the general stock of Christian ethical teaching."[110] James appropriated the themes of Jesus' preaching through the ecclesiastical paraenetic tradition which both he and Matthew possessed. It is unnecessary to assume contact with one or more of the Synoptic gospels.

4.0 James preserves independently of Matthew and Luke the memory of a tradition of the *logia* of Jesus.[111] This is authenticated primarily by the fact that in James' conscious allusions to the sayings of Jesus, there is no single tradition that James consistently reproduces. Instead the form of these sayings is influenced by particular Jamesian emphases as well as the paraenetic teaching of the early church.[112] The commonalities between James and Luke can be explained by their corporate knowledge of the teachings of Jesus and their opposition to the same social evils.[113] The parallels with Matthew center primarily upon their common theological understanding of such themes as the law, righteousness, perfection, and the relationship between faith and works. The differences in their theology of wealth, Matthew's peculiar emphasis with regard to oaths, and the divergent use of beatitude themes and eschatological vocabulary substantiate our conclusion of independent traditions. It is highly plausible that James and Matthew appropriated their similar theological views through their upbringing in Judaism and their experience in the Jewish-Christian community. Furthermore, the similar placing of loose sayings (often connected by catchwords) into lengthy discourses of *logia* by Matthew and extended paraenetic paragraphs by James accounts for the fact that the Sermon on the Mount is often said to be the primary source of parallels between James and the gospels. Therefore, we cannot accept any hypothesis which attempts to prove either oral (Shepherd) or written (Gryglewicz) dependence of James upon one of the gospels. Neither does the theory of geographical origin explain both the distinct similarities and yet the obvious divergencies of the Epistle of James with the Synoptic gospels.[114] The Epistle of James embodies an independent tradition of the teachings of Jesus embedded in Jewish concepts and background and intricately absorbed into the ethical teaching of the early church.

(Jas. 1:21; 3:13; Mt. 5:41), the taming of the tongue (Jas. 1:26; Mt. 5:22), the judgment on the unmerciful (Jas. 2:13; Mt. 7:2), friendship with the world being enmity with God (Jas. 4:4; Mt. 6:24), dependence upon God (Jas. 4:13-16; Mt. 6:25), and the unresisting spirit of the righteous (Jas. 5:6; Mt. 5:39ff).

[109]Feine, Jakobusbrief, 75-76 enumerates the following: the advantages of benevolence (Lk. 12:33; 16:1-6; Jas. 2:15-17; 1:27; 3:17), warnings against making plans without seeking the will of God (Lk. 12:16-21; Jas. 4:13-15), the view that the famine in Elijah's time lasted three and a half years (Lk. 4:25; Jas. 5:17), the enthusiastic striving after the lost (Lk. 15:1-32; 19:10; 23:43; Jas. 5:19-20), the teaching that God requires more of some than others (Lk. 12:48; Jas. 3:1), the evil of knowledgeable sinning (Lk. 12:47; Jas. 4:17), and God's goodness in giving (Lk. 11:13; Jas. 1:17).

[110]Laws, James, 14.

[111]Cf. Davids, "James and Jesus," 68.

[112]Cf. below, pp. 222-223,226.

[113]Cf. Knowling, James, xxii; R. Leconte, Les Epitres Catholiques, 12; Laws, James, 12-15; Davids, James, 49; and Williams, John and James, 86.

[114]Cf. above, pp. 152,162,165 and Laws, James, 15.

Chapter 5

HYPOTHESES ACCOUNTING FOR THE FORM OF THE SAYINGS OF JESUS IN THE EPISTLE OF JAMES

1.0 We have assembled compelling evidence (chapter 4) that the form of the sayings of Jesus in the Epistle of James is not dependent upon the Matthean or Lucan traditions. Moreover, we have already established (chapters 2 and 3) that James does not cite the sayings of Jesus in the same manner as his OT quotations i.e. with introductory formulations and almost verbatim transcription for the purpose of grounding his arguments in the recognized authority of scripture.[1] Neither is the authority of Jesus himself appealed to as when Paul and the Apostolic Fathers introduce allusions to dominical sayings with an introductory formula. The examples of sayings of Jesus in the Epistle of James must likewise be distinguished from the use of Jesus' *logia* in the genre of gospel where the transmission of the words and works of Jesus is the stated objective. James' allusions to sayings of Jesus are more comparable to the manner in which OT allusions are treated. On several occasions[2] James repeats phraseology from the OT, not to appeal to an outside authority, but rather to transmit the accepted ethical teachings in traditional language. No *formulae citandi* are employed in the OT allusions, and the wording of the saying is molded to fit the context within the new body of literature as well as the specific purposes of the author. These same characteristics typify the ethical exhortations reminiscent of the teaching of Jesus. Where are we to seek a solution to this peculiarity of James?[3]

The Postulation of Progressive Stages in the Transmission of the Sayings of Jesus

2.1 Kittel has concluded that the solution lies in the postulation of progressive stages in the transmission of the sayings of the Jesus-tradition. He perceives the end product of this process in the writings of Justin Martyr and the later church fathers who often quote Jesus' sayings as scripture[4] or at least introduce citations as dominical sayings with all the authority that this implied.[5] The beginning of this process is supposedly illustrated in the Epistle of James where only allusions without any introductory formulations are encountered. In between these two periods Kittel deduces a second stage which clearly progresses from an early employment of allusions to a later use of citations. For the most part Paul employs only allusions to the Jesus-tradition in a manner similar to James though occasionally he prefaces a *verbum Christi* with a *formula citandi*.[6] On the other hand, the

---

[1]The quoting of the sayings of Jesus as scripture begins in the middle of the second century (Rudolf Bultmann, Theology of the New Testament, II: 140).

[2]Cf. ch. 2, sections 3.1-3.6.

[3]Some commentators believe that the similarities and divergencies with the form of the sayings in the gospels is explained by the personal memory of Jesus' brother, James of Jerusalem, who as a disciple of the earthly Jesus reproduced what he had heard and took over his mode of speaking. We have discarded this thesis since there is no scriptural evidence that Jesus' brothers were close to his earthly ministry until after the resurrection (Mk. 3:21,31; Jn. 7:5; Acts 1:14; 1 Cor. 15:7). Cf. ch. 1, section 3.1.

[4]Just., Dial. 100:1; 103:6,8; 104:1; 105:6; 106:3,4; 107:1.

[5]Just., 1 Apol. 15:1,8,9,10; 16:1,5,6,9; Dial. 17:3,4; 35:3,7 etc.

[6]1 Cor. 7:10 is the clearest example and the only one mentioned by Kittel, "Der geschichtliche Ort," 93.

Apostolic Fathers regularly quote the sayings of Jesus with an introductory formula and only seldom allude to dominical sayings in the manner of the Epistle of James.[7] Thus one encounters according to Kittel an increasing utilization of citations and a decreasing of the free, loose employment of Jesus' words in the form of mere allusions. In this process the Epistle of James is "ein besonders anschauliches und echtes Beispiel dieser früher Form."[8]

In addition to appealing to these progressive stages, Kittel calls attention to signs which indicate that the Epistle of James was written at an early date. He specifically refers to the strong eschatological expectations in the Epistle of James (pp. 83-84), the social situation of poverty and trials whose description conforms to the experience of the church during the famine at the time of the Apostolic Council (pp. 81-82), the evidence for a Palestinian, preHellenistic background for the Epistle of James (pp. 78-81), and the psychological fact that James' failure to mention his kinship with Jesus is best explained as an indication that the actual brother of Jesus wrote this epistle at an early date (pp. 73-74). Kittel believes that if an early dating can be established, then attestation for an early stage of *logia* transmission would logically follow.

In his second article on this subject[9] Kittel continues his arguments for an early dating by contrasting the Apostolic Fathers with the teachings of James on the subjects of faith and works (pp. 56-68) and eschatology (pp. 68-83). Here, however, criticism regarding his first article[10] has forced him to modify his argument about progressive stages and to recognize the magnitude of allusions in the writings of many Apostolic Fathers. Therefore Kittel no longer contrasts the complete lack of quotation formulas in James with the regular employment of citation formulas by the Apostolic Fathers but concentrates instead on the frequency of the employment of allusions in each. Following the study made by the Committee of the Oxford Society of Historical Theology,[11] Kittel gathers the following statistics concerning the frequency of allusions to the Synoptic gospels.[12]

book	number of words	citations	allusions
James[13]	1500	0	18-20
Didache	2250	4	23 (48)
1 Clement	10,500	2	7 (14)
Ignatius' epistles[14]	8000	0	14 (32)
Polycarp to Phil.	1700	4	4 (17)
Barnabus[15]	6750	4	3 (19)
2 Clement	1800	12-14	4 (30)
Shepherd of Hermas[16]	27,000	1	5 (52)

[7]Kittel, "Der geschichtliche Ort," 93.

[8]Ibid., 94.

[9]Gerhard Kittel, "Der Jakobusbrief und die Apostolischen Väter, ZNW 43(1950-1951): 54-112.

[10]Specifically Kurt Aland, "Der Herrenbruder Jakobus und der Jakobusbrief," ThLZ 69(1944): 97-104.

[11]The New Testament in the Apostolic Fathers.

[12]Aland, "Herrenbruder Jakobus," 104 discerns considerably more allusions in these writings. His calculations are put in parenthesis after the figures of Kittel.

[13]In his earlier article, "Der geschichtliche Ort des Jakobusbriefes," Kittel lists 26 allusions, but here (p. 84) he admits that six to eight are doubtful.

[14]Kittel, "Jakobusbrief und Apostolischen Väter," 95 gives a breakdown of Ignatius' letters with the epistle, number of words, and number of allusions: Eph. 1800 6; Mag. 1100 1; Trall. 1000 1; Rom. 1100 1; Phld. 1050 1; Smyr. 1200 2; Pol. 850 2.

[15]The four citations consist of OT quotations put into the mouth of Jesus.

[16]Kittel, "Jakobus und Apostolischen Väter," 105-108 lists about 16 other uncertain allusions as well as six other occasions where the imagery in the Shepherd's parables is similar to Jesus' illustrations.

Kittel contends that by comparing the length of each book with the number of allusions to Synoptic material, the only writing of the Apostolic Fathers which contains a comparable number of allusions with the Epistle of James is the Didache.[17] James' greater frequency in using allusions is thus utilized to substantiate Kittel's claim of an early authorship of James, since a greater tendency to allude to the Jesus-tradition without *formulae citandi* characterizes the first stage of the transmission of the *logia* of Jesus.

2.2 Kittel's thesis has not received much positive affirmation within the scholarly world.[18] The recurring argument against Kittel is the continuing employment of allusions without an introductory formula within the writings of not only James but also Paul, Peter, and the Apostolic Fathers. In the Pauline epistles, as Allison[19] points out, there are six explicit citations of a word of Christ or a command of the Lord: 1 Cor. 7:10-11 (Mk. 10:11-12; Mt. 5:32; 19:9; Lk. 16:18); 1 Cor. 7:25; 1 Cor. 9:14 (Mk. 6:8-9; Mt. 10:10; Lk. 9:3; 10:7); 1 Cor. 11:23-26 (Mk. 14:22-25; Mt. 26:26-29; Lk. 22:14-20); 1 Cor. 14:37; and 1 Thess. 4:15-17. The allusions, on the other hand, are difficult to enumerate since the definition of an allusion differs from author to author.[20] Furnish[21] will admit less than ten purposeful allusions to the sayings of Jesus in the whole Pauline corpus whereas Resch[22] discovers over a thousand. Davies' catalogue[23] of about thirty is a more average estimate, yet Furnish is critical of all of these except eight: Rom. 12:14=Mt. 5:44; 12:17=Mt. 5:39ff; 13:7=Mt. 22:15-22; 14:13=Mt. 18:7; Mk. 9:42; Lk. 17:1-2; 14:14=Mt. 15:11; Mk. 7:15; 1 Thess. 5:2=Mt. 24:43; Lk. 12:39; 5:13=Mk. 9:50; 5:15=Mt. 5:38-48.[24] With regard to other NT literature outside the gospels, only one citation of a saying of Jesus is found (Acts 20:35), and that reference appears to be extra-canonical. On the other hand, similar to the Epistle of James, allusions to the gospel tradition are much more frequently discerned. Selwyn believes that *verba Christi* lie just below the surface of the text of 1 Peter.[25] Chase discovers twenty-six parallels between 1 Peter and the Synoptic gospels and concludes that "his mind

---

[17]Cf. below, p. 173.

[18]Cf. ch. 1, section 3.6.

[19]Dale C. Allison Jr., "The Pauline Epistles and the Synoptic Gospels: The Pattern of the Parallels," NTS 28(1982): 2. Cf. also David L. Dungan, The Sayings of Jesus in the Churches of Paul.

[20]For distinctions between citations, allusions, and parallels of content and vocabulary see ch. 7, section 1.1.

[21]Victor P. Furnish, Theology and Ethics in Paul, 51-59. Bultmann, Theology, 35 maintains that the teaching of the historical Jesus played no role in Paul's thought.

[22]Alfred Resch, Der Paulinismus und die Logia Jesu in ihren gegenseitigen Verhältnis untersucht, 35-154,468-507. William D. Davies, Paul and Rabbinic Judaism, 137 compiles Resch's results giving 1) the number of parallels to the Synoptics and 2) parallels to the agrapha: 1 Thess. 63, 8; 2 Thess. 25, 1; 1 Cor. 214, 21; 2 Cor. 99, 9; Gal. 88, 11; Rom. 270, 35; Col. 81, 4; Eph. 127, 14; Philemon 10, 0; Phil. 58, 4; Acts 61, 3; total 1096, 110.

[23]Davies, Paul and Rabbinic Judaism, 138-140.

[24]Furnish, Theology and Ethics, 53-54. With Allison, "Pauline Epistles and Synoptic Gospels," 10 we should also include 1 Cor. 13:2=Mk. 11:23; Mt. 21:21. David M. Stanley, "Pauline Allusions to the Sayings of Jesus," CBQ 23(1961): 26-39 contends that Paul is familiar with many of Jesus' parables (pp. 34-38) and his doctrine of prayer (pp. 30-32) but his conclusions are highly improbable and overexaggerated.

[25]Selwyn, First Peter, 366.

was saturated with the words of Christ."[26] Admittedly, this list is considerably too lengthy, but at least twelve deliberate allusions to the sayings of Jesus should be recognized in 1 Peter.[27] Furthermore, Davies discovers ten echoes of the words of Jesus in 1 John,[28] and Vos convincingly locates twenty-five diverse sayings of Jesus in the book of Revelation.[29] Moreover, as with the Epistle of James, the Apocalypse and 1 Peter at no point explicitly quote a saying of Jesus.[30] Therefore throughout the documents of the NT we encounter the identical phenomenon of the dominance of allusions to the sayings of Jesus. In fact there are as many allusions in a late book such as the Apocalypse as in a presumably early epistle such as James. Thus Kittel's hypothesis that the presence of allusions is an indication of an early state in the transmission of the sayings of Jesus cannot be sustained with regard to NT literature.

If we turn to the literature of the Apostolic Fathers, we detect an identical predominance of allusions to the sayings of the Jesus-tradition. Although Aland's statistics differ dramatically from those of Kittel,[31] we can still safely conclude that in the time of the Apostolic Fathers the predominant manner of referring to Jesus' words was through the use of allusions. Moreover, with the exception of 2 Clement[32] we encounter an unexpected low

---

[26]F.H. Chase, "Peter, First Epistle," A Dictionary of the Bible III: 787-788. 1 Pet. 1:4=Mt. 5:5; 25:34; 6:20; 1:6,8 and 4:13=Mt. 5:12; 1:10=Lk. 10:24; 1:11=Lk. 24:26,44; 1:13=Lk. 12:35; 21:34; 1:17=Mt. 6:9; Lk. 11:2; 2:2=Mt. 18:2f; 19:14; Lk. 18:17; 2:4=Mt. 11:28; 2:5=Mt. 16:18; 2:7=Mt. 21:42; 2:12=Mt. 5:16; 2:13,17=Mt. 22:21; 2:21=Mt. 10:38; 2:23=Lk. 23:46; 2:25=Mt. 9:36; Lk. 15:4; 3:9=Lk. 6:28; 3:13=Lk. 10:19; 21:18; 3:14=Mt. 10:26ff; 3:16=Lk. 6:28; 4:7=Mt. 24:42; 25:13; 26:41; Lk. 12:37; 21:34; 4:14=Mt. 5:11; 4:19=Mt. 6:25ff; 5:1=Lk. 24:47; Mt. 19:28; Lk. 22:28; 5:3=Mt. 20:25f; 5:6=Mt. 23:12. Cf. also Gerhard Maier, "Jesustradition im 1 Petrusbrief?" Gospel Perspectives, 5: 127-128 who includes more than 30 possible allusions.

[27]Grouped according to source: 1 Pet. 5:2-4=Lk. 12:32; 1:4=Lk. 12:33; 1:13=Lk. 12:35; 4:10f=Lk. 12:42. 1 Pet. 4:14=Lk. 6:22; Mt. 5:11; 3:16=Lk. 6:38; 2:19f=Lk. 6:32f; 3:14=Mt. 5:10; 2:12b=Mt. 5:16b. 1 Pet. 1:18f=Mk. 10:45; 5:6=Lk. 14:11; 18:14; Mt. 23:12; 5:7=Mt. 6:25.

[28]Davies, Setting, 412. 1 Jn. 1:5-6 and 2:9-11=Mt. 6:22-23; Lk. 11:34-36; 2:17=Mt. 7:21; 3:1-3=Mt. 5:8-9; 3:13=Lk. 6:22; 3:15=Mt. 5:21-22; 3:17=Mt. 5:48; 3:22=Mt. 7:8; Lk. 11:10; 4:7=Mt. 5:44-45; 4:11=Mt. 28:23; 4:21=Mk. 12:29-31.

[29] Louis A. Vos, The Synoptic Traditions in the Apocalypse, 218-219. Rev. 1:3a=Lk. 11:28; 1:3b=Lk. 21:8; 1:7=Mt. 24:30; 2:7,11=Mt. 13:9; (Mk. 4:23); Lk. 8:8; 3:2f and (16:15)=Mt. 24:42,43; (Mk. 13:35; Lk. 12:37); 12:39; 3:5c=Mt. 10:32; Lk. 12:8; 3:20=Mt. 24:33; (Mk. 13:29); Lk. 12:36; 3:21=(Mt. 19:28); Lk. 22:28f; 6:4=Mt. 10:34; (Lk. 12:51); 6:16=Lk. 23:30; ch. 6=Mt. 24 par. (cf. Vos, 186); 11:2b=Lk. 21:24; 11:3,6=Lk. 4:25; 13:9= (Mt. 13:9); Mk. 4:23; (Lk. 8:8); 13:10=Mt. 26:52b; 13:11,13=Mt. 7:15; 24:24; Mk. 13:22; 14:4b=(Mt. 8:19; Lk. 9:57); 14:6=Mt. 24:14; (Mk. 13:10); 14:14-19=Mt. 26:64; (24:29-31); 13:24-43; (Mk. 14:62; 13:26f; Lk. 21:25f); 17:4b=Mt. 23:25; (Lk. 11:39); 18:4=Mt. 24:15ff; (Mk. 13:14ff); 18:21=(Mt. 18:6; Mk. 9:42); Lk. 17:2; 18:24=Mt. 23:35; (Lk. 11:50); 19:6ff=(Mt. 9:14-17); 22:1-13; 25:1-13; 22:14; (Mk. 2:18-22; Lk. 5:33-39); 22:12=Mt. 16:27. ( ) indicates parallel passages with less similarity.

[30]Cf. Vos, Synoptic Traditions in Apocalypse, 8,54.

[31]Cf. above, p. 168 and n. 12.

[32]In 2 Clement references both to the OT (6:8; 14:1; 14:2) and the Synoptic gospels (2:4) are prefixed with the term γραφή. Likewise, the introductory formula λέγει (present tense), never employed elsewhere in the Apostolic Fathers to refer to the NT writings (with the possible exception of Barn. 6:13), is applied to both the OT (3:5; 11:2; 13:2; 15:3) and the NT (3:2; 4:2; 5:2; 6:1; 8:5; 13:4). These facts indicate the late date of 2 Clement whose references to the Jesus-tradition fit better with Justin Martyr than with the rest of the Apostolic Fathers.

proportion of citations, roughly comparable to that of Paul. Kittel argued that a substantially greater use of allusions occurred in the earliest days of the transmission of the Jesus-tradition, while the number of citations continually increased. This hypothesis, as indicated by the data above, cannot be substantiated. Furthermore, Kittel's list of allusions between the Epistle of James and the Synoptic gospels is exaggerated.[33] If this list is reduced, the frequency of allusions is more in harmony with the literature of the Apostolic Fathers than in contrast with it. Therefore, a more valid conclusion would be that the employment of allusions without *formulae citandi* remained popular in the Christian church from the very beginning. The employment of citations also continued throughout this period, especially when the authority of Jesus was appealed to in order to add significant weight to the author's argument. The sayings of Jesus are finally cited as scripture with the emergence of the Marcionite heresy and the writings of Justin Martyr.[34] It should be conceded that there was a gradual increase in the use of introductory formulations as the written gospels began to be utilized. Yet no clear stages of transmission of the sayings of Jesus can be substantiated.

Aland has offered the most thorough rebuttal of Kittel's views by attempting to counter his arguments at every point, including Kittel's suggestions concerning authorship, date, place of origin, and the use of the sayings of Jesus. Aland even turns Kittel against himself. Kittel had admitted:

> Keines dieser Beispiele an sich ist irgendwie durchschlagend. Viele von ihnen sind sogar, wenn man sie für sich allein nimmt, ganz unerhebliche Kleinigkeiten, auf die niemand etwas geben würde, wenn die irgendwo vereinzelt stünden.[35]

If James' allusions to the Synoptic tradition are so weak that they cannot individually stand on their own feet, how can a whole theory of stages in the transmission of the sayings of Jesus be built upon such an insecure foundation? asks Aland. Furthermore, regarding Kittel's supportive arguments for an early dating of the Epistle of James, Aland undercuts each argument by attempting to demonstrate that the eschatological expectations, the presumed social situation, the theology of faith and works, and the lack of ritualism in the author's concept of law coincide with the writings of 1 Clement and the Shepherd of Hermas equally as well as with the historical data we know of the person of James and an early date near the Apostolic Council.[36]

Lohse likewise counters Kittel's claim about the greater frequency of allusions in the Epistle of James but progresses a step further than Aland by offering a counter hypothesis to that of Kittel. Within each of the stages which Kittel had proposed Lohse notices that the allusions specifically occur within paraenetic sections, i.e. in most parts of James, within the Pauline corpus at 1 Thess. 5 and Rom. 12-14, and in the Two Ways section of the Didache. Kittel had argued that the similar use of allusions in the Epistle of James and the Didache stemmed from the older material present in the Two Ways as well as its Pales- tinian background.[37] Yet recent studies have shown that the section most

---

[33]See our findings in ch. 7, section 1.1.

[34]Cf. above, notes 1, 4 as well as James M. Robinson, "From Quotation Formula to Collection of Sayings," Trajectories Through Early Christianity, 99-100. With Justin, 2 Cl. 2:4 refers to Jesus' sayings as scripture although the term could possibly apply to the OT reference at 2:1. Barn. 4:14 is disputed since some discern a Judaic apocalyptic saying (4 Ezr. 8:3; 9:15). Cf. Bultmann, Synoptic Tradition, 110; Köster, Synoptische Überlieferung, 125-126; Zahn, Geschichte Kanons, I: 847f.

[35]Aland, "Herrenbruder Jakobus," 103 quotes Kittel, "Der geschichtliche Ort," 90.

[36]Kittel counters Aland's arguments in "Jakobus und Apostolischen Väter," 109-112.

[37]Kittel, "Der geschichtliche Ort," 93.

saturated with allusions to the Jesus-tradition, Did. 1:3-2:1, is a later addition.[38] Lohse's thesis of a common genre of paraenesis[39] accounts more adequately for the accumulation of allusions to the *logia* of Jesus at Did. 1:3-2:1 as well as the close resemblance to the Sermon on the Mount found in both Did. 1:3-2:1 and the Epistle of James.[40] In fact, the Sermon on the Mount is itself an accumulation of paraenetic teaching material grouped together by catchwords.[41] Lohse also discerns a connection between paraenesis and eschatology.[42] The eschatology in James is not in the first place concerned with the immediacy of the *parousia* as Kittel contends but with an attitude of patient waiting (5:7ff). Did. 16 is likewise concerned with the moral qualities present in the life of the catechumen, in this case watchfulness. Thus a recognition of the role that the genre of paraenesis plays in the quoting of sources is essential in explaining the phenomenon of allusions in the transmission of the sayings of Jesus according to Lohse.[43]

2.3 It is possible to describe the history of the transmission of dominical sayings in three ways: 1) as a series of stages; 2) as a settled, fixed tradition from the very beginning; or 3) as a fluid, living, flexible phenomenon where individual authors apply the *logia* to diverse and multiform contexts. To demonstrate further that the transmission history does not consist in a series of three stages as Kittel suggested, we will now investigate the remaining alternatives. Some posit an alternative two stage approach which distinguishes an early oral stage in which memorization reigned from a later standardized period when the sayings became stereotyped through the influence of the written gospels. The Epistle of James would thus belong to the former stage with the explanation for the form of the sayings being James' memory of the oral tradition if not the preaching of Jesus itself. Rendall, for example, explains:

> They correspond to the stage of fluid oral reminiscence, during which the *logia* of Jesus were for a generation preserved and handed down, until gradually through Q and other sources they were combined by M in the traditional form exhibited in the Sermon on the Mount. This gives a natural explanation of the close and numerous resemblances between the Epistle and the Gospel, agreeing so closely in substance and content, yet with a marked absence of verbal borrowing or reproduction.[44]

Elliot-Binns is a second witness to this type of analysis:

> Furthermore although the epistle is full of reminiscences of the sayings of Jesus as contained in the Synoptics, there is seldom verbal agreement, a circumstance which

---

[38]Cf. Cyril C. Richardson, "The Teaching of the Twelve Apostles, Commonly Called the Didache," Early Christian Fathers, I: 165. The discovery of a Latin document (*Doctrina apostolorum)* consisting of Did. 1-6 without 1:3-2:1 gave considerable weight to this argument.

[39]Lohse, "Glaube und Werke," 10-11.

[40]This section of the Didache consistently refers to the Sermon on the Mount except at 1:2 where the love command (also common in paraenetic literature at Rom. 13:9; Gal. 5:14; Jas. 2:8) of Mt. 22:37-39 par. is mentioned (cf. n. 154). All of James' deliberate allusions except Jas. 4:10 find their home in the sermon.

[41]Some catchwords in Mt. 6-7 include: 6:6,7 προσεύχομαι; 6:7,9 προσέυχομαι; 6:12,14 ἀφίημι; 6:16,19 ἀφανίζω; 6:31-33,34 μὴ οὖν μεριμνήσητε; 7:5,6 ἐκβάλλω, βάλλω; 7:6,7,11 δίδωμι; 7:8,9 αἰτέω; 7:9,12 ἄνθρωπος. For the catchwords in the Epistle of James see pp. 32-33.

[42]Lohse, "Glaube und Werke," 12-13.

[43]Lohse's thesis is taken up in section 3.0.

[44]Rendall, James and Judaic Christianity, 68.

strongly suggests that they came from a period before the sayings had become stereotyped in literary form.[45]

The postulation of an oral fluid stage followed by a written fixed era rests upon the false presupposition that later, at the time of the Apostolic Fathers, the citing of the sayings of Jesus became standardized. Koester demonstrates that even after the written gospels had appeared, the sayings of Jesus were not always transmitted in this standardized form.[46]

writing	from the gospels	from a free tradition
1 Clement	-	13:2; 46:8
Ignatius	Smyr. 1:1	Eph. 5:2; 6:1; 14:2; 17:2; 19:2; Trall. 11:1; Phld.3:1; Smyr. 3:2f; Pol. 2:1; 2:2
2 Clement	2:4; 3:2; 4:2,5; 5:2-4; 6:1,2; 9:11; 13:4	4:5; 5:2ff; 8:5; 12:2
Pol. Phil.	2:3; 7:2; 12:3	2:3
Barnabas	-	5:8f,11; 12:10ff; 21:2
Didache	1:3,4,5; 9:5?; 15:3?	1:2a,5; 8:1,2; 9:5; 11:4f,7; 13:1f; 14:2; 16:1,3-8
Shepherd of Hermas	-	Vis. 4,2,6; Mand. 4,1,6; Sim. 9,20,2f; 9,29,3; 9,31,2

The results indicate that the citing of the sayings of Jesus in a free, flexible manner remained popular in the church's life. The context and the author's peculiar emphasis and intention control the wording of the allusion as much as the standard inherited terminology found in the written gospels. As Wright explains,

> The presumption that with the increasing authoritative definition of the canon of the New Testament there arose a corresponding reverence for the *ipsissima verba* of the new sacred corpus, at least with reference to patristic treatment of this text, will be seen to require some revision.[47]

Therefore, postulating a temporary stage where memory dominated the citing of Jesus' words does not adequately account for the form in which these sayings were transmitted. We must search elsewhere for a more convincing solution.

2.4 Scandinavian scholars have emphasized the fixed, static nature of the history of the transmission of the sayings of Jesus. Gerhardsson insists that early Christian development is more comparable to the Pharisaic-Rabbinic tradition than that described by the form critics:

> The form-critics regarded the process of tradition as being one of gradual solidification of a hitherto plastic body of material. The final phase in this process, the actual transfer from memory to manuscript, they called the redaction-history of the material. This scheme cannot be applied to the Pharisaic-Rabbinic Tradition. Here the basic material always had a 'fixed' form, being transmitted as memorized texts.[48]

---

[45]Leonard E. Elliott-Binns, Galilean Christianity: Studies in Biblical Theology, 47.

[46]Köster, Synoptische Überlieferung, 259-260.

[47]Leon Wright, Alterations of the Words of Jesus as Quoted in the Literature of the Second Century, 8.

[48]Birger Gerhardsson, Tradition and Transmission in Early Christianity, 38.

Gerhardsson appeals especially to the role of memory and the importance of tradition in the ancient Near East. He points out that the Western art of reproducing another's statements in one's own vocabulary and of abstracting ideas and theories from these words was not practiced in ancient Israel.[49] No attempt was made to give a synopsis of the views of the old masters; instead the *ipsissima verba* of each authority remained unaltered.[50] Likewise, Riesenfeld notes that the ideal Semitic pupil never lost one iota of the tradition being passed on.[51] Thus the tireless Rabbi was exceedingly praised. Rabbi Perida, for instance, was regarded as exemplary since he would repeat every passage four hundred times for slow learners and on one occasion when a pupil had still failed to absorb the text, Rabbi Perida proceeded to repeat the passage four hundred more times.[52] Based upon these Jewish precedents, it is reasonable to suppose that the Christian catechumen had to memorize a number of important OT texts, sayings of Jesus, and summaries of apostolic doctrine.[53] This is substantiated by the memory technique utilized by Irenaeus[54] and the description of Peter's recollection process found in the Pseudo-Clementine Recognitions (2,1,6).[55] According to the Scandinavian school this evidence establishes a continuity between the apostolic and post-apostolic traditions, which in turn entails a fixed "Holy Word" rather than stages or a fluid transmission of Jesus' sayings.

---

[49]Birger Gerhardsson, Memory and Manuscript: Oral Tradition and Written Transmission in Rabbinic Judaism and Early Christianity, 130. Cf. pp. 134-135 for examples from Rabbi Eliezer ben Hyrkanos and Rabbi Aquiba.

[50]Ibid., 131.

[51]Riesenfeld, Gospel Tradition and Beginnings, 18. He admits, however, that even the Oriental mind was not a tape recorder.

[52]Gerhardsson, Memory and Manuscript, 134-135.

[53]Ibid., 203. Bruce M. Metzger, The Text of the New Testament, 87, n. 1 mentions examples of memorization in ecclesiastical circles: "According to the ostracon, Samuel, Jacob, and Aaron, who applied to Bishop Abraham to be ordained as deacons, were required 'to master the Gospel according to John and learn it by heart by the end of Pentecost and to recite it.' Aphou, Bishop of Oxyrhynchus, is said to have required a deacon at ordination to know twenty-five Psalms, two Epistles of Paul, and a portion of a Gospel by heart; a priest had to know in addition, portions of Deuteronomy, Proverbs, and Isaiah .... According to the Rules of St. Pachomius, applicants for entrance into the monastery were required to know twenty Psalms or two Epistles of Paul ...."

[54]Irenaeus explains how he memorized Polycarp's conversations with him: "I can even name the place where the blessed Polycarp sat and taught (καθεζόμενος διελέγετο), where he went out and in. I remember his way of life (τὸν χαρακτῆρα τοῦ βίου), what he looked like, the addresses (τὰς διαλέξεις) he delivered to the people, how he told (ἀπήγγελλε) of his intercourse with John and with the others who had seen the Lord, how he remembered their words (ἀπεμνημόνευε τοὺς λόγους αὐτῶν) and what he heard from them about the Lord, about his miracles, and about his teaching (τῆς διδασκαλίας). As one who had received this from eye-witnesses of the word of life (ὡς παρὰ αὐτοπτῶν τῆς ζωῆς τοῦ Λόγου παρειλῆφως) Polycarp retold everything in accordance with the Scriptures (σύμφωνα ταῖς Γραφαῖς). I listened to this then, because of the grace of God which was given me, carefully, copying it down, not on paper, but in my heart (ὑπομνηματιζόμενος αὐτά· οὐκ ἐν χάρτῃ ἀλλ' ἐν τῇ ἐμῇ καρδίᾳ). And I repeat it (ἀναμαρυκῶμαι) constantly in genuine form by the grace of God." HE 5:20 in MPG, XX: 485 cited in Davies, Setting, 468 and Gerhardsson, Memory and Manuscript, 204.

[55]"I have adopted the habit of recalling in my memory (*revocare ad memoriam)* the words of my Lord which I heard from himself, and because of my longing for them I force my mind and my thoughts to be roused, so that, awaking to them, and recalling and repeating each one of them, I may keep them in memory (*ut evigilans ad ea et singula quaeque recolens ac retexens possim memoriter retinere)*." Rehm, GCS 51, pp. 51-52, lines 18-19,1 cited in Davies, Setting, 468 and Gerhardsson, Memory and Manuscript, 207.

Besides recalling the Semitic desire for an exact, oral transmission, Gerhardsson also points to the important role that tradition played in Judaism and the early church. Imitation of teachers and reliance on authorities were values which the church took over from Judaism. The care and exactness with which the Masoretic recension of the OT text was preserved proves the reverence afforded to a source of authority in Judaism.[56] Gerhardsson finds this same reverence for the words of Jesus and the apostles in the early church.[57] Since the apostles were continually with the Lord from the time of John the Baptizer (Acts 1:21-22), they possessed the necessary knowledge to correctly preserve, transmit, and apply this "Holy Word". The two NT terms παραλαμβάνω and παραδίδωμι are specifically used to express this truth. Paul transmitted the Christian tradition (παράδοσις 2 Thess. 2:15; 3:6; 1 Cor. 11:2); he delivered it (παραδίδωμι 1 Cor. 11:2,23; 15:3), and it[58] was therefore received (παραλαμβάνω 1 Cor. 11:23; 15:1,3; Gal. 1:9; Phil. 4:9; Col. 2:6; 1 Thess. 2:13; 4:1; 2 Thess. 3:6). Gerhardsson and his Scandinavian colleagues contend that this double emphasis upon precise memorization and authoritative tradition necessitates that a fixed transmission of the sayings of Jesus must be assumed.

2.5 Most scholars demand that the work of Gerhardsson and Riesenfeld must be qualified. Allison's response is typical:

> But, although many of their emphases are salutary, the gospels do not permit the thesis that the tradition was fixed as was the later Mishnah. The editorial activity of the evangelists, even if today often exaggerated, puts this beyond all doubt. Further, the freedom of the redactional level cannot be radically discontiguous with the oral stage, which implies for that period also some degree of fluidity.[59]

When the fathers of the church quote a passage more than once, divergent forms are regularly employed. Metzger states that "Origen is notorious in this regard, for he seldom quotes a passage twice in precisely the same words."[60] The frequent occurrence of deviations from the Biblical record likewise offers evidence for a fluid tradition. Gildersleeve remarks of Justin Martyr, "Suffice it to say that Justin's citations from the Memoirs of the Apostles do not tally exactly, save in a few instances, with the parallel passages in our Gospels."[61] It is striking that Lk. 6:36 γίνεσθε οἰκτίρμονες is cited in six different formats in later Greek writings:[62]

---

[56]Gerhardsson, Memory and Manuscript, 43.

[57]He refers to Papias who explains, "And then whenever someone came who (as a disciple) had accompanied the elders (εἰ δέ που καὶ παρηκολουθηκώς τις τοῖς πρεσβυτέροις ἔλθοι), I used to search for (ἀνέκρινον) the words of the elders: what Andrew or what Peter had said (εἶπεν) or what Philip or what Thomas or what James or what John or what Matthew or any other disciple of the Lord, or what Aristion or what John the Elder, the disciples of the Lord say (λέγουσιν). Patrum Apostolicorum Opera, 70 cited in Davis, Setting, 467-468 and Gerhardsson, Memory and Manuscript, 206.

[58]The objects of παραλαμβάνω in Paul's writings include "the gospel" (1 Cor. 15:1; Gal. 1:9), "the word of the message ... the word of God" (1 Thess. 2:13), "the things which were learned, heard, and seen" (Phil. 4:9), "the tradition" (2 Thess. 3:4), and "Christ" (Col. 2:6).

[59]Allison, "Pauline Epistles and Synoptic Gospels," 23. Cf. Davies, Setting, 468-469 who argues that a struggle with Gnosticism would not have been credible if the tradition was not somewhat ambiguous.

[60]Metzger, Text, 87.

[61]Basil L. Gildersleeve, The Apologies of Justin Martyr (New York: Harper, 1877), xxxv.

[62]Cf. Bellinzoni, Sayings of Jesus in Justin, 10-12 where the locations in primary literature are given. Cf. also Resch, Aussercanonische Paralleltexte, II: 91-93 and above, ch. 3, n. 260.

γίνεσθε ἀγαθοί	Epiph., Adv. Haer. 66,22,4
γίνεσθε ἀγαθοὶ καὶ χρηστοί	Macarius of Egypt, Hom. 19:2; De Custodia Cordis 13
γίνεσθε ἀγαθοὶ καὶ οἰκτίρμονες	Pseudo-Clementine Homilies 3:57
γίνεσθε οἰκτίρμονες καὶ ἀγαθοί	Ps.-Athan., Quaest. ad Ant. 89
γίνεσθε χρηστοὶ καὶ οἰκτίρμονες	Just., 1 Apol. 15:13
γίνεσθε ἐλεήμονες καὶ οἰκτίρμονες	Cl. Alex., Strom. 2,100,4

Moreover, the textual tradition of the NT, especially within the Western text type, displays a freedom which does not harmonize with a strict interpretation of what a "fixed tradition" implies.[63] We must, therefore, assume that the classical authors' manner of quotation also influenced Christian writers. There "one finds a deliberate freedom in quoting, a kind of poetic license which seems to have been the sign of mastery in the treatment of the material."[64] Thus we encounter additional motivations[65] in the transmitting of the gospel tradition beyond that of maintaining a fixed tradition. Specifically we confront examples of 1) the adaptation of a saying to a new context;[66] 2) a harmonizing motivation;[67] 3) an explanatory motivation;[68] 4) stylistic changes;[69] 5) ethical and practical motivational

[63]Gerhardsson, Memory and Manuscript, 201 explains this phenomenon by the fact that private copyists were employed whose precision could not compete with Jewish Scripture specialists.

[64]Krister Stendahl, The School of St. Matthew and its Use of the Old Testament, 157.

[65]The following categories (with the exception of the last two) are taken from Wright, Alterations of the Words of Jesus. The examples are mostly drawn from Wright and Bellinzoni, Sayings of Jesus in Justin.

[66]Mt. 5:6 in Cl. Alex., Strom. 5,70,1; Lk. 16:9 in Iren., Adv. Haer. 4,30,3; Mt. 15:8 (Mk. 7:6) in Cl. Alex., Paed. 2,62,5; Mt. 26:41 in Tert., Pat. 13:7; Jn. 14:27 in Cl. Alex., Dives 37:4.

[67]Mt. 6:25-26 with Lk. 12:22-24 in Just., 1 Apol. 15:14; Mt. 7:22-23 with Lk. 13:26-27 in Just., 1 Apol. 16:11; Dial. 76:5; 2 Cl. 4:2,5; Lk. 6:36 with Mt. 5:48,45 in Just., 1 Apol. 15:13; Dial. 96:3; Lk. 9:22 (Mk. 8:31) with Lk. 24:7 in Just., Dial. 76:7; 100:3; 51:2; Mt. 23:23 with Lk. 11:42 in Just., Dial. 17:4; Lk. 4:8 with Mt. 4:10; 16:23 in Just., Dial. 125:4; 103:6; Mk. 2:7 with Lk. 5:32 in Just., 1 Apol. 15:8a; Mt. 5:42 with Lk. 6:30 in Just., 1 Apol. 15:10a; Mt. 5:29 with Mk. 9:47 and perhaps Mt. 18:9 in Just., 1 Apol. 15:2; Mt. 16:26; 6:20 with Lk. 9:25 in Just., 1 Apol. 15:12; Cl. Alex., Strom. 6,112,3; Mt. 10:28 with Lk. 12:4,5 in Just., 1 Apol. 19:7; 2 Cl. 5:4; Mk. 11:17b with Mt. 21:13a (Lk. 19:46a) in Just., 1 Apol. 17:3a; Mt. 27:46b with Mk. 15:34b in Just., Dial. 99:1; Orig., Mt. 16:23; Eus., Dem. Ev. 10,8,8; Lk. 16:16 with Mt. 11:12b-15 in Just., Dial. 81:4; Mt. 22:30 (Mk. 12:25) with Lk. 20:36 in Just., Dial. 81:4; Mt. 5:39-40 with Lk. 6:32 in Did. 1:4; Mt. 5:46 with Lk. 6:29 in Did. 1:3; Mt. 12:49-50 with Lk. 8:21 in 2 Cl. 9:11; Mt. 26:28 with Lk. 22:20 in Iren., Adv. Haer. 5,33,1; Mt. 8:11 with Lk. 13:29 in Iren., Adv. Haer. 4,8,1; Mt. 13:16-17 with Lk. 10:23-24 in Iren., Adv. Haer. 4,29,1; Mk. 10:18 (Lk. 18:19) with Mt. 19:17 in Just., Dial. 101:2; Epiph., Adv. Haer. 69:19; Iren., Adv. Haer. 1,20,2; Orig., Adv. Haer. 5:7; Pseudo-Clementine Homilies 18:3.

[68]Mt. 24:42 in Did. 16:1; Mt. 5:28 in Just., 1 Apol. 15:1; Mt. 15:8 (Mk. 7:6) in Cl. Alex., Paed. 2,62,5; Mt. 10:29 in Tert., Monog. 9:1; Mt. 5:46 (Lk. 6:32) in Just., 1 Apol. 15:9.

[69]Mt. 5:45 in Cl. Alex., Strom. 7,85,2: ἐπιλάμπει for ἀνατέλλει, ἀγαθός for καλός; Mk. 10:25 in Cl. Alex., Dives 4:9: βελόνης for ῥαφίδος; Mt. 6:19 in Just., 1 Apol. 15:11: λῃσταί for κλέπται, ἐν τοῖς οὐρανοῦς for ἐν οὐρανῷ, θησαυρίζητε for θησαυρίζετε θησαυρούς (suppress a Semitism); Mk. 9:47 in Just., 1 Apol. 15:2 βασιλεία τῶν οὐρανῶν for βασιλεία τοῦ θεοῦ; Mt. 6:21 in Just., 1 Apol. 15:16b: νοῦς for καρδία; Mt. 17:11-12 in Just., Dial. 49:5: ἐλεύσεται for ἔρχεται, absence of ἐν before αὐτῷ (suppress a Semitism).

changes;[70] 6) dogmatic or apologetic changes;[71] 7) changes to fit a new audience[72] 8) liturgical changes;[73] and 9) literary improvements.[74] From these examples it is safe to conclude that a fixed, static transmission of the sayings of Jesus without variation is excluded.

In more recent publications Gerhardsson appears to have modified his position somewhat, admitting that several Synoptic texts have been treated with "artistic freedom" by later interpreters.[75] In fact already in his earlier work he distinguishes between transmitting allusions to the sayings of Jesus and employing *logia* of the Jesus-tradition. When a saying is only alluded to, then there is no direct quotation in the strict sense of the word, but only a freely reproduced wording adapted in some way to the context.[76] Thus Gerhardsson too is close to acknowledging the truth of two seemingly mutually exclusive considerations in the history of the transmission of *verba Christi*. At the same time as one encounters a demonstrably lax method of quotation, there is still a high degree of authority and priority accorded to the words of Jesus in the Christian community. The holding together of these two conclusions speaks against those who accept a fluid view of the tradition which allows the church to create "sayings of Jesus", to project utterances of the early prophets back into the life of Jesus, and to assign wisdom sayings and folk legends from various traditions to the authorship of Jesus by inserting his name in place of the traditional subject.[77] If we accept this conclusion that the tradition was at the same time fluid and authoritative, then it is possible to contend that the traditions have been marked by the milieu through which they have passed without accepting the claim that they were created by the secondary milieu. The tradition was surely rooted in Jesus' words, yet this fact did not create a legalism which prohibited these sayings from being adapted to fit various new situations and the peculiar emphases of different authors. As Schweizer states, "The community had no sacred texts in the sense of ones that had to be repeated without the slightest change."[78] The authority of the words was not established by an exact verbal repetition of the sayings but in the putting into practice of the lifestyle and faith commitment demanded by these words through the inspired presence of the Holy Spirit. By accepting the fluid nature of this transmission process, we reject a theory of stages to explain the form of the sayings of Jesus in the Epistle of James and turn to a second solution, one already hinted at in our discussion of Lohse's critique of Kittel.

---

[70]Mt. 5:39 in Did. 1:4; Mt. 5:36 in Cl. Alex., Paed. 3,16,4; Tert., Cult. Fem. 2,6,3; Mt. 4:4 (Lk. 4:4) in Cl. Alex., Paed. 2,7,2.

[71]Mt. 26:24 (Mk. 14:21) and Mt. 18:6-7 in 1 Cl. 46:7-8; Mt. 5:47 (Lk. 6:34) in Just., 1 Apol. 15:10; Mt. 11:27 (Lk. 10:22) in Just., 1 Apol. 63:11; Cl. Alex., Strom. 7,109,4; Iren., Adv. Haer. 2,14,7; Tert., Adv. Marc. 2,27,4; Lk. 11:42 in Tert., Adv. Marc. 4,31,5; Mt. 11:19 (Lk. 7:33-34) in Cl. Alex., Strom. 3,52,4; Mt. 24:11 (Mk. 13:22) in Just., Dial. 35:3; Lk. 24:39 in Ig., Smyr. 3:2; Mk. 10:17-18 par. in Just., 1 Apol. 16:7. Cf. also Metzger, Text, 201-203.

[72]Mt. 6:32 in Just., 1 Apol. 15:15; Mt. 5:28 in Just., 1 Apol. 15:1; Mt. 6:1 in Just., 1 Apol. 15:17; Mt. 13:42a in Just., 1 Apol. 16:12; Mt. 6:33 in Just., 1 Apol. 15:16; Mt. 5:22 in Just., 1 Apol. 16:2; Mt. 5:16 in Just., 1 Apol. 16:2; Mk. 13:22 (Mt. 24:24) in Just., Dial. 35:3d.

[73]Mt. 6:9-13 in Did. 8:2; Mt. 28:19 in Did. 7:1.

[74]Mt. 7:15 in Just., 1 Apol. 16:13; Dial. 35:3a, the addition of ἔξωθεν (μέν) for parallelism; Mt. 6:1 in Just., 1 Apol. 15:17, the use of the genitive; Lk. 6:29 in Just., 1 Apol. 16:1, avoiding τύπτειν ἐπί with the accusative; Lk. 12:48 in Just., 1 Apol. 17:4, a compound verb; Lk. 6:28 in Just., 1 Apol. 15:9, the use of ὑπέρ.

[75]Birger Gerhardsson, The Origins of the Gospel Traditions, 87-89.

[76]Gerhardsson, Memory and Manuscript, 198.

[77]Therefore, we disagree with Köster, Synoptische Überlieferung, 261 when he states that "eine große Anzahl dieser Logien den AVV noch nicht als Jesusworte überliefert waren." (AVV = Die apostolischen Väter)

[78]Schweitzer, Matthew, 147.

3.0 The Genre Paraenesis as the Explanation for the Form of the Sayings of Jesus in the Epistle of James

James does not regularly employ the familiar language of the kerygma.[79] Nor do we encounter theological instruction, διδαχή, derived from the events of the death and resurrection of Jesus and employed to ground the Christian community in the fundamentals of faith and conduct. For these reasons the Christian character of the Epistle of James is sometimes even questioned.[80] Instead we observe purely ethical exhortations of practical wisdom with no immediately apparent theological or Christological undergirding.[81] The abundance of ethical exhortations has led scholars since Dibelius[82] to describe the genre of James by the term paraenesis (transliterated from the Greek word παραίνεσις, meaning exhortation).[83] Since paraenesis consists in its simplest form of imperatival sentences[84] and 54 imperatives occur in the 108 verses of the Epistle of James,[85] this appears to be an appropriate title. Lohse[86] uses the genre of paraenesis to explain James' prevalent employment of allusions to the sayings of Jesus. He contends that allusions to the Jesus-tradition regularly occur without an introductory formula within the paraenetic sections of Paul and the Didache.[87] Could the use of a particular genre, therefore, explain the form in which the sayings of Jesus are transmitted in the Epistle of James? In order to answer this question, we will examine in more detail the various suggestions concerning the genre of James and attempt to discern which hypothesis of genre coincides most accurately with the exegetical data.

3.1 As will become evident, the particular genre employed by James has been widely disputed. The dominant theory throughout church history, which has formed the very vocabulary with which we converse about the book, is the supposition that James is an epistle.[88] The main argument in favor of this traditional opinion is the acknowledged fact that the book is introduced as a letter: "From James, a servant of God ... to the Twelve Tribes dispersed throughout the world" (1:1 NEB). However, Jas. 1:1 can be "fully accounted for by the literary custom of the time without the necessity of supposing either a real epistolary aim on the part of the author or the addition by a later and inept hand of an

---

[79]Except for 1:17-18,21b. Cf. ch. 7, section 2.2.

[80]Cf. ch. 1, section 3.4.

[81]Harold S. Songer, "The Literary Character of the Book of James," REx 66(1969): 382 says, "James does not spell out the theological foundations on which his ethical demands are made."

[82]Supported by Blackmann, Hahn, Kümmel, Lohse, Mußner, Schnackenberg, Schrage, Songer, Wanke, Windisch etc.

[83]In the NT it occurs only as a verb at Acts 27:9,22; Lk. 3:18D.

[84]Songer, "Literary Character of James," 384. This is most clearly manifested in Jas. 4:7-10.

[85]Provided one includes participles which follow imperatives in a series.

[86]Lohse, "Glaube und Werke," 9-11.

[87]Esp. Rom. 12-14, 1 Thess. 5, and Did. 1:3-2:1; ch. 16.

[88]Citing examples from 1 Corinthians, Adamson, James: Man and Message, 97 entitles James a pastoral epistle, but pastoral epistles, as evidenced by Paul's epistles to Timothy and Titus and Ignatius' epistle to Polycarp, 1) are written to individuals; 2) mention duties in connection with church office; 3) address groups in the church as in the *Haustafeln* (1 Tim. 2:1-3:13; 5:1-6:2; Tit. 1:6-9; 2:1-3:2; Ig. Pol. 4:1-6:1); 4) include personal items (1 Tim. 1:12-14,18; 2:7; 3:15; 5:23; 6:12; 2 Tim. 1:4-6,15-18; 2:8-9; 3:11,15; 4:9-21; Tit. 1:5; 3:12-13; Ig. Pol. 7-8); and 5) warn against heresy (1 Tim. 1:3-4,6-7,19-20; 4:1-7; 6:3-5,20; 2 Tim. 2:17-19; 3:1-9; Tit. 1:10-16; 3:9-11), elements missing in the book of James.

alien epistolary preface."[89] Just as the book of Hebrews appears to be a group of homilies or exhortations (λόγου τῆς παρακλήσεως Heb. 13:22; Acts 13:15; 15:32) attached together and circulated as a short epistle (διὰ βραχέων ἐπέστειλα 13:22), so James could be a grouping together of ethical exhortations by a recognized teacher (Jas. 3:1) merely published in the form of a letter.[90] Outside Jas. 1:1 this document has little to recommend it as an epistle,[91] especially with the omission of a typical epistolary conclusion[92] and the impersonal and general manner in which James describes his audience.[93] Recently, however, Francis has attempted to prove that James is an epistle "from start to finish".[94] He contends that many Hellenistic letters have no closing formulas[95] but often conclude with the regular repeated themes of eschatology (Jas. 5:7-11), oath formulas (Jas. 5:12), and prayer (Jas. 5:13-18). This argument would be convincing if it were not for the fact that catechetically oriented paraenesis also habitually embraces eschatological sections introduced or concluded with exhortations advocating some moral virtue (Jas. 5:8-11 patience; Rom. 13:11-14 decency: 1 Thess. 4:13-18 encouragement; 1 Thess. 5:1-12 sobriety; Did. 16 watchfulness) as well as a section with church order themes such as prayer, confession of sins, and the functions of leaders.[96] Therefore, the best solution is to regard Jas. 5:7-20 as paraenetic material grouped together in the form of a primitive church order[97] rather than the regular conclusion of an epistle.

3.2 Others have claimed that James is a homily[98] or a series of homiletic-didactic discourses. Elliot-Binns contends that Jas. 1:1 was added to turn a homily into an epistle.[99] Shepherd divides the material into eight homiletic-didactic discourses,[100] while Meyer perceives twelve short homilies based allegorically upon the twelve patriarchs.[101] Wessel believes that the writing was originally a synagogue sermon.[102] As in a sermon James

---

[89]Ropes, James, 9-10.

[90] Richard Bauckham, "Pseudo-Apostolic Letters," JBL 107 (1988): 473 states, "The fact that only a letter opening is required to make a letter a letter means that a letter could easily be written that *also* belonged to *another* literary genre." Consider the Apocalypse which is given an epistolary form (Rev. 1:4-7), 2 Clement which is a homily but categorized as a letter in the early church (Eus., HE 3,38,4), the Epistle of Jeremiah which is really a tract against idolatry, the epistles of Enoch (1 En. 92-105) and Baruch (2 Bar. 78-87) as well as 2 Peter which are really testaments, and the Apocryphon of James and Epistle of the Apostles which belong to the very popular 2nd-3rd century genre of postresurrection dialogues between Christ and the disciples.

[91]Cf. Stowers, Letter Writing in Antiquity, 20-22 for the characteristic features of an epistle.

[92]Esp. if compared with the Pauline epistles.

[93]Cf. Kittel, "Der geschichtliche Ort," 102; William G. Doty, Letters in Primitive Christianity, 11-12.

[94]Francis, "Opening and Closing Paragraphs," 126.

[95]Ibid., 125 where Francis offers examples. Davids, James, 25-26 follows his lead.

[96]Cf. Did. 7-15. In the catechetical sections of 1 Peter we also perceive the themes of eschatology (4:7), prayer (4:7), forgiveness of sins (4:8), counsel for times of suffering (4:12-19), and the mention of the tasks of elders (5:1-4) in a somewhat similar fashion to Jas. 5:7-20.

[97]Cf. above, p. 131.

[98]For authors who support this position see Adamson, James: Man and Message, 94, n. 44.

[99]Elliott-Binns, Galilean Christianity, 47f.

[100]Shepherd, "James and Matthew," 41-42. Cf. above, p. 57.

[101]Meyer, Rätsel, 179-194.

addresses his audience as brethren and proceeds to teach the ethical applications of the Christian faith. The problem with this suggestion is the unfulfilled expectation that in a sermon the name of Christ would be mentioned more often or at least the kerygma recited, neither which is characteristic of James' writing.[103] Furthermore, there is no clear unifying theme to indicate that a single homily is in view.[104] Finally, there is no evidence of an oral address,[105] the application of scripture passages,[106] or the use of hortatory sections beginning with the cohortative "let us" as in other homilies of this time.[107]

3.3 The Hellenistic secular alternative to the homily is the diatribe. Ropes in particular promotes the thesis that the diatribe "serves to explain much, both of the form and the content, of the Epistle of James."[108] Some of the more characteristic traits of a diatribe include:[109]

A. Certain formal means of recognition:

1) the use of dialogue with an imaginary interlocutor[110] or a hypothetical opponent (2:18f; 5:13f) often introduced by ἀλλ' ἐρεῖ τις, ἀλλ' ἐροῦνται, ἔρουντ' ἄν ἡμᾶς, or simply φησί;

2) objections are anticipated and answered (2:8,14);[111]

3) the presence of rhetorical questions (2:4,5,14-16; 3:11-12; 4:4-5);

4) a row of short parallel questions and answers (5:13);

5) statements commencing with a paradox (1:2) and incorporating yet other paradoxes (1:10; 2:5) as well as serious irony (2:14-19; 5:1-6);

6) numerous imperatives (54 in 108 verses) which are often ironical (5:1; perhaps 4:9);

102W.W. Wessel, An Inquiry into the Origin, Literary Character, Historical and Religious Significance of the Epistle of James, 73-89. Cf. Davids, James, 12.

103Cf. 2 Cl. 1:1; Melito, Peri Pascha, 4-5,100-105; and the manner in which the homilies in Hebrews interpret the person and work of Christ. James only mentions Jesus Christ twice (1:1; 2:1) and the kerygma is almost absent (1:18,21).

104Adamson, James: Man and Message, 95 contends that the theme of the homily is "faith without works is dead", but this is limited to Jas. 2:14-26. Cf. above, ch. 3, section 1.3.

105Cf. 2 Cl. 17:3; 19:1; Heb. 2:1,5; 5:11; 6:9; Melito, Peri Pascha 46.

106Cf. 2 Cl. 2; 12; Heb. 2:6-8; 3:7-11; 5:6; 8:8-12; 10:5-7; 10:37-38; Melito, Peri Pascha 1. We have refuted Shepherd's claim that James contains a central gnomic saying in each of his discourses. Cf. ch. 4, section 1.2.

107Cf. 2 Cl. 4:1; 5:1; 7:1; 8:1; 10:1; 11:1; 12:1; 13:1; 16:1; 17:1; 18:1; Heb. 2:1; 4:1,11,14; 6:1; 10:22,23; 12:1,28.

108Ropes, James, 12.

109These traits are gleaned mostly from Ropes, James, 12ff and Wifstrand, "Stylistic Problems in James," STh 1(1948): 170-182. Cf. Ropes (p. 11) for a larger esp. German bibliography and Stanley K. Stowers, The Diatribe and Paul's Letter to the Romans, 7-48 for a history of the problems connected with the diatribe.

110Cf. Stowers, Diatribe and Romans, 85-93.

111Cf. Ibid., 119ff for a description of what Stowers calls "objections and false conclusions".

7) harsh addresses to the audience (2:20; 4:4);

8) certain familiar formulas such as μὴ πλανᾶσθε (1:16), θέλεις δὲ γνῶναι (2:20), βλέπεις (2:22), ὁρᾶτε (2:24), ἴστε (1:19), τί ὄφελος (2:14,16), οὐ χρή to introduce a conclusion (3:10), διὸ λέγει with a quotation (4:6), and ἰδού (3:4,5; 5:4,7,9,11);

9) "The form of the diatribe and the way it functions presupposes a student-teacher relationship" (3:1).[112]

B. Characteristics of content:

1) the apostrophizing of people (the merchants and the rich 4:13-5:6);

2) references to already known phenomena by appealing to analogy (2:14-17), experience (3:5; 4:1-3), and common sense (1:3; 3:1; 4:4);

3) an abundance of conventional figures (rudder, bridle, forest fire 3:3-6);

4) the citation of historical examples who are well-known representatives of certain virtues (Abraham, Rahab, Job, Elijah in 2:21-23,25; 5:11,17 respectively).

C. Contextual connections:

1) no clear logical structure unifying the whole but only individual sections fitted together by certain key words (πειρασμός 1:2-14; σοφία 3:13-18; ζῆλος 3:13-4:2; χαλιναγωγεῖν γλῶσσαν 1:26; 3:2; λόγος 1:18-23; νόμος ἐλευθερίας 1:25; 2:12; κρίνειν 4:11-12) and concluded by sharp antitheses (1:26; 2:13,26; 3:15-18; 4:12), questions (4:12; 5:6), quotations (5:20), or the expression οὐ χρή (3:10);

2) transitions made by the raising of an objection (2:8), a question (2:14; 4:1; 5:13), or by ἄγε (4:13; 5:1).

Yet Ropes himself admits that the Epistle of James embodies several striking divergencies from the style found in Greek diatribes:[113]

1) A greater seriousness and restraint of tone are evident in James; the bitter laugh and ridiculing abuse characteristic of a diatribe are missing;

2) A more intense and intimate tone is present in James; the Greek preacher addresses individuals (not "my brethren" as in James) and is not bonded by a relationship of love;

3) The prohibition of oaths in Jas. 5:12 is in no way comparable with the frequent oaths occurring in diatribes;

4) The range of metaphors and illustrations is noticeably narrowed in James' epistle.

Furthermore, Wifstrand[114] discovers additional elements in James which are not characteristic of a diatribe including: 1) James' greater frequency of imperatives; 2) the abundance

---

[112]Ibid., 175.
[113]Ropes, James, 15-16.
[114]Wifstrand, "Stylistic Problems in James," 177.

of abstract substantives, especially nouns that denote certain qualities or mental conditions; 3) quotations from the OT; and 4) Christian vocabulary. Ropes accounts for this disparity by proposing that "the specific character of this Christian Jew led him to develop the type of these tracts."[115] Thus James would be applying the specific genre of diatribe to his own experience, background, and way of thinking. On the other hand, as we shall see, another genre such as paraenesis can also account for most of the similarities listed above. The decisive argument centers on the ingredients of the epistle itself. Rather than encountering Hellenistic Cynic and Stoic philosophy on the pages of this document, we confront Jewish-Christian religious and ethical teaching.[116] It is only the specific discourses of James, i.e. those sections where a more logical and extensive structure is employed, that contain characteristics approaching those encountered in a diatribe.[117] Three such extensive, thematic discourses have been identified (2:1-13; 2:14-26; 4:1-10),[118] but the similarities of 4:1-10 with the catechetical material in 1 Pet. 5:5-10 as well as its contextual connection with the general paraenesis of Jas. 4:7-10 disqualify this pericope from being categorized as a diatribe. It is better to follow Dibelius' diagnosis[119] and include James' discourse on the tongue in 3:1-12 while eliminating 4:1-10.[120] In any case, the description "diatribe" should not be used to characterize the entire writing as is done by Ropes and his followers.

3.4 The Epistle of James exhibits a vital connection with wisdom literature as exemplified by the many parallels of content with Sirach and the Wisdom of Solomon.[121] Before settling upon a background in the genre of diatribe, Ropes surprisingly admits that with regard to the deeper roots of his thought James displays a closer kinship with Jewish wisdom literature than with Hellenistic diatribe.[122] Halson is a chief advocate of this position and maintains that the Epistle of James is "cast in the mould of the wisdom tradition as a conscious attempt to use a teaching form with Jewish antecedents yet with an 'international flavour' suitable for use in the Hellenistic world."[123] He points to:

1) the similar vocabulary: of the NT *hapax legomena* situated in James, 34 (65%) appear in the wisdom books of the OT and the Apocrypha;[124] with regard to the 21

---

[115]Ropes, James, 15.

[116]Cf. Grosheide, Jakobus, 338-339.

[117]Therefore Wifstrand, "Stylistic Problems in James," 178 goes too far when he concludes that it is "a grotesque overstatement ... to call the Epistle of James a Greek diatribe."

[118]Wilfred L. Knox, "The Epistle of St. James," JThS 46(1945): 10-17; Blackman, James, 23; Hoppe, Hintergrund Jakobusbriefes, 9.

[119]Dibelius and Greeven, James, 1. Cf. Songer, "Literary Character of James," 385 ("Jas. 2:1-3:12 appears to be three *topoi* in diatribe style."). Halson, "James: 'Christian Wisdom'?" 309-310 accepts only 2:14-26 as diatribe.

[120]In 4:4-5 we encounter rhetorical questions as in sections sometimes described as diatribe (2:1-3:12 at 2:4,5,6,7,14, 22,25; 3:11-12). Our author appears to slip into diatribe style in the middle of this section although the whole section cannot be entitled diatribe. The rhetorical question at 4:1b is an answer to the question of 4:1a rather than a diatribe characteristic.

[121]Cf. ch. 2, section 4.1. Jas. 4:6 and 5:20 both refer to texts from the book of Proverbs as well.

[122]Ropes, James, 16.

[123]Halson, "James: 'Christian Wisdom'?" 313. For other representatives of this opinion see Popkes, Adressaten, Situation, Form Jakobusbriefes, 23-27.

[124]25 (48%) from non-wisdom Apocryphal books; 18 (35%) from the prophets; 15 (29%) from the Pentateuch; 12 (23%) from the historical books; 9 (17%) from the Psalms.

words in common with only one other NT writer, 19 (90%) appear in wisdom literature.[125]

2) the literary form: this includes an abundance of isolated aphorisms,[126] a similar personal address (a wise man to his pupil, "my son" and a wisdom teacher to his flock, "my beloved brethren"[127]), and a marked use of picturesque imagery.[128]

3) the shared basic theme of practical guidance for everyday godly living.

In addition to Halson's three main arguments one could also assert that the subject of wisdom itself is an undergirding theme in James' theology (1:5; 3:13-18). In fact James repeats several themes which are identical with the emphases of contemporary Jewish wisdom literature as exemplified in the Sentences of Pseudo-Phocylides: rich and poor (Jas. 1:9-11; 2:5-7; 5:1-6; Ps.-Phoc. 5, 10, 19, 22, 28, 29, 53, 62, 83, 109, 199),[129] judging unjustly (Jas. 2:4; 4:11-12; Ps.-Phoc. 9), partiality (Jas. 2:1,9; Ps.-Phoc. 10), oaths (Jas. 5:12; Ps.-Phoc. 16-17), the tongue (Jas. 1:26-27; 3:1-12; Ps.-Phoc. 20, 124) mercy (Jas. 2:13; Ps.-Phoc. 25-26), anger (Jas. 1:19-20; Ps.-Phoc. 57,63), the uncertainty of tomorrow (Jas. 4:13-14; Ps.-Phoc. 116), wisdom (Jas. 3:13-17; Ps.-Phoc. 129-131), and the decalogue (Jas. 2:11; Ps.-Phoc. 3-8). Finally, the sayings are loosely connected with a minimum of mutual interconnection as is common in wisdom literature. We support those arguments above which affirm the importance of wisdom literature in understanding the ethical exhortations of James. However, James is not poetry but prose throughout. Furthermore, paraenesis runs parallel with the OT wisdom tradition[130] in that to a large extent it is likewise concerned with practical instruction on the everyday affairs of the godly and, therefore, can account for the same phenomena that a connection with wisdom literature explains. The advantages for accepting paraenesis as the genre of James will now be enumerated.

3.5 Since Dibelius' commentary an increasing number of Biblical scholars[131] are contending that the genre of paraenesis best accounts for the language, style, subject matter, and organization of the Epistle of James. We will now attempt to define the various elements which make up paraenesis, and in doing so, demonstrate its applicability in explaining the character of the book of James.[132]

---

[125] 13 (62%) from non-wisdom Apocryphal books; 13 (62%) from the prophets; 8 (38%) from the Pentateuch; 8 (38%) from the historical books; 7 (33%) from the Psalms. The statistics are taken from Halson, "James: 'Christian Wisdom'?" 308-309.

[126] Halson, "James: 'Christian Wisdom'?" 311 identifies 23 of these.

[127] Ropes, James, 17 disputes this as well as any close formal contact with the books of Proverbs, Sirach, Tobit, or the Wisdom of Solomon.

[128] Halson, "James: 'Christian Wisdom'?" 310, n. 3 states that typical wisdom similies can be found in Jas. 1:6b,10,23f; 3:3-5; 5:7-8.

[129] Especially warnings against economic injustice (Jas. 2:6; 5:4 = Ps.-Phoc. 5,10), pride in riches (1:10 = 53), and putting off meeting the needs of the poor (2:15-16 = 22) as well as the general convictions that riches will perish with you (5:2-3 = 110) and fighting and murder come from the lust for more (4:2 = 46).

[130] Cf. the end of n. 140, the 11th characteristic of paraenesis on p. 248, and Ernst Baasland, "Der Jakobusbrief als neutestamentliche Weisheitsschrift," STh 36(1982): 135, n. 3.

[131] Cf. above, n. 82. For opposition to Dibelius' thesis see the discussion in Popkes, Adressaten, Situation, Form Jakobusbriefes, 12.

[132] Combining most of the following elements into one definition we could say that paraenesis consists of an eclectic conglomeration of admonitions loosely strung together without a theological substructure whose purpose is the transmission of traditional material of universal applicability for the socialization of the audience.

1) Paraenesis consists of a fusion of eclectic material from diverse origins[133] and, therefore, accounts for the multiform traditions which one encounters in James: OT allusions, wisdom sayings, popular maxims, sayings of Jesus, and ecclesiastical moral reflection.

2) Paraenesis is composed primarily, although not exclusively, of traditional and unoriginal material.[134] This helps explain why the background questions pertinent to our epistle are so difficult to answer.

3) Paraenesis is addressed to those who have already known or heard such things before.[135] Hearing-forgetting and knowing-doing are therefore important topics of discussion, and it is precisely these themes which frequently surface in the Epistle of James (1:19-27; 2:14-26; 4:13-17).

4) Paraenetic precepts have universal applicability.[136] Therefore James does not consist of concrete solutions to ethical problems in a given situation as exhibited, for instance, in 1 Corinthians, a book dominated by ethical instruction although not paraenesis. Instead one encounters exhortations in favor of general virtues (perseverence in suffering 1:2-4; purity 4:8; humility 4:10; patience 5:7 etc.) and decrying various vices whose specific circumstances remain vague and nonspecific (doubt 1:6; anger 1:19-20; quarreling 4:1-3; slander 4:11 etc.).

5) Although assuming that a friendly relationship exists between the teacher and the recipients,[137] paraenesis "is an impersonal writing, not a confession in which reminiscences would be expressed."[138] Thus James continually addresses his audience with the words, "my beloved brethren" (1:16,19; 2:5) or "my brethren" (1:2; 2:1,14; 3:1,11; 5:7,10,12,19), and yet nowhere reveals his personal memories, character traits, or the relational interaction that has taken place between the teacher and the pupils.

6) The primary function of paraenesis is the socialization of the audience or the refashioning of those who were supposedly already socialized.[139] To accomplish this purpose norms and values are rehearsed to enable each member of the group to realize and perform his/her proper role and function. Thus through verbal chastisement (2:21; 4:4,8,10) and appeals to reason (1:3; 2:6; 2:14-17), James as "the significant other" (3:1) demonstrates the positive consequences of virtue (1:4,12,25; 3:18; 5:20 etc.) and the negative results of vice (1:6-7,11,15; 2:13 etc.). In this way the existing social world (the Christian community) is legitimized, a group identity and cohesion is strengthened, and boundaries are established which demarcate this group from other social worlds. In the paraenesis of James the church is differentiated from the world in general (1:27; 4:4) and from the wealthy oppressive landowners in particular (5:1-6; 2:5-7; 1:10-11). Those who are not totally socialized into the new community include the double-minded (1:8; 4:8), the adulterous people (4:4), and those who neglect to allow God's will to influence their business plans (4:13-17).

---

[133]Hahn, "Begründung urchristlicher Paränese," ZNW 72(1981): 89; Dibelius and Greeven, James, 24; Songer, "Literary Character of James," 385-386.

[134]Leo G. Perdue, "Paraenesis and the Epistle of James," ZNW 72(1981): 241; Dibelius and Greeven, James, 21; Kamlah, Form der katalogischen Paränese, 1.

[135]Perdue, "Paraenesis and James," 244. He supplies examples from Seneca, 13th Epistle 15; 94th Epistle 21,25; Dio Chrysostom, 17th Discourse 2:5.

[136]Ibid., 243; Songer, "Literary Character of James," 382-383.

[137]Perdue, "Paraenesis and James," 246.

[138]Dibelius and Greeven, James, 17.

[139]This section is taken from Perdue, "Paraenesis and James," 251-255.

7) Renowned human paradigms of virtue are repeatedly referred to in paraenesis for the emulation of the audience.[140] James mentions Abraham and Rahab (2:21-25), the Hebrew prophets and Job (5:7-11), and Elijah (5:14-18).

8) The simplest form of paraenesis is the command or summons.[141] This accounts for the nearly 60 imperatives within the 108 verses of James.

9) This conglomerate of admonitions which typifies paraenesis is loosely strung together by similar ethical content or by formal connections, especially through the device of catchword. This accounts for the difficulty exegetes encounter in unearthing a logical structure for the paraenesis of James.[142] Catchwords appear to connect sayings drawn from different sources at 1:3,5, 6,12,13,20; 2:13; 3:2,5,18; 4:10,12.[143]

10) Characteristic of paraenesis is the repetition of identical motifs in different places within the same writing.[144] Thus one discovers exhortations about endurance in times of tribulation at Jas. 1:2-4,12 and 5:7-11, praise of wisdom at 1:5 and 3:13-18, instruction about faith in prayer at 1:5-8; 4:2-3; and 5:16-18, cautions against wealth at 1:9-11; 2:1-7; and 5:1-6, recommendations for meekness at 1:21 and 3:13, advocation of duty at 1:22-25 and 2:14-16, and warnings about the tongue at 1:26 and 3:3-12.

11) In paraenesis the poetical tradition of gnomic literature is transmitted in prose form.[145] Thus paraenesis can easily be confused with wisdom literature as indeed has happened with the Epistle of James.

12) Paraenesis provides little opportunity for the development and elaboration of religious preconceptions and theological substructures. Instead they are presupposed or at best only touched upon.[146] Consequently, the human side of the sanctification process is emphasized. Moral freedom and responsibility are inscribed in capital letters whereas divine initiative and God's sovereignty stand in the background. The paraenesis of James thus "presupposes man's power to be a doer, to put aside all filthiness, to resist the devil, to draw near to God, to cleanse one's hands etc."[147] The divine action is not completely missing ("Every good and perfect gift is from above" 1:17), but the accent of James certainly coincides with this general characteristic of paraenesis.

---

[140]Ibid., 245. Perdue illustrates from Pseudo Isocrates, To Demonicus 8; Seneca, 95th Epistle 70-73; Test. Reuben 4:8f; Dio Chrysostom, 17th Discourse 16f.

[141]Dibelius and Greeven, James, 3. Hahn, "Begründung urchristlicher Paränese," 90 desires to remove from the concept of paraenesis any characteristics of law since its Christological undergirding is the love command (Rom. 12:9; 13:8-10; 1 Thess. 4:9; Gal. 5:14; Col. 3:14; Eph. 5:2; 1 Pet. 1:22; 2:17; 4:8; Jas. 2:8) and the message of the kingdom of God (Jas. 2:5; Gal. 5:21; 1 Cor. 6:9f; Rom. 14:17), yet the imperatival nature of paraenesis always demands that it be closely tied with ethical norms and moral laws. In fact, paraenesis could be described as the command of legal literature put into the master-student structure of wisdom literature.

[142]Cf. Songer, "Literary Character of James," 383-384.

[143]Cf. above, pp. 32-33 and Dibelius and Greeven, James, 7.

[144]Dibelius and Greeven, James, 11 offer examples from Tobit 4 and Rom. 12-13.

[145]Ibid., 27.

[146]Ibid., 21.

[147]Cadoux, Thought of James, 65.

13) "Paraenesis contains fewer religious and theological proof-texts than do other writings,"[148] since allusions rather than citations with introductory formulations are the general rule. This accounts for the form of the sayings of Jesus within the paraenesis of James where no quotations, no references to Jesus, and no exact wording are employed. The reason, therefore, for the particular form of the dominical sayings in James is not memory failure or the hypothesis of a first stage in the transmission of the Jesus-tradition but instead the characteristics of the genre of paraenesis. We will now attempt to substantiate this claim with examples from paraenetic texts.

3.6 Exegetes have noticed that when the NT writers turn their attention to general ethical exhortations, they display a remarkably homogeneous style. The following passages have been categorized under the genre of paraenesis: 1 Thess. 4:1-9; 5:1-22; Gal. 5:14-6:10; Phil. 4:4-9; Rom. 12:9-13:14; Col. 3:5-4:6; Eph. 4:17-6:17; Heb. 13:1-9,17; 1 Pet. 2:11-4:11; 5:1-11; Jas. 1:1-5:11.[149] In speaking specifically about paraenetic passages in Paul, Dibelius offers some enlightening comments on the uniqueness of these sections:

> As a rule this section is in a style widely differing from that of the rest of the letter. It contains no far-reaching discussions based on religion or theology, but special caveats often in the form of proverbs either loosely strung together or simply following one another without connection .... In particular they lack an immediate relation with the circumstances of the letter. The rules and directions are not formulated for special churches and concrete cases but for the general requirements of earliest Christendom. Their significance is not factual but actual -- not the momentary need but the universal principle .... Thus we see that the hortatory sections of the Pauline epistles have nothing to do with the theoretic foundation of the ethic of the Apostle, and very little with other ideas peculiar to him. Rather they belong to tradition.[150]

With the exception of the last comment which redaction critics have modified so that even the paraenetic sections are now seen to be affected by an author's theological foundation,[151] these observations coincide perfectly with our conclusion that the Epistle of James is paraenetic literature. The question now before us is whether passages categorized as paraenesis indicate the presence of sayings of Jesus in the same manner. If we recheck the eight certain allusions to the sayings of Jesus in the Apostle Paul which Furnish catalogues,[152] we discover that all are located within two paraenetic sections of Paul, Romans 12-14 and 1 Thess 5, and each saying is alluded to without an introductory formula. Likewise, the ties of the Epistle of James with 1 Peter are explained by the use of the paraenetic tradition for catechetical purposes. As Perrin explains,

> It is not that James necessarily knows 1 Peter, but rather that there is a Christian paraenetical tradition into which sayings ascribed to Jesus in the gospels have been taken up, although not in the form of sayings of Jesus, and of which both James and 1 Peter make use.[153]

---

[148]Dibelius and Greeven, <u>James</u>, 53.

[149]Hahn, "Begründung urchristlicher Paränese," 89, n. 13. In our opinion Rom. 14 could be included as well as Jas. 5:12-20. The only sections of James that one might exclude from the genre of paraenesis are the discourses in Jas. 2:1-3:12 which display characteristics of a diatribe or homily. However, these sections can be seen as extended paraenesis so that the whole book can be rightly entitled, the Paraenesis of James.

[150]Martin Dibelius, <u>From Tradition to Gospel</u>, 238-239.

[151]Cf. ch. 1, section 4.0.

[152]Cf. above, p. 169.

[153]Norman Perrin, <u>The New Testament: An Introduction</u>, 255.

Finally, the most obvious paraenetic section from the Apostolic Fathers, Did. 1-6, illustrates that when specific material from the Jesus-tradition is referred to,[154] it consistently takes the form of allusions without *formulae citandi.*[155] Therefore, it is no coincidence that the form of James' allusions follow a similar pattern.

If we investigate the referents to these allusions within the Synoptic gospels, we discover that they are not scattered randomly throughout the gospels but "come from a handful of relatively brief well-defined sections which are widely held to reproduce early blocks of tradition."[156] With regard to Paul the three main sections involved are the Sermon on the Mount/Plain (esp. Lk. 6:27-38), the missionary discourse (Mt. 10:1-16 par.), and Mark's collection of sayings in Mk. 9:33-50.[157] Regarding 1 Peter the allusions to the *verba Christi* primarily derive from two collections: Lk. 6:20b-38 which is also important to Paul (and James) and Lk. 12:32-45 which emphasizes the ethical implications of a series of eschatological sayings and parables.[158] Of vital significance to our argumentation is the realization that these collections in the gospels were also employed for paraenetic purposes in the early church.[159] The popularity of the Gospel of Matthew in the early church is probably accounted for by the fact that Matthew (like James) wishes to develop the ecclesiastical ethical tradition and thus groups together sayings of Jesus into long discourses.[160] Likewise, the close parallels between the Epistle of James and the Shepherd of Hermas (esp. the Mandates) are explained by both authors' wish to transmit the paraenetic tradition, although Hermas evidences a later homilized form of this paraenesis.[161] Thus we are con-

---

[154]Did. 1:2 = Mt. 22:37-39 par.; 1:2 = Mt. 7:12; Lk, 6:31; 1:3 = Mt. 5:44,46,47; Lk. 6:27,28,32,33; 1:4 = Mt. 5:39,48; Lk. 6:29; 1:4 = Mt. 5:41,40; 1:4-5 = Lk. 6:30; Mt. 5:42; 1:5 = Mt. 5:26. Taken from the footnotes of Karl Bihlmeyer, Die Apostolichen Väter (Tübingen: Mohr, 1956), 1-2.

[155]Cf. Lohse, "Glaube und Werke," 10. Some of the references to sayings of Jesus in Did. 7-16 (cf. Did. 8:3; 11:3; 15:3,4) contain introductory formulations since specific problem areas within the church are being dealt with (as in 1 Corinthians) and the authority of Jesus' words is being appealed to (as in 1 Cor. 7:10-11,25: 9:14; 11:23-26; 14:37).

[156]Allison, "Pauline Epistles and Synoptic Gospels," 11.

[157]Fifteen of Allison's 24 parallels (p. 20) can be accounted for if one assumes that Paul employed the sources mentioned: (Rom. 8:15 = Lk. 22:2; Mt. 6:9); Rom. 12:14 = Lk. 6:28; Mt. 5:44; Rom. 12:17 = Lk. 6:27-36; Mt. 5:38-48; Rom. 12:21 = Lk. 6:27-36; Mt. 5:38-48; Rom. 13:7 = Mk. 12:13-17; (Rom. 13:8-10 = Mk. 12:28-34); Rom. 14:10-11 = Lk. 6:37; Mt. 7:1-2; Rom. 14:13-14 = Mk. 9:42; Rom. 14:14 = Mk. 7:15; (Rom. 16:19 = Mt. 10:16); 1 Cor. 4:14 = Lk. 6:28; Mt. 5:44; 1 Cor. 7:10 = Mk. 10:12; Mt. 5:32; 1 Cor. 8:13 = Mk. 9:42; 1 Cor. 9:14 = Lk. 10:27; Mt. 10:10; Mk. 6:8-9; 1 Cor. 11:23-27 = Lk. 22:19-20; 1 Cor. 13:2 = Mk. 11:23; Col. 3:5 = Mk. 9:43-48; (Col. 3:12 = Lk. 6:35); (Col. 4:6 = Mk. 9:50); 1 Thess. 4:8 = Lk. 10:16; 1 Thess. 5:2,4 = Lk. 12:39-40; Mt. 24:43-44; 1 Thess. 5:13 = Mk. 9:50; 1 Thess. 5:15 = Lk. 6:27-36; Mt. 5:38-48; (2 Thess. 3:3 = Mt. 6:13). The more uncertain parallels are in parenthesis.

[158]Cf. Best, "1 Peter and the Gospel Tradition," 112-113.

[159]The catchwords in Mk. 9:37-50, for instance, indicate that paraenesis is being employed: 1) in my name: 9:37,38,39,41; 2) cause to sin: 9:42,43,45,47; 3) good or better: 9:42,43,45, 47,50; 4) fire and hell: 9:43,45,47,48,49; 5) salt: 9:49a,49b,50a,50b.

[160]Cf. Lohse, "Glaube und Werke," 11; Hagner, "Sayings of Jesus in Apostolic Fathers," 256; Edouard Massaux, L'influence de l'Evangile de Saint Matthieu sur la littérature Chrétienne avant Saint Irénée (Louvain: Un. de Louvain, 1950); and Erich Fascher's review in ThLZ 78(1953): 281-283 for the importance of Matthew's gospel in the early church's teaching.

[161]Cf. Lohse, "Glaube und Werke," 16.

fronted with a group of documents or sections of documents whose similarity to each other is determined by the genre of paraenesis.[162]

In contrast to the allusionary manner in which the sayings of Jesus are employed within paraenetic literature, citations with introductory formulas are regularly used in situations where specific (rather than general) moral guidance is presented. Confronted with the specific problems in the Corinthian church, Paul grounds his arguments in the authority of a saying of Jesus. In dealing with the question of marriage in 1 Cor. 7:10 (=Mk. 10:11-12 par.), Paul specifies that it is "not I but the Lord" who commands this authoritative injunction about divorce. Likewise in 1 Cor. 9:14 (=Mt. 10:10 par.) Paul argues for the financial support of missionaries by stating that "the Lord commanded that those who proclaim the gospel should get their living by the gospel." Since Paul appeals to *verba Christi* from the gospel tradition rather than from paraenesis, one can differentiate between two strands of tradition, both of which employed the sayings of Jesus in different ways.[163] The comments of Hahn concur with this opinion,

> Die Ausbildung der Paränese vollzog sich auf doppeltem wege. Einerseits wurden die überlieferten Worte Jesu zunehmend der Christlichen Unterweisung dienstbar gemacht, wie beispielhaft die Komposition der Bergpredigt im Matthäus evangelium erkennen lässt. Anderseits wurde paränetisches Gut aus sehr verschiedenen Überlieferungsbereichen zusammengetragen, unter einheitliche Leitmotive gestellt und zum Gebrauch in den Gemeinden weitergegeben, wie die ermahnenden Teils der neutestamentlichen Briefe zeigen.[164]

When the gospel tradition is utilized by the leaders of the early church, the words of Jesus are employed to authenticate arguments[165] and to ground the church's life in the authoritative utterances of the historical Jesus, the Lord of the church. When the paraenetic tradition is employed, the words of Jesus are intertwined with Jewish wisdom, illustrations from nature, and the peculiar emphases of the author in order to transmit the authoritative ethical tradition of the church.

---

[162]Ibid. Lohse explains, "In dieser Gestalt und Abfolge der Mahnungen, die in vielen Fällen ohne eine gedankliche Verknüpfung sich aneinander anschliesen, ist der Jac Schriften wie den Proverbien, den Sprüchen des Jesus Sirach, paränetischen Abschnitten der paulinischen Briefe ... sowie der zwölfapostellehre nah verwandt."

[163]Cf. Dibelius, Tradition to Gospel, 241 and below, ch. 7, section 1.5.

[164]Hahn, "Begründung urchristlicher Paränese," 89.

[165]Cf. Joachim Wanke, "Die urchristlichen Lehrer nach dem Zeugnis des Jakobusbriefes," Die Kirche des Anfants, 501.

Chapter 6
BACKGROUND QUESTIONS SURROUNDING THE EPISTLE OF JAMES

1.0 We began this study by labeling the Epistle of James an enigma.[1] The question before us now is whether our discussion of the relationship between the sayings of Jesus and the Epistle of James has contributed any insights into the background questions surrounding the Epistle of James such as date, provenance, and authorship. Some authors claim that no conclusions can be reached regarding questions of introduction either from the epistle itself or by studying its relationship with other writings. Dibelius, for example, contends that the nature of paraenesis, the stylized examples within the Epistle of James, and the lack of any character of correspondence as in a normal epistle rules out any inferences about the nature of the community, the situation addressed by the author, or the particular geographical climate assumed from the examples and imagery utilized.[2] However, with the rise of redaction criticism some of Dibelius' views of the nature of paraenesis have been challenged,[3] and again evidence for a particular *Sitz im Leben* is being investigated.[4]

In our rehearsal of the history of interpretation of the Epistle of James we outlined four strands of interpretation with regard to the difficult questions of background.[5] Already in chapter 1 we dismissed the alternative of a preChristian authorship advocated originally by Spitta and Massebieau by pointing to the Christian references inherent in the epistle. In chapter 4 we countered arguments aimed at proving a tie with the Gospel of Matthew and his community in Syria.[6] Therefore yet to be investigated are the possibilities that the Epistle of James is a mid-first century writing of James of Jerusalem, the brother of Jesus, or a late (post) apostolic document written by an unknown or pseudonymous author from Rome. We will examine these two options in turn, discussing in each the introductory questions of date, geographical location, and authorship.

2.0 The thesis that James of Jerusalem, the brother of Jesus, wrote this epistle is a well-founded hypothesis, since as the traditional interpretation it has stood the test of time

---

[1]Cf. ch. 1, section 1.1.

[2]Dibelius and Greeven, James, 2,47,129.

[3]Cf. ch. 1, section 4.0.

[4]Kittel, "Der geschichtliche Ort," 81-82 and Robinson, Redating, 120-124 believe that the situation described in James' epistle is the poverty and suffering experienced during the time of the Apostolic Council in Jerusalem (AD 48). Ralph P. Martin, "The Life-Setting of the Epistle of James in the Light of Jewish History," Biblical and Near Eastern Studies, 97-103 argues that because James sided with the lower Jewish clergy, the high priests under Ananus II found it to their advantage to execute him in AD 62. James' sympathy for the lower class poor without an acceptance of the Zealot's violent approach is discerned by Martin in the Epistle of James. Davids, James, 28-34 emphasizes the economic situation in Palestine which caused James to admonish the wealthy landowners and encourage his community to endure difficult situations with joy and patience. Reicke, James, 6-7 contends that the Epistle of James is a circular homily urging political passivism on the part of Christians during the reign of Domitian. Laws, James, 25,35 envisions a *Sitz im Leben* in Rome as the church is on the verge of experiencing moral laxity. See also n. 46 and n. 189 below.

[5]Cf. ch. 1, section 1.3.

[6]Cf. ch. 4, sections 1.1-1.2.

and fits much of the evidence derived from the epistle. However, this traditional standpoint has continuously encountered opposition since other theories coincide as well with the exegetical facts. What then are the pros and cons favoring this traditional solution to the enigma of James? We will consider first the "Jewishness" of the epistle, then its Palestinian environment, the evidence for an early date, and finally the question of authorship by James of Jerusalem.

2.1 Written by a Jew

The Jewish character of the Epistle of James is supported by the fact that several prominent interpreters have concluded that this epistle was originally a Jewish document and only later Christianized.[7] The enormous number of parallels with the sayings of Jesus[8] is also best explained by a common background in Jewish thought patterns and verbal expressions.[9] These Jewish roots can be detected in such teachings as the fundamental Jewish doctrine of a monotheistic creed (2:19), the indication that Abraham is "our father" (2:21), the use of the Torah as the norm for all moral precepts (2:8-12; 4:11), the vital connection between healing and forgiveness of sins (5:15),[10] the acquisition of forgiveness through the human acts of prayer (5:14-15), confession (5:16), and reconciliation (5:20), the application of the term "righteousness" to human actions (1:19; 2:23-24; 3:18),[11] the condemnation of double-mindedness (1:8; 4:8),[12] the theme of the pious poor (1:9; 2:5; 5:6), and finally the close bond between the practice of good works and a just reward (1:22,27; 2:24; 5:9,11,20).[13] James' acquaintance with nonscriptural Jewish traditions also indicates a thorough knowledge of Jewish thinking.[14] At 2:23 James has attached to his quote of Gen. 15:6 the fact that Abraham was called a friend of God, a familiar designation in Jewish intertestamental works.[15] The famine mentioned in 1 Kings 18:1 is said in Jas. 5:17 to have endured three and a half years, a Jewish tradition also found in Lk. 4:25.[16] The address to the twelve tribes in the Dispersion (1:1) presumes an application of peculiarly Jewish concepts. Finally, "there is no reference to idolatry, to slaves, to a generally accepted low standard of sexual morality, to any surrounding heathenism,"[17] as would be expected if Gentiles were being addressed.

The Jewish flavor of James is likewise discernible in the grammatical constructions and word usage. The expression προσευχῇ προσηύξατο (5:17) is clearly an imitation of the Hebrew infinitive absolute.[18] The phrase ακροατης ἐπιλησμονῆς (1:25) displays the Semitic conjunction of two nouns in the construct state with the second term best translated

---

[7]Cf. ch. 1, sections 3.4 and 3.9.

[8]Over 180 parallels have been discerned. Cf. Appendix I, section 1.0.

[9]Cf. ch. 4, section 3.3.

[10]Cf. Dibelius and Greeven, James, 255.

[11]Cf. ch. 4, section 3.5.

[12]Cf. Laws, James, 3-4; Jean Daniélou, The Theology of Jewish Christianity, 364.

[13]Robinson, Redating, 121 points out that "social justice, prayer, almsgiving, and sick-visiting are the (characteristically Jewish) scope of Christian good works." Ropes, James, 31 states that "the religious attitude of the average rabbinical Jew would in most respects well sum up the fundamental ideas of the Epistle of James."

[14]Cf. Davids, "Tradition and Citation in James," 113-126 and Cadoux, Thought of James, 11.

[15]Cf. ch. 2, section 2.3.

[16]Cf. Appendix I, section 3.8.

[17]Ropes, James, 41.

[18]Cf. BDF 198.6.

in an adjectival sense.[19] The use of a passive construction to avoid the mention of God's name (1:5,12,17; 5:15) is a common Jewish device.[20] Typical patterns of Semitic parallelism can be discerned at 1:5,9,11,13; 3:9; 4:8,9; 5:4.[21] The employment of the prophetic perfect tense in Jas. 5:2-3a is reminiscent of the Jewish prophets,[22] and the numerous Biblicisms[23] reveal an unmistakeable familiarity with Biblical expressions. Oesterley has even attempted to trace many of James' phrases back to a Hebrew equivalent.[24] With regard to word choice the address "go in peace" (2:16) is a typical Hebrew greeting.[25] Whereas in normal Greek usage ποιητής indicates a maker or composer[26] and ποιητής λόγου a writer, poet, or orator (2 Macc. 2:30), in Jas. 1:22 these expressions are best translated as "a doer" or "a doer of the word", thus displaying Semitic influence.[27] In particular the expressions "Lord of Sabaoth" (5:4) and "Gehenna" (3:6) are distinct marks of Jewish authorship since these terms could have easily been replaced by expressions more Greek in outlook.[28] Finally, in contrast to the practice of every other NT author (except the author of the Apocalypse), the title "Lord" is more frequently a title for God as in OT usage than a reference to Jesus Christ.[29] Therefore, the influence of Jewish thought patterns and means of expression can best be accounted for by the hypothesis that James was a Jew steeped in Semitic culture.[30]

2.2 Written in Palestine

Scholars who have postulated Palestine as the geographical origin for the Epistle of James have concentrated their attention on the imagery utilized by James. In a frequently quoted article Hadidian contends that the nature imagery in Jas. 1:6,11; 3:11; and 5:7 supplies conclusive proof for a Palestinian background.[31] The two terms ἀνεμιζομένῳ and ῥιπιζομένῳ (1:6) are said to describe a familiar scene on the Sea of Galilee. The scorching heat (καυσών) in Jas. 1:11 portrays a familiar weather pattern in Palestine as evidenced by the frequent employment of this term in the LXX[32] in comparison with its rare use in ordinary Greek.[33] Although καυσών can describe either the scorching heat (Mt. 20:12; Lk. 12:55; Is. 49:10) or the forceful southeast wind (Jer. 18:17),

---

[19]Other examples are found in 2:1,4; 3:13; and probably 5:15. Cf. Dibelius and Greeven, James, 36-37.

[20]Cf. Kittel, "Jakobusbrief und Apostolischen Väter," 110.

[21]Mußner, Jakobusbrief, 30-31.

[22]Is. 44:23; 53:5-10; 60:1-2. Cf. above, pp. 122-123.

[23]Cf. Mußner, Jakobusbrief, 31 and Oesterley, "James," 392-393.

[24]Oesterley, "James," 393-396.

[25]Cf. Smits, OT Citaten in het NT, 347.

[26]Plato, Rep. 597; Phaed. 234; Her. 2:53. Cf. Davids, James, 96.

[27]For further examples see the excellently organized presentation of Mußner, Jakobusbrief, 30-33 and Chaine's detailed discussion, Jacques, xci-xcix.

[28]This is the only NT occurrence of the term "Gehenna" outside the sayings of Jesus.

[29]Cf. above, pp. 115-116 and Laws, James, 3.

[30]The excellent Greek utilized in the epistle should not be used to disprove authorship by a Jew but rather deals more specifically with the problem of the geographical location of the author.

[31]Dikran Y. Hadidian, "Palestinian Pictures in the Epistle of James," ExT 63(1952): 227-228.

[32]Gen. 31:40; Jud. 8:3; Job 27:21; Is. 49:10; Jer. 18:17; 28:1; Ezk. 17:10; 19:12; Dan. 3:67 θ; Hos. 12:1; 13:15; Jon. 4:8; Sir. 18:16; 34:16; 43:22. Is. 49:10 brings together καυσών and ἥλιος as in Jas. 1:11.

[33]Hadidian. "Palestinian Pictures," 228.

those who advocate a Palestinian milieu prefer the latter, stating that "no one who has ever lived in Palestine can forget the Sirocco (Shargiya) -- the blasting, scorching southeast wind which blows there in the spring."[34] An allusion to the fresh and salt springs by the Dead Sea is seen in Jas. 3:11, "Does a spring pour forth from the same opening fresh water and brackish?"[35] The mentioning of the early and late rains in Jas. 5:7 is frequently reported as the decisive witness for a Palestinian location since the former rains fall in Palestine after the sowing of the crops and the latter rains just before their ripening.[36] Finally, the figs, olives, and grapevines mentioned in Jas. 3:12 are sometimes associated with the geographical features of Palestine,[37] although such crops can be found throughout the Near East.

Many scholars, however, have remain unconvinced that this geographical imagery points to a Palestinian environment. The waves of the sea driven and tossed by the wind (1:6), the scorching heat accompanying the rising of the sun (1:11),[38] and the abundance of grapevines, fig trees, and olives (3:12) are pictures applicable to the whole of the Mediterranean region and not Palestine alone. Certainly James was not referring to the springs around the Dead Sea at 3:11 since "James' argument would hardly be assisted by pointing to a situation where these opposites in fact co-exist."[39] However, the piece of evidence concerning the former and latter rains[40] is not so easily dismissed. Laws has argued that a recognition of the traditional character of James' vocabulary in 5:1-6, where he has deliberately archaicized and Biblicized the language, makes it doubtful that the details of 5:7 should be interpreted literally,[41] but the change in context at 5:7 does not substantiate her argument.[42] The familiarity of the phrase "early and late rains" could indicate that James' language was derived from Jewish worship[43] or reading the OT rather than from his own personal experience within the geographical area from the Taurus mountains south to the Judean Negeb[44] where this pattern of rainfall is experienced. On the other hand, because of the restrictiveness of this meteorological phenomenon, Jas. 5:7 offers the strongest evidence for a Palestinian provenance.[45] Davids offers four grounds:

> 1) the ellipsis of ὑετόν is more likely as part of James's habitual vernacular style (e.g. 3:11) than as part of a reference to scripture; 2) there is no evidence in rabbinic liter-

---

[34]Adamson, James, 63.

[35]Mayor, James, 120; Rendall, James and Judaic Christianity, 38.

[36]Dt. 11:14; Prov. 16:15; Jer. 5:24; Hos. 6:3; Joel 2:23; Zech. 10:1.

[37]Cf. Adamson, James, 147.

[38]We agree with Dibelius and Greeven, James, 86 that because of the "with" (σύν), καυσῶν is not to be translated "east wind" but "heat" since the sun brings with it scorching heat. However, a dogmatic opinion on this point is excluded by the fact that in Jonah 4:8 the rising of the sun is coupled with a sultry east wind.

[39]Laws, James, 157.

[40]The ambiguous reading πρόϊμον καὶ ὄψιμον caused copyists to insert an appropriate noun such as ὑετόν (A, P, Ψ, the Byzantine text tradition, $syr^{p.h}$, and most minuscules).

[41]Laws, James, 96.

[42]Jas. 5:7 begins a new section of primitive catechetical material. Cf. ch. 3, section 6.0.

[43]Mußner, Jakobusbrief, 202 notes that this phrase was recited regularly in Jewish worship as part of the Shema (in Dt. 11:14).

[44]Denis Baly, The Geography of the Bible: a Study in Historical Geography (New York: Harper, 1957), 47-52; Dalmon, Die Worte Jesu, 115ff, 172ff, 291ff. The fact that certain MSS (ℵ, 255, 398, 1175, it^{ff}, syr^{hmg}) read καρπόν instead of ὑετόν probably is evidence that some scribes were not familiar with Palestinian climate patterns. Cf. Metzger, Textual Commentary, 685.

[45]Adamson, James, 191; Cadoux, Theology of James, 30; Kittel, "Der geschichtliche Ort," 81; Mayor, James, 162; Oesterley, "James," 329ff,401.

ature, other Jewish materials, the Apostolic Fathers, or early apologists (Ropes, 297) that this image was used outside Palestine or in Christian tradition; 3) the themes of the passages cited do not match the theme of patience in James, so at least the application is novel; and 4) the whole context both here and in 5:1-6 fits the agricultural situation in Palestine before AD 70.[46]

It is difficult to dismiss this line of argumentation although one must admit that the geographical picture painted by James does not offer sufficient evidence to pinpoint a particular location. An author's knowledge of the Palestinian terrain is not necessarily an indication that the letter was written from Palestine. The frequent travel of many of the church's teachers as exemplified in the Acts of the Apostles warns against equating references to Palestinian pictures with a Palestinian milieu for authorship. Our author, for instance, could very well have been born and raised in Palestine and later moved to a Hellenistic city to continue his Christian ministry.[47]

Besides the geographical arguments, other indicators of a Palestinian provenance include the employment of the term "synagogue" (2:2), the mention of three and a half years as the extent of the famine during the time of Elijah (5:17), the exhortation aimed at endurance in times of stress (1:2,12), and the condemnation of the rich oppressors (1:9-11; 2:5-7; 5:1-6). Since James mentions the Jewish place of worship, the synogogue, rather than the normal Greek designation ἐκκλησία, some commentators[48] have argued that a Palestinian frame of reference is definitely envisioned. Yet evidence from the Apostolic Fathers and Apologists conclusively proves that the word συναγωγή was chosen to describe the Christian meeting place in various major centers of the Roman world.[49] Furthermore, archeologists have discovered a Marcionite assembly hall near Damascus with the superscription συναγωγὴ Μαρκωνιστῶν.[50] Finally, the Epistle to the Hebrews (written either from or to Italy[51]) employs the term ἐπισυναγωγή, a word "scarcely to be differentiated from συναγωγή",[52] to designate the assembly of a church. These reports from varous Jewish-Christian centers within the Roman world as well as the fact that James utilizes the term ἐκκλησία at 5:14 indicate that these words were used interchangeably throughout the first few generations of the church. Therefore the occurrence of συναγωγή at Jas. 2:2 cannot point to any certain geographical center.

Jeremias[53] contends that a distinct Palestinian tradition is reflected in the alteration of the period of the famine during the time of Elijah to three and a half years in Jas. 5:17; Lk. 4:25. If the six month period from the latter Palestinian rains in April until the former rains in October was attached to the three years of the famine in 1 Kings 18:1,[54] then Palestinian geography would be the determining factor. However, other hypotheses likewise account for the change in time designation. The modification to three and a half

---

[46]Davids, James, 183-184. Elliot-Binns, Galilean Christianity, 125 has used the fact that James "breathes a rural rather than a metropolitan air" to argue for a *Sitz im Leben* in Galilee.

[47]On the mobility of early Christians see Abraham Malherbe, Social Aspects of Early Christianity, 62-68.

[48]Mentioned in Mayor, James, 79; Cadoux, Thought of James, 27.

[49]In Antioch (Ig. Pol. 4:2), Rome (Herm., Mand. 11:9,13,14; Just., Dial. 63:14), and Lyons (Iren., Adv. Haer. 4,31,2).

[50]BAGD, s.v. συναγωγή, 783.2b.

[51]Heb. 13:24 "Those who come from Italy send you greetings."

[52]BAGD, s.v. ἐπισυναγωγή, 301.

[53]Joachim Jeremias, s.v. Ἠλ(ε)ίας, TDNT, II: 934. Cf. Kittel, "Der geschichtliche Ort," 58 and Aland, "Herrenbruder Jakobus," 99 for a rebutal of Kittel.

[54]Eric F.F. Bishop, "Three and a Half Years?" ExT 61(1949-50): 126f; Cf. Ellis, Luke, 98; Laws, James, 236-237.

years could be an attempt to round off the time designation to half of the number seven.[55] However, the hypothesis that the typical Jewish eschatological time period of three and one-half years (or 42 months or 1260 days) is being referred to is backed by more exegetical data. In later Jewish literature (Dan. 7:25; 12:7; Jos., Bell. 1:32) as well as the NT Apocalypse (Rev. 11:2f; 12:6,14; 13:5) the period of three and a half years was used symbolically to envision distress and world-changing upheavals. The description of a severe famine during the time of idolatrous king Ahab could easily have been identified with this apocalyptic designation.[56] Thus this eschatological time period was applied to events of Elijah both inside (Rev. 11:6,3) and outside the apocalyptic tradition (Lk. 4:25; Jas. 5:17). Therefore, although a Jewish tradition provides the background for this time designation, no geographical limitation to Palestine can be proven.

Finally, some[57] have argued that the trials described in the Epistle of James as well as its condemnation of wealthy landowners traces back to the famine during the reign of Claudius (AD 41-54) which caused severe suffering to the inhabitants of Palestine.[58] This thesis, however, cannot be verified by "hard exegetical facts". Acts 11:28 states that this famine would be spread over the entire Roman world, not Palestine alone. Furthermore, James offers no indications of the nature of the trials which he envisages. In his woe upon the rich (esp. 5:1-6) he enlists traditional OT language so that his descriptions are applicable to any time and any place in history. Therefore, no solid arguments can be produced to establish beyond a reasonable doubt that a Palestinian origin for the Epistle of James is necessary, although it is certainly a good hypothesis. The grounds produced by Gryglewicz[59] such as 1) dependence upon the OT; 2) the designations: the twelve tribes (1:1), Abraham our father (2:21), the fruit of justice (3:18), adulteresses (4:4), the just one (5:6), and the plural, heavens (5:18); 3) the Semitic notions; 4) the examples; 5) the ideas and the warnings; and 6) the fact that some theologians find the epistle to be preChristian cannot prove a Palestinian background but more appropriately indicate a Jewish-Christian author. The absolute certainty with which some authors propound a Palestinian background overlooks completely the contrary arguments produced above.

2.3 An Early Dating for the Epistle of James

In calling for a redating of the NT documents, Robinson has argued for the primitive character of the Epistle of James. The arguments basically fall into two categories: 1) the undeveloped nature of the contents of the epistle and 2) the absence of certain characteristics expected in a late Christian manuscript. Robinson[60] contends that the reference to wealthy landowners who withhold the salaries of their workers (5:4) describes a situation which disappeared in Palestine after the siege and destruction of Jerusalem in AD 66-70. Furthermore, James' address to the twelve tribes is best understood as a greeting to only Jewish Christians,[61] thus reflecting a situation where "the believing Israel constituted the entire church".[62] Since a church without Gentiles was a

---

[55]StrB III: 760f; Marshall, Luke, 189 appears to support this conclusion.

[56]Cf. Appendix I, section 3.8.

[57]Karl Holl, Gesammelte Aufsätze zur Kirchengeschichte (Tübingen: Mohr, 1928), II: 60; Hans Lietzmann, Geschichte der alten Kirche (Berlin: DeGruyter, 1936), I: 54.

[58]Physical poverty was especially evident in Palestine (Gal. 2:10; 2 Cor. 8:9; Acts 11:29).

[59]Gryglewicz, "Jacques et Matthieu," 33-34.

[60]Robinson, Redating, 120. Cf. Mayor, James, cxvi-cxviii.

[61]Cf. Adamson, James: Man and Message, 10, n. 63 for the scholarly support for various meanings of the Dispersion.

[62]Robinson, Redating, 122. Therefore, he distinguishes Jas. 1:1 from 1 Pet. 1:1, Acts 26:7, and Herm., Sim. 9,17,1f where a Jewish and Gentile Christian audience is in mind.

phenomenon of limited extension in the earliest years of the Christian movement, the Epistle of James must have emanated from this time frame. The undeveloped nature of the Christology is then used to reinforce this conclusion. Because the Epistle of James makes no mention of the sufferings, death, and resurrection of Jesus, the incarnation, atonement, or future life (doctrines which abound in the other epistles of the NT), an early Jewish-Christian theology as yet uninfluenced by the theological implications of Christ's death is detected.[63] Furthermore, the primitiveness of the church order discloses an early date. Elders are mentioned (5:14-15) without any evidence of one central leader as bishop.[64] The ministry of healing is still in full force, a phenomenon peculiar to primitive charismatic Christianity.[65] A strong and vital fellowship is disclosed in the fact that almost every paragraph is introduced with the address, "my (beloved) brethren" reminiscent of Paul's earliest writing, 1 Thessalonians,[66] and other descriptions of earliest Christianity.[67] The early eschatological expectations of the church are evident in the description of the return of the Lord "as at hand" (5:8). An early dating can also explain why the epistle does not identify James as the brother of Jesus[68] since "the simplicity of the address suggests no crisis of authority or need to resort to credentials".[69] Finally, Kittel contends that the nature and form in which the sayings of Jesus are transmitted (i.e. as allusions with no *formulae citandi*) reveal that the epistle was written at an early date.[70]

In addition to the undeveloped nature of the epistle, many commentators point to certain historical and theological developments whose absence in the Epistle of James betray an early date. Robinson[71] reports the following omissions:

1) There is no polemic directed against Judaism whereby we can assume that the church had already begun to separate itself from its Jewish origins.[72]

2) In a similar vein, there are no suggestions of a Gentile presence in the Christian community.[73]

---

[63]Cf. Cadoux, Thought of James, 5.

[64]Cf. Mayor, James, cxxiii.

[65]Ibid., cxxii.

[66]1 Thess. 1:4; 2:1,9,14,17; 3:7; 4:1,10,13; 5:1,4,12, 14,25 with every major new paragraph containing this address except 1:2 (where it is placed instead at 1:4) and 2:13 (where the second sentence at 2:14 uses this address). The frequency of this word in Pauline literature is greater only in the much lengthier epistle, 1 Corinthians (39x). James, Romans, and 1 Thessalonians all have 19 occurrences.

[67]Acts 2:42-47; 4:32-35.

[68]Kittel, "Der geschichtliche Ort," 73-75 and Davids, James, 9, n. 31 contend that the familial relationship of James to Jesus is stressed only after James' death. However, the mention of their relationship in Mk. 6:3 is certainly an important early tradition.

[69]Robinson, Redating, 124. Cf. Kittel, "Jakobusbrief und Apostolischen Väter," 110.

[70]Cf. ch. 5, section 2.2.

[71]Robinson, Redating, 120,122-124,137-138.

[72]Adamson, James: Man and Message, 161 explains that whereas Matthew is definitely anti-Jewish (Mt. 20:1-16; 21:28-34; 22:1-14; 28:15), "James is wholeheartedly interested in promoting a Christianity uncritical of and firmly grafted on Judaism."

[73]For instance, there are no references to fornication and pollution by idolatry, the two characteristic dangers associated with a Gentile environment. Knowling, James, xiii contrasts these omissions with a later document, the Didache.

3) Coupled with the omission of a Gentile mission, the absence of any mention of the circumcision controversy could point to a very early date of origin.[74]

4) There are no signs of heresy or schism as in later Pauline and Johannine writings.

5) There is no hint of the reappraisal of the nature of eschatology promoted by the delay of the *parousia*.

6) The complete lack of references to the fall of Jerusalem is striking.

7) There are substantial differences with the Apostolic Fathers. On this last point Ropes claims that "when we make a comparison with the Apostolic Fathers the positive traits which give definite character to the thinking of everyone of them are all lacking in James."[75]

A good case can thus be presented for an early dating of the Epistle of James. Yet there are other equally valid solutions that account for the undeveloped nature of Christianity as well as each of the omissions mentioned above. The omission of the Jew/Gentile controversy[76] and the orthodoxy/heresy apologetic can be explained by the fact that James is a moralist whose enemies are attitudes and behavior patterns rather than specific groups or theological heresies.[77] Likewise, James' deletion of the circumcision issue could reflect his Hellenistic view of the law whereby the cultic aspects of Jewish ceremonialism were minimized to a point that the ethical law equalled the Torah. Finally, a later date (in the 80's) outside Palestine could account for the omission of the fall of Jerusalem and James' accusation of the wealthy landowners. Similarly an early date is not the only solution accounting for the undeveloped nature of James' Christology and the omission of specifically Christian elements. Paraenesis, by definition, concentrates on human moral behavior. Therefore, we would expect to encounter exhortations describing the human response to salvation rather than soteriological statements concerning the sufficiency of the cross for forgiveness of sins. We would expect ethical demands rather than Christological propositions.[78] Finally, some of the arguments adduced for an early date are thoroughly invalid. The reference to the twelve tribes in Jas. 1:1 most naturally applies to both Jewish and Gentile Christians, based on the close similarities between 1 Peter and James.[79] The church order is not as primitive as often assumed since the church officers are petitioned to care for the sick rather than those with charismatic gifts of healing. The anointing with oil appears to have developed into an established ceremony rather than a spontaneous inspiration of the Holy Spirit. James' eschatological statements also betray a struggle with the length of time required between Jesus' first and second comings. No

---

[74]Adamson, James: Man and Message, 29 conjectures that the epistle was written before Paul was a Christian.

[75]Ropes, James, 37. For our discussion see below, pp. 216-217.

[76]Dibelius and Greeven, James, 24 state that "the most one can conclude from the absence of anti-Gentile warnings is that Jas does not have in mind recently converted Gentile Christians."

[77]One encounters behavior patterns which characterize the rich (1:9-11; 2:5-7; 5:1-6), those who hear without responding with actions (1:22-25), and those who cannot control their emotions in difficult circumstances by means of endurance (1:2-4), bridling the tongue (1:26; 3:2), and refraining from accusing God of evil (1:13-17); James criticizes general behavioral patterns such as judging (2:4), slander (4:11), grumbling (5:9), and swearing (5:12).

[78]Cf. ch. 7, section 2.3 and the 12th characteristic of paraenesis on pp. 185-186.

[79]Cf. Appendix I, section 2.3. 1 Pet. 1:18 indicates that Peter's audience in the Dispersion included Gentiles.

longer as in Mk. 13:37 are exhortations "to watch" primary, but now an explanation for "why we must wait" is presented. Jas. 5:7 explains that patience is necessary since the harvest must necessarily wait until both the early and late rains have prepared the earth. Likewise in 2 Peter 3, Christians must wait (3:12-13) for the coming judgment, recognizing that with the Lord one day is as a thousand years (3:8).[80] Aland demonstrates that James' eschatological conceptions coincide just as well with the Shepherd of Hermas.[81] Furthermore, the frequent address "my (beloved) brethren" is used regularly by certain Apostolic Fathers.[82] Finally contrary to Kittel, we have proven that the form of the allusions to dominical sayings does not substantiate an early dating for James' epistle since this identical phenomenon abounds in the Apostolic Fathers.

2.4 Authorship by James, the Brother of Jesus

Now we move to the most difficult question, i.e. whether James of Jerusalem, the brother of Jesus, wrote the Epistle of James. A large amount of evidence can be produced to substantiate the attractive hypothesis that the James whom we encounter in the Acts of the Apostles (12:17; 15:13-21; 21:18-25), in Paul's epistles (Gal. 1:19; 2:9,12; 1 Cor. 15:7), in the introduction to the Epistle of Jude (1), and in the gospels along with his brothers (Mk. 6:3; 3:32; Jn. 7:3ff) was the author of the document the church entitled "the Epistle of James". For the sake of clarity we will outline these arguments:[83]

1) The author identifies himself as James, and since James the son of Zebedee was martyred by Herod in AD 44 (Acts 12:2) and James the son of Alphaeus (Mk. 3:18 par.; Acts 1:13) is practically unknown in the NT,[84] James the brother of Jesus is the most logical choice.

2) The simplicity of the description, "a servant of God and of the Lord Jesus Christ," most likely implies that a well-known James[85] is intended and speaks decisively against pseudonymity. James the brother of Jesus is the only James who could speak without need of introduction or explanation as evidenced in Jude's introduction of himself as simply the "brother of James".[86]

3) Origen testifies that the epistle was identified with James of Jerusalem.[87]

---

[80]For differences with 2 Peter 3, see below, p. 216.

[81]Aland, "Herrenbruder Jakobus," 103 lists Vis. 2,2,5ff; 3,4,2; 3,5,5; 3,8,9; 3,9,5; 4; Sim. 1; 3; 4; 5,5,3; 6; 8,8,3ff; 8,9,4; 9,12,3; 9,19,2; 9,20,4; 9,21,4; 9,26,6; 9,32,1.

[82]1 Cl. 1:1; 4:7; 13:1; 14:1; 33:1; 37:1; 43:4; 62:1 at the beginning of paragraphs; also Barn. 2:10; 3:6; 4:14; 5:5; 6:15.

[83]The strongest arguments are presented in Guthrie, NT Introduction, 736-758; Robinson, Redating, 128-135; Kittel, "Der geschichtliche Ort," 73-84 and "Jakobus und Apostolischen Väter," 109-112.

[84]James the son of Alphaeus is consistently designated by means of the addition of his father's name, whereas James of Jerusalem is simply called James (Acts 12:17; 15:13; 21:18; Gal. 2:9,12) as in the epistle.

[85]Mitton, James, 230 states, "There is an unmistakable note of authority in the epistle which suits well the position of James of Jerusalem but is not so appropriate to an unknown James, of so little importance that his identity was soon totally forgotten."

[86]Robinson, Redating, 129.

[87]Cf. Hom. Gen. 13:2 (GCS 29, p. 115, line 27); Hom. Ex. 8:4 (GCS 29, 224, 6-7); Hom. Lev. 11:3 (GCS 29, 453, 8-9); Hom. Josh. 7:1 (GCS 30, 328, 3); Joann. 19:6 (MPG 14, 569-570).

4) The Jewish nature of the epistle supports the suggestion that a pious Jew (Eus., HE 2,23,esp. 5,6,19), such as one who would head a thoroughly Jewish church (Jerusalem), was the author.

5) The similarities to the teaching of Jesus reveal a close relationship between the two figures. Being Jesus' brother, James could have personally heard the teaching of Jesus or their common upbringing would have given them similar vocabularies and modes of thought.

6) James' speech to the Apostolic Council (Acts 15:13-21) and the composition of the resulting letter (Acts 15:23-29) exhibit similarities with the Epistle of James.[88]

a) χαίρειν as a salutation is found in the NT only at Jas. 1:1; Acts 15:23; and Acts 23:26.

b) Jas. 2:7 τὸ καλὸν ὄνομα τὸ ἐπικληθὲν ἐφ' ὑμᾶς ("the honorable name which was invoked over you") is paralleled in Acts 15:17: ἐφ' οὓς ἐπικέκληται τὸ ὄνομά μου ἐπ' αὐτούς ("who are called by my name").

c) The word ὄνομα occurs in Jas. 2:7; 5:10,14; and Acts 15:14,26 in a specifically pregnant sense, occurring nowhere else in the NT in quite the same sense.

d) Both quote the OT frequently: Acts 15:14,16-18,21.

e) The affectionate address ἀδελφός popular with James is also chosen in Acts 15:13,23.

f) There are several examples of similar vocabulary: ἀκούσατε with the address "my brethren" (Jas. 2:5; Acts 15:13); ἐπισκέπτεσθαι (Jas. 1:27; Acts 15:14); τηρεῖν and διατηρεῖν (Jas. 1:27; Acts 15:29); ἐπιστρέφειν (Jas. 5:19,20; Acts 15:19); ἀγαπητός (Jas. 1:16,19; 2:5; Acts 15:25).

The forcefulness of these arguments is undercut when we examine more closely the validity of these claims. This is especially applicable to the last piece of evidence comparing Acts 15:13-29 with the Epistle of James. The greeting χαίρειν is the standard Greek epistolary greeting[89] and is prevalent among many Jewish writers as shown by its occurrences in Esther 8:12b LXX; 1 Esd. 6:7b-8a; 8:9; 1 Mac. 10:18,25; 11:30,32; 12:6,20; 13:36; 14:20; 15:2,16; 2 Mac. 1:1,10; 9:19; 11:16,22,27,34; 3 Mac. 3:12; 7:1; Arist. 35,41.[90] The standardized nature of this address is verified by comparing the structure of Jas. 1:1, Acts 15:23, 23:26, and the Jewish apocraphal texts above. The overwhelming majority contain three distinct parts each in the exact sequence: the specifying of the author followed in the dative case by the intended audience and concluded with the single word, χαίρειν.[91] There-

---

[88]These similarities are taken from Oesterley, "James," 392. Cf. also Adamson, James: Man and Message, 18-20; Grosheide, Jakobus, 327; Knowling, James, xxv; Mayor, James, iii-iv.

[89]Even a proponent of traditional authorship like Robinson, Redating, 130 admits this.

[90]Cf. also Jos., Vita 217; 365 and the inscriptions to Ignatius' epistles (Eph., Mag., Pol., Rom., Smyr., Trall.) which contain the greeting πλεῖστα χαίρειν. 2 Jn. 10-11 also employs the infinitive form in speaking about refusing to greet heretics.

[91]The only exceptions are 2 Mac. 1:1; 9:19 which follow the order: intended audience, greeting, author; 1 Mac. 1:30 which attaches an additional audience after the greeting; and 2 Mac. 1:1; 9:19; 3 Mac. 3:12; 7:1; Arist. 35 which add a greeting of good health.

fore, no exclusive connection between Jas. 1:1 and Acts 15:23 can be established through their similar greetings.

The argument that Acts 15:17 compares remarkably with Jas. 2:7 is also misleading. Acts 15:17 is an OT quotation (Amos 9:11-12 LXX) in the speech of James, and the vocabulary of a source cannot be said to typify the usual vocabulary of an author citing the quotation. Furthermore, Robinson himself admits that the invoking of the name of God upon people is "quite unremarkable in a Jewish writer",[92] since the regular OT usage is here exhibited (Dt. 28:10; Is. 63:19). Unless we fail to understand Oesterley's argument for contending that the word ὄνομα is used in a special pregnant sense, our verdict is that his judgment is imprecise. In fact, the specific sense given to the term ὄνομα in Acts 15:14 is clearly distinguishable from its content and usage in Acts 15:26. In the first instance the word "name" is a circumlocution for God, while a few verses later Jesus Christ is being referred to and the translation "for the sake of" is more appropriate than "for himself". Furthermore, when Jas. 5:10,14 mention "speaking in the name of the Lord," the meaning corresponds much better with other passages of Acts like 10:48 "being baptized in the name of the Lord" and 16:18 where demons are cast out in the name of the Lord. Oesterley is correct in contending that both Acts 15:13-29 and the Epistle of James frequently quote the OT, yet this is expected in Acts 15 since the authority needed to ground a decision would naturally be the OT scriptures. The only deduction that logically flows from this evidence is the conclusion that both speakers are Jewish Christians or at least strongly influenced by the OT.

Oesterley and others call attention to a group of terms common to both Acts 15 and James' epistle, yet the arbitrariness of their claims is especially evident at this point. The address ἀκούσατε ἀδελφοί μου (Jas. 2:5; Acts 15:13) is not uniquely Jamesian. Robinson even admits that a fixed formula is being utilized which "is more exactly paralleled in Stephen's speech in Acts 7:2 and Paul's address in Acts 22:1 than in Jas. 2:5."[93] The address ἄνδρες ἀδελφοί coupled with the imperative ἀκούσατε at Acts 15:13 is certainly Lucan since numerous parallels in the book of Acts can be cited (1:16,29; 2:37; 7:2; 13:15, 26,38; 15:7). The term ἐπισκέπτεσθαι is also Lucan since seven out of eleven occurrences are located in Lucan literature (Lk. 3x; Acts 4x). Along with ἐπιστρέφειν it occurs in "markedly different contexts in Acts and James and represents in fact characteristic Lukan usage rather than anything distinctive of James."[94] This is proven by the fact that half of the occurrences of ἐπιστρέφειν in the NT appear in Luke's gospel (7x) and Acts (11x). Regarding ἀγαπητός any similarities with the Epistle of James must be dismissed since this address is employed as a popular term of endearment to defend the authority of Paul and Barnabas (Acts 15:25) and not because it is characteristic Jamesian vocabulary. Furthermore, διατηρεῖν is unique to Lucan writings (cf. Lk. 2:5), and the phraseology in Jas. 1:27 (ἄσπιλον ἑαυτὸν τηρεῖν) is closer to other writings where moral instruction is emphasized than to Acts 15:29.[95] Finally, whereas Acts 15 focuses on ceremonial pollution (eating blood, food sacrificed to idols, and meat of strangled animals), James nowhere mentions any ceremonial requirements regarding food, circumcision, the Sabbath, or even the one ethical absention cited in Acts 15:29, πορνεία (sexual immorality).

Contrary to Guthrie it is not that "these parallels are remarkable,"[96] but what is truly remarkable is the differences between the speech and letter assigned to James in Acts

---

[92]Robinson, Redating, 130-131.

[93]Ibid., 130.

[94]Ibid., 131. Robinson argues against his fellow proponents of a traditional authorship; his honest conclusion is that "nothing therefore can be built on such parallels."

[95]Wis. 10:5 ἐτήρησεν αὐτὸν ἄμεμπτον; 1 Tim. 5:22 σεαυτὸν ἁγνὸν τήρει; 1 Tim. 6:14 τηρῆσαί σε τὴν ἐντολὴν ἄσπιλον; 2 Cl. 8:4 τὴν σάρκα ἁγνὴν τηρήσαντες; 2 Cl. 8:6 τηρήσατε τὴν σάρκα ἁγνὴν καὶ τὴν σφραγῖδα ἄσπιλον. Cf. BAGD, s.v. τηρέω, 815.2b.

[96]Guthrie, NT Introduction, 742.

15 and the epistle supposedly written by the same brother of Jesus. Much of the vocabulary employed in the speech and letter is completely absent from the Epistle of James but characteristic of Luke. The following list is enlightening:

A. The relationship between the Epistle of James and the terminology employed in the message of James (Acts 15:13-21).[97]

1) Acts 15:13 ἀκούειν: Acts and Luke rank first and second in the frequency with which this verb is used.

2) Acts 15:14 ἐξηγεῖσθαι: not in James but five out of six occurrences in the NT are found in Lucan literature.

3) Acts 15:14 καθώς: not in James yet 28x in Luke-Acts.

4) Acts 15:14,19 ἔθνος: not in James yet 56x in Luke-Acts.

5) Acts 15:14 λαός: not in James yet 84x in Luke-Acts.

6) Acts 15:15 συμφονεῖν: not in James but half of the occurrences in the NT appear in Lucan literature (3 of 6).

7) Acts 15:19: κρίνειν is a favorite Jamesian term (6x), yet it is always used in an unfavorable sense, "to find fault with, criticize, condemn," whereas in Acts 15:19 a positive sense is required as in Acts 4:19; 16:15; and 26:8.[98]

8) Acts 15:20,29 ἀπεχεῖν: not in James.

9) Acts 15:20 εἴδωλον and πορνεία: not in James.

10) Acts 15:21 γενεά: not in James whereas Luke's gospel has the most occurrences in the NT (15 out of 33).

11) Acts 15:21 ἀρχαῖος: not in James whereas 5 out of 11 occurrences appear in Lucan literature.

12) Acts 15:21 πόλις: once in James whereas Acts (42x) and Luke (39x) by a wide margin rank first and second in the frequency of occurrence (Paul only four times).

13) Acts 15:21 κηρύσσειν: not in James but 17x in Luke-Acts.

14) Acts 15:21 σάββατον: not in James whereas it occurs most frequently in Luke (20x).

15) Acts 15:21 ἀναγινώσκειν: not in James whereas Acts (along with Paul) has the most occurrences (8x).

---

[97]We do not include terminology from the OT quotes since this would be source material rather than the author's characteristic vocabulary. The statistics are gleaned from Robert Morgenthaler, Statistik des neutestamentlichen Wortschatzes (Zürich: Gotthelf, 1982).

[98]Cf. BAGD, s.v. κρίνω, 451.2.

B. The relationship between the Epistle of James and the terminology employed in the letter allegedly written by James (Acts 15:23-29).

1) Acts 15:24 ἐπειδή: not in James but one-half of the occurrences in the NT appear in Luke-Acts (5 out of 10).

2) Acts 15:24 ταράσσειν: not in James; 5x in Lucan literature.

3) Acts 15:25,28 δοκεῖν: The impersonal use "it seems best to me" is Lucan as in Lk. 1:3.[99]

4) Acts 15:25 ὁμοθυμαδός: 10 out of 11 occurrences in Acts.

5) Acts 15:25 ἐκλέγεσθαι: one-half of the NT occurrences (11 out of 22) are found in Lucan literature.

6) Acts 15:25 πέμπειν: not in James; 11x in Acts.

7) Acts 15:25 πρός with the accusative: twice in James; 164x in Luke and 133x in Acts.

8) Acts 15:25 σύν: once in James; 52x in Acts.

9) Acts 15:26 παραδιδόναι: not in James; 30x in Luke-Acts.

10) Acts 15:26 ψυχή: James 2x; Luke 13x; Acts 15x. Bauer[100] places Jas. 1:21 and 5:20 under the heading "the soul as seat and center of life that transcends the earthly" whereas Acts 15:26 with Lk. 12:22f; Acts 20:24; 27:10,22 refer to "earthly life itself".

11) Acts 15:27 ἀποστέλλειν: not in James; 30x in Luke-Acts.

12) Acts 15:27 δία with the genitive: once in James; 54x in Acts.

13) Acts 15:28 πνεῦμα: in James πνεῦμα is not employed for the Holy Spirit (2:26; 4:5) whereas the word is a favorite term of Luke (106x Luke; 70x Acts).

14) Acts 15:28 μηδέν: not in James.

15) Acts 15:28 ἐπιτιθέναι: not in James; 14x in Acts.

16) Acts 15:28 πλήν: not in James; more than one-half of the NT occurrences appear in Lucan literature (19 out of 31).

17) Acts 15:29 πράσσειν: not in James; 13x in Acts.

One might attempt to counter this lengthy list of evidence with the claim that the Epistle of James is not written to Gentiles as the letter from James in Acts 15:23ff, and therefore the vocabulary is greatly divergent. However, the list above includes prepositions and commonly used verbs which are not controlled by the audience addressed. Thus, a comparison between Acts 15:13-29 and the Epistle of James cannot be employed to prove that James of Jerusalem is the figure behind the letter beginning "James, a servant of God and of the

---

[99]Cf. BAGD, s.v. δοκέω, 202.3b.
[100]Cf. BAGD, s.v. ψυχή, 893.1c vs. 893.1aβ.

Lord Jesus Christ." Oesterley's conclusion that the similarities between Acts 15 and the Epistle of James "almost compels us to recognize the same mind at work in each"[101] is totally misleading.

Proponents of the traditional view of authorship further claim that the verbal and content similarities with the Synoptic gospels reveal that our author personally knew Jesus and heard his teaching. Yet we have demonstrated that the allusions to sayings of Jesus are in most cases quite different from the exact wording of the Synoptic tradition.[102] No direct relationship with Jesus is necessarily presupposed since our author could have received his knowledge of the sayings of Jesus through contact with the church's paraenetic tradition. Furthermore, the obvious Jewish nature of the epistle could point to any Jew named James and does not necessarily specify James of Jerusalem. The view that the unmistakable note of authority in the epistle suits well the position of James of Jerusalem[103] is countered by Henshaw who states,

> The idea that he speaks with authority is the exact opposite of the truth; he says nothing for which he cannot find warrant in previous recognized authorities.[104]

The fact that within early church history the epistle was regarded as "spurious" [105] indicates that the identity of Ἰάκωβος with James of Jerusalem was not a natural deduction. The strongest argument for the traditional view of authorship is unmistakeably the fact that we have so little information about other men named "James" in the early church.

There are three pieces of evidence which fail to harmonize with the traditional view of authorship and force the exegete to rethink his/her assumptions: 1) the excellent Greek style; 2) the purely ethical content given to the law; and 3) the delayed acceptance into the canon. The picture we deduce of James of Jerusalem from the NT is that of an Aramaic-speaking, Galilean peasant who spent his whole life within the Jewish, Palestinian, first-century culture. On the other hand, the impression we derive from reading the Greek version of the Epistle of James is that the writer was a cultured stylist with a large Greek vocabulary whose diction is shaped by Hellenistic culture and a first-hand knowledge of the Greek language.[106] Greek rather than Aramaic or Hebrew would appear to be his primary language. In a guarded manner Turner will admit that "some of his vocabulary belongs to the higher reaches of the literary koine."[107] More boldly Mayor states that "the author comes nearer to the classical standard than any NT author, except perhaps Hebrews, which has a larger variety of constructions."[108] An added paradox lies in the fact that the content of the epistle appears thoroughly Jewish while its style with a large amount of rhyme and

---

[101]Oesterley, "James," 392. Instead the vocabulary of Acts 15:13-29 reveals the hand of Lucan redaction.

[102]Cf. below, pp. 222-223,226.

[103]Cf. above, n. 85.

[104]Thomas Henshaw, New Testament Literature in the Light of Modern Scholarship, 359.

[105]Mentioned in Eus., HE 2:23; Jerome, De Virus Illustribus, 2. Cf. Brooke F. Westcott, A General Survey of the History of the Canon of the New Testament, 452.

[106]Martin Dibelius, A Fresh Approach to the New Testament and Early Christian Literature, 229-230 states, "The style is frequently cultured, the Greek vocabulary large, the entire diction not of a man whose real language was Aramaic."

[107]Moulton and Turner, Grammar, IV: 115. Turner cites these examples: "give birth to (Plutarch, Lucian), entice (2 Peter, Josephus, Philo), gloominess (Plutarch, Philo)."

[108]Mayor, James, ccxvi.

alliteration,[109] the use of rare compounds[110] and particles placed in the second position in the sentence,[111] similarities with the Stoic-Cynic diatribe,[112] and certain niceties of grammatical distinctions[113] suggests a Hellenistic writer. Patry concludes, for example, that if one considers only the contents of James, an acceptance of authorship by Jesus' brother would be fitting, but the Greek form, on the other hand, speaks against this view.[114]

How can we account for these opposing tendencies encountered in this document? An increasingly popular supposition suggests that James learned Greek from his youth in a bilingual Galilean environment. Easton asserts, for instance, that because "Nazareth lay on a thronged trade route, it may be assumed that most Nazarenes would pick up more or less Greek of some sort or other."[115] But it was Sevenster's work more than any single influence that pushed scholarly opinion to accept the fact of a bilingual Galilee.[116] He explains,

> It is no longer possible to refute such a possibility by recalling that these were usually people of modest origins. It has now been clearly demonstrated that a knowledge of Greek was in no way restricted to upper circles, which were permeated with Hellenistic culture, but was to be found in all circles of Jewish society, and certainly in places bordering on regions where Greek was much spoken, e.g. Galilee.[117]

Exegetical support for a knowledge of Greek throughout Palestine derives from the fact that the crowd in Acts 22:2 expected to hear Paul speak in the Greek language. Therefore we affirm the hypothesis that James as well as Jesus[118] could understand and converse in Greek. Yet whether someone without Hellenistic experience, who spoke Greek only infrequently as a second language, could write in the quality literary Greek which we encounter in the Epistle of James is another question. Some argue that "acquainted with Greek from boyhood, his position of leadership in the Jerusalem church would make it necessary for him to develop proficiency in its use."[119] Certainly there were Greek-speaking Hellenists in the Jerusalem church from the very beginning (Acts 6:9). Therefore, it is possible that "daily contact with these Hellenists, as well as frequent practice in public speak-

---

[109]Rhyme at 1:6,14; 2:12; 4:8; alliteration on the sound p at 1:2,3,11,17,22; 3:2; m at 3:5; d at 1:1,6,21; 2:16; 3:18; d and p at 1:21; l at 1:4; 3:4; k at 1:26f; 2:3; 4:8.

[110]Cf. Mayor, James, ccxviii-ccxix. These rare compounds have been explained by the employment of a professional interpreter by some commentators who support the traditional view of authorship (cf. p. ccxxxvii).

[111]Cf. the table prepared by Turner in Moulton and Turner, Grammar, IV: 119.

[112]Cf. ch. 5, section 3.3 and Moulton and Turner, Grammar, IV: 114-115.

[113]Bruce M. Metzger, "The Language of the New Testament," The Interpreter's Bible, VII: 47 states, "The author observes certain niceties of grammatical distinctions (such as the correct usage of the two negatives in Greek, οὐ and μή) and maintains a high degree of precision in the idiomatic choice of moods and tenses."

[114]Patry, Jacques, 121.

[115]Easton, "The Epistle of James," The Interpreter's Bible, XII: 6.

[116]Jan N. Sevenster, Do You Know Greek? How Much Greek Could the First Jewish Christians Have Known? A complete list of literature supporting this view can be found in Robinson, Redating, 133, n. 46. Cf. also Gerald Mussies, "The Greek as the Vehicle of Early Christianity," NTS 29(1983): 356-369 and Charlesworth, OT Pseudepigrapha and the NT, 86 who states that "the works in the Pseudepigrapha reveal that Jews, including those in Palestine, could write in excellent Greek."

[117]Sevenster, Do You Know Greek? 190.

[118]Cf. Moulton, Grammar I: 8, n. 1.

[119]Hiebert, James, 19.

ing and debate, would give James ample opportunity to develop proficiency in the use of the language."[120] Furthermore, if Jude, another brother of Jesus could write an epistle in quality literary Greek, why could not also James?

The explanation of a bilingual Palestine, however, can only be categorized as one possibility among many.[121] Another recognized hypothesis states that James used an amanuensis.[122] Recently Davids has argued that

> In the light of the Greek idiom used in the work, it is likely that either James received assistance in the editing of the work or that his teaching was edited at a later date (perhaps after his death) as the church spread beyond Jerusalem and began to use Greek more exclusively.[123]

However, there are no specific indications of the employment of an amanuensis as in the epistles of Paul (Tertius in Rom. 16:2) and Peter (Silvanus in 1 Pet. 5:12). Furthermore, scholars have arrived at contrary conclusions over the popularity of scribal redactors in the ancient world. On the one hand, Beasley-Murray concludes that "in the Hellenistic age in which the New Testament was written, scarcely an author gave even his letters their final form in language and style; the dependence of authors on the art of the scribes was well-nigh universal."[124] On the other hand, Sevenster asserts that the employment of an educated scribe "probably seldom occurred".[125] With such a lack of consensus with regard to both the utilization of an amanuensis and the amount of freedom given to such a person in composing an epistle, it is practically impossible to support this line of argumentation convincingly.

Others explain the excellent Greek by referring to James' intellectual qualifications rather than the bilingual environment of Galilee or the thesis of an amanuensis. Mitton states that "James must have been a man of quite extraordinary intelligence and ability to have risen so quickly to the position he achieved."[126] This argument, however, can be countered by the hypothesis that James received his position in the Jerusalem church not because of personal qualifications but because of Jesus' revelation to him (1 Cor. 15:7). Another equally supportable deduction from the paradox of Semitic content and Hellenistic style is the conclusion that James was a non-Palestinian Jew "whose rhetorical training was Hellenistic, but whose religious background was firmly Hebraic."[127] The excellent rhetorical features and stylistic development could reveal the well-rounded Hellenistic education and upbringing of our author. The best solution is to affirm that the high literary Greek alone cannot disprove the authorship of James of Jerusalem, but coupled with the next two problems we will present, it offers one clue that the evidence for the traditional view that James, the brother of Jesus, wrote the epistle is not nearly as conclusive as sometimes assumed.

---

[120] Ibid.

[121] Even Sevenster, Do You Know Greek? 191 states his thesis only as a possibility.

[122] Cf. Mayor, James, ccxxxvii; Kittel, "Der geschichtliche Ort," 79f; and Lohse, "Glaube und Werke," 20 who criticizes Kittel's views.

[123] Davids, James, 22.

[124] George R. Beasley-Murray, The General Epistles: James, 1 Peter, Jude, and 2 Peter, 19.

[125] Sevenster, Do You Know Greek? 12. He points to the use of key words, word plays, alliteration, and the arrangement of the epistle's content into short pericopes to refute such a claim (pp. 13-14).

[126] Mitton, James, 228.

[127] Easten, "The Epistle of James," The Interpreter's Bible, XII: 5.

Dibelius insists that "the decisive argument against James as the author arises from the position of our document with regard to the Law."[128] We will first trace the view of the law traditionally assigned to James of Jerusalem in the Biblical record and the writings of the church fathers; then we will contrast these results with the interpretation of the law encountered in the Epistle of James. The legalistic piety of James is described by Hegesippus through the pen of Eusebius.[129]

> He drank no wine or strong drink, nor did he eat flesh; no razor went upon his head; he did not anoint himself with oil, and did not go to the baths. He alone was to enter into the sanctuary, for he did not wear wool but linen, and he used to enter alone into the temple and be found kneeling and praying for forgiveness for the people, so that his knees grew hard like a camel's because of his constant worship of God, kneeling and asking forgiveness for the people.[130]

The Biblical record offers supportive backing to the claim that James was chiefly concerned with the ceremonial dimensions of the law. In Gal. 2:12 James is regarded as the spiritual leader of those who advocated that Jews should not break bread with Gentile Christians.[131] Likewise in Acts 21:24 James encourages Paul to practice the ritual injunction of shaving the head. Finally in Acts 15 James insists that Gentiles abstain from certain types of forbidden food, namely sacrifices offered to idols, blood, and the meat of strangled animals (15:29). Thus in each prominent reference to James in the NT the importance of the Jewish ceremonial law is underlined.

With this in mind one would naturally expect to be confronted with the significance of ritual laws when reading an epistle from James of Jerusalem. However, although the keeping of the moral law is of paramount importance to the Epistle of James, nowhere are there prescriptions about ceremonial laws. The content of the law consists completely of ethical injunctions similar to the expected emphasis of a Hellenistic Jew. There is no talk of food laws, circumcision, the Sabbath, purification,[132] or eating with Gentiles even though the injunction at 1:27, to keep oneself unstained from the world, would have been an ideal opportunity for such ceremonial prescriptions. James mentions oaths in 5:12 but offers no examples of legitimate oath ceremonies.[133] Neither are there any injunctions promoting the ideals which according to Eusebius and Hegesippus James championed: abstinence from wine and meat, avoiding the razor, and refraining from anointing oneself with oil[134] or going to the baths. There is teaching about prayer (1:5-8; 4:2-3; 5:14-18) but never about kneeling in prayer; the importance of clothing is stressed (2:2-4,15-16), but the appropriate type of clothing (wool vs. linen) is never discussed. Instead, moral and social sins are emphasized: evil desire (1:14), anger (1:20), moral filth

---

128Dibelius and Greeven, James, 17.

129The truth of these legends is called into question by Dibelius and Greeven, James, 16 and Davids, James, 19, n. 71, while Daniélou, Theology of Jewish Christianity, 370 says that there "does not appear to be any ground for calling in question the historical validity of the text." We will only reproduce those aspects of Hegesippus' account which are analogous to the scriptural descriptions of James in Galatians and Acts.

130Eus. HE 2,23,6-7 in Kirsopp Lake, Eusebius: Ecclesiastical History, LCL, I: 171.

131Yet this detail does not prove that James agreed with those Judaizers on this point or was the real leader of the circumcision party since a consensus with Paul in these matters is expressed in Gal. 2:9 and Acts 15:13-21.

132Jas. 4:8 does not refer to ritual purification but to the fact that both overt conduct and inner motives must be set right. Cf. Seitz, "James and the Law," 481-482.

133Cf. above, pp. 137-140.

134In fact, the use of oil is advocated for healing (5:14).

(1:21), sins of evil speech (1:26; 3:1-12), favoritism (2:1), the injustice wrought by the rich (2:5-7; 5:1-6), adultery and murder (2:11), coveting and quarreling (4:2), slander (4:11), and boasting (4:16). It is true that Hegesippus' description of James as "famous among all for righteousness" and "no respecter of persons"[135] corresponds with two emphases within the Epistle of James. However, righteousness is connected with moral attributes like the absence of anger (1:20) and the presence of peace (3:18) rather than with any ritual ceremonies. Furthermore, the Greek expression used by Hegesippus to describe favoritism (πρόσωπον οὐ λαμβάνεις) is not the term employed by James at 2:1,9 (προσωποληψίαις, προσωποληπτεῖτε) but fits much better the pattern of Lk. 20:21 (οὐ λαμβάνεις πρόσωπον) since in each case the statement is used by opponents as a covering for evil motives (i.e. part of the plot to kill Jesus or James). Finally, the expression "law of freedom" (1:25; 2:12) does not coincide with the apparent emphases of James of Jerusalem expressed in Gal. 2:12, Acts 15:29, and Acts 21:24.[136] If James wrote prior to Paul, as many advocates of an early date and authorship by James of Jerusalem maintain, how can one account for the inconsistency between the prominence given by James to ceremonial laws in Galatians and Acts and the complete omission of this emphasis in his epistle. If James conceded to the demands of Paul and Barnabas at the Apostolic Council described in Acts 15, certainly before this circumcision conflict he must have been more demanding with regard to ritual laws.[137]

Most supporters of the traditional view of authorship[138] challenge the assumption that James the Just was legalistic by pointing to James' spirit of conciliation in his approach toward circumcision (Acts 15:22f) and in his relationship with Paul (Gal. 2:9).[139] Robinson contends that the ritual observations urged by James were not a matter of principle but only of tact (Acts 21:21-26).[140] Therefore a discussion about ritual purity could easily be omitted in James' development of his religious principles in the epistle. The particular audience to which the epistle is directed might explain James' omission of the ceremonial law. Davids, for instance, states that "one would not expect him to stress this form of piety when writing to Jewish Christians who held the same position."[141] However, the postulation of a Hellenistic audience in the Dispersion might also explain this omission. Since Hellenistic Jews emphasized the ethical dimensions of the law to make their religious faith more attractive to the Greeks, it would be quite natural for James to omit the mentioning of the ceremonial law, especially if he possessed a mediating personality.[142]

---

[135]Eus., HE 2,23,19 and 10 in Lake, Eusebius: Ecclesiastical History, LCL, I: 177,173.

[136]Therefore Mayor, James, ii-iii is far from the truth when he states, "If we turn now to the Epistles of St. Paul and to the Acts of the Apostles we find mention of a James who exactly fulfils the conditions required in the writer of the Epistle."

[137]Robinson, Redating, 132 insists that James' attitude toward the law is only an argument against placing the date in the context of the controversy with the Judaizers and not a general objection to his authorship.

[138]Jean Cantinat, "The Catholic Epistles," in André Robert and André Feuillet, Introduction to the New Testament, 562; Davids, James, 19; Guthrie, NT Introduction, 751.

[139]Kittel, "Der geschichtliche Ort," 99 offers the less convincing solution that James omitted the ceremonial aspects of the law to distance himself from the raving, wild Judaizers.

[140]Robinson, Redating, 132.

[141]Davids, James, 20. Cf. Adamson, James: Man and Message, 23.

[142]Another solution might be the genre of paraenesis. H. Dixon Slingerland, The Testaments of the Twelve Patriarchs: A Critical History of Research (Missoula: Scholars, 1977), 110 perceives a "curious absence of references to the ritual elements of the Law, i.e. Sabbath and circumcision" in the paraenetic passages of the Testaments of the Twelve Patriarchs. However, this does not seem to be universally applicable since Paul speaks about circumcision (Gal. 5:1-4) and the Sabbath (Rom. 14:5-6) in or near paraenetic sections.

These explanations are plausible although it must be admitted that this discrepancy has caused some writers to conclude that "no one would dream that the apostle James was meant by the James of ver. 1 merely by reading the contents of the epistle."[143] Even a staunch supporter of the traditional authorship like Zahn admits that the epistle "does not bring out a single one of those characteristics by which James is distinguished in history and legend."[144]

A third argument against the traditional view of authorship is the late acceptance of the Epistle of James into the canon. If the Epistle of Jude was accepted from an early date,[145] why would another epistle assigned to a brother of Jesus have had such a rocky history before finally being accepted into the canon? The Epistle of James was neither accepted into the Muratorian Canon believed to represent the judgment of the church at Rome (AD 170-200)[146] nor included in the so-called "Cheltenham List" depicting the opinion of the church of Africa as late as AD 360.[147] Nothing in the writings of Irenaeus (185),[148] Tertullian (200), or Cyprian (250) indicates any awareness of the epistle's existence. Josephus (100) and Hegesippus (180) preserve traditions about James of Jerusalem yet reveal no knowledge of an epistle. In the east there is no explicit mention of the letter until the time of Origen (230).[149] Clement of Alexandria comments only upon 1 Peter, Jude, and 1 and 2 John in his Hypotyposeis.[150] In Caesarea Eusebius categorized it among the disputed books (ἀντιλεγόμενα), although he harbored no reservations about its authenticity. In Syria the Peshitta (c. 412) is the first witness of the inclusion of the Epistle of James into the canon. Probably the earliest incontrovertible quotation of James is found

---

143Moffatt, Historical NT, 582. Cf. Aland, "Herrenbruder Jakobus," 100.

144Theodore Zahn, Introduction to the New Testament, I: 140. Cf. Robinson, Redating, 130.

145Accepted by the Muratorian Canon, Clement of Alexandria, Origen, and Tertullian but in Eusebius' disputed list (HE 3,25,3; 2,23,25).

146Edgar Hennecke, New Testament Apocrypha, I: 42 states that the catalogue originated around AD 200, but Westcott, History of the Canon, 212 contends that it cannot be placed much later than AD 170. Guthrie, NT Introduction, 737 appeals to "the obviously corrupt state of the text of that canon" to argue that little weight may be attached to it as evidence for exclusion from the canon of the Roman church. Westcott (pp. 530-534) describes the errors in the Muratorian Canon, yet at this particular point in the text there is no evidence of its corrupt state.

147Cf. Mitton, James, 219.

148Cf. Dibelius and Greeven, James, 34. Adamson, James: Man and Message, 126 believes that Irenaeus knew of the Epistle of James.

149In Joann. 19:23 (A.E. Brooke, The Commentary of Origen on S. John's Gospel (Cambridge: Un. Press, 1896), 32) and Mt. 10:17 on Mt. 13:55-56 (Robert Girod, SC 162, pp. 216-218) he refers to James' epistle explaining that the author is usually understood to be the Lord's brother. Laws, James, 24 thinks that Origen knew of James' epistle only after moving to Caesarea, but two third century Egyptian papyri, p^{20} and p^{23}, contain parts of James' epistle. For further references see Dibelius and Greeven, James, 52, n. 199.

150Eusebius (HE 6,14,1) states that Clement did not pass over even the disputed writings, i.e. the Epistle of Jude and the remaining Catholic epistles. Yet it is questionable whether Eusebius intended to include James in the category, "Catholic epistles." Cassiodorus, chief minister of Theodoric, in his "Introduction to the Reading of Holy Scripture" says that Clement made comments on 1 Peter, 1 and 2 John, and James. However, as Westcott, History of the Canon, 357-358 explains, "There can be little doubt that the reading in Cassiodorus is false, and that 'Jude' should be substituted for 'James'." Clement's silence as to the contents of James prove that he was unacquainted with the epistle. Cf. also Ropes, James, 91-93.

in the Pseudo-Clementine tractate De Virginitate (1,11,4) in the third century.[151] The place of the Epistle of James in the canon was finally assured when it was included in the lists of Athanasius (367) and Cyril of Jerusalem (378) and recognized as canonical by the Third Council of Carthage (397).[152]

How can we account for this late and gradual acceptance into the Christian canon? If the epistle was written by James, one of the reputed pillars of the church along with Peter and John (Gal. 2:9), why was it not quickly accepted into the recognized Holy Writings of the churches? Harnack[153] thought the hypothesis of an anonymous writing with a secondary prescript (Jas. 1:1) would explain why the epistle was not earlier recognized as canonical. However, Dibelius has argued that the play on words in 1:1 and 1:2 (χαίρειν / χαράν) makes this thesis unlikely.[154] In its place Dibelius, following his custom of explaining every unique aspect of the Epistle of James by means of its genre,[155] suggests that since the language of paraenesis quickly becomes obsolete, the epistle was not accepted until the authority of its patron became important to the church.[156] A similar opinion is proposed by Sparks who believes that the practical attitude evident in the letter was viewed to be of little consequence by those who were more interested in theological and Christological statements.[157] This might explain its lack of popularity, but surely would not account for the disputed nature of the epistle if it was believed to have the authority of James of Jerusalem. A third solution[158] points to a limited circulation and sphere of influence among a Jewish-Christian audience as the explanation for the obscurity surrounding the letter, and the fact that James did not claim apostolic authority as the solution for the disputed history of the epistle. Yet the Jewish audience of the Gospel of Matthew did not result in that book's obscurity, nor did Jude's failure to claim apostolic authority result in omission from the Muratorian Canon. A fourth recommendation contends that James' late acceptance into the canon was due to "the apparent contradiction between its teaching concerning the relationship of faith and works and that of St. Paul."[159] We believe this is the most likely explanation if one accepts an authorship by James of Jerusalem. Yet its disputed nature and delayed acceptance into the canon could have been caused by the early

---

[151]Dibelius and Greeven, James, 51. M.B. Riddle, "Two Epistles Concerning Virginity," The Ante-Nicene Fathers, VIII: 59, column 1, lines 3ff translates, "And they hearken not to that which the Scripture has said: 'Let not many be teachers among you, my brethren, and be not all of you prophets.' For 'he who does not transgress in word is a perfect man able to keep down and subjugate his whole body!" In addition to alluding to Jas. 3:1-2, there is a second reference to Jas. 1:5 later in the same chapter, "Blessed be God, who helps every man without grudging -- that God who gives to every man and does not upbraid him" (column 2, lines 1ff).

[152]Based upon the information of this paragraph the opinion of Mayor, James, cxxi cannot be sustained: "it was apparently commented on, along with the other Catholic Epistles, by Clement of Alexandria, and is referred to anonymously by Irenaeus, Theophilus, Justin Martyr, the writers of the Epistle to Diognetus, and the so-called second epistle of Clement, by Ignatius, Polycarp ... during the second century; by Clement of Rome, and the author of the Didache during the first century, also by Barnabas, and the author of the Testaments of the Twelve Patriarchs."

[153]Adolf von Harnack, Geschichte der altchristlichen Litteratur bis Eusebius (Leipzig: Hinrichs, 1897), part 2, vol. 1, 487f.

[154]Dibelius and Greeven, James, 53.

[155]Cf. above, p. 24.

[156]Dibelius and Greeven, James, 53-54.

[157]Hedley F.D. Sparks, The Formation of the New Testament, 129. Cf. Mitton, James, 227.

[158]Mayor, James, li; Knowling, James, liii.

[159]Tasker, OT in NT, 125.

recognition that this book was not written by James the Just. This was certainly the fate of the Shepherd of Hermas which is excluded from the Muratorian Canon since "Hermas wrote the Shepherd quite lately in our time in the city of Rome."[160] Is it not also possible that Hebrews and James were omitted from this list because the church at Rome was familiar with the authors and did not classify Apollos[161] and "James, a servant of God and of the Lord Jesus Christ" as apostles around the year AD 180?[162] Their recognition as canonical would then only take place in a distant location by those unfamiliar with the authors so that in Alexandria Hebrews would be accepted as Pauline and the Epistle of James as from James of Jerusalem.[163] This particular suggestion is undoubtedly hypothetical; however, the combined force of the contrasts between the cultured literary Greek of the epistle vs. the Aramaic-speaking James of Jerusalem, the ethical law of freedom of the epistle vs. the emphasis of James of Jerusalem upon ceremonial rituals, and the delayed and disputed acceptance of the epistle vs. the obvious authority given to the figure of James, the brother of Jesus, compel us to consider other hypotheses of authorship and provenance which might account for these difficulties.

We will then turn to consider a second solution, a Roman origin in the late apostolic period, and investigate if more of the pieces of the enigma of the Epistle of James come together into a well-integrated whole.

3.1 Written by an Unknown James

Could "James, a servant of God and of the Lord Jesus Christ" be a different James than the brother of Jesus who headed the Jerusalem church? Kümmel does not think so. He asserts, "Without doubt James claims to be written by him, and even if the letter is not authentic, it appeals to this famous James and the weight of his person as authority for its content."[164] Yet the discrepancies with the person of James whom we encounter in the NT and the ecclesiastical tradition indicate that Kümmel is overstating the case. Nowhere does our author claim to be the brother of Jesus. Naturally this omission would lead to the identification with the most well-known James, namely James of Jerusalem, just as the anonymity of the Epistle to the Hebrews led to the identification with Paul and the unspecified John of Revelation became John, the Son of Zebedee, author of the gospel and epistles, even though the style of the Greek in each case is manifestly dissimilar. On the other hand, one might argue that this omission in the case of James was a gesture of humility and reserve common to the brothers of Jesus, since Jude also labels himself the brother of James rather than the brother of Jesus. Yet Jude's pattern is not so convincing if we compare the acceptance of each epistle into the canon. Is it reasonable that the authority of Jude, the less important brother of Jesus, was sufficient to have his document included in the Muratorian Canon while James' epistle was not accepted? As Moffatt

---

[160]Cf. Hennecke, New Testament Apocrypha, I: 45.

[161]For evidence that Apollos wrote the Epistle to the Hebrews see Harrison, Introduction to NT, 378-379.

[162]Alternative hypotheses include those of 1) Zahn, Geschichte Kanons, 963 who thinks that as the Gentile element increased in Rome, this Judaic epistle fell into the background; and 2) Westcott, History of the Canon, 219, "The cause of the omissions cannot have been ignorance or doubt. It must be sought either in the character of the writing or in the present condition of the text." He opts for a corruption in the Muratorian Canon, but the character of the writing is a more defensible hypothesis.

[163]Likewise, Jude, 2 John, and 3 John, although originating in the east, were accepted in the Western church but omitted in the Peshitta. Cf. Westcott, History of the Canon, 353. An admitted flaw in this theory is the fact that it does not explain the omission of 1 Peter from the Muratorian Canon of Rome.

[164]Werner G. Kümmel, Introduction to the New Testament, 412.

states. "Had the revered head of the Jerusalem church written such a manifesto, it is difficult to understand its comparative oblivion for two centuries."[165] We must at least consider the possibility that another James was the author of this epistle.[166]

Many commentators have posited a pseudonymous document which appealed to the authority of James of Jerusalem.[167] In this case the murdered "righteous man" of Jas. 5:6 would be a hidden reference to James himself whose nickname was "the just".[168] The foremost argument for pseudonymity is the experienced divergency between the real James, the brother of Jesus, and the James of the epistle where the literary Greek, the omission of the ceremonial law, and the tardiness of acceptance into the canon offer the impression that the epistle is an unsophisticated attempt at imitating an already deceased authority of the early church. This argument is overridden, however, by the totally surprising absence of a motive for such a pseudonymous production. If the author were appealing to the apostle's reputation to ground his own teaching, why is there no clearer indications of James' personality and authority? Certainly the fact that James was Jesus' brother would be mentioned as well as more specifics about the controversy between James and Paul over justification by works in 2:14-26. Even Dibelius admits that "1:1 constitutes the only mark of pseudonymity".[169] Therefore Dibelius contends that "in choosing this name, the author did not have in mind some special purpose such as those behind the artistic fictions of style or situation in the pseudepigraphical literature". The author merely thought that "James the 'Just', who was known to be zealous for the law, seemed the appropriate literary patron for such a document."[170] Yet Guthrie's question is very appropriate at this point, "If the letter is merely a moralizing tract, why should he be chosen?"[171] Furthermore, those who advocate pseudonymity for the Epistle of James usually ascribe the same situation to Jude, 2 Peter and often 1 Peter. Dibelius, for example, states that "it seems to me very probable that the author of the Letter of Jude would not have chosen this obscure brother of the Lord as his patron unless the more well-known brother of the Lord already had a reputation as the author of a letter."[172] Thus among some modern scholars James is thought to be based upon a pseudonymous 1 Peter, Jude upon a pseudonymous James, and 2 Peter upon a pseudonymous Jude. This chain of pseudonymity in no way fits the short time period (a few decades at the most) involved in the writing of these documents. The popularity of a pseudonymous writing must first be assumed before another writer would appeal to its authority or contents. Therefore, "it would seem easier to believe that it was the work of another completely unknown James"[173] than that the Epistle of James was pseudonymous.

In addition to James of Jerusalem and James the son of Zebedee (died AD 44), we read in the NT of James the younger (Mk. 15:40), James the father of Judas (Lk. 6:16),

---

[165]Moffatt, Introduction to NT, 468.

[166]Moffatt, General Epistles, 2 states that a composition by some teacher of the church called James, of whom we know nothing, "meets the facts of the case adequately."

[167]Laws, James, 41-42 and Dibelius and Greeven, James, 19-21 are good examples.

[168]Cf. The Gospel of Thomas 12; Hegesippus quoted by Eusebius, HE 2,23,4; Dibelius and Greeven, James, 240, n. 58; and Mußner, Jakobusbrief, 4-5. Other possibilites include a reference to Jesus Christ who is called the just one in Acts 3:14; 7:52; 22:14; 1 Pet. 3:18; 1 Jn. 2:1,29; 3:7, or more likely the "righteous one" is a generic collective term as in Wis. 2:20; Prov. 1:11; Ps. 37:28ff; 4QpPs37. Cf. Appendix I, n. 34.

[169]Dibelius and Greeven, James, 20.

[170]Ibid. As a parallel Dibelius appeals to the Epistle of Barnabas.

[171]Guthrie, NT Introduction, 754. Cf. also Robinson, Redating, 130.

[172]Dibelius and Greeven, James, 33.

[173]Robinson, Redating, 130.

and the apostle James, the son of Alphaeus (Mk. 3:18 par.; Acts 1:13).[174] It is impossible to link any of these men with the Epistle of James because of the lack of information we possess concerning their life and work. However, "James was a common name and it might well have happened that some later James wrote the Epistle and that he was subsequently mistaken for James of Jerusalem."[175] This theory does not carry much conviction unless a particular *Sitz im Leben* can be described which accounts for the writing of the epistle and blends the author into a specific time frame and place of origin.[176] We will attempt in the next section to describe such an environment of origin in the city of Rome as the apostolic age was progressing into the moralism of the Apostolic Fathers.

3.2 Written in Rome

Some evidence supporting an origin in a Hellenistic center has already been presented: the excellent literary Greek, characteristics of the Stoic-Cynic diatribe, a totally ethical concept of the law,[177] and the conventional manner of greeting in a Hellenistic center.[178] Likewise James utilizes the LXX or at least a paraenetic tradition influenced by the LXX.[179] In Jas. 2:11 the seventh commandment is placed before the sixth following the LXX tradition.[180] In Jas. 5:12 the accusative τὸν οὐρανόν is a classical Greek construction whereas Mt. 5:34-36 (ἐν plus the dative) conforms to Semitic usage.[181] Verbal parallels with Philo, a renowned Hellenistic Jew, are numerous.[182] Moule concludes that the epistle "betrays a considerable acquaintance with the Greek moralists and sophists."[183] In particular James employs technical religious and philosophical expressions of the Greek language without adopting the underlying Stoic or Orphic concepts behind them: 1:18 λόγος ἀληθείας; 1:21 ἔμφοτος λόγος; the ship metaphors at 3:3; 3:6 τροχὸς τῆς γενέσεως; 3:15 ψυχικός.[184] From such evidence Kennedy concludes,

> It seems difficult for any unprejudiced enquirer to evade the conclusion that the Jewish writer of this Epistle moved with more than ordinary freedom in the region of Hellenistic culture.[185]

---

[174]Since James the son of Alphaeus is consistently mentioned along with the name of his father, one might assume that he is not the author of the Epistle of James, unless the possibility of confusion was eliminated after the death of the other apostle named James.

[175]Guthrie, NT Introduction, 755.

[176]Davids, James, 22 has argued that the discrepancies with the character of James of Jerusalem are explained if we posit a later redaction of the Epistle of James. Yet this position is as hypothetical as the suggestion of an unknown James without any particular *Sitz im Leben* to account for the origin of the writing.

[177]Cf. Dibelius and Greeven, James, 23.

[178]Cf. Laws, James, 5.

[179]Kennedy, "Hellenistic Atmosphere," 39. Cf. above, p. 52.

[180]Cf. ch. 2, section 2.2.

[181]Cf. above, pp. 140-141.

[182]Cf. Kennedy, "Hellenistic Atmosphere," 40-52 for examples spread throughout the epistle.

[183]Moule, Birth of the NT, 166.

[184]Cf. Dibelius and Greeven, James, 21.

[185]Kennedy, "Hellenistic Atmosphere," 51.

If a Hellenistic environment is conjectured, then the city of Rome is the likely choice.[186]

Rome was a Jewish-Christian center. In his study of the Christian beginnings in Rome, Brown accepts the estimated figure that 40,000-50,000 Jews lived in Rome in the first century AD.[187] Most of these Jewish residents had originally come as immigrants from the Palestine/Syria area.[188] This historical information could account for the agricultural imagery encountered in the Epistle of James which is admittedly the most difficult exegetical detail to fit into a Roman provenance. The tossing waves of the sea (1:6), flowers of the field (1:10), scorching heat (wind) (1:11), horses being harnessed (3:3), great forests set on fire (3:18), fig trees and grapevines (3:12), sowing and harvest (3:18), mowing the fields (5:4), and the fall and spring rains (5:7) could either be standardized traditional metaphors not indicating any specific geographical setting or else reveal the former experiences of an immigrant from the Near East.[189] Furthermore, from the combined works of Romans, 1 Peter, Hebrews, and 1 Clement, Brown contends that a consistent picture of Christianity can be deduced which reveals "a Jewish/Gentile Christianity more conservative in its preservation of the Jewish law and cult than the Christianity of Paul in Galatians."[190] This description coincides with the centrality of the concept of the law in the Epistle of James.[191]

If we investigate the relationship of the Epistle of James to the Christian literature written to or from the Christian community at Rome, we discover that these documents bear the closest resemblance to the Epistle of James in both content and vocabulary. In James and 1 Peter[192] the similarities of terminology and subject matter as well as the parallel order of the material betray common patterns of teaching.[193] Both epistles are addressed to the believers living in the Diaspora which could have been a standard procedure among Roman Jewish-Christians.[194] James (2:23-25), 1 Clement (10:7; 12:1), and Hebrews[195] (11:8-19, 31) all single out Abraham and Rahab as examples of faithful obedience. The parallels with the Shepherd of Hermas are so striking that one is forced to acknowledge that Hermas utilized a copy of James' manuscript at Rome. Both emphasize the ethical paraenetic dimensions of the gospel.[196] Both embody a Jewish-Christian tradi-

---

[186]S.G.F. Brandon, The Fall of Jerusalem and the Christian Church (London: SPCK, 1951), 238 and Goodspeed, Introduction to NT, 291 assign the origin to Alexandria and Antioch respectively because of their stance on the provenance of Matthew, but we have shown in chapter 4 that the differences between the Gospel of Matthew and the Epistle of James make such a position unlikely.

[187]Raymond Brown and John P. Meier, Antioch and Rome, 94.

[188]Harry J. Leon, The Jews of Ancient Rome, 240. Cf. Brown, Rome, 95.

[189]On the subject of imagery, Streeter, Primitive Church, 196 contends that the gold ring (2:2-4) was an official class distinction in Rome signifying membership in the Equestian order. Cf. also Reicke, James, 27.

[190]Brown, Rome, 90.

[191]Cf. below, p. 217 for a qualification of this statement.

[192]The reference to Babylon in 1 Pet. 5:13 as in Rev. 18 leads us to accept a Roman origin for 1 Peter.

[193]Cf. Appendix II, section 2.3.

[194]Mayor, James, cxiv-cxv contends that the reason why both Peter and James address the Diaspora is that 1 Peter used the Epistle of James as source material. For evidence against this conclusion see pp. 2-3,341-343 in this dissertation.

[195]Hebrews also was written either from or to Rome (13:24).

[196]The important parallels are located in Hermas' section entitled "The Mandates". Cf. Appendix II, section 8.2.

tion[197] which has absorbed the teaching of Jesus into its thought patterns to such an extent that it is difficult to determine when a saying of Jesus is being alluded to.[198] Both picture worship in a synogogue (Mand. 11:9,13,14; Jas. 2:2). Snyder contends that the debate with those who have faith without works (Jas. 2:14-26) is reflected frequently in the Shepherd.[199] A situation of moral laxity where business affairs have taken priority over faith (Jas. 4:13-16; Herm. Vis. 3,6,5) and double-mindedness has resulted (Jas. 1:7-8; 4:8; Mand. 11:5-8) is evident in both documents. Hermas' description of Christians who "continued in the faith, though they wrought not the works of the faith" (Sim. 8,9,1) expresses precisely the sort of nominal Christianity warned against by James.

Of prominent importance are the common quotations in these documents. Along with the Shepherd of Hermas (Vis. 2,3,4) and Clement of Rome (23:3), James (4:5) recites as scripture an unknown book which within the limitations of our present knowledge can best be identified as the book of Eldad and Modad.[200] Secondly, the exhortation against oath making in Jas. 5:12 suggests that the transmission of the sayings of Jesus by James is related to the tradition passed on by Justin Martyr in the city of Rome. Justin's citation (1 Apol. 16:5) appears to be a harmony of the Gospel of Matthew with the tradition found in James.[201] Since Justin specifically states that he is quoting Jesus' teaching, he is probably not dependent upon the Epistle of James itself, but is transmitting a tradition familiar to his community in Rome.[202] More remarkable is the common quotation of Prov. 3:34 and 10:12 by James (4:6; 5:20), 1 Peter (5:5b; 4:8), and 1 Clement (30:2; 49:5) as well as the allusion to Is. 40:4 by both Jas. 1:10-11 and 1 Pet. 1:24. Without the use of each other's writings,[203] such a coincidence of citation is statistically improbable unless all the documents emanated from a common geographical area where these texts were "in the air", being employed in a somewhat uniform Christian catechism or common teaching pattern.

Another literary connection involves James' relationship to Paul and the theme of justification by faith developed in the Epistle to the Romans. James' employment of the phrase "justification alone" (2:24) certainly entails a knowledge of Paul's unique doctrine.[204] Ropes, for example, states,

> That James wrote after Paul's doctrine had become well known to the church must be admitted, for he quotes exactly Paul's formula (2:21,24; cf. Gal. 2:16; Rom. 3:28) and

---

[197]Brown, Rome, 203 in speaking about the Shepherd of Hermas explains, "Virtually all agree that while the author does not speak of the Jews or their customs, or even quote the OT, he has been deeply influenced by Jewish traditions. For some this means he was a convert Jew; for others, that he belonged to a select Jewish congregation at Rome."

[198]Köster, Synoptische Überlieferung, 254 describes Hermas in these words: "Die jüdisch Tradition spielt oftenbar in dieser Schrift eine große Rolle, und aus ihr erlären sich auch sehr viele Berührungen des Herm. mit den Synoptikern."

[199]Graydon F. Snyder, The Apostolic Fathers: The Shepherd of Hermas, 6:15. He refers to Sim. 8,9,1; 8,10,3; 9,19,2; 9,21,2; Vis. 3,6,1-4; Mand. 10,1,4f.

[200]Cf. ch. 2, section 2.4.

[201]Cf. above, pp. 148-149 and Leslie L. Kline, The Sayings of Jesus in the Pseudo-Clementine Homilies, 87.

[202]Cf. Bellinzoni, Sayings of Jesus in Justin, 100,141.

[203]The different emphases prove that one document is not the source of the others. Cf. Appendix II, section 2.3.

[204]Throughout Jas. 2:14-26 James is concerned about a type of teaching that separates faith and works. On the other hand, Jewish thinking always closely combines faith and works, as Dibelius and Greeven, James, 179 explain. Laws, James, 131 adds that "even in 2 Esd. ix. 7f., xiii. 23, where works and faith seem to be distinguished, they are seen as alternative possible means of salvation and not as opposed." Cf. also Mußner, Jakobusbrief, 17-18.

this formula was the outgrowth of the most original element of Paul's system and is alien to earlier Jewish thought.[205]

In Romans Paul defends himself against the claim that his gospel leads to a freedom that nullifies the law (3:31) and is overly gracious toward sin (6:1).[206] This concern seems to be identical with James' apprehensiveness about the implications of a teaching that places the emphasis on justification by faith alone. Maybe Paul's clarification of his teaching (Rom. 3:31; 6:1) as well as James' discourse on faith and works (2:14-26) were both aimed at a freedom party (set over against the circumcision party -- Titus 1:10; Gal. 2:4-5,12; Acts 11:2) which had adherents in Rome. Therefore we are not saying that James opposed Paul,[207] but only that James was disquieted over the possible implications of an unbalanced doctrine of justification by faith in the hands of members of this "freedom party" in Rome. A similar balance of faith and works is advocated in AD 95 by Clement of Rome. In the same section (29:1-33:8) he teaches a doctrine of justification through faith without any resort to one's own piety and works (32:4) like Paul as well as a justification by works and not through words (30:3) like James.[208] If these documents emanate from a common Christian community in Rome, then this controversy over justification by faith and works as evidenced in Jas. 2:14-26 has been solved by the time of 1 Clement.

What is the explanation for the similarities between these documents? Some have argued for a literary dependence upon the Epistle of James.[209] Peter, Clement, and Hermas would then have employed the Epistle of James of Jerusalem which had been sent to Rome. This is an attractive hypothesis since the traditional view of authorship can be maintained and, at the same time, a relationship with the city of Rome can be postulated. However, if this letter did not originate in Rome but at a distant Jerusalem, then it would be impossible to maintain that:

1) the use of the term "double-mindedness" witnesses to a particular emphasis of the church at Rome;
2) the harmony between justification by faith and works in 1 Clement demonstrates the solution to a struggle within the Christian community of Rome which was personally experienced by James;
3) the wording of Jas. 5:12 illustrates the particular form of a saying of Jesus (Mt. 5:33-37) in the Roman church;
4) the common use of OT texts (Prov. 3:34; 10:12; Is. 40:4) and the book of Eldad and Modad is caused by their employment in the ethical (catechetical) instruction of the Roman church; and
5) the similar address of 1 Peter and the Epistle of James (to the Dispersion) has become a standard means of addressing the Jewish-Christian community from the city of Rome.

Those who deny literary dependency have either abandoned any search for the place of composition by comparing James with other early Christian writings or have settled upon a Roman provenance. Dibelius relinquishes any hope of fixing the place of the composition of James by explaining that "We cannot say whether or not the paraenetic material common to Jas and Hermas circulated only in Rome."[210] Laws, on the other hand, states,

---

[205]Ropes, James, 35.

[206]Cf. also Gal. 3:21 where Paul refuses to admit that he sets the law over against the promises of God.

[207]Cf. Appendix II, section 3.3.

[208]Cf. Appendix II, section 7.3.

[209]Cf. ch. 1, n. 16,27,32; Appendix II, n. 25.

[210]Dibelius and Greeven, James, 47. Kümmel, Introduction to NT, 410 claims that "no clearly perceptible literary connection with other early Christian writings exists".

> If literary interdependence is not the link between the several documents' use of δίψυχος, then the likely explanation is familiarity with it as current in a common place of origin.[211]

One of the most satisfying conjectures to explain this common environment of thought and terminology is the postulation of a Roman origin. Someone might contend that a Roman provenance would necessitate that the Epistle of James be found in the Muratorian Canon of Rome, whereas James is first accepted as canonical in the distant Eastern city of Alexandria. However, it is often true that disputed books are initially accepted only at a place distant from their place of origin as in the case of Hebrews and the Shepherd of Hermas.[212] Thus Streeter's solution is surely a possibility: "Of this the only explanation I can see is that the Roman Church originally knew the names of the actual authors, and therefore never thought of ascribing their works to Apostles."[213] Then James, "a servant of God and of the Lord Jesus Christ," and Apollos, the probable author of Hebrews, did not attain to the strict apostolic expectations of the writer(s) of the Muratorian Canon. Whatever the case, it is a reasonable explanation that the geographical location of Rome explains many of the similarities between the documents of James, 1 Peter, 1 Clement, and the Shepherd of Hermas.

3.3 An Approximate Date for the Epistle of James

Are there any indications of an approximate date when James could have recorded his paraenesis from Rome? As we have noted earlier, exegetes who favor an authorship by James of Jerusalem often place the date very early before any conflicts over circumcision and the place of the Gentiles within the church. Yet several factors attest that a significant period of time has elapsed since the cross and resurrection event launched the kerygma of a crucified Lord into the Graeco-Roman world. First of all, there is a complete absence in the epistle of any concern about laying the foundations of the faith. Powell contends that

> The many references to teaching and to teachers ... suggests that it is not written to a community (or communities) still in the missionary stage, but to a settled group. What the community now needs is sound moral teaching to prevent deterioration.[214]

The distinctively kerygmatic tenets of the atonement, the person of Jesus, and the Holy Spirit are assumed rather than proclaimed.[215] The ethical demand is now called upon to remedy the crisis of the present situation. Since this is reminiscent of the moralism encountered in the Apostolic Fathers, it is possible that the beginning of this process can be detected in the short epistle under our microscope. James' emphasis on the evils of double-mindedness (1:8; 4:8), instability (1:8; 3:8,16), and friendship with the world (4:4; 1:27) suggests a protest against secularist tendencies which are for the first time emerging in the history of Christianity. It is the morally lax who are the adulterous people (4:4), the double-minded, and the real sinners (4:8). Exhortations aimed at disciples who are hearers

---

[211]Sophie S. Marshall (Laws), "Δίψυχος: A Local Term?" SE 6:350.

[212]Eusebius (HE 6,20,3) reports that the hesitation of Rome with regard to Hebrews lasted to his own time (AD 311). However, Hebrews and the Shepherd of Hermas were treated as canonical in the east (Orig. Rom. 16:14 (10:31) in MPG, 14, 1252).

[213]Streeter, Primitive Church, 192.

[214]Cyril H. Powell, "Faith in James and its Bearing on the Problem of the Date of the Epistle," ExT 62(1950): 312.

[215]Cf. Moffatt, Introduction to NT, 471 although his suggestion of a second century date is misleading.

of the message without being doers call attention to a situation where nominal Christianity has become a problem. James' emphasis upon waiting patiently for the coming of the Lord (5:7-8) without grumbling (5:9) assumes that his audience has been diverted from an attitude of watchfulness by their present circumstances. To solve this dilemma of moral laxity, an intimate interconnection between faith and works is presented at the heart of James' doctrine of justification.[216]

The second indication of a later date is the form in which the sayings of Jesus are transmitted. Kittel argued that their allusionary character attests to an early period before introductory formulations were employed. However, we have shown that the genre of paraenesis is the determining factor for James' use of allusions.[217] Furthermore, the process of standardization within the ethical instruction of the church must have taken a considerable amount of time. Finally, James' employment of the Pauline formulation "justification by faith alone" (2:24) implies that Jas. 2:14-26 cannot "be imagined without the Pauline mission."[218] A date before the circumcision controversies is, therefore, untenable. Certainly a date within the second or third generation of Christians must be postulated.[219]

These factors, however, do not compel one to acknowledge a post-apostolic, second century date. Striking contrasts with the Apostolic Fathers are also evident. Ropes has enumerated the following omissions in the Epistle of James:[220] 1) no inclination to asceticism; 2) no sacramental theology; 3) no speculative interests; 4) no "intellectualistic" view of faith in the acceptance of certain propositions;[221] 5) no allegorical interpretations; nor 6) does James "carry what might readily have become a doctrine of works and of the human will a step beyond the simple expression of sincere moral earnestness." We could add to this list the fact that a harmonization of the various gospel traditions encountered in the Didache (1:3-2:1) and Justin Martyr is missing in James.[222] Furthermore, the rich are primarily outside the Christian community whereas in Hermas the rich have thoroughly infiltrated the church.[223] If we compare the eschatology of James and 2 Peter, we perceive that:

> While 2 Peter admits and interprets delay in the fulfilment of eschatological hope (iii. 8f), James affirms its imminence (v. 8f); and while 2 Peter writes in the knowledge of some collection of Paul's letters, James' contact with Paul is in 'oral tradition'.[224]

Finally, the heated controversy over faith and works in Jas. 2:14-26 has been solved by the time of Clement of Rome (1 Cl. 30-34). Thus if one decides that the geographical environment explains the similarities between James, 1 Peter, and the Shepherd of Hermas, then the Epistle of James stands in the gap between the writings of Paul and the correspondence of Clement with the Corinthians, between 1 Peter and the Shepherd of Hermas. A date in the 80's is therefore about as precise as one could hope to posit. Thus, within this

---

[216]For additional arguments against an early date see above, pp. 196-197.

[217]Cf. ch. 5, sections 2.1 and 3.6.

[218]Dibelius and Greeven, James, 179. Cf. Appendix II, section 3.3.

[219]Lohse, "Glaube und Werke," 13 concludes, "Erkennen wir somit ander Verwendung der Herrenworte in den paränischen Teilen sowie an der Stellung der Eschatologie innerhalb der Katechismusstücke, daß wir in die Zeit derzweiten und dritten christlichen Generation versetzt werden."

[220]Ropes, James, 37-38.

[221]Ropes is mistaken here since an intellectualistic view of faith is opposed by James in Jas. 2:14-26.

[222]Cf. ch. 5, n. 67 for examples of harmonizing.

[223]Vis. 3,9,5-6; Sim. 2:5. For James' view of wealth see above, pp. 128-130.

[224]Laws, James, 35. For similarities between the eschatological expectations of James and 2 Peter, see above, p. 197.

hypothesis it is conjectured that a teacher in Rome by the name of James in a crisis of moral laxity instructed his Christian group and all the new Israel scattered throughout the Diaspora on the ethical implications of their faith.

4.0 The Ambivalent Nature of our Conclusions

We have drawn attention to the insufficient evidence supporting an authorship by James of Jerusalem around the time of the Apostolic Council. As an alternative we have postulated an authorship by an unknown James from Rome between the time of the apostles and 1 Clement. However, this theory is also based on an unsturdy foundation since all the evidence which supports it is used by other authors to support a contrary conclusion.

First of all, a Hellenistic provenance remains a point of contention since the ambiguous evidence causes authors to interpret the exegetical data in different directions. Jeremias identifies the three and a half year famine of Jas. 5:17 as a Palestinian tradition while Lohse argues for a Hellenistic environment.[225] Kirk contends that "the list of adjectives by which Wisdom is described is part of a current practice of Hellenism adopted by a Greek-speaking James,"[226] but the similar list in 1QS 4:3 at Qumran indicates that this practice had also found a home in Palestinian territory.[227] Laws points out that "some of his striking metaphors have little biblical background, but are commonplace in Greek and Latin literature,"[228] while other authors are insistent that the imagery is strikingly Palestinian.[229] There is evidence that Palestinian as well as Hellenistic Jews could employ excellent literary Greek and use the conventional greetings of Hellenistic letters as well as the LXX.[230]

Secondly if we posit a Roman provenance for the Epistle of James, we would expect to encounter there a Jewish Christianity which emphasized the ethical dimensions of the law rather than ritual. Yet ancient Roman writers "allude to the scrupulousness of the Roman Jews in observing the Sabbath, abstaining from pork, and practicing the rite of circumcision."[231] Furthermore, the similarities between the books of James, 1 Peter, 1 Clement, and the Shepherd of Hermas could also point to a standard ethical teaching in the Jewish-Christian community rather than a tradition limited to the geographical area of Rome. We just do not have enough information about Jewish Christianity in Palestine to connect the Epistle of James with documents from this area.

Thirdly, one is not compelled to postulate a time of origin at the beginning of the Apostolic Fathers. The conflict between justification by faith and works can be interpreted not only against a background of Paul's theology but, as Knowling contends, with reference to "a Jewish acceptance of faith as purely intellectual, and to an antinomianism which might at any time invade the church, and which St. Paul, nay our Lord Himself, rebuked and condemned,"[232] as evidenced in Rom. 2:13-24 and Mt. 7:21ff. Other sup-

---

[225]Jeremias, s.v. 'Ηλ(ε)ίας, TDNT, II: 934 vs. Lohse, "Glaube und Werke," 19-20.

[226]James A. Kirk, "The Meaning of Wisdom in James: Examination of a Hypothesis," NTS 16(1969): 26.

[227]Cf. Davids, James, 54.

[228]Laws, James, 5 mentions the horse and the ship in Jas. 3:3f, the images of human control over the animal kingdom in 3:7, and the mist in 4:14.

[229]Cf. above, section 3.2.

[230]Cf. above, n. 116 and Martin Hengel, Judaism and Hellenism, tr. John Bowden (London: SCM, 1974), 100-102.

[231]Leon, Jews of Ancient Rome, 244.

[232]Knowling, James, lxiii. Robinson, Redating, 126 believes that James is "taking up an attack, begun by Jesus and the Baptist before Him, on the inadequacies of contemporary Judaism." Scriptures like Mt. 3:8-10; 7:16-27; 12:33-35; 21:28-31; 25:31-46 are referred to.

porters of the traditional view of authorship admit that James was written in "a period when faith had lost some of its original fervour and was in danger of developing into a barren orthodoxy,"[233] yet perceive no problem in assigning the letter to a time just before the death of James of Jerusalem.[234] The development of a standard ethical tradition ("catechism") must have taken a period of time to develop, but this is fully possible in the three decades between Jesus' death and the murder of James the Just. With regard to the development of ecclesiastical structure, the exhortation in Jas. 5:14 to call the elders could merely refer to elders in a Jewish-Christian setting without implying an organized hierarchy.

Finally, the decision which a modern reader of the Epistle of James arrives at with regard to its authorship appears to be dependent upon the reader's particular emphasis. If the Palestinian imagery is emphasized,[235] then James of Jerusalem is the recognized author. If the relationship with 1 Peter, 1 Clement, and the Shepherd of Hermas is emphasized, then authorship by a Jewish Christian in Rome is the logical conclusion. The exact same evidence is interpreted in different ways to support each of the above hypotheses. It is impossible to choose decisively for one thesis while denying any truth to the arguments of the opposing side.[236] Therefore any conclusion must be tentative. However, if we choose for an authorship by James of Jerusalem, then we must admit that the traditional picture of an ascetic, legalistic James who spoke primarily Aramaic and emphasized the ceremonial dimensions of the law does not fit the givens of this epistle. Therefore, we must either adjust our image of James, the brother of Jesus, or assign the epistle to an unknown James in the provenance of Rome. Since the traditional assumption of authorship has stood the test of time and explains most of the exegetical givens of the text, a decision to adjust our image of James of Jerusalem is probably a preferable solution.

---

[233]Tasker, OT in NT, 124. Cf. Mitton, James, 233.

[234]Hegesippus, as preserved in Eus., HE 2:23, says that the martyrdom of James took place after the outbreak of the Jewish War because Christians refused to participate in this struggle against Rome, thus making James' death about AD 67. A more authentic tradition appears in Jos., Ant. 20,9,1 which assigns his death to AD 62.

[235]Cf. above, section 3.2.

[236]Oesterley, "James," 404-405 observes, "Against every argument adduced in favour of either view serious objections can be urged; but then these objections, again, can for the most part be upset by counter-arguments."

Chapter 7

CONCLUDING PERSPECTIVES

The Relationship of the Epistle of James to the Synoptic Tradition

1.1 The number of allusions to the sayings of the Jesus-tradition in the Epistle of James has been greatly exaggerated. Over the last two centuries commentators have identified over 180 possible references to the teaching of Jesus.[1] Yet two-thirds of these authors agree on only six parallel texts. These statistics indicate the arbitrariness involved in the selection process as well as the complete lack of distinction between different types of parallels. In a recent article Davids has attempted to correct this tendency by distinquishing between indirect citations, close allusions, possible allusions, basic concepts, concepts of parable, and ideas of narrative.[2] Since any clear demarcation between the categories of indirect citation, close allusion, and possible allusion is almost impossible to define, we prefer to differentiate the following categories:[3] 1) quotations or citations; 2) allusions or intended reminiscences; 3) parallels of both common content and similar terminology; 4) parallels of content; 5) parallels of terminology; 6) common references to other writings or sources. The most important category for determining literary dependence between two documents is, of course, the presence of quotations with an introductory formula citing the source. The presence of (almost) exact wording likewise reveals that one is transmitting the work of a previous writer. To define a saying as an allusion, there must be substantial verbal similarities as well as a common context and emphasis of content. Other allusions in the immediate context help to establish with greater certainty the presence of an allusion.[4] Parallels with both similar terminology and common content provide the closest category to that of allusion, although a difference of emphasis or an author's peculiar usage of similar material indicates that no intended reminiscence can be substantiated. Parallels with only analogous subject matter as well as instances of mere verbal correspondence are far less helpful in determining literary dependence. Their importance lies in the valuable information they contribute for a comparison of the theology and distinctive vocabulary of the various authors. The employment of these categories can facilitate a classification of the abundance of parallels so that the precise relationship between the teaching of Jesus and the moral exhortations of James can be determined.

1) Citations: On six occasions the Epistle of James quotes the OT with introductory formulas but never the sayings of Jesus.

2) Allusions: (8)

a) to Q:

Jas. 1:5 = Mt. 7:7; Lk. 11:9	Ask and you will receive
Jas. 4:2c-3 = Mt. 7:7; Lk. 11:9	Ask and you will receive

---

[1]Cf. Appendix I, section 1.0.

[2]Davids, "James and Jesus," 66-67.

[3]In German a quotation = *Zitat*; an allusion or reminiscense = *Anklang* or *Anspielung*; a parallel = *Parallel* or *Berührung*.

[4]For Kittel's criteria for an allusion see ch. 3, n. 28. It must be admitted that allusions by their very nature are somewhat elusive, and therefore it is often difficult to decide assuredly what is an allusion and what is not.

b) to a Q saying where the Lucan parallel is closer to James:
Jas. 2:5 = Lk. 6:20b; Mt. 5:3 the kingdom belongs to the poor

c) to a Q saying where the M tradition is closer to James:
Jas. 5:2-3a = Mt. 6:19-20; Lk. 12:33b against the treasuring up of wealth

d) to peculiarly Lucan material:
Jas. 4:9 = Lk. 6:21,25b those who laugh will mourn
Jas. 5:1 = Lk. 6:24 woe to the rich

e) to peculiarly Matthean material:
Jas. 5:12 = Mt. 5:33-37 on oaths and truth-telling

f) to independent sayings used by both Matthew and Luke:
Jas. 4:10 = Mt. 23:12; Lk. 14:11; 18:14b the humble are exalted

3) Parallels of both content and wording: (6)

a) listed in chapter 3: (4)
Jas. 1:6 = Mt. 21:21; Mk. 11:23 the prayer of faith without doubting
Jas. 1:22-25 = Mt. 7:24-27; Lk. 6:47-49 being doers of the word
Jas. 3:12 = Mt. 7:16; Lk. 6:44 employing fruit tree imagery to express the impossibility of an event
Jas. 5:10-11a = Mt. 5:11,12b; Lk. 6:22,23b blessed are those who endure

b) listed in Appendix I: (2)
Jas. 1:12 = Mt. 5:11-12a; Lk. 6:22-23a blessed are those who endure trials
Jas. 1:17 = Mt. 7:11; Lk. 11:13 God the Father gives good gifts

4) Parallels of terminology: (9)

a) listed in chapter 3: (0)

b) listed in Appendix I: (9)
Jas. 1:21 = Mt. 13:19-23; Lk. 8:11-15 λόγος able to save; ἔμφυτος and φύω
Jas. 2:15 = Mt. 25:36,41 naked and hungry
Jas. 4:4a = Mt. 12:39a; 16:4a; Mk. 8:38 adulteresses
Jas. 4:8 = Mt. 5:8 purifying the heart
Jas. 4:12 = Mt. 10:28 save and destroy
Jas. 4:17 = Lk. 12:47 knowing something but not doing it
Jas. 5:9a = Mt. 7:1 that you may not be judged
Jas. 5:9b = Mt. 24:33b; Mk. 13:29b at the doors
Jas. 5:17 = Lk. 4:25 three years and six months

5) Parallels of content: (12)

a) listed in chapter 3: (7)
Jas. 1:2 = Mt. 5:11-12a; Lk. 6:22-23a joy in tribulation
Jas. 1:4 = Mt. 5:48 be perfect
Jas. 1:19b-20 = Mt. 5:22a exhortation against anger
Jas. 2:13 = Mt. 5:7 being merciful results in mercy
Jas. 3:18 = Mt. 5:9 peacemakers

Jas. 4:4 = Mt. 6:24; Lk. 16:13 serving two masters
Jas. 4:11-12 = Mt. 7:1-2a; Lk. 6:37 against judging

b) listed in Appendix I: (5)
Jas. 1:12 = Mt. 10:22 endurance
Jas. 2:10 = Mt. 5:19 a restricting of the law
Jas. 2:14 = Mt. 7:21; Lk. 6:46 faith and works
Jas. 5:6 = Lk. 6:37b; Mt. 12:7,37 judgment according to works
Jas. 5:14 = Mk. 6:13 anointing with oil

6) Common source: (1)[5]
Jas. 2:8 and Mt. 22:39-40 par. = Lev. 19:18b the love command

1.2 We have detected eight conscious allusions to the Synoptic gospels in the Epistle of James. One could also attempt to locate extra-canonical sayings of Jesus within the Epistle of James[6] or delve into the parallels with the Gospel of John,[7] but those projects lie outside the bounds of this study. Compared with the short length of James' epistle and the relative infrequency in which sayings of Jesus are alluded to in the NT epistles, the presence of eight allusions is not insignificant. However, the primary parallels are those of common theme or subject matter rather than intended allusion or citation. Furthermore, it is not true, as many have erroneously suggested,[8] that the Epistle of James contains more allusions to the Synoptic tradition than any of the other NT epistles. Paul alludes to the *logia* of Jesus between eight and twenty-four times.[9] 1 Peter echoes twelve sayings of Jesus,[10] while James is in approximately the same vicinity with eight allusions. The book of Revelation probably possesses the greatest number of allusions to the sayings of Jesus with about twenty-five examples.[11]

It is difficult to determine with any certainty how James received the sayings of Jesus. Commentators who postulate an authorship by James, the brother of Jesus, favor

---

[5]The common catechetical material between James and 1 Peter might also be included here. Yet the hypothetical nature of this area of study cautions us against drawing any dogmatic conclusions. Cf. Davies, Setting, 370.

[6]James H. Ropes, Die Sprüche Jesu die in den kanonischen Evangelien nicht überliefert sind, 37-38,40-41,75-76,124 disputes Resch's claim that Jas. 1:12; 4:5; 4:7; and 5:20 are extra-canonical sayings of Jesus. Jas. 1:12 has received the most attention. Adamson, James, 68; Mayor, James, 47, n. 1; Oesterley, "James," 427; and Vos, Synoptic Traditions in Apocalypse, 192 claim that the same *logion* of Jesus is being alluded to at 2 Tim. 4:8; 1 Pet. 5:4; Rev. 2:10. Resch, Agrapha, 253 regards this frequency of quotation by subsequent writers as a sure proof that the passage was originally uttered by Christ, but from the findings of our study there is equal likelihood that the ethical teaching of the church is being referred to especially since Jas. 5:11 repeats the same teaching (ch. 3, section 6.1) and the crown is described differently in each passage. On the other hand, Davids, James, 80 finds the source of Jas. 1:12 in Jewish thought. Resch's hypothesis is therefore unnecessary (cf. Laws, James, 69). The relationship of Jas. 5:20 to the OT has been examined in ch. 2, section 3.6.

[7]Jas. 1:17 = Jn. 3:3; 1:18 = 6:39 and 17:17; 1:18,25 = 8:31-32; 1:22 = 8:47; 1:25 and 4:17 = 13:17; 2:1 = 5:44; 2:10 = 7:19; 5:20 = 5:24; 4:4 = 15:19 where Chaine, Jacques, LXVIII hypothesizes dependence. For lists of parallels see Knowling, James, xxiii-xxiv and Moffatt, Historical NT, 578.

[8]Cf. above, pp. 13-15.

[9]Cf. ch. 5, p. 169 and n. 157.

[10]Cf. ch. 5, n. 27.

[11]Cf. ch. 5, n. 29.

the view that James heard the preaching with his own ears.[12] Yet the antagonism of Jesus' brothers to his ministry (Mk. 3:21,31; Jn. 7:5) and the divergent wording of the sayings from the Synoptic tradition do not support this thesis. A few scholars contend that James utilized the Gospel of Matthew either through the hearing of it read in worship services[13] or by reading the Greek version itself.[14] We have shown in chapter 4 that this thesis is indefensible. The solution which best coincides with the form of the sayings as well as the particular genre of James is the thesis that the author was transmitting the paraenetic tradition of the church which included both specific sayings of Jesus as well as ethical themes extracted from Jesus' preaching. The words of Jesus could be said to be "in the air".[15]

The development of certain sayings displays the hand of the church applying Jesus' words to new situations which emerged as salvation history moved onward. Two *logia* on the subject of prayer portray situations where Jesus' saying about confidence in prayer ("ask and you will receive") is no longer applicable, i.e. when asking with wrong motives to satisfy one's own pleasures (4:3) and when one is double-minded (1:5-8). The eschatological mourning and weeping of Lk. 6:25 is applied to the present state of the church in Jas. 4:9, a sign according to Jeremias of a later development in the sayings of Jesus.[16] The additional contrast (poor in worldly goods vs. rich in faith) inserted into the promise of the kingdom to the poor in Jas. 2:5 (=Mt. 5:3) displays the experience of the church as witnessed in 1 Cor. 1:27 and Rev. 2:9. Furthermore, the fact that most of the Jamesian parallels with the Synoptic tradition derive from the Sermon on the Mount/Plain[17] reveals the hand of the church in the arrangement of this material to serve the paraenetic needs of the community. The popularity of the Gospel of Matthew in the early church is most surely caused by the fact that the Matthean discourses provided paraenetic material to serve the church in establishing her ethical teachings.[18] The Epistle of James is intended to meet this identical need and thus consists largely of short exhortations grouped together by catchwords as in the Matthean discourses.

1.3 In addition to allusions to the sayings of the Jesus-tradition, we also encounter in the Epistle of James certain themes from the preaching of Jesus which have been incorporated into the paraenetic tradition of the church. The following ethical themes are paralleled emphatically in the Synoptic gospels:

1) joy in tribulation (Jas. 1:2; 5:10-11a; Mt. 5:11-12a; Lk. 6:22-23a);[19]

2) faith and doubting (Jas. 1:6; Mt. 21:21; Mk. 11:23);

3) exhortations against anger (Jas. 1:19-20; Mt. 5:22);[20]

4) hearing and doing (Jas. 1:22-25; Mt. 7:24-26; Lk. 6:46-49; 8:21) and faith and action (Jas. 2:14; Mt. 7:21; Lk. 6:46);

---

[12]Cf. ch. 1, sections 3.1 and 3.8.

[13]Shepherd, "James and Matthew," 55. Cf. above, ch. 4, sections 1.1-1.2.

[14]Gryglewicz, "Jacques et Matthieu," 55. Cf. above, ch. 4, sections 2.0-2.3.

[15]Davies, <u>Setting</u>, 404.

[16]Jeremias, "The Hortatory Use of the Parables," <u>Parables of Jesus</u>, 42-48.

[17]Cf. above, p. 150. In Did. 1:2-2:1 (cf. ch. 5, n. 154) and in Justin's <u>1 Apol</u>. 15-17 we encounter this same phenomenon (cf. Bellinzoni, <u>Sayings of Jesus in Justin</u>, 54).

[18]Cf. ch. 5, n. 160.

[19]This catechetical tradition was also developed in Rom. 5:3-5 and 1 Pet. 1:6; 4:13.

[20]This ethical tradition is also developed in Did. 3:2-3, in passages describing the qualifications of leaders (Tit. 1:7; Pol. 6:1), and by Paul in Eph. 4:26,31.

5) the love commandment (Jas. 2:8; Mt. 22:39; Mk. 12:31; Lk. 10:27);[21]

6) mercy (Jas. 2:13; Mt. 5:7; 9:13; 12:7; 18:33ff; 1 Cl. 13:2; Pol. Phil. 2:3);[22]

7) serving God vs. loving the world (Jas. 4:4; Lk. 16:13; Mt. 6:24);[23]

8) refraining from judging (Jas. 4:11-12; 5:9; Mt. 7:1; Lk. 6:37);

9) those who persevere in trial will receive a blessing (Jas. 1:12; 5:10-11a; Mt. 5:11-12a; 10:22; Lk. 6:22-23a).

The church, then, adopted many of the important themes in the preaching of Jesus and employed them as a foundation for its ethical paraenesis. These themes, however, were developed in the individual author's own words and directed at each one's unique situation. Thus James describes doubting by referring to "a wave of the sea that is driven and tossed by the wind" (1:6) rather than through Jesus' imagery of a mountain (Mt. 21:21; Mk. 11:23) or a mulberry tree (Lk. 17:6) cast into the sea. James pictures hearing without doing by the analogy of peering into a mirror and forgetting immediately what one has seen (1:22-23) rather than Jesus' verbal portrait of wise and foolish people building their homes upon rock and sand respectively (Mt. 7:24-27 par.). Jas. 3:12 utilizes the imagery of a fruit tree producing different kinds of fruit (a fig tree bearing olives; a grapevine yielding figs) rather than Jesus' imagery (Mt. 7:16; Lk. 6:44) of wild (evil) trees producing edible fruit (thorn bushes bearing grapes, thistles yielding figs) to teach the same lesson about the impossibility of doing good and evil at the same time. Both Jesus and James call attention to the blessedness of those who endure tribulation, but Jesus condemns Israel's persecution of the prophets (Mt. 5:12; Lk. 6:23) while James exalts the prophets as examples of patience in suffering (Jas. 5:10). This development of the themes of Jesus' preaching by employing different imagery and unique emphases explains the perceptive observation of various exegetes who state that "the imagery belongs to James, but the thoughts are more of Jesus,"[24] or again "James says less about the Master than any other writer in the NT, but his speech is more like that of the Master than the speech of any one of them."[25] The double use of the preaching of Jesus in the paraenesis of the church (i.e. as allusions and as themes derived from Jesus' teaching) explains both the similarities and the differences between the sayings of Jesus and the exhortations of James. Thus the Jesus-tradition forms the foundational rule of conduct for the early church by providing both specific *logia* and the thematic raw material for the church's ethical paraenesis.[26]

1.4 We have concluded in chapter 4 that the Epistle of James is an independent witness to the sayings of the Jesus-tradition. James does not employ our Synoptic gospels;

---

[21]This also becomes the heart of Paul's ethical teaching at Rom. 13:8-10 and Gal. 5:14. Cf. also Did. 1:2.

[22]This example is placed hesitantly into our list since this theme could just as easily have entered the church's ethical tradition through Jewish wisdom. Cf. ch. 3, section 3.3.

[23]Cf. also 1 Jn. 2:15-17; Rom. 8:7-9; Gal. 5:16-26; 6:14-15; 2 Tim. 3:4.

[24]Michaels, "James -- The Royal Law," 332.

[25]Doremus A. Hayes, "James, Ep. of," ISBE, 1564.

[26]Davies, Setting, 404 probably had this in mind when he explained that the words of Jesus "moulded the life of the Christian community both indirectly by supplying, on occasion, specific halakah as in Jas. 5:12, and indirectly by supplying a climate of and a form for a 'Christian' moral awareness."

instead his epistle witnesses to an additional community for which the ethical teaching of Jesus was influential. Was James aware of any preSynoptic collections of the sayings of Jesus? Knowledge of Q is a possibility since four out of James' eight allusions are drawn from Q material. However, in one case the wording (Jas. 2:5) corresponds more exactly with the Lucan version (Lk. 6:20b), while in a second instance (Jas. 5:2-3a) the saying is closer to M (Mt. 6: 19-20) than to the Lucan recension of Q (Lk. 12:33b). Shepherd's assessment[27] that the Epistle of James is closer to the Matthean interpretation of Q overlooks the instances where James matches Luke both in tone and language. Streeter[28] postulates that James has read Q in the recension known to Luke, yet the inclusion of M material in James (Jas. 5:12=Mt. 5:33-37; 5:2-3a= Mt. 6:19-20?) makes this hypothesis highly remote and definitely unnecessary. Davies' suggestion[29] that the eschatological (rather than the catechetical) nature of Q explains why James did not employ this sayings source is also a supposition that cannot be proven. Someone might argue that James was aware of the M tradition since James' most obvious allusion (Jas. 5:12) is only found in the Gospel of Matthew (5:33-37). Yet we have demonstrated that certain striking dissimilarities between Jas. 5:12 and Mt. 5:33-37 confirm that the Biblical writers employed two separate traditions which Justin Martyr in his characteristic fashion harmonized.[30] Therefore, no conclusive evidence pointing to a knowledge of the Q or M traditions can be derived from the Epistle of James.

A more fruitful investigation might concentrate on discerning preSynoptic blocks of material which were orally transmitted. Allison has argued decisively that Paul has drawn from such preexistent blocks of material as Lk. 6:27-39, Lk. 10:1-16, and Mk. 9:33-50.[31] Best has likewise demonstrated that 1 Peter utilized Lk. 12:32-45 and Lk. 6:20b-38 as well as certain isolated sayings of Jesus.[32] We contend that James displays familiarity with a list of beatitudes as well as woes. Riesenfeld has proposed that James alludes to four Matthean beatitudes cited in the exact order of the Gospel of Matthew.[33] A much less hypothetical suggestion offered by Shepherd maintains that James is acquainted with a list of beatitudes more extensive than those preserved in Luke.[34] The clearest example for Shepherd is the blessing upon the merciful in Jas. 2:13 (Mt. 5:7). Less conclusive are the references to meekness (3:13=Mt. 5:3), peacemaking (3:18=Mt. 5:9), and purity of heart (4:8=Mt. 5:8). However, we have argued in chapter 3 that Jas. 3:18 (on peacemaking) is a Jewish proverb and that the theme of mercy (Jas. 3:13) is either derived from Jewish wisdom or the paraenesis of the church rather than from a collection of beatitudes of the M tradition. The exhortations to meekness and purity of heart are familiar themes in ethical writings and the wording in each case diverges from the Matthean beatitudes.[35] Instead the only unmistakable allusions to the beatitudes bear the closest resemblance to Luke (Jas. 2:5=Lk. 6:20b concerning the poor; Jas. 4:9=Lk. 6:21 about those who weep). It is enlightening to realize that James also contains a pair of woes in common with Luke. In fact, God's promise of a kingdom for the poor found in James' second discussion of wealth

---

27Shepherd, "James and Matthew," 44-45. He cites Jas. 1:6,17,22-25,26-27; 4:13-14; 5:2-3 as closer to Matthew, but only the last instance is a true allusion to a gospel saying.

28Streeter, Primitive Church, 183.

29Davies, Setting, 403.

30Bellinzoni, Sayings of Jesus in Justin, 139-141.

31Cf. ch. 5, n. 157.

32Cf. above, pp. 187-188.

33Cf. ch. 4, section 3.2 where we have demonstrated the erroneousness of his claims.

34Cf. ch. 4, section 3.2.

35Jas. 3:13 ἐν πραΰτητι σοφίας / Mt. 5:5 μακάριοι οἱ πραεῖς; Jas. 4:8 ἁγνίσατε καρδίας / Mt. 5:8 μακάριοι οἱ καθαροὶ τῇ καρδίᾳ.

(2:5-7) is balanced with the corresponding claim that eschatological miseries are coming upon the rich in James' third pericope about wealth (5:1-6). This is parallel to Luke's double reference to a beatitude (6:20) and woe (6:24) against the rich. Although the contexts in James are separated by several discourses, it is customary for James to revert to previous themes,[36] and on one occasion he even repeats a saying of Jesus on the subject of answered prayer (1:5; 4:3). Furthermore, the expected application of the beatitude to the Christian community and the woe to the wicked world is reversed when James applies the woe of Lk. 6:25b to the Christian community, exhorting them to mourn and weep and change their laughter into repentant sorrow (Jas. 4:9). The placing of a woe upon those who would normally expect a blessing indicates that James knew both a beatitude and a curse about those who laugh. The Epistle of James offers some proof that Luke was not the first to place the woes alongside the beatitudes but was instead transmitting an already established tradition (Lk. 6:20-49). We thus have evidence for a preLucan combination of beatitudes and woes[37] which in all probability was also found (in the same order?) in Q. Matthew's redactionary reason for omitting the woes in the Sermon on the Mount[38] may have been motivated by a desire to include only paraenetic material which was easily applicable to the church. Thus the woes in Matthew are aimed against the scribes and Pharisees (Mt. 23) and not directed at the disciples as in Lk. 6:20-26. James demonstrates creativity by de-eschatologizing these woes and applying them to God's chosen people as a disciplinary call to repentance. Thus, even though the sayings of Jesus in James' epistle are of an allusionary nature and therefore somewhat unhelpful in determining the original wording of the dominical sayings, they do provide indications of the extent of James' knowledge of the *logia* of the Jesus-tradition.

1.5 The sayings of Jesus were foundational for two genre of literature -- the gospel and church paraenesis. How did these two streams of literature employ the sayings of the Jesus-tradition differently? First of all, the form of the sayings differ in the two genre. It is evident from the Epistle of James, the paraenetic sections of Paul (esp. Rom. 12-13 and 1 Thess. 5), and Did. 1:3-2:1 that allusions rather than citations are the customary means of transmitting the sayings of Jesus in paraenesis. Therefore we cannot label the Epistle of James a fifth gospel as Patry suggested in his 1899 dissertation[39] and as Haslehurst entitled his article on the gospel material in James.[40] Instead a discussion of the sayings of Jesus within the Epistle of James must concentrate upon the question of the use of dominical sayings within paraenesis.

A second difference between the genres of gospel and paraenesis centers in the purpose of alluding to the Jesus-tradition. For the genre of gospel the teaching of Jesus is the end product; the primary purpose is to rehearse what Jesus said and did. On the other hand, for paraenesis the sayings of Jesus are only the raw material; they provide the themes and vocabulary necessary to develop an ethical tradition which can practically be applied to each new context which the church encounters. For example, in Jas. 4:3 Jesus' saying that those who ask will receive is shown not to apply to certain situations in the believing community, namely when people desire answered prayers to satisfy their own lust for pleasure. Such a situation had not emerged in Jesus' preaching, but now in the ethical teaching of the church new situations are addressed by means of traditional sayings. The sayings of Jesus are transmitted in the author's own words and combined with the emphases of his own

---

[36]Cf. above, p. 185.

[37]Cf. Marshall, Luke, 247. James does not employ the terms μακάριος and οὐαί as Luke does, yet we have argued in ch. 3, sections 4.3 and 4.4 that the nature of the sayings is similar even though these specific terms are missing.

[38]For Matthew's knowledge of the woes see Gundry, Matthew, 68f.

[39]Patry, Jacques, 112.

[40]Haslehurst, "The Fifth Gospel," esp. 102-103.

theology. Thus Jesus' same promise of answered prayer is attached to James' favorite theme of wisdom (1:5-6; 3:13-18) so that Jesus' word is now addressed to those who lack wisdom (1:5). The saying about the exaltation of the humble (Jas. 4:10) is transmitted apart from the parallel statement that the exalted will be humbled since the rewarding of the humble is the special emphasis of Jas. 4:6-10. James' paraenetic intent is apparent here when the gospel saying is changed into the second person plural address familiar to paraenesis. James' distinctive term "be wretched" (ταλαιπωρήσατε 4:9) or "wretchedness" (ταλαιπωρίαις 5:1) is inserted into two woes from the Jesus-tradition. Finally, James' common address "my (beloved) brethren" is employed to introduce two gospel allusions (2:5; 5:12). All of these alterations are allowable within the paraenetic tradition since its primary purpose is not the preservation of Jesus' words but the practical need of the church for ethical exhortations. This does not entail that the Jesus-tradition within paraenesis was ever emerging, constantly altered, and nonauthoritatively transmitted while that of the gospels was standard and fixed. There is flexibility in the midst of a well-defined core of teaching, redaction alongside tradition, in both of these genre. Yet as to degree, a much greater freedom to alter, add to, and apply the established traditions is evident in paraenesis.[41] Furthermore, within paraenesis the reader encounters not only allusions to specific sayings of Jesus but also the employment of the themes of Jesus' preaching to develop the Christian's moral awareness. The exegete who does not distinguish between these two usages of the Jesus-tradition will discern in the Epistle of James countless allusions to the sayings of Jesus when in reality only certain themes of the Jesus-tradition are developed separately from the precise words which Jesus spoke. While admitting the importance of the sayings of Jesus to James' teaching, we have argued against an overestimation of the role these sayings played in James' theology.

If two means of transmitting the sayings of Jesus need to be distinguished -- gospel and paraenesis,[42] what role does the authority of Jesus play in each stream? First of all, in paraenesis the allusions to Jesus' sayings are not given the authority of scripture. In the Epistle of James the sayings of Jesus function differently from the OT citations. James quotes the OT to authoritatively ground his arguments: 1) in chapter 2:8 James employs Lev. 19:18b to defend the claim that his audience has exhibited partiality; 2) the citation of Gen. 15:6 at Jas. 2:23 proves that Abraham was justified by works; 3) an unknown scripture[43] at 4:5 substantiates James' claim that friendship with the world is contrary to the divine intention; and 4) the quoting of Prov. 3:34 at 4:6 demonstrates that God gives more grace to the humble. On the other hand, James never designates Jesus' sayings as scripture[44] nor are they appealed to in order to authoritatively ground his arguments. It is not the formal authority of Jesus' sayings but their material authority that is critical. The sanctifying effect of Jesus' words upon people's lives gave these sayings authority; James' emphasis is always practical.

Typical of paraenesis James collects material from multifarious sources: the traditional language of Judaism and the OT, the sayings and themes of Jesus' preaching,

---

[41]Cf. Allen Verhey, The Great Reversal: Ethics and the New Testament, 71: "In the paraenetic tradition that evolved, the early church began the continuing task of assimilating, transforming, and fulfilling the moral wisdom of its time."

[42]Supported among others by Allison, "Pauline Epistles and Synoptic Gospels," 23 and Piper, Love Your Enemies, 139 and 134 where he follows Leonhard Goppelt, "Jesus und die 'Haustafel'-Tradition," Orientierung an Jesus, ed. Paul Hoffmann (Freiburg: Herder, 1973), 93-106.

[43]Cf. ch. 2, section 2.4 for evidence that the book of Eldad and Modad is referred to.

[44]We do not encounter any introductory formulas such as "according to the scripture" (Jas. 2:8), "the scripture was fulfilled which says" (2:23), "the scripture says" (4:5), or "he said" (2:11) or "it says" (4:6).

everyday maxims and wisdom sayings, analogies from nature, logical arguments, and the author's particular emphases. No single strand (i.e. the sayings of Jesus) supplies the needed authority and inspiration; instead the interaction and combination of all these factors form the authoritative teaching of the church. We therefore disagree with David's contention that the allusions to the Jesus-tradition are the basic authority behind almost every section of James' moral teaching.[45] He claims that "of 22 sections in the Epistle 15 have close allusions, 5 others 'possible' allusions and the 2 remaining ones have less verbally exact parallels in the narrative and sayings tradition."[46] On the other hand, we can only substantiate eight instances where James intentionally alludes to sayings of Jesus, and these are situated primarity in his more paraenetic sections where short exhortations dominate. In James' discourses located in 2:1-3:12 logical arguments, analogies from nature, and OT citations dominate. Throughout the epistle Jesus' sayings are intertwined with James's own terminology and related maxims from Jewish wisdom and do not by themselves provide the ground of authority for James' teaching. This identical phenomenon is experienced in the paraenesis of Paul at Rom. 12:14,17 and 1 Thess. 5:13,15 where allusions to sayings of Jesus do not substantiate Paul's teaching or give authority to his ideas. Rather a whole group of exhortations, one after another, are presented with each one able to stand on its own authority. That is the nature of paraenesis. Only when Paul is dealing with specific moral problems (and not a list of general exhortations indigenous to paraenesis) will he appeal to the gospel tradition and the formal authority which the sayings of Jesus there possessed to defend his own judgment on such issues as marriage (1 Cor. 7:10) or a financially supported ministry (1 Cor. 9:14).[47] Thus the sayings of Jesus had authority in themselves when the gospel tradition was cited, but in paraenesis the authority of the moral exhortations depended not upon their source but upon the simple fact that this was the teaching of the church which in its totality was inspired by the Holy Spirit.[48]

Implications for the Importance of Genre in the Interpretation of Scripture

2.1 Dibelius is renowned for his categorization of the Epistle of James as paraenesis. Yet in his application of this finding he has misrepresented its importance by assigning to almost every problem of this epistle the solution of paraenesis.[49] Yet we should not allow a misuse of the importance of genre to cause us to underestimate the role played by paraenesis in the Epistle of James. The genre explains, first of all, the form of the sayings of Jesus. As we have explained earlier, the allusionary character of quotations is inherent to paraenesis. No introductory formulations are employed, and the wording of the saying is strongly governed by the author's own vocabulary. This influence of paraenesis upon the sayings of Jesus should not surprise us since the writer of the apocalypse also allows his genre to influence the form of the sayings of Jesus. As Vos explains, "While the Apocalyptist often couches such sayings in apocalyptic dress, the actual forms of the promises themselves display much similarity with the sayings of Jesus as they have been recorded in the Synoptics."[50] Just as the Lord speaks to his church through the inspired prophet in the book of Revelation,[51] so Jesus Christ speaks through the wisdom of

---

[45]Davids, "James and Jesus," 70,72-73. This is also the contention of Shepherd (cf. above, p. 57) and Adamson, James: Man and Message, 163.

[46]Davids, "James and Jesus," 69-70.

[47]Cf. above, pp. 244-245.

[48]Dibelius, Tradition to Gospel, 241 states, "Thus all of them appeared as exhortations 'in the Lord', if not as exhortations 'of the Lord'." Cf. Hahn, "Begründung urchristlicher Paränese," 89.

[49]Cf. ch. 1, section 3.5.

[50]Vos, Synoptic Traditions in the Apocalypse, 217.

[51]Sayings found in the third person in the gospels are placed in the prophetic first person in the Apocalypse: Rev. 3:3 (Mt. 24:42-43), 3:5 (Mt. 10:32), 3:20 (Mt. 24:33), 3:21 (Mt. 19:28), 16:15 (Mt. 24:42-43), and 22:12 (Mt. 16:27).

the church in the genre of paraenesis. Just as the Apocalyptist "does not hesitate to adapt the themes and expressions to the apocalyptic form,"[52] so James does not hesitate to adapt the sayings of Jesus to the paraenetic form. Just as the apocalyptic sayings play a prominent role in the book of Revelation,[53] so the short wisdom sayings of Jesus play a major role in the paraenesis of James. The Epistle of James does not refer to Jesus as risen savior, Son of God, or exalted Son of Man, but the appeal to his ethical teachings indicates that Jesus, the teacher of wisdom, is standing in the background behind the paraenesis of James. Thus in paraenetic literature the threefold anointing of Christ as prophet, priest, and king is expanded into a fourfold anointing including that of teacher of wisdom.

2.2 The almost complete omission of Christology in the Epistle of James has been variously explained by theologians:

1) Some believe that the lack of Christology and the undeveloped nature of Christian theology indicate an early date of composition;[54]

2) Others like Spitta and Massebieau have used this omission of Christology to postulate a Jewish origin to the Epistle of James;[55]

3) A third position perceives the solution in James' evangelistic method.[56] James does not overtly press the claims of Christ's words or redemptive actions since he is attempting to conciliate non-Christian Jews and remove objections to the new way by demonstrating the effect of this faith on conduct.

4) Tasker connects the lack of Christology with the problem of authorship stating that Jesus' own brother would not stress Christology.[57]

5) Adamson believes that the lack of Christology is dependent upon the conditions under which James was written, i.e. "in a hostile environment and at a time when Christianity was a forbidden religion and proselytizing (or even the hint of it) was unlawful."[58]

6) Riesenfeld appeals to the holiness of the gospel tradition and to the assumption that the Jesus-tradition was presumed in James' epistle.[59]

---

[52]Vos, Synoptic Traditions in the Apocalypse, 216. He is referring here to the parabolic sayings of Jesus.

[53]Ibid., 217. Rev. 1:6; ch. 6 (cf. Vos' diagram on p. 186); 11:26; 13:13; 14:6,14-19.

[54]Rendall, James and Judaic Christianity, 88,108; Robinson, Redating, 123-124; Davids, James, 22.

[55]Cf. ch. 1, section 3.4.

[56]Cadoux, Thought of James, 88; Moule, Birth of NT, 219; James H. Moulton, "The Epistle of James and the Sayings of Jesus," Ex 7,4(1907): 54.

[57]Tasker, James, 28.

[58]Adamson, James: Man and Message, 222,10.

[59]Riesenfeld, Gospel Tradition and Beginnings, 23. "Here we have the reason why the words and deeds of Jesus were probably never quoted verbally in the missionary preaching and only on rare occasions in the community instruction. The tradition which was recited was holy and hence, in contrast to present-day practice, was not readily mentioned by word of mouth. Mission preaching, indeed, pointed and led to it. The instruction in the community presuppossed it and linked itself up with it. But in its verbal form, in its *Sitz im Leben* in the community, it was *sui generis*."

7) We choose rather for the view that the genre of paraenesis explains the unusually slim amount of references to Christology and Christ's life and work. Paraenesis is ethical teaching emphasizing the human response to the gospel and not the kerygma itself. The kerygma surfaces only momentarily in the Epistle of James at 1:18 ("of his own will he brought us forth by the word of truth") and 1:21b ("receive with meekness the implanted word which is able to save your souls"). Then immediately in 1:22 the human response to the kerygma is again emphasized by utilizing the same term λόγος, "But be doers of the word." The Epistle of James is ethical throughout. Even near the end of the book when he deals with eschatology (5:7-11) and questions of church order (5:12-20), the ethical implications of eschatology (patience, waiting steadfastly, no grumbling) and the ethical demands of the church order (not swearing, praying, confession of sins) are emphasized. Therefore, a Christological section is not necessary in a Christian paraenetic writing.

Yet it is not inherent to paraenesis that Christology is omitted. Paul has ingeniously grounded his ethics upon the death and resurrection of Christ. In the *Haustafeln* we repeatedly encounter the phrases "as to the Lord" (ώς τῷ κυρίῳ Eph. 5:21; Col. 3:23; ώς τῷ Χριστῷ Eph. 6:5; ώς ἀνῆκεν ἐν κυρίῳ Col. 3:18) or "in the Lord (ἐν κυρίῳ Col. 3:20). In his personal ethics Paul bases his moral teaching upon the union of the believer with the death of Christ (Eph. 4:22ff; Col. 2:20ff) and his resurrection (Col. 3:1ff). Likewise, 1 Peter emphasizes the example of Christ[60] which believers should follow (1 Pet. 2:21-25).[61] In the Epistle of James, however, only OT characters such as Abraham (2:21-24), Rahab (2:25), the prophets (5:10), Job (5:11), and Elijah (5:17) are highlighted as paradigms. There is no attempt to constuct a moral theology around specifically Christological claims. Instead the moral virtues of love (2:8) and wisdom (3:13-18) are held up as norms along with the ethical precepts of the law, which now become the law of freedom under the influence of Christian reinterpretation. If there is any theological core or governing principle to James' moral theology,[62] it is this last point concerning the perfect (1:25), royal (2:8) law of liberty (1:25; 2:12).[63] James' paraenesis consists of moral obligations which follow from a Christian rendering of the ancient Jewish law. Yet nowhere in the Epistle of James does one perceive the personalization of the ethical tradition as is so prevalent in Paul. In Paul the I-Thou relationship provides the foundation for the ethical demand. The mystery for Paul is that the demands of God have been fulfilled in the person of Jesus. For James the I-it relationship is dominant. The Christian is impinged upon by a code of moral behavior which he must obey and is capable of obeying. This difference has justifiably accounted for the greater impact of Paul's theology upon the church's moral teaching. Yet it must not be forgotten that the paraenesis of James is also the wisdom of God. His proclamation of a personal and social righteousness which permeates the very fabric of human nature and cultural development will always be relevant.

---

[60]Paul also grounds his exhortation to selflessness on the example of Jesus in Phil. 2:1-11.

[61]For a description of Peter's manner of grounding the imperative in the indicative of the kerygma, see Eduard Lohse, "Paränese und Kerygma im 1 Petrusbrief," ZNW 45(1954): 68-89.

[62]Sophie S. Laws, "The Doctrinal Basis for the Ethics of James," SE, 7:301 believes that the oneness of God governs the development of James' ethics although she admits (p. 304) that there are no examples in current thought indicating that God's oneness was a quality able to be imitated. Verhey, Great Reversal 133 believes that "if there is any theological basis to be discerned in James, it seems to be the memory of Jesus' proclamation of a 'great reversal'." However, this is much more obvious in Jesus' preaching than it is in James' ethical exhortations. J.L. Houlden, Ethics and the New Testament, 66 and Jack Sanders, Ethics, 126, on the other hand, contend that no governing principle undergirds the ethics of James.

[63]The word "law" occurs ten times in the epistle: 1:25; 2:8,9,10,11,12; 4:11 (4x).

Thus the Epistle of James is a witness to the importance of genre in the interpretation of scripture. The presence of paraenesis best accounts for the form of the sayings of Jesus, the lack of Christology, and the overlap between Jewish and Christian ideas.[64] The title of the Epistle of James could in fact be more appropriately called the Paraenesis of James. Our study has shown that the sayings of the Jesus-tradition could find a home in every genre which the NT produced -- not only in the gospels, epistles, and apocalyptic literature of the early church but also embedded in the collection of ethical exhortations which we call the paraenetic tradition.

---

[64]Dibelius, Tradition to Gospel, 240 offers a suggestion on how Jewish wisdom and the sayings of Jesus became the two main sources for paraenesis. "The primitive Christian Churches were prepared for the disappearance of this world and not for life in it. They were therefore in no way prepared for the the necessity of bringing forward hortatory sentences for every-day life. However, Judaism had been at work. Often dependent upon Hellenistic models, its teachings as given to proselytes required only slight change or filling-out of a Christian character in order to become usable among Christians. And with their special treasure in the words of Jesus, Christians had a storehouse of warnings and teachings directed, or at least capable of being directed, towards the most varied everyday relationships, even when their teachings were by no means sufficient for all requirements of exhortation."

Appendix I

SUGGESTED PARALLELS BETWEEN THE EPISTLE OF JAMES AND THE SYNOPTIC GOSPELS[1]

Authors	Publication Year	Page	Total Number of Sayings
60 authors			184
1. Thiele	1833	44-45	15
2. Credner	1836	608-609	18
3. deWette	1848	187	10
4. Reuss	1853	130	9
5. Schmid	1853	135-137	26
6. Huther	1865	20	18
7. Schmidt	1869	73	6
8. Blom[2]	1869	193-196	24
9. Holtzmann[3]	1871	180	16
10. Werner	1872	263-264	5
11. Brückner[4]	1874	537	14
12. Beyschlag	1874	142-143	14
13. Riedel	1875	7	9
14. Schenkel	1879	117	9
15. Holtzmann	1882	294	19
16. von Soden[5]	1884	169	28
17. Salmon	1886	482	10
18. Weizsäcker[6]	1886	378-379	18
19. Mayor[7]	1892	lxxxii-lxxxiv	65
	1897	lxxxiv-lxxxvi	
20. Feine	1893	133	29
21. Davidson	1894	295	9

---

[1]These are only possible parallels since some authors (Spitta etc.) offer a list of parallels but then critically dismiss them as invalid.

[2]There appears to be a typographical error on p. 195 of Blom's work where Jas. 2:4 is identified with Mt. 5:19 rather than 5:9.

[3]Since Holtzmann does not mention the gospel references in his 1871 article in Schenkel's Bibel-Lexicon, we have included the most likely possibilities. Jas. 3:17 is not included since we cannot identify which parallel was in Holtzmann's mind. Concerning Jas. 2:13-16 we can only identify Jas. 2:13 = Mt. 5:7.

[4]Brückner's less probable references are included in parenthesis.

[5]In a footnote von Soden lists as doubtful Jas. 4:4 = Mt. 6:24; 1:12 and 5:11 = Mt. 10:22; 1:4 = Mt. 5:48.

[6]Weizsäcker offers three lists: 1) a group of sayings saturated with the words of Jesus; 2) sayings of doubtful character (marked with parenthesis); 3) sayings definitely belonging to a later time (marked with a double parenthesis).

[7]Mayor's less important parallels, unstarred in his list, are here put in parenthesis.

22. Rose	1896	528	10
23. Spitta[8]	1896	158-177	50
24. B. Weiss	1897	390	13
25. Plumptre[9]	1901	8	16
26. Cone	1903	2322	9
27. Grafe	1904	23	7
28. Knowling	1904	xxi-xxii	17
29. Fulford[10]	1906	847	19
30. Zahn	1906	81	22
31. Toxopeus	1906	181-182	22
32. Ermoni	1910	1089	18
33. Ropes	1916	31	6
34. Moffatt	1918	466	14
35. Dibelius	1921		
and Greeven	1964	28-29	11
36. Hauck	1926	13	9
37. Grosheide	1927; 1955	417-418; 342	24
38. Chaine[11]	1927	LXIV-LXIX	29
39. Schlatter[12]	1932	10-21	57
40. Kittel	1944	84-90	25
41. McNeille	1953	208	4
42. Hayes	1955	1564	12
43. Shepherd	1956	42-47	30
44. Wikenhauser	1956	343	5
45. Lohse[13]	1957	9-11	4
46. Gryglewicz[14]	1961	43-54	13
47. Leconte	1961	11-12	22
48. Guthrie	1962	67-68	19
49. Grant	1963	221	6
50. Eleder[15]	1964	54	16

---

[8]Spitta supplies a detailed list of possible parallels to the gospels and then precedes to deny any connection betweeen the sayings. At Jas. 1:20 Spitta's reference to Mt. 6:23 should be corrected to Mt. 6:33.

[9]Plumptre only refers to parallels with the Sermon on the Mount.

[10]Fulford's less important parallels are placed in parenthesis. He adds three parallels from the Gospel of John: Jas. 1:17=Jn. 3:3; 1:25=Jn. 8:31-33; 4:17=Jn. 13:17.

[11]Chaine's list includes three categories: 1) general reminiscences to the gospels (marked by parenthesis); 2) probable dependence on the sayings of Jesus (no marking); 3) certain dependence upon the sayings of Jesus (marked by a star *). In this third category Chaine includes a parallel with the Gospel of John (Jas. 4:4=Jn. 15:19).

[12]Schlatter has both a discussion concerning parallels of content (pp. 10-16) and a list of mere verbal reminiscences (pp. 19-21, marked by parenthesis). References found in both of Schlatter's categories are marked with a star *.

[13]Lohse (p. 9) states that his list could be augmented but that these four examples already prove that James is consciously employing sayings of Jesus.

[14]The references listed are those in which Gryglewicz finds direct dependence of James upon Matthew. He also distinguishes other categories: 1) similar verbal expressions (p. 35); 2) similar themes developed differently (pp. 37-40); and 3) coinciding themes where the direction of dependence is impossible to establish (pp. 40-43).

[15]Because of the extent of his dissertation, Eleder only includes references to the Sermon on the Mount.

51. Davies[16]	1964	402	24
52. Stott	1964	102-103	25
53. Williams	1965	84-86	13
54. Cantinat	1965	558-559	11
55. Mußner	1967	48-50	24
56. Sidebottom	1967	8-11	39
57. Gromacki[17]	1974	340	6
58. Hiebert	1979	17	16
59. Kugelman	1980	9	9
60. Davids[18]	1985	66-67	52

Jas. 1:2=Mt. 5:11-12; Lk. 6:22-23: 5, 6, 8, 9, 15, 16, 19, 20, 22, 23, 25, 28, 29, 30, 32, 38, 40, 48, 50, 51, 52, 53, 54, 56, 57, 58, 59, 60.
Jas. 1:3=Lk. 21:19: (19), 23.
Jas. 1:3-4=Lk. 8:15: (29).
Jas. 1:4=Mt. 5:48: 6, 9, (11), 12, 15, 17, (19), 23, 25, 32, 39*, 40, 42, 48, 50, (51), 52, 56, 58, 60.
Jas. 1:4=Mt. 10:22; 24:13: 30.
Jas. 1:4=Mt. 19:21: (19).
Jas. 1:5=Mt. 7:7; Lk. 11:9: 1, 2, 5, 6, 8, 9, 11, 12, 15, 16, 17, 19, 20, 21, 23, 24, 25, 27, 28, 29, 30, 31, 32, 33, 34, 35, 36, 37, 38, 39*, 40, 42, 43, 45, 46, 47, 48, 49, 50, 51, 52, 53, 55, 56, 58, 59, 60*.
Jas. 1:5=Mt. 11:21-22: 1.
Jas. 1:6=Mt. 7:1: 47.
Jas. 1:6=Mt. 21:21; Mk. 11:23: 2, 5, 9, 12, 15, 16, 17, (18), (19), 20, 21, 23, 24, 26, 31, 37, 38, 40, 42, 43, 46, 48, (51), 52, 55, 56, 59, 60*.
Jas. 1:7=Lk. 11:13: 34.
Jas. 1:6-8=Mt. 14:30; 17:20; Lk. 8:24-25: (19).
Jas. 1:9=Mt. 5:3: 6, 9, 25, 39, 58.
Jas. 1:9=Lk. 1:52: 16, 20, 23, (38), 52.
Jas. 1:9-10=Mt. 18:4: 8, 19, (60).
Jas. 1:9-10=Mt. 23:12; Lk. 14:11; 22:26: (60).
Jas. 1:10-11= Mt. 13:6: (19).
Jas. 1:10-11=Lk. 12:15-21: 39.
Jas. 1:11=Mt. 6:29: (19), 23.
Jas. 1:12=Mt. 5:10-12; Lk. 6:22-23: 32, 38, 43, 47, 54, 56, 59.
Jas. 1:12=Mt. 10:22: 8, (11), 19, 23, 60.
Jas. 1:13=Mt. 26:41; Mk. 14:38; Lk. 22:40,46: 23.
Jas. 1:13-14=Mt. 6:13; Lk. 11:4: 43, 60.
Jas. 1:14=Mt. 15:19: 6, 32.
Jas. 1:16=Mt. 22:29: (39).
Jas. 1:17=Mt. 5:16: (19).
Jas. 1:17=Mt. 7:11; Lk. 11:13: 3, 4, 7, 13, 16, (19), 20, 22, 26, 31, 32, 37, 40, 43, 52, 55, 56, 60*.

---

[16]Davies' less important parallels (which he leaves unstarred) are here placed in parenthesis.

[17]Gromacki limits himself to parallels with the Sermon on the Mount.

[18]We will follow the more detailed categorization found in David's article, "James and Jesus," 66-67 rather than the list in his commentary, pp. 47-48. The asterisk * means a close allusion; the double asterisk ** designates an indirect citation; no marking indicates a possible allusion; parenthesis are used for Davids' other distinctions entitled basic concept (5), concept of parable (4), and idea of narrative (1).

Jas. 1:19 = Mt. 12:36: 19.
Jas. 1:19-20 = Mt. 5:22: 3, 4, 5, 6, 7, 9, 13, 15, 16, 20, 23, 25, 26, 28, 29, 32, 37, 39, 40, 43, 48, 50, 51, 53, 56, 58, 60*.
Jas. 1:20 = Mt. 5:6,20: 23.
Jas. 1:20 = Mt. 6:33: (19), 23.
Jas. 1:21 = Mt. 5:5: 5, 39.
Jas. 1:21 = Mt. 13:19-23; Lk. 8:11-15: 16, 20, 23, (39), 56, (60).
Jas. 1:21 = Mt. 15:13: (19).
Jas. 1:21 = Mt. 16:25: (39).
Jas. 1:21 = Lk. 2:28: 16.
Jas. 1:22 = Mt. 5:19: (19).
Jas. 1:22-25 = Mt. 7:24-26; Lk. 6:46-49: 1, 2, 3, 4, 5, 8, 9, 10, 11, 12, 13, 14, 15, 16, 17, 18, 19, 20, 22, 23, 24, 26, 27, 28, 29, 30, 31, 34, 36, 37, 38, 40, 41, 42, 43, 45, 46, 47, 48, 50, 51, 52, 53, 54, 55, 56, 57, 59, 60*.
Jas. 1:25 = Mt. 5:17: (19).
Jas. 1:25 = Mt. 5:19: 10.
Jas. 1:25 = Mt. 22:36f: 15, 23.
Jas. 1:26 = Mt. 5:22: 5.
Jas. 1:26-27 = Mt. 15:4-9: 47
Jas. 1:26-27 = Mt. 7:21-23: 19, 23, 43, (60).
Jas. 1:26-27 = Mt. 12:7; 23:2-4,23-26; Mk. 12:40: 30.
Jas. 1:27 = Mt. 18:7: 38*, 54.
Jas. 1:27 = Mt. 25:24: 56.
Jas. 1:27 = Mt. 25:36: 39, 43.
Jas. 1:27 = Mt. 16:26; 18:5; 25:40: 39.
Jas. 1:27 = Lk. 20:46-47: (19).
Jas. 2:1ff = Mt. 25:31ff: 54.
Jas. 2:1-4 = Mt. 23:6-12; Mk. 12:38f: 30.
Jas. 2:2 = Lk. 20:46-47: (19).
Jas. 2:2 = Lk. 23:11: (39).
Jas. 2:4 = Mt. 15:19: 8, (39).
Jas. 2:4 = Mt. 21:21: (19), (39).
Jas. 2:4 = Lk. 5:22: (19), 23.
Jas. 2:5 = Mt. 4:23; 25:34: (39).
Jas. 2:5 = Mt. 5:3,5; Lk. 6:20b: 2, 3, 5, 7, 8, 11, 12, 14, 15, 16, 17, 19, 20, 21, 22, 23, 27, 28, 29, 30, 31, 33, 34, 36, 37, 38, 39, 40, 41, 42, 43, 44, 47, 49, 50, 51, 52, 54, 55, 56, 59, 60*.
Jas. 2:5 = Mt. 11:2; Lk. 7:22: (19), 60*.
Jas. 2:5 = Lk. 12:21; 16:19f: 31
Jas. 2:6 = Lk. 6:24-25: 19, 31.
Jas. 2:6 = Lk. 18:3: 55, (60).
Jas. 2:8 = Mt. 7:12; Lk. 6:29-31: 1, 2, 8, 14, 28, 29.
Jas. 2:8 = Mt. 22:39; Mk. 12:31; Lk. 10:27: 1, 2, 3, 4, 5, 8, 12, 13, 15, 16, 19, 20, 21, 22, 23, 24, 26, 30, 31, 35, 37, (38), 40, 44, 48, (51), 52, 56, 60*.
Jas. 2:8-10 = Mt. 19:17: (39), 43.
Jas. 2:10 = Mt. 5:19: (19); 43, 48, 52, 53, 56, 60*.
Jas. 2:11 = Mt. 5:21f: 40, 50, (51), 60.
Jas. 2:12 = Mt. 7:16: 2.
Jas. 2:13 = Mt. 5:5; 25:34f: 1, 2, 8.
Jas. 2:13 = Mt. 5:7; Lk. 6:33: 3, 4, 5, 6, 7, 9, 12, 13, 15, 16, 19, 20, 22, 23, 24, 25, 26, 28, 29, 30, 32, 35, 37, 38, 39, 40, 43, 44, 47, 48, 51, 52, 53, 54, 55, 56, 58, 59, 60.
Jas. 2:13 = Mt. 6:14-15: 6, 25, 32, 58.
Jas. 2:13 = Mt. 7:1-2: 16,21.

Jas. 2:13 = Mt. 12:7; Lk. 6:37: (19).
Jas. 2:13 = Mt. 18:33f: 24, 52.
Jas. 2:13 = Mt. 23:23; Lk. 1:72: (39).
Jas. 2:14 = Mt. 7:21; Lk. 6:46: 6, 25, 32, 43, 56, 57, 58, 60.
Jas. 2:14 = Mt. 17:20: (39).
Jas. 2:15 = Mt. 6:25: 40, 44, 51, (60).
Jas. 2:15 = Mt. 25:36,41: 15, 23, 43, 56, (60).
Jas. 2:15f = Lk. 3:11; 12:33; 16:9: 34.
Jas. 2:15f = Lk. 6:29f: 14.
Jas. 2:15-16 = Mt. 6:16: 19, 28.
Jas. 2:16 = Mk. 5:34: (39).
Jas. 2:17 = Mt. 21:28f: 43.
Jas. 2:19 = Mt. 8:29: 19, 23, 56.
Jas. 2:19 = Mt. 19:7: (39).
Jas. 2:24 = Mt. 12:37: 23.
Jas. 2:26 = Mt. 7:21: 50.
Jas. 3:1 = Mt. 12:36-37: 19, 23, (29), 60.
Jas. 3:1 = Mt. 23:8: 21, 38, 47, 48, 56.
Jas. 3:1 = Mk. 12:40: 2, 8, 30, 39*.
Jas. 3:1 = Lk. 12:48: 34.
Jas. 3:1 = Lk. 20:46-47: 2, (19).
Jas. 3:2 = Mt. 5:48; 19:21: (19).
Jas. 3:2 = Mt. 12:35f: (38), 43, 48, 56.
Jas. 3:6 = Mt. 15:11: (38), 43, 56.
Jas. 3:9 = Mt. 11:25: (39).
Jas. 3:9-10 = Mt. 12:34: (19), 23.
Jas. 3:9-10 = Lk. 6:28: 47.
Jas. 3:10 = Mt. 15:11,18: (39), 46.
Jas. 3:12 = Mt. 7:16; Lk. 6:44: 1, 2, 5, 8, 11, 15, 16, 18, 19, 20, 21, 23, 28, 29, 30, 31, 35, 37, 39*, 40, 42, 43, 46, 47, 50, 51, 52, 53, 55, 56, 57, 60*.
Jas. 3:12 = Mt. 12:33-34: 18, 47.
Jas. 3:13 = Mt. 5:5: 5, 39, 43.
Jas. 3:13 = Mt. 11:19: (19), 23, 38, 60.
Jas. 3:14-15 = Mt. 7:21-23: 19.
Jas. 3:17 = Mt. 11:29: (19).
Jas. 3:17 = Mt. 12:33: 56.
Jas. 3:17f = Lk. 3:11; 12:33; 16:9: 34.
Jas. 3:18 = Mt. 5:9; Lk. 6:43: 1, 2, 5, 6, 8, 9, 11, 12, 15, 16, (19), 20, 21, 23, 25, 27, 28, 29, 30, 31, 32, 33, 34, 37, 39, 40, 41, 43, 48, 49, 50, 51, 52, 53, 55, 56, 58, 60*.
Jas. 3:18 = Mt. 13:8: 18.
Jas. 4:2 = Mt. 5:21-22: 8.
Jas. 4:2 = Mt. 21:22; Mk. 11:24: 39.
Jas. 4:2-3 = Mt. 7:7-8; Lk. 11:9-10: 5, 8, 11, 15, 16, 18, 19, 20, 22, 23, 24, 28, 31, 35, 37, (39), 40, 43, 46, 51, 52, 55, 56, 60.
Jas. 4:4 = Mt. 6:24; Lk. 16:13: 1, 2, 5, 6, 8, 9, 10, (11), 12, 15, 18, 19, 24, 25, 27, 28, 29, 30, 31, 32, 34, 43, 48, 52, 53, 55, 56, 58, 60*.
Jas. 4:4 = Mt. 12:39; 16:4; Mk. 8:38: 1, 2, 16, (19), 20, 23, 27, 30, 31, 33, 35, 36, 37, (38), 40, 49, (51), 60.
Jas. 4:5 = Mt. 26:53; Lk. 13:2: (39).
Jas. 4:6 = Mt. 18:4: (29).
Jas. 4:7,9 = Mt. 23:39: 39.
Jas. 4:8 = Mt. 5:8: 5, 19, 23, (38), 43, 47.
Jas. 4:8 = Mt. 5:30: 46

Jas. 4:8 = Mt. 6:22: 60.
Jas. 4:8 = Mt. 7:3,7: 18.
Jas. 4:8 = Mt. 18:8: 46.
Jas. 4:9 = Lk. 6:25: 5, 8, 17, ((18)), 19, 20, 22, 23, 30, 37, (38), (39), 40, 42, 47, 50, (51), 55, 56, 60*.
Jas. 4:10 = Mt. 5:3-5: 6, 25, 32, 48, 53, 58.
Jas. 4:10 = Mt. 18:4: 19, (39), 46.
Jas. 4:10 = Mt. 23:12; Lk. 14:11; 18:14: 5, 12, 16, 17, 20, 22, 23, 24, 30, 31, 36, 37, 38, 39*, 40, 42, 46, (51), 52, 55, 56, 60*.
Jas. 4:10 = Lk. 1:15: (39).
Jas. 4:11-12 = Mt. 6:12; Mk. 11:25: 39.
Jas. 4:11-12 = Mt. 7:1; Lk. 6:37: 5, 6, 11, 12, 16, 17, 18, 19, 20, 23, 25, 28, 29, 30, 31, 32, 36, 37, 39, 40, 42, 43, 45, 47, 48, 50, 51, 52, 53, 56, 57, 58, 60*.
Jas. 4:12 = Mt. 10:22: 30, 56.
Jas. 4:12 = Mt. 10:28: 3, 4, 6, 13, (19), 23, 26, 32, 38, (39).
Jas. 4:13-14 = Mt. 6:34; Lk. 12:16-21: 1, 2, 5, ((18)), 19, 20, 23, (29), 31, 34, 37, 38, 39, 43, 52, 55, 56, 60.
Jas. 4:17 = Mt. 7:24-26; Lk. 6:47-49: 38, 59.
Jas. 4:17 = Lk. 12:47: 16, 19, 20, 23, 24, 30, 34, 37, 56, 60.
Jas. 4:19 = Lk. 6:25: 12, 16, 20.
Jas. 5:1 = Lk. 6:24: 12, 14, 16, 17, 19, 20, 23, (29), 31, 32, 33, 34, 37, (38), 40, 42, 47, 49, 50, (51), 52, 54, 55, 56, 60*.
Jas. 5:1 = Lk. 16:19-31: 52.
Jas. 5:1 = Lk. 21:26: (39).
Jas. 5:2 = Mt. 6:19-20; Lk. 12:33b: 1, 2, 3, 4, 5, 6, 7, 8, 9, 10, 11, 13, 15, 16, 18, 19, 20, 23, 25, 28, 29, 30, 31, 32, 35, 36, 37, (38), 40, 43, 46, 47, 48, 50, 51, 52, 53, 55, 56, 57, 58, 60.
Jas. 5:2 = Lk. 6:37: 60*.
Jas. 5:3 = Mt. 8:4: (39).
Jas. 5:3 = Mt. 10:9: 56.
Jas. 5:3 = Lk. 12:16-21: 16, 20.
Jas. 5:5 = Mt. 5:3: 22.
Jas. 5:5 = Mt. 7:13; 21:41; 24:2,21; Lk. 13:1-5: 39.
Jas. 5:5 = Lk. 16:19: (38), 55, 56, 60.
Jas. 5:5 = Lk. 19:27: (39).
Jas. 5:6 = Mt. 5:21-22: 8.
Jas. 5:6 = Mt. 5:39: 1, 2.
Jas. 5:6 = Mt. 12:7,37; Lk. 6:37: 5, 16, (19), 20, 23, 37, (38), 40, 43, (51), 60.
Jas. 5:7 = Mk. 4:26-29: ((18)), 55, (60).
Jas. 5:7-8 = Mt. 24:3,27,37,39: 2, (19), 22, 23, (39), (60).
Jas. 5:7-9 = Mt. 7:21-23; 16:27: 5.
Jas. 5:7-9 = Lk. 12:35-40: 52.
Jas. 5:8 = Mt. 3:2; 4:17: (19), 23, (39).
Jas. 5:9 = Mt. 5:22: 60*.
Jas. 5:9 = Mt. 6:12; Mk. 11:25: 39.
Jas. 5:9 = Mt. 7:1: 19, 23, 24, 28, 39*, 47, 55, 56, 60*.
Jas. 5:9 = Mt. 24:33; Mk. 13:29: 1, 5, 18, 19, 20, 30, 35, 37, 38*, 40, 42, 47, 48, (51), 52, 54, 55, 60*.
Jas. 5:9 = Lk. 13:25: (18), 60.
Jas. 5:10 = Mt. 23:29-31: 47.
Jas. 5:10-11 = Mt. 5:11-12; Lk. 6:22-23: 5, 6, 9, 11, 15, 16, 19, 20, 23, 25, 31, 32, 35, 37, 39, 40, 47, 48, 50, 51, 55, 56, 58, 60.
Jas. 5:11 = Mt. 10:22: 8, (11), (39), 56.

Jas. 5:11=Lk. 21:19: (29).
Jas. 5:12=Mt. 5:33-37: 1, 3, 4, 5, 6, 7, 8, 9, 10, 11, 12, 13, 14, 15, 16, 17, 18, 19, 20, 21, 22, 23, 24, 25, 26, 27, 28, 29, 30, 31, 32, 33, 34, 35, 36, 37, 38, 39, 40, 41, 42, 43, 44, 45, 46, 47, 48, 49, 50, 51, 52, 53, 54, 55, 56, 57, 58, 59, 60**.
Jas. 5:12=Lk. 6:37: 14
Jas. 5:13=Lk. 6:38: 14
Jas. 5:14=Mt. 9:1: 3, 9.
Jas. 5:14=Mk. 6:13: 8, 9, 15, (19), 23, 26, (39), (60).
Jas. 5:15=Mt. 7:7: 6, 9, 25, 58.
Jas. 5:15=Mt. 9:2f; Mk. 2:5f; Lk. 5:20f: 4, 13, 23, 39.
Jas. 5:15=Mt. 12:32: 19, 38, (39), 46, 54.
Jas. 5:16=Mt. 3:6; 5:13: (39).
Jas. 5:16=Mt. 18:18f: (18).
Jas. 5:16=Lk. 15:21; 18:13: 39.
Jas. 5:16f=Lk. 6:38: 14.
Jas. 5:17=Lk. 4:25: 8, 16, (19), 20, 23, 28, 31, 34, 35, 36, 37, 43, 47, 55, 60.
Jas. 5:19=Mt. 18:15; Lk. 17:3: (18), 55, 60.
Jas. 5:19=Lk. 1:16: (39).
Jas. 5:20=Mt. 7:13: (19), 23, 38.
Jas. 5:20=Mt. 18:12-14,24; 25:24-30: 39.

The Twenty-five Most Frequently Mentioned Parallels

The following list indicates the most frequently quoted parallels between James and the gospels. Those couplets above the line have been dealt with in chapter 3 while those below the line will be discussed in this appendix. The double starred entries we have classified as deliberate allusions to specific sayings of Jesus. The single starred entries consist of important themes in the preaching of Jesus drawn from the church's paraenetic tradition. Jas. 3:18 and probably 2:13 find their source in Jewish wisdom and are employed as transitions between paragraphs whereas Jas. 3:12 is an everyday wisdom saying also used transitionally.

	Parallel	Number of Authors
**	Jas. 5:12= Mt. 5:33-37	59
*	Jas. 1:22-25=Mt. 7:24-26; Lk. 6:47-49	49
**	Jas. 1:5=Mt. 7:7; Lk. 11:9	45
**	Jas. 2:5=Mt. 5:3; Lk. 6:20	43
**	Jas. 5:2=Mt. 6:19-20; Lk. 12:33b	42
*?	Jas. 2:13=Mt. 5:7; Lk. 6:36	40
	Jas. 3:18=Mt. 5:9; Lk. 6:43	38
*	Jas. 4:11-12=Mt. 7:1-2a; Lk. 6:37	33
	Jas. 3:12=Mt. 7:16; Lk. 6:44	32
*	Jas. 2:8=Mt. 22:39; Mk. 12:31; Lk. 10:27	29
*	Jas. 4:4=Mt. 6:24; Lk. 16:13	29
	Jas. 1:19b-20=Mt. 5:22a	27
*	Jas. 1:6=Mt. 21:21; Mk. 11:23	27
*	Jas. 1:2=Mt. 5:11-12a; Lk. 6:22-23a	27
**	Jas. 5:1=Lk. 6:24,25b	25
**	Jas. 4:2-3=Mt. 7:7; Lk. 11:9	24
*	Jas. 5:10-11a=Mt. 5:11,12b; Lk. 6:22,23b	24

**	Jas. 4:10 = Mt. 23:12; Lk. 14:11; 18:14b	22
**	Jas. 4:9 = Lk. 6:21,25b	20
	Jas. 1:4 = Mt. 5:48	20
	Jas. 4:4a = Mt. 12:39a; 16:4a; Mk. 8:38	18
	Jas. 1:17 = Mt. 7:11; Lk. 11:13	18
	Jas. 4:13-14 = Mt. 6:34; Lk. 12:16-21	18
	Jas. 5:9b = Mt. 24:33b; Mk. 13:29b	18
	Jas. 5:17 = Lk. 4:25	15

2.0 It is frequently remarked that the Epistle of James contains more reminiscences to the *logia* of Jesus than any NT book outside the gospels. As witnessed by the length of this appendix, the parallels between James and the Synoptic gospels are extensive. Over 180 possible parallels have been compiled by 60 authors in the last two centuries. The agreement of results, however, is substantially less extensive.

One-tenth of the authors (6 or more) agree on 40 parallels.
One-fourth of the authors (15 or more) agree on 25 parallels.
One-third of the authors (20 or more) agree on 20 parallels.
One-half of the authors (30 or more) agree on 9 parallels.
Two-thirds of the authors (40 or more) agree on 6 parallels.
Three-fourths (45 or more) agree on three parallels.
Nine-tenths (54 or more) agree on only one parallel.

Furthermore, there are several texts in the Epistle of James whose likeness to the Synoptic tradition is so vague that they are compared to numerous passages in the gospels. Jas. 1:21; 2:15; 3:1; and 4:8, for instance, are said to parallel five different texts in the gospels; 2:13 and 5:9, seven; and 1:26-27 is compared with nine different gospel references. If we omit the extended discourses of 2:1-3:12, only nine verses in James (out of 70 total verses) are unparalleled in the Synoptic gospels. This extensive divergence of opinion raises doubts over the usefulness of the great majority of these parallels. In order to understand the nature of these parallels, this dissertation has been written. We have included in the main body of this book the gospel parallels listed by at least one-third of the various authors (i.e. those mentioned at least 20 times). In this appendix we will undertake a short more superficial study of those parallels that are referred to by one-tenth of the authors (at least six occurrences) paying the most attention to the more important parallels listed at least ten times (by one-sixth of the authors).

3.0 Eight texts in the Epistle of James are listed between 10 and 19 times as parallels with the sayings of Jesus: Jas. 1:17 = Mt. 7:17; Lk. 11:13; 4:4a = Mt. 12:39a; 16:4a; Mk. 8:38; 4:12 = Mt. 10:28; 4:13-14 = Mt. 6:34; Lk. 12:16-21; 4:17 = Lk. 12:47; 5:6 = Mt. 12:7,37; Lk. 6:37b; 5:9b = Mt. 24:33b; Mk. 13:29b; 5:17 = Lk. 4:25.

3.1 Jas. 1:17	Mt. 7:11	Lk. 11:13
13b ὁ γὰρ θεὸς	εἰ οὖν ὑμεῖς	εἰ οὖν ὑμεῖς
ἀπείραστός ἐστιν κακῶν	πονηροὶ ὄντες	πονηροὶ ὑπάρχοντες
17 πᾶσα δόσις ἀγαθὴ	οἴδατε δόματα ἀγαθὰ	οἴδατε δόματα ἀγαθὰ
καὶ πᾶν δώρημα τέλειον	διδόναι τοῖς τέκνοις	διδόναι τοῖς τέκνοις
ἄνωθέν ἐστιν καταβαῖνον	ὑμῶν, πόσῳ μᾶλλον	ὑμῶν, πόσῳ μᾶλλον
ἀπὸ τοῦ πατρὸς	ὁ πατὴρ ὑμῶν	ὁ πατὴρ
τῶν φώτων, παρ' ᾧ	ὁ ἐν τοῖς οὐρανοῖς	ὁ ἐξ οὐρανοῦ
οὐκ ἔνι παραλλαγὴ	δώσει ἀγαθὰ τοῖς	δώσει πνεῦμα ἅγιον
ἢ τροπῆς ἀποσκίασμα.	αἰτοῦσιν αὐτόν.	τοῖς αἰτοῦσιν αὐτόν.

Throughout this paragraph we will offer exegetical data that argues for an allusion to the gospel references and then in each case explain why this evidence is invalid. First of all, both the gospels and James present the teaching that God the Father gives good gifts. The purpose of the author, however, is different in each case: the gospels place the accent upon God's willingness to give to those who ask, while James defends his claim that God cannot be blamed for causing the trials which the righteous are encountering. Therefore James does not include a comparison with earthly fathers but offers only a statement about the character of God. This basic difference of emphasis proves that no connection with the gospels can be established. Instead, James is addressing a specific situation of bitterness in the midst of trials which has arisen in the experience of his audience. Secondly, in each case the words πατήρ and ἀγαθά coincide. The remaining vocabulary, however, is divergent: 1) the word for gift is different in each case; 2) the use of the adjective τέλειος is characteristic of James;[19] 3) in the gospels God is described as a Father in (the) heaven(s), while in James the designation "Father of lights" is employed. Ropes contends that James' phrase stems from a Jewish background since the benediction employed before the familiar *Shema* states, "Blessed be the Lord our God who hath formed the lights."[20] Dibelius, on the other hand, envisions Hellenistic influence.[21] Whatever the case, this terminology was apparently not employed by Jesus. Therefore, even though common content and some coinciding vocabulary are present, it is unnecessary to assume a source in the sayings of Jesus. Thirdly, the allusion to Mt. 7:7 par. at Jas. 1:5 increases the possibility that James would refer to another verse from Mt. 7 within the same context. One possible verbal tie is the word ἄνωθεν, since the theme of wisdom mentioned in 1:5 is described as "from above" (ἄνωθων) at 3:17 just as every good gift comes from above in 1:17.[22] Yet this connection is somewhat far-fetched. Jas. 1:17 is more likely influenced by the immediate context than by the more remote reference to Mt. 7:7-11 par. at Jas. 1:5. At v. 13 James has proclaimed that God is not tempted with evil. Now to continue his defense of God's character, he states the opposite, positive truth that only good proceeds from God. Thus 1:13 belongs with 1:16-18 as well as the middle section (1:14-15) which explains where temptations originate. Since James' context has changed from asking in prayer (1:5-8), to riches (1:9-11), and finally to a description of the wrong response to temptation (1:12-18), the assumption of an identical context is questionable. There is, therefore, no allusion to the gospels but only the employment of similar themes and vocabulary: the Father gives good gifts. Because of the hexameter meter Ropes believes an unknown source is being quoted.[23] The same phrase μὴ πλανᾶσθε (Jas. 1:16) introduces a quote of Menander at 1 Cor. 15:33. On the other hand, since James employs rhyme, alliteration, and excellent literary Greek[24] throughout his epistle, he could have composed this poetical section himself rather than have borrowed source material.

---

[19]Five out of 19 times in the NT: Jas. 1:4 (2x),17,25; 3:2.

[20]Ropes, James, 160. Cf. also Ps. 136:7.

[21]Dibelius and Greeven, James, 100. In n. 160 Dibelius cites the Assumption of Moses 36,38 where the phrase "Father of lights" is employed (but see Laws, James, 73). On the other hand, Davids, James, 87 contends that Hellenistic thought did not use φῶς to designate heavenly bodies. Therefore, it cannot be proven whether the author's Jewish thinking or Hellenistic vocabulary shapes this passage.

[22]Cf. Davids, James, 88.

[23]Cf. Ropes, James, 159 for the division of syllables. He supports his argument by referring to the unusual and poetical word δώρημα and the imperfect antithesis to vv. 13-15. Spitta, Zur Geschichte, II: 41,162 suggests the Sibylline Oracles 3:278 but also illustrates from other apocryphal literature. Adamson, James: Man and Message, 118 refers to the Odyssey 6:153.

[24]Ch. above, p. 203.

3.2 Jas. 4:4a	Mt. 12:39a; 16:4a	Mk. 8:38
		ὅς γὰρ ἐὰν ἐπαισχυνθῇ με
	γενεὰ πονηρὰ	... ἐν τῇ γενεᾷ ταύτῃ
μοιχαλίδες,	καὶ μοιχαλὶς	τῇ μοιχαλίδι
οὐκ οἴδατε ὅτι		καὶ ἁμαρτωλῷ,
ἡ φιλία τοῦ κόσμου	σημεῖον ἐπιζητεῖ	καὶ ὁ υἱὸς τοῦ ἀνθρώπου
ἔχθρα τοῦ θεοῦ ἐστιν;		ἐπαισχυνθήσεται αὐτόν

In chapter 4:1-10 James omits his usual greeting "my (beloved) brethren" and addresses his audience as "unfaithful creatures" (4:4), "you sinners", and "you men of double mind" (4:8). This section's purpose, therefore, is the disciplining of the audience. James points out that his readers' prayer life is polluted by a pursuit of pleasure (4:3) which expresses itself in friendship with the world (4:4b). Thus they are designated as "adulteresses". The use of this feminine pejorative address is strange if one assumes that actual adultery is taking place.[25] But since this phrase has an extensive history as figurative language,[26] the commentators have almost universally chosen for a symbolic meaning.[27] Although Hosea (ch. 1-3) was the first prophet of Israel to apply a metaphorical understanding of adultery to the covenantal relationship between God and his people, a closer parallel to James is encountered in Ezekiel. Ezk. 16:1-34 records an allegorical interpretation of history describing Israel's idolatry, while 16:35 employs the parallel term "harlot" (πόρνη) in a vocative address similar to Jas. 4:4, "Wherefore, O harlot, hear the word of the Lord."

The parallel expression "evil and adulterous generation" is found in the gospels at Mk. 8:38, Mt. 12:39a, and 16:4a. Since these are the only places in the NT where μοιχαλίς is used in a figurative sense (adjective in the gospels, substantive in James), the gospels are possibly the source from which James gleaned the expression "adulteresses". Because neither Matthew nor Luke follow Mark's use of this harsh phraseology in the parallel passages, it is difficult to determine if this term traces back originally to Jesus. In all likelihood Matthew and Luke decided that such language was not appropriate to a context teaching the meaning of discipleship.[28] This hypothesis is supported by the parallel saying in Q (Lk. 12:8-9; Mt. 10:32-33) which also fails to include this specific application to an "adulterous and sinful generation" in a context about discipleship. Matthew appears to transfer this phrase to conflict situations where it understandably makes more sense (12:39a; 16:4a). Whereas the Q saying about the sign of Jonah in Lk. 11:29 begins with the words "this is a wicked generation" (ἡ γενεὰ αὔτη γενεὰ πονηρά ἐστιν), Mt. 12:39 inter-

---

[25]Therefore ℵ[2], P, Ψ, M, sy[h] add μοιχοὶ καὶ. They probably understood the verse literally and were thus trying to include both sexes. However, the substantive μοιχαλίδες already implies both sexes as BAGD 526.2b points out. The RSV translation "unfaithful creatures" thus avoids the difficulties created by more literal translations.

[26]This phrase is used figuratively in Is. 1:21; 50:1; 54:1-6; 57:3; Jer. 3:9; 13:27; Ezk. 16:38; 23:45. Spitta denies the influence of these OT images since individual persons are James' mind, but Dibelius and Greeven, James, 220 counter this argument. Laws, James, 174 points to Ps. 73:27 and possibly 1 Cor. 6:15.

[27]Hort, James, 91 is the exception even though he enumerates the reasons supporting a figurative reading: 1) adulterers are omitted; 2) friendship with the world seems too slight and inappropriate a charge to bring against adultery; 3) adultery was not likely to be found in early Christian societies.

[28]Matthew omits the whole verse and substitutes a saying about reward according to works (16:27). Lk. 9:26 erases only this phrase to generalize its application beyond this evil and adulterous generation.

poses the term "adulterous" (γενεὰ πονηρὰ καὶ μοιχαλὶς).[29] There is a doublet to this expression in Mt. 16:4 where Matthew inserts this term into similar Markan material (8:11-12) about asking for signs. Thus on two occasions Matthew introduces this phrase into contexts concerned with the giving of signs, probably indicating that Matthean vocabulary is being employed. Therefore, even though we possess only one certain witness that Jesus spoke of an adulterous generation (Mk. 8:38), we are left with the impression that "this wicked and adulterous generation" is a set formula since in all three occurrences in the gospels the identical term "generation" appears. Therefore the omission of this formula in James probably indicates that he was not alluding to a saying of Jesus. Instead, James' particular address is understandable within the subject matter of the verse. They are adulteresses since friendship with the world adulterizes any relationship with God (Jas. 4:4b). The choice of the vocative, "you men of double-mind," at 4:8 likewise illustrates the pollution of a standard of conduct. Thus both addresses can be accounted for within the concepts used by James. He was, of course, influenced by the frequent employment of the term "adulteresses" in the OT, the teaching of Jesus, and the early church as witnessed by Matthew's addition of the term μοιχαλίς to his sources. Yet this similar wording in no way establishes a dependence upon the gospel parallels.

3.3 Jas. 4:12	Mt. 10:28
εἷς ἐστιν ὁ νομοθέτης καὶ κριτὴς	καὶ μὴ φοβεῖσθε ἀπὸ τῶν ἀποκτεννόντων τὸ σῶμα, τὴν δὲ ψυχὴν μὴ δυναμένων ἀποκτεῖναι· φοβεῖσθε δὲ μᾶλλον
ὁ <u>δυνάμενος</u> σῶσαι καὶ <u>ἀπολέσαι</u>· σὺ δὲ τίς εἶ ὁ κρίνων τὸν πλησίον;	τὸν <u>δυνάμενον</u> καὶ ψυχὴν καὶ σῶμα <u>ἀπολέσαι</u> ἐν γεέννῃ.

Both Jas. 4:12 and Mt. 10:28 are eschatological sayings with a practical ethical application. Jas. 4:12 speaks about a judge who has the power to save or destroy at the final judgment in order to outlaw judging and speaking evil against a fellow believer. Likewise in Mt. 10:28 an eschatological judgment scene describing the destruction of soul and body in Gehenna is envisioned to indicate that fear of bodily harm by earthly enemies is unnecessary. Therefore, the form of the saying as well as some vocabulary (δυνάμενος ἀπολέσαι) is similar. However, the content is too divergent to assume a deliberate allusion to this gospel tradition. James exhorts the Christian fellowship to put themselves under the law and not speak evil against each other if they wish not to be destroyed. The exhortation in Matthew, on the other hand, is directed at the outside oppressor and fear, not judging, is spoken against. Moreover with regard to vocabulary, the additional positive element of salvation is included in James while the descriptions "soul and body" and "in Gehenna" are omitted. The insignificance of this parallel is reinforced by the fact that in the last fifty years Jas. 4:12=Mt. 10:28 has not appeared in the list of any commentator. The primary source for James' saying is probably the OT description of God as the one who "kills and makes alive" (Dt. 32:39; 1 Sam. 2:6; 2 Kings 5:7), although the LXX does not employ the exact wording as James.[30]

---

[29]Matthew switches the order of the "sign of Jonah" saying and the "evil spirit" *logion* so that the evil spirit returns to this wicked and adulterous generation. He adds this phrase without the word "adulterous" as a conclusion at 12:45b.

[30]Dt. 32:39 ἀποκτενῶ καὶ ζῆν ποιήσω; 1 Sam. 2:6 θανατοῖ καὶ ζωογονεῖ; 2 Kings 5:7 τοῦ θανατῶσαι καὶ ζωοποιῆσαι.

3.4 Jas. 4:13-14: "Come now, you who say, 'Today or tomorrow we will go into such and such a town and spend a year there and trade and get gain,'whereas you do not know about tomorrow (αὔριον). What is your life? For you are a mist that appears for a little time and then vanishes."

Mt. 6:34: "Therefore do not be anxious about tomorrow (εἰς τὴν αὔριον) for tomorrow will be anxious for itself. Let the day's own trouble be sufficient for the day."

Lk. 12:16-21 The parable of building bigger barns -- the rich fool. Verse 19 says "Soul, you have ample goods laid up for many years" (εἰς ἔτη πολλά).

In this case it is unnecessary to transcribe these texts into Greek to indicate verbal similarities; the terminology of James and Luke is completely incongruous, while the only similarity between James and Matthew is the word "tomorrow". Shepherd contends, however, that Matthew underscores the same emphasis "of being without anxiety for the morrow."[31] Although all three passages involve the future, the differences with the gospels dwarf any similarities. Whereas Mt. 6:34 is against future plans altogether, James exhorts his audience to plan their future within the will of the Lord. The unique wording of Jas. 4:13, "Come now you," stands in parallelism with 5:1, "Come now you rich." Although both Jas. 4:13-17 and Lk. 12:16-21 contain a similar warning against building a future for yourself and leaving God out, the future involves an active life of trading and business in Jas. 4:13-14 whereas a retirement of ease and pleasure is described in Lk. 12:19. Furthermore, the imagery of the narrative is completely divergent: a farmer vs. a merchant; barns vs. a journey of buying and selling; life as a mist vs. life as a fool. Such exhortations about the future are common in Jewish wisdom; Prov. 27:1 warns "Do not boast about tomorrow, for you do not know what a day may bring forth." Therefore a popular Jewish wisdom tradition underlies James' text rather than a specific saying of Jesus.

3.5 Jas. 4:17	Lk. 12:47
	ἐκεῖνος δὲ ὁ δοῦλος
εἰδότι οὖν καλὸν ποιεῖν	ὁ γνοὺς τὸ θέλημα τοῦ κυρίου αὐτοῦ
καὶ μὴ	καὶ μὴ ἑτοιμάσας
ποιοῦντι,	ἢ ποιήσας πρὸς τὸ θέλημα αὐτοῦ
ἁμαρτία αὐτῷ ἐστιν.	δαρήσεται πολλάς·

Jas. 4:17 and Lk. 12:47 both emphasize that the distinguishing mark of sin is knowing what is right and not doing it. In describing sin both seem to imply levels or degrees of wrongdoing, although only Luke specifically distinguishes between a severe beating for premeditated misconduct and a light beating for unconscious sin. Furthermore, both Jas. 4:17 and Lk. 12:47 appear in stories about journeys; in James a merchant will embark on a trading expedition and in Luke the master of a household has departed on a trip. Yet these similarities in content are too superficial to establish any close connection between the texts. The eschatological nature of Jesus' parable is missing in James' story. We do encounter some similar terminology, but the theme of "not doing" is characteristic of James. Having already discussed hearing without doing (1:22-25) and faith without doing (2:14-26), James now condemns knowing without doing. Moreover, teaching on degrees of sin is a common feature in the NT church (1 Jn. 5:16-17; Heb. 6:4-6; 10:26). This verse can be best categorized as a traditional wisdom saying[32] which serves a transitional purpose in

---

[31]Shepherd, "James and Matthew," 46.

[32]The fact that εἰδότι does not have a grammatical reference point in the context could be evidence of preexistent material which does not fit well in its new context.

the framework of James' epistle similar to 2:13, 3:11-12, and 3:18. Even an exegete like Mitton who continually discerns allusionary material to the gospels admits that here we encounter only "a superficial resemblance to the saying of Jesus in Lk. 12:47."[33]

3.6 Jas. 5:6	Lk. 6:37b	Mt. 12:7	Mt. 12:37
		εἰ δὲ ἐγνώκειτε	ἐκ γὰρ τῶν λόγων
		τί ἐστιν·	σου δικαιωθήσῃ,
		ἔλεος θέλω καὶ	καὶ ἐκ τῶν λόγων
	καὶ μὴ	οὐ θυσίαν, οὐκ	
κατεδικάσατε,	καταδικάζετε,	ἂν κατεδικάσατε	σου καταδικασθήσῃ.
ἐφονεύσατε			
τὸν δίκαιον,		τοὺς ἀναιτίους.	
οὐκ ἀντιτάσσεται	καὶ οὐ μὴ		
ὑμῖν.	καταδικασθῆτε.		

All of the above texts embrace the common subject matter of condemning. This accounts for the one term that is similar in each column. Furthermore, all these references emphasize the reciprocal interaction between a person's actions and what is received in return. Since the rich of Jas. 5 have condemned and oppressed the righteous, disastrous miseries are coming upon them (5:1-3). The Pharisees in Mt. 12:7 have condemned the disciples because of Sabbath transgression, and in return Jesus condemns the Pharisees for their lack of mercy. Likewise in Mt. 12:37 Jesus teaches that the cause of condemnation (or justification) is the manner with which people handle their words. It could be argued that all of these examples are specific applications of the more general principle of Lk. 6:37b, "condemn not and you will not be condemned." All are different movements upon the same theme of judgment according to works. However, this Jewish principle is applied to completely different situations with James addressing the rich man's behavior while Jesus speaks out about sabbath observance and the use of the tongue. Therefore, it is doubtful whether James was consciously thinking of a specific saying of Jesus or reflectively grasping the connection between all of the above verses. He appears to be merely describing the means of oppression which the rich normally employ against the righteous.[34] Spitta claims that Wis. 2:20 is the specific source for Jas. 5:6.[35] Wis. 2:12 specifically refers to the righteous like Jas. 5:6 ("But let us lie in wait for the righteous man"[36]), and Wis. 2:20 describes the plan of attack executed by the oppressing rich against the rightous poor ("Let us condemn him to a shameful death"). However, it is more likely that only traditional language similar to Wis. 2:18-20; Prov. 1:11,18; and Mt. 12:7b is being utilized given the fact that traditional language is also employed at Jas. 5:4-5.[37]

---

[33]Mitton, James, 173.

[34]It is possible that a worker in James' community actually suffered martyrdom since murder is exposed as a actual temptation at 4:2 and 2:11. However, at Jas. 5:6 the "just one" (τὸν δίκαιον) is in the singular while the possible referents in the context are in the plural: workmen (τῶν ἐργατῶν 5:4) or harvesters (τῶν θερισάντων 5:4). For other options see ch. 6, n. 150.

[35]Spitta, Zur Geschichte, II: 135. Wis. 2:20a θανάτῳ ἀσχήμονι καταδικάσωμεν αὐτόν.

[36]Charles, APOT, I: 538.

[37]Cf. ch. 2, sections 3.3 and 3.4.

3.7 Jas. 5:9b	Mk. 13:29b	Mt. 24:33b
	γονώσκετε	γινώσκετε
ἰδοὺ ὁ κριτὴς	ὅτι ἐγγύς ἐστιν	ὅτι ἐγγύς ἐστιν
πρὸ τῶν θυρῶν ἕστηκεν.	ἐπὶ θύραις.	ἐπὶ θύραις.

The obvious tie between these texts is the common use of the term "gates" within an eschatological context.[38] In Mark and Matthew this saying is found in the eschatological discourse; Jesus is exhorting his disciples to read the signs of the times which reveal that the coming of the Son of Man is near.[39] James uses the eschatological facts that "the coming of the Lord is at hand" (5:8) and "the Judge is standing at the doors" (5:9) to ground his exhortations in favor of patience (5:7) and establishing the heart (5:8) and against grumbling (5:9). Therefore the French commentator Chaine has put this parallel in his short list entitled "Rapprochements qui établissent une dépendance certaine de Jacques à l'égard de l'enseignement de Jésus."[40] This seems to us an overestimate on Chaine's part; it is more likely that the phraseology of both James and Jesus is dependent upon the common background of Jewish eschatological language. This is confirmed by both the parable of the ten virgins (Mt. 25:10) and the parable of the householder (Lk. 13:24-25) where the imagery of the eschatological door reappears as a shut door. If direct dependence on a word of Jesus were to be discerned, there would have to be more similarity between the ethical exhortations (grumbling vs. discerning the times) and the specific nature imagery employed (early and late rains vs. a fig tree budding leaves). One can only establish a common eschatological outlook on the part of James and Jesus, not an intentional allusion.

3.8 Jas. 5:17	Lk. 4:25
	πολλαὶ χῆραι ἦσαν
Ἠλίας ἄνθρωπος ἦν ὁμοιοπαθὴς	ἐν ταῖς ἡμέραις Ἠλίου
ἡμῖν, καὶ προσευχῇ προσηύξατο	ἐν τῷ Ἰσραήλ,
τοῦ μὴ βρέξαι,	ὅτε ἐκλείσθη ὁ οὐρανὸς
καὶ οὐκ ἔβρεξεν ἐπὶ τῆς γῆς	
ἐνιαυτοὺς τρεῖς καὶ μῆνας ἕξ·	ἐπὶ ἔτη τρία καὶ μῆνας ἕξ,
	ὡς ἐγένετο λιμὸς μέγας
	ἐπὶ πᾶσαν τὴν γῆν

In contrast to the OT account (1 Kings 18:1) where the famine prophesied by Elijah persisted for three years, both Lk. 4:25 and Jas. 5:17 describe the famine as enduring for three years and six months. Could James be literally following Jesus' example in this time designation? Aland[41] contends that this parallel raises the possibility that James drew his material from Luke's gospel. However, other explanations account equally well for the divergent time designations. Some interpreters follow the calculation theory whereby the usual six month dry period of Palestine is added to the time reference of 1 Kings 18:1 upon

---

[38]It is not the place of temporal judgment, i.e. the city gate, which is spoken of as Cantinat, Jacques, 237 maintains, but rather the eschatological door leading to the future age.

[39]Whereas in Matthew and Mark the Son of Man is at the gates, at Lk. 21:31 the kingdom is near. In Rev. 3:20 the exalted Lord stands ἐπὶ τὴν θύραν, but this is the door to salvation probably based on the imagery of Mt. 7:7 par. and not the eschatological door.

[40]Chaine, Jacques, LVIII.

[41]Aland, "Herrenbruder Jakobus," 104.

the supposition that Elijah's prophecy was spoken at the beginning of the rainy season.[42] On the other hand, in the Jewish apocalyptic tradition three and one-half years had become a typical symbolic period in Jewish thought.[43] The two witnesses of Rev. 11:6 have the identical power of Elijah to shut the sky that no rain will fall during the three and a half years of their prophecying. This eschatological time period could very easily have been applied to the events of Elijah outside the apocalyptic tradition to suggest a time of disaster or calamity.[44] Since Luke emphasizes Elijah's going to the Gentiles while James demonstrates Elijah's righteousness through answered prayer, any close connection between Lk. 4:25 and Jas. 5:17 must be minimized. The differences in content and context argue in favor of a common Jewish oral tradition. Even an exegete like Mitton who repeatedly finds allusions to sayings of Jesus admits that traditional language is here the connecting link.[45]

4.0 There are twelve more parallels which are listed at least one-tenth of the time (6-9 occurrences) in the history of interpretation: Jas. 1:12=Mt. 5:11-12a; Lk. 6:22-23a; 1:12=Mt. 10:22; 1:21=Mt. 13:19-23; Lk. 8:11-15; 2:8=Mt. 7:12; Lk. 6:31; 2:10=Mt. 5:19; 2:14=Mt. 7:21; Lk. 6:46; 2:15=Mt. 25:36,41; 4:8=Mt. 5:8; 4:10=Mt. 5:3-5; 5:7-8=Mt. 24:3,27,37,39; 5:9a=Mt. 7:1; 5:14=Mk. 6:13. For these we will merely indicate how each pair has been tied together.

4.1 Both Jas. 1:12 and Mt. 5:11-12a; Lk. 6:22-23a promise a reward to those who endure trials. Furthermore, each is expressed in the form of a blessing -- a μακάριος statement followed by a ὅτι clause. However, both the trials and the rewards are expressed differently. Whereas James speaks generally about trials, the gospels refer specifically to the disciples being reviled, spoken evilly about (Mt. and Lk.), persecuted (Mt.), excluded, and hated (Lk.). In James a crown of life is promised while in the gospels the kingdom of heaven is the reward. James could have been thinking about a cluster of Jesus' blessings upon the "underdog", but the wording is just too general to establish any positive parallel with the suggested texts above. The reference to a crown of life could point to an unknown saying of Jesus since Jas. 1:12, Rev. 2:10b, and 2 Tim. 4:8 all employ similar terminology.[46] However, we believe that Jas. 1:12 as well as Jas. 5:10-11a[47] expresses a popular motif in the church's paraenesis which in turn was probably based on themes from Jesus' preaching. Whatever the case, it must be admitted that these parallels are too superficial to establish a deliberate allusion. This is surely the reason why this parallel is only found in a few (French) 20th century authors. In the 19th century Jas. 1:12 was paralleled more closely with Mt. 10:22.

4.2 The theme of endurance in times of trial is present in both Jas. 1:12 and Mt. 10:22. Whereas James describes the trials in a general manner, Matthew specifies the problem as the hatred of fellow Jews toward their close relatives who have been converted to Christianity. In both a reward for endurance is specified; yet Matthew is very general ("he will be saved") while James specifically promises a crown of life. The similar verb ὑπομένω should not be overemphasized since endurance was a common paraenetic theme.[48] Jas. 1:12 and 5:10-11a (cf. also Herm., Vis. 2,2,7) are evidence of this paraenetic

---

[42]Cf. Laws, James, 236-237 and the midrashic passages referred to.

[43]Dan. 7:25; 12:7; Rev. 11:2; 12:6,14.

[44]Jeremias, s.v. Ἠλ(ε)ίας, TDNT, II: 934 contends that "its use in the Elijah tradition has no connection with its use as an apocalyptic number from Daniel onwards," but Rev. 11:6 is proof against this hypothesis.

[45]Mitton, James, 208.

[46]Cf. ch. 7, n. 6.

[47]Cf. ch. 3, section 6.1.

[48]Cf. above, pp. 63-64.

tradition which probably originated in the themes of Jesus' preaching as indicated in the similar subject matter in Mt. 10:22 and Mt. 5:11-12 par. No direct allusion to a specific saying of Jesus is necessary.

4.3 Jas. 1:21 and Mt. 13:19-23; Lk. 8:11-15 both speak about the word which is first planted and then bears results. Comparing Jas. 1:21 with the interpretation of Jesus' parable of the sower, Davids explains:

> The interesting fact is that only in Luke 8:12 is the word (λόγος) said or implied to have been able to save. Furthermore, the parable of the sower may also be indicated in the idea of receiving the word (Luke 8:13) and by the strange use of ἔμφυτος which is likely influenced by the use of φύω in the parable.[49]

Davids' thesis, however, is not supportable. First of all the genre is different. James employs an ethical exhortation, "receive with meekness the implanted word, which is able to save your soul," while Jesus speaks a parable where the planted seed yielding fruit represents "he who hears the word and understands it" (Mt. 13:23). Secondly, the use of ἔμφυτος is not strange but is paralleled in Barn. 9:9, "He has placed within us the implanted gift of his teaching"[50] (τὴν ἔμφυτον δωρεὰν τῆς διδαχῆς αὐτοῦ). Finally, this word can better refer to the church's preaching and teaching than the planting (φύω) of the seed in Lk. 8. Since the church's kerygma is alluded to in the use of λόγος at Jas. 1:18 ("the word of truth"), it would be consistent to also describe the kerygma at Jas. 1:21.[51] Carrington's work on the early church's catechism[52] has established that such exhortations as "put off" and "put on" found in Jas. 1:21 were standard teaching patterns of the early church. It is the preached word that saves; no reference to Lk. 8:12 is necessary.

4.4 Both Jas. 2:8 and Mt. 7:12; Lk. 6:31 speak about treating another person in the same manner that you treat yourself. Although similar subject matter is evident, each saying has its own separate history. As the introductory formula indicates, Jas. 2:8 originated in the OT and is passed on by Jesus (Mt. 22:39 par.) unconnected with the golden rule. Whereas Jas. 2:8 mentions the neighbor as the object of love, Luke places the golden rule within a context of love for the enemy. Therefore the OT passage Lev. 19:18b is in James' mind and not any NT references. If James' teaching is colored by the preaching of Jesus, surely Mt. 22:36-40 par. is the primary reference and not the golden rule of Mt. 7:12; Lk. 6:31.

4.5 Both Jas. 2:10 and Mt. 5:19 contain a similar increasing of the demands of the law. This restriction, however, is expressed uniquely in each case. Whereas Matthew warns against relaxing even the least of the commandments, James proclaims that breaking the law at one point makes one "guilty of all of it". Although James and Matthew witness to a similar attitude toward the law,[53] no direct dependence can be established. The necessity of keeping every commandment was a generally accepted teaching at this time as witnessed by Paul in Gal. 5:3, "every man who receives circumcision is bound to keep the whole law".[54] The insufficient scholarly backing for this parallel is indicated by the fact that only

---

[49]Davids, "James and Jesus," 71.

[50]We have attempted a more literal translation since Lightfoot's version is inaccurate: "He who placed within us the innate gift of His covenant knoweth."

[51]Cf. above, pp. 84-85.

[52]Carrington, Primitive Christian Catechism, 43.

[53]Cf. ch. 4, section 3.4.

[54]Paul, however, uses this truth as evidence against the continuing function of the law rather than as a prod to keep the whole law as James does.

authors from the English-speaking world have included this reference in their list of parallels between the Epistle of James and the sayings of Jesus.

4.6 In both Jas. 2:14 and Mt. 7:21; Lk. 6:46 we encounter a contrast between unresponsive talk and appropriate action. Yet the verbal details and examples of application diverge in each case. In the gospels the hearer responds saying "Lord, Lord" while in James the hypothetical subject replies that he has faith. Whereas the examples in Mt. 7:22 display both inappropriate verbal responses (prophesying and casting out demons) and actions (doing mighty works), in the Epistle of James only words of comfort and encouragement are offered when actions to relieve hunger and nakedness are required. Inappropriate actions in Matthew are contrasted with the omission of good works in James; thus there is no dependence. Jesus' important preaching theme of talk without obedient action (Mt. 7:15-27 par.) has probably been taken over by the paraenetic tradition since James' exhortations both here and at 1:22-25 have been closely identified with motifs in Jesus' preaching.[55] However, James applies this teaching to the specific problem of justification by faith or works which the preaching of Jesus did not encounter. Jas. 2:14ff is thus a combination of the paraenetic tradition with a problem peculiar to James' experience. There is no conscious allusion to a specific saying of Jesus.

4.7 Both Jas. 2:15 and Mt. 25:36,41 employ the term γυμνός in describing situations of economic poverty where there is hunger (Mt. 25:35) and a lack of daily food (Jas. 2:15). It is common subject matter, therefore, which explains why the parable of the sheep and goats "affords so many parallels to this section in James".[56] To confirm an allusion to the Synoptic tradition, either more of the situations described by Jesus (thirst, a stranger, sickness, in prison) would have to be specified by James or Jesus' words, "as you did it not to one of the least of these, you did it not to me" would have to be hinted at. We agree with Davids that James is illustrating from "a typical situation of need portrayed in numerous OT passages."[57]

4.8 Jas. 4:8 and Mt. 5:8 link together being pure in heart and seeing God (Mt.) or drawing near to God (Jas.). However, whereas the interplay between the two concepts in Matthew is direct and straightforward, in James the two ideas are in separate sentences creating only a vague and arguable connection: "Draw near to God and <u>he will draw near to you</u>. Cleanse your hands, you sinners, and <u>purify your hearts</u>, you men of double mind." In Jas. 4:9,10 we do encounter allusions to the sayings of Jesus,[58] an indication that more of the section might be influenced by dominical words. Yet the ethical call to purity of heart is a common paraenetic theme, "a call that John, Hebrews, 1 Peter, and the Pastorals take up."[59] Clean hands and a pure heart are also OT virtues (Ps. 24:4). Therefore the employment of similar terminology in paraenetic sections is the connecting link.

4.9 Both Jas. 4:10 and Mt. 5:3-5 indicate that good things will happen to those who have such character qualities as poverty of spirit (Mt. 5:3-4), meekness (Mt. 5:5), and humility (Jas. 4:10). However, the divergent vocabulary and subject matter prove that the

---

[55]Cf. above, pp. 112-113.

[56]Mitton, <u>James</u>, 101.

[57]Davids, <u>James</u>, 121. He refers to Job 22:6; 24:7; 31:9; Is. 20:5; 58:7. Knowling, <u>James</u>, 54 misses the mark when he states, "Both our Lord's words, Matt. xxv. 36,43 and the solemn scene of the Last Judgment may well have been present to the mind of St. James, especially when we remember that his thoughts were dwelling upon mercy and judgment."

[58]Cf. ch. 3, sections 4.3 and 4.5.

[59]Davids, <u>James</u>, 167.

supposition of an allusion is unwarranted. A much closer parallel with the saying of Jesus in Mt. 23:12; Lk. 14:11; 18:14b[60] makes the proposal of a relationship with Mt. 5:3-5 unnecessary.

4.10 Mt. 24:3,27,37,39 and Jas. 5:7,8 all employ the term παρουσία to describe the eschatological event which will inaugerate the new age. This is the extent of the similarities involved. In Matthew the term "Son of Man" is chosen whereas in James the title "Lord" is utilized. Jesus is describing the signs of his coming in Matthew while James is interested in patience and firmness of heart. Furthermore, as Laws explains, "*parousia* becomes a technical term in Christian eschatology, found frequently elsewhere in the NT."[61] Therefore one would expect this word to appear when James exhorts his readers about the eschatological future; no allusion to a saying of Jesus is necessary.

4.11 In section 3.7 we have already connected Jas. 5:9b with Mt. 24:33b and Mk. 13:29b which picture the door to the eschatological future. To a lesser extent in the tradition (since Mayor in 1892) Jas. 5:9a has been positioned alongside Mt. 7:1. Both verses speak about the eschatological judgment: therefore the common phrase ἵνα μὴ κριθῆτε. On the other hand, each verse warns against a different vice: Matthew speaks against judging while James exhorts his readers not to grumble. These exhortations reveal the same moral principle that we discussed under Jas. 5:6=Lk. 6:37b etc. There we saw that this emphasis upon the reciprocal interaction between a person's actions and what is received in return is common to both James and Jesus as well as Jewish thought. Therefore James has internalized a common religious assumption found in both Judaism and Christianity: one will be held accountable for his vices at the final judgment. The fact that the judgment is an important ethical deterrent for James (2:12; 3:1; 4:12; 5:9,12) demonstrates that we are encountering Jamesian theology here.

4.12 Jas. 5:14 and Mk. 6:13 illustrate the healing technique of anointing with oil. Both the twelve disciples on their missionary journey and the elders of the assembly of James' day anointed people with oil while invoking the name of the Lord. Since the laying on of hands for healing[62] as well as the use of oil[63] was popular in the Jewish tradition, it is possible that we are encountering here a common environment of religious thought not limited to Christian contexts.[64] However, because we know of the impact of Jesus' healing ministry upon the early church (Acts 3:7; 5:15 etc), it is more probable that a continuation of the healing ministry of Jesus by the church is being illustrated. Jesus' frequent procedure of the laying on of hands (Mk. 1:41; 7:32) would then be implied in James' instruction to pray "over them". Therefore, Jesus' example is in the mind of James, but certainly no specific example of anointing with oil such as Mk. 6:13 needs to be specified.

5.0 A Categorization of Parallels

No allusions to the sayings of the Jesus-tradition have been discerned in the Jamesian passages investigated in this appendix. Most of the parallels are limited to the employment of common terminology. Two texts (Jas. 1:12=Mt. 5:11-12a; Lk. 6:22-23a; Jas.

---

[60]Cf. ch. 3, section 4.5.

[61]Laws, James, 15.

[62]Pss. 35:13; 41:4; Job 2:11; Tobit 1:19; Sir. 7:35; 31:9-15; Baba Bathra 116a; Berakoth 34b; Sanhedrin 101; 1QapGen. 20:21-22,29.

[63]Is. 1:6; Jer. 8:22; Jos., Ant. 17:172; Bell. 1:657; Apoc. Mos. 9:3; 2 En. 22:8-9; 8:35; Philo, Som. 2:58.

[64]For a list of examples of the medicinal quality of oil see Dibelius and Greeven, James, 252-253, n. 63 and Ropes, James, 306.

1:17=Mt. 7:11; Lk. 11:13) contain both similar content and vocabulary. There are several instances where the similarities are so minimal that even the category of parallel does not apply. These include 1) Jas. 2:8=Mt. 7:12; Lk. 6:31 where James specifically cites Lev. 19:18b; 2) Jas. 4:10=Mt. 5:3-5 where the saying of Jesus in Mt. 23:12; Lk. 14:11; 18:14b is alluded to; 3) Jas. 4:13=Mt. 6:34; Lk. 12:16-21 where the single word "tomorrow" ties these passages together; and 4) Jas. 5:7-8=Mt. 24:3,27,37,39 where the familiar term for the eschatological coming, παρουσία, is employed. Finally, there are a couple of texts where the themes of Jesus' preaching contributed to the inclusion of these topics in the church's paraenesis: 1) the call to endurance in trials in Jas. 1:12 (Mt. 5:11-12a par.; 10:12); and 2) the theme of faith and action in Jas. 2:14 (Mt. 7:21; Lk. 6:46). For a complete categorization of all the parallels see the charts in chapter 7.

6.0 In addition to setting forth the minor parallels in this appendix, we will attempt to analyze the complicated history of the listing of parallels between James and the Synoptic gospels. The presence of parallels with the Synoptic tradition has been noticed by scholars for a long time; already in 1886 Weizsäcker[65] noted that the connection was a long observed fact. Most exegetes handle the similarities by first listing the individual parallels and then examining a few of the most important occurrences.[66] When an author simply lists the various parallels, it is difficult in most cases to determine if the author personally decided on this set of parallels or has merely repeated an established tradition. A few scholars indicate indebtedness to others. Riedel notes that he is simply repeating Reuss' list. Davies takes over Kittel's list but specifies which parallels he considers most important, thus revealing some personal judgment on his part.[67] Toxopeus indicates both that he purposely narrowed down the list of Spitta and that he expressly differs with certain specifics of Holtzmann's list, thus maintaining a more critical attitude than some. On the opposite end of the spectrum, von Soden attempts not to shorten the list but to draw together "eine möglichst vollständige Uebersicht"[68] by combining the lists of Reuss, Holtzmann, Beyschlag, and Brückner. It is this combined list of von Soden that many scholars seem to employ in their decision about the legitimate parallels between the Epistle of James and the Synoptic gospels.[69] All the major parallels were already recognized in the 19th century. In our century commentators have given special attention to the list of Kittel, although particularly two of his parallels are of poor quality (Jas. 2:11=Mt. 5:21; Jas. 2:15=Mt. 6:25) and have not been followed except by those who uncritically transmit his list. Shepherd has offered a couple new creative parallels and has been followed by many recent English commentators as well as Mußner in the German tradition. For a detailed description of the major parallels examine chapter 3 of this dissertation. For a general overview of the history of interpretation see chapter 1.

As can be gleaned from the divergent lists, commentators have operated with different standards in determining what is a reminiscence to the Jesus-tradition. The four biggest exaggerators of possible parallels are Davids, Spitta, Mayor, and Schlatter who produce 52, 50, 65, and 57 respectively. Spitta has a certain purpose in mind; one by one he points out closer parallels in Jewish literature, thus completely negating the seeming authority of a lengthy list of parallels to the gospels. Davids subdivides his list into six different rubrics wherein 20 out of the 52 are described as close allusions, thus indicating that he is not naively assuming that James is consciously referring to dominical sayings on more than fifty occasions. Mayor and Schlatter, on the other hand, have lists of reminiscenses

---

[65]Weizsäcker, Apostolische Zeitalter, 378.

[66]Cf. above, p. 15.

[67]Davies seems to have accidentally skipped Kittel's parallel, Jas. 1:17=Mt. 7:11; Lk. 11:13.

[68]von Soden, "Jacobusbrief," 169.

[69]Cf. Feine, Jakobusbrief, 133.

that are ridiculously long. One similar word in some cases indicates a parallel. In contrast, other writers like McNeille, Lohse, Wikenhauser, Grant, and Ropes have very high standards and dismiss most similarities as merely indicating a common cultural or religious background. We hope that the various categories which we have enumerated[70] will facilitate the difficult process of distinguishing between true allusions to source material and mere incidental parallels of content or terminology. The mean number of entries in a list of parallels is about 18. We have recognized eight conscious allusions to Jesus' sayings and nine important themes of Jesus' preaching which have been mediated to James through the paraenetic tradition of the church.[71]

[70]Cf. ch. 7, section 1.1.
[71]Cf. above, pp. 219-220,222-223.

Appendix II

OTHER LITERARY PARALLELS WITH THE EPISTLE OF JAMES[1]

1.0 In categorizing the literary parallels between James and the Synoptic tradition, we have distinguished the following groupings:[2] 1) quotations or citations; 2) allusions without an introductory formula (also called reminiscences[3]); 3) parallels of content; 4) parallels of terminology; 5) parallels of both common content and similar terminology; 6) common references to other writings or oral traditions such as the OT, sayings of Jesus, a possible Christian catechism, or commonly recited wisdom sayings. In the following lists we have underlined the similar vocabulary and designated the divergent content in parenthesis after the textual parallels.

2.1 Parallels between James and 1 Peter

James	1 Peter
1:1 ταῖς δώδεκα φυλαῖς ταῖς ἐν τῇ διασπορᾷ (the whole Dispersion)	1:1 ἐκλεκτοῖς παρεπιδήμοις διασπορᾶς (the Dispersion in Asia Minor)
1:2 πᾶσαν χαρὰν ἡγήσασθε ... ὅταν πειρασμοῖς περιπέσητε ποικίλοις, 1:3 γινώσκοντες ὅτι τὸ δοκίμιον ὑμῶν τῆς πίστεως κατεργάζεται ὑπομονήν. (temporal result)	1:6 ἐν ᾧ ἀγαλλιᾶσθε, ὀλίγον ἄρτι εἰ δέον ἐστὶν λυπηθέντες ἐν ποικίλοις πειρασμοῖς, 1:7 ἵνα τὸ δοκίμιον ὑμῶν τῆς πίστεως ... εὑρεθῇ εἰς ἔπαινον καὶ δόξαν ... ἐν ἀποκαλύψει Ἰησοῦ Χριστοῦ· (eschatological result)
1:2 πᾶσαν χαρὰν ἡγήσασθε ... ὅταν πειρασμοῖς περιπέσητε ποικίλοις, 1:3 γινώσκοντες ὅτι τὸ δοκίμιον ὑμῶν τῆς πίστεως κατεργάζεται ὑπομονήν. (temporal result of patience)	4:13 ἀλλὰ καθὸ κοινωνεῖτε τοῖς τοῦ Χριστοῦ παθήμασιν χαίρετε, ἵνα καὶ ἐν τῇ ἀποκαλύψει τῆς δόξης αὐτοῦ χαρῆτε ἀγαλλιώμενοι. (eschatological result of glory)

[1]The parallels of this appendix have been derived from the lists of Dibelius, Mayor, Meyer, Moffatt, Mußner, Spitta, and Toxopeus.

[2]Cf. ch. 7, section 1.1.

[3]Sometimes a reminiscence suggests an unconscious repetition or imitation, but we will use it to refer to an intentional recalling of something said or done in the past.

James	1 Peter
1:10b-11 ὅτι ὡς ἄνθος χόρτου παρελεύσεται. 11 ἀνέτειλεν γὰρ ὁ ἥλιος ... καὶ ἐξήρανεν τὸν χόρτον καὶ τὸ ἄνθος αὐτοῦ ἐξέπεσεν καὶ ἡ εὐπρέπεια τοῦ προσώπου αὐτοῦ ἀπώλετο· οὕτως καὶ ὁ πλούσιος ... (about the rich)	1:24 διότι πᾶσα σὰρξ ὡς χόρτος καὶ πᾶσα δόξα αὐτῆς ὡς ἄνθος χόρτου· ἐξηράνθη ὁ χόρτος καὶ τὸ ἄνθος ἐξέπεσεν· 1:25 τὸ δὲ ῥῆμα κυρίου μένει εἰς τὸν αἰῶνα. (about the word of God)
1:12 μακάριος ἀνὴρ ὃς ὑπομένει πειρασμόν, ὅτι δόκιμος γενόμενος λήμψεται τὸν στέφανον τῆς ζωῆς (blessing upon enduring sufferers of a crown of life)	3:14 εἰ πάσχοιτε διὰ δικαιοσύνην, μακάριοι. — 4:14 εἰ ὀνειδίζεσθε ἐν ὀνόματι Χριστοῦ, μακάριοι (blessing upon righteous sufferers) 5:4 τὸν ἀμαράντινον τῆς δόξης στέφανον. (crown of glory)
1:18a βουληθεὶς ἀπεκύησεν ἡμᾶς λόγῳ ἀληθείας (brought forth by gospel)	1:22 τὰς ψυχὰς ὑμῶν ἡγνικότες ἐν τῇ ὑπακοῇ τῆς ἀληθείας ... 23 ἀναγεγεν- νημένοι ... διὰ λόγου ζῶντος θεοῦ (born anew by gospel)
1:21 διὸ ἀποθέμενοι πᾶσαν ῥυπαρίαν καὶ περισσείαν κακίας ἐν πραΰτητι, δέξασθε τὸν ἔμφυτον λόγον τὸν δυνάμενον σῶσαι τὰς ψυχὰς ὑμῶν. (putting away two evils)	2:1 ἀποθέμενοι οὖν πᾶσαν κακίαν καὶ πάντα δόλον καὶ ὑποκρίσεις καὶ φθόνους ... 1:25b τοῦτο δέ ἐστιν τὸ ῥῆμα τὸ εὐαγγελισθὲν 2:2 ... ἵνα ἐν αὐτῷ αὐξηθῆτε εἰς σωτηρίαν (putting away 5 different evils)
1:26 εἴ τις δοκεῖ θρησκὸς εἶναι ... τούτου μάταιος ἡ θρησκεία. 1:27 θρησκεία καθαρὰ καὶ ἀμίαντος παρὰ τῷ θεῷ καὶ πατρὶ αὕτη ἐστιν (vain religion vs. pure religion)	1:18 ... ἐλυτρώθητε ἐκ τῆς ματαίας ὑμῶν ἀναστροφῆς 2:5 ... πνευματικὰς θυσίας εὐπροσδέκτους τῷ θεῷ (vain lifestyle vs. spiritual sacrifices)
2:1 μὴ ἐν προσωπολημψίαις ἔχετε τὴν πίστιν τοῦ κυρίου ἡμῶν Ἰησοῦ Χριστοῦ τῆς δόξης. (show no impartiality)	1:17a τὸν ἀπροσωπολήμπτως κρίνοντα 1:21 τοὺς δι᾽ αὐτοῦ πιστοὺς εἰς θεὸν τὸν ἐγείραντα αὐτὸν ἐκ νεκρῶν καὶ δόξαν αὐτῷ δόντα (God judges impartiality)
2:7 οὐκ αὐτοὶ βλασφημοῦσιν τὸ καλὸν ὄνομα τὸ ἐπικληθὲν ἐφ᾽ ὑμᾶς; (blaspheme Christ or God)	4:4 βλασφημοῦντες 4:14 εἰ ὀνειδίζεσθε ἐν ὀνόματι Χριστοῦ, μακάριοι (blaspheme the people)
2:8 ἀγαπήσεις τὸν πλησίον σου ὡς σεαυτόν (Lev. 19:18b)	1 Pet.1:22 ἀλλήλους ἀγαπήσατε — 2:17 τὴν ἀδελφότητα ἀγαπᾶτε — 4:8 πρὸ πάντων τὴν εἰς ἑαυτοὺς ἀγάπην ἐκτενῆ ἔχοντες (church instruction)

James	1 Peter
Jas. 3:13b δειξάτω ἐκ τῆς καλῆς ἀναστροφῆς τὰ ἔργα αὐτοῦ ἐν πραΰτητι σοφίας (show works by good conduct)	1 Pet. 2:12a τὴν ἀναστροφὴν ὑμῶν ἐν τοῖς ἔθνεσιν ἔχοντες καλήν (good conduct among Gentiles)
4:1b οὐκ ἐντεῦθεν, ἐκ τῶν ἡδονῶν ὑμῶν τῶν στρατευομένων ἐν τοῖς μέλεσιν ὑμῶν; (passions at war within)	2:11b ἀπέχεσθαι τῶν σαρκικῶν ἐπιθυμιῶν αἵτινες στρατεύονται κατὰ τῆς ψυχῆς· (desires at war with soul)
4:6b διὸ λέγει· ὁ θεὸς ὑπερηφάνοις ἀντιτάσσεται, ταπεινοῖς δὲ δίδωσιν χάριν. (emphasis on humility)	5:5b ὅτι ὁ θεὸς ὑπερηφάνοις ἀντιτάσσεται, ταπεινοῖς δὲ δίδωσον χάριν. (emphasis on grace)
4:7 ὑποτάγητε οὖν τῷ θεῷ, ἀντίστητε δὲ τῷ διαβόλῳ καὶ φεύξεται ἀφ᾽ ὑμῶν (submit to God; devil will flee)	5:5a ὑποτάγητε πρεσβυτέροις· 5:9 ἀντίστητε στερεοὶ τῇ πίστει 5:8 ὁ ἀντίδικος ὑμῶν διάβολος περιπατεῖ ζητῶν τινα καταπιεῖν· (submit to elders; devil will devour)
4:8c ἁγνίσατε καρδίας, δίψυχοι. (clean hands and hearts)	1:22a τὰς ψυχὰς ὑμῶν ἡγνικότες (clean souls)
4:10 ταπεινώθητε ἐνώπιον κυρίου καὶ ὑψώσει ὑμᾶς. (before the Lord)	5:6 ταπεινώθητε οὖν ὑπὸ τὴν κραταιὰν χεῖρα τοῦ θεοῦ, ἵνα ὑμᾶς ὑψώσῃ ἐν καιρῷ (under the mighty hand of God)
5:3a ὁ χρυσὸς ὑμῶν καὶ ὁ ἄργυρος κατίωται (about material riches)	1:18a οὐ φθαρτοῖς, ἀργυρίῳ ἢ χρυσίῳ, ἐλυτρώθητε (about spiritual riches)
5:6 ἐφονεύσατε τὸν δίκαιον, οὐκ ἀντιτάσσεται ὑμῖν. (the oppressed one as the righteous dead)	3:18b δίκαιος ὑπὲρ ἀδίκων ... θανατωθεὶς μὲν σαρκὶ (Jesus as the righteous dead man)
5:8b ἡ παρουσία τοῦ κυρίου ἤγγικεν. (with an exhortation to be patient)	4:7 πάντων δὲ τὸ τέλος ἤγγικεν. (connected with an exhortation to pray)
5:9b ἰδοὺ ὁ κριτὴς πρὸ τῶν θυρῶν ἕστηκεν. (against grumbling)	4:5b τῷ ἑτοίμως ἔχοντι κρῖναι ζῶντας καὶ νεκρούς. (against wild profligacy)
5:10 ὑπόδειγμα ... τῆς κακοπαθίας καὶ τῆς μακροθυμίας (prophets as examples of patient suffering)	2:21 ὑπολιμπάνων ὑπογραμμὸν 2:19 πάσχων ἀδίκως. 2:20 πάσχοντες ὑπομενεῖτε (Jesus as the example of patient suffering)

Jas. 5:12a πρὸ πάντων δέ ... μὴ ὀμνύετε (against swearing)	1 Pet. 4:8a πρὸ πάντων ... ἀγάπην ἐκτενῆ ἔχοντες (in favor of loving)
5:16a ἐξομολογεῖσθε ... ἁμαρτίας καὶ εὔχεσθε ὑπὲρ ἀλλήλων ὅπως ἰαθῆτε. (healing by confession of sins and prayer)	2:24c οὗ τῷ μώλωπι ἰάθητε. (healing by Jesus' suffering)
5:19 ἐάν τις ... πλανηθῇ ... καὶ ἐπιστρέψῃ τις αὐτόν (return to the truth after backsliding)	2:25 ἦτε γὰρ ... πλανώνενοι, ἀλλὰ ἐπεστράφητε νῦν ἐπὶ τὸν ποιμένα (return to the Shepherd in conversion)
5:20 γινωσκέτω ὅτι ὁ ἐπιστρέψας ἁμαρτωλὸν ... καλύψει πλῆθος ἁμαρτιῶν. (reconverting a sinner covers a multitude of sins)	4:8b ὅτι ἀγάπη καλύπτει πλῆθος ἁμαρτιῶν. (love covers a multitude of sins)

2.2 The Categories

1) Quotations or Citations: none.

2) Allusions: none.

3) Parallels of both terminology and content: Jas. 1:1 = 1 Pet. 1:1; 1:2 = 1:6; 1:3 = 1:7; 1:21 = 1:25-2:2; 4:7 = 5:8-9; 4:10 = 5:6; 5:8b = 4:7.

4) Only similar content: Jas. 1:2 = 1 Pet. 4:13; 1:12 = 3:14; 4:14; 1:18a = 1:22-23; 1:27 = 2:5; 2:8 = 1:22; 2:17; 4:8; 5:9b = 4:5b; 5:10 = 2:19-21.

5) Only similar terminology: Jas. 1:12 = 1 Pet. 5:4; 1:26 = 1:18; 2:1 = 1:17,21; 2:7 = 4:4,14; 3:13b = 2:12a; 4:1b = 2:11b; 4:7 = 5:5a; 4:8c = 1:22a; 5:3a = 1:18a; 5:6 = 3:18b; 5:12a = 4:8a; 5:16a = 2:24c; 5:19 = 2:25.

6) Common references to other material:

a) OT: Jas. 1:10b-11 = 1 Pet. 1:24-25 (Is. 40:6); 4:6b = 5:5b (Prov. 3:34); 5:20 = 4:8b (Prov. 10:12).

b) Sayings of Jesus: Jas. 4:10 = 1 Pet. 5:6 (Mt. 23:12; Lk. 14:11; 18:14b); 1 Pet. 3:14 = Mt. 5:10 and 1 Pet. 4:13-14 = Mt. 5:11 but not in Jas. 1:12; possible extra-canonical saying: 1:12 = 5:4.[4]

c) Possible primitive catechism:
"rejoicing in trials" Jas. 1:2 = 1 Pet. 1:6; 1:3 = 1:7.
"putting off vices" 1:18 = 1:23; 1:21 = 2:1.
"subjection in humility but resisting subjection to the devil" 4:7 = 5:8-9; 4:10 = 5:6.

[4]Cf. above, ch. 7, n. 6.

2.3 Conclusions

Since James' style is in the form of terse proverbial sayings while Peter uses homiletical exhortations,[5] the probability that James or Peter directly employed the other's material is small.[6] The best explanation for the similarities is the thesis that both James and Peter drew from a primitive catechism developed either in the Jewish-Christian community or within the geographical region of Rome.[7] The parallels of terminology and content betray common teaching patterns on the subjects of rejoicing in trials, putting off certain vices, and being humbly subject to God and human authorities while resisting the subjection of the devil.[8] The same general ordering of material is also apparent.[9] It appears that both James and Peter drew from this primitive oral catechism or established church teaching in order to remind the Christians of the Diaspora what they had formerly memorized and should have put into action. The phrase γινώσκοντες ὅτι in Jas. 1:3, for example, implies that a known saying is being referred to.[10] Furthermore, the parallels with 1 Peter are most visible precisely where James employs typical paraenetic material containing traditional ethical exhortations and wisdom. None of these parallels occurs in Jas. 2:1-3:12 where James' peculiar style, vocabulary, and employment of extended discourse are most visible. Also in 1 Peter many of the commonly mentioned parallels occur in the very sections which are most frequently identified as church catechetical teaching. Halson explains,

> There are definite affinities with some of the catechetical sections of 1 Peter, e.g. Jas. 1,2-3 with 1 Pet. 1,6-7; Jas. 1,10-11 with 1 Pet. 1,24 in which the same passage from LXX Isaiah 40 is used; Jas. 1,18 with 1 Pet. 1,23; Jas. 1,21 with 1 Pet. 2,1 a catechetical summary; Jas. 4,1 with 1 Pet. 2,11; Jas. 4,6 with 1 Pet. 5,5 in which the same quotation from LXX Proverbs 3 appears with the same substitution of θεός for κύριος; Jas. 4,7 with 1 Pet. 5,9; Jas. 5:20 with 1 Pet. 4,8 in which the same passage from LXX Proverbs 10 is used.[11]

It is remarkable that both James and Peter utilize three identical verses form the OT, indeed too remarkable to be considered merely an accident. Selwyn, Carrington, and Halson have argued that these verses belonged to the primitive Christian catechism. These traditional texts were then employed by different authors to expound upon their characteristic emphases. With regard to Is. 40:6 James compares the withering flower of the field to the rich while Peter calls attention to the abiding word of God, a phrase employed as a catchword tying 1 Pet. 1:23, 24, and 25 together. Concerning Prov. 3:34 James concentrates on the word "grace" to support his conclusion that God gives more grace (4:6a) while Peter emphasizes the theme of humility. Likewise, with regard to Prov. 10:12 James observes that the retrieving of the sinner covers a multitude of sins while Peter asserts that love covers a multitude of sins. In each case a different segment of the verse is emphasized by James and Peter. The most logical conclusion is that all three of these passages were popular and beloved sayings of the OT which had found a home in the ethical

[5]Cf. Jas. 1:18=1 Pet. 1:23; 1:10=1:24; 1:21=2:1-2; 4:7=5:8-9.

[6]For examples of authors who discern literary dependence see ch. 1, n. 16-17.

[7]Cf. ch. 6, section 3.2. Laws, James, 25 supports a common geographical background but admits that "the contrasts between the distinctive concerns of James and Peter are too strong for it to be probable that they derived their common material in the same situation."

[8]Cf. Carrington's diagram, Primitive Catechism, 42-43.

[9]See the chart of Cadoux, Thought of James, 39.

[10]Cf. above, pp. 31-32.

[11]Halson, "James: 'Christian wisdom?'" SE 4:313-314, n. 3.

tradition of the church and were quoted by various authors with their own particular emphasis.

3.1 Parallels Between James and Paul's Early Epistles

James	Paul	
1:2-4 πᾶσαν χαρὰν ἡγήσασθε ... ὅταν πειρασμοῖς περιπέσητε ποικίλοις, 3 γινώσκοντες ὅτι τὸ δοκίμιον ὑμῶν τῆς πίστεως κατεργάζεται ὑπομονήν. 4 ἡ δὲ ὑπομονὴ ἔργον τέλειον ἐχέτω, ἵνα ... ἐν μηδενὶ λειπόμενοι. (testing of faith works endurance)	Rom. 5:3-5 καυχώμεθα ἐν ταῖς θλίψεσιν, εἰδότες ὅτι ἡ θλῖψις ὑπομονὴν κατεργάζεται, 4 ἡ δὲ ὑπομονὴ δοκιμήν ... 5 ἡ δὲ ἐλπὶς οὐ καταισχύνει (suffering works endurance)	
1:6a αἰτείτω δὲ ἐν πίστει μηδὲν διακρινόμενος· (prayer for wisdom)	Rom. 4:20 εἰς δὲ τὴν ἐπαγγελίαν τοῦ θεοῦ οὐ διεκρίθη τῇ ἀπιστίᾳ ἀλλ' ἐνεδυναμώθη τῇ πίστει (Abraham's faith for a son)	
1:13 μηδεὶς πειραζόμενος λεγέτω ὅτι ἀπὸ θεοῦ πειράζομαι· (God does not tempt)	1 Cor. 10:13b πιστὸς δὲ ὁ θεός, ὃς οὐκ ἐάσει ὑμᾶς πειρασθῆναι (God not allow you be tempted beyond your strength)	
1:15b ἡ δὲ ἁμαρτία ἀποτελεσθεῖσα ἀποκύει θάνατον. (context is temptation)	Rom. 5:12b διὰ τῆς ἁμαρτίας ὁ θάνατος (context about justification)	6:23 τὰ γὰρ ὀψώνια τῆς ἁμαρτίας θάνατος
1:18b ἀπαρχήν τινα τῶν αὐτοῦ κτισμάτων. (firstfruits of his creatures)	Rom. 8:23 τὴν ἀπαρχὴν τοῦ πνεύματος ἔχοντες (first fruits of the Spirit)	
1:21 διὸ ἀποθέμενοι πᾶσαν ῥυπαρίαν καὶ περισσείαν κακίας (specific exhortation)	Rom. 13:12b ἀποθώμεθα οὖν τὰ ἔργα τοῦ σκότους (general exhortation)	
1:25 ὁ δὲ παρακύψας εἰς νόμον τέλειον ... οὐκ ἀκροατὴς ἐπιλησμονῆς γενόμενος ἀλλὰ ποιητὴς ἔργου, οὗτος μακάριος ἐν τῇ ποιήσει αὐτοῦ ἔσται. (hearing and doing problem)	Rom. 2:13 οὐ γὰρ οἱ ἀκροαταὶ νόμου δίκαιοι παρὰ τῷ θεῷ, ἀλλ' οἱ ποιηταὶ νόμου δικαιωθήσονται. (Jew and Gentile problem)	
Jas. 1:26 εἴ τις δοκεῖ θρησκὸς εἶναι ... τούτου μάταιος ἡ θρησκεία. (pride in religion)	1 Cor. 3:18 εἴ τις δοκεῖ σοφὸς εἶναι ... μωρὸς γενέσθω (pride in wisdom)	Gal. 6:3 εἰ γὰρ δοκεῖ τις εἶναί ... φρεναπατᾷ ἑαυτόν. (pride in self)

James	Paul	Paul
2:2,4 ἐὰν γὰρ εἰσέλθῃ εἰς συναγωγὴν ... πτωχὸς ἐν ῥυπαρᾷ ἐσθῆτι, 4 οὐ διεκρίθητε ἐν ἑαυτοῖς καὶ ἐγένεσθε κριταὶ διαλογισμῶν πονηρῶν; (poorly dressed enter the synagogue)	1 Cor. 14:23 ἐὰν συνέλθῃ ἡ ἐκκλησία ... εἰσέλθωσιν δὲ ἰδιῶται ἢ ἄπιστοι (outsiders enter church)	Rom. 14:1 τὸν δὲ ἀσθενοῦντα τῇ πίστει προσλαμβάνεσθε, μὴ εἰς διακρίσεις διαλογισμῶν. (welcome weak in faith)
2:5 οὐχ ὁ θεὸς ἐξελέξατο τοὺς πτωχοὺς τῷ κόσμῳ πλουσίους ἐν πίστει (God chose the poor)	1 Cor. 1:27b ἐξελέξατο ὁ θεός, 27a ἀλλὰ τὰ μωρὰ τοῦ κόσμου 27c ἵνα καταισχύνῃ τοὺς σοφούς (God chose what is foolish)	
2:6b κριτήρια (rich take poor to court)	1 Cor. 6:2,4 κριτηρίων ... κριτήρια (Christian goes to unchristian court)	
Jas. 2:8 εἰ μέντοι νόμον τελεῖτε βασιλικὸν κατὰ τὴν γραφήν· ἀγαπήσεις τὸν πλησίον σου ὡς σεαυτόν, καλῶς ποιεῖτε· (completing the royal law)	Rom. 13:8b,9c ὁ γὰρ ἀγαπῶν τὸν ἕτερον νόμον πεπλήρωκεν ... ἀγαπήσεις τὸν πλησίον σου ὡς σεαυτόν. (fulfilling the OT law)	Gal. 5:14 ὁ γὰρ πᾶς νόμος ἐν ἑνὶ λόγῳ πεπλήρωται, ἐν τῷ·
2:10 ὅλον τὸν νόμον τηρήσῃ (breaking the moral law)	Gal. 5:3 ὅλον τὸν μόμον ποιῆσαι. (keeping the law, esp. circumcision)	
2:11 ὁ γὰρ εἰπών· μὴ μοιχεύσῃς...φονεύεις δέ γέγονας παραβάτης νόμου. (breaking one law while keeping another)	Rom. 2:22-23 ὁ λέγων μὴ μοιχεύειν μοιχεύεις; ... 23 διὰ τῆς παραβάσεως τοῦ νόμου τὸν θεὸν ἀτιμάζεις· (breaking a command you believe in)	
2:19 σὺ πιστεύεις ὅτι εἷς ἐστιν ὁ θεός ... (demons believe in one God) καὶ τὰ δαιμόνια πιστεύουσιν καὶ φρίσσουσιν. (demons believe in God)	1 Cor. 8:4 οἴδαμεν ὅτι ... οὐδεὶς θεὸς εἰ μὴ εἷς. (we believe in one God) 2 Cor. 11:14 αὐτὸς γὰρ ὁ σατανᾶς μετασχηματίζεται εἰς ἄγγελον φωτός. (Satan is an angel of light)	
2:21,23 Ἀβραὰμ ... ἐξ ἔργων ἐδικαιώθη ... 23 καὶ ἐπληρώθη ἡ γραφὴ ἡ λέγουσα· ἐπίστευσεν δὲ Ἀβραὰμ τῷ θεῷ, καὶ ἐλογίσθη αὐτῷ εἰς δικαιοσύνην (Abraham justified by works)	Rom. 4:2-3 εἰ Ἀβραὰμ ἐξ ἔργων ἐδικαιώθη, ἔχει καύχημα ... τί γὰρ ἡ γραφὴ λέγει; ἐπίστευσεν δὲ Ἀβραὰμ τῷ θεῷ καὶ ἐλογίσθη αὐτῷ εἰς δικαιοσύνην. (Abraham not justified	Gal. 3:6 καθὼς Ἀβραὰμ ἐπίστευσεν τῷ θεῷ, καὶ ἐλογίσθη αὐτῷ εἰς δικαιοσύνην· by works)

Jas. 2:24	Rom. 3:28	Gal. 2:16a
ὁρᾶτε ὅτι ἐξ ἔργων δικαιοῦται ἄνθρωπος καὶ οὐκ ἐκ πίστεως μόνον. (not justified by faith alone)	λογιζόμεθα γὰρ δικαιοῦσθαι πίστει ἄνθρωπον χωρὶς ἔργων νόμου. (justification by faith	εἰδότες δὲ ὅτι οὐ δικαιοῦται ἄνθρωπος ἐξ ἔργων νόμου ἐὰν μὴ διὰ πίστεως without works)

3:15 οὐκ ἔστιν αὕτη ἡ σοφία	1 Cor. 2:6b σοφίαν δὲ οὐ
ἄνωθεν κατερχομένη ἀλλὰ ἐπίγειος, ψυχική, δαιμονιώδης. (wisdom from above vs. unspiritual wisdom)	τοῦ αἰῶνος τούτου 2:14 ψυχικὸς δὲ ἄνθρωπος (wisdom of this age vs. hidden wisdom of the Spirit)

3:16 ὅπου γὰρ	1 Cor. 3:3 ὅπου γὰρ ἐν	1 Cor. 14:33
ζῆλος καὶ ἐριθεία, ἐκεῖ ἀκαταστασία καὶ πᾶν φαῦλον πρᾶγμα. (jealousy and strife produce evil)	ὑμῖν ζῆλος καὶ ἔρις, οὐχὶ σαρκικοί ἐστε καὶ κατὰ ἄνθρωπον περιπατεῖτε; (jealousy and strife are of the flesh)	οὐ γάρ ἐστιν ἀκαταστασίας ὁ θεὸς ἀλλὰ εἰρήνης. (context about worship)

4:1b ἐκ τῶν ἡδονῶν	Rom. 6:13	Rom. 7:23 ἕτερον νόμον
ὑμῶν τῶν στρατευομένων ἐν τοῖς μέλεσιν ὑμῶν; (passions warring in members)	μηδὲ παριστάνετε τὰ μέλη ὑμῶν ὅπλα ἀδικίας τῇ ἁμαρτίᾳ (sin in members)	ἐν τοῖς μέλεσίν μου ἀντιστρατευόμενον τῷ νόμῳ τοῦ νοός μου (two laws warring in members)

4:4 ἡ φιλία τοῦ κόσμου	Rom. 8:7 τὸ φρόνημα τῆς σαρκὸς
ἔχθρα τοῦ θεοῦ ἐστιν; (love of the world)	ἔχθρα εἰς θεόν (the flesh is the enemy of God)

4:5b πρὸς φθόνον	Gal. 5:17 ἡ γὰρ σὰρξ	Rom. 8:9b
ἐπιποθεῖ τὸ πνεῦμα ὃ κατῴκισεν ἐν ἡμῖν (human spirit)	ἐπιθυμεῖ κατὰ τοῦ πνεύματος (divine Spirit vs. flesh)	πνεῦμα θεοῦ οἰκεῖ ἐν ὑμῖν. (Spirit of God)

Jas. 4:11b	Rom. 2:1b ἐν ᾧ γὰρ	Rom. 14:4
κρίνων τὸν ἀδελφὸν αὐτοῦ καταλαλεῖ νόμου καὶ κρίνει νόμον· (judging another = judging the law)	κρίνεις τὸν ἕτερον, σεαυτὸν κατακρίνεις (Judging another = condemning yourself)	ὁ κρίνων ἀλλότριον (not judging the servant of another)

4:15 ἐὰν ὁ κύριος θελήσῃ	1 Cor. 4:19 ἐὰν ὁ κύριος θελήσῃ
(economic travel plans)	(ecclesiastical travel plans)

Jas. 5:12b	2 Cor. 1:17b
 ἤτω δὲ ὑμῶν τὸ ναὶ ναὶ καὶ τὸ οὒ οὔ, ἵνα μὴ ὑπὸ κρίσιν πέσητε. (concerning oaths)	ἢ ἃ βουλεύομαι κατὰ σάρκα βουλεύομαι, ἵνα ᾖ παρ' ἐμοὶ τὸ ναὶ ναὶ καὶ τὸ οὒ οὔ; (concerning making plans)

3.2 The Categories

1) Quotations: none.

2) Allusions: Jas. 2:21=Rom. 4:2; 2:24=Rom. 3:28; Gal. 2:16.

3) Parallels of both content and terminology: Jas. 1:2-4=Rom. 5:3-5; 1:13=1 Cor. 10:13b; 1:15b=Rom. 5:12b; 6:23; 1:25=Rom. 2:13; 2:5=1 Cor. 1:27; 3:16=1 Cor. 3:3b.

4) Parallels of content alone: Jas. 1:21=Rom. 13:12b; 2:2,4=1 Cor. 14:23; 2:6=1 Cor. 6:2,4; 2:19=1 Cor. 8:4; 2 Cor. 11:14; 3:15=1 Cor. 2:6b; 4:1b=Rom. 6:13; 7:23; 4:11b=Rom. 2:1b; 14:4.

5) Parallels of terminology alone: Jas. 1:6a=Rom. 4:20; 1:18=Rom. 8:23; 1:26=Gal. 6:3; 1 Cor. 3:18; 2:2,4=Rom. 14:1; 2:10=Gal. 5:3; 3:15=1 Cor. 2:14; 3:16=1 Cor. 14:33; 4:4=Rom. 8:7; 4:5b=Rom. 8:9; Gal. 5:17; 4:15=1 Cor. 4:19; 5:12b=2 Cor. 1:17b.

6) Parallels caused by common source material:

a) OT: Jas. 1:15b=Rom. 5:12; 6:23 (derived from Gen. 3); 2:8=Rom. 13:8b,9c; Gal. 5:14 (Lev. 19:18); 2:11=Rom. 2:22-23 (Ex. 20:13; Dt. 5:17); 2:23=Rom. 4:3; Gal. 3:6 (Gen. 15:6).

b) Paraenetic material based on important themes in Jesus' preaching: Jas. 1:25=Rom. 2:13 (Mt. 7:24-26; Lk. 6:46-49); 2:5=1 Cor. 1:27 (Jas. 2:5 from Mt. 5:3; Lk. 6:20; 1 Cor. 1:27 from Mt. 11:25; Lk. 10:21); 2:8=Rom. 13:8b; Gal. 5:14 (Mt. 22:39 par.).

c) Possible primitive catechism:
"rejoicing in trials" Jas. 1:2-4=Rom. 5:3-5
"putting off vices" 1:21=Rom. 13:12; 3:16=1 Cor. 3:3b.

d) Well-known wisdom sayings: Jas. 1:26=Gal. 3:6; 1 Cor. 3:18.

3.3 Conclusions

Some differences emerge in the manner in which Paul and 1 Peter are related to the Epistle of James. Whereas the parallels in 1 Peter follow the same general order of James, the Pauline parallels are scattered randomly throughout the epistle. Whereas in 1 Peter no significant parallels are detected in the discourse sections of James (2:1-3:12), it is precisely in the second of these discourses (Jas. 2:14-26 treatise on faith and works) that the most significant parallels between Paul and James are located. Paul appears to be the first person in the Jewish-Christian tradition to have concluded that the law is impossible to keep and that faith alone apart from obedience to the law can justify someone. There is no evidence to indicate that preChristian Judaism posited a contrast between justification by faith alone and salvation by works or even that prePauline Christianity was conscious of such a distinction.[12] A Jew would point to Gen. 15:6 to prove that Abraham's works proceeded from his trust in God, but James insists against certain opponents that faith and works cooperate to bring about the justification of Abraham. Dibelius is correct when he observes that this is "intelligible only if this whole 'non-Jewish' tearing apart of faith and works had already been posed."[13] Paul was the creative force in bringing about this new

---

[12]Cf. Dibelius and Greeven, James, 178-180 and above, p. 214.
[13]Ibid., 179.

situation; his teaching of justification by faith apart from the works of the law must have influenced the Jewish-Christian community before the situation described in James' epistle could take place. Although some have concluded that James is deliberately countering Rom. 3,[14] we agree with Dibelius when he explains,

> For though the section in Jas. 2:14-26 seems to me to presuppose an acquaintance with definite Pauline slogans, it also demonstrates precisely the fact that any penetrating reading of the letters of Paul upon the part of Jas is out of the question. He is familiar with only the slogans, not the concepts, and one would think that such a familiarity was rather caused by transmission through non-literary channels.[15]

Although Paul and James employ identical terminology, they presuppose a different understanding of faith, works, the law, and justification. For Paul faith assumes obedient trust in God, but the definition of faith employed by James in his discourse on faith and works (2:14-26) involves a mere verbal assent to certain beliefs.[16] For Paul faith by itself is positive, understood as containing everything necessary to receive salvation. For James faith by itself is negatively conceived as mere intellectual assent isolated from a life of good works. Therefore, for Paul James' phrase "dead faith" (2:26) would have been a contradiction of terms. Secondly, for Paul the designation "works" indicates "works of the law" which means primarily the vast complex of cultic regulations of which circumcision is the initiatory demand.[17] On the other hand, James understands the ἔργα νόμου as moral prescriptions and acts of charity grounded in love and mercy (1:27; 2:1-13; 3:18; 5:4). What James calls works are described by Paul as the fruit of the Spirit (Gal. 5:22).[18] Therefore, the law for Paul is a yoke of slavery (Gal. 5:1) while James entitles it "the law of liberty" (1:25; 2:12). Finally, for Paul justification is an initiatory act of union with Christ while for James justification is the same as salvation (2:14, 24).[19] Whereas Paul in Phil. 2:12 exhorts to "work out your salvation with fear and trembling", James could just as easily have said "work out your justification".

Not only is the content of their terminology disparate, but they speak to different audiences. Paul is wrestling with a legalistic Judaism where circumcision and keeping the law of Moses are considered the conditions for justification. On the other hand, James addresses an audience where faith has become sterile and incapable of producing good works. Therefore, James' allusions to Paul's doctrine of faith and works (Jas. 2:21=Rom. 4:2; Jas. 2:24=Rom. 3:28) are not based upon any particular writing of Paul but rather on certain phraseology (justification by faith alone) which has either been used by libertines to deny the necessity of certain acts of obedience or at least, in the mind of James, has the potential to condone this sort of behavior if justification by faith is not

---

[14]Cf. Sanders, Ethics in the NT, 119-121.

[15]Dibelius and Greeven, James, 50-51.

[16]There are two definitions of faith running through the Epistle of James. In the 13 verses of James' discourse on faith and works the noun πίστις is employed 12 times and the verb πιστεύω twice to indicate a theoretical assent to teachings such as God is one (2:19). Throughout the rest of the epistle we encounter a totally different understanding of faith. In 1:3,6; 2:5; 5:15 πίστις is conceived as vital trust in God and in 2:1 as the content of such trust. We take this to be James' normal understanding of faith. The alteration of his definition of faith in Jas. 2:14-26 proves that James is influenced by source material foreign to his own thought.

[17]Cf. Davids, James, 50-51.

[18]Cf. Schrenk, s.v. δικαιοσύνη, TDNT, II: 201.

[19]Ibid., 198. Schrenk states that "δικαιοσύνη is almost always used ... in the NT for the right conduct of man which follows the will of God and is pleasing to Him ...." James and not Paul is true to this dominant line of NT usage (p. 201).

balanced with a teaching of justification by works. In Rom. 3:8 and 6:1-2 Paul warns against this twisting of his teaching to give license to libertinism. James too appears to be fearful about such a misunderstanding of Paul's teaching. Since Paul's epistle is directed at the Romans, it is possible that a discussion about justification by faith apart from the works of the law was raging in the city of Rome.[20] However, this conflict could have been broader than just the geographical area of Rome since it was a problem that all Jewish Christians faced.

4.1 Parallels Between James and Paul's Later Epistles[21]

James	Paul
1:4b ἵνα ἦτε τέλειοι καὶ ὁλόκληροι ἐν μηδενὶ λειπόμενοι. (context about endurance)	Col. 1:28b ἵνα παραστήσωμεν πάντα ἄνθρωπον τέλειον ἐν Χριστῷ. (context about teaching wisdom)
1:4b,6b ἵνα ἦτε τέλειοι ... ἔοικεν κλύδωνι θαλάσσης ἀνεμιζομένῳ καὶ ῥιπιζομένῳ. (the results of endurance)	Eph. 4:13b,14a εἰς ἄνδρα τέλειον ... ἵνα μηκέτι ὦμεν νήπιοι, κλυδωνιζόμενοι καὶ περιφερόμενοι παντὶ ἀνέμῳ τῆς διδασκαλίας (the results of gifted leaders)
1:12 μακάριος ἀνὴρ ὃς ὑπομένει πειρασμόν, ὅτι δόκιμος γενόμενος λήμψεται (endure in trials) τὸν στέφανον τῆς ζωῆς ὃν ἐπηγγείλατο τοῖς ἀγαπῶσιν αὐτόν. (crown of life)	2 Tim. 2:11a,12 πιστὸς ὁ λόγος ... εἰ ὑπομένομεν, καὶ συμβασιλεύσομεν· (endure in the Christian faith) 4:8 ὁ τῆς δικαιοσύνης στέφανος ... τοῖς ἠγαπηκόσι τὴν ἐπιφάνειαν αὐτοῦ. (crown of righteousness)
1:18a βουληθεὶς ἀπεκύησεν ἡμᾶς λόγῳ ἀληθείας (in the work of regeneration)	2 Tim. 2:15c ὀρθοτομοῦντα τὸν λόγον τῆς ἀληθείας. (in preaching)

Jas. 1:21a διὸ ἀποθέμενοι πᾶσαν ῥυπαρίαν καὶ περισσείαν κακίας (put away two evils)	Col. 3:8 νυνὶ δὲ ἀπόθεσθε καὶ ὑμεῖς τὰ πάντα, ὀργήν, θυμόν, κακίαν, βλασφημίαν, αἰσχρολογίαν (put away 5 different evils)	Eph. 4:25 διὸ ἀποθέμενοι τὸ ψεῦδος (put away falsehood)

1:22 ποιηταὶ λόγου ... μὴ μόνον ἀκροαταὶ παραλογιζόμενοι ἑαυτούς. (delude self with only hearing)	Col. 2:4 ἵνα μηδεὶς ὑμᾶς παραλογίζηται ἐν πιθανολογίᾳ. (delude with beguiling speech)

---

[20]However, we do not know the degree to which Paul is informed about the Roman church, nor if the book of Romans is a reply to reports which have come to Paul from Rome.

[21]By dividing Paul's epistles into earlier and later we do not mean to imply that the later epistles are spurious. However, one should recognize certain changes in Paul's style.

1:27c ἄσπιλον ἑαυτὸν τηρεῖν ἀπὸ τοῦ κόσμου. (keep oneself unstained)	1 Tim. 6:14a τηρῆσαι σε τὴν ἐντολὴν ἄσπιλον (keep commandment unstained)
2:14 πίστιν ... ἔργα δὲ μὴ ἔχῃ; μὴ δύναται ἡ πίστις σῶσαι αὐτόν; (faith and works)	Eph. 2:8-9 τῇ γὰρ χάριτί ἐστε σεσωσμένοι διὰ πίστεως ... 9 οὐκ ἐξ ἔργων (faith not works)
3:1 μὴ πολλοὶ διδάσκαλοι γίνεσθε, ... ὅτι μεῖζον κρίμα λημψόμεθα. (context over sins of the tongue)	1 Tim. 1:7 νομοδιδάσκαλοι, μὴ νοοῦντες ἅ λέγουσιν (context about heresy)
4:7b ἀντίστητε δὲ τῷ διαβόλῳ (resist the devil)	Eph. 6:11b στῆναι πρὸς τὰς μεθοδείας τοῦ διαβόλου· (take the armor of God)
5:3c ἐθησαυρίσατε ἐν ἐσχάταις ἡμέραις. (against the rich)	2 Tim. 3:2 φιλάργυροι 3:1 ἐν ἐσχάταις ἡμέραις (against various evil people)
5:8 μακροθυμήσατε καὶ ὑμεῖς...ὅτι ἡ παρουσία τοῦ κύριου ἤγγικεν. (advocating patience)	Phil. 4:5 τὸ ἐπιεικὲς ὑμῶν γνωσθήτω .... ὁ κύριος ἐγγύς. (advocating forbearance)

4.2 The Categories

1) Quotations: none.

2) Allusions: Jas. 2:14 = Eph. 2:8-9.

3) Parallels of both content and terminology: Jas. 1:12 = 2 Tim. 4:8; 1:21a = Col. 3:8; Eph. 4:25.

4) Only similar content: Jas. 1:4b = Col. 1:28b; 3:1 = 1 Tim. 1:7; 4:7b = Eph. 6:11b; 5:8 = Phil. 4:5.

5) Only similar terminology: Jas. 1:4b = Eph. 4:13b; 1:6b = Eph. 4:14a; 1:12 = 2 Tim. 2:12; 1:18a = 2 Tim. 2:15c; 1:21a = Eph. 4:25; 1:22 = Col. 2:4; 1:27c = 1 Tim. 6:14a; 5:3c = 2 Tim. 3:1-2.

6) Common references to other material:

a) Possible extra-canonical saying of Jesus: Jas. 1:12 = 2 Tim. 4:8; cf. 1 Pet. 5:4.

b) Possible primitive catechism:
"putting off vices" Jas. 1:21 = Eph. 4:22; Col. 3:9
"resisting subjection to the devil" 4:7b = Eph. 6:11b.

4.3 Conclusions

Discussing the relationship of justification to faith and works, James alludes to Paul's teaching as exemplified in Eph. 2: 8-9. Although we categorize Jas. 2:14 as an allusion, one should not assume that James had read the book of Ephesians. Instead he is merely alluding to Pauline terminology very similar to that found in this reference in Ephesians. Other connections with Paul's later letters are in the form of common teaching patterns.

5.1 Parallels Between James and Hebrews

James	Hebrews
1:4 ἡ δὲ ὑπομονὴ ἔργον τέλειον ἐχέτω, ἵνα ἦτε τέλειοι (believer made perfect)	2:10c διὰ παθημάτων τελειῶσαι. (Jesus made perfect)
1:12 ὅς ὑπομένει πειρασμόν ... λήμψεται ... ὃν ἐπηγγείλατο (promise to those who love God)	10:36 ὑπομονῆς γὰρ ἔχετε χρείαν ἵνα ... κομίσησθε τὴν ἐπαγγελίαν. (promise to those who have faith)
1:21a διὸ ἀποθέμενοι πᾶσαν ῥυπαρίαν καὶ περισσείαν κακίας (put away all filth and evil)	12:1b ὄγκον ἀποθέμενοι πάντα καὶ τὴν εὐπερίστατον ἁμαρτίαν (put away every hindrance and sin)
1:25 εἰς νόμον τέλειον (praising the law)	7:19 οὐδὲν γὰρ ἐτελείωσεν ὁ νόμος (condemning the law)
2:21-22 Ἀβραὰμ ... ἀνενέγκας Ἰσαὰκ ... 22 βλέπεις ὅτι ἡ πίστις συνήργει τοῖς ἐγροῖς (evidence of works)	11:17 πίστει προσενήνοχεν Ἀβραὰμ τὸν Ἰσαὰκ (sacrifice is evidence of faith)
2:25 Ῥαὰβ ἡ πόρνη οὐκ ἐξ ἔργων ἐδικαιώθη ὑποδεξαμένη τοὺς ἀγγέλους καὶ ἑτέρᾳ ὁδῷ ἐκβαλοῦσα; (by works)	11:31 πίστει Ῥαὰβ ἡ πόρνη ... δεξαμένη τοὺς κατασκόπους μετ᾽ εἰρήνης. (by faith)
2:26b ἡ πίστις χωρὶς ἔργων νεκρά ἐστιν. (condemns dead faith)	6:1c μετανοίας ἀπὸ νεκρῶν ἔργων καὶ πίστεως ἐπὶ θεόν (condemns dead works) 9:14c καθαριεῖ ... ἀπὸ νεκρῶν ἔργων εἰς τὸ λατρεύειν θεῷ ζῶντι. (condemns dead works)
3:13 καλῆς ἀναστροφῆς (about wisdom)	13:18 καλῶς ... ἀναστρέφεσθαι. (about a clear conscience)
3:18 καρπὸς δὲ δικαιοσύνης ἐν εἰρήνῃ σπείρεται τοῖς ποιοῦσιν εἰρήνην. (about peace)	12:11b ὕστερον δὲ καρπὸν εἰρηνικὸν τοῖς δι᾽ αὐτῆς γεγυμνασμένοις ἀποδίδωσιν δικαιοσύνης. (about discipline)
4:12b ὁ δυνάμενος σῶσαι καὶ ἀπολέσαι· (save and destroy)	5:7b τὸν δυνάμενον σῴζειν αὐτὸν ἐκ θανάτου (save Jesus from death)

5.2 The Categories

1) Quotations and allusions: none.

2) Parallels of both content and terminology: Jas. 1:12=Heb. 10:36; 3:18=12:11b.

3) Only similar terminology: Jas. 1:4=Heb. 2:10c; 1:21a=12:1b; 1:25=7:19; 2:26b=6:1c; 9:14c; 3:13=13:18; 4:12b=5:7b.

4) Common references to other material:

a) OT: Jas. 2:21-22=Heb. 11:17 (Gen. 22:9); 2:25=11:31 (Josh. 2).

b) Well-known wisdom sayings: Jas. 1:12=Heb. 10:36; 3:18=12:11b.

5.3 Conclusions

The chief connections between James and Hebrews lie in their common references to the OT examples of Abraham and Rahab.[22] We frankly doubt the possibility that James was alluding to Hebrews 11 in his discussion of faith and works. Since the citing of OT models for faith and conduct would be understandable against a common upbringing and education in Judaism, it is more likely that these examples were "in the air" in the Jewish-Christian community. This is substantiated by the fact that 1 Clement also refers to Abraham and Rahab. However, it is possible that the geographical center of Rome is the connecting link since Hebrews was either written from Italy or to the Roman churches (13:24). Therefore, 1 Clement, Hebrews. and James could be drawing from examples current in the churches of Rome.[23] Jas. 3:18 also manifests close ties with Heb. 12:11. There are sufficient vocabulary parallels to classify this verse as an allusion to James, yet the different contexts (the theme of wisdom in James and spiritual discipline in Hebrews) argues against such a conclusion. Furthermore, in Hebrews discipline yields the peaceful fruit of righteousness whereas in James peace results in a harvest of righteousness. Since this verse is employed in James as a transitional saying connected to the preceding and following contexts by catchwords, the source is in all likelihood a well-known piece of wisdom quoted in proverbial form by James but expanded into a homiletical exhortation in Hebrews.

6.1 Parallels Between James and Revelation

James	Revelation
1:12 μακάριος ἀνὴρ ὃς ὑπομένει πειρασμόν, ὅτι δόκιμος γενόμενος λήμψεται τὸν στέφανον τῆς ζωῆς (general trials)	2:10b ἵνα πειρασθῆτε καὶ ἕξετε θλῖψιν .... γίνου πιστὸς ἄχρι θανάτου, καὶ δώσω σοι τὸν στέφανον τῆς ζωῆς. (the trial of prison)
1:18 ἀπεκύησεν ἡμᾶς ... ἀπαρχήν τῶν αὐτοῦ κτισμάτων. (disciples are the first fruits)	14:4c ἠγοράσθησαν ... ἀπαρχὴ τῷ θεῷ καὶ τῷ ἀρνίῳ (celebate are the first fruits)

[22]Pfleidener, Urchristentum, II: 541 concludes from this fact that James also knew Hebrews. Cf. Mayor, James, ciii.

[23]Cf. ch. 6, section 3.2.

Jas. 2:5 οὐχ ὁ θεὸς ἐξελέξατο τοὺς πτωχοὺς τῷ κόσμῳ πλουσίους ἐν πίστει (rich in faith)	Rev. 2:9a οἶδά σου τὴν θλῖψιν καὶ τὴν πτωχείαν, ἀλλὰ πλούσιος εἶ (unspecified riches)
5:9b ἰδοὺ ὁ κριτὴς πρὸ τῶν θυρῶν ἕστηκεν. (eschatological door)	3:20a ἰδοὺ ἕστηκα ἐπὶ τὴν θύραν (realized eschatological door of fellowship)

6.2 The Categories

1) Quotations or allusions: none.

2) Parallels of content and terminology: Jas. 1:12 = Rev. 2:10b; 2:5 = 2:9b.

3) Only similar terminology: Jas. 1:18 = Rev. 14:4c; 5:9b = 3:20a.

4) Common references to other material:

a) Possible extra-canonical saying of Jesus: Jas. 1:12 = Rev. 2:10 (cf. 1 Pet. 5:4).

b) Common church instruction based on the important themes of Jesus' preaching: Jas. 2:5 = Rev. 2:9a (also 1 Cor. 1:27) based on Mt. 5:3; 11:25 par.

6.3 The only connections between these two documents are 1) the common ecclesiastical teaching patterns with regard to enduring in times of trial and the exaltation of the poor and 2) the similar vocabulary employed in eschatological settings.[24]

7.1 Parallels Between James and 1 Clement

James	1 Clement	
1:8 ἀνὴρ δίψυχος 1:6 ὁ διακρινόμενος (about prayer)	11:2 οἱ δίψυχοι καὶ οἱ διστάζοντες (about judgment with Lot's wife as example)	23:3 οἱ δίψυχοι, οἱ διστάζοντες (scriptural quote about the future)
1:12 μακάριος ἀνὴρ ὃς ὑπομένει πειρασμόν, ... λήμψεται ... ὃν ἐπηγγείλατο (a promise to those who love God)	35:4b τῶν ὑπομενόντων, ὅπως μεταλάβωμεν τῶν ἐπηγγελμένων δωρεῶν. (a promise to those who patiently await)	5:5 ὑπομονῆς βραβεῖον ἔδειξεν (Paul's example)
2:21 'Αβραὰμ ὁ πατὴρ ἡμῶν οὐκ ἐξ ἔργων ἐδικαιώθη ἀνενέγκας 'Ισαὰκ τὸν υἱὸν αὐτοῦ ἐπὶ τὸ θυσιαστήριον; (Abraham's works)	31:2-3 ὁ πατὴρ ἡμῶν 'Αβραάμ; οὐχὶ δικαιοσύνην καὶ ἀλήθειαν διὰ πίστεως ποιήσας; 3 'Ισαὰκ ... προσήγετο θυσία. (Abraham's righteousness and faith)	

[24]Pfleiderer is mistaken in his contention that James used the Apocalypse since Jas. 1:12 is the ground for Rev. 2:10. Cf. Knowling, James, xlviii.

2:23 ἐπίστευσεν δὲ
Ἀβραὰμ τῷ θεῷ, καὶ
ἐλογίσθη αὐτῷ εἰς δικαιοσύνην
καὶ φίλος θεοῦ
ἐκλήθη.
(Abraham, example of faith and works)

10:6d ἐπίστευσεν δὲ
Ἀβραὰμ τῷ θεῷ, καὶ
ἐλογίσθη αὐτῷ εἰς δικαιοσύνην.
10:1 ὁ φίλος 17:2 φίλος
προσαγορευθείς προσηγορεύθη
(Abraham, example of obedience)

2:24 ὁρᾶτε ὅτι ἐξ ἔργων
δικαιοῦται ἄνθρωπος
καὶ οὐκ ἐκ πίστεως μόνον.
(justified by works and not faith alone)

30:3c ἔργοις
δικαιούμενοι
καὶ μὴ λόγοις.
(justified by works and not words)

2:25 Ῥαὰβ ἡ πόρνη
οὐκ ἐξ ἔργων ἐδικαιώθη
(Rahab's works)
ὑποδεξαμένη τοὺς ἀγγέλους
καὶ ἑτέρᾳ ὁδῷ ἐκβαλοῦσα;

(spies sent out another way)

12:1 διὰ πίστιν καὶ φιλοξενίαν
ἐσώθη Ῥαὰβ ἡ ἐπιλεγομένη πόρνη.
(Rahab's faith and hospitality)
12:4c οἱ ἄνδρες ... ἀπῆλθον
καὶ πορεύονται τῇ ὁδῷ·
ὑποδεικνύουσα αὐτοῖς ἐναλλάξ.
(representatives of the king pointed
in another direction)

3:13 τίς σοφὸς καὶ ἐπιστήμων
ἐν ὑμῖν; δειξάτω
ἐκ τῆς καλῆς ἀναστροφῆς τὰ
ἔργα αὐτοῦ ἐν πραΰτητι σοφίας.
(wisdom vs. jealousy 3:14)

38:2c ὁ σοφὸς
ἐνδεικνύσθω τὴν σοφίαν αὐτοῦ
μὴ ἐν λόγοις
ἀλλ' ἐν ἔργοις ἀγαθοῖς·
(words vs. good deeds)

4:1 πόθεν πόλεμοι καὶ
πόθεν μάχαι ἐν ὑμῖν;
(consider cause of fighting)

46:5 ἱνατί ἔρεις... καὶ σχίσματα
πόλεμός τε ἐν ὑμῖν;
(consider results of fighting)

4:6 μείζονα δὲ δίδωσιν χάριν;
διὸ λέγει· ὁ θεὸς
ὑπερηφάνοις ἀντιτάσσεται,
ταπεινοῖς δὲ δίδωσιν χάριν.
(emphasis on grace)

30:3 κολληθῶμεν...οἷς ἡ χάρις...
δέδοται· 30:2 θεὸς γάρ, φησίν,
ὑπερηφάνοις ἀντιτάσσεται,
ταπεινοῖς δὲ δίδωσιν χάριν.
(emphasis on pride)

4:14b ποία ἡ ζωὴ ὑμῶν·

ἀτμὶς γάρ ἐστε
ἡ πρὸς ὀλίγον φαινομένη,
ἔπειτα καὶ ἀφανιζομένη.
(ἀτμίς as mist)

17:5c-6 τίς εἰμι ἐγώ, ὅτι με πέμπεις; ... καὶ
πάλιν λέγει·
ἐγὼ δέ εἰμι ἀτμὶς
ἀπὸ κύθρας.

(ἀτμίς as smoke)

4:16a καυχᾶσθε
ἐν ταῖς ἀλαζονείαις ὑμῶν·
(concerning those who neglect to say,
"if the Lord wills")

21:5b ἐγκαυχωμένοις
ἐν ἀλαζονείᾳ τοῦ λόγου αὐτῶν
(concerning foolish and
senseless people)

5:10 ὑπόδειγμα ... τῆς
μακροθυμίας τοὺς προφήτας
(the prophets as
examples of patience)

5:7c ὑπομονῆς γενόμενος μέγιστος
ὑπογραμμός. 5:4 Πέτρον 5:5 Παῦλος
(Paul and Peter as
examples of patient endurance)

5:20 ὁ ἐπιστρέψας ἁμαρτωλὸν ἐκ πλάνης ... <u>καλύψει</u> <u>πλῆθος</u> <u>ἁμαρτιῶν</u>. (bringing back a sinner covers sin)	1 Cl. 49:5 ἀγάπη <u>καλύπτει</u> <u>πλῆθος</u> <u>ἁμαρτιῶν</u> (love covers sin)

7.2 The Categories

1) Quotations or allusions: none.

2) Parallels of both content and terminology: Jas. 1:12=1 Cl. 35:4b; 2:24=30:3c; 3:13=38:2.

3) Only similar content: Jas. 1:12=1 Cl. 5:5; 5:10=5:7c.

4) Only similar terminology: Jas. 1:8=1 Cl. 11:2; 23:3; 4:1=46:5; 4:14b=17:5c-6; 4:16a=21:5b.

5) Common references to other material:

a) OT: Jas. 2:23a=1 Cl. 10:6d (Gen. 15:6); 2:23b=10:1; 17:2 (like 2 Chr. 20:7; Is. 41:8); 2:25b=12:4c (tradition from Josh. 2); 4:6=30:2 (Prov. 3:34); 5:20=49:5 (Prov. 10:12).

b) NT authors: Jas. 2:21=1 Cl. 31:2-3 (Rom. 4:2 or for Clement, Heb. 11 in addition); 2:24=30:3c (James is like Rom. 3:28; Gal. 2:16 while Clement resembles Rom. 2:13 or even Jas. 1:22-23 and Mt. 7:21); 2:25a=12:1 (traditions like Heb. 11).

c) Common wisdom saying: Jas. 1:12=1 Cl. 35:4b.

7.3 Conclusions

The quality rather than the quantity of the parallels between James and 1 Clement is impressive. In both we encounter an emphasis on faith and action working together. Like Paul Clement of Rome explains that we "are not justified through ourselves or through our own wisdom or understanding or piety or works which we wrought in holiness of heart, but through faith" (32:4). But also like James he believes that Christians are "justified by works and not by words" (30:3), that wisdom is displayed in good works (Jas. 3:13=1 Cl. 38:2), and that Christians must "work the work of righteousness" (33:8). In quoting the OT Clement again emphasizes both faith (like Paul) and works (like James). In 1 Cl. 9:3-10:2 he speaks about the faithful obedience of Enoch, Noah, and Abraham, while in 10:7, 11:1, and 12:1 he points out that Abraham, Lot, and Rahab were saved through both faith and hospitality. Thus some have concluded that Clement is consciously attempting to reconcile the teaching of Paul and James.[25] However, the exegetical evidence is against such a conclusion. Clement is specifically contrasting works and words, not works and faith. This is a familiar contrast in both Paul (Rom. 2:13)[26] and James (1:22-23) as well as Jesus (Mt. 7:21). Instead of quoting James, Clement (30:4) illustrates from Job

---

[25]Knowling, <u>James</u>, xlix explains, "It is very difficult to believe that St Clement, as one who reverenced St Paul, would have used such expressions as 'being justified by works and not by words', xxx.3 cf. James ii. 14-17,21,24, unless he had some high authority behind him, to say nothing of the fact that the whole context in St Clement reminds us of words and expressions in St James' letter." Cf. also Mayor, <u>James</u>, lii-liii.

[26]1 Clement connects justification with works in the manner of Rom. 2:13 rather than Rom. 3:28.

11:2f. Therefore, the important word "justified" receives its content from Job ("Does the braggart think that he is justified?") rather than from James.[27] Similarly, Clement's stress upon hospitality is not derived from James' mention of Rahab's "receiving the messengers" but is an essential part of Clement's polemic against the Corinthian Christians (1:2). If Clement were attempting to argue that the teaching of Paul and James should be synthesized, he certainly would have openly mentioned their names or at least elaborated the problem.

The chief connections between James and 1 Clement are encountered in their common references to other material. The identical two OT passages are quoted by James and Clement as well as Peter (Prov. 3:34; 10:12). Yet no allusion to another's document is probable since all three writers emphasize a different word in their citation of Prov. 3:34 (Peter, humility; James, grace; Clement, pride). In their rehearsal of paradigms both James and Clement, after mentioning the example of Abraham, skip over Isaac, Jacob, Joseph, Moses, and Joshua (unlike Heb. 11) and immediately recite the example of Rahab. Referring to the story of Rahab in 1 Cl. 12 Young notes, "This particular emphasis (the sending of the antagonists in opposite directions) although absent from Jewish literature and early Christian literature until Augustine, is found in one passage,"[28] i.e. Jas. 2:25b. Young contends that James is indebted to 1 Clement since Clement often offers unique alterations of the OT text.[29] Yet in 1 Clement the representatives of the king of Jericho are pointed in another direction while in James the spies[30] are sent out another way.[31] Moreover, the term ἐναλλάξ is unique to 1 Clement. Therefore, no dependence can be proven. The more probable solution is that each author is reproducing a Jewish tradition. However, it is possible that within the specific geographical locale of Rome the church emphasized not only the fact that Rahab hid the spies underneath the flax (the usual emphasis), but also that the spies and the messengers of the king of Jericho were sent off in opposite directions. It could be hypothesized that a rigorous discussion of the themes of justification, faith, and works was taking place in the city of Rome. Some (like James) were afraid that Paul's emphasis on faith alone could be easily misunderstood and lead to a laxity of good works on the part of the community. However, by the time of Clement (95 AD) the Roman church has sufficiently integrated these various opinions so that a polemic such as that found in Jas. 2:18 is no longer necessary. Instead, we encounter in 1 Clement a synthesis where both faith and obedient works are integral parts of justification. This geographical thesis, however, is not the only solution; the chief connection between James, Peter, and Clement could be the common teaching patterns in the broader Jewish-Christian community.

---

[27]Jas. 5:11 also uses the example of Job but not in connection with faith and works.

[28]Franklin W. Young, "The Relation of 1 Clement to the Epistle of James," JBL 67(1948): 342.

[29]Ibid., 345.

[30]The word ἀγγέλους, messengers, is ambiguous. Young, "1 Clement to James," 342-343 hesitantly affirms that the king's messengers are in mind even though he recognizes that ὑποδεξαμένα in both Classical and Hellenistic Greek meant "receive as a guest". We contend that Rahab's guests were the spies.

[31]Mayor, James, 102 (also Laws, James, 139) believes that "another way" indicates the use of the window instead of the door (Josh. 2:11,15,16), yet the term ὁδός would more naturally refer to a road, highway, or direction of a return journey than to the window through which the spies exited. 1 Clement and James would thus derive from a common tradition that the spies and the messengers of the king went in different directions. However, the following dissimilarities exclude any dependence of one author upon the other: 1) 1 Clement is unique in its hidden reference to Christ's blood in the scarlet thread; 2) 1 Clement as well as the Epistle of Hebrews labels the men κατασκόποι, spies, while James calls them ἀγγέλοι, messengers.

8.1 Parallels Between James and the Shepherd of Hermas

James	Hermas	
1:3-4 τὸ δοκίμιον ὑμῶν τῆς πίστεως κατεργάζεται ὑπομονήν. ἡ δὲ ὑπομονὴ ἔργον τέλειον ἐχέτω, ἵνα ἦτε τέλειοι καὶ ὁλόκληροι (endurance produces completeness)	Mand. 5,2,3 αὕτη ἡ μακροθυμία κατοικεῖ μετὰ τῶν τὴν πίστιν ἐχόντων ὁλόκληρον. (patience is for those with complete faith)	
1:5 εἰ δέ τις ὑμῶν λείπεται σοφίας, αἰτείτω παρὰ τοῦ διδόντος θεοῦ ... καὶ δοθήσεται αὐτῷ. (answered prayer if have faith)	Sim. 5,3,9 καὶ ὅσα ἂν αἰτήσωνται παρὰ τοῦ κυρίου λήψονται. (answered prayer if fasting)	Sim. 5,4,3 αἰτεῖται παρ᾽ αὐτοῦ σύνεσιν καὶ λαμβάνει (receive interpretation of the parable)
Jas. 1:5 αἰτείτω παρὰ τοῦ διδόντος θεοῦ πᾶσιν ἁπλῶς (God gives generously)	Mand. 2:4 πᾶσιν ὑστερουμένοις δίδου ἁπλῶς (human giving)	Sim. 5,4,4 καὶ πᾶσι τοῖς αἰτουμένοις παρ᾽ αὐτοῦ ἀδιαλείπτως δίδωσι (God gives unceasingly)
1:5 αἰτείτω παρὰ τοῦ διδόντος θεοῦ ... καὶ δοθήσεται αὐτῷ. 1:6 αἰτείτω δὲ ἐν πίστει μηδὲν διακρινόμενος ... 1:7 μὴ γὰρ οἰέσθω ὁ ἄνθρωπος ἐκεῖνος ὅτι λήμψεταί τι παρὰ τοῦ κυρίου, 1:8 ἀνὴρ δίψυχος 1:4 ἵνα ἦτε τέλειοι καὶ ὁλόκληροι 1:6 αἰτείτω δὲ ἐν πίστει μηδὲν διακρινόμενος· (without doubting) 1:13 μηδεὶς πειραζόμενος λεγέτω ὅτι ἀπὸ θεοῦ πειράζομαι· (not blame God for temptation)	Mand. 9:4 καὶ αἰτοῦ παρὰ τοῦ κυρίου, καὶ ἀπολήψῃ πάντα ... ἐὰν ἀδιστάκτως αἰτήσῃς παρὰ τοῦ κυρίου. 9:5 ἐὰν δὲ διστάσῃς ἐν τῇ καρδίᾳ σου, οὐδὲν οὐ μὴ λήψῃ τῶν αἰτημάτων σου. ... οὗτοί εἰσον οἱ δίψυχοι ... 9:6 οἱ δὲ ὁλοτελεῖς ὄντες ἐν τῇ πίστει ... ἀδιστάκτως αἰτοῦνται, μηδὲν διψυχοῦντες. (without wavering) 9:8d σεαυτὸν αἰτιῶ καὶ μὴ τὸν διδόντα σοι. (blame yourself for unanswered prayer)	
1:8 ἀκατάστατος ἐν πάσαις ταῖς ὁδοῖς αὐτοῦ. (about a double-minded man) 1:12 μακάριος ἀνὴρ ὃς ὑπομένει πειρασμόν (endure trials in general)	Mand. 5,2,7 ἀκαταστατεῖ ἐν πάσῃ πράξει αὐτοῦ (about a person's angry temper) Vis. 2,2,7 μακάριοι ὑμεῖς ὅσοι ὑπομένετε τὴν θλῖψιν τὴν ἐρχομένην τὴν μεγάλην (endure the great tribulation)	

James

1:14-15 ἕκαστος δὲ πειράζεται
ὑπὸ τῆς ἰδίας ἐπιθυμίας
ἐξελκόμενος καὶ δελεαζόμενος·
εἶτα ἡ ἐπιθυμία συλλαβοῦσα
τίκτει ἁμαρτίαν,
ἡ δὲ ἁμαρτία ἀποτελεσθεῖσα
ἀποκύει θάνατον.
(not blame God for temptation)

Hermas

Mand. 4,1,2 ἐὰν γὰρ αὕτη ἡ ἐνθύμησις
ἐπὶ τὴν καρδίαν σου ἀναβῇ,
διαμαρτήσεις,
καὶ ἐὰν ἕτερα οὕτως πονηρά,
ἁμαρτίαν ἐργάζῃ ... ἐὰν δέ τις
ἐργάσηται τὸ ἔργον πονηρὸν τοῦτο,
θάνατον ἑαυτῷ κατεργάζεται.
(about extra-marital affairs)

Jas. 1:14-15

ἕκαστος δὲ πειράζεται
ὑπὸ τῆς ἰδίας ἐπιθυμίας ...
εἶτα ἡ ἐπιθυμία συλλαβοῦσα
τίκτει ἁμαρτίαν,
ἡ δὲ ἁμαρτία ἀποτελεσθεῖσα
ἀποκύει θάνατον.
(emphasis on the cause of temptation)

Vis. 1,1,8 ἢ οὐ δοκεῖ σοι ἀνδρὶ δικαίῳ πονηρὸν
πρᾶγμα εἶναι
ἐὰν ἀναβῇ αὐτοῦ ἐπὶ τὴν καρδίαν
ἡ πονηρὰ ἐπιθυμία;

ἁμαρτία γέ ἐστιν, καὶ μεγάλη ...
οἱ δὲ πονηρὰ βουλευόμενοι ἐν ταῖς
καρδίαις αὐτῶν θάνατον
(emphasis on righteousness)

1:17 πᾶσα δόσις ἀγαθὴ
καὶ πᾶν δώρημα τέλειον
ἄνωθέν ἐστιν καταβαῖνον
ἀπὸ τοῦ πατρὸς τῶν φώτων
3:15 αὕτη ἡ σοφία ...
ἐπίγειος, ψυχική,
δαιμονιώδης.

(gift from above)

Mand. 11:5-6 πᾶν
γὰρ πνεῦμα ἀπὸ θεοῦ
... ἄνωθέν ἐστιν
ἀπὸ τῆς δυνάμεως...
6 τὸ δὲ πνεῦμα ...
ἐπίγειόν ἐστι καὶ
ἐλαφρόν,
δύναμιν μὴ ἔχον·
(Spirit from above)

Mand. 9:11
ὅτι ἡ πίστις
ἄνωθέν ἐστι
παρὰ τοῦ κυρίου...
ἡ δὲ διψυχία
ἐπίγειον πνεῦμά ἐστι
παρὰ τοῦ διαβόλου,
δύναμιν μὴ ἔχουσα.
(faith from above)

1:20 ὀργὴ γὰρ ἀνδρὸς
δικαιοσύνην θεοῦ
οὐκ ἐργάζεται.
(anger)

Mand. 5,2,1 τὴν ἐνέργειαν τῆς
ὀξυχολίας ... ἀποπλανᾷ αὐτοὺς
ἀπὸ τῆς δικαιοσύνης.
(evil temper)[32]

1:21b τὸν ἔμφυτον λόγον τὸν
δυνάμενον σῶσαι τὰς ψυχὰς ὑμῶν.
(implanted word able to save)

Sim. 6,1,1 περὶ τῶν ἐντολῶν ...
δυνάμεναι σῶσαι ψυχὴν ἀνθρώπου
(commandments able to save)

1:22a,25 γίνεσθε δὲ ποιηταὶ λόγου
καὶ μὴ μόνον ἀκροαταὶ ...
οὗτος μακάριος
ἐν τῇ ποιήσει αὐτοῦ ἔσται.
(context about hearing and doing)

Sim. 5,3,9 ὅσοι ἂν ἀκούσαντες
αὐτὰ τηρήσωσι,
μακάριοι
ἔσονται
(context about fasting)

Jas. 1:27 θρησκεία
καθαρὰ καὶ ἀμίαντος
... ἐπισκέπτεσθαι
ὀρφανοὺς καὶ χήρας
ἐν τῇ θλίψει αὐτῶν
(pure religion; content of pure religion)

Mand. 2:7 ἡ καρδία σου
καθαρὰ καὶ ἀμίαντος.
Sim. 1:8 χήρας καὶ ὀρφανοὺς
ἐπισκέπτεσθε
καὶ μὴ παραβλέπετε αὐτούς
(pure heart; content of the works of God)

---

[32]Laws, James, 23 states, "In Mandate v Hermas discusses irascibility, *oxucholia*, a word peculiar to him. One of its effects is that it leads men astray from righteousness (Mand. v. 2. 1), as James says of *orgē*, anger, that it cannot effect righteousness (i. 20)."

2:5 ἀκούσατε, ἀδελφοί ... οὐχ
ὁ θεὸς ἐξελέξατο τοὺς πτωχοὺς τῷ κόσμῳ
πλουσίους ἐν πίστει
(poor but rich)

Sim. 2:5 ἄκουε, φησίν·
ὁ μὲν πλούσιος ἔχει χρήματα πολλά,
τὰ δὲ πρὸς τὸν κύριον πτωχεύει
(rich but poor)

2:5 τοὺς πτωχοὺς τῷ κόσμῳ

πλουσίους ἐν πίστει
(rich in faith)

Sim. 2:6 ἡ ἔντευξις τοῦ πένητος
προσδεκτή ἐστι καὶ
πλουσία πρὸς τὸν θεόν.
(rich in intercession)

2:7 οὐκ αὐτοὶ βλασφημοῦσιν
τὸ καλὸν ὄνομα
τὸ ἐπικληθὲν ἐφ᾽ ὑμᾶς;
(about the rich)

Sim. 8,6,4 βλασφημήσαντες ...
ἐπαισχυνθέντες τὸ ὄμομα κυρίου
τὸ ἐπικληθὲν ἐπ᾽ αὐτούς.
(about heretics)

2:26b οὕτως καὶ ἡ πίστις χωρὶς ἔργων
νεκρά ἐστιν.
2:26a ὥσπερ γὰρ τὸ σῶμα
χωρὶς πνεύματος νεκρόν ἐστιν,
(about faith without works)

Sim. 9,21,2 τὰ ῥήματα αὐτῶν μόνα ζῶσι,
τὰ δὲ ἔργα αὐτῶν νεκρά ἐστιν.
οἱ τοιοῦτοι
οὔτε ζῶσιν οὔτε τεθνήκασιν.
(about the double-minded)

3:2b εἴ τις
ἐν λόγῳ οὐ πταίει ...
δυνατὸς χαλιναγωγῆσαι καὶ
ὅλον τὸ σῶμα.
3:8 τὴν δὲ γλῶσσαν
οὐδεὶς δαμάσαι δύναται ἀνθρώπων
(over the tongue)

Mand. 12,1,1
μισήσεις τὴν πονηρὰν ἐπιθυμίαν
καὶ χαλιναγωγήσεις
αὐτὴν καθὼς βούλει.
12,1,2 ἀγρία ἐστιν ἡ ἐπιθυμία ἡ
πονηρὰ καὶ δυσκόλως ἡμεροῦται·
(over evil desire)

Jas. 3:8
τὴν δὲ γλῶσσαν ...
ἀκατάστατον κακόν,
μεστὴ ἰοῦ
θανατηφόρου.
(tongue: a restless poison)

Mand. 2:3
πονηρὰ ἡ καταλαλιά,
ἀκατάστατον
δαιμόνιόν ἐστιν
(slander: a restless demon)

Sim. 9,26,7
7d τὰ ῥήματα διαφθείρει
τὸν ἄνθρωπον καὶ ἀπολλύει.
7c διαφθείρει τῷ ἑαυτῶν ἰῷ
τὸν ἄνθρωπον καὶ ἀπολλύει
(words are poison)

3:15 οὐκ ἔστιν αὕτη ἡ σοφία
ἄνωθεν κατερχομένη
ἀλλὰ ἐπίγειος, ψυχική,
δαιμονιώδης.
(true vs. false wisdom)

Mand. 9:11 ὅτι ἡ πίστις
ἄνωθέν ἐστι παρὰ τοῦ κυρίου, ...
ἡ δὲ διψυχία ἐπίγειον πνεῦμά ἐστι
παρὰ τοῦ διαβόλου
(faith vs. double-mindedness)

3:17 ἡ δὲ ἄνωθεν σοφία
πρῶτον μὲν
ἁγνή ἐστιν,
ἔπειτα εἰρηνική, ἐπιεικής...
(Seven qualities of wisdom from above)

Mand. 11:8 πρῶτον μὲν
ὁ ἔχων τὸ πνεῦμα τὸ θεῖον τὸ ἄνωθεν
πραΰς ἐστι
καὶ ἡσύχιος καὶ ταπεινόφρων ...
(Seven qualities of the Spirit from above)

3:18 καρπὸς δὲ δικαιοσύνης
ἐν εἰρήνῃ σπείρεται
(about peace)

Sim. 9,19,2 μὴ ἔχοντες
καρπὸν δικαιοσύνης·
(about hypocrates)

Jas. 4:3
αἰτεῖτε
καὶ οὐ λαμβάνετε
διότι κακῶς αἰτεῖσθε
(not receive if ask wrongly)

Sim. 4:6 πῶς οὖν, φησίν, ὁ τοιοῦτος
δύναταί τι αἰτήσασθαι
παρὰ τοῦ κυρίου καὶ λαβεῖν,
μὴ δουλεύων τῷ κυρίῳ;
(not receive if not serve the Lord)

4:5b πρὸς φθόνον
ἐπιποθεῖ τὸ πνεῦμα
ὃ κατῴκισεν
ἐν ἡμῖν.
(envious spirit)

Mand. 3:1
τὸ πνεῦμα, ὃ ὁ θεὸς
κατῴκισεν
ἐν τῇ σαρκὶ ταύτῃ
(about truth)

Sim. 5,6,5
τὸ πνεῦμα τὸ ἅγιον ...
κατῴκισεν
ὁ θεὸς εἰς σάρκα
(about the holy spirit)

Jas. 4:7

ὑποτάγητε οὖν τῷ θεῷ
ἀντίστητε δὲ

τῷ διαβόλῳ καὶ
φεύξεται ἀφ᾽ ὑμῶν

(submit to God and
resist the devil)

Mand. 12,2,5 ἐὰν δουλεύσῃς
τῇ ἐπιθυμίᾳ τῇ ἀγαθῇ
καὶ ὑποταγῇς αὐτῇ
2,4 ἀντίστηθι αὐταῖς.
2,2 ἡ ἐπιθυμία ἡ πονηρὰ
τοῦ διαβόλου θυγάτηρ ἐστίν.
2,4 φεύξεται ἀπὸ σοῦ μακράν,
καὶ οὐκ ἔτι σοι ὀφθήσεται
(evil desire vs. good desire)

Mand. 12,5,2
ὁ διάβολος ...
ἐὰν οὖν
ἀντισταθῆτε
αὐτῷ, νικηθεὶς
φεύξεται
ἀφ᾽ ὑμῶν
κατῃσχυμμένος.
(mastered by devil
vs. resist devil)

4:8b καθαρίσατε χεῖρας,
ἁμαρτωλοί,
καὶ ἁγνίσατε καρδίας,
δίψυχοι.
(command to the double-minded
to purify themselves)

Vis. 3,2,2 πάντες δὲ οἱ
μὴ διψυχοῦντες καθαρισθήσονται
ἀπὸ πάντων τῶν ἁμαρτημάτων
εἰς ταύτην τὴν ἡμέραν.
(promise of purification
for those not double-minded)

4:8b καθαρίσατε χεῖρας, ἁμαρτωλοί, καὶ ἁγνίσατε καρδίας,
δίψυχοι.
(adds "cleanse your hands")

Mand. 9:7 καθάρισον οὖν
τὴν καρδίαν σου
ἀπὸ τῆς διψυχίας
(adds "put on faith")

4:8 δίψυχοι.
4:9 ταλαιπωρήσατε
καὶ πενθήσατε
(the double-minded must grieve)

Vis. 3,7,1 ἀπὸ δὲ τῆς διψυχίας
αὐτῶν ἀφίουσιν τὴν ὁδὸν ...
πλανῶνται καὶ ταλαιπωροῦσιν
(double-minded lose their way)

4:11 μὴ καταλαλεῖτε ἀλλήλων ...
ὁ καταλαλῶν ἀδελφοῦ ἢ κρίνων τὸν
ἀδελφὸν ... καταλαλεῖ νόμου
(context about judging the law)

Mand. 2:2 πρῶτον μὲν μηδενὸς
καταλάλει, μηδὲ ἡδέως ἄκουε
καταλαλοῦντος·
(context about slander)

4:12 ὁ δυνάμενος
σῶσαι καὶ ἀπολέσαι·
(theme: against judging)

Mand. 12,6,3 τὸν πάντα δυνάμενον,
σῶσαι καὶ ἀπολέσαι
(theme: fear God, not the devil)

5:1 ἄγε νῦν οἱ πλούσιοι, κλαύσατε ὀλολύζοντες ἐπὶ ταῖς ταλαιπωρίαις ὑμῶν ταῖς ἐπερχομέναις. 5:4b καὶ αἱ βοαὶ τῶν θερισάντων εἰς τὰ ὦτα κυρίου σαβαὼθ εἰσεληλύθασιν. 5:9b ἰδοὺ ὁ κριτὴς πρὸ τῶν θυρῶν ἕστηκεν. (the rich will suffer ruin)	Vis. 3,9,6 βλέπετε οὖν ὑμεῖς οἱ γαυρούμενοι ἐν τῷ πλούτῳ ὑμῶν... 3,9,5 βλέπετε τὴν κρίσιν τὴν ἐπερχομένην. 3,9,6 καὶ ὁ στεναγμὸς αὐτῶν ἀναβήσεται πρὸς τὸν κύριον, καὶ ἐκκλεισθήσεσθε ... ἔξω τῆς θύρας τοῦ πύργου. (ungenerous shut outside tower)
5:11a ἰδοὺ μακαρίζομεν τοὺς ὑπομείναντας· (a general exhortation)	Vis. 2,2,7 μακάριοι ὑμεῖς ὅσοι ὑπομένετε τὴν θλῖψιν τὴν ἐρχομένην (about the final tribulation)
5:11c ὅτι πολύσπλαγχνός ἐστιν ὁ κύριος καὶ οἰκτίρμων. (about God's good purpose)	Mand. 4,3,5 πολύσπλαγχνος οὖν ὢν ὁ κύριος ἐσπλαγχνίσθη ἐπὶ τὴν ποίησιν (an opportunity for repentance)

8.2 The Categories

1) Quotations: none.

2) Allusions: Jas. 1:5-7 = Mand. 9,4,4-6; 3:15 = Mand. 9:11; probably 1:17 and 3:15 = Mand. 11:5-6; 3:17 = Mand. 11:8; 4:8b = Mand. 9:7.

3) Parallels of content and terminology: Jas. 1:3-4 = Mand. 5,2,3; 1:5 = Sim. 5,4,3; 5,4,4; 5,3,9; 1:12 and 5:11a = Vis. 2,2,7; 1:14-15 = Mand. 4,1,2; Vis. 1,1,8; 3:8 = Mand. 2:3; 4:7 = Mand. 12,2,2-5; 12,5,2; 4:8b = Vis. 3,2,2; 5:1,4b,9b = Vis. 3,9,5-6.

4) Only similar content: Jas. 1:13 = Mand. 9:8d; 1:22-25 = Sim. 5,3,9; 3:8 = Mand. 12,1,2; Sim. 9,26,7; 4:3 = Sim. 4:6; 4:11a = Mand. 2:2.

5) Only similar terminology: Jas. 1:4 = Mand. 9:6; 1:5 = Mand. 2:4; 1:8 = Mand. 5,2,7; 1:17 = Mand. 9:11; 11:5-6; 1:20 = Mand. 5,2,1; 1:21b = Sim. 6,1,1; 1:27 = Mand. 2:7; Sim. 1:8; 2:5 = Sim. 2:5-6; 2:7 = Sim. 8,6,4; 2:26 = Sim. 9,21,2; 3:2b = Mand. 12,1,1; 3:18 = Sim. 9,12,2; 4:5b = Mand. 3:1; Sim. 5,6,5; 4:9 = Vis. 3,7,1; 4:12 = Mand. 12,6,3; 5:11c = Mand. 4,3,5.

6) Common references to other material:

a) Sayings of Jesus: Jas. 1:5 = Vis. 5,4,3; 5,4,4; Sim. 5,3,9; and Jas. 4:3 = Sim. 4:6 (Mt. 7:7; Lk. 11:7).

b) Possible Christian catechism (established teaching pattern): Jas. 4:7 = Mand. 12,2,2-5; 12,5,2 like 1 Pet. 5:8-9.

c) Well-known wisdom saying: Jas. 1:12 = Vis. 2,2,7.

8.3 Conclusions

Whereas the parallels between James and 1 Clement are concentrated in the area of allusions to other writings, the parallels with the Shepherd of Hermas lie primarily in similar terminology. The Shepherd nowhere admits dependence upon James; it seems rather that Hermas has internalized the Epistle of James so that James' terminology has become his own.[33] Only in one pericope can we positively affirm an allusion to James -- Mand. 9. Here Hermas draws together three references from the Epistle of James into one of his paragraphs. In a discourse over doubting in prayer he apparently is reminded what James (1:5-7) said on this subject. Similar to James Hermas includes Jesus' saying about the certainty of answered prayer (Jas. 1:5=Mand. 9:5), an exhortation aimed at asking in faith without wavering (Jas. 1:6=Mand. 9:5), a statement identifying those who waver as the double-minded (Jas. 1:8=Mand. 9:5) who will receive nothing from the Lord (Jas. 1:7=Mand. 9:5), and an explanation why Jesus' promise of answered prayer is sometimes not fulfilled (Jas. 1:6-7 and 4:3=Mand. 9:8-9). In addition, Hermas emphasizes being complete in the faith (9:6) just as James has begun this section with the theme of being "perfect and complete, lacking in nothing" (1:4). Finally, Hermas warns against blaming God when prayers are not answered (Mand. 9:8) just as James had warned against blaming God for causing temptations (1:13). Temptation begins from within the human being (Jas. 1:13); therefore, one can only blame one's self (Mand. 9:8). Thus Hermas has incorporated the content of Jas. 1:4-7 into Mand. 9 and, at the same time, sharpened the contrast between "complete in faith" and "wavering because of double-mindedness".

While thinking about James' teaching on prayer, Hermas' mind apparently wandered to other terminology of James later in the epistle. He states that faith is from above while double-mindedness is an earthly, devilish spirit (Mand. 9:11) just as James had contrasted wisdom from above with that which is earthly, unspiritual, devilish (3:15). Since Hermas employs this same terminology in another context about double-mindedness (Mand. 11:5-8), it is likely that in Mand. 11 we encounter another allusion to Jas. 3:15,17 although new content is put into James' terminology. An allusion to a third passage of James (4:8) is also possible at Mand. 9:7 where both authors combine a call to purity of heart with a warning against double-mindedness. We believe that this cluster of references to Jamesian terminology and subject matter at Mand. 9 establishes the fact that Hermas had previously read the Epistle of James, although at the time of writing James' epistle is probably not before him in written form.[34]

Once we have established one certain allusion, then the numerous other examples of similar phraseology confirm our suspicion that Jamesian terminology is present in other parts of this writing. In both documents we encounter the following phraseology: a sevenfold description of qualities that come from above (Mand. 11:8; Jas. 3:17); a condemnation of the rich (Vis. 3,9,5-6; Sim. 2:5; Jas. 2:5; 5:1,4); a blessing upon those who endure trials (Vis. 2,2,7; Jas. 1:12; 5:10-11a); warnings against instability (Mand. 5,2,7; Jas. 1:8) and blaspheming the honorable name which was invoked over them (Sim. 8,6,4; Jas. 2:7); and exhortations aimed at bridling desire (Mand. 12,1,1; Jas. 3:2), visiting the widow and orphan (Sim. 1:8; Jas. 1:27), and praying for wisdom and understanding (Sim. 5,4,3; Jas. 1:5) in confidence of receiving it (Sim. 5,3,9; Mand. 9:4; Jas. 1:5). In addition each document contains similar descriptions of the fruit of righteousness (Sim. 9,19,2; Jas. 3:18), the spirit who was made to dwell in us (Mand. 3:1; Sim. 5,6,5; Jas. 4:5), good as coming from above but evil being earthly and devilish (Mand. 11:5-6; Jas. 1:17), desire leading to sin and

---

[33]Charles Taylor, "The Didache Compared with the Shepherd," JPh 18(1890): 320-321 offers five examples of how Hermas has adapted the Epistle of James.

[34]It is far less likely that James utilized Hermas and transferred two or three sayings from one paragraph (Mand. 9) into different settings. Cf. the use of Jonah 4:2 and 3:9 in Joel 2:13-14.

sin in turn bringing forth death (Mand. 4,1,2; Vis. 1,1,8; Jas. 1:14-15), evil speaking described as a restless evil (Mand. 2:3; Jas. 3:8), and God as the one able to save and destroy (Mand. 12,6,3; Jas. 4:12), who is full of compassion (Mand. 4,3,5; Jas. 5:11) and generous in his giving (Mand. 2:4; Jas. 1:5). Within these general similarities of phraseology, the common utilization of infrequently used vocabulary is especially striking: δίψυχος, ἀκατάστατος, ἐπίγειος, χαλιναγωγέω, καρπὸς δικαιοσύνης, πολύσπλαγχνος, ἁπλῶς. Finally, in both documents the oneness of God is acclaimed (Mand. 1:1; Jas. 2:19), the law and the commandments are emphasized (Sim. 5,5,3; 5,6,3; 8,3,2; Vis. 1,3,4; Jas. 1:25; 2:8-12; 4:11-12), a blessing upon those who both hear and observe is encountered (Sim. 5,3,9; Jas. 1:22-25), a similar eschatological perspective is present,[35] the glorification of long-suffering and its relation to perfection is posited (Mand. 5,2,3; Jas. 1:3-4), and the resisting of the devil and his subsequent fleeing are connected (Mand. 12,5,2; 12,2,4; Jas. 4:7).

The important themes of wealth, faith and works, and double-mindedness are developed along similar lines. Riches are regarded by both authors as an enemy to faith (Sim. 8,9,1[36] Jas. 1:9-11; 2:5-7; 5:1-6), although the rich have already entered the community in Hermas (Vis. 3,6,5)[37] whereas this is more doubtful in James. In both documents wealth itself and not the desire for riches must be cut away before someone can become useful to the Lord (Vis. 3,6,6). Both epitomize the oppression of the wealthy through picturing their fields (Sim. 1:1,8; Jas. 5:4), although Hermas offers positive advice to the rich about their fields (Sim. 1:8)[38] while James only illustrates the oppression involved (5:4). The same accusation about the rich (Vis. 3,9,6; Jas. 5:4) ascends to the Lord through the mourning of the oppressed. In Hermas the consequence is exclusion outside the gate of the tower (church), whereas in Jas. 5:9 the judge is standing at the eschatological gates ready to condemn. Finally, Vis. 3,6,5[39] could refer to Jas. 4:13-5:6 where the business affairs of the merchants and the riches of the oppressing landowners are warned against. The same view of faith "as recognition and acceptance of Christian teaching as such"[40] is witnessed in Sim. 8,9,1; Vis. 3,6,5 and Jas. 2:14,17,18,20,22,24,26. Furthermore, double-mindedness is a prominent evil in both James and Hermas.[41] Not only are the double-minded addressed in the vocative case in Jas. 4:8; Sim. 1:3, but the identical term "wretched" (ταλαιπωρέω) is employed in the immediate context (Jas. 4:9; 5:1; Sim. 1:3; Vis. 3,7,1). Furthermore, in each case the definition of double-mindedness presupposes a situation where faith is separated from works. In Sim. 9,21,2 the double-minded are described as those whose "words only live, but their works are dead" which is reminiscent of Jas. 2:26 where faith apart from works is dead. Certainly for James this contradictory attitude would characterize double-minded people who are unstable in all their ways and able to receive nothing from the Lord (Jas. 1:7-8).

None of these similarities alone establishes a direct dependence of the Shepherd of Hermas upon James, but taken together they present a strong case supporting

---

[35]Cf. above, ch. 6, n. 81.

[36]"... these are men who have been believers but grew rich and became renowned among the Gentiles."

[37]"These are they that have faith, but have also riches of this world." Dibelius and Greeven, James, 45 state that the parable of the elm and the vine (Sim. 2) is the clearest indication that the wealthy were already members of the Christian community.

[38]"Therefore, instead of fields buy ye souls that are in trouble, as each is able, and visit widows and orphans, and neglect them not; and spend your riches and all your displays, which ye received from God, on fields and houses of this kind." Cf. Vis. 3,9,5.

[39]"When tribulation cometh, they deny their Lord by reason of their riches and their business affairs."

[40]BAG, s.v. πίστις, 669.2dδ. These are the only texts which Bauer positions under this category of faith.

[41]The adjective is chosen 19x in Hermas, the verb 20x, and the substantive 16x. Only in Jas. 1:8; 4:8 is the term employed in the NT.

our supposition that Hermas employed the Epistle of James. The only other major alternatives are that both utilized well-known Jewish hortatory teaching[42] possibly emanating from the church of Rome, or that both drew material from a common source. Although it has been conjectured that this common document was the book of Eldad and Modad which is quoted in Vis. 2,3,4,[43] certainly the immense list of Jamesian parallels cited above suggests that the Shepherd of Hermas provides a commentary on the Epistle of James. As Dibelius remarks,

> This is especially the case with regard to the sphere of thought related to faith and doubt. Herm. Mand. 9 is the best interpretation of Jas. 1:5-8 imaginable.[44]

The Shepherd of Hermas then furnishes the *terminus ad quem* for the composition of the Epistle of James.

9.0 General Conclusions Concerning all the Parallels

Within this appendix we have discovered a remarkable relationship between James, 1 Peter, 1 Clement, and the Shepherd of Hermas. Only with Hermas can a definite dependence upon the Epistle of James be established, but the utilization of common material among 1 Peter, Clement, and James is conspicuous. All three quote Prov. 3:34 and 10:12. Clement and James along with Hebrews include the examples of Abraham offering Isaac (Paul too in Romans) and Rahab's hospitality when they discuss the theme of faith and works. 1 Peter and James are both addressed to the Diaspora and include similar material in the same general order. We can perceive here established teaching patterns whose order and similarity of terminology give the impression of a primitive Christian catechism.[45] Furthermore, James (1:8; 4:8), 1 Clement (11:2; 23:3), and the Shepherd of Hermas on many occasions exhort against double-mindedness. In our estimation these similarities are best explained by common teaching patterns within the Jewish-Christian community or with a hypothesis which ties these documents to the same geographical

---

[42]Cf. Ropes, James, 89ff.

[43]Seitz, "Relationship of Hermas to James," 131-140. Seitz postulates that the source of 1 Cl. 23:3 and 2 Cl. 11:2 is also Eldad and Modad since there is a similar reference to double-mindedness. Then the Epistle of James is linked to these texts by 1) the use of the unknown source at Jas. 4:5 which is identified as from Eldad and Modad; 2) the close association between ταλαιπωρεῖν and δίψυχοι at Jas. 4:8-9 as in 1 Cl. 23:3 and 2 Cl. 11:2; 3) the tie between double-mindedness and purity of heart in Mand. 9:7 and Jas. 4:8; 4) the fact that both epistles of Clement connect doubting (ὁ διστάξων is employed rather than ὁ διακρινόμενος) with the heart (1 Clement, the soul) in a context about double-mindedness (Jas. 1:6-8); 5) the almost exact order of vocabulary in Mand. 9 as well as Jas. 1:5-8 and 4:3,6-8 (αἰτεῖν meaning "to pray"; λαβεῖν in answer to prayer; ὁ θεός as the subject of διδόναι, all preceding δίψυχος) together with the common phrases αἰτεῖν παρὰ τοῦ θεοῦ, τι παρὰ τοῦ κυρίου λαβεῖν, and ἀνὴρ δίψυχος. In our opinion, much of the above material could just as easily be utilized to demonstrate a dependence upon Jamesian vocabulary. However, the frequent use of δίψυχος language by the above authors argues against the opinion of Hort, James, 12 and Mayor, James, 42 who contend that James himself coined the term. Cf. Marshall (Laws), "Διψυχος," 349.

[44]Dibelius and Greeven, James, 31. Cf. also Martin Dibelius, Der Hirt des Hermas, 529.

[45]Cf. Carrington, Primitive Catechism, 42-43. Davies, Setting, 370 is correct when he states that Carrington (and Selwyn) have "too much systematized what was often fluid and amorphous, but their data do at least reveal clearly what the main body of that teaching was which was transmitted through the medium of catechesis."

area.[46] If underneath all these documents are the teachings of the church at Rome, then faith and works, faith and doubt with regards to prayer, double-mindedness and wisdom, and wealth and poverty were subjects of lively discussion in Rome. If we assume an authorship by James of Jerusalem, then the Epistle of James would have arrived in Rome sometime near the death of James and maybe in response to certain discussions happening there. The Epistle of James was known and used in Rome (by Hermas, for example) until it lost its popularity and was not included in the Muritorian Canon. Although not always able to account for the commonalities of perspective, this appendix has established the presence of a common ethical tradition which James and the other prominent teachers of the church share.

[46]If the latter is the case, then double-mindedness became a standard phrase in Rome to describe the moral laxity which began to cool the initial firey spirit of the Christian movement.

TABLE OF ABBREVIATIONS

I. Apostolic Fathers:

Barn.	The Epistle of Barnabas
1 Cl.	1 Clement (of Rome), To the Corinthians
2 Cl.	2 Clement or An Ancient Homily
Did.	Didache or The Teaching of the Twelve Apostles
Dg.	The Epistle to Diognetus
Herm.	The Shepherd of Hermas
Mand.	The Shepherd of Hermas, Mandates
Sim.	The Shepherd of Hermas, Similitudes
Vis.	The Shepherd of Hermas, Visions
Ig.	Ignatius
Eph.	To the Ephesians
Mag.	To the Magnesians
Phld.	To the Philadelphians
Pol.	To Polycarp
Rom.	To the Romans
Smyr.	To the Smyrneans
Trall.	To the Trallians
Pol. Phil.	Polycarp, To the Philippians

II. Ancient Writers:

Cicero	
Parad.	*Paradoxa Stoicorum*
Cl. Alex.	Clement of Alexandria
Dives	*Quis Dives Salvetur*; Who is the Rich that shall be Saved?
Paed.	*Paedagogus*; The Instructor
Strom.	*Stromateis*; The Stromata or Miscellanies
Epict.	Epictetus
Diss.	Arrian's Discourses of Epictetus
Epiph.	Epiphanius
Adv. *Haer*.	*Adversus Haereses*; Against Heresies
Eus.	Eusebius
Adv. *Haer*.	*Adversus Haereses*; Against Heresies
HE	*Historia Ecclesiastica*; Ecclesiastical History
Dem. *Ev*.	*Demonstration Evangelica*; Demonstration of the Gospel
Iren.	Irenaeus
Adv. *Haer*.	*Adversus Haereses*; Against Heresies
Jos.	Josephus
Ant.	Jewish Antiquities
Bell.	*Bellum*; War
Vita	The Life of Flavius Josephus
Just.	Justin Martyr
1 Apol.	First Apology
2 Apol.	Second Apology
Dial.	Dialogue with Trypho the Jew

Orig.	Origen
Cels.	Contra Celsum; Against Celsius
Hom.	Homilies
Joann.	In Johannem Commentarius; Commentary on John's gospel
Mt.	Commentariorum in Mt., Libri 10-17; Commentary on the Gospel of Matthew
Rom.	Commentary on Romans
Philo	
Abr.	De Abrahamo; On Abraham
Conf. Ling.	De Confusione Linguarum; On the Confusion of Tongues
Dec.	De Decalogo; On the Decalogue
Deus. Immut.	Quod Deus Immutabilis sit; On the Unchangeableness of God
Ebr.	De Ebrietate; On Drunkenness
Flacc.	In Flaccum; On Flaccus
Fug.	De Fugo et Inventione; On Flight and Finding
Leg. Alleg.	Legum Allegoriae; Allegorical Interpretation
Mut. Nom.	De Mutatione Nominum; On the Change of Names
Omn. Prob. Lib.	Quod Omnis Probus Liber sit; Every Good Man is Free
Op. Mund.	De Opificio Mundi; On the Creation of the World
Post. Cain.	De Posteritate Caini; On the Posterity and Exile of Cain
Praem. Poen.	De Praemiis et Poenis; On Rewards and Punishments
Rer. Div. Her.	Quis Rerum Divinarum Heres; Who is the Heir?
Sac. Abel.	De Sacrificiis Abelis et Caini; On the Sacrifices of Abel and Cain
Sobr.	De Sobrietate; On Sobriety
Som.	De Somniis; On Dreams
Spec. Leg.	De Specialibus Legibus; On the Special Laws
Vit. Mos.	De Vita Mosis; The Life of Moses
Plato	
Her.	Heraditus
Phaed.	Phaedrus
Rep.	Republic
Theaet.	Theaetetus
Plutarch	
Tranq.	De Tranquillate Animi; On Tranquility of Mind
Ps.-Athan.	Pseudo-Athanasius
Quaest. ad Ant.	Quaestiones ad Antiochum
Ps.-Phoc.	The Sentences of Pseudo-Phocylides
Ps.-Plato	Pseudo-Plato
Def.	Definitiones
Seneca	
Ep.	Epistulae Morales; The Epistles of Seneca
Vit. Beat.	De Vita Beata; On the Happy Life
Tert.	Tertullian
Adv. Iud.	Adversus Iudaeos; Against the Jews
Adv. Marc.	Adversus Marcionem; Contra Marcion
Cult. Fem.	De Cultu Feminarum; The Apparel of Women
Monog	De Monogamia; On Monogamy
Pat.	De Patientia; On Patience
Pud.	De Pudicitia; On Modesty

III. Books, Series, and Periodicals:

APOT	The Apocrypha and Pseudepigrapha of the Old Testament, R.H. Charles, 2 Vols.
BAG	Bauer, Arndt, and Gingrich, A Greek Lexicon of the New Testament, 1957 ed.
BAGD	Bauer, Arndt, Gingrich, and Danker, A Greek Lexicon of the New Testament, 1979 ed.
BDF	Blass, Debrunner, and Funk, A Greek Grammar of the New Testament
BFTh	Beiträge zür Förderung der christlichen Theologie
Bib.	Biblica
BJGZ	Beilage zum Jahresberichte des Gymnasiums zu Zittau
BJRL	Bulletin of the John Rylands Library
BTr	Bible Translator
BZ	Biblische Zeitschrift
CBQ	Catholic Biblical Quarterly
Con. Neot.	Coniectanea Neotestamentica
CQ	Constructive Quarterly
CQR	Church Quarterly Review
EvQ	Evangelical Quarterly
EvTh	Evangelische Theologie
Ex	The Expositor
ExT	Expository Times
GCS	Die Griechischen Christlichen Schriftsteller
HCNT	Hand-Commentar zum Neuen Testament
HNT	Handbuch zum Neuen Testament
HTR	Harvard Theological Review
ICC	International Critical Commentary
ISBE	The International Standard Bible Encyclopaedia
JBL	Journal of Biblical Literature
JQR	Jewish Quarterly Review
JPh	Journal of Philology
JR	Journal of Religion
JrDTh	Jahrbücher für Deutsche Theologie
JrPrTh	Jahrbücher für Protestantische Theologie
JSNT	Journal for the Study of the New Testament
JSS	Journal of Semitic Studies
JThS	Journal of Theological Studies
KEK	Kritisch-exegetischer Kommentar über das Neue Testament
KNT	Kommentar zum Neuen Testament
LCL	Loeb Classical Library
LThJ	Lutheran Theological Journal
MPG	J.P. Migne, Patrologia Graeca
MPL	J.P. MIgne, Patrologia Latina
NCBC	New Century Bible Commentary
NF	Neue Folge
NHL	The Nag Hammadi Library, ed. James M. Robinson
NICNT	New International Commentary on the New Testament
NIGTC	New International Greek Testament Commentary
NovT	Novum Testamentum
NTD	Das Neue Testament Deutsch
NTS	New Testament Studies

OT Pseud.	*The Old Testament Pseudepigrapha*, ed James H. Charlesworth, 2 Vols.
PRR	*The Presbyterian and Reformed Review*
PrKZ	*Protestantische Kirchenzeitung*
PVTG	Pseudepigrapha Veteris Testamenti Graece, ed. A.M. Denis and M. de Jonge
RB	*Revue Biblique*
RCh	*Revue Chrétienne*
REx	*The Review and Expositor*
RGG	*Die Religion in Geschichte und Gegenwart*
RHE	*Revue d'Histoire Ecclésiastique*
RHR	*Revue d'Histoire des Religions*
RTK	*Roczniki Teologicano-kanoniczne*
SBL	Society of Biblical Literature
SC	Sources Chrétiennes
SE	*Studia Evangelica*
SJTh	*Scottish Journal of Theology*
SNT	Supplements to Novum Testamentum
StrB	Strack und Billerbeck, *Kommentar zum Neuen Testament*, 5 Vols.
STh	*Studia Theologica*
SVTP	Studia in Veteris Testamenti Pseudepigrapha
SWJTh	*Southwestern Journal of Theology*
TDNT	*Theological Dictionary of the New Testament*, ed. Gerhard Kittel and Gerhard Friedrich, 10 Vols.
Th	*Theology*
ThD	*Theology Digest*
ThG	*Theologie und Glaube*
Th. Handk. NT	Theologischer Handkommentar zum Neuen Testament
ThLBl	*Theologisches Literaturblatt*
ThLZ	*Theologische Literaturzeitung*
ThQ	*Theologische Quartalschrift*
ThSKr	*Theologische Studien und Kritiken*
ThT	*Theologische Tijdschrift*
ThZ	*Theologische Zeitschrift*
ThZS	*Theologische Zeitschrift aus der Schweiz*
TU	Texte und Untersuchungen zur Geschichte der altchristlichen Literatur
TZTh	*Tübinger Zeitschrift für Theologie*
ZKG	*Zeitschrift für Kirchengeschichte*
ZKTh	*Zeitschrift für katholische Theologie*
ZNW	*Zeitschrift für die neutestamentliche Wissenschaft und die Kunde der älteren Kirsche*
ZWTh	*Zeitschrift fUr wissenschaftliche Theologie*

IV. Other Abbreviations:

ASV	American Standard Version
b.	Babylonian Talmud
c.	circa; approximately
cf.	confer; compare
ch.	chapter
diss.	dissertation
ed.	editor, edited by
e.g.	exempli gratia; for example
esp.	especially, in particular
f,ff	following
i.e.	id est; that is
JB	Jerusalem Bible
KJV	King James Version
LXX	Septuagint
MT	Masoretic Text
n.	note, footnote
NASB	New American Standard Bible
NEB	New English Bible
NIV	New International Version
par.	parallel(s) in other Synoptic gospels
p(p)	page(s)
RSV	Revised Standard Version
s.v.	sub verbo; under the word
TEV	Today's English Version
t.r.	textus receptus
tr.	translator
trans.	translation
Un.	University
Vol(s).	Volumn(s)
vs.	versus; in opposition to
v(v).	verse(s)
x	number of occurrences, times

BIBLIOGRAPHY

Aalen, S. "St Luke's Gospel and the Last Chapters of 1 Enoch." NTS 13(1966-67): 1-13.

Adamson, James B. The Epistle of James. NICNT. Grand Rapids: Eerdmans, 1976.

________. An Inductive Approach to the Epistle of James. Unpub. diss. Cambridge, 1954.

________. James: The Man and His Message. Grand Rapids: Eerdmans, prepublication edition.

Aland, Kurt. "Der Herrenbruder Jakobus und der Jakobusbrief." ThLZ 69(1944): 97-104.

________. s.v. "Jakobusbrief." RGG. 1959 ed.

Alford, Henry. The Greek Testament. Vols. 1-4. London: Rivertons, 1859.

Allen, Willoughby C. Gospel Acc. to S. Matthew. ICC. Edinburgh: Clark, 1912.

Allison, Dale C. Jr. "The Pauline Epistles and the Synoptic Gospels: The Pattern of the Parallels." NTS 28(1982): 1-32.

The Ante-Nicene Fathers. Vols. 1-10. ed. Alexander Roberts and James Donaldson. Grand Rapids: Eerdmans, reprinted 1970's and 80's.

Apocalypsis Henochi Graece. ed. Matthew Black. PVTG. ed. Albert M. Denis and Marinus deJonge. Leiden: Brill, 1970.

Audet, Jean P. La Didache: instructions des apostres. Etudes bibliques. Paris: Gabalda, 1958.

Baasland, Ernst. "Der Jakobusbrief als neutestamentliche Weisheitsschrift." STh 36(1982): 119-132.

The Babylonian Talmud. ed. I. Epstein. London: Soncino, 1935.

Bacon, Benjamin. "Jesus and the Law." JBL 47(1928): 203-231.

Bammel, Ernest. s.v. πτωχός. TDNT VI: 885-915.

Barth, Gerhard. "Matthew's Understanding of the Law." in Bornkamm, Gunther; Barth, Gerhard; and Held, Heinz J. Tradition and Interpretation in Matthew. tr. Percy Scott. Philadelphia: Westminster, 1963.

Bauckham, Richard. "The Study of Gospel Traditions Outside the Canonical Gospels: Problems and Prospects." Gospel Perspectives. ed. David Wenham. Sheffield: JSOT, 1985, 5: 369-403.

Bauer, Walter; Arndt, William F.; and Gingrich, F. Wilbur. A Greek-English Lexicon of the New Testament and Other Early Christian Literature. 2nd ed. F. Wilbur Gingrich and Frederick W. Danker. Chicago: Un. of Chicago, 1979.

Bauernfeind, Otto. s.v. σής. TDNT VII: 275-278.

Beasley-Murray, George R. The General Epistles: James, 1 Peter, Jude, and 2 Peter. Bible Guides. London: Lutterworth, 1965.

Bellinzoni, Arthur J. The Sayings of Jesus in the Writings of Justin Martyr. SNT. Leiden: Brill, 1967.

Berger, Klaus. Die Gesetzesauslegung Jesu. Assen: Neukirchener, 1972.

Bertram, George. s.v. ὕφος. TDNT VIII: 602-613.

Best, Ernest. "1 Peter and the Gospel Tradition." NTS 16(1969-70): 95-113.

Beyschlag, Willibald. Der Brief des Jacobus. KEK. Göttingen: Vandenhoeck und Ruprecht, 1897.

________. "Der Jakobusbrief als urchristliches Geschichtsdenkmal." ThSKr 48(1874): 105-166.

Bishop, Eric F.F. "Three and a Half Years?" ExT 61(1949-50): 126f.

Black, Matthew. An Aramaic Approach to the Gospels and Acts. Oxford: Clarendon, 1954.

Blackman, Edwin C. The Epistle of James. Torch Bible Commentaries. London: SCM, 1957.

Blass, Friedrich; Debrunner, Albert; and Funk, Robert W. A Greek Grammar of the New Testament and Other Early Christian Literature. Chicago: Un. Press, 1961.

Blom, A.H. De brief van Jacobus. Dordrecht: Braat, 1869.

Blondel, Jean-Luc. "Theology and Paraenesis in James." ThD 28 (1980): 253-256.

Bowker, John. The Targums and Rabbinic Literature. Cambridge: Un. Press, 1969.

Bradley, David G. "The *Topos* as a Form in the Pauline Paraenesis." JBL 72(1953): 238-246.

Braumann, Georg. "Der Theologische Hintergrund des Jakobusbriefes." ThZ 18(1962): 401-410.

Braun, Herbert. Spätjüdisch-häretischer und frühchristlicher Radikalismus. Vols. 1-2. Tübingen: Mohr, 1957.

________. s.v. ποιέω. TDNT VI: 458-484.

Brooks, James A. "The Place of James in the New Testament Canon." SWJTh 12(1969): 41-55.

Brown, John P. "Synoptic Parallels in the Epistles and Form-History." NTS 10(1963): 27-48.

Brückner, Wilhelm. "Zur Kritik des Jakobusbriefes." ZWTh 17 (1874): 530-541.

Büchsel, Friedrich. s.v. διακρίνω. TDNT III: 946-949.

Bultmann, Rudolf. s.v. ἔλεος. TDNT II: 477-487.

________. s.v. πένθος. TDNT VI: 40-43.

________. History of the Synoptic Tradition. tr. John Marsh. New York: Harper and Row, 1963.

________. Der Stil der paulinischen Predigt und die Kynischstoische Diatribe. Göttingen: Vandenhoeck und Ruprecht, 1910.

________. Theology of the New Testament. Vols. 1-2. tr. Kendrick Grobel. London: SCM, 1951, 1955.

Bunsen, Christian C.J. Vollständiges Bibelwerk für die Gemeinde. Vols. 1-8. Leipzig: Brockhaus, 1866.

Burney, Charles F. The Poetry of our Lord. Oxford: Clarendon, 1925.

Cadoux, Arthur. The Thought of St. James. London: Clarke, 1944.

Calvin, John. Commentaries on the Catholic Epistles. tr. John Owen. Grand Rapids: Eerdmans, 1948.

Campenhausen, Hans von. The Formation of the Christian Bible. tr. J.A. Baker. Philadelphia: Fortress, 1972.

Cantinat, Jean. "The Catholic Epistles." in Robert, André and Feuillet, André. Introduction to the New Testament. tr. Patrick Skehan. New York: Deschee, 1965.

________. Les Epitres de Saint Jacques et de Saint Jude. Sources bibliques. Paris: Gabalda, 1973.

Carrington, Philip. The Primitive Christian Catechism. Cambridge: Un. Press, 1940.

Carroll, Kenneth L, "The Place of James in the Early Church." BJRL 44(1961-62): 49-67.

Chaine, Joseph. L'Epitre de Saint Jacques. Etudes bibliques. Paris: Gabalda, 1927.

Charles, Robert H. The Apocrypha and Pseudepigrapha of the Old Testament in English. Vols. 1-2. Oxford: Clarendon, 1963.

________. The Greek Versions of the Testaments of the Twelve Patriarchs. Oxford: Clarendon, 1908.

Charlesworth, James H. The Old Testament Pseudepigrapha and the New Testament. Cambridge: Un. Press, 1985.

Chase, Frederic H. "Peter, First Epistle." A Dictionary of the Bible. ed. James Hastings. 1900 ed.

Cohn, Leopold and Wendland, Paul. Philonis Alexandrini Opera Quae Supersunt. Vols. 1-7. Berlin: DeGruyter, 1930.

Connolly, Richard H. "The Didache in Relation to the Epistle of Barnabas." JThS 33(1932): 237-253.

Conzelmann, Hans. s.v. χαίρω. TDNT IX: 359-372.

Cooper, Robert M. "Prayer: a Study in Matthew and James." *Encounter* 29(1968): 268-277.
Court, John M. "The Didache and St. Matthew's Gospel." *SJTh* 34 (1981): 109-120.
Craddock, J.G. "A Possible Connection between the Letter of James and the Events of John 7 and 8." *SE* 7:141-144. Berlin: Akademic-Verlag, 1982.
Credner, Karl A. *Einleitung in das Neue Testament*. Halle: Waisenhauses, 1836.
Dalman, Gustaf H. *Die Worte Jesu: mit Berücksichtigung des nachkanonischen jüdischen Schrifttums und der aramäischen Sprache erördert*. Leipzig: Hinrichs, 1930.
Danby, Herbert. *The Mishnah*. Oxford: Un. Press, 1933.
Daniélou, Jean. *The Theology of Jewish Christianity*. tr. John A. Baker. Philadelphia: Westminster, 1964.
Dautzenberg, Gerhard. "Ist das Schwurverbot Mt. 5, 33-37; Jak. 5,12 ein Beispiel für die Torakritik Jesu?" *BZ* 25(1981): 47-66.
Davids, Peter H. *The Epistle of James*. NIGTC. Grand Rapids: Eerdmans, 1982.
________. "James and Jesus." *Gospel Perspectives*. ed. David Wenham. Sheffield: JSOT, 1985, 5:63-84.
________. "Jesus-Paraenesis in the Catholic Epistles." read at the Society of Biblical Literature Meeting, Dec. 1984.
________. "Tradition and Citation in the Epistle of James." *Scripture, Tradition, and Interpretation*. ed. W.W. Gasque and W.S. Laser, Grand Rapids: Eerdmans, 1978, 113-126.
Davidson, Samuel. *An Introduction to the Study of the New Testament*. Vols. 1-2. London: Kegan, 1894.
Davies, William D. *The Setting of the Sermon on the Mount*. Cambridge: Un. Press, 1964.
________. *Paul and Rabbinic Judaism*. London: SPCK, 1955.
Davison, James E. "*Anomia* and the Question of an Antinomian Polemic in Matthew." *JBL* 104(1985): 617-635.
de Jonge, Marinus and Hollander, Harm W. *The Testaments of the Twelve Patriarchs: A Commentary*. SVTP8. Leiden: Brill, 1985.
________; Hollander, Harm W.; de Jonge, H.J.; Korteweg, Th. *The Testaments of the Twelve Patriarchs: A Critical Edition of the Greek Text*. PVTG1.2. Leiden: Brill, 1978.
________. "Christian Influence in the Testaments of the Twelve Patriarchs." *Studies on the Testaments of the Twelve Patriarchs*. Leiden: Brill, 1975, 183-246.
________. *Testamenta XII Patriarcharum*. PVTG1. Leiden: Brill, 1970.
________. *The Testaments of the Twelve Patriarchs: A Study of their Text, Composition, and Origin*. Assen: van Gorcum, 1953.
de Wette, Wilhelm M.L. *Kurze Erklarung der Apostelgeschichte*. Leipzig: Weidmann, 1848.
Dibelius, Martin. *Der Brief des Jakobus*. KEK. Göttingen: Vandenhoeck und Ruprecht, 1921.
________. *A Fresh Approach to the New Testament and Early Christian Literature*. New York: Scribner, 1936.
________. *From Tradition to Gospel*. tr. Bertram Woolf. London: Redwood, 1971.
________. *Der Hirt des Hermas*. HNT. Die Apostolischen Väter IV. Tübingen: Mohr, 1923.
________. *James: A Commentary on the Epistle of James*. Hermaneia. Revised by Heinrich Greeven. tr. Michael Williams. Philadelphia: Fortress, 1976.
Dittmar, Wilhelm. *Vetus Testamentus in Novo: Die alttestamentlichen Parallelen des Neuen Testaments*. Göttingen: Vandenhoeck und Ruprecht, 1903.
Dods, Marcus. *An Introduction to the New Testament*. London: Hodder and Stoughton, 1889.
Doty, William G. *Letters in Primitive Christianity*. Philadelphia: Fortress, 1973.
Draper, Jonathon. "The Jesus Tradition in the Didache." *Gospel Perspectives*. ed. David Wenham. Sheffield: JSOT, 1984, 5:269-288.

Dungan, David L. The Sayings of Jesus in the Churches of Paul. Philadelphia: Fortress, 1971.

DuPlessis, Paul J. ΤΕΛΕΙΟΣ : The Idea of Perfection in the New Testament. Kampen: Kok, 1954.

Easton, Burton S. "The Epistle of James." The Interpreter's Bible. New York: Abingdon, 1957, XII: 3-74.

Eichholz, Georg. Glaube und Werke Bei Paulus und Jakobus. Theologische Existenz Heute. NF 88. München: Kaiser, 1961.

Eleder, P. Felix. Jakobusbrief und Bergpredigt. Unpubl. diss. Wein, 1966.

Elliott-Binns, Leonard E. Galilean Christinaity: Studies in Biblical Theology. London: SCM, 1956.

_______. "James 1:18: Creation or Redemption?" NTS 3(1956-57): 148-161.

Ellis, E. Earle. The Gospel of Luke. NCBC. London: Oliphants, 1974.

_______. Paul's Use of the Old Testament. Grand Rapids: Baker, 1957.

Ermoni, V. s.v. "Jacques (Épitre de Saint)." Dictionaire de la Bible. III. 1910 ed.

Feine, Paul. Der Jakobusbrief nach Lehranschauungen und Entstehungsverhältnissen. Eisenach: Wilckens, 1893.

Ferris, T.E.S. "The Epistle of James in Relation to 1 Peter." CQR 128(1939): 303-308.

Feuillet, André. "Le sens du mot Parousie dans l'Evangile de Matthieu: Comparaison entre Matth. XXIV et Jac V, 1-11." Studies in the Background of the New Testament and its Eschatology. ed. W.D. Davies and D. Daube. Cambridge: Un. Press, 1956, 261-280.

Fichtner, Johannes. s.v. ὀργή. TDNT V: 394-412.

Flusser, David. "Do not commit adultery, Do not murder." Textus. ed. S. Talmon. Jerusalem: Magnes, 1964, IV: 220-224.

Foerster, Werner. s.v. εἰρήνη. TDNT II: 406-417.

Forbes, P.B.R. "The Structure of the Epistle of James." EQ 44 (1972): 147-153.

Francis, Fred O. "The Form and Function of the Opening and Closing Paragraphs of James and 1 John." ZNW 61(1970): 110-126.

Fry Euan. "The Testing of Faith: A Study of the Structure of the Book of James." BTr 29(1978): 427-435.

Fulford, Henry W. "James." A Dictionary of Christ and the Gospels. ed. James Hastings. 1906 ed.

Funk, Franciscus X. ed. Didascalia et Constitutiones Apostolorum. Paderbornae: Schoeningh, 1905.

Furnish, Victor P. The Love Command in the New Testament. Nashville: Abingdon, 1972.

_______. The Moral Teaching of Paul. Nashville: Abingdon, 1979.

_______. Theology and Ethics in Paul. Nashville: Abingdon, 1968.

Gass, D.W. "Betrachtungen über dem Jacobusbrief." PrKZ (1873): 956-965,981-986,1002-1009.

Gaugusch, Ludwig. Der Lehrgehalt der Jakobusepistel: Eine Exegetische Studie. Freiburg: Herder, 1914.

Gerhardsson, Birger. Memory and Manuscript: Oral Tradition and Written Transmission in Rabbinic Judaism and Early Christianity. tr. Eric Scharpe. Uppsala: Almquist and Wiksells, 1961.

_______. The Origins of the Gospel Traditions. trans. of Evangeliernas Förhistoria. London: SCM, 1979.

_______. Tradition and Transmission in Early Christianity. Con. Neot. XX. tr. Eric Sharpe. Lund: Haken Ohlssans, 1964.

Gerrevink, G. van. De brief van Jakobus in zijne denkbeelden. Utrecht: Kemink, 1875.

Gertner, M. "Midrashim in the New Testament." JSS 7(1962): 267-292.

Glover, Richard. "The Didache's Quotations and the Synoptic Gospels." NTS 5(1958-59): 12-29.

Goodspeed, Edgar J. The Apocrypha. New York: Random House, 1959.

________. An Introduction to the New Testament. Chicago: Un. Press, 1937.

Gordon, Robert P. "ΚΑΙ ΤΟ ΤΕΛΟΣ ΚΥΡΙΟΥ ΕΙΔΕΤΕ (JAS. V. 11)." JThS 26(1975): 91-95.

Gotaas, Daniel S. The Old Testament in the Epistle of the Hebrews, the Epistle of James, and the Epistle of Peter. Unpub. diss. Northern Baptist Theological Seminary. Chicago, 1958.

Grafe, Eduard. Die Stellung und Bedeutung des Jakobusbriefes in der Entwicklung des Urchristentums. Tübingen: Mohr, 1904.

Grant, Robert M. A Historical Introduction to the New Testament. New York: Harper and Row, 1963.

Grimm, Wilibald, "Zur Einleitung in den Brief des Jacobus." ZWTh 13(1870): 377-394.

Gromacki, Robert G. New Testament Survey. Grand Rapids: Baker, 1974.

Grosheide, Frederick W. De Brief aan de Hebreën en de Brief van Jakobus. Commentaar op het Nieuwe Testament. Amsterdam: Bottenburg, 1927 and Kampen, Kok, 1955.

Grundmann, Walter. Das Evangelium nach Lukas. Th. Handk. NT. Berlin: Evangel, 1974.

________. Das Evangelium nach Matthäus. Th. Handk. NT. Berlin: Evangel, 1972.

________. s.v. ταπεινος. TDNT VIII: 1-26.

Gryglewicz, Feliks. "L'Épitre de St. Jacques et l'Évangile de St. Matthieu." RTK 8,3(1961): 33-55.

Guelich, Robert A. The Sermon on the Mount. Waco, Texas: Word, 1982.

Gundry, Robert H. Matthew: A Commentary on his Literary and Theological Art. Grand Rapids: Eerdmans, 1982.

________. "'Verba Christi' in 1 Peter: Their Implications Concerning the Authorship of 1 Peter and the Authority of the Gospel Tradition." NTS 13(1966): 336-350.

Gutbrod, Walter. s.v. νόμος. TDNT IV: 1036-1091, esp. 1080-1082.

Guthrie, Donald. New Testament Introduction. London: Tyndale, 1970.

Hadidian, Dikran Y. "Palestinian Pictures in the Epistle of James." ExT 63(1952): 227-228.

Hagner, Donald A. "The Sayings of Jesus in the Apostolic Fathers and Justin Martyr." Gospel Perspectives. ed. David Wenham. Sheffield: JSOT, 1984, 5:233-268.

Hahn, Ferdinard. "Die christologische Begründung urchristlicher Paränese." ZNW 72(1981): 88-99.

Halson, B.R. "The Epistle of James: 'Christian Wisdom?'" SE 4:308-314. TU 102. Berlin: Akademie, 1968.

Hamaan, Henry P. "Faith and Works in Paul and James." LThJ 9 (1975): 33-41.

Harder, Gunther. s.v. πονηρός. TDNT VI: 546-566.

Harnack, Adolf von. Die Chronologie der Altchristlichen bis Eusebius I. Leipzig: Hinrichs, 1897.

Harrison, Everett F. Introduction to the New Testament. Grand Rapids: Eerdmans, 1971.

Hartmann, Gert. "Der Aufbau des Jakobusbriefes." ZKTh 66(1942): 63-70.

Haslehurst, R.S.T. "The Fifth Gospel." Th 35(1937): 96-103.

Hauck, Friedrich. Der Brief des Jakobus. KNT. Leipzig: Deichert, 1926.

________. s.v. μοιχεύω. TDNT IV: 729-735.

Haupt, Erich. "F. Spitta, der Brief des Jakobus." ThSKr 69(1896): 747-768.

Hayes, Doremus. "James, Ep. of." The International Standand Bible Encyclopaedia. 1955.

Hennecke, Edgar and Schneemelcher, Wilhelm. New Testament Apocrypha. tr. A.J.B. Higgins. Vols. 1-2. Philadelphia: Westminster, 1963.

Henshaw, Thomas. New Testament Literature in the Light of Modern Scholarship. London: Allen and Urwin, 1952.

Hiebert, D. Edmund. The Epistle of James. Chicago: Moody, 1979.

Hilgenfeld, Adolf. "Der Brief des Jakobus." ZWTh 16(1873): 1-33.

________. "Das Urchristenthum und seine neuesten Bearbeitungen." ZWTh 1(1858): esp. 405f.

Hill, David. The Gospel of Matthew. NCBC. London: Marshall, Morgan, and Scott, 1972.
Holtzmann, Heinrich J. "Die Zeitlage des Jakobusbriefes." ZWTh 25(1882): 292-310.
_______. "Jakobusbrief." Bibel-Lexikon III. ed. Daniel Schenkel. Leipzig: Brodhaus, 1871.
_______. Lehrbuch der historisch-kritischen Einleitung in das Neue Testament. Freiburg: Mohr, 1892.
_______. Lehrbuch der neutestamentlichen Theologie. Tübingen: Mohr, 1911.
_______. Die Synotiker. HCNT 1. Tübingen: Mohr, 1901.
Hoppe, Rudolf. Der theologische Hintergrund des Jakobusbriefes. Wurzburg: Echter, 1977.
Horst, Friedrich. "Der Eid im Alten Testament." EvTh 17(1957): 366-384.
Horst, Pieter van der. The Sentences of Pseudo-Phocylides. SVTP 4. Leiden: Brill, 1978.
Hort, Fenton J.A. The Epistle of St. James. London: MacMillan, 1909.
Houlden, James L. Ethics and the New Testament. London: Mowbrays, 1979.
Hunter, Archibald M. Introducing the New Testament. Philadelphia: Westminster, 1947.
Hunzinger, Claus-Hunno. s.v. συκῆ. TDNT VII: 751-757.
Huther, Johannus E. Kritisch exegetisches Handbuch über den Brief des Jakobus. Meyer's Kommentar zum Neuen Testament. Göttingen: Vandenhoeck und Ruprecht, 1865.
Jeremias, Joachim. New Testament Theology. tr. John Bowden. New York: Scribner, 1971.
_______. s.v. ʼΗλ(ε)ίας. TDNT II: 928-941.
_______. "Jac. 4,5: *epipothei*." ZNW 50(1959): 137-138.
_______. The Parables of Jesus. tr. S.H. Hooke. London: SCM, 1972.
Johnson, Luke T. "The Use of Leviticus 19 in the Letter of James." JBL 101(1982): 391-401.
Jones, Peter R. "Approaches to the Study of the Book of James." REx 66(1960): 425-434.
Jülicher, Adolf. Einleitung in das Neue Testament. Tübingen: Mohr, 1906.
Kamlah, Erhard. Die Form der katalogischen Paränese im Neuen Testament. Tübingen: Mohr, 1964.
Kennedy, Harry A.A. "The Hellenistic Atmosphere of the Epistle of James." Ex 82(1911): 37-52.
Kern, Friedrich H. Der Brief Jacobi. Tübingen: Fues, 1838.
_______. "Der Charakter und Ursprung des Briefs Jakobi." TZTh (1835, 2 Heft): 3-132.
Keulers, J. De Katholieke Brieven en het Boek der Openbaring. Roermand: Romen, 1956.
Kilpatrick, George D. The Origins of the Gospel Acc. to St. Matthew. Oxford: Clarendon, 1946.
Kirk, James A. "The Meaning of Wisdom in James: Examination of a Hypothesis." NTS 16(1969): 24-38.
Kirn, Otto, "Noch einmal Jakobus 4,5." ThSKr 77(1904): 593-604.
Kistemaker, Simon. The Gospels in Current Study. Grand Rapids: Baker, 1972.
Kittel, Gerhard. "Der Brief des Jakobus." (review of Martin Dibelius, Der Brief des Jakobus). ThLBl 44(1923): 3-7.
_______. "Der geschichtliche Ort des Jakobusbriefes." ZNW 41 (1942): 71-105.
_______. "Der Jakobusbrief und die Apostolischen Väter." ZNW 43 (1950-51): 54-112.
_______. "Die Stellung des Jakobus zu Judentum und Heidenchristentum." ZNW 30(1931): 154-156.
_______. s.v λέγω. TDNT IV: 91-136.
Kline, Leslie L. The Sayings of Jesus in the Pseudo-Clementine Homilies. Dissertation Series 14. Missoula, Scholars, 1975.
Klostermann, Erich. Das Matthäus-Evangelium. HNT. Tübingen: Mohr, 1938.
Knowling, Richard J. The Epistle of St. James. London: Methven, 1904.
Knox, Wilfred L. "The Epistle of St. James." JThS 46(1945): 10-17.
Köhler, Albert. Glaube und Werke im Jakobusbrief. BJGZ. Zittau: Menzel, 1913.
Köhler, Kaufmann, s.v. "James, General Epistle of." The Jewish Encyclopedia. 1925 ed.
Köster, Helmut. s.v. σπλάγνον. TDNT VI: 548-559.
_______. Synoptische Überlieferung bei den Apostolischen Vätern. TU 65. Berlin: Akademie, 1957.

Kraft, Robert. The Apostolic Fathers: Barnabas and the Didache. Vol. 3. New York: Nelson, 1965.

Kübel, Robert. Über das Verhältnis von Glauben und Werken bei Jakobus. Tübingen: Tübingen Un., 1880.

Kugelman, Richard. James and Jude. New Testament Message. Wilmington, Delaware: Glazier, 1980.

Kümmel, Werner G. Introduction to the New Testament. tr. Howard Kee. Nashville: Abingdon, 1975.

Kutsch, Ernst. "Der Eid der Essener." ThLZ 81(1956): 495-498.

_______. "Eure Rede aber sei ja ja, nein, nein." EvTh 20(1960): 206-218.

Ladd, George E. A Theology of the New Testament. Grand Rapids: Eerdmans, 1974.

Lane, William L. The Gospel According to Mark. NICNT. Grand Rapids: Eerdmans, 1974.

Laws, Sophie S. A Commentary on the Epistle of James. Black's New Testament Commentaries. London: Black, 1980.

_______. "Δίψυχος: A Local Term?" SE 6:348-351. Berlin: Akademie, 1973.

_______. "The Doctrinal Basis for the Ethics of James." SE 7: 299-306. Berlin: Akademie, 1982.

_______. "Does Scripture Speak in Vain? A Reconsideration of James IV. 5." NTS 20(1973-74): 210-215.

Layton, Bentley. "The Sources, Date, and Transmission of Didache 1,3b-2,1." HTR 61(1968): 343-383.

Lechler, Gotthard. Das apostolische und das nachapostolische Zeitalter. Stuttgart: Besser, 1857.

Leconte, R. Les Épitres Catholiques. Paris: Cerf, 1961.

Leon, Harry J. The Jews of Ancient Rome. Philadelphia: Jewish Publication Society, 1960.

Lieberman, Saul. Greek in Jewish Palestine. New York: Jewish Theological Seminary, 1942.

Lightfoot, Joseph B. The Apostolic Fathers. ed. J.R. Harmer. Grand Rapids: Baker, 1978.

Littmann, Enno. "Torrey's Buch über die vier Evangelien." ZNW 34(1935): 20-34.

Lohse, Eduard. "Glaube und Werke: Zur Theologie des Jakobusbriefes." ZNW 48(1957): 1-21.

_______. "Paränese und Kerygma im 1 Petrusbrief." ZNW 45(1954): 68-87.

Lohmeyer, Ernst. Das Evangelium des Matthäus. Göttingen: Vandenhoeck, 1956.

Longenecker, Richard N. Biblical Exegesis in the Apostolic Period. Grand Rapids: Eerdmans. 1975.

Luck, Ulrich. Die Vollkommenheitsforderung der Bergpredigt: ein aktuelles Kapitel der Theologie des Matthäus. München: Kaiser, 1968.

Maier, Gerhard. "Jesustradition im 1 Petrusbrief?" Gospel Perspectives. ed. David Wenham. Sheffield: JSOT, 1985, 5:85-128.

Malherbe, Abraham. Social Aspects of Early Christianity. Baton Rouge: LSU Press, 1977.

Manen, Willem C. van. "Jacobus Geen Christen?" ThT 31(1897): 398-427.

Manson, Thomas W. "The Sayings of Jesus," in Major, H.D.A.; Manson, T.W. and Wright, C.J. The Mission and Message of Jesus. London: MacMillan, 1940.

_______. The Sayings of Jesus. London: SCM, 1964.

Marshall, I. Howard. Commentary on Luke. NIGTC. Grand Rapids: Eerdmans, 1977.

Martin, Ralph P. "The Life-Setting of the Epistle of James in the Light of Jewish History." Biblical and Near Eastern Studies. ed. G.A. Tuttle. Grand Rapids: Eerdmans, 1978, 97-103.

_______. New Testament Foundations. Vos. 1-2. Grand Rapids: Eerdmans, 1978.

Marxsen, Willi. Introduction to the New Testament. tr. G. Buswell. Philadelphia: Fortress, 1968.

Massibieau, L. "L'Épitre de Jacques est-elle l'oeuvre d'un Chrétien?" RHR 32(1895): 249-283.

Mayor, Joseph B. The Epistle of St. James. London: MacMillan, 1892.

________. The Epistle of St. James. Grand Rapids: Baker, 1978 reprint from the 1897 edition.

McNeile, Alan H. An Introduction to the Study of the New Testament. ed. C.S.C. Williams. Oxford: Clarendon, 1953.

________. The Gospel Acc. to St. Matthew. London: MacMillan, 1955.

Meier, John P. Law and History in Matthew's Gospel. Rome: Biblical Institute, 1976.

Metzger, Bruce M. "The Formulas Introducing Quotations of Scripture in the NT and the Mishnah." JBL 70(1951): 297-307.

________. "The Language of the New Testament." The Interpreter's Bible. New York: Abingdon, 1951, VII: 43-59.

________. The Text of the New Testament: Its Transmission, Corruption, and Restoration. Oxford: Un. Press, 1968.

________. A Textual Commentary on the Greek New Testament. London: United Bible Societies, 1971.

Meyer, Arnold. Das Rätsel des Jacobusbriefes. Gießen: Topelmann, 1930.

Michaelis, Wilhelm. Einleitung in das Neue Testament. Bern: Evangel, 1946.

Michaels, J. Ramsey. "James -- The Royal Law." in Barker, Glenn W.; Lane, William L.; and Michaels, J. Ramsey. The New Testament Speaks. New York: Harper and Row, 1969.

Michel, Otto. s.v. ἰός. TDNT III: 334-336.

Michl, Johann. Die katholischen Briefe. Regensburger Neues Testament. Regensburg: Pustet, 1968.

________. "Der Spruch Jakobusbrief 4,5." Neutestamentliche Aufsatze (für J. Schmid). ed. J. Blinzler, O. Kuss. F. Mußner. Regensburg: Pustet, 1963, 167-174.

Midrash Rabbah. ed. H. Freedman and Maurice Simon. Vols 1-10. London: Soncino, 1939.

Mielziner, Moses. Introduction to the Talmud. New York: Bloch, 1968.

Minear, Paul S. "Yes or No, The Demand for Honesty in the Early Church." NovT. 13(1971): 1-13.

Mitton, Charles L. The Epistle of James. Grand Rapids: Eerdmans, 1966.

Moffatt, James A. An Introduction to the Literature of the New Testament. Edinburgh: Clarke, 1918.

________. The General Epistles. The Moffatt New Testament Commentary. London: Hodder and Stoughton, 1928.

________. The Historical New Testament. Edinburgh: Clarke, 1901.

Montefiore, Claude G. and Herbert Loewe. A Rabbinic Anthology. London: MacMillan, 1938.

Montefiore, Claude G. Rabbinic Literature and Gospel Teachings. London: MacMillan, 1930.

________. The Synoptic Gospels. London: MacMillan, 1927.

Moore, George F. Judaism in the First Centuries of the Christian Era. Cambridge: Harvard Un. Press, 1962.

Moule, Charles F.D. The Birth of the New Testament. London: Black, 1962.

________. An Idiom Book of New Testament Greek. Cambridge: Un. Press, 1959.

Moulton, James H. "The Epistle of James and the Sayings of Jesus." Ex 7,4(1907): 45-55.

________. A Grammar of New Testament Greek. Vols. 1-4. ed. Wilbert Howard and Nigel Turner. Edinburgh: Clark, 1979.

________. "Synoptic Studies: The Beatitudes." Ex 7,2(1906): 95-110.

Muilenburg, James. The Literary Relations of the Epistle of Barnabas and the Teaching of the Twelve Apostles. Marburg, Germany, 1929.

Mußner, Franz. Der Jakobusbrief. Herders Theologischer Kommentar Zum Neuen Testament. Freiburg: Herder, 1967.

The Nag Hammadi Library. ed. James M. Robinson. San Francisco: Harper and Row, 1977.

Nauck, Wolfgang. "Freude im Leiden." ZNW 46(1955): 68-80.

________. "*Lex inculpta* in der Sektenschrift." ZNW 46(1955): 138-140.

The New Testament in the Apostolic Fathers. Committee of the Oxford Society of Historical Theology. Oxford: Clarendon, 1905.

Nickelsburg, George W.E. "Riches, the Rich, and God's Judgment in 1 Enoch 92-105 and the Gospel according to Luke." NTS 25(1978-79): 324-344.

Nissen, Andreas. Gott und der Nächste im antiken Judentum. Tübingen: Mohr, 1974.

Nösgen, Karl F. "Der Ursprung und die Entstehung des dritten Evangeliums." ThSKr 53(1880): 49-140.

Nötscher, Friedrich. "Gesetz der Freiheit im NT und in der Mönchsgemeinde am Toten Meer." Bib 34 (1953): 193-194.

Oepke, Albrecht. s.v. ἀνήρ. TDNT I: 360-363.

Oesterley, William O.E. "The General Epistle of James." The Expositor's Greek Testament IV. Francker, Holland: Wever, 1910.

The Old Testament Pseudepigrapha. Vols 1-2. ed. James H. Charlesworth. New York: Doubleday, 1983.

Old Testament Quotations in the New Testament. Helps for Translators. ed. Robert Bratcher. London: United Bible Societies, 1967.

Orchard, J. Bernard. "Thessalonians and the Synoptic Gospels." Bib 19(1938): 19-42.

Palmer, Christian. "Die Moral des Jacobusbriefes." JrDTh 10(1865): 1-36.

Patrologia Graeca. ed. Jacques P. Migne. Vols. 1-162. Montrouge: Seu Petit, 1857.

Patrum Apostolicorum Opera. ed. Oscar de Gebhardt, Adolfus de Harnack, Theodorus Zahn. Lipsiae: Hinrichs, 1920.

Patry, Raoul. L'Epitre de Jacques dans ses rapports avec la prédication de Jésus. diss. Paris. Alencon: Guy, 1899.

Percy, Ernst. Die Botschaft Jesus. Lund: Gleerup, 1953.

Perdue, Leo G. "Paraenesis and the Epistle of James." ZNW 72 (1981): 241-256.

Perrin, Norman. The New Testament: An Introduction. New York: Jovanovich, 1974.

Pesch, Wilhelm. "Zur Exegese von Mt. 6, 19-21 und Lk. 12, 33-34." Bib 41(1960): 356-378.

Pfleiderer, Otto. Das Urchristentum: seine Schriften und Lehren II. Berlin: Riemer, 1862.

Piper, John. Love Your Enemies: Jesus' Love Command in the Synoptic Gospels and in the Early Christian Paraenesis. Cambridge: Un. Press, 1979.

Pisikta Rabbati. Vols. 1-2. tr. William G. Braude. New Haven: Yale Un. Press, 1968.

Plummer, Alfred. Gospel According to S. Matthew. London: Elliot Stock, 1909.

Plumptre, Edward H. St. James. Cambridge: Un. Press, 1901.

Pohill, John B. "The Life-Situation of the Book of James." REx 66 (1969): 369-378.

Popkes, Wiard. Adressaten, Situation und Form des Jakobusbriefes. Stuttgarter Bibelstudien 125/126. Stuttgart: Katholisches Bibelwerk, 1986.

Poss, Richard H. The Articular and Anarthrous Construction in the Epistle of James. Unpub. diss. Southwestern Baptist Theological Sem., 1948.

Powell, Cyril H. "'Faith' in James and its Bearing on the Problem of the Date of the Epistle." ExT 62(1950): 311-314.

Reicke, Bo. The Epistles of James, Peter, and Jude. The Anchor Bible. Garden City, New York: Doubleday, 1964.

Rendall, Gerald H. The Epistle of St. James and Judaic Christianity. Cambridge: Un. Press, 1927.

Rendtorff, Heinrich. Hörer und Täter: Eine Einführung in den Jakobusbrief. Die urchristliche Botschaft. Hamburg: Furche, 1953.

Rengstorf, Karl H. s.v. γελάω. TDNT I: 658-662.

________. s.v. κλαίω. TDNT III: 722-726.

Resch, Alfred. Agrapha: Außercanonische Schriftfragmente. TU 30.2. Leipzig: Hinrichs, 1906.

________. Außercanonische Paralleltexte zu den Evangelien. Vols. 1-3. TU 10. Leipzig: Hinrichs, 1893-1896.

________. Der Paulinismus und die Logia Jesu in ihren gegenseitigen Verhältnis untersucht. Leipzig: Hindrichs, 1904.
Reuss, Eduard. Die Geschichte der Heiligen Schriften Neuen Testaments. Braunschweig: Schwetschke, 1853.
Richardson, Cyril C. "The Teaching of the Twelve Apostles Commonly Called the Didache." Early Christian Fathers. The Library of Christian Classics. London: SCM, 1953.
Riddle, Donald W. and Hutson, Harold H. New Testament Life and Literature. Chicago: Un. Press, 1946.
Riedel, Petrus A. De zedeleer van den brief van Jacobus vergeleken met de zedeleer van Jezus. diss. Un. Groningen. Groningen: Schierbeek, 1875.
Rienecker, Fritz. A Linguistic Key to the Greek New Testament I. ed. Cleon L. Rogers Jr. Grand Rapids: Zondervan, 1980.
Riesenfeld, Harold. "'ΑΠΛΩΣ: ZU Jak. 1, 5." Con. Neot. 9(1944): 33-41.
________. The Gospel Tradition and its Beginnings. London: Mowbray, 1961.
________. The Gospel Tradition: Essays. Philadelphia: Fortress, 1970.
________. "Vom Schätzesammeln und Sorgen -- ein Thema urchristischer Paränese zu Mt. VI. 19-34." Neotestamentica et Patristica. Leiden: Brill, 1962, 47-58.
Robertson, Archibald T. A Grammar of the Greek New Testament in the Light of Historical Research. New York: Hoder and Stoughten, 1919.
________. Studies in the Epistle of James. New York: Doran, 1915.
Robinson, James M. and Koester, Helmut. Trajectories Through Early Christianity. Philadelphia: Fortress, 1971.
Robinson, John A.T. Redating the New Testament. London: SCM, 1976.
Ropes, James H. Epistle of St. James. ICC. Edinburgh: Clark, 1916.
________. Die Sprüche Jesu die in den kanonischen Evangelien nicht überliefert sind. TU 14. Leipzig: Hindrichs, 1896.
Rose, R. Vincent. "L'Épitre de Saint Jacques est-elle un ecrit Chrétien?" RB 5(1896): 519-535.
Ross, Alexander. The Epistles of James and John. NICNT. Grand Rapids: Eerdmans, 1954.
Salmon, George. A Historical Introduction to the Study of the Books of the New Testament. London: Murray, 1886.
Sanders, E.P. The Tendency of the Synoptic Tradition. Cambridge: Un. Press, 1969.
Sanders, Jack. Ethics in the New Testament. Philadelphia: Fortress, 1975.
Sandmel, Samuel. A Jewish Understanding of the New Testament. London: SPCK, 1977.
Sasse, Hermann. s.v. κόσμος. TDNT III: 868-895.
Schenkel, Daniel. Das Christusbild der Apostel und der nachapostolischen Zeit. Leipzig: Brockhaus, 1879.
Schillebeeckx, Edward. Jesus: An Experiment in Christology. tr. Hubert Hoskins. New York: Vintage, 1981.
Schlatter, Adolf von. Der Brief des Jakobus. Stuttgart: Calwer, 1932.
________. Der Evangelist Matthäus. Stuttgart: Calwer, 1963.
________. Das Evangelium des Lukas. Stuttgart: Calwer, 1960.
Schmid, Christian F. Biblical Theology of the New Testament. tr. G.H. Venables. Edinburgh: Clark, 1877.
________. Biblische Theologie des Neuen Testamentes II. Stuttgart: Gottlieb, 1853.
Schmidt, Karl L. s.v. βασιλεία and βασιλικός. TDNT I: 574-593.
Schmidt, Woldemar G. Der Lehrgehalt des Jacobusbriefes. Leipzig: Hinrichs, 1869.
Schmithals, Walter. Paulus und Jacobus. Göttingen: Vandenhoeck und Ruprecht, 1963.
Schnackenburg, Rudolf. The Moral Teaching of the New Testament. tr. J. Holland-Smith and W.J. O' Hara. London: Burns and Oates, 1965.
Schneider, Johannes. s.v. ὀμνύω. TDNT V: 176-185.
________. s.v. ὅρκος. TDNT V: 457-467.

Schniewind, Julius. Das Evangelium nach Matthäus. NTD. Göttingen: Vandenhoeck und Ruprecht, 1968.
Schoeps, Hans J. "Exkurs I: Die Stellung des Jakobusbriefes." Theologie und Geschichte des Judenchristentums. Tübingen: Mohr, 1949.
Schrage, Wolfgang. "Der Jakobusbrief." in Balz, Horst und Schrage, Wolfgang. Die katholischen Briefe. NTD. Göttingen: Vandenhoeck und Ruprecht, 1973.
Schrenk, Gottlob. s.v. γραφή. TDNT I: 749-761.
_______. s.v. δικαιοσυνη. TDNT II: 192-210.
Schwegler, Albert. Das nachapostolische Zeitalter in den Hauptmomenten seiner Entwicklung I. Tübingen: Mohr, 1846.
Schweizer, Eduard. The Good News According to Matthew. tr. David Green. Atlanta: John Knox, 1975.
Seesemann, Heinrich. s.v. πεῖρα. TDNT VI: 29-30.
Seitz, Oscar J.F. "Afterthoughts on the Term *'DIPSYCHOS'*." NTS 4 (1957-58): 327-334.
_______. "James and the Law." SE 2:472-486. Berlin: Akademie, 1964.
_______. "The Relationship of the Shepherd of Hermas to the Epistle of James." JBL 63(1944): 131-140.
Selwyn, Edward G. The First Epistle of St. Peter. London: MacMillan, 1947.
Septuaginta. ed. Alfred Rahlfs. Stuttgart: Privilegierte Württembergische Bibelanstalt, 1952.
The Septuagint Version, Greek and English. ed. Lancelot C.L. Brenton. Grand Rapids: Zondervan, 1970.
Sevenster, Jan N. Do You Know Greek? How Much Greek Could the First Jewish Christians Have Known? SNT. Leiden: Brill, 1968.
Shepherd, Massey H. "The Epistle of James and the Gospel of Matthew." JBL 75(1956): 40-51.
Sidebottom, E.M. James, Jude and 2 Peter. The Century Bible. London: Nelson, 1967.
Sigal, Phillip. "The Halakhah of James." Intergerini Parietis Septum (Eph. 2:14): Essays presented to Markus Barth on his sixty-fifth birthday. ed. Dikran Hadidian. Pittsburgh: Pickwick, 1981.
Smelink, Evert L. De brief van Jakobus. Nijkerk: Callenbach, 1963.
Smit Sibinga, Joost. "Ignatius and Matthew." NovT 8(1966): 263-283.
Smits, C. Oud-Testamentliche Citaten in het Nieue Testament. Collectanea Franciscana Neerlandica. s'Hertogenbosch: Malmberg, 1955.
Snyder, Graydon F. The Apostolic Fathers: The Shepherd of Hermas. Vol. 6. Camdon, New Jersey: Nelson, 1968.
Soden, Hermann von. "Der Jacobusbrief." JrPrTh 10(1884): 137-192.
_______. Hebraerbrief, Briefe des Petrus, Jakobus, Judas. HCNT. Leipzig: Mohr, 1899.
Songer, Harold S. "The Literary Character of the Book of James." REx 66(1960): 379-389.
Soucek, Josef B. "Zu den Problemen des Jakobusbriefes." EvTh 18(1958): 460-468.
Sparks, Hedley F.D. The Formation of the New Testament. New York: Philosophical Library, 1953.
Spitta, Friedrich. "Der Buch des Jacobus." Zur Geschichte und Literatur des Urchristentums II. Göttingen: Vandenhoeck und Ruprecht, 1896.
Stählin, Gustav. s.v. αἰτεω. TDNT I: 191-193.
_______. s.v. ὀργή. TDNT V: 419-447.
_______. "Zum Gebrauch von Beteuerungsformeln im Neuen Testament." NovT 5(1962): 115-143.
Stanley, David M. "Pauline Allusions to the Sayings of Jesus." CBQ 23(1961): 26-39.
Steck, R. "Die Konfession des Jakobusbriefes." ThZS 15(1898): 169-188.
Stendahl, Krister. The School of St. Matthew and its Use of the Old Testament. Uppsala: Almquist and Wiksells, 1954.
Stott, John R.W. Basic Introduction to the New Testament. Downers Grove: Inter-Varsity, 1970.

Stowers, Stanley K. The Diatribe and Paul's Letter to the Romans. Chico: Scholars, 1981.

______. Letter Writing in Greco-Roman Antiquity. Philadelphia: Westminster, 1986.

Strack, Hermann L. and Billerbeck, Paul. Kommentar zum Neuen Testament. Vols. 1-4. München: Beck, 1926.

Strecker, Georg. "Die Antithesen der Bergpredigt (Mt. 5, 21-48 par)." ZNW 69(1978): 36-72.

________. The Sermon on the Mount: An Exegetical Commentary. tr. O.C. Dean Jr. Nashville: Abingdon, 1988.

________. Der Weg der Gerechtigkeit: Untersuchung zur Theologie des Matthäus. Göttingen: Vandenhoeck und Ruprecht, 1971.

Streeter, Burnett H. The Four Gospels: A Study of Origins. London: MacMillan, 1924.

________. The Primitive Church: Studied with Special Reference to the Origins of the Christian Ministry. The Hewett Lectures 1928. London: MacMillan, 1930.

Tasker, Rudolph V.G. The General Epistle of James. Tyndale New Testament Commentaries. Grand Rapids: Eerdmans, 1957.

________. The Old Testament in the New Testament. London: SCM, 1946.

Taylor, Charles. "The Didache Compared with the Shepherd." JPh 18 (1890): 297-325.

Taylor, Vincent. The Gospel according to St. Mark. London: MacMillan, 1966.

Theile, Carl G.W. Commentarius in Episolam Jacobi. Impensis Librariae Baumgaertheriae, 1833.

Theological Dictionary of the New Testament. ed. Gerhard Kittel and Gerhard Friedrich. tr. Geoffrey W. Bromiley. Vols. 1-10. Grand Rapids: Eerdmans, 1964-1974.

Thiessen Henry C. Introduction to the New Testament. Grand Rapids: Eerdmans, 1943.

Thyen, Hartwig. Der Stil der jüdisch-hellenistischen Homilie. Göttingen: Vandenhoeck und Ruprecht, 1955.

Torrey, Charles C. The Four Gospels. New York: Harper, 1933.

Toxopeus, Hendrik J. Karakter en Herkomst van den Jacobusbrief. diss. Amsterdam: Clausen, 1906.

Travis, Arthur E. "James and Paul, A Comparative Study." SWJTh 12(1960): 57-79.

Treuett, Christine. "Approaching Matthew from the Second Century: The Under-Used Ignatian Correspondence." JSNT 20(1984): 59-67.

Turner, Nigel. Grammatical Insights into the New Testament. Edinburgh: Clark, 1966.

Usteri, Leonhard. "Glaube, Werke, und Rechtfertigung im Jakobusbrief." ThSKr 62(1889): 211-256.

van der Horst (see Horst).

Verhey, Allen. The Great Reversal: Ethics and the New Testament. Grand Rapids: Eerdmans, 1984.

Vermès, Géza. The Dead Sea Scrolls in English. Baltimore: Penguin, 1968.

Via, Dan O. Jr. "The Right Strawy Epistle Reconsidered: A Study in Biblical Ethics and Hermeneutic." JR 49(1969): 253-267.

Vokes, F.E. "The Ten Commandments in the New Testament and in First Century Judaism." SE 5:146-154. Berlin: Akademie, 1968.

von Soden (see Soden).

Vos, Louis A. The Synoptic Traditions in the Apocalypse. diss. Vrije Universiteit. Kampen: Kok, 1965.

Vowinkel, Ernst. Die Grundgedanken des Jakobusbriefes verglichen mit den ersten briefen des Petrus und Johannes. BFTh. Gutersloh: Bertelsmann, 1879.

Wanke, Joachim. "Die urchristlichen Lehrer nach dem Zeugnis des Jakobusbriefes." Die Kirche des Anfants. Festschrift für Heinz Schurmann. Leipzig: St. Benno, 1977, 489-511.

Warfield, Benjamin B. "'It Says': 'Scripture Says': 'God Says'." PRR 10(1899): 472-510.

Weiss, D. Bernhard. Lehrbuch der Einleitung in das Neue Testament. Berlin: Hertz, 1897.

Weissman, Moshe. The Midrash Says. Vols. 1-5. Brooklyn: Benei Yakov, 1983.

Weizsäcker, Carl. Das Apostolische Zeitalter der christlichen Kirche. Freiburg: Mohr, 1886.
Wenham, David. "Paul's Use of the Jesus Tradition: Three Samples." Gospel Perspectives. ed David Wenham. Sheffield: JSOT, 1985, 5:7-38.
Werner, Karl. "Ueber den Brief Jacobi." ThQ 54(1872): 246-279.
Wessel, W.W. An Inquiry into the Origin, Literary Character, Historical and Religious Significance of the Epistle of James. Unpub. diss. Edinburgh, 1953.
Westcott, Brooke F. A General Survey of the History of the Canon of the New Testament. London: MacMillan, 1889.
Wiefel, Wolfgang. "The Jewish Community in Ancient Rome and the Origins of Roman Christianity." The Romans Debate. ed. Karl P. Donfried. Minneapolis: Augsburg, 1977, 100-119.
Wifstrand, Albert. "Stylistic Problems in the Epistles of James and Peter." STh 1(1948): 170-182.
Wijbelingh, H. De vraag of Jacobus polemiseerdt: beoordeld en beantwoord. Groningen: van Wicheren, 1860.
Wikenhauser, Alfred. Einleitung in das Neue Testament. Freiburg: Herder, 1956.
Wilckens, Ulrich. s.v. σοφία. TDNT VII: 524-525.
Williams, Robert R. The Letters of John and James. The Cambridge Bible Commentary. Cambridge: Un. Press, 1965.
Windisch, Hans. Die katholischen Briefe. HNT. Tübingen: Mohr, 1930.
Wohlenberg, Gustav. Die Lehre der zwölf Apostel in ihrem Verhältnis zum neutestamentlichen Schriftum. Erlangen: Deichert, 1888.
Wright, Leon. Alterations of the Words of Jesus as Quoted in the Literature of the Second Century. Harvard: Un. Press, 1952.
Yarnold, Edward J. "Τέλειος in St. Matthew's Gospel." SE 4:269-273. Berlin: Academie, 1968.
Young, Franklin W. "The Relation of 1 Clement to the Epistle of James." JBL 67(1948): 339-345.
Zahn, Theodor. Einleitung in das Neue Testament I. Leipzig: Deichert, 1906.
________. Evangelium des Matthäus. KNT. Leipzig: Deichert, 1910.
________. Geschichte des neutestamentlichen Kanons. Erlangen: Deichert, 1888.
Zeller, Eduard. "Ueber Jakobus 1, 12." ZWTh 6(1863): 93-96.

SAMENVATTING IN NEDERLANDS

De gangbare opvatting, dat de Brief van Jacobus meer toespelingen op de woorden van Jezus bevat dan enig ander geschrift in het Niewe Testament, afgezien van de evangeliën, wordt in deze studie op haar juistheid onderzocht.

Ten einde de stand van het onderzoek in kaart te brengen zijn uit de laatste twee eeuwen een zestigtal auteurs, die zich met de vraag naar de relatie van de Jezustraditie tot de Brief van Jacobus hebben beziggehouden, op hun inzichten onderzocht (vgl. Appendix I). Uit dit onderzoek bleek dat in de loop van de genoemde periode 180 mogelijke verwijzingen naar de woorden van Jezus in de synoptische traditie zijn geregistreerd. Daarbij viel echter dadelijk in het oog hoe groot de divergentie in hun beoordelingen was. Tweederde van de onderzochte geleerden blijkt het onderling eens te zijn over slechts zes parallel-plaatsen, terwijl driekwart van hen overeenstemt ten aanzien van drie parallellen. Daaruit zou kunnen blijken, dat er bij het selectie-proces een zekere mate van willekeur is. Ook laat zich een gebrekkige differentiatie van parallellen gemakkelijk uit het onderzochte materiaal aflezen. In de door ons gevolgde werkwijze wordt onderscheid gemaakt tussen de volgende categorieën: 1) citaten; 2) toespelingen of bewuste reminiscenties; 3) parallellen van inhoudelijke en terminologische aard; 4) zuiver inhoudelijke parallellen; 5) zuiver terminologische parallellen; 6) gemeenschappelijke stof die teruggaat op andere bronnen.

Voor het vaststellen van literaire afhankelijkheid is het voorkomen van dezelfde of bijne dezelfde bewoording in citaten voorafgegaan door een formule met bronvermelding uiteraard de belangrijkste categorie. Om een *logion* als toespeling te kunnen kwalificeren dient er sprake te zijn van een wezenlijke woordelijke overeenkomst, waarbij uiteraard ook analoge contekst of gelijke inhoudelijke accentuering van gewicht is. De waarschijnlijkheid van het voorkomen van een toespeling wordt verhoogd, wanneer er ook andere toespelingen in de tekst aanwezig blijken te zijn. In zeker opzicht staat dichtbij de categorie van de toespeling die van de parallel met overeenkomstige terminologie en gemeenschappelijke inhoud, al kan een verschil in accentuering aanduiden dat er geen sprake is van een bewuste reminiscentie. Parallellen met alleen woordelijke overeenkomst geven veelal minder houvast voor het vaststellen van literaire afhankelijkheid. Door het gebruik van deze verschillende categorieën kan een classificatie binnen de overvloed aan parallellen aangebracht worden, waardoor wellicht een beter beeld verkregen kan worden van de verhouding tussen het onderwijs van Jezus zoals wij die uit de synoptische evangeliën kennen en de morele aansporingen van Jacobus.

Hoofdstuk 1 geeft een verslag van de geschiedenis van het onderzoek naar de relatie tussen de Brief van Jacobus en de traditie van de *logia* van Jezus. De oudste theorie die veel aanhangers heeft gehad, en tot op heden vooral in de Engelse en Amerikaanse wereld nog op veel crediet kan rekenen, is dat de bron van de in dit opzicht relevante teksten in de brief geen andere is dan het geheugen van Jacobus, de broer van Jezus. De opvatting dat Jacobus voor zijn vermaningen met name gebruik maakte van het Evangelie naar Mattheüs is in de negentiende eeuw door Brückner gelanceerd. Deze mogelijkheid is recentelijk opnieuw aan de orde gesteld door Shepherd en Gryglewicz, zij het dat eerstgenoemde haar nader kwalificeert door aan te nemen dat Jacobus dit evangelie slechts uit de voorlezing in de eredienst heeft leren kennen. In de periode 1895-1896 komen Massebieau en Spitta onafhankelijk van elkaar tot de these, dat de Brief van Jacobus van origine een joods document was dat pas later met name door toevoeging van interpolaties tot een christelijk document zou zijn omgewerkt. Er is in de brief dan ook geen relatie tot het onderwijs van Jezus, daar de overeenkomst voldoende verklaard wordt door een gemeenschappelijke afhankelijkheid van joodse begrippen en vocabulaire. De overheersende opvatting op het Europese continent gedurende de hier onderzochte periode is, tenslotte, dat de orale traditie van de woorden van Jezus binnen de vroeg-christelijke gemeenten zowel de overeenkomsten als de verschillen tussen Jacobus en de synoptische overlevering verklaart. Een nuancering die door Dibelius werd voorgesteld gaat er van uit dat de bizondere vorm van de *logia* in Jacobus (toespelingen zonder inleidende formule en exacte aanhaling van de woorden) te danken is aan het gebruik van het overleveringsmateriaal binnen het genre van de paraenese. Kittel echter verklaarde deze bijzondere vorm door aan te nemen dat hier sprake is van een eerste stadium van de geschiedenis van de overlevering van woorden van Jezus.

Deze terugblik op de geschiedenis van het onderzoek plaatst ons voor twee reeksen problemen: 1) de problemen rondom het zogenaamde 'raadsel' van Jacobus, met name de vragen betreffende de datering, het auteurschap, herkomst en lezers, en 2) de problemen rondom de geschiedenis van de overlevering van de woorden van Jezus. Bij de eerste reeks van problemen gaat het onder meer om de vraag of uit de verhouding tussen Jacobus en de synoptische evangeliën ook licht valt op de datering en herkomst. Daarbij speelt vooral een rol of uit een mogelijke relatie tussen de theologische posities van Mattheüs en Jacobus iets valt af te lezen voor een gemeenschappelijke herkomst van beide documenten. Bij de tweede reeks van problemen komen de volgende vragen naar voren: citeerde Jacobus bewust uit een bepaalde traditie van *logia* van Jezus? En indien dat het geval is, welke tekstuele elementen kunnen dan worden aangemerkt als toespelingen op deze *logia*? Zijn er bepaalde ontwikkelingen binnen de traditie (Mattheüs, Lucas, Q of eventueel 'Sondergut') die de formulering van de traditie bij Jacobus benaderen, of treffen we nu juist in Jacobus een geheel onafhankelijke traditie aan? Is er een verklaring voor de specifieke overeenkomsten èn verschillen tussen Jacobus en de synoptische traditie? In hoeverre spelen factoren als de toepassing van overgeleverde stof in een concrete situatie, het persoonlijk geheugen van de auteur, de ontwikkeling van divergerende orale tradities, of het gebruikmaken van een literair genre (bijv. paraenese) hierbij een rol? Tenslotte laat zich de vraag stellen, in hoeverre de *logia* bij Jacobus ons in staat stellen de hypothese te toetsen dat er verschillende stadia zijn geweest in de traditie van woorden van Jezus.

Om deze vragen te kunnen beantwoorden wordt eerst nagegaan in hoeverre Jacobus gebruik gemaakt van reeds bestaand materiaal. Met het oog daarop wordt in hoofdstuk 2 onderzocht hoe en in welke vorm Jacobus herkenbaar materiaal uit het Oude Testament en de intertestamentaire literatuur heeft aangehaald. Zesmaal hanteert Jacobus teksten uit het Oude Testament met *formulae citandi* om zich ter staving van zijn argumentatie te beroepen op het gezag van de Schrift. Ook elders zinspeelt hij op teksten uit het Oude Testament en andere joodse geschriften, niet zozeer om zijn argumentatie in de Schrift te funderen, maar veeleer om zich van bekende religieuze taal en traditionele begrippen te bedienen.

In hoofdstuk 3 worden de parallellen tussen de Jacobusbrief en de Jezus-logia onderzocht, om na te gaan of Jacobus zich op dezelfde wijze op het gezag van de stichter van het Christelijk geloof beroept als op het Oude Testament door middel van inleidingsformules, of dat hij slechts op het onderwijs van Jezus zinspeelt door zich van 'traditionele' terminologie te bedienen. Dit hoofdstuk is de kern van de dissertatie. Daarin beperken wij ons tot een onderzoek naar de twintig meest geciteerde parallellen tussen de Jacobusbrief en de *logia* van Jezus. Eerst onderzoeken wij de struktuur van het Jacobusboek en daarna exegetiseren we elk onderdeel van de brief als basis voor de nadere analyse van de parallelle vermaningen. Bij elke parallel bedienen wij ons van de criteria van 1) vergelijkbare materie en context; 2) overeenkomstige woordkeus en vorm; 3) parallellen in andere literatuur; en 4) de steun die de geschiedenis van de interpretatie biedt om vast te stellen of het onderwijs van Jacobus dichter stond bij resp. uitingen van joodse wijsheid of bij morele uitspraken in de literatuur van de Grieks-Romeinse wereld, óf dat het aansloot bij een specifiek *logion* van Jezus. In geen enkel geval citeert Jacobus de *logia* van Jezus d.m.v. inleidingsformules; doch in acht passages kunnen wij bewuste toespelingen op de *logia* van Jezus onderscheiden (cf. pp. 219-221). Hoewel er kennelijk een belangrijk verband bestaat tussen Jacobus en de woorden van de Jezus-traditie, is het onjuist, zoals het door velen gesuggereerd werd, dat de Jacobusbrief meer toespelingen op de synoptische traditie bevat dan enig andere NT brief. Paulus zinspeelt tenminste achtmaal, maar wellicht zelf vierentwintig maal op woorden van Jezus, terwijl in 1 Petrus twaalf van *logia* van Jezus worden gevonden (cf. p. 169). Naast toespelingen op de woorden van Jezus komen wij in Jacobus ook bepaalde thema's tegen uit de prediking van Jezus die opgenomen zijn in het paraenetisch onderwijs van de gemeente (cf. pp. 222-223). Uitleggers, die nalaten te onderscheid bemaken tussen deze twee categorieën (i.e. toespelingen èn thema's van Jezus' prediking) hebben onvermijdelijk een veel langere lijst van toespelingen op de woorden van Jezus dan redelijkerwijs uit de inhoud en formulering van Jacobus kan worden afgeleid.

Vele geleerden vestigen regelmatig de aandacht op de nauwe relatie tussen de Brief van Jacobus en het Evangelie naar Mattheus, en met name de Bergrede. In hoofdstuk 4 bespreken wij het exegetisch bewijsmateriaal van Shepherd en Gryglewicz, dat zou wijzen op Jacobus' afhankelijkheid van het onderwijs van Mattheus. In onze bespreking weerleggen wij deze opvatting stap voor stap met gegevens die veeler op een onafhankelijke overdracht van de *logia* van Jezus wijzen. Door het overeenkomstig gebruik van zaligsprekingen, van analoge beeldspraak, en van de thema's van wet, gerechtigheid, van geloof en werken, en van rijkdom, te analyseren pogen wij aan te tonen dat de band tussen Jacobus en Mattheus veeleer bestaat in hun gemeenschappelijke opvoeding in het Jodendom en in hun ervaring in de Joods-Christelijke gemeenschap, dan in een literaire afhankelijkheid, of in dezelfde geografische oorsprong in Syrie samen met de Didache en de geschriften van Ignatius.

In hoofdstuk 5 wordt onderzoek gedaan naar het specifieke probleem dat met de overdracht van de Jezus-logia verband houdt. Ligt de verklaring van de uiteenlopende verschillen in vorm én van het gebrek aan inleidingsformules in het poneren van verschillende stadia in het overleveringsproces? Of ligt de sleutel tot het begrip van deze wijzingen in het gemeenschappelijke genre van de paraenese? Ten eerste onderzoeken wij de veronderstelling van Kittel dat de Jacobusbrief een eerste stadium in de overdracht van de *logia* van Jezus vertegenwoordigt waarin alleen toespelingen zonder inleidende formulering aangetroffen worden. In het tweede stadium neemt het benutten van citaten toe en vermindert het vrije, losse gebruik van Jezus' woorden in de vorm van louter toespelingen. Het eind-product van dit proces wordt tenslotte aangetroffen in de geschriften van Justinus en de latere patres waar de *logia* van Jezus geciteerd worden als woorden van den Heer of worden gekwalificeerd als Schrift. Door aan te tonen dat verwijzing naar de woorden van Jezus in Jacobus, 1 Petrus, Paulus, èn de apostolische vaders veelal geschiedt in de vorm van toespelingen, wordt Kittel's theorie van stadia kwestieus gesteld; zij kan beter worden vervangen door de voorstelling van een flexibele, maar gezaghebbende, overdracht van de Jezus-traditie. Vervolgens komt de oplossing van Dibelius en Lohse aan de orde, waarin aandacht gerraagd wordt voor het feit dat toespelingen op *logia* van Jezus regelmatig plaatsvinden zonder een inleidingsformule binnen paraenetische stukken. Na het bewijs voor het categoriseren van Jacobus resp. als brief, homilie, diatribe, of als specimen van wijsheidliteratuur te hebben onderzocht, wordt aangetoond dat de kenmerken van de paraenese de verschillende aspecten van het Jacobusboek kunnen verklaren. Paraenese kan gedefinieerd worden als een eclectisch conglomeraat van vermaningen die los, zonder een sluitende theologische onderbouw, met elkaar verbonden worden, met als doel de overdracht van algemeen toepasbaar traditioneel materiaal voor de socialisatie van de toehoorders. Door aan te tonen dat toespelingen specifiek gevonden worden in de paraenetische delen van Paulus' briefen, 1 Petrus, en de Didache, concluderen wij dat Jacobus zich van toespelingen bedient, omdat dit het normale middel was om de *logia* van Jezus over to dragen in de paraenese. De Brief van Jacobus zou wellicht juister getypeerd kunnen worden als de Paraenese van Jacobus.

In hoofdstuk 5 worden de resultaten van hoofdstuk 3 op de overdracht van de Jezus-*logia* toegepast. In hoofdstuk 6 wordt onderzocht wat een en ander berekent voor de achtergrondsproblemen van de Brief van Jacobus zoals auteurschap, herkomst en datering. Aangezien reeds in hoofdstuk 4 de opvatting van een nauwe verwantschap tussen de gemeente van Jacobus en die van Mattheus in Syrie werd afgewezen, overwegen wij hier de twee resterende mogelijkheden: 1) die van een vroeg, in het midden van de eerste eeuw tot stand gekomen, geschrift van Jacobus, de Jacobus van Jeruzalem, de broeder van Jezus; of 2) een laat (post-) apostolisch document door een ons onbekende, mogelijk pseudonieme auteur te Rome geschreven. Het Joodse karakter van de brief, de waarschijnlijkheid dat Jac. 1:1 van de meest bekende Jacobus spreekt, en vooral de Palestijnse geografische trekken, begunstigen de traditionele interpretatie. Er zijn echter drie gegevens die niet stroken met een auteurschap van Jacobus, de broeder van Jezus, namelijk: 1) de voortreffelijke Griekse stijl; 2) de zuiver ethische inhoud aan de wet geschonken; en 3) de vertraagde opname van dit boek in de canon. Wanneer we nagaan welke documenten het meest, qua woordenschat en inhoud, met Jacobus overeenkomen, dan blijken dat documenten te zijn die uit Rome stammen, nl. 1 Petrus, 1 Clemens, en de Herder van Hermas. Zie daarvoor Appendix II. Op grond daarvan is de suggestie dat de Brief van Jacobus in Rome geschreven is door een onbekende Jacobus, «een dienstknecht van God en van den Here Jezus Christus,» ook een verdedigbare veronderstelling. Indien wij een keuze doen voor een auteurschap door Jacobus van Jeruzalem moeten we erkennen dat het traditionele beeld van een ascetische Jacobus, die primair Aramees sprak en de nadruk legde op de ceremoniële aspecten van de wet, niet overeenkomt met de gegevens van deze brief en dan ook moet worden gewijzigd.

Hoofdstuk 7 geeft een samenvatting van de resultaten. Daar de parallellen met de synoptische traditie worden gecategoriseerd, de verhouding van Jacobus tot de pre-synoptische *logia*-verzamelingen onderzocht, en wordt het verschillend gebruik van de woorden van Jezus binnen de genres van paraenese en evangelie verklaard. Deze studie poogt aan to tonen dat een identificatie van de inhoud van de Brief van Jacobus als paraenese zowel de vorm van de *logia*, het totaal ontbreken van een Christologie, alsook de bijzondere structuur van de Jacobusbrief, verklaart.